Ner
T0089761

Neruda

THE BIOGRAPHY OF A POET

MARK EISNER

ecco
An Imprint of HarperCollinsPublishers

HarperCollins books may be purchased for educational, business, or sales promotional use. For information please e-mail the Special Markets Department at SPsales@harpercollins.com.

A hardcover edition of this book was published in 2018 by Ecco, an imprint of HarperCollins Publishers.

FIRST ECCO PAPERBACK EDITION PUBLISHED 2019.

Designed by Michelle Crowe

Library of Congress Cataloging-in-Publication Data has been applied for.

ISBN 978-0-06-269421-8

19 20 21 22 23   RS/LSC   10 9 8 7 6 5 4 3 2 1

CONTENTS

AUTHOR'S NOTE

In the first chapters a difficulty presents itself whether to use Pablo Neruda, the pen name he assumed at age sixteen, or Neftalí, from his given name, Ricardo Eliecer Neftalí Reyes Basoalto. When events jump ahead of those first sixteen years, I refer to him as Pablo Neruda. When writing about him during the time before he changed his name, I use Neftalí or some combination of his original first, middle, and last names.

All translations of the poems in this book are mine unless otherwise indicated, most often in the endnotes. I also translated most of the source material. I take responsibility for any inadequacies or errors in these translations. It should be noted that strict literal fidelity to the original, especially with the poetry, wasn't always maintained. Modest, appropriate liberties were sometimes taken in order to best convey the true intents and richness of the original.

Megan Coxe and Jessica Powell provided invaluable help. Those passages and poems fully translated by them are cited with their names; these were graciously crafted for this book and thus are previously unpublished.

If you ask me what my poetry is, I'd have to say: I don't know. But if you ask my poetry, she'll tell you who I am.

—PABLO NERUDA, 1943

Neruda

INTRODUCTION

> The word
> was born in the blood,
> grew in the dark body, beating,
> and flew through the lips and the mouth.
> —"The Word"

At the break of dawn on September 11, 1973, generals of the Chilean armed forces launched a coup d'état against the democratically elected government of President Salvador Allende, a Marxist-Socialist. The air force bombed the presidential palace; soldiers swarmed the grounds. Allende shot himself rather than face capture.

Twelve days later, Pablo Neruda, central figure of the Chilean Left and beloved poet, died in a Santiago hospital. He had been gravely ill with metastatic prostate cancer. Many say he died of a broken heart as well, as terror swept across his beloved country, as his friends were tortured, as all the social progress they had struggled for was quickly destroyed. While he lay in the hospital, the military ransacked his home.

Neruda's funeral became the first public act of resistance against the military dictatorship of Augusto Pinochet. As thousands of Chileans were being arrested by the regime and many more were beaten or "disappeared," Neruda's friends and fans, his people—those who had not already been forced into hiding—marched through the streets of Santiago with his coffin, crying out his name. Throughout his life, Neruda had fought for peace and justice for his people both on the page and off. Now that the military had stripped them of their liberties, he spoke for them—even in death—once more.

His close friends and foreign ambassadors escorted Neruda's coffin from his poetically distinctive home to the cemetery. Word spread like wildfire through Santiago that morning, about the growing crowds joining Neruda's funeral procession. Hundreds came out—despite the soldiers who lined the streets armed with automatic rifles—to invoke him as a champion of courage and truth, and to give voice to their pain over what had happened in the thirteen days since the coup. The marchers mourned the death of their poet, they mourned the death and disappearance of friends and family members, and they mourned the death of their democracy.

Neruda had become a symbol. Throughout his life, he had actively positioned himself to play this role. From his arrival in Santiago in 1921 as a shy, young anarchist, through his sudden designation by the student movement as the voice of his generation, through Allende's election and Chile's turbulent transition to socialism, Neruda had fulfilled his own sense of the poet's calling. This sense encompassed the poet's duty, a social obligation, a vocation and impulse. In turn, many working people and progressive activists—not just in Chile, not just in Latin America, but all over the world—had adopted him as their hero, claimed him as their own. He was the quintessential "people's poet."

From all walks of life, from all corners of the sprawling city of Santiago, citizens joined the long procession. They marched with their grief and sang their way through the streets, in resistance, fists raised in solidarity. With their sadness came a unifying strength. The soldiers may have held their guns as if they were ready, but they could only watch. Pinochet didn't dare do anything, because this was Pablo Neruda, and international news cameras were capturing the streets. The world was watching.

The mourners walked beside the hearse and lined the narrow streets. The flower-covered casket rode atop the vehicle rather than within it, so that his *pueblo* could see the Poet one last time. Solemnly, defiantly, they sang the Socialist anthem, "The Internationale," fists in the air: "Arise, ye prisoners of starvation! Arise, ye wretched of the earth! For justice thunders condemnation: A better world's in birth!"

Over the grief came the chants: "He isn't dead, he isn't dead! He has only fallen asleep, just like the flowers sleep when the sun has set. He isn't dead, he isn't dead! He has only fallen asleep!"

When the procession reached Santiago's main cemetery, the coffin was carried to the grave, draped in the red, white, and blue of the Chilean flag. With her hand like a megaphone up to her mouth, a woman unflinchingly yelled, *"¡Jota! ¡Jota! Juventudes Comunistas de Chile!"* "Communist Youth of Chile!" Then she yelled, *"¡Compañero Pablo Neruda!"*

The crowd answered, *"¡Presente!"* "He is present!"

"¡Compañero Pablo Neruda!"

★

In film footage of this historic moment, its intense emotion is crystallized in the image of a grief-stricken man with a timeworn face, carefully groomed hair, and missing teeth, whose eyes fill with tears as he struggles to choke out the word *"¡Presente!"* along with the crowd. This man embodies the love Chile had for Neruda—not just the literati or the militant Communists, but the everyman, the everywoman. Beyond the political, for many, this march was about Chile's soul, the hope and pride of the people, and Neruda was its catalyst.

★

This biography was born twenty-one years later in 1994, the year I turned twenty-one. Fascinated by Latin America, I studied abroad in Central America as part of my junior year at the University of Michigan, where I was majoring in political science and English literature.

I had been introduced to Neruda before my trip, and I'd packed a bilingual edition of his selected poems that would accompany me on a spectacular set of voyages to come.

That year, I found myself doing fieldwork in the highlands of El Salvador, observing as the National Association of Agricultural Workers helped set up coffee cooperatives among the campesinos. This was following the first rounds of land reform, two years after peace accords had ended the country's horrific civil war. Reading Neruda's poetry at night made the history—the human experience of it—palpably real to me. The depth and simplicity of Neruda's portrayal of humanity in the poems hit my soul.

A few years after I graduated, I headed south again, with the same weathered book in my tattered green pack. Eventually I reached Chile, that slender country sliding off toward Antarctica. Somehow I found myself working on a ranch in its Central Valley, nestled between the Andes and the sea. This was certainly part of Neruda's territory, his terroir: here grew the grapes that made his velvet red wine and the red poppies that flower in his verse.

The ranch was close to the Pacific coast, the source of so many of his metaphors. His fabled eccentric house at Isla Negra was not too far up the rocky shoreline. It spread out like a boat, for he was, as he liked to say, "a sailor on land"; this was the vessel from which he wrote most of his poetry in the second half of his life. Its walls, often curved, were covered in his endless collections, everything from ship figureheads to butterflies, all overlooking the beach.

I also spent time in Neruda's home in Chile's capital, Santiago. Like Isla Negra and La Sebastiana—another small home he had in the funky port city of Valparaíso—it is preserved as a *casa-museo,* a house-museum. La Chascona was named for the wild curly hair of his third wife, Matilde Urrutia. They built the home as a refuge while he was still living with his second wife, Delia del Carril.

When I approached La Chascona from the street for the first time, adrenaline surged through me. Amid thick green vegetation, I saw that the house had been painted in a color like French blue and rested atop a street-level wall of warm gray and gold stones. A steep hill rose behind, with what seemed like rooms and outcroppings coming off a stepped path.

I entered a room behind heavy brown doors. To my dismay, it was a gift shop. I resigned myself to the limitations of the moment and bought my ticket.

Then I found myself on an open patio canopied by a wooden trellis covered in grapevines. From the patio, stairs climbed up to the living room and other rooms on both sides of the stairs. His library and writer's cabin were situated at the top of the hill, above the bedroom. The

floors alternated in color, blue and yellow, like the tiers of a multicol-
ored and unusually shaped wedding cake; the yellow floor had rounded
walls, while the blue floor above was a charming box perched among
the treetops. One white door in a white wall featured a rough stone
mosaic. This was clearly the house of an artist.

There were sculpted metal frames on two windows off of one of the
rooms on the patio; one held a *P* for Pablo, the other an *M* for Matilde,
both set against a pattern of white iron waves. I wanted to run my fin-
gers along them, but such intimacy was prohibited within the confines
of the tour.

As I walked from one room to another, I realized Neruda had in-
tricately decorated his home so that he was actually living inside of a
visual poem: a double-faced painting of Matilde by friend Diego Rivera
next to the stairs leading to their small bedroom; antique maps of the
world and many of Chile in one room and a collection of East Asian
statues in another; art deco furniture in the living room; a grand photo
of Walt Whitman in one of the house's two bars; several enchanting
women figureheads from the prows of old boats; and a collection of
books ranging from the maritime history of Chile to Allen Ginsberg's
poetry in his library, along with his Nobel Prize medal.

As I walked out of Neruda's library toward his little writer's cabin,
the sunset turned the distant Andes into a glowing rigid curtain of
breathtaking orange, blending into the white of the snow covering the
sheer mountains.

I returned to the patio to soak it all in. There I met Verónica, who
was working for the Pablo Neruda Foundation while doing graduate
work in feminist Latin American literature at the University of Chile,
Neruda's alma mater. We started up a conversation, which turned into
a friendship. Later that week I met her for lunch at one of the old bo-
hemian spots near Neruda's house. Afterward, she let me sit at Pablo's
desk, with his framed picture of Walt Whitman on it.

Neruda seemed to be everywhere. My life became saturated by his
poetry, to a degree I've never experienced with any literature. With my
Spanish now at a much more agile and precise level of fluency, I felt
closer to his words than ever before and took up the art of translating

his poetry at night in the little cabin I lived in on the ranch. Although there were many beautiful translations, and I had grown to love Neruda through the translations in that book brought from Ann Arbor, I now began to realize that many did not flow as I felt they should, and I often had interpretive differences with them.

I reached out to Verónica about this. She introduced me to two of her professors and the executive director of the foundation, and there was a consensus validating the dictum that Edmund Keeley, prominent translator of Greek poetry, put so well: "Translation is a moveable feast . . . there must always be room for retouching and sharpening that image as new taste and new perception may indicate." These conversations, combined with a few I had with people back in the States, prompted me to create a new book of dynamic translations that would serve as a fresh voice of Neruda in English, involving an unprecedented collaboration with academics to better empower the translator-poets. This book was *The Essential Neruda: Selected Poems,* with a preface by one of my greatest literary heroes, Lawrence Ferlinghetti, published by City Lights Books in April 2004 in coordination with celebrations of Neruda's centennial birthday.

That experience was a fluid bridge to this biography, for collaboration was the precept. I worked closely with Neruda scholars— Nerudianos—as well as luminary poets and translators, both in Chile and in the United States. I owe them a tremendous debt, as the acknowledgments at the end of this volume attest in further detail. These leading minds and generous souls not only made *The Essential Neruda* possible but helped pave the way for this biography as well.

With the work of all of those involved in *The Essential Neruda,* we came closer to the bones of his words, enabling new translations that are faithful to both the original meaning and inherent beauty of Neruda's poems. The intimacy I gained with his words, character, and world allowed me to work further toward Neruda's core.

Based on the success of *The Essential Neruda,* I was asked to write this book. At first I thought, *Why another book?* So much had already been written on Neruda, including many works I admired. What would mine bring that others hadn't?

I came to see a valid need for another approach, one that aims to bring Neruda's gripping story to life in a new way. This volume is neither unbiased nor hagiographic; rather, it aims to offer a compelling narrative version of Neruda's life and work, undergirded by exhaustive research, designed to bring this towering literary figure to a broader audience. My goal is to present the nuances of this complex, seemingly larger-than-life figure, to show all his vastness, to show both the redeeming and the cruel sides of his personal life, to show both the inspirational and the deeply troublesome sides of his political life.

In addition, I felt it was vital to unite, in a single volume, the three inseparable strands of Neruda's legacy: his personal history, the entire canon of his poetry, and his social activism and politics both on and off the page. Each of these components depends on the other two. Each is shaped by the other two. No single thread can be understood fully without understanding the others. This book aims to deeply explore each of these three aspects of his life, while also highlighting the phenomenon behind their interrelationship. Without examining each of them extensively, the true expanse of Neruda's story can't be told.

From this, I also want to explore the multifaceted ways a reader can interpret Neruda as a figure in history. He was a man who gained celebrity status assuming the role of the "people's poet," while also acting as what some call a "Champagne Communist." The contradictions are inherent within his multitudes, to paraphrase his hero Whitman. As Alastair Reid, Neruda's favorite English-language translator, said to me, "Neruda is seven different poets, if not nine": there is a Neruda for everyone. His legacy can be appreciated in different ways, but it is best understood in the context of the startling historical events in which he took part and the intense complexities of his life—from the shockingly shameful to the inspiringly heroic—while still absorbing the beauty and innovation of his poetry.

Within the examination of those three strands—poetry, personality, and politics—is an exploration of the nature of political poetry's power and effectiveness, and how Neruda's role as a people's poet, a political poet, connects to the shifting political climates of this new millennium. Because Neruda was so linked, so involved with major phenomena of the twentieth century, this book takes the reader through major historical events, including the South American student, labor, and anarchist movements of the 1910s, which tied into similar ones in Europe; the Spanish Civil War; the Battle of Stalingrad; Fidel Castro, the cult of Che Guevara, and the Cuban Revolution; and Richard Nixon's interventions in Chile and Vietnam.

*

There was another impetus, inspiration, and source for this book: in celebration of the centennial of Neruda's birth in 2004, not only did *The Essential Neruda* come out, but I also premiered a documentary film on him that I had produced. That initial version has led to a more ambitious feature-length documentary film that is currently in production. Work on the film has produced brilliant, unique gems for this biography, this text nourished by interviews and conversations with a diverse array of characters.

Unfortunately, some of the subjects have passed since I first talked to them. Neruda was born in 1904, so many of those who knew him for most of his life are no longer with us. One of these people was Sergio Insunza, minister of justice under Allende. Insunza was in his twenties when he first met Neruda, when the Chilean Communist Party brought the poet-senator to hide out in his apartment—then-president Gabriel González Videla had ordered Neruda's arrest for speaking out against his antidemocratic, oppressive measures on the Senate floor. Another interviewee, Juvenal Flores, was ninety-two when I spoke to him. He worked on a ranch in southern Chile and helped guide the fugitive Neruda on horseback across a snowcapped peak in the Andes, safely into exile.

Then there was an afternoon I spent at one of Santiago's main produce markets. When I asked an effusive woman in front of a vegetable stand about Neruda's love poetry, she spontaneously burst out, "I like it when you're quiet. It's as if you were absent"—the iconic first lines of Neruda's Poem XV in *Twenty Love Poems*. And then, with the biggest smile and half-laughing, she said, "That's as far as I get, but it's a beautiful book!" She told me that although she had read the poem as a young girl, in school, it gained a heightened significance for her six years before, when, at thirty-two, she had fallen in love with a Bolivian doctor. He eventually left Chile, giving her a copy of *Twenty Love Poems* as a departing gift.

I turned to Mario Fernández Núñez and asked him what he thought of Neruda. The whole time we had been talking, he had been preparing bundles of cilantro for his market stand. His hands did not pause in their work when he answered, "Well, he's our national poet. He won the Nobel Prize."

"And what does that mean to you?" I asked.

"Well, first, it's pride, an honor. And secondly, for us, Pablo Neruda, beyond all the poetry, was a very good person. Remember that he was practically the ambassador—he brought the Spanish over here when Spain was in a dictatorship."

These experiences provided breathing insight that could not be found on the printed pages of the books I found at the Stanford Library, the Biblioteca Nacional de Chile, the Library of Congress, or Neruda's own archives, or in so many key sources I've been grateful for in between.

★

In 2004, Isabel Allende, the globally renowned Chilean author, provided the narration for my documentary. Isabel lives in Marin County, and on a spectacular day, I drove her over the Golden Gate Bridge to the recording studio in my beat-up, graffiti-tagged old Subaru. My creative collaborator, Tanya Vlach, was in the back seat, and we listened, exhilarated, to Isabel's enthusiastic account of her young granddaughter's ability to invent tales of magical realism, and then she switched back to Neruda, to what he meant to her.

Isabel was thirty-one at the time of the coup. President Salvador Allende was her father's cousin. She was an ambitious young journalist, writing humor articles for Chile's first feminist magazine. She had met Neruda personally, at his home in Isla Negra, and his suggestion that she write novels rather than articles, as she had a penchant for exaggeration, would one day prove prophetic in her life. When the poet died, Isabel braved the streets for his funeral, though she stayed close to the tall Swedish ambassador, believing if the soldiers were to start firing, they wouldn't shoot at leading diplomats. She stayed in Chile for another year, but freedom of the press ended the day of the coup. Despite all her efforts, in the new climate of censorship, her attempts to work as a journalist were futile. And eventually the dictatorship became too threatening: "The circle of repression was closing around my neck."

An opportunity arose where she and her family could flee safely into exile if they acted quickly. They did. Isabel could not take much with her. As she recounted to us, she took with her a small bag with dirt from her garden and just two books. One was Eduardo Galeano's *Open Veins of Latin America,* a history of the centuries of exploitation by foreign governments and multinational corporations that left countries like Chile so vulnerable to the horrors that had just occurred. The other was an old edition of Neruda's poetry, a volume of his odes—not his typical love poems or political verses, but rather these utterly unique, beautiful, and brilliant poems that convey the social utility in everyday objects. "With Neruda's words," she has said, "I was taking a part of Chile with me, for Neruda was such a part of the country"—and such a part of the political dreams that had just been destroyed.

She took the soil of the country she loved, and she took Neruda.

Earth and poetry: two powerful, enduring sources of identity, inspiration, and hope, as seen in Isabel's suitcase, as well as in the continued endurance of Neruda's work. Earth and poetry: grounding, yet fertile.

Crystallized in Isabel's story is a sentiment that runs through Neruda's work and legacy: that poetry serves a purpose. Poetry is not only for the elite or for intellectuals, but for everyone—from the people in the market to Justice Minister Sergio Insunza and Isabel Allende, from Verónica studying feminist literature while working at Neruda's house to that grief-stricken man with missing teeth, tearfully calling out *"¡Presente!"* Neruda's life is nothing less than a testimony to poetry's power to be so much more than pretty words on paper; it is an essential part of the fabric of human existence, one that mirrors culture and plays a role in shaping it. Yes, it evokes emotions, but it can also shift social consciousness, sparking both individual and collective change.

★

I am finishing the writing of this biography just at the end of the first hundred days of Trump's presidency. Ever since his election, "resistance" has become the operative word in our new political reality, including for poets: on April 21, 2017, for example, the *New York Times* featured an article—on the front page, the first time the art form had been featured there in decades—titled "American Poets, Refusing to Go Gentle, Rage Against the Right." What does one of the most iconic and important resistance poets of the past century give us now, both in the utility of his actual words and in his example? How can his words stir people to action, or provide space for reflection, even healing? What might this poet's tumultuous and influential journey through political upheavals, uprisings, and exiles offer us as we continue to shape the next chapter in our own cultural story? In our current, unprecedented times, what is the relationship between literature and politics, between artists and social change? My hope is that this book will offer readers an opportunity to explore these questions alongside the vivid details of Neruda's life and work, which find renewed purpose and relevance every day.

CHAPTER ONE

TO TEMUCO

A man was born
among many
who were born.
He lived among many men
who also lived,
and that alone is not so much history
as earth itself,
the central part of Chile, where
vines unwind their green tresses,
grapes feed on the light,
wine is born from the feet of the people.
    —"The Birth"

Pablo Neruda's father, José del Carmen Reyes Morales, grew up in the late nineteenth century on a farm outside the town of Parral, two hundred miles south of the Chilean capital, Santiago. The landscape there was picturesque: well-irrigated orchards, flower farms, and vineyards stretching across fields at the foothills of the Andes. In this long, thin country, never more than 110 miles wide, Parral sat in the shadows of the mountains some sixty miles east of the Pacific Ocean. The area was short on rainfall but long on hot, dry sun, unusual for the fertile Central Valley. So all that beauty didn't count for much when it came to feeding an extensive family from land that lacked good access to water, which was the case for José del Carmen's parents on their hacienda-type farm. They had named it Belén, the Spanish spelling for Bethlehem.

José del Carmen had inherited his mother's striking blue eyes, but she, Natalia Morales, barely had time to look into them; she died shortly after giving birth, in 1872. He was left to his imposing father, José Angel Reyes Hermosilla. The authoritarian patriarch wanted to instill the fear of God in José del Carmen and the thirteen more children he'd have with a new wife. His booming voice was frightening. He rarely cracked a smile.

Their property had a little more than 250 cultivable acres, which was rather modest compared with other haciendas of that type in Chile at the time. They struggled to eke out a subsistence living farming its soil. The family had little money to invest in crops and animals, or in rich rootstock for vines. With fourteen children, there were simply too many mouths to feed on a farm that didn't have enough hands of age to successfully work the stubborn soil.

As José del Carmen grew, so did his frustration with farm life. Despite all their acreage, he felt claustrophobic with so many siblings and an overbearing father. In 1891, at the age of twenty, he took his dreams for a different life to the burgeoning salty port town of Talcahuano, 150 miles by steam train to the southwest, where a great public works project had just begun. It was a whole new world, and a stark contrast to the confines of repressive religion back at Belén. Here the future was open and his responsibilities were few, and shortly after he arrived he joined a team building dry docks down by the wharf.

José del Carmen's home in Talcahuano was a cold pension run by a Catalan widow with three young daughters. The pension was only a few blocks from the port, and it housed a few other dockworkers who had come from the provinces for work. José del Carmen's sense of possibilities was sparked further by the social interaction within this urban society in an international port—so different from the enclosed, rigid world of Belén and the small, provincial Parral. Meanwhile, he was witnessing a historic period of transformation in southern Chile, with the import of machinery to exploit the land and turn it into an agricultural region, and the export of some of the first products.

His time at the port moved him further away from the influence of his father, allowing him to find his own identity and instilling in him a nonreligious, rational outlook on life. At the pension down by the docks, he came to know the owner's teenage daughter Aurelia Tolrá, who would become a close confidante. As José wandered between Parral and Talcahuano in search of work, the pension would be an important location to which he'd return often.

★

Charles Sumner Mason was born in Portland, Maine, in 1829. He would come to play a fundamental role in Neruda's life. While many Europeans immigrated to Chile, especially the south, very few North Americans did. Though his exact motivation for traveling to South America isn't certain, after a supposed stop in Peru, he came to Parral in 1866 at the age of thirty-seven. He arrived with another American (Henry "Enrique" St. Clair), who was enticed by Chile's rich mineral deposits. At one point the two would formally set up a business venture to explore silver deposits in the hills.

Mason would soon involve himself in many matters in Parral. By 1891, when José del Carmen was starting his adventures and coming and going from the farm outside Parral, Mason marked his twenty-fifth anniversary of living in Chile. He was a well-settled family man, husband to Micaela Candia, the daughter of an important Parral businessman. He was the father of eight. He was so widely respected during his life that people would often ask him to arbitrate disputes. He even represented José del Carmen's father in a lawsuit in 1889.

Eventually Mason headed to the newly founded pioneer town of Temuco, some two hundred miles to the south. There, he and his family could expand on what they had established in Parral, taking advantage of all the opportunities that the exciting frontier could offer. Temuco and its surroundings were Chile's "Far West," as Neruda would describe it in his memoirs. Just two decades earlier, the indigenous Mapuche people of the region—an area of ancient forests, snowcapped volcanoes, and breathtaking volcanic lakes—had finally submitted to the Chilean military. The Mapuche's three-century-long resistance, dating back to 1535, had constituted the longest continual war of indigenous people defending their native lands and rights against colonial encroachment in the history of the Americas. With the Mapuche defeated, the town of Temuco was formed in 1881 next to a Chilean fort, where the peace accords were finally signed that same year.

The virgin territory now being relatively safe for settlement and exploitation, Mason, among others, wanted to be sure to get in on the opportunity. In 1888, shortly after his father-in-law died (there's no record of the date of his mother-in-law's death), Mason began to act in earnest toward his new ambition. That year he placed a small ad in a regional newspaper offering his services as a bookkeeper. Through this work, he was able to provide critical help to all the entrepreneurs setting up new businesses in the south who had little formal business experience. With his skill and integrity, he earned trust and respect among the key players in Temuco. Combining this with his ease at establishing personal relationships, he quickly ascended to the top of the city's social and political scene.

Mason was still going back and forth between Temuco and Parral when his seventh child, Laura, was born in 1889. By 1891, the whole family had moved to Temuco for good. Nearly all of his wife Micaela's seven siblings moved there with him.

The national railroad arrived in Temuco in 1893, a seminal event in a burgeoning frontier town. In 1897, Mason built the Hotel de la Estación right in front of the station—fifty meters from the ticket window, to be exact—on land he had managed to obtain at a significant discount or perhaps even through a free land grant. It advertised itself with the English title THE PASSENGER'S HOME, and noted SE HABLA INGLÉS, ALEMÁN Y FRANCÉS. The hotel allowed Mason to further strengthen his social and political influence in up-and-coming Temuco, as government functionaries, businessmen, important members of the state railroad company, political candidates on their campaigns, and tourists all would either stay or at least eat at the hotel. It also became a meeting place for local politicians.

Not long after he turned twenty-one, José del Carmen traveled by train to Temuco. Its population had just passed ten thousand, with some twenty-five thousand people pioneering the countryside around it. The town was dominated by a recent wave of mostly Swiss German immigrants. The Chilean government wanted to set up an agricultural economy, particularly to help meet the growing food demands of miners in the arid north, where the mining industry was booming. In order to attract people who had enough capital and capability to exploit the virgin frontier, the Chilean government enacted the Law of Selective Immigration—"selective" as in only upstanding European citizens looking for new opportunities and of a sufficient socioeconomic level who would be able to colonize and enrich the area. Toward this end, these immigrants were granted swaths of land, tax exemptions, and other incentives. They would form a broad society, founding new towns and cities and dominating local politics, while establishing ties between the region and the national political scene as never before. They would dominate the social and class structure of the region for decades.

José del Carmen would also witness the domestic migration of adventurous Chileans of all economic stripes to the incipient town, people looking for the excitement of uncharted territory and the opportunities that come from expansion, as Mason and his relatives had done. The remainder of the population was mostly former soldiers who settled down after the war against the Mapuche and the War of the Pacific, hoping to find jobs, and people teetering on the edge of tenement life in Santiago who had enough to head south to try their luck. These latter groups offered a striking contrast to the European colonials and other more "dignified" citizenry. The recently incarcerated, the desperate and jobless, and the former soldiers often drank excessively, which frequently led to fist and knife fights. Newcomers dealt with a variety of new challenges, including the need to fortify themselves against the cold of seemingly endless winters drenched in rain, now being so close to the southern tip of South America.

Temuco was colorful and studded with diverse characters both within its borders and outside of town, such as the *huasos*, the gentlemen of the countryside who would ride their white horses into town for supplies and drink. These men were extremely skilled horsemen, often landowners, and they distinguished themselves with their short, colorful ponchos decorated in broad primary-color stripes and their flat-brimmed black straw hats rimmed with ribbon, called *chupallas*. Even the stirrups of their saddles were carved by hand. They had maintained this artisan craft as they migrated from the north over the previous decades.

When José del Carmen first stepped off the train onto the muddy platform, he saw a station crowded with women wearing floor-length dresses and ornate bonnets escorted by men in suits, the local gentry. There were also people in simpler clothes, those in laborers' threads, and a few vendors in well-worn sombreros selling bread and cheese for those about to take the train north.

José would have been amazed to see another kind of people: the Mapuche. These indigenous people were so low on the social scale that they weren't considered part of the town's population and were forbidden to live within its confines. The women wore beautiful, distinctive silver jewelry over their wide black ponchos; the men wore ponchos of many colors. The majority of Chilean citizens, including those in power, treated the Mapuche as outcasts.

Because they were not allowed to live within the boundaries of Temuco itself, the Mapuche came into town from the fields and forests to trade and left at night, the men on horseback, the women on foot. Most of the Mapuche couldn't read Spanish, and their native language, Mapudungun, had no written form. Thus, as José walked the streets that first day, he kept looking up at the enormous representations of objects hanging outside stores to convey what goods they sold: "an enormous cooking pot, a gigantic padlock, an Antarctic spoon," as Neruda would later recount in his memoirs. "Farther along the street, shoe stores, a colossal boot."

Mason knew of José del Carmen from José's father, but José del Carmen was just one of his friend's fourteen children. José may have spent a few nights in Temuco, but he wouldn't have been able to just stay for free at the hotel, nor would Mason have had a job waiting for him.

So José continued his travels back and forth between Talcahuano and Parral, scraping together work as he found it. It was an austere but free life. But then, on a visit to Temuco in 1895, José had an intimate encounter with Trinidad, Mason's sister-in-law. He had a wanderer's charm, and the twenty-six-year-old Trinidad, whose long, angular face was more interesting than beautiful, had little to entertain her in Mason's frontier compound.

It was a short-lived passion, but it had lifelong ramifications for both. This affair would be one of several clandestine relationships conducted by people with some relation to Charles Mason. Neruda's childhood was undeniably influenced by these unspoken histories and their repercussions.

Trinidad knew the consequences of taking a lover. Four years earlier, the first of several secret scandals had occurred. Trinidad had a son, Orlando, from an earlier affair with Rudecindo Ortega, a twenty-two-year-old seasonal farm laborer whom Mason had invited down from Parral to help him get things started in Temuco. Micaela and Mason, the boy's aunt and uncle, were irate at Trinidad's indiscretion and quickly adopted Orlando. The circumstances of Orlando's birth were never mentioned outside Mason's household.

Rudecindo Ortega never lost the grace of his employer, as Mason had been so fond of him before the scandal and apparently found him less culpable than Trinidad. Later, Mason would even allow Ortega to marry his youngest daughter, Telésfora.

Trinidad and José del Carmen hid their affair from Mason and Micaela, but Trinidad became pregnant, forcing the secret to light. Mason and Micaela were furious that she had been so reckless under their roof; each adopted baby came with the risk of social disgrace, and they searched for the right punishment for the young woman who, it seemed, could not accept that she was supposed to remain chaste until marriage. Trinidad revealed who the father was, and word was sent to him. José del Carmen was in Belén or Talcahuano when he found out, and he replied quickly, unmoved and refusing to marry Trinidad. Unlike with her first child, Micaela and Mason made it clear that under no circumstances would they see or raise this baby.

Far along in her pregnancy, Trinidad returned to Parral to give birth, most likely because there she would have the support of her local relatives and friends. She would be kept from the public scrutiny of Temuco, and, as she had left Parral many years before, none of the townsfolk would know that she was not married.

In 1897, Trinidad gave birth to her second son, Rodolfo, but Micaela and Mason (supposedly) prohibited her from keeping him. The baby was handed off to a midwife in the village of Coipúe, along the banks of the silver Toltén River. It was far enough away from Temuco and close enough to Parral so that it was easy for the Masons to keep tabs on him and send the midwife support.

For the next five years, José del Carmen drifted between working at the dry docks of Talcahuano, visiting Temuco to see if there were any good railroad jobs available, and occasionally returning home to Belén to rest and perhaps pick up a little work around Parral. Then, in the town he had left nearly a decade ago, he found the love of his life. Her name was Rosa Neftalí Basoalto Opazo. She was a schoolteacher who wrote poetry. In 1899 she had moved to Parral from the open countryside to be closer to a doctor, as she had struggled with pulmonary problems since childhood. José del Carmen saw her for the first time shortly after she had arrived and approached her. Rosa Neftalí may not have been beautiful, but there was something in the modest grandeur of her face that radiated a simple sweetness. Though not stern in nature, her expression did convey an unmistakable seriousness. She was the kind of woman who carried herself with intent and purpose, perhaps in part because she doubted how long her health would allow her to live an active life.

For José, who had grown rough from his life of hard work and constant movement, Rosa's sweet, practical demeanor was enchanting. He was in love, but he still wasn't sure he was ready to start a family, so for the following four years José didn't stay in Parral. Each time he visited, however, he would see Rosa as often as he could. In 1903, he finally asked her to be his wife. They were married in a simple ceremony on October 4, 1903. José del Carmen was thirty-two; Rosa was thirty. They moved into their own home—a long, narrow adobe house with curved tiles ornamenting the roof—near the town limits of Parral. About nine months later, at close to nine o'clock on the night of July 12, 1904, Rosa gave birth to a son, Ricardo Eliecer Neftalí Reyes Basoalto, who would one day be known throughout the world as Pablo Neruda.

Two months and two days after the boy was born, Rosa died from tuberculosis. José, alone with his infant son, retreated into himself. His own mother had died shortly after his own birth, and this repeated misfortune threw José into a deep despair. He returned to Belén, and his stepmother took charge of the new baby. She searched for a wet nurse among the local campesinas and put Neftalí in the care of María Luisa Leiva. On September 26, twelve days after his mother's death, Neftalí was baptized in Parral's San José Church. The anguished José set off again, now not just to wander, but having to provide for someone besides himself. In contrast with the ambivalence he felt toward his firstborn from his affair with Trinidad, he felt a paternal closeness and responsibility to his new, legitimately born son.

Hearing of cattle work on the other side of the Andes, he headed to Argentina, but returned six months later, in March 1905, penniless. With Neftalí still in his parents' care, José took the train to Talcahuano, which continued to boom with port business fourteen years after he had first arrived there. He worked the docks as he had previously, following the rhythm of the big boats that came to and went from the harbor, laden with machinery that would help to cultivate the newly settled southern countryside or timber and grains for export.

José stayed at the same pension where he had first lived in Talcahuano. Back then, the owner's daughter, Aurelia Tolrá, had been a budding teenage beauty. Now she was a young woman with a watchful face, framed by long black hair and punctuated by curving cheekbones. She and José quickly became close friends, and he spoke openly with her of his sadness and uncertainty. José was thirty-three, mourning his wife, and still working as a laborer as he had for fourteen years. He was hardened by experience, and now he had a goal to work toward: the train trips back to Parral to visit his son. On weeknights at the pension, José would often uncork a bottle of wine and talk with Aurelia, the sounds of the port whistling and clanging a few blocks away. One night, seeing his present and future in disarray, José asked Aurelia what he should do with his life. "Go back to Trinidad," she told him. "She's the mother of your firstborn."

Nearly a decade had passed since Trinidad Candia Malverde had given birth to Rodolfo. José had kept in touch with her to some extent, keeping tabs on his oldest son, who was being raised in the woods by someone outside the family. He may have been harboring the hope that Mason would help him out if he reunited with Trinidad and also with his being the widowed son of Mason's old friend José Angel back in Parral. Mason certainly had the connections and influence to get him a job on the railroad or something similar. Plus, José might have believed he'd find the comfort he sought in Trinidad; he would bring Neftalí from Belén and Rodolfo back from the forest to complete their family.

With a plan set at last, José returned to Temuco. He had a long, sincere discussion with Trinidad, now homey and sweet. He expressed his intentions to Mason and received his blessing to marry her. At 7:30 on the evening of November 11, 1905, the two were wed in the home of Mason and Micaela.

The newlyweds made their home next to the Mason-Candia homestead. It belonged to Trinidad, who had received the plot fifteen years prior as a free land grant, quite likely with Mason pulling a few strings. While Mason must have been supportive of José del Carmen, as he was making an honest woman of Mason's sister-in-law, he wasn't nearly as involved with him as José del Carmen would have hoped: Mason didn't pull any strings for him; there was no new job.

Still, Neftalí, now two years old, was brought down from Parral to Temuco as planned. From the beginning, and for the rest of her life, Trinidad treated him with nurturing warmth. In a portrait of him taken at a Temuco studio in 1906, standing with his hand resting on a cushioned chair, wearing his white cambric baby dress and black boots, Neftalí looks poised and angelic. His cheeks are full, and he seems to have the composure of someone very sure of himself.

A few months after settling himself and Neftalí into their new Temuco home, José's next move was to reclaim Rodolfo, or rather to claim him for the first time. José had never felt any obligation or affection toward his son until now, when he made it his mission to assemble the family together for the good of all. José del Carmen set off on the path of the Toltén River, to Coipúe. The small village where the boy was being raised was a wild place, with a smattering of houses along the riverbank, and surrounded by a thick oak forest and a few small, isolated farms. José, who had come dressed in a formal jacket and vest, must have seemed impossibly foreign to the barefoot eight-year-old. The only resemblance between the two was their blue eyes. When the only mother he had known told "Rodolfito" to greet his father, the barefoot, semiwild son drew back from the stranger. It would take a series of visits for the boy to become accustomed to his father and agree to join him in Temuco, and even then a sense of unease remained between them.

José del Carmen and Trinidad settled into their wood-plank house that was in a continual state of construction. José began to realize that he was just a minor player in Mason's huge, active world. There would be little special treatment from his wife's brother-in-law, forty-three years his senior. Meanwhile, he continued to mourn for Rosa Neftalí profoundly and often returned to her grave in Parral. On those trips he would occasionally visit Aurelia Tolrá in Talcahuano. As a man who was accustomed to the freedom of solitude, he quickly found himself straining against the confines of family life. It had been hardly a year since Aurelia had counseled him to return to Trinidad, but now José found himself longing for her instead.

He had known the attractive Aurelia for years now, during which time they had developed a special, intimate friendship. Now in his mid-thirties, José looked and acted more dignified than he had in the past. He had taken on the familial responsibility that Aurelia herself had urged him to. With his solid body, handsome face, and hypnotic, rare blue eyes, José was a charmer. Thus on one of his visits to Talcahuano, after one of their long conversations at the pension over a bottle or two of wine, José del Carmen's maturity made a deep impression on Aurelia. Their mutual attraction was undeniable. Aurelia was now a grown woman, with an endearing charm and a stern yet striking beauty. With a full moon shining on the water in the port below and everyone else in the pension asleep, the two joined each other in bed. Near the end of that year, 1906, she became pregnant with his child.

To avoid a scandal, Aurelia left the pension to her sisters and moved to San Rosendo, a railroad village at the juncture of two lines. There she gave birth to Neftalí's half sister, Laura, on August 2, 1907. Aurelia set up a new pension house in San Rosendo and courageously cared for Laura alone, though José del Carmen would often take the train up from Temuco to visit. Trinidad had no idea about the relationship or the birth.

Aurelia was devoted to her daughter and in love with José. But despite her strong character, evidenced by the self-sufficiency and discipline that it took to run a pension while raising a child by herself, Aurelia's situation became increasingly difficult to manage. Her Catholic faith— she always wore a crucifix around her neck—gave her strength, but it was also the source of great anxiety. How could she, in good conscience, continue to see a married man who was also the father of her illegitimate child? After two anguished, isolated years in San Rosendo, Aurelia, convinced she was unfit to raise a daughter alone, told José it was time for him to make a choice: either come back with her to Talcahuano and claim his daughter, or, if he had to stay with the family he established in Temuco, take Laura to his home with Trinidad. Aurelia would even have her daughter drop her last name, Tolrá, and take up Trinidad's; she would be known as Laura Reyes Candia.

From Temuco, José del Carmen answered her call. He brought his son Neftalí, now seven or eight, along with him to pick up his new half sister. A hard rain fell as they took the train to San Rosendo, where Aurelia was waiting for them. It was the first time she and Neftalí had ever seen each other. His clothes were soaked; Aurelia helped him change and dried his clothes, then she put him and Laura to sleep in the same bed. Bewildered from this strange trip, Neftalí fell asleep wondering who in the world this skinny girl was, in bed beside him, and why he was there. An unshakable bond soon formed between the two of them.

The next morning, he awoke to see Laura's bags were already packed. Aurelia's eyes swelled with tears as José del Carmen took her daughter away with him. Laura too was struck by the sudden separation.

The father and the two half siblings rode the rickety steam train back to Temuco, seeing the endless forests and pastures passing outside the window. José reflected on his life and the change to come. It was the last time he would visit Aurelia.

When the train arrived in Temuco and the three travelers reached the wooden house, José finally confessed to his affair with Aurelia. Trinidad was outwardly neither angry nor hurt. Instead it seemed as if she had known about it all along, or at least suspected it. Trinidad had a certain equanimity, the source of which couldn't be traced, but her inner nature was sweet, diligent, with a campesina's sense of humor. Her compassion was limitless. Without a word, though perhaps with some resignation, she agreed to take care of Laurita. In their Temuco house, Trinidad thus would raise three children: her own Rodolfo, Rosa's Neftalí, and Aurelia's Laura. This family, with its complex origins and unique dynamics, would shape Neftalí's formative years; its secrets and transgressions would mark the future poet for his entire life.

CHAPTER TWO

WHERE THE RAIN WAS BORN

I first saw trees, ravines
decorated with flowers of wild beauty,
humid territory, forests that flame,
and winter behind the world, flooded.
My childhood is wet shoes, broken trunks
fallen in the dense forest, devoured by vines
and beetles, sweet days above the oats,
and the golden beard of my father leaving
towards the majesty of the railways.
  —"The Frontier (1904)"

Trinidad and her stepson had a close, confiding relationship. Trinidad not only nurtured Neftalí affectionately, but protected him as much as she could from the flares of his father's increasingly short-fused temper, much as José's stepmother had done for him as a child. In his memoirs, Neruda calls Doña Trinidad his "guardian angel," and notes tenderly that her "gentle shadow watched over my childhood."

She governed the Reyes family home, which was always in a state of flux. The interior patio of the house was a familiar, essential setting in Neftalí's social development growing up. The extended Mason family, as well as neighbors and friends, constantly interacted on the patio and, as Neruda later said, shared everything: "tools or books, birthday cakes, rubbing ointments, umbrellas, tables and chairs."

Gloomy moss and various vines grew freely on the patio and up the two-story walls. Overflowing potted red geraniums sat atop a five-foot-tall armoire on one side of the patio, and a young palm tree was situated in the center. There were other fruit trees by the fence, and a patch of grass where cilantro, mint, and some medicinal herbs grew. There was a chicken coop. The gate dangling from the fence was rendered irrelevant by the constant circulation of people as the Ortegas, the Masons, and other relatives, friends, and neighbors passed through.

Many of the Mason clan, in which Charles served as paterfamilias, all lived on the same block with interconnecting backyards. José del Carmen's house adjoined Charles Mason's larger and much nicer home. The Masons by then had a very full house with six children (two had died in infancy), plus the adopted Orlando, whose parentage was still a secret. Another adjoining home was that of Rudecindo Ortega, who had fathered Orlando and later married Mason's youngest daughter, Telésfora. In 1899, Telésfora gave birth to Rudecindo Ortega Mason. José del Carmen's half brother Abdías also lived nearby. He had married Mason and Micaela's daughter Glasfira, and they had six children who grew up alongside Neftalí.

Like the families that inhabited them, these houses were always being augmented. Consequently, they seemed perpetually under construction. Incomplete staircases led to floors that were equally unfinished, and a conglomeration of objects populated the compound: saddles lined up by the entrances, large wine barrels sat in corners, and ponchos, sombreros, horseshoes, and horse spurs lined the walls. This atmosphere of constant evolution helped to ignite Neftalí's prodigious creativity. Decades later, Neruda would fill his own homes with unique collections of objects, from ships' figureheads, glass bottles, and countless seashells to Asian masks and Russian dolls.

There was some pragmatism behind José del Carmen's efforts and design. A purposeful path cut through the rectangular property, directly linking the street to the patio. Other than the particularities of the objects all around, the walls lacked any creative, artistic sensibility.

The second floor was built quickly out of the need to expand when all the children came together at once. Its construction was thrifty and basic, yet the windows were large.

Neftalí's room looked out over the patio, where he'd get lost in the rain raking the leaves of the avocado tree or the coal-colored smoke disappearing into the sky as it rose from the pipe jutting out from the kitchen's wood-burning stove. Near the window stood the little desk on which he would start to write his first poems in his arithmetic book.

Right across from the house was a no-name bar, just some shack with hitching posts outside where Mapuche would exchange whatever money they made from whatever wares they managed to sell that day for *aguardiente*—firewater—in Chile made from grapes like a harsh grappa. Not all Mapuche were drunks, but Neftalí saw how Temuco disenfranchised all of them. The injustices they faced made many Mapuche despondent. Witnessing their condition instilled in Neftalí a lifelong empathy for the oppressed. Their downtrodden state mirrored the mental state that was now descending upon him.

Neftalí seemed to embody a natural melancholy, which would slowly begin to slip into serious sorrow as he progressed through childhood. His figure cut thin, a reflection of his weak constitution. His demanding father inflicted a hefty emotional toll, and the relentless rain of Temuco's long winters made him restless.

The railroad ran through his childhood, as constant as the rain. Charles Mason's foresight into the new railroad's potential for bringing development to the country around Temuco proved accurate. Business at his hotel was steady, as people continued to migrate south. José, now integrated into Mason's family, must have felt he had proven himself to be a steady, mature, and reliable head of household. Whether he got it from pressing Mason or not, José finally got a job with the railroad company.

It was a line of work that allowed José to travel as he labored, satisfying his desire to be on the move. He was quickly promoted to be the conductor in charge of a ballast train, which spread crushed rocks, river stone, and sand to form the foundational bed between the rails, all the while making repairs along the tracks. It was unforgiving work, especially during the winter months, when José had to make sure that the wooden ties wouldn't be washed away by the torrents of rain that often lasted for hours. José del Carmen had been a reluctant farmer and a mediocre dockworker, but he was good with the trains, which he had ridden so frequently in their nascent development. He soon found that he was a railroader at heart.

By the time he was five years old, young Neftalí would often join his father on the rails, one of the very few places the two could bond. As they steamed through the virgin forests of the south, crossing over emerald rivers flowing down from the Andes and passing by small frontier outposts, impoverished Mapuche villages, freshly cleared pastures, and a variety of volcanoes, the natural world as a wealth of untamed possibilities unfolded before the child's eyes.

A lifetime later, Neruda opened his memoirs with this impression, highlighting its significance as the origin of his poetic path: "Below the volcanoes, beside the snowcapped mountains, among the great lakes, the fragrant, the silent, the tangled Chilean forest . . . I have come out of that earth, that mud, that silence, to roam, to go singing throughout the world." The fundamental curiosity that would augur the creation of his poetry stemmed from these early journeys.

"The essential Neruda was a human being," his translator Alastair Reid once said. "In his eyes he never forgot that he was born naked into a world he didn't understand, into a world of wonder."

His father's train and the laborers aboard it fascinated Neftalí. First was the locomotive engine, then a car or two for the workers, rough from the life they had lived before coming here. They usually wore heavy, thick raincoats provided by the state railroad company. Often their gaits and their hardened faces, many of which were lined, some with scars, were all that distinguished one from the other. Then there was the caboose in which José del Carmen lived during long trips along the rails, which could last a week or more. Finally, an open flatbed car at the rear carried the crushed stones and all the workers' tools and equipment.

Neftalí would spend hours watching the men shovel the ballast off the end of the train and then work it into the tracks. The stones improved drainage and their sharp edges gave the workers a grip to anchor the rickety wooden ties to—which, in turn, kept the rails in place. The harsh rains wreaked havoc on the railbeds. The rapidly expanding rail network in the south was key to the area's growth (and, increasingly, the economy of the entire country). José del Carmen and his crew bore the responsibility to keep it functional, and they were committed to making sure their assigned tracks were constantly maintained, no matter the weather or amount of labor involved.

Once the car was empty, they would travel to Boroa, in the wild heart of the frontier, or other quarries in whatever corner of the wild forests, where workers would labor on the "terrestrial core," the enormous rocks, breaking them down for ballast and loading the train with the finished product. They could be there for over a week. Once they had shoveled the car full of stones, they were on the move again, straightening the rails, spreading the ballast, resetting the iron spikes that held the steel to the wooden rail ties, and repairing the tracks where needed.

It was all fantastic, if not bizarre, Neruda wrote later in a 1962 autobiographical article for a Brazilian newspaper. All the action of the train and the rain and the forest and the workers was taking place "in the middle of green and red glass lanterns and lampposts, flags and signals and storm blankets, the smell of oil and rusted iron, and with my father, small sovereign with a blond beard and blue eyes, like the captain of a boat, commanding his crew, commanding the voyage."

Immersed in these smells and colors, Neftalí witnessed the social aspects of the train as well. He observed the workers shyly, in awe. They seemed like giants to him, muscular men from the tenements of Santiago, from the fields of the Central Valley, from prison, from the recent War of the Pacific. They were children of the elements, often arriving in the south dressed in rags, their faces battered, as Neruda would later lyricize, by the rain or the sand, their foreheads divided by rough scars. The camaraderie and solidarity that Neftalí saw among them, out on the tracks or around the dining room table telling long, unlikely tales, thrilled him.

Most of the crew had come to Temuco looking for something better than their difficult pasts, and now they toiled for subsistence wages.

Neftalí was the son of their boss, and the young boy's particular frailty contrasted sharply with their brute strength. These disparities widened the aperture of his impressionable mind, affecting how he would interpret class and society for the rest of his life, creating the foundation of his sociopolitical convictions. This would become central to his poetry and his politics, identifying with and championing the working class.

> My father with the dark dawn
> of the earth, towards what lost archipelagos
> did he slide in his howling trains?
> . . . the grave train crossing the extended winter
> over the earth, like a proud caterpillar.
> Suddenly the doors trembled.
>   It's my father.
>
> . . . .
>
> The centurions of the road surround him:
> rail-workers wrapped in their wet blankets,
> the steam and rain with them covered
> the house, the dining room was filled with hoarse
> tales, glasses were poured,
> and even me, of the beings, like a separated
> barrier, where the sorrows lived,
> and the anguishes and scowling scars,
> the men without money,
> the mineral claw of poverty,
> arrived . . .
>   —"La Casa"

By the time he was ten years old, when the train would stop somewhere in the middle of the virgin forests, Neftalí would go out and explore, feeling an instant connection to nature. The birds and the beetles fascinated him. Partridge eggs were wonders; he wrote later that it "was miraculous to find them in the nooks and crannies of the forest floor, greasy, dark, gleaming, gunmetal gray." The insects' "perfection" amazed him too. Neftalí spent many of his childhood days in the "vertical world" of the forests, "a nation of birds, a mass of leaves," surrounding Temuco. Rotten logs were full of treasures: fungi, insects, and red parasite plants. As he reflected in a poem he wrote later in life, Neruda felt quite literally "immersed" in the natural world:

> I lived with the spiders,
> I was damp from the forest,
> the beetles knew me
> and the tri-colored bees,
> I slept with the partridges
> immersed in the mint.
>   —"Where Can Guillermina Be?"*

Neftalí's explorations piqued the workers' curiosity; some became interested in his discoveries. Many of the crew took to Neftalí, whose physical characteristics were so completely different from their own, his frailty perhaps inspiring something in them. José del Carmen referred to one of the men, named Monge, as "the most dangerous knife fighter." A scar from a knife slash ran down the dark skin of Monge's cheek. A white smile complemented the scar, mischievous yet charming and welcoming. It brightened his toughness. Monge, more than the others, would slip off into the forest to use his strength and size to get to places that Neftalí could not. He brought him back incredible treasures—magnificent mushrooms, moon-colored beetles, brilliant flowers, green snails, birds' eggs from crevices—all delivered from his gigantic, worn hands to the smooth palms of the child. These materials would become elemental nutrients of Neftalí's creative experience.

Much later, Neruda would write: "Along endless beaches or thicketed hills, a communication began between my spirit—that is, my poetry—and the loneliest land in the world. This was many years ago, but that communication, that revelation, that pact with the wilderness, has continued to exist throughout my life."

The treasure for Neftalí, though, wasn't just the natural objects

---

*   Complete poem in Appendix I.

Monge would bring him, but the fact that the worker did so. It was a gesture not done to please his boss, for José del Carmen wouldn't stand for one of his employees feeding his son's imagination at the expense of work. Later, Monge's death would have a profound impact on Neftalí. Though he did not witness Monge's fall from a moving train off a cliff, José told Neftalí that the man's remains were "just a sack of bones." The toughest man Neftalí knew had been brought down by the dangers inherent in his world.

Neftalí learned to measure the distance between his father and the workers. He realized that he effectively came from a family of modest means, and that his father had once been a vagabond looking for work in the Andes or on the docks. They had a cook, a local lady who would help prepare meals, easing the workload of Doña Trinidad in her five-person household—a service a railroad conductor could afford. José del Carmen consistently pushed—or tried to steer—his sons toward a dignified vocation, life, social class. Secondary school wasn't mandatory and only a small number of children attended after finishing grammar school around age twelve. Most young men went to trade schools or to work instead, but there was no question that José del Carmen's sons would attend and study with discipline.

Neftalí was puzzled by his father's desire to have a good piano for the house, something grand to come home to after traveling on the train for days. It didn't seem in line with his personality; he punished Rodolfo for pursuing a musical path. Perhaps more than anything, it had a dignifying presence in the house. It was a status symbol.

The Mason clan and José del Carmen's brothers, who visited often from Parral, influenced Neftalí with their traditions, which by turns could be flamboyant, ritualistic, and macho. Big parties and dinners were regularly held at the Masons', where the blue-eyed *Norteamericano* with flowing white hair, "looking like Emerson," presided over the bountiful table: turkeys stuffed with celery, grilled lamb, and, for dessert, floating islands—*leche nevada*, literally "snowcapped milk"— where white poached meringues float in a creamy custard, decorated with mint leaves. Red wine flowed through the night. An immense Chilean flag with its red and white bands and lone white star set in a block of blue hung behind Mason, to which he had pinned a tiny U.S. flag as well.

One evening when Neftalí was a young adolescent, just as the night train clanged into the wooden station a block away, his uncles called him out to the patio. Neftalí knew what was about to take place: the great ritual slaughtering of the lamb. His uncles and other family friends were all gathered around, strumming guitars and playing with knives underneath a tree, their singing interrupted only by the blowing of the train whistle and the gulps of crude wine. Neftalí was a skinny, innocent-faced presence at these events, with his boyish wave of dark hair swept back from a gentle widow's peak. He dressed, as he often did in these years, formally in black, already with what he considered to be his necessary "poet's tie," a thin, tightly knotted black accent on his narrow frame. He was dressed, as he'd reflect later, "like a man in mourning, mourning for nobody in particular, for the rain, for the universal pain."

His uncles slit open the throat of the quivering lamb. The blood fell into a basin filled with potent spices. They motioned to Neftalí to come closer and lifted the goblet of hot blood to his lips, gunfire and songs going off. Neruda later explained that he felt as agonized as the lamb itself, but he wanted to become a centaur, like the other men, as barbarian as they seemed just then. So, pale and indecisive, he overcame his fear and drank with them. By drinking the blood, he began his passage to manhood.

From his first verses, blood was a symbol in his poetry, a symbol of the poetry itself. At one of his greatest peaks, in the poem "The Heights of Macchu Picchu," imploring the Incan slaves to rise up, the final two lines of the poem's twelve sweeping cantos read:

Come to my veins and my mouth.

Speak through my words and my blood.

★

Neftalí from the outset had a close relationship with his half sister, Laura, three years his junior. As they grew older, she would be one of his closest friends, confidantes, and supporters. The bond between them, born in the room the night before her mother gave her away, remained constant throughout their lives. He would always be protective and tremendously tender toward her. Laura was sweet and reserved, simple yet complicated, devoted to her parents and even more so to Neftalí.

Rodolfo, on the other hand, was always off on his own and would never have a close relationship with either of his siblings. Now a teenager, he found it hard to integrate himself within the confining structure of the family after his life in the forest and was mostly silent, except for his singing. Whereas Neftalí would soon seek refuge in his poetry, Rodolfo found his in song. He had an extraordinary voice, but he sang alone behind the closed door of his tiny room.

All three siblings sought Trinidad's protection to shield them from their father's impatience. José del Carmen had a stern attitude toward his children, perhaps inherited from his own father's example. Over Neftalí's childhood and into his adolescence, José del Carmen had coarsened. Though they weren't as poor as Neruda would later often portray them as having been, José's wages from the state-run railroad never led to economic prosperity and comfort, and there was little hope for advancement. But despite these frustrations and his possible yearnings, he never abandoned his responsibilities again. He was never known to have another affair.

Neruda called southern Chile the land "where the rain was born." During the winter, it rains copiously for days on end, a constant lyric. That melancholic music accompanied Neftalí's childhood. The Temuco of his memories was of mud streets, worn-out shoes, cold, rain, and a general lack of happiness that hovered over the town.

School for Neftalí was similarly gloomy. It was in a vast house with dilapidated classrooms. Neftalí was always the last in line to enter the school or exit class for the playground. He was not particularly tall for his age, and he was noticeably thin. He wore his sadness like the formal uniform he chose to wear: a long wool-blend dress jacket, matching pants, and boots. Already at this age he had the countenance of a much older person, one who had seen more than he should have, one who understood that life was not just play, but was full of hardship as well.

Compounding his melancholy was the fact that Neftalí's constitution was fragile. He was constantly ill with something—a cold, the chills, the flu. His classmate Juvencio Valle was one of his first and only true friends at the *liceo,* the secondary school. Neftalí had drifted to the margins, away from the other kids. But the introspective and thoughtful Juvencio was drawn to Neftalí's "mysterious inner halo," and they bonded. The first time Neftalí invited him over to his house, Trinidad gave them coffee, but she served Neftalí's with milk but not Juvencio's, leaving it just black. This made Neftalí uncomfortable. "He wanted to give me his cup as a gift, in deference to me, being the guest. But when Doña Trinidad saw, she opposed: 'No, don't change the cups. I don't have any more milk right now so at this moment the coffee with milk is for Neftalí, because he's weak.'"

Because he was so sickly, Neftalí often stayed home from school. When he was confined to his bed, he'd ask Laura to stick her head out the window and tell him everything that was going on in the street—*everything,* even the most insignificant detail. "There goes a little Indian selling ponchos," she'd report from the window, or "There are four little kids playing on the other side of the street." Neftalí would keep insisting on more detail. He was obsessed with observing the world around him.

Neftalí was fascinated by the school's dark basement, which felt like a tomb to him. He would often go down alone, sometimes lighting a candle, absorbed in the damp odor of his hidden world. Juvencio Valle, who shared his curiosity, would often join him. Valle, who would become a significant poet himself, would later muse that already in these childhood years he could sense that Neftalí was truly a unique individual, with "an imperceptible vibration, an air that was his alone and made him different. To the ordinary observer it was a nonexistent aura, but to me it was powerfully effective and real."

While the other kids ran around, jumped, and shouted in a group,

Juvencio and Neftalí would spend their days in the forest together, exploring, observing the world's little things—a leaf, an insect, a path in the woods—trails of exploration forged through curiosity. The other kids didn't want much to do with them. They took "refuge in [their] own particular territory, that marvelous universe of dreams," where the two were always the "undisputed champions."

Sometimes they would walk down to the cold Cautín River that ran through town near the school and dip their feet into its water, then lose themselves simply watching the rippling current from the bank. Often they did not get back to class on time.

Neruda saw those early days as a period of discovery. He began his lifelong friendship with Valle and explored the natural world, but also poetry found him. As Neruda versed in *Memorial de Isla Negra:*

> And it was at that age . . . poetry arrived
> in search of me. I don't know, I don't know where
> it came from, from winter or a river.
> I don't know how or when,
> no, they were not voices, they were not
> words, nor silence,
> but from a street it called me,
> from the branches of night,
> abruptly from the others,
> among raging fires
> or returning alone,
> there it was, without a face,
> and it touched me.
>   —"Poetry"

Two weeks before he turned eleven, some unknown thought, emotion, or experience sparked the kindling that had been developing in him, and Neftalí wrote his "first, faint line" of poetry of which there is a record. Upon writing this original poem, according to his memoirs, he was overcome by emotion, racked by "a kind of anguish and sadness," emotions that were already familiar to him. The language on the page was revelatory and strange, "different from every-day language."

When he was finished, he took the poem to his father. Trembling from the experience, he held the paper out to the man, who took it absently, then returned it, saying, "Where did you copy this from?" Then he resumed a conversation with Trinidad.

That poem appears to be hardly a poem at all. It is a dedication to his stepmother, written in a fine, cursive hand on the back of a postcard of an alpine lake surrounded by snowy trees:

> From a landscape of aureate
> > regions
> I chose
> to give you, dear mamá,
> this humble postcard. *Neftalí*

It is more than just a note. Armed with the basic tools of prosody he was learning in his progressive education, supplemented by his own reading, he had composed a structured, if basic, poem. The nuanced versecraft, with internal rhymes and rhythms and thematic words, is remarkable.[*] In this humble, tender gift to his stepmother,

---

[*]   The original Spanish of Neftalí's earliest recorded poem, on the postcard to his stepmother, is indeed a poem of true complexity. Besides the themes mentioned in the text, when one reads the original Spanish, there is a sublime rhythm of internal rhymes:

> *De un paisaje de áureas*
> > *regiones,*
> *yo escogí*
> *para darle querida mamá*
> *esta humilde postal.* Neftalí

The internal rhyme runs around the *j* in front of the short *e* vowels in *paisaje*, pronounced *paee-sah-heh*, a similar inflect with the combination of *gi*, which sounds like *hee: regiones* and *escogi*. Then there are the *ee* sounds (as the *i* in Spanish sounds like English's long *e*), sometimes accented, sometimes milder: *regiones, escogí, querida, humilde, Neftali*. As well, there are the last two lines' short *ahs: para, dar, querida, mamá, esta, postal, Neftali*.

he has reversed the cold Alpine scene to create a warm, golden place of nature. Neftalí is looking out from himself, the "I"—"I chose"— into this space. Creating such a perspective in prosody at the age of ten, he demonstrates the beginnings of a cosmic vision. A poet was emerging.

CHAPTER THREE

AWKWARD ADOLESCENCE

I was fourteen
and proudly bleak,
thin, taut and brooding,
funereal and formal.
—"Where Can Guillermina Be?"

Neftalí's adolescence was marked by isolation, unrequited love, sadness, and frequent illness, exacerbated by the confines of his harsh father's home and the hard weather and poverty of the frontier. Poetry became a way to express his frustrations and angst, as is clear in the aptly titled poem "Desperation," which he wrote in his notebook as a teenager. The language may not flow as beautifully as in his mature work, but the young man's yearning is palpable, as is his inherent sense that, as poet-observer, vision is vital:

They have closed my eyes. My God!
and I don't know the sorrow where I am.
. . . sorrow has cruelly nailed my soul.
Where do I look? My eyes! My eyes!
Who suffocates my voice in my mouth?
I'm alone, Lord, I'm alone
and I don't feel the beat of my heart.

Who calls for me in the shadows? Who feels
my howls of rage and pain?
Impotence squeezes me. They don't come!
But black desperation comes.
Who do I call, Lord, who do I call?
It's useless to call You!
I smash my fingers in vain,
still I know You haven't come to my soul.
. . . And the wind carries my voices,
and the abyss brings me obscurity!

The narrator seems lost at the bottom of the world, so frustrated as he struggles to use his pen to write himself out of the darkness. Neftalí, however, would encounter several key adults who would support him throughout his teens. He developed relationships with mentors in Temuco and the surrounding area who introduced him to influential literature and convinced him of his potential as a poet. Furthermore, his mentors also encouraged the social awareness and political stance that would mark so much of his verse.

Additionally, during this time Neftalí fell deeply in love, more than once. Poetry became more than just an outlet to help diffuse his predisposition toward gloominess and to help ease the confusion in his mind by ordering it on paper; poetry now became an expression of his exuberant romantic and sexual feelings, a way to soothe his struggling heart. Neftalí's experiences of rejection during these years would shape the development of his character, and he would find a cutting-edge poetic expression to communicate the aching lyricism of unfulfilled love. It was here, in Temuco, that the seeds for Neruda's monumental *Veinte poemas de amor y una canción desesperada (Twenty Love Poems and a Desperate Song)* were planted.

In the summers of his adolescence, after the cold muck of winter had passed, Neftalí would often wander Temuco's dirt streets alone, lost in thought. He was often oblivious to the sources of inspiration around him: the stunning snowcapped Llaima volcano off in the distance or the stimulating wild blue Cautín River running through town. His gaze was turned inward and only occasionally would something strike his eye, like the life-sized brown wooden horse in the saddlery shop. He'd stop and look at it through the window: it was precious, he'd write later, stoic in its stillness, seemingly "proud of its shiny skin and first-rate tack." When he grew bold enough, Neftalí would even go inside, stretch out his little hand, and touch its soft snout.

This timid boy's bond with this wooden horse was quite remarkable, as his detour to touch it on his way to school became an almost daily ritual. His innocent imagination drew him to this horse, which, un-like strong, fast, flesh-and-blood horses—working or wild—was "too precious to be exposed to the winds and rains of the world's southern reaches." This sheltered horse was always there for him, always quiet and still just like him, but also "proud" in its wooden stature.

One of Neftalí's favorite places in Temuco was Orlando Mason's rickety wooden office. Neftalí thought of Orlando as *un tío,* an uncle, though they were in fact stepbrothers (as Orlando was Trinidad's son, adopted by the Masons). Orlando was now in his early twenties. A noted poet and journalist, he spent his days running a radically progressive newspaper in Temuco. Orlando was a boisterous anarchist, which was a relatively common ideology then in Chile. His small paper, *La Ma-ñana* (The Morning), lashed out against injustices, such as the plight of the middle class, the continued oppression of the indigenous Mapuche (in particular the plunder of their land by crooked lawyers), and the abusive power of the police.

Orlando was young and unruly, but he had enormous talent, drive, and intellect. Beyond the newspaper, he was gaining prestige as an ora-tor and poet, being invited to social events and even Temuco's theater to speak with his dramatic flair. Neftalí would watch, mesmerized. Or-lando's passionate idealism struck a chord in Neftalí. He was more than just an uncle: he was a hero and a romantic, revolutionary inspiration. As Neruda wrote later in life, "Orlando Mason protested against every-thing. It was beautiful to see that paper, among such brutal and violent people, defending the just against the cruel, the weak against the ar-rogant, the overbearing."

What Orlando was protesting, defending, and reacting to on and off the pages of his newspaper—and in turn inspiring Neftalí to recognize—were issues that many Chileans were concerned about at the time. In Temuco, specifically, Orlando and others were disturbed by the horrific treatment of coal miners, many of them Mapuche, toiling in the small town of Lota, in tunnels that extended under the Pacific Ocean. Their workday extended from six A.M. to six P.M., with a twenty-four-hour shift on the weekends. Workers were often paid in tokens that could be used only in the company store.

The barbaric conditions seemed even more outrageous in contrast to the immense wealth flaunted by the owners of the mine, the Cousiño family, one of the country's richest. Matías Cousiño, the patriarch, had started his enterprise with silver mines in the north, and now he was making a fortune off of the Lota mines and other exploitations he extended through the region. The great steamships that came across the Strait of Magellan would stop off in Lota to refill their coal. Cousiño's family designed an elaborate, refined French-style park, more than thirty acres, filled with Greek statues and flora from all over the world.

In contrast to the park was the tragedy of child labor: pale kids between eight and sixteen years old, with emaciated faces and bodies, worked for twelve hours a day. The smallest were put to work in the mines as lamp holders and porters, often huddled in a corner in the darkness, inhaling poisonous fumes.

The groundbreaking social activist writer Baldomero Lillo, whose father was a coal miner in Lota, wrote stunningly stark firsthand accounts of these conditions. His classic short-story collection *Sub-Terra* shows the social condition in stirring prose:

> With a glance, the penetrating eyes of the foreman judged the feeble body of the boy. His slender appendages and his childlike lack of awareness . . . gave him an unfavorable impression . . . He didn't consider him apt to work in the mine. His father begged, arguing that among six people in his family, only one was working. Finally, the foreman placed him at a sluice gate, replacing the cart driver, squeezed in

a tunnel . . . The mine never let go of those who chose it, and like new chain links that replaced the old and withered ones in a never-ending chain, there below, children replaced their parents.

The book was published in 1904, the year Neftalí was born. Years later, little progress had been made, and Orlando worked tirelessly to spread the same message. He wrote in defense of those beaten down by the wrenching poverty of Temuco and the surrounding area. Poverty beat those souls down just as the rain beat down as they walked through muddy streets, holes in their shoes.

Influenced by Orlando and others, Neftalí's social conscience grew apace. Tío Orlando was showing him how to express his concerns through his writing, not just poetry, but prose as well. Orlando inspired him with stories about his hero, Luis Emilio Recabarren, who had organized the miners in the north and founded the Socialist Workers Party of Chile in 1912. Orlando's perspective on the written word would help define Neruda's sense of social obligation as a poet.

The powerful root of these convictions can be traced in part to the fact that Neftalí's political and philosophical thought as an adolescent emerged during an especially vital, transformational period in the history of Chilean thought in the 1910s. It was a time that incubated a new generation of philosophical and political ideas (including anarchism, socialism, and, slowly, Marxism). This important segment of Chilean history was sparked by Chile's 1910 centennial as an independent republic. The event led to a significant amount of soul-searching—the country was not in a celebratory mood. Chileans had achieved a hundred years of independence, but the economy was in a dismal state, and society was rife with disease, poverty, crime, and squalor, leading to mushrooming tenements in Santiago and labor unrest from pent-up demands not being met by a rather aristocratic-led government. These were the years of the "social question," the pre-paralysis of the political system, with many Chileans asking, "Who are we?"

Alejandro Venegas, a thirty-nine-year-old schoolteacher who traveled the length of Chile in search of an answer to this question, perhaps put it the most passionately in his book, *Sinceridad: Chile íntimo en 1910* (Sincerity: Intimate Chile in 1910):

> A deplorable neglect continues toward the people: we have armies, warships, fortresses, cities and ports, theaters and racetracks, clubs, hotels, buildings and public promenades, monuments and (we've got the most vain of them all) opulent magnates, lords of true dominions, who live in stately, sumptuous palaces . . . but not far from the theaters, gardens, and lordly residences live the people, that is to say nine-tenths of the population of Chile, plunged in the most atrocious economic, physiological, and moral poverty, and degenerating rapidly through excessive work, poor diet, lack of hygiene, extreme ignorance, and the most vulgar vices.

There had been a remarkable rise of liberalism in Chile during the previous century, its strength and breadth relatively unique to Chile among its neighbors. It resulted in a deepening debate regarding the role of church and state, within politics and society in general and within the educational system most acutely. Such was the stage on which positivism appeared, a philosophy that aimed to secularize society. It was a primarily anticlerical philosophy that emphasized human thought instead of religious thought; the word "positive" denoted knowledge obtained from the observable world. Championed by intellectuals such as José Victorino Lastarria, positivism espoused that man should seek happiness within the finite boundaries of the known world.

The first fusion of Neftalí's literary ability with sociopolitical thinking notably tapped directly into this special, fluid period of new thought in Chile. On the very day he turned thirteen, perhaps on the back patio of their adjoining houses before his *fiesta de cumpleaños*, an excited Neftalí, with faint mustache hair barely starting to appear on his skinny face, handed Orlando an op-ed piece he had just written.

Orlando, dark skinned and short, read it over quickly, then more slowly. With a brimming smile, he told his nephew that, yes, he would publish it in *La Mañana*. It was the best possible gift for Neftalí, dispelling at least for a moment the habitual unhappiness that haunted him.

The work impressed Orlando with its idealistic and stylistic merits, and also because the thoughts came from someone so young. Entitled "Entusiasmo y perseverancia" ("Enthusiasm and Perseverance"), it began:

> These two are the factors that contribute principally to the rising and enhancement of the people.
>
> How many times do beneficial ideas and work fall to the ground, victims of little enthusiasm and perseverance, which put into practice would bring forward an abundance of goods for the countries that would adopt them!

He goes on to write:

> There are philosophies in this present century that just try to spread enthusiasm and perseverance, and their books are true, sincere, and eloquent, which if read by all, especially by the working class, would bring great benefits to humanity.

Neftalí was reflecting on the realities he saw around him, from the railroad workers to those struggling in the shanties on the outskirts of town, from the mistreatment of the Mapuche he witnessed every day to the injustices he'd heard about in Lota. Furthermore, despite his youth, some aspects of Neftalí's piece relate directly to the crisis of conscience sparked by the centennial, vocalizing in his personal manner the fact that there was something seriously wrong with the country and that the new philosophies were more humane. In broad, abstract terms, he was laying down a solid foundation, both for the reader and for himself as a writer and thinker.

Neftalí was directly in tune with this vanguard liberal vision that would continue to develop intellectually and politically in a manner unique to Chile. Despite periods of harsh repression of those who subscribed to it, this tendency would continue to flourish, taking on different forms at different stages, until it crested with the democratic election of the Marxist-Socialist president Salvador Allende in 1970, a victory in which the poet from Temuco played a public part.

★

In his early teenage years, there was another social struggle that captured Neftalí's attention: girls.

Upon first sight, Amelia Alviso provoked an acute anxiety within Neftalí that would not ameliorate. The two met when he was about thirteen. A friend who knew her later in life described her as "a very beautiful woman, dark skinned, with . . . black eyes . . . a charming personality. Sexy. She played the piano very well, and she was very artistic." In Temuco, her parents owned an electric plant that lit up the city.

Amelia's parents were in fact one of the wealthiest couples in town, and they forbade their daughter to spend time alone with Neftalí because his father was a lowly conductor on the state railroad. Crushed, Neftalí took refuge in poetry. The paper was a mirror in which he could now see, decipher, and share his emotions and thoughts. He soon discovered poetry's nurturing, healing power.

Neftalí displayed a remarkable skill in working with the traditional forms of meter and rhyme, cutting his teeth by pushing the envelope of what could be composed within a chosen construction. In the *liceo*, he would have been hearing the amorous verses of Garcilaso de la Vega, who in the early sixteenth century brought the innovations of the Italian Renaissance into the world of Spanish poetry. Among his most important innovations was extending the lines of stanzas from eight syllables or fewer to eleven syllables, allowing for a notable increase in flexibility.

Neftalí was also reading the "historical cadences" of Francisco de Quevedo's baroque sonnets, their rapid rhythms often in epigrams. As an avid reader both in and out of class, Neftalí was seduced by these traditional metered forms. He used them first as a primary exercise in his composition; the impulse to do so sprang forth spontaneously. Other than some side instruction from his various mentors, he was writing of his own volition, without a formal creative writing class. He worked within the patterns just as a painter might start off doing simple exercises, even a paint by numbers. It was a way to practice and sharpen his skills and to gain confidence by finding success within the established, sometimes quite complicated, forms that he would push the boundaries of later.

His disciplined and constant practice during these teenage years produced some very successful poems and proved to be essential training for *Twenty Love Poems,* which he would start writing about five years later. Part of that book's power derives from Neruda's deft use of a diverse set of forms and poetic techniques to intensify the expressions of emotion, squeezing them into the set structure, the confinement pressurizing the sentiments, increasing their potency. And the frequent use of rhythmic repetition within these poems helped pop the emotion off the page, off the reader's tongue. As the poet Robert Hass has written, form is "the way the poem embodies the energy of the gesture of its making."[*]

As René de Costa argues in his book *The Poetry of Pablo Neruda,* there was an additional, purposeful effect caused by using these disciplined styles. The form of successive symmetrical stanzas, often quartets, falls down the page, giving the reader the impression that it wasn't just a quickly written piece, but rather a measured, classically composed poem, a true literary construction. The sentimental value of a poem—or an entire book—is then elevated, even glorified, by association with the classics. Neftalí definitely wanted to do everything he could to add glory to his verse.

---

[*]   In these early works, Neruda often employs the alexandrine, a classic form found in both French and Spanish poetry (among others) for centuries. It is composed of five symmetrical quartets of flexible fourteen-syllable lines that rhyme alternately. Neruda also built upon recent trends with the form. This is most notable in Poem XV, from *Twenty Love Poems,* and its famous lyrics: "I like it when you're quiet . . ." Allowing himself the flexibility to break out of the traditional patterns of where the stresses fell in each line, he could dynamically accentuate specific words, intensifying their impact. As author René de Costa highlights, in Poem XV, for instance, Neruda actually targets stress on phrases that hit on the poem's themes of absence, distance, and the inability to communicate with one's lover. Sometimes he compounds the effect by repeating a line's resonant pattern a little later, adding just a slight variation. The second line of Poem XV reads: *"y me oyes desde lejos, y* mi voz no te toca" (and you hear me from afar, and *my voice does not touch you*). Then two quatrains later he writes, *"Y me oyes desde lejos, y* mi voz no te alcanza" (And you hear me from afar, and *my voice does not reach you*).

During Neftalí's transformative thirteenth year, he started craving something beyond just the urgent, crucial flight he felt in the basic act of writing. Possibly also as a consequence of Orlando's influence, Neftalí started to feel strongly—if not desperately—that if others weren't reading his poetry, it lacked purpose. He became preoccupied with his poetry being shared and promoted, primarily so that both he and his work could be accepted, approved, and validated. Despite his shyness, Neftalí was so certain that poetry was the one positive thing that he had inside of him that he summoned up the courage to submit his work for publication. Encouraged by Orlando, he sent one of his poems to the popular Santiago magazine *Correvuela* (Run-Fly). The magazine was considered by contemporary readers to be somewhat frivolous and vulgar compared with other publications, but it did have a section dedicated to highlighting young poets from the provinces.

When its reply came, Neftalí ran to the offices of *La Mañana,* yelling, "Tío, Tío, they're going to publish my poem! They're going to publish my poem!"

On October 30, 1918, just a few months after his fourteenth birthday, his poem "My Eyes" was published:

> I wish my eyes were hard and cold,
> that they wounded deep inside the heart,
> that they didn't express anything from my empty dreams
>   or hope, or illusion.
>
> Forever indecipherable to the sacrilegious,
> deep blue and smooth with tranquil sapphire
> and that they didn't glimpse human pain
>   or the joy of being alive.
>
> But these eyes of mine are naive and sad:
> not how I want them nor how they should be.
> It's that my heart dresses these eyes of mine,
>   and makes them see its pain.

Like many of his poems in these years, "My Eyes" is concerned with finding escape from his personal desolation. He is aware, importantly, that his perception of the world isn't unfiltered reality. His heart that pumps his blood, his emotions, and his sensitivity add a human element to the vision, which causes the eyes not just to perceive their surroundings but also to cause these scorching sensations.

Within the next two years, before graduating from the *liceo*, he would publish nearly thirty poems: fifteen more in *Corre-vuela*, as well as pieces in *Selva austral* (Austral Forest), Temuco's own literary journal; the *Cultural Review* of Valdivia, the biggest city to the south; and *Siembra* (Sowing) in Valparaíso, the port city seventy-five miles northwest of Santiago. Most of the journals that took his work were of rather radical tendencies.

Neftalí received these successes modestly, but with great satisfaction. His early achievements further drove his determination to be a poet, not only because he wanted to rise above his physical and social awkwardness, but also because he already felt he was on a path to hold the *oficio*, or vocation, of poet for all his life.

CHAPTER FOUR

THE YOUNG POET

I come from a dark region, from a land separated from
all others by the steep contours of its geography. I was
the most forlorn of poets and my poetry was provin-
cial, oppressed and rainy.
—"Toward the Splendid City," Nobel lecture, 1971

Chile has a long history of reverence for poetry. From the early
sixteenth-century epic poetry of Alonso de Ercilla to the strong
roots of oral poetics in indigenous Mapuche culture, Chile has
earned its reputation as a "nation of poets," where poetry is not only
enjoyed by the elite, but also recited by campesinos, factory workers,
miners, and ordinary people around their campfires or kitchen tables.
This unique environment nurtured Neftalí's passion for poetry from
the beginning.[*] Even though he was extremely timid, he entered po-
etry competitions throughout the region. Tiny towns in the middle of
nowhere would have such contests as part of their fairs. In 1919, at the
age of fifteen, Neftalí traveled north some 250 miles by train, probably
alone, to read a poem in the tiny, dusty town of Cauquenes. He took
third prize for best poem at the Maule Flower Games.

The following year, his poem "Salutation to the Queen" won first
place at Temuco's Fiesta de la Primavera. Teresa León Bettiens won the

_____

[*] See Appendix II for more on this history.

title of Fiesta Queen. She looked like a Byzantine angel with her large black eyes and curly black hair, complemented by an intelligence apparent in her intriguing speech that immediately attracted Neftalí's attention. The young queen and her salutation's scribe were each eccentric in her or his own way. They soon fell in love.

Teresa's family vacationed in Puerto Saavedra, a primitive, misty town on the Pacific coast with just about fifteen houses braced by high cliffs. It was approximately fifty miles west of Temuco. As it happened, that year Neftalí's family would be summering in Puerto Saavedra too. On the first day of vacation, Neftalí's father blew his whistle at four in the morning to wake everybody up. Preparation was prodigious work, as Neruda would describe in his memoirs, with each family member scurrying around the house gathering what was needed, a candle in hand to see in the predawn darkness, the flames flickering with each burst of wind in the drafty house. The family stayed in a house owned by a friend of José del Carmen's, Señor Pacheco. The house was large but didn't have enough beds for all five of them, so they carried their own mattresses with them on the train, rolled into giant balls.

The train took them as far as the little town of Imperial, where they took a small steamship down the Imperial River. When Neftalí finally stood in front of the ocean for the first time, it held him in thrall, with its immense waves and its colossal roar that seemed, to him, the heartbeat of the universe itself: "There's nothing more stirring to a fifteen-year-old heart than navigating down a wide and unknown river, among mountainous banks, on the mysterious path to the sea." The ocean would take an important place in both Neruda's heart and his poetry; it would serve as a principal vehicle in many of his metaphors. One of the first times we see this is in "The Desperate Song," which ends *Twenty Love Poems*, written at a time when he had lost all hope for Teresa during his university days:

> You swallowed everything, like distance.
> Like the sea, like time. In you everything sank!

Later in the same poem he reminisces on their first days:

It was the happy hour of assault and the kiss.
The hour of the spell that blazed like a lighthouse.

Up until then, Neruda's poetic expression of nature had focused on
the forest, which, in contrast to the constant motion of the churning
ocean, was steadfast and immovable, a soliloquy of ancient trees and
rotted trunks. It could make Neftalí feel as if nothing else existed ex-
cept for himself and the orange-throated chucao bird's coos, nothing
"but that cry of all the wilds combined / like that call of all the wet
trees." The only movement was the occasional rush of leaves from a
flutter of wind or the flow of a waterfall.

Conversely, in the sea, Neftalí discovered a masculine model, a vor-
tex of aggression and accelerated action, a paternal figure, as the noted
Neruda scholar Hernán Loyola has suggested.

By the time he was fifteen or sixteen, Neftalí's restlessness and sense
of self, tightly confined by Temuco's smallness, provoked him to write
lines like these:

> This lead-colored city wraps me in its
> disease, makes me suffer in my solitude
> giving me the bitter sip
> of remaining in life with neither love nor kindness
> . . . gray and monotonous city beneath my disappointments,
> beneath the turbulent rain of my first tears,
> in the desolation of the first path.
>
> . . . City which by the song of the blue spring
> is hostile and tired like any day
> with its men whose stunted spirits have left me
> to bleed out all of my hopeful tears.
> —"Hate"

The escape to Puerto Saavedra and his relationship with Teresa
León Bettiens thus brought Neftalí a kind of liberation. "Puerto Saa-

vedra had the smell of honeysuckle and the ocean wave," Neruda rem-
inisced in an article he wrote for the magazine *Ercilla* on the occasion
of his sixty-fifth birthday. "Behind every house there were gardens
with arbors that delivered the aroma of the solitude of those transpar-
ent days." Teresa wore flamenco dresses as they talked and walked
and flirted on the shore and in the woods, Neftalí almost always with
his black cape and wide-brimmed black sombrero (inspired by his
uncle Orlando's dress, that of the poet). Once, Teresa dressed up as
an indigenous Mapuche woman—scandalous. Like the piano-playing,
heartbreaking Amelia Alviso, Teresa was artistic. She'd break out in
song, recite poetry; she was spontaneous and intellectual. In Teresa,
Neftalí had finally found requited love. He called her "Marisol," as in
mar (sea) and *sol* (sun).

Like Amelia, Teresa came from a family of a higher social rank than
Neftalí's; her parents were well respected among Temuco's upper crust.
The young lovers were doomed from the start, because Teresa's par-
ents didn't want their daughter to have anything to do with him. They
called him *un jote,* a vulture, because of his buzzard-like look with his
hat and cape, the flaps, the wings. And if he continued his sole pursuit
of being a poet, "they'd both starve to death." Teresa's parents ordered
her not to see Neftalí anymore.

This time, despite his pain, Neftalí showed a new level of resolution
that he would continue to demonstrate in years to come. The teenag-
ers continued to see each other, if not on moonlit beaches, then by the
exchange of poems when apart.

Neftalí made other new friends that summer. The Parodi family had
made their money by using their sawmill to process the virgin forests
around Puerto Saavedra into timber. Their home, in which they lived
year-round, was a hub for social gatherings among the rich and influ-
ential families who came to summer in the increasingly fashionable
seaside community. No one needed an invitation; the town was small
enough that everyone knew when the gatherings would be. Sometimes
they would read poetry or have intellectual discussions about society
or art. Neftalí would show up and take in the flow of ideas as he sat off
in a corner.

He was surprised and struck by the "black and sudden eyes" of the Parodis' youngest daughter, Maria. They exchanged little pieces of paper, folded up so as to disappear in the hand. Neruda would write what would be the nineteenth poem in *Twenty Love Poems* for her.

> Girl *morena* and agile, the sun that grows the fruits
> that plumps the grains, that twists the seaweed
> made your joyous body, your luminous eyes
> and your mouth that has the smile of water.
>
> A black and eager sun is braided into the strands
> of your black mane, when you stretch your arms.
> You play with the sun like with a little creek
> and it leaves two dark pools in your eyes.

In Puerto Saavedra, Neftalí also began a great friendship with Augusto Winter, widely considered to be Chile's first ecological poet. His venerability was accented by his beautiful beard, which cascaded like the stacks of bookshelves along the walls of his library, a tiny room in his house crammed with books from floor to ceiling. Winter had the best library Neruda ever knew. He so loved literature and wanted to share his passion with others that he simply lent his books to everyone. On his first visit, Neftalí was immediately drawn to books by Jules Verne and the Italian adventure and science fiction author Emilio Salgari. There was a sawdust-burning stove in the center of the room, and he would settle himself next to it as if he were "condemned to read in the three summer months all the books that were written through the long winters of the world." "Have you read this one yet?" Winter would ask, passing him one of Pierre Alexis Ponson du Terrail's nineteenth-century adventure novels, starring the intrepid hero Rocambole. Or perhaps Winter would press on him Vargas Vila's latest novel, *Ante los bárbaros: Los Estados Unidos y la guerra* (In the Face of the Savages: The United States and the War), in which the radical Colombian writer denounced the United States for its imperialism in the Spanish-American War. Whatever book Neftalí was reading, this library by the sea was a sanctuary where he found new ideas and myths, which would inflame his imagination and richly inform his writing.

Neftalí spent plenty of time exploring the local wilderness in Puerto Saavedra, including the sublime green shores of the expansive Lake Budi, often stippled with swans (as long as no one was hunting them). He might sit on the hillside above Señor Pacheco's second house, where he was staying, and watch the light blue ocean pulse its universal heartbeat for hours. From that slope, he could pivot from watching the waves hit the beach to an overhead view of the river meeting the sea, as he first did upon his arrival, miniature boats like toys in the distance. He rode his horse through rolling fields, sometimes daring into the limits of the Mapuche lands. Or he headed down to town, near Winter's library, and walked to where the river met the sea, sand dunes sloped smooth, small to huge. Riding his horse on the beach, he could lose himself in the backdrop of deep green pines, which complemented the colors of sand and sea. Neruda once noted in an interview that in his twenties, when home alone composing, he couldn't write without seriously thinking of the sound of Temuco's rain and the waves crashing on the sand of Puerto Saavedra.

At the end of summer, Neftalí would leave Winter and his library, the relaxed time spent with Teresa in the open air, and all the other wonders of the coast. He dreaded the start of another anxiety-provoking school year. But in 1920 Neftalí found a fascinating new teacher who would become another essential mentor for him, opening up new literary worlds while inspiring his writing and intellect. The poet Gabriela Mistral had left her teaching post in Punta Arenas, at the southern tip of Patagonia, and moved to Temuco to head its girls' *liceo*. Twenty-five years later she would become the first Latin American to win the Nobel Prize in Literature. When she arrived in Temuco, at the age of thirty-one, she was already one of the country's best-known poets. Mistral's "Sonetos de la muerte" ("Sonnets of Death") had won first place in the most important national poetry competition in Santiago in 1914. Neftalí was thrilled that a poet of her stature had come to Temuco.

Shortly after her arrival in town, he dressed himself in a white collared shirt, black vest, and black cloth pants, and knocked on the door to her house, hoping that she would read some of his poetry. A young artist, just nineteen, answered the door. She was Laura Rodig Pizarro, who had met Mistral in Punta Arenas and became her assistant, while Rodig herself developed into a nationally acclaimed activist painter and sculptor. Neftalí wasn't the only one in Temuco who had called on Mistral; many other writers, intellectuals, and pseudo-intellectuals wanted the attention and blessing of such an accomplished poet living in the isolation of the frontier. Rodig told Neftalí that Mistral wasn't in, so Neftalí waited for three hours, saying nothing. Finally, saddened, he walked back home, poetry in hand. But he returned the next day. Rodig informed him that Mistral had a terrible headache and could not see him. Impressed by his persistence despite his obvious shyness, however, she told him to leave his notebook and she'd give it to Mistral. He could come back later that day to see if her headache had passed and they could meet.

When he returned that afternoon, it was Mistral who opened the door. She was tall and wore a long dress. He bowed to her. "I have fixed myself up to receive you," Mistral said. "I was sick, but I began to read your poems and I've gotten better, because I am sure that here there is indeed a true poet. I have never made a statement like that ever before."

The two became lifelong friends. Neftalí often ran to her house in the afternoon after classes were finished for the day. The two would drink tea together next to the wood-burning stove in her modest house. "Here, read this," Mistral would say. She would introduce him to the "terrible vision" of Tolstoy, Dostoyevsky, and Chekhov.

Neftalí's young, colorful French teacher, Ernesto Torrealba, was another important literary influence. A writer and critic himself, he told Neftalí, "If you want to write, don't just read Spanish and follow its rules, because you'll never free yourself of the pedagogy." Instead, he pushed Neftalí to read, among others, Arthur Rimbaud, Charles Baudelaire, and Paul Verlaine; reading French would help him write better Spanish. Like Mistral, Torrealba also promoted the importance of Russian literature and lent him several books by Maksim Gorky.

Neftalí's special skills with language could be seen in the translations from French to Spanish that he was doing in school, which greatly impressed Torrealba, though none of these survives today.

Neftalí and his classmates were inspired by Torrealba's persona as well as his intellectual prowess. He was a flamboyant man for the southern frontier who dreamed of Paris; he dressed in an elegant tie and with suede gaiters over his high boots, and he always used an ornamental cane. Torrealba would eventually make it to Paris, where he'd publish a few daring books, including *Paris sentimental y pecador* (Sinful and Sensual Paris). He died at the age of thirty-five in Santiago from unknown causes. Neruda would dedicate his Nobel Prize in part to him: "my French teacher now up in heaven."

Neftalí first publicly referred to himself as not just *a* poet but *the* poet in a sonnet written on July 30, 1919: "The Poet Who Is Neither Bourgeoisie nor Humble."

> A kid who just turned fifteen,
> who writes verses punctuated by bitterness
> who tasted the salts of disappointment
> when many others know laughter and kindness.
>
> and goes on sadly through life
> (The men haven't discovered that in him exists
> the poet who as a child was not childish.)
>
> and he waits proudly with his pains,
> unknown and alone, for better days
> which he imagines, crazily, are to come.

Notable, along with the date, is the location where it was written: "in Chemistry class." He was known to his classmates to be a lazy student, and he struggled especially with math and science. His obvious disinterest didn't help.

While Neftalí thought poetry would be his salvation, José del Carmen certainly did not. He admonished Neftalí about his writing; José didn't want his child to be a starving artist or bohemian; he wanted him to have a stable middle- or upper-class lifestyle, and unlike his son he was certain that lyrical lines of verse were no source of wealth.

Neftalí's half brother, Rodolfo, also suffered their father's scorn of artistic vocation. As Rodolfo would later tell his grandson, one day the *liceo* called José del Carmen to come to an urgent meeting at the school. Irritated at the disruption, he was surprised when the music teacher came in, beaming. Then Rodolfo entered. The teacher explained that Rodolfo was divinely blessed: he had an extraordinary talent for singing. The teacher insisted that Rodolfo must set forth on a path toward becoming a professional singer. The teacher took a piece of paper from one of his pockets and passed it to José del Carmen: it was a telegram stating that Rodolfo, who had started his life deep in a forest village, had been accepted into the prestigious Conservatorio Nacional de Música de Santiago, with a full scholarship. José del Carmen was quiet, which indicated that the matter would be settled privately at home.

After a few days of silence had passed, Rodolfo timidly approached his father. José del Carmen turned on him, listing Rodolfo's faults as he saw them: idleness, singing, and a lack of common sense. The coronation of this violent explosion was a kick with sharp-pointed shoes that knocked Rodolfo to the floor. José then whipped his son's back with his belt. "Damn slackers, the sons I had to have," Rodolfo later recalled hearing him grunt. "First, one goes around joining anarchists and drunks, and then the other, an overgrown fool, wants to follow the same path."

Neftalí feared that this violence would be wielded against him as well, and it was not long before those fears came true. One day, José del Carmen burst into Neftalí's room and kicked over his shelves of books and writings. He threw them out the window, onto the familial patio below. José then went down and burned it all as Neftalí watched, trembling, the rest of the family staring in astonishment.

Neftalí was crestfallen after the incident, falling further into his gloom, until one day when Laura took him to her room without anyone else noticing. She pulled out a few notebooks she had hidden away, filled with poetry that he had written and asked her to write out legibly. He had forgotten about them. To this date they serve as the only record of many of his childhood poems. This tender gesture permanently sealed the bond between the siblings. She would always be his loyal confidante, perhaps his most loyal, because he knew for certain that she would never betray him, even to their father.

Despite his father's duress, Neftalí was undeterred from expressing his emotion through poetry. On July 12, 1920, his sixteenth birthday, he wrote at least two poems. One was the sonnet "Sensación autobiográfica" ("Autobiographic Sensation"):

> I was born sixteen years ago in a dusty
> town, distant and white which I still don't know,
> and as this is a bit vulgar and naive,
> wandering brother, let's go to my youth.
>
> You are very few things in life. Life
> hasn't given me all I've delivered to her,
> equative and proud I laugh at the wound:
> sorrow is to my soul like two is to three!
>
> Nothing more. Ah! I remember when I was ten
> I drew my path against all the harms
> that could defeat me down that long trail:
>
> to have loved a woman and written
> a book. I haven't succeeded, because the book
> is handwritten and I loved not one, but five or six . . .

Neftalí displays a surprising level of confidence here and also a playfulness in his sorrowful circumstance—even self-deprecation in the recognition of his own innocence. The poem marks a light departure from the largely dark imagery of those years. It also lacks the desperation of "El liceo," the second poem he wrote when he turned sixteen.

"El liceo" is one of the sharpest of his teenage years. It showcases how Neftalí was approaching his creative craft more consciously. Less submerged in his inner world, he is aware of the realities of the outside world, of where and how he fits in it, and thus the travails it will present to him. Here we see him firmly plant his position that poetry can be a profession, not just a diversion. In his critique of the doldrums of Temuco, he clearly starts to set his sights on leaving the provinces.

> ¡El liceo! ¡El liceo! All my poor life
> in a sad cage . . . My lost childhood!
> But it doesn't matter, let's go!, for tomorrow or the next day
> I'll be bourgeois, the same lawyer,
> like any little doctor with glasses, keeping
> the paths closed toward the new moon . . .
> What hell, and in life, like in a magazine,
> a poet has to graduate from dentistry!

About three months later, in October 1920, Ricardo Neftalí Reyes Basoalto began to sign his poems as Pablo Neruda. This was partly to hide the poems from his father as his poetry became more public. It was also partly for the sheer romance of having a pen name. Above all, it was a proclamation that he was no longer just Neftalí Reyes Basoalto, schoolboy, but rather Pablo Neruda, poet.

The origins of the name are debatable. Through most of his life Neruda wouldn't reveal the precise details or would claim that he couldn't remember them exactly. The working theory is that he read a short story by the Czech writer Jan Neruda in a magazine and felt it would throw his father "completely off the scent." In 1969, four years before his death, when Brazilian writer Clarice Lispector asked him in an interview if it did indeed come from the Czech, Neruda responded: "No one until now has been able to figure it out." Some believe it actually came from the dazzling Moravian violinist Wilhelmine Neruda, whose picture appeared in a Chilean magazine in 1920. Pablo, most likely, was for the poet Paul Verlaine.* In a poem written a few months before he

---

* Since Neruda never gave a definitive answer, scholars like Hernán Loyola have speculated the choice could also relate to Dante's *Divina commedia* and Paolo with his star-crossed lover, Francesca. Around the time Neruda came

changed his name, entitled "La chair est triste, hélas!" ("The Flesh Is Sad, Alas!"), he wrote:

> My poor, poor, poisoned, dreadful life!
> When I was thirteen I read Juan Lorrain*
> and then I squeezed the emotion of my wings
> spreading my pain with the verses of Verlaine.†

The poet Pablo Neruda forged onward. In 1920, Neruda and his friends organized an *ateneo literario* in Temuco. In Chile, literary athenaeums were popular societies that held conferences and long debates over the art of words. They had formal rules and regular meetings, but were open to everybody, unlike the exclusive aristocratic literary societies prevalent throughout Chile at the time. Neruda was the obvious choice for president, as he had already become the town's most successful writer of his generation. His classmate and friend Alejandro Serani was the secretary. At first, the meetings in Temuco were tiny, held in members' houses or occasionally at a restaurant. The members weren't wealthy, especially the students. Neruda himself never hosted a meeting: Orlando Mason's newspaper office was too small, and José del Carmen would never have let his son host at his own house.

Neruda began to lead discourses on the importance of the Russian writers, the avant-garde, and what was being written in Santiago. This was a significant breakthrough considering his usual shyness. He was

---

up with his new name, he wrote "Ivresse" (the title being the French word for "exalted intoxication"): "Let the passion of Paolo dance in my body today / and my heart will shake, drunk with a merry dream." At the end of his teenage years, he would write "Paolo" next to "Teresa," his lover's name, in the sand of Puerto Saavedra.

* Lorrain's first name is actually "Jean," not "Juan," as Neruda puts it. He was a prolific French poet, journalist, and novelist, a member of the decadent movement closely in line with Verlaine. He was famously flamboyant, a dandy during the Belle Époque. He died in 1906 at the age of fifty.

† Lost here in translation from the original Spanish, the first and third lines rhyme just like the second and fourth.

beginning to gather the first glimmers of a unique self-assurance that would emerge more and more (though sometimes retreat) in the coming years.

The *ateneo* was increasingly excited by the literary voices of the revolutionary student movement in the capital. Members read about it in the nascent newspaper *Claridad* (Clarity), published by the Federación de Estudiantes de la Universidad de Chile (University of Chile Student Federation, or FECh), which, in October 1920, circulated in Temuco and elsewhere.

The FECh—Latin America's very first student organization—had been founded in 1906. It emerged out of students' desire to better defend their rights and perspectives. *Claridad* took its name from the Clarté movement, started by French intellectuals in 1919, born of a hatred of war and its horrors, which they had just experienced, World War I having ended the year before. Their biweekly journal, *Clarté,* promoted internationalism, pacifism, and political action.

Over time, the "Student" part of the FECh's name lost some of its relevance as artists and writers participated and the group's alliance with labor strengthened. Within the organization, there was a wide variety of ideologies. According to one of the student leaders, FECh was a mix of "radicals, masons, anarchists, vegetarians, liberals, socialists, collectivists, Nietzscheans, and Catholics, among the more well-known strands."

As an alliance representing several movements, FECh was increasingly seen as a threat to the Chilean aristocracy, which still maintained a powerful grip on the country. By 1920, the Chilean oligarchy and the rest of the ruling class were having trouble managing the crisis that was cresting in the wake of a critical economic downturn. Food shortages were becoming more common, especially of staples such as wheat (and therefore bread). The wages of those who still had jobs were not keeping up with widespread inflation. Strikes and protests persisted. Meanwhile, the emerging middle class was entering politics to an unprecedented degree, while at the same time the working class was becoming more directly involved in the formal political process, especially through elections.

Chile's 1920 elections further exacerbated the tense situation. The stranglehold that Chile's conservative upper class had maintained on Congress and the presidency for nearly three straight decades was under serious threat. In that year's presidential election, the liberal Arturo Alessandri barely lost the popular vote to the conservatives' candidate, but won a majority of the electoral college. Congress set up a special Tribunal of Honor to determine the outcome. Liberals were skeptical. In the meantime, Chile's president, the conservative Juan Luis Sanfuentes, suddenly announced that his administration had reason (which it wouldn't make public) to believe that Peru and Bolivia were planning a major attack on Chile in order to reclaim the territory they had lost in the War of the Pacific (1879–1883). He mobilized the army and, with the help of the press and other conservatives, fomented war fever throughout the country. The goal was to distract the public from the election, call into question Alessandri's patriotism, and harness the newly intensified nationalist fervor to quash pockets of popular dissent.

Much of that dissent was coming straight from the student-labor movement. One of its leaders, Juan Gandulfo, was an outstanding orator, an anarchist, and a member of the Industrial Workers of the World. He would be very influential in Neruda's life in the years to come. Gandulfo delivered a dramatic speech from the balcony of the FECh's headquarters, criticizing many of the failed political policies but primarily blasting the government for its warmongering. He laid out a passionate plea for pacifism, demanding the release of more information about the supposed threats and urging people not to partake in the "patriotic" marches and events and to see that the government was using the threat of war to manipulate the public.

In the midst of this economic and political crisis, the oligarchy was perturbed by the threat to the social order posed by the surge of the student movement and its alliance with labor. On the chilly winter night of July 19, 1920, a multitude of "patriotic" young Chileans, many the children of oligarchs—and more than a few wildly drunk on whiskey—descended on the FECh headquarters looking for the "traitor" and communist Juan Gandulfo. One of them vomited on the federation's piano, then wiped his mouth with the corner of a Chilean flag that a fellow young patriot had draped in his hands. They beat up Gandulfo until a few policemen appeared on the scene and escorted him away. No members of the attacking gang were arrested.

In the next two days, anti-FECh propaganda increased. An article in Chile's largest newspaper, *El Mercurio,* criticized the group and actually placed the blame for the assault on Gandulfo's "inflammatory" balcony speech. At the same time, various "respectable persons" had come out calling for the removal of the federation's legal status. The tension built to the point that on July 21, a multitude of conservative youth descended on the FECh headquarters. A police report filed later noted nearly three thousand agitators advancing upon the students and their building. Six members of the police tried to hold them off at the door but were unable to prevent their entry. This time they didn't just vomit on the piano; they destroyed it. They destroyed everything: windows, furniture, a pool table, paintings. They threw out onto the street the entire archive of *Claridad*'s precursor, the journal *Juventud,* and burned it. The FECh's headquarters was in the center of the city on high-traffic streets. Agents from Santiago's version of the FBI, Sección de Seguridad (Security Section), arrived in the midst of the chaos and collected documents and archives as intelligence on the "subversive" students. Yet the police commander wrote in his report that due to the "tumultuous nature of this assault, personnel in my charge were unable to take down the name of any of the assailants." However, they did manage to arrest some of the students, especially their leaders. In fact, after the assault on the FECh headquarters, police and other government officials persecuted so-called subversives for four months in Santiago and Valparaíso. There was no set definition of what a subversive was. According to former student leader Daniel Schweitzer, who was a lawyer during this time, anything "that aspired to give human and social content to the actions of the State or of groups was labeled 'subversive.'"

One of the student leaders, the poet José Domingo Gómez Rojas, was arrested for his involvement with the Industrial Workers of the World in Chile. Under harsh prison conditions, his mental condition deteriorated quickly. After only three months behind bars he was moved to a psychiatric home where he died, officially of meningitis, which the student movement did not necessarily dispute but saw as directly linked to his incarceration and poor treatment.

Gómez Rojas's death was one of the most important events in the further radicalization of students at the University of Chile. It clearly shook Neruda, all the way down in Temuco. He had looked up to Gómez Rojas as an early contemporary example of a commitment to "the poet's duty." As Neruda wrote years later, "Within the national context of a small country, the repercussions of this crime were as profound and far-reaching as [would be] those of Federico García Lorca's assassination" in Spain.

Claridad was born as a direct result of the headquarters' destruction. A group of students rallied around the idea of launching a paper of protest, one that was "aggressive, combative, destined to show the public that the assault wasn't enough to quiet the youth gathered at the Federación," as Raúl Silva Castro, one of the magazine's founders, wrote four decades later. The first issue was published on October 12, 1920, about three months after the attack, and it was so well received by the public that the edition was reprinted twice. *Claridad* would soon become one of the most significant publications of its time, with a total of 140 issues until 1934. It was a vital vehicle of expression for students, young poets, and intellectuals and enjoyed a broad readership.

Rudecindo Ortega Mason, the legitimate son of Charles Mason's daughter Telésfora and Rudecindo Ortega, was the delegate for the FECh in Cautín Province (Temuco was its major town). His role was mainly to relay information from the headquarters in Santiago, keeping the federation in the south current on what was going on in the capital. The local FECh assemblies took place in the Teatro Tepper, the biggest theater in Temuco, which the owners, the Tepper brothers, let the group use free of charge. The group was a significant presence in the quiet social landscape of the region; its gatherings were jubilant cultural soirees in the vein of European salons.

Toward the end of 1920, Ortega had impressed upon some of *Claridad*'s editors the significance of Neruda's work, telling them the poet was still at the Liceo de Temuco but would be coming up to Santiago in the next year or so. They were eager to read his work. At their request

Ortega soon returned with a whole file of Neruda's poems and some press clippings about the prizes he had won.

On January 22, 1921, in the magazine's twelfth issue, *Claridad* published five of Neruda's poems, along with a laudatory introduction, which was written by Raúl Silva Castro. It begins:

> Through these verses, Pablo Neruda reveals himself as a complex figure, whose writing portrays his fantasies marked by essential, ordinary reality.
>
> His youth is a shield for him. Still an adolescent, he knows the anonymous contortions of human pain, he studies in the founts of the most modern thought, lives what he says, and he heralds the most beautiful lyrical harvests.

The poems that the editors chose from Ortega's selection were "Campesina," "Pantheos," "Railroad Roundhouses at Night," "The Words of a Blind Man"—all written shortly before Ortega delivered them—and the first of three sonnets that make up "In Praise of Hands," from 1919.

The chosen poems are especially reflective of Neruda's inner life. Some of them deal with his internal emotions, such as "The Words of a Blind Man," another about eyes and vision. Silva Castro quite astutely put forth that the poems reveal a "complex" young poet "tortured by a deep, almost inhuman anxiety."

Beyond those interior notes, the social concern that stands out through most of the five poems is congruent with *Claridad*'s roots and mission, and it exemplifies that not all the poems of his teenage years revolve around concerns of his desolate mental state. "Maestranzas de noche" ("Railroad Roundhouses at Night") is still considered to be one of the most emotionally effective of all the humanitarian-political verse of his career. The poem shows how Neruda already possessed the ability to translate his keen perception of injustice into affecting poetry. Its inspiration is the heroic Monge, the knife-scarred railroad worker who sought treasures in the forests for the young Neftalí, until his fateful fall off the train and down the cliff. In the poem, Neruda imagines a roundhouse—a structure built around a turntable to service and store locomotives—haunted by the souls of dead workers. He seamlessly illustrates the deep effect that the "desperate . . . souls of the dead workers" have on him. The spotlight shines on *him* to be the witness and act upon what he sees: "Each locomotive has an open pupil / to look at me." There's a call for justice: "On the walls hang the interrogations"— questions he is putting to the public through the poem, stirring empathy throughout.

> Black iron that sleeps, black tool that groans
> an inconsolable cry through every pore.
>
> The burnt ashes over the sad earth,
> the broths in which the bronze melted its pain.
>
> Birds from which distant, misfortuned country
> cawed in the painful and endless night?
>
> And the cry tenses me like a coiled nerve
> or like a violin's broken string.
>
> Each locomotive has an open pupil
> to look at me.
>
> On the walls hang the interrogations,
> on the anvils bloom the souls of the bronzes
> and there is a tremor of steps in the deserted rooms.
>
> And into the black night—desperate—the souls
> of the dead workers run and sob.

Eerily, just a week after Neruda's words about "the dead workers" were published by the FECh, the San Gregorio massacre took place: sixty-five nitrate miners were killed and thirty-four injured when government troops fired into a crowd organized by the Federación Obrera de Chile (Chilean Workers Federation) to protest conditions at the mine.

The FECh recognized Neruda's talent as a poet and sympathized with his political leanings. Besides publishing his work in *Claridad,* where he'd contribute poems, criticisms, and op-ed pieces for years to come, it named him the secretary of the Cautín Province chapter. While Alejandro Serani was the secretary of the *ateneo,* of which Neruda was president, Serani served as the FECh local chapter's president. It wouldn't have been permitted for the same person to be president of both. Serani ended up having to deal with the minutes for both organizations, as well as other menial administrative tasks to which Neruda simply wasn't disposed, but apparently Serani didn't mind. Neruda, energized, threw himself into the literature and drama of the movement.

Shortly after the government began to crack down on the "subversive" students in Santiago, one of the leaders of the movement, José Santos González Vera, fled the capital to escape the repression. He ended up in Temuco. After just a couple of days in town, González Vera, seven years older than Neruda, went to meet Temuco's young star poet:

> I waited for him in the *liceo*'s door, around five o'clock. He was the skinniest kid. His skin had an earthen pallid color, and he had a big nose. His eyes were little black points. Despite his feebleness, he had something firm and decisive. He was quite a quiet one, and his smile was in between sorrowful and cordial.

González Vera noted that Neruda carried around Jean Grave's *La société mourante et l'anarchie* (*Moribund Society and Anarchy*) under his arm; Grave was a French shoemaker turned anarchist editor and propagandist who disapproved of the violent tendencies of earlier generations.

Soon after González Vera moved to Temuco, in December 1920, Neruda graduated from the *liceo,* allowing him the freedom to leave behind the provincial frustrations of Temuco and his father's domination. He was more than ready to take both his activism and his poetry to a real city.

After spending a final summer unsuccessfully courting Teresa in Puerto Saavedra, Neruda prepared for his departure to Santiago. Just before he left, depressed, he wrote:

> When I was born my mother died
> with a saintly soul in shame.
> She was her transparent body. She had
> an illumination of stars under her flesh.
> For this I carry
> an invisible river within my veins,
>
> . . . .
>
> . . . This yellow moon of my life
> makes me a sprout of death.
>   —"Moon"

The poem was in a newly prepared notebook along with forty-six others, both old and new. The cover read, "HELIOS, Poemas de Pablo Neruda." Helios, the Greek god of the sun, gave light to both the gods and man. Neruda prepared the notebook meticulously, in his best calligraphy, even including some artwork in the pages. The product of all the poetry of his youth, it would serve as a calling card, an introductory letter to the capital's literary types—work so well developed that it almost seemed ready for a publisher.

Notebook in hand, Neruda bought a third-class ticket and boarded a night train to Santiago. He couldn't sleep; with every passing station, his sense of freedom expanded and the painful memories of his childhood in the provinces seemed to fall away. The pulse of the big city awaited him at daybreak.

CHAPTER FIVE

BOHEMIAN TWILIGHTS

the long rails continued afar,
following on, following on
the Night Train among the vineyards.
. . . when
I looked backward
it was raining,
my childhood was disappearing.
The thundering train entered
Santiago de Chile, the capital,
I felt the sorrow of the rain:
something was separating me from my blood
and as I went out frightened
to the street,
I knew, because I was bleeding,
that my roots had been cut off.
—"Night Train"

Neruda arrived in bustling Santiago in March 1921 with a metal trunk and "the indispensable black suit of the poet, so skinny and sharp as a knife," according to his memoirs. Despite his tendency toward shyness, he now asserted his identity quite audaciously through his clothing, including the large, wide-brimmed black sombreros he liked to wear. Over the next three years, the sometimes sullen, introverted yet ambitious student from the south ascended to the apex of the capital's progressive poetry scene. Inside, though, he harbored a troubled psyche.

Santiago, a city of just over a half million people, was a world away from Temuco. Neruda was intimidated by the "thousands of buildings housing strangers and bedbugs" and was immediately impressed by new sights: the luxurious coaches drawn by elegant horses, their drivers with boots of folded yellow leather or oilcloth, as well as the new electric trams that were starting to crisscross the city.

One of the capital's outstanding features was reminiscent of Temuco: inequality. The deep divisions between social classes seemed even more punctuated here than in the provinces. In Santiago, the important families had aristocratic roots in Europe, especially Paris, London, and Italy. These families maintained an entrenched elitism, which Neruda mulled over as he walked from their elegant neighborhoods into the surrounding tenements and squalor.

Neruda hoped that Santiago would take him into "her enormous womb, where the expectations, the ideas, the lives, and almost all of our country's struggles were digested." Upon his arrival, he took his reference papers to his first lodging in Santiago, a boardinghouse at 513 Maruri Street. He arrived with just the smallest allowance from his father for his studies, but this neighborhood seemed much poorer than he was, a dense block of harsh concrete that made Temuco's slums seem quaint in comparison. The odor of gas fumes and coffee hung in the air; the barks of old dogs echoed down empty streets.

At least the boardinghouse itself was handsome amid the drab surroundings. It occupied the second floor of an old colonial-style mansion, with an arch in the center and columns on each side. Neruda was fortunate enough to have a room facing west, with windows open to a wide and peaceful sky. The sunsets were prodigiously colorful, enhanced by the coastal mountain range lit up in the distance. In the late afternoons, the view of "magnificent sheaves of colors, partitions of light, immense orange and scarlet fans" unfolded at his balcony.

The colors evoked his creativity but couldn't do the same for his mood, which, despite his long-sought escape from Temuco, remained fitfully bleak:

> I open my book. I write
> imagining myself
> in a mine
> shaft, a humid
> abandoned tunnel,
> I know that there's nobody now,
> in the house, in the street, in the bitter city.
> I'm a prisoner with the door open,
> with the world open.
> I am a sad student lost in the twilights,
> and I climb to the noodle soup
> and descend to my bed and the following day . . .
> —"The Pension House on Calle Maruri"

On the wall of his room in the pension, Neruda had a print of the oil painting *The Death of Chatterton*. It depicts the body of the tortured English poet Thomas Chatterton stretched out on a bed. He supposedly poisoned himself with arsenic at the age of seventeen, seemingly unable to escape his despair and dire poverty in a materialistic society that had turned its back on him. The year was 1770. The painting is haunting as it glorifies the pain of the beautiful, prodigious, and radical political writer. Chatterton's story deeply affected the romantic poets, many of them born around the time of his death. They martyrized him; Neruda did so as well. He realized the similarities in Chatterton's short life and his own. The print may have also served as a cautionary reminder of the risks of depression.

After he returned to Santiago from his first summer vacation, spent in Temuco, Neruda found new lodgings close to the University of Chile's Pedagogical Institute. He had enrolled there to become a French teacher, a career that pleased his father enough that he would pay the tuition. It would also allow Neruda to connect even more deeply with the spirit of his admired *poètes maudits*, the "cursed poets" Verlaine,

Baudelaire, Mallarmé, and others who reflected his own personal de-
mons and romance.

But Neruda was an undisciplined student, just as he had been in high
school; he would never graduate from the university. At first he often
skipped classes to spend time in his room reading and writing, drinking
cup after cup of tea. He took to reading beneath a sugar magnolia tree
in Santiago's main cemetery. Still depressed, still feeling alone, Neruda
continued to find respite in the act of writing poetry. The freedom of
being a student in Santiago did not ease his mental and emotional dis-
tress. Despite being in a more "civilized" setting, he could not escape
the "sorrow of the rain" from his youth.

He continued to feel emotionally impotent—creatively as well, de-
spite the rich poetry he was producing. His dreams of establishing him-
self as an active poet in Santiago were washed out by pessimism. As he
walked through the city, deflated, surrounded by endless concrete, any
thought of lyrically affecting the drabness around him seemed futile.
Meanwhile, building after building filled with offices seemed to shout
out his fear of a desk job and a boss. This frustration, this sinking help-
lessness, is apparent in "Neighborhood Without Light."

> Yesterday—watching the last twilight—
> I was a moss stain among the ruins.
>
> The cities—soot and vengeances—
> the suburb's pig-filthy grayness,
> the office that bends backs,
> the boss with turbid eyes.
>
> Blood of the clouds at sunset above the hills,
> blood on the streets and plazas,
> sorrow of broken hearts,
> pus of weariness and tears . . .

The poem's speaker seems to long for the purity and tranquility
of the rural life he left behind, no snowcapped volcanoes or virgin

forests in his view. His move to the city appears to have been detrimental:

> Far away . . . the mist of forgets
> . . . and the countryside, the green countryside! where
> the oxen and sweaty men pant.
>
> And here I am, sprouted among the ruins,
> alone, biting all sadness,
> as if weeping were a seed,
> and I, the only furrow in the earth.

His isolation was relieved by two other poets who had lived alongside Neruda in his first pension house: Romeo Murga, the same age as Neruda, and Tomás Lago, a year older. Lago would become one of Neruda's close lifelong friends; six years later they would write a book of prose poetry together, and both would be part of the social and intellectual circle that gestated during Neruda's student days in Santiago. Murga, like Neruda, had just begun his studies in French pedagogy at the University of Chile. Their dispositions were similar; in many ways they mirrored and could be a calming presence for each other. Murga was tall and lean. He often wore a wide-brimmed hat, like Neruda's, framing his dark brown face and green eyes. When he spoke, he did so gently. He always seemed to be worried about something not of this world. Within a year or so the three poets would be swept up in the whirlwind of their university world, engaging in furious literary discussion, jubilant student bedlam, debates over all the new ideologies, and political protests. But Murga tended to remain on the margins of the activity, as Neruda had in the beginning.

Murga was seen as an enlightened member of what was to be known as the *generación poética del año 20* (the poetic generation of 1920), but his time was cut short. He committed suicide in 1925, one month before he would have turned twenty-one years old. Like the French poets who preceded them, this *generación poética* would be struck with the loss of at least five of its brightest talents, either to suicide or illnesses aggravated by poverty and alcoholism.

Ever so gradually, the camaraderie of his new circle of friends and intellectual sparring partners drew Neruda into his new life. He ventured into the bohemian quarters of Santiago and became absorbed in socializing, discussing radical politics, philosophy, love, and literature in small cafés and smoky bars. Walt Whitman, James Joyce, and Victor Hugo were all subjects of constant conversation, as well as the French *poètes maudits* and the Bengali Nobel laureate Rabindranath Tagore. The French writer André Gide was also a popular subject, especially his *Les caves du Vatican* (1914; *The Vatican Cellars*), an early surrealistic farce of religious moralism. It resonated with Neruda's generation. Chilean society had become much more secularized over the past decades, yet the Catholic Church's conservative social values still permeated deeply throughout the country's culture.

They were eager to dig into the most cutting-edge literature that came out each year. The year 1922, for instance, featured the publication of three modern masterpieces: T. S. Eliot's "The Waste Land," James Joyce's *Ulysses,* and the Peruvian poet César Vallejo's *Trilce.* To one degree or another, each work would influence Neruda.

The group also gravitated toward contemporary Nordic literature, as the Chileans in their southern isolation could identify with its characters, snow-covered landscapes, and, increasingly, anti-establishment tendencies. Selma Lagerlöf's *The Saga of Gösta Berling* was a fundamental example. Full of magical realism, the Swedish novel touches on themes of emotional depression and economic poverty and features a rebellious pastor-poet out in the countryside. Lagerlöf's descriptions of the story's young countess seem narratively parallel to Neruda's *Crepusculario* (*The Book of Twilights*): "What she had hoped, what she had loved, what she had ever done seemed to her also to be enshrouded in the gray twilight. It was an hour of fatigue, defeat, powerlessness, for her, for her as for all of nature."

Another favorite was the Norwegian neorealist novelist Knut Hamsun. His prevalent images of darkness and eroticism, in particular, undoubtedly had some effect on Neruda's composition within *Twenty Love Poems.* Hamsun won the Nobel Prize in 1920; *Twenty Love Poems* was published in 1924.

Neruda found a particular bond with Rainer Maria Rilke's German-language writing, translating a fragment of his only novel, *Die aufzeich-nungen des Malte Laurids Brigge* (*The Notebooks of Malte Laurids Brigge*), for *Claridad*. Published in 1910, the book is a fragmented, highly experimental exploration by a destitute twenty-eight-year-old poet yearning to find his individuality, not unlike Neruda himself.

As eager as Neruda and his cohort were to obtain the most recent work from foreign lands, they also reached back centuries. They still regarded seventeenth-century Spanish poet Francisco de Quevedo as highly relevant. His simultaneously serious and satirical verse had a significant influence on Neruda. And the great bard Shakespeare was still present; Julius Caesar's rebellious role as a tragic hero was especially ripe and popular among the young revolutionary Chileans.

The group's literary tastes changed with the ebb and flow of international influence. People were always arriving in Santiago from abroad, as transportation and communication improved for this country that had seemed so trapped in a lost corner of the world during the previous century. Bars like El Hércules, El Jote, and El Venezia were hubs for the exchange of these new books and ideas. The intertwined worlds of politics and literature were flourishing in fertile ground, and Neruda became a part of it.

The FECh, which had recouped from the attacks and persecution of 1919 and 1920, was a major impetus for Neruda's integration into this circle. These incorrigible bohemians were trying to envision another kind of country. Their interest in politics was more romantic and idealistic than practical or direct. Socialist anarchism was still the most popular political ideology among them, and many were members of the Industrial Workers of the World (a group the government continued to repress).

Very slowly and still somewhat restrained, Neruda became a fixture in Santiago's circle of young leftist poets, artists, and student activists. Compared to his "semi-mute" childhood in Temuco, here he found life and conversation and the society of people like himself. Yet he still spoke little, and when he did, it was in a smooth, even voice, monotone and rather nasal, a stark contrast to his lyrical expression on the page.

In photos of the time, while surrounded by others clearly enjoying cabaret shows, banquets, or poetry events, Neruda tended to look serious, despondent, or lost in thought. His new friends, though, found him to have a sweet smile. He was tall and slim. Especially with his prominent nose, some wondered if his facial traits might have been Arab in origin, not uncommon in Chilean families from Spain.

As he emerged into prominence within his student circle, Neruda met people who'd be significant to his work, including mentors who took to him immediately. One of them was the prestigious Chilean poet Pedro Prado, a transcendent talent, thirty-three years old when they met. Prado's support would be instrumental to Neruda in the years to come. A more immediate and direct influence on Neruda's poetry at the time was the Uruguayan poet Carlos Sabat Ercasty, whom he revered for his intense lyricism and the depth of his connection to both nature and the human condition. Neruda expressed his raw excitement for Sabat to the readers of the December 5, 1923, issue of *Claridad,* in a review of his recent books:

> Carlos Sabat is a great river of expressive energy linked together in athletic succession, dragging it through invading undertows, separating it into diaphanous necklaces of syllables . . . All of this under the pressure of an . . . active conscience skilled in the primary elements of reason and enigma . . . He is victory's trumpet, the song dividing darkness . . .

With a bravado somewhat reminiscent of how he first knocked on Gabriela Mistral's door, Neruda wrote to Sabat directly. In his first letter, dated May 13, 1923, from Santiago, he began:

> Carlos Sabat. From the first line of yours that I read, you have not had a greater admirer nor more heartfelt sympathy. I'm also a poet, I write and I've read about three centuries[' worth of literature], but nothing of anybody else has car-

ried me so far away. Receive, Sabat, my embrace, through all these tongues that separate us.

The letter concluded with these curiously bold lines: "Send me all your books . . . Write me. How old are you? I'm eighteen . . ." Considering his usual timidity and the fact that he still, at the time of writing this letter, had not published his first book, the familiar tone reveals either courage or mania. Sabat's intermittent responses to the younger poet, sometimes encouraging, sometimes double edged, would haunt Neruda throughout his career.

Just as important as his literary mentors were the fellow writers who exposed Neruda to new subjects and stylistic approaches. There were enigmatic members of the group like Alberto Rojas Jiménez, four years older than Neruda, one of the main directors of *Claridad*. Despite his poverty, he gave off the air of a bohemian dandy with "the eccentricity of a storybook prince." He had a custom of giving away everything to his friends: his hat, his shirt, his jacket, even his shoes. Perhaps most important, he dispelled Neruda's somber moods by playfully teasing him, though always with tact. His joy was contagious, and in those first years in Santiago, Neruda certainly needed it.

In October 1921, six months after his arrival in the capital, Neruda earned his greatest accolade yet at the FECh's spring festival. The festival filled the streets of Santiago, especially around the University of Chile's School of Fine Arts, known as the "School of the Bohemia." This ability to exercise such a celebration, complete with the election of their queen of the fiesta, was a much-needed validation for the students. They had taken a marginalized, risky path; this was their manifestation after being so often denigrated by the older, more conservative generation.

The fiesta was full of ceremony and revelry. One highlight was the Grand Bacchanalia, a masquerade ball at the federation's headquarters. Entrance for *las señoritas* was "absolutely free," three pesos for the young men. Students got into the bacchanalia fantasy theme by dressing up as demons and angels, Columbuses and Mapuche, Gypsies and Arabs, pirates and Pierrots (after the sad-faced mime pining for love).

They promenaded through Santiago, ending up at the dance, where the punch, beer, and wine fueled the sensation of self-expression, sexual passion, and freedom. The students embraced their own identity as the confetti fell like snow, as the alcohol quenched the embers that smoldered in their throats. All of Santiago watched as they rejoiced "in the midst of so much despicable garbage of the world" in which they lived, as Diego Muñoz, a childhood friend of Neruda's, phrased it.

In the midst of the festivities, Neruda rose above the twenty-five or so other poets involved with the FECh to win the revered poetry competition. The next day, October 15, his "Song of the Fiesta" was published in a beautiful sixteen-page edition by *Claridad*. It was read aloud in classrooms and bars across Santiago. The poem captured the surging political pulse of the students at the time:

> Today as the ripe earth shakes
> in a dusty and violent quake
> our young souls go forth filled
> like the sails of a boat in the wind.

Before the festival, Neruda was little known outside of his artistic, bohemian student circle. With "Song of the Fiesta," there on the main stage, Neruda was suddenly proclaimed one of the country's greatest literary talents. *"La juventud tenía a su poeta."* This generation had its poet. The prize ceremony was held at the Politeama Theater, two nights after the fiesta, as part of a larger program that included symphonic music and dance. Neruda, though, was simply too shy to read his poem to the huge crowd, and the winner from preceding years had to read it for him.

In the days and weeks that followed, Neruda was asked to read "Song of the Fiesta" all the time, everywhere. The youth were identifying strongly with those verses. But Neruda was not ready to step into the shoes of the celebrity he had become.

Neruda reflected back on it in a poem forty years later:

> Song of the fiesta . . . October,
> Spring's

reward:
a full-throated Pierrot unleashes
my poetry above the madness
and I, the fine edge
of a black sword among masks and jasmine
still walking about scowling alone,
cutting through the crowd with the melancholy
of the South wind, beneath the bells
and the unfurling streamers.
        —"1921"

Between 1921 and 1926, *Claridad* published nearly 150 works by Neruda: poems, literary criticism, and political pieces. As it was a student paper, he did not receive payment for his contributions. He got by on a small allowance from his father, who, for now, knew little about his son's writing.

As a way to differentiate his short essays from his poetry, Neruda published his *Claridad* literary criticisms under the pseudonym Sachka Yegulev, from the Russian Leonid Andreyev's novella of the same name, chosen for ideological reasons along with a twinge of romanticism. Sachka leads a bloody rebellion but loses his life in the fight for liberty. The fictional character was a hero to many young Latin Americans. Neruda's fascination with him would fade, especially as he became more of a pacifist. Other students also assumed Russian pen names as an homage both to that country's literary heritage and to its revolution.

Neruda's articles of the early 1920s demonstrate that he was already a highly politicized leftist humanist. On August 27, 1921, *Claridad* published a gloss by Neruda that epitomizes the activist prose he was producing during these years, this one aimed at the working class, entitled "Employee":

You don't know that they exploit you. That they've robbed you of happiness, that in return for the dirty money they give you, you gave the portion of beauty that fell over your soul. The cashier who pays your wages is an arm of *el patrón* [owner-boss]. *El patrón* is also the arm of a brutal body that keeps killing you just like many other men. But don't hit the cashier, no, it's someone else [you should hit], the body, the assassin's body.

We call it exploitation, capital, abuse. The newspapers that you read, hurried in the streetcar, they call it order, law, patriotism, etc. Perhaps you find yourself weak. No. Here we are, we who now aren't alone, we who are equal to you and, like you, are exploited and hurt, but we rebel . . .

In a 1922 editorial, he made an early allusion to his sense of a poet's calling. The text, on the front page of *Claridad*, runs next to an illustration of what's evidently a workingman and workingwoman, huddled in the cold, the hardship they've endured evident in their postures and facial expressions. The narrator of the piece writes of how he looks at this "miserable and mute" couple, but nothing comes to him; he's perplexed, wondering, "Why doesn't the bonfire of my rebellion ignite in my lips? In front of these two beings tied together by the very symbol of my pain, why doesn't the red word that whips and condemns crack in my heart and mouth?" He keeps looking at the paper, "but nothing!" Until all of a sudden the man in the picture comes to life, grabs the narrator with his hands, looks him in the eyes, and says:

Friend, brother, why do you keep silent? . . . You who know the gift of illuminating the words with your internal flame; you can only sing and sing your small pleasures and forget the abandonment of our hearts, the brutal wound of our lives, the terror of the cold, the scourge of hunger? . . . If you don't say it and don't say it in every moment of every hour, you will fill the earth with lying voices that amplify the bad and silence the protest . . .

The man's discourse continues for a handful of lines until the author, Neruda, writes: "The man stops speaking. His *compañera* looks at me. And I begin to write . . ."

As for his verse, Neruda was dedicated to completing and publishing his first book, *Crepusculario* (*The Book of Twilights*), its title referencing the scarlet fans of the sun's last rays as seen from his window on Maruri Street. His friends at *Claridad* offered to publish the book, but under the condition that he come up with the money to print it himself. This was Neruda's only option at the time. So he sold the few cheap pieces of furniture he had and pawned his black "poet's suit," as well as the watch that José del Carmen had solemnly given to him as a gift (how insulted he would have been had he known!). It was only enough to start the printing process, and the inexorable printer wouldn't hand over any copies until Neruda paid in full.

It was at this critical moment that Hernán Díaz Arrieta entered Neruda's life. Arrieta, who went by the pen name Alone (using the English word), would become one of Chile's most influential literary critics. At the time he met Neruda, he was writing for the Santiago newspaper *La Nación*. Though Alone wasn't part of the younger crowd, he already knew of Neruda and recognized him by sight one day on one of Santiago's main avenues, La Alameda.

As Alone wrote in a book nearly fifty years later, Neruda struck him as "pale, with a melancholy air, visibly malnourished, inclined to be silent." A bit scatterbrained, with "perfunctory manners," Neruda described his circumstances to Alone: he couldn't get the printed edition in his hands until he paid the full amount in advance, which he couldn't afford. The *muchacho,* the kid, as he appeared to Alone, didn't ask for anything; he just related the situation.

The timing of the encounter was fortuitous: Alone had just cashed in on some nice capital gains from a stock tip his friend had given him. The money, Alone later admitted, made him feel powerful. With a slight show of grandeur, he generously offered to help fund the printing. Neruda accepted the gift with modesty and gratitude.

Thanks to Alone's donation, *The Book of Twilights* was released to the public in June 1923, a month before Neruda turned nineteen. As he wrote in his memoirs, "That moment when the first book appears, with the ink fresh and the paper tender, that enchanted and ecstatic moment, with the sound of beating wings and of the first flower opening on the conquered height, that moment comes only once in the poet's lifetime."

The book itself marks a significant moment in Neruda's advancement in both his self- and social cognition since arriving in Santiago. Neruda's achievement in *The Book of Twilights* derives from that growth, from his ability to capture not just the moods of the poet himself, but also the essential characteristics of his generation. It was a generation—not just in Chile—that had been tremendously affected by the monumental global events of the past decade, coming of age during the destruction and inhumanity of World War I, the October Revolution, and the surging movements of socialist anarchism, syndicalist anarchism, and communism around the world.[*] This series of global changes moved writers and all kinds of artists to develop new styles to express the new realities of mass society: postwar desolation, disillusionment, and sexual disappointment.[†]

While these world events were churning in the exterior, at home in Santiago the events of the century's first two decades were quickly changing the city. It was exciting to some, but provoked anxiety among many of Neruda's generation. As Raymond Craib, an expert on Chile's student movements at the time, writes:

> The dizzying array of technological changes that pumped
> elite self-confidence also primed consternation. Mass cul-

---

[*]   The radical environment of the time is even captured, in a sense, on the book's cover, stamped in time by the illustrations that Juan Gandulfo, the anarchist leader whose name was synonymous with revolution, volunteered to make from his wood engravings. (His images were used only on the first edition.)

[†]   T. S. Eliot's "The Waste Land" (1922) and D. H. Lawrence's novel *Kangaroo* (1923) are two major products of this trend. Chileans were also participating in this literary experimentation, most notably the avant-garde leader Vicente Huidobro. José Domingo Gómez Rojas's bohemian poetry—though cut short by his death after the attacks on the student movement—fits in as well. Many other Latin Americans were also writing in a similar vein at the time, most notably the Peruvian César Vallejo.

ture could appear threatening, and not "culture" at all. In the new world of the cinemas, social classes mixed. New forms of association between workers and students created feelings of disassociation among others accustomed to more rigid class boundaries. The "death of God" and the crisis in artistic representation had its corollary in the rise of a politics that questioned the very possibility of representation. The continuous influx of migrants from the north, the concomitant growth of the city, and the networks of mobility within it meant that Santiago's neighborhoods were increasingly traversed by a teeming raif of urban strangers.

Thus *The Book of Twilights* wasn't an illustration of a generation caught in the drunken excesses of bohemia, but rather of youths unable to grip all these convulsive changes around them—paralyzed, if you will, in their moment of crisis. Their enthusiasm was equally mixed with despair, and their idealism was inhibited by an apathy, often to the point of inertia.

This sentiment is portrayed in an article Neruda wrote for *Claridad* several months after *The Book of Twilights* was published, so emblematic that it was printed on the front page:

We are wretched. We play at living, we pretend to live, every day; every day we expose our skin to the sun, reflections of so much ignominy crawling beneath the sun, tainted by all the lepers on earth, torn to shreds by so much scratching at the filth that surrounds us; throw-away, sterile, useless, filled with unsatisfied anxiety and sacrificed dreams. In that daily piece of existence, peering out to receive malice and give it back, friends, we are whole. With our ruin uselessly patched over by old heroic illusions of other men in other times. With our roots, feverish with mud, mixing the swamp with the junkyard, futilely covered by the awning of the infinite sky. That's what we are, friends, and less than that. What have we done with our life, friends? Disgust and

tears, tears slip out as I ask you, what have you done with
your lives?

In *Book of Twilights,* Neruda joined the vanguard writers of the 1920s
in his own way. He wrote skillfully with emotional complexity. To
paint this portrait of his generation, he used landscapes of poor barrios
and sad fields. Within them he employed succinct phrases to create im-
ages that seem to be out of an impressionist painting: dead leaves, ach-
ing flesh, a poor tambourine, painful eyes, sad earth, sick bridges, the
moss stain among the ruins. Neruda acutely feels his inability to slow
the degradation of all these things around him.

And the poems' speaker—Neruda himself—is constantly fearful,
sad, fatigued, poor, distant. We see the purity of the youth's dreams
darkened by the unbearable strains of adolescence. From the poem "I'm
Scared":

(In my troubled mind there's no room for dreams
like the sky that has no space for a star.)

Not all is lost in the depths, though. The lines above are followed by:

But in my eyes a question exists
and there's a scream in my mouth that my mouth does not scream.
There are no ears on this earth that hear my sad moan
abandoned in the middle of the infinite earth!

The scream stays paralyzed in the mouth, reflecting the generation's
paralyzed state. But the fact that the scream exists, a question exists,
that there exists the potential to articulate and move beyond suggests
that an escape is apparent on the horizon—the speaker just hasn't been
able to break through to it yet.

Despite the richness of this portrayal, *The Book of Twilights'* public
reputation rests mainly on the fact that it was Neruda's first work, with
negligible enduring acclaim for the poetry and little attention to how it
captured the zeitgeist of his generation. Even then, most of the critical

reception—outside the positive promotions from *Claridad* and Neruda's friends—was unenthusiastic. "Overall, the work seems to contain more literature than feeling," wrote Salvador Reyes, a contemporary of Neruda's, in *Zig-Zag*.

Except for its most famous poem, "Farewell," several of the book's outstanding poems are hardly known today and have been left out of most anthologies. "Railroad Roundhouses at Night," his lament to Monge ("into the black night—desperate—the souls / of the dead workers run and sob"), is one example. It resounds above the book's other sociopolitical poems, because here the sympathy with the proletariat Neruda wants to express originates from a true personal relationship with the subject. That connection enables the poem's sublimity. It became Neruda's first poem to be published outside of Chile: in 1923, his old mentor Gabriela Mistral, then in Mexico, included it in an anthology.[*]

Neruda's Santiago desolation poem, "Neighborhood with No Electricity," is also in *The Book of Twilights*, as well as the one-liner "My Soul." Like many lines in the book, and the next few to follow, it was a mournful description of how he felt at the time:

My soul is an empty *carrousel* in the twilight.

The one poem that received real popular notice was "Farewell" (Neruda wrote the title in English). The lines that are still often quoted today are the first poetic reveals of Neruda's *machismo*:

I love the love of sailors
who kiss, then leave.

---

[*] Mistral included "Railroad Roundhouses at Night" in what became an enormously successful anthology of Latin American and European writers, *Lecturas para mujeres* (Readings for Women), intended to be a primer for girls' schools. The same progressive secretary of education who had brought her to Mexico commissioned and printed twenty thousand copies. It was also published in Madrid, one year later.

Diego Muñoz wrote that shortly after *Book of Twilights'* publication, he and Neruda took a liking to two female performers at their favorite cabaret club, La Ñata Inés. Sarita was the mixed-race daughter of a famous black drummer. As a child, she had performed with her father, and Muñoz vividly remembered seeing her dance when they were both young, in Concepción, before he moved to Temuco and entered Neruda's grammar school. Annie, the other dancer, had Asian ancestry, unusual in Chile at the time, making the two an exotic combination for Chileans, who were most commonly of European descent.

One night Diego had some money in his pocket after getting paid for a short story. He invited Pablo to the cabaret—but only Pablo, not their other friends, so that they'd be able to talk to Sarita and Annie by themselves. They arrived after midnight, just in time for the women's number of sultry and—especially for Chile—risqué dancing.

After the girls' performance and the frenetic cheers they received, Diego gave a message to the maître d' to pass on to the ladies: "Your amigos the painter Muñoz and the poet Pablo Neruda are here. Would you like to come to our table? We'd really like you to." The girls came over after their second act.

"Are you Pablo Neruda?" Annie inquired of the poet. "May I ask you for something?"

"What would that be?" he answered.

"I want you to recite that pretty verse, named 'Farewell.'"

When Neruda answered that he couldn't remember all the lines, Annie, according to Muñoz, recited most of the verses from memory:

> I love the love that's served
> in kisses, bed, and bread.
>
> Love that can be eternal
> and can be fleeting.
>
> Love that wants to free itself
> so it can return to love again.

Exalted love that draws near,
Exalted love that goes away . . .

They all went out to dinner afterward and continued drinking. Diego and Pablo suggested they go dancing, but the two women weren't interested. Instead, they took some bottles of liquor to Annie's house. They opened one and had a round of shots, then another, followed by another. Diego sat talking with Sarita while Annie was fastened to Pablo's lips. Finally, Annie stretched out her arm and turned out the light.

The narrative of the poem Annie loved so much is rooted in betrayal; it is about a man saying "farewell" as he abandons his pregnant lover:

From deep inside you, on his knees,
a sad child, like myself, watches us.

For that life that will burn in your veins,
they would have to tie our lives together.

For those hands, daughters of your hands,
they would have to kill my hands.
. . . .
From your heart a child says good-bye to me.
And I say good-bye to him.

★

While *The Book of Twilights* did not have the sensational impact that *Twenty Love Poems* would the following year, it did much for Neruda's reputation. At nineteen, such was his stature that he had disciples who would dress like him, copy his metaphors, and, especially when *Twenty Love Poems* began to garner substantial acclaim, follow him around the city. Younger poets would approach him so frequently in bars that, according to Muñoz, he and other friends prescreened these disciples' verses to see if they were worth Neruda's time. The importance of poetry in the Chilean culture allowed Neruda to gain popular recognition early on, which eventually evolved into widespread fame.

Despite all the initial excitement and attention surrounding the publication of *Book of Twilights,* Neruda's spirits sank yet again. Adding to the psychological pressure of constant recognition was the fact that, just as his father had predicted, the book did nothing to improve Neruda's finances. In truth, having discovered how much attention his son was paying to his poetry rather than his studies, José del Carmen reduced Neruda's allowance. *La mamadre* (the more-mother), as Neruda called his stepmother, Trinidad, managed to sneak him some much-needed cash through his sister, Laura. Early in 1924, Neruda ran into Pedro Prado, the older poet who had so warmly embraced Neruda when he arrived in Santiago. When Prado asked him where he was currently living, Neruda answered, "In an alley with a lot of people; I'm not going to give you the address, because I haven't paid the rent and they're going to kick me out tomorrow or the next day."

He had just published a significant book of poetry, but he was nervous and forlorn. He saw himself standing at a significant crossroads, unsure and anxious over what direction to free his emotion, to take his poetry, the two always interconnected. In an op-ed that appeared on the front page of *Claridad* several months after *The Book of Twilights* had been published, he asked his generation: "What have we done with our life?"

He provided, as the article continued, his own interpretation: "All of you, everyone, the best, the brightest, you have consented to mutually annihilate yourselves," Neruda answers, "like the person who completes a task, who works toward his destiny. I have seen you kissing, biting, eating away at yourselves, dirtying yourselves, belittling yourselves, always equally monotonous and brutal . . . Water that returned to the earth. Cloud that the gust of wind turned to ashes."

He, though, is a poet, and turns to explain what has become his personal manifesto of 1923, at the age of nineteen:

> And me? Who is this that you challenge, what purity and entirety can you claim? I, too, am like you. Like you belittled,

tainted, dirty, wasted, guilty. Like you. We are swallowed by the same ferocious throat, the same terrible monster. But, listen to me, I must free myself. Do you understand? The leap to a great height, the flight into the infinite sky, it will be I who takes it, and before you do. Before I rot I must be different, transform myself, free myself. You can continue the show. Not me. I'm leaving all of this, I'll tear off these clothes in which you met me yesterday, and, crazy in turmoil, drunk with liberty, convulsed with threats, I shout out to you: *Miserables!*

He was now fixed on making a decisive turn at this crossroads to take his poetry in a different direction, in search of his true voice; to take the leap out of the misery that his previous work didn't relieve; to find personal liberation through lyrical transformation. The route he set for himself was "provoked by an intense love passion." The goal: "to encompass man, nature, the passions, and specific events, all into one work."

Around the time he published that exposition in *Claridad,* feeling especially anxious about his poetry, Neruda made another trip to Temuco to restore his strength; his hometown served as a refuge, despite the ever-present tension with his father. One night, in the second-floor bedroom he grew up in, Neruda had what he'd later call a "curious experience." Sometime past midnight, just before going to bed, he opened the window and looked out into an extraordinarily silent night. Then, as he described it in his memoirs, "The sky dazzled me. The entire sky was alive with a swarming multitude of stars. The night was newly cleansed by the rain and the Antarctic stars unfurled above my head."

As if possessed by some sort of cosmic euphoria, he went to his desk, the same desk where he wrote his first poems in his math books. He wrote a poem, deliriously, as if trying to transcribe a dictation. The next morning he read it over with pure joy. Neruda felt he had discovered the new style he had been searching for: dramatically more exuberant, more open, just like the night sky under which it was composed.

When he returned to Santiago, he showed one of the new poems to his friend Aliro Oyarzún, who was well respected for his literary knowledge. "Are you sure those lines haven't been influenced by Sabat Ercasty?" Oyarzún asked. Anxious, but ready to roll the dice, Neruda sent the poem to the Uruguayan poet himself, the man he had so boldly written to soon after he arrived in Santiago. He was just as bold this time:

> Read this poem. It's called "The Enthusiastic Sling-Shooter." Someone told me that he saw your influence in it. I am very content with the poem. What do you think? I'd burn it [if it were true.] I admire you more than anyone, but how tragic is this racking my brain for words and symbols and turns of phrase. It is the greatest pain, greater still, more than ever, and for the first time (like in other things that I sent you) I thought I was in uncharted territory, in a place [land] that was destined to be mine alone.

The reply from Montevideo, according to Neruda, was: "Seldom have I read such a poem so significant, so magnificent, but I have to say it: yes, there is something of Sabat Ercasty in your verse."

Sabat's letter contained high praise, yet to Neruda, his hero's words sounded a death knell for the new voice he had been pursuing. He carried around Sabat's reply in his pocket for days until it fell apart. Neruda was at a crossroads with his writing, and, as he would one day explain in his memoirs, "Sabat Ercasty's letter ended my cyclic ambition for an expansive poetry. I closed the door on an eloquence that I could never go on with; I deliberately toned down my style and my expression. Looking for more sensitive traits, for my own harmonic world, I began to write another book. *Twenty Love Poems* was the result."

CHAPTER SIX

DESPERATE SONGS

You hear other voices in my aching voice.
The weeping of old mouths, the blood of old prayers.
Love me, *compañera*. Don't abandon me. Follow me.
Follow me, *compañera,* on that wave of anguish.
   —Poem V

Along with Teresa León Bettiens in Temuco, Neruda's muse for the majority of *Twenty Love Poems* was Albertina Rosa Azócar. She was the sister of his new friend Rubén, a brilliant and charming student he'd met through the student scene. Albertina was studying French at the Pedagogy Institute. Although she was two years older than Neruda, she had entered the school just a year before. In the autumn of 1921, Neruda's first year, they had classes together. Neruda was instantly attracted to her. Albertina knew of his intelligence, his reputation in the student circles, and his poetry.

Ninety-six female and eighty-eight male students, including Neruda, were enrolled in the French pedagogy program that year, all ensconced in the one brick building. Neruda could not have avoided Albertina if he had wanted to. She was affectionate, comforting, calm, sensual yet reserved, smart, and engaged. She ignited romantic and sexual fantasies in him that would explode in his heart, mind, and poetry.

They saw each other at the Saturday get-togethers where student poets would read their poetry. Albertina often attended with her friends. Reluctantly, Neruda began to participate. Albertina enjoyed his "sleepy reading voice," which she and a friend would imitate afterward. They liked him, and Albertina was physically attracted to him too, despite the fact that he often "looked ill." She found charm in how he was "always delicate," in his wistfulness and melancholy. "He was so young, so romantic," Albertina recalled a half century after they met. "I don't know, a lot of girls like poets." Neruda had, in fact, outgrown his adolescent gawkiness. While his thinness and gaunt face were remarkable, Neruda was developing a handsomeness, looking tall and smooth in his thin dark ties and the railroad worker's jacket from his father. Confident from the prestige of winning the festival prize and the respect he had from her brother, Neruda made the move to sit next to her in class.

Soon after, on the rainy autumn afternoon of April 18, 1921, Neruda walked Albertina home to her boardinghouse and their romance began. They strolled down Avenida Cumming, through the heart of the university neighborhood. He continued to walk her home after classes, sometimes delighting her with fantastic tales. He gave her French books with yellow bindings, at least one by the writer Colette, which Albertina kept her entire life. Most often, though, the two walked silently, sometimes for hours, through the narrow Parque Forestal that lined the statuesque downtown streets of Santiago alongside the Mapocho River. He was very tender with her. He would love her like few others in his life.

Albertina was smart but not brilliant, and there was a charm to her but not an overwhelming allure. Her personality wasn't as dynamic, exciting, and eccentric as others who had slipped in and out of his life, or those he would encounter over the next two decades. Her demeanor, in fact, made her seem almost "absent," as Neruda would describe her in his famous Poem XV: "a butterfly in mourning," "as if you weren't here now." She seemed especially flat compared with the naturally vibrant Teresa León Bettiens, whom he still loved and longed for. Albertina's beauty was subtle as well: pale skin, almost ceramic; a refined, large nose; shapely lips; cheekbones that sat high near her sad, dark eyes; and tightly curled black hair that was often held in some type of chignon. Her figure, though, was strong and seductive.

Neruda saw her as a delicious, delicate lover who excited his sexual urges, conquering his timidity. And unlike Amelia and Teresa, those daughters of wealthy Temuco families who'd crushed his heart, Albertina was present and available.

Albertina's significance for Neruda went beyond their romance. Neruda was still struggling to find his personal poetic path, to find his own language, and in this struggle his need for sexual release had become a driving force. As a primary object of his sexual desire at the time, Albertina became a source of poetic energy, and this only intensified when he lost her.

But her role in his writing went beyond that of the basic muse. At first, he may have been writing poems that were sympathetic in nature, like hymns or odes. But her absent answers to his desperate craving would convert her from muse to antagonist, provoking in him a terrorizing sensation of being caught in a tragedy. Just as he took to pen and paper to write about his desperation as a schoolkid, so he did now. He found release in his lyricism, saving him from emotional implosion, while also creating a medium for self-reflection.

At first, their relationship was limited to silent walks with only limited acts of physical intimacy. Albertina's older sister, Adelina, kept a watchful eye on the two, worried about the bad influence of a rawboned bohemian poet. Adelina was repressive, almost tyrannical in her oversight of her little sister, whom she perceived as delicate, who was only in the big city because the University of Concepción was not yet teaching French pedagogy. Rubén interceded to help the couple. He would accompany Albertina, walk with her until they were out of sight of the house, and then depart so she and Pablo could be together.

Sexual relations between lovers in Neruda's generation were not uncommon. In fact, the anarchist students were practically advocating a free-love movement, as shown in some of the pieces published in *Claridad*. A couple of months after his relationship with Albertina began, Neruda wrote an article that was typical not just of his own nature, but also of the predominating chauvinistic attitude in the male-dominated socialist circles. It lashed out against "bourgeois" traditions like marriage and chastity while designating women as means for sexual gratification.

His piece, simply entitled "Sex," opened with a prefatory note from the editors of *Claridad:* "We publish this article because it reflects a fatal state of mind in all young people and because it contains a manifestation of protest against Christian morality."*

The article begins: "He is strong. And young. The ardent flash of sex courses through his veins in electric shocks." After his "first friend" shared with him the secret of masturbation, "the solitary pleasure went on corrupting the purity of his soul and opening him up to unknown pleasures." But that time has passed. "Now, strong and young, he searches for an object in whom to empty out his goblet of virility. He is the animal that simply searches for an outlet for his natural potency. He is a male animal and life must give him the female in whom he's made complete, growing stronger." (Just two months earlier, he had found that female in Albertina, though she thus far insisted on remaining chaste.)

When the man finds a woman to be with, he "discovers that the arrival of one of these women brings with it something curious and strange: the dishonor of the one he wanted, like him, enjoying a pleasure for which nature gave him an organ. So the young male, who is honorable, becomes aware of the hypocritical morality they've invented to impede the full blooming of his physical inclinations."

Seemingly with no other recourse, he goes to a "house of pleasure," but the young male, "who is pure, limits his natural need and spurns, pitying the machine that delivers pleasure for an hourly rate." Despis-

---

* A piece Neruda wrote in his sixties, destined for his memoirs, provides light on Neruda's attitude toward religion in his twenties, one that aligns with the "protest against Christian morality" within a very Catholic country. In the text, Neruda explains that for centuries, priests of all rites and languages have sold pieces of heaven, along with all its commodities: water, electricity, great television, the comforts of a clear conscience. The curious thing about this property, however, "inhabited by a terrible being named God," is that it has never been visited by anyone. Yet they keep selling it, as the price per square meter "of the celestial air or divine earth" just keeps climbing. "Since I was very young," he contends, "I have rebelled against this always invisible kingdom and the strange ways of the ruling gods."

ing the laws, "he feels an urge to vent his rage against those who gave him the ancestral desire that ties him, like a giant hook, to life."

About two months after the article was published, Albertina agreed to consummate their relationship. His eyes fixated on her entire length, seeing that body of woman, as he'd pen later in *Twenty Love Poems,* with her white hills, white thighs spreading open for the first time. He attempted to plow through her and reach the depths of the earth.

Yet, in what would become a pattern, while he had one lover he still longed for another in a distant location: in this case, Teresa León Bettiens, still living in Temuco. The queen of that town's 1920 spring fiesta was still intrigued by the curious poet, despite the fact that her parents had called him a "vulture." They would sometimes see each other when Neruda returned south for vacation, as he did over the first months of 1923 (the summer season in South America).

That would be a pivotal year for Neruda: he had fully established himself in the capital and was entering into the profound production of *Twenty Love Poems.* Yet nearly half of them pertained to Teresa, verses fostered by their time together in Puerto Saavedra and the longing that followed. Because of his time with her there, Neruda had elevated Puerto Saavedra to near-mythic stature in his poetry. Dreams, love, and sex combined in this landscape, ocean and forest fused, as Teresa's body and womanhood bloomed. She was poetic, natural, eccentric, almost exotic in her Andalusian spirit, so different from the women he knew in the sprawls of Santiago. She defied her parents to be with him, on patios full of poppies, where the river that first took him to the sea flowed into the waves of the ocean.

His letters to Teresa speak for themselves:

> And as you know, I can all of a sudden fall into fits of loneliness, fatigue, and sadness that don't let me do anything and make me bitter about life. Why would I write you in these moments? Then, in these times that come upon me so unexpectedly, how sweet it is to receive letters from far away, from the woman I love, from you, and return to love life and return to happiness! —Pablo

Another one, written to Teresa from Santiago in 1923:

> It rained yesterday, today too. It's filled me with nostalgia.
> Oh, my faraway life! Everything I have is so far away, my
> childhood, my thoughts, now you, and the eternal rains
> falling on the roof, all of that abandoned world has filled my
> head with old musings and memories.
> Love me, Little One. —Pablo

A more desolate missive, in which he professed devotion to only her,
runs parallel to his continual profession of the very same to Albertina:

> I confess to you my disenchantment with everything,
> when you have the right—or do you?—to be my only en-
> chantment . . . Tell me, you've never thought of these things
> that smash my heart into a thousand pieces? You've never
> left your girlish thoughts to feel the pain of abandonment of
> this boy who loves you? —Pablo

Sometime around May 1923, Albertina required urgent surgery. It
seemed that a case of appendicitis infected and subsequently inflamed
the thin tissue lining the interior of her abdominal wall. This acute
condition, called peritonitis, can be fatal. The emergency surgery was
especially complicated at the time; she stayed in the hospital for over a
month. Her lover proved devoted; Neruda came to her bedside every
day throughout her recovery.

During her stay he wrote "Hospital," a short prose piece for *Clari-
dad*, part of a series of twelve impressionistic pieces under the title "The
Distant Life":

> The sole center of my existence was often just a yellow
> sliver of sun that pierced the curtains. I watched it glim-
> mer, stretch, and scatter. My roommates' moans sometimes
> snapped me out of that obsessive observation, and all the

mortal sadness of those sickrooms suddenly leaked out on my defeated heart.

Convalescing, I walked the strangely silent corridors with slow steps. The sisters passed by me with their daily hustle and bustle, and sometimes, a trembling, anguished cry would stop me near a window or against the crack of a doorway . . . In the center of the courtyard the nuns had an altar to the Virgin: a stony grotto, covered in climbing vines. It was the only bright spot in the hospital filled with shadows. Night and day, the candles of that alcove were lit, and I would light my cigarettes one by one in those sacred flames flickering in the wind.

Once Albertina was fully recuperated, her parents commanded her to return home to Lota. Even before her illness they had never liked the idea of her being in such a threatening city, some 350 miles away. Furthermore, the University of Concepción's School of Education, only twenty-five miles from Lota, had just started a French program of its own. As far as they were concerned, there was no longer any reason for her to be in Santiago. After all of Neruda's constancy, the swell of so much love, he was suddenly told to keep his distance.

Neruda was crushed by this turn of events. His frustration raged, and he found few ways to ameliorate it. Yet while he often suggested it, he never moved to Concepción, and Albertina's fate was fixed for now. He turned to poetry, of course, and his despair at her absence led to the most famous poem in *Twenty Love Poems*.

His exasperation also came out in more than a hundred surprising letters that he wrote to Albertina between 1923 and 1932 (which she saved). Prior to her departure, he had written to her about minute details of daily life and profound thoughts. Yet immediately after she moved to Concepción, nearly every letter desperately and aggressively declared how much he needed her. They became quite nasty. Most of them started with an attack on her, a reproach, almost always followed by placation and a soft expression of how much he loved her. These were combined with cute illustrations, such as patterns drawing out the word *beso* (kiss). Perhaps he hoped that he could make her feel guilty for inspiring his obsession and causing him such pain. He called her an "ugly cockroach," simply "ugly" on several more occasions, a "bad woman." His nicknames for Albertina seemed to harken back to his discovery of the forest as a child: Princess Worm. Pesky little worm. Girl of the secrets. Frog. Snake. Spider. Beetle. Malicious whore. Adored doll. Little scoundrel. My ugly little girl. My pretty little girl. Little rat. Seashell. Bee. Beloved brat of my soul.

In the earliest of the letters, we can see the emotional and linguistic ingredients of some of the poems in *Twenty Love Poems*. While Albertina was in Concepción, in a letter dated September 16, 1923, Neruda confided to her that "spread out on the moist grass, in the afternoons, I think of your gray beret, of your eyes that I love, of you." Later, in Poem VI, he took that very imagery from the letter and deepened it, turning it into a dynamic, multileveled poem:[*]

> I can feel your eyes, voyaging away, distant as that autumn,
> Grey beret, voice of a bird, heart of a huntress—
> Where all my deep agony migrated,
> Where my happy kisses fell like embers.
>
> The skies from shipboard. Fields from the hills.
> Your memory is of light, of smoke, of a still pool.
> Deep in your eyes the twilight burned.
> The dry leaves of autumn whirled in your soul.

In that same letter in which Neruda mentions her gray beret, he states: "Little One, yesterday you must have received a newspaper, and in it the *poem of the absent one. (You are the absent one.)*"

---

[*]   The poem's rhyme scheme gets lost in translation:

> *Te recuerdo como eras en el último **otoño**.*
> *Eras la boina gris y el corazón en **calma**.*
> *En tus ojos peleaban las llamas del **crepúsculo**.*
> *Y las hojas caían en el agua de tu **alma**.*

The poem he refers to had just been published in *Claridad* six days before:

> This lullaby is for you, Little One, wherever you are, wherever you go.
> Trembling warm river, the tenderness wets my voice, my voice that speaks your name.
> For you, further than the distant red clouds, and the distant mountains, distant because of you I look farther, farther still.
> . . . .
> The absent one, who closes the eyelids, on the other side of the shadow. I speak to you, and my voice calls out to you, Little One. Don't leave, don't you ever leave.

This idea, that by invoking her absence he will make them both more present, is evident in the letter after he mentions the poem and her role in it: "Did you like it, Little One? Does it convince you that I remember you? And on the other hand, you. In ten days, one letter." He admits, "Given that I am very vain, I'm very sensitive [to the fact that she isn't writing him]."

True to its raw autobiographical nature, *Twenty Love Poems* seems composed directly from many of these letters, both the words and the psychology. This is evident in a similar, subsequent letter to Albertina, which contains the opening to Poem XV:

> Almost always I feel like writing to you, so if I don't receive your letter I become troubled. It's as if you were thinking about something else while I talk to you, or as if I talked to you through a wall and didn't hear your voice.

The beginning of Poem XV:

> I like it when you're quiet. It's as if you were absent,
> and you heard me from a distance, and my voice couldn't reach you.

It's as if your eyes had flown away from you,
and that a kiss had sealed your mouth.*

Albertina, years later, would relate that during their days together in Santiago, "when we went for walks, he'd be silent, but I'd be quiet too."

In the years since the book was published, Poem XV may be considered the most popular poem in the book, alongside Poem XX ("I can write the saddest verses tonight"). Albertina herself said that "I like it when you're quiet" was her favorite. The poem is powered by Neruda's glorification of the absence of his lover, which is idealized as we find him, the poem's speaker, struggling to accept that he and his lover are not together.†

Neruda had several muses/subjects for *Twenty Love Poems*, though Albertina and Teresa were the two most important and prevalent. In each poem, the loved one is not present; each verse is a failed call to have her right next to him. Those to Teresa express a heartache that became wrung ever tighter as the futility of his desire for her increased with time. By the end of 1923, Teresa's parents' opposition to their relationship became too much for her. Neruda sent her one final letter from Santiago with the hope of changing her mind:

Your life, God, if he exists, will want to make good and sweet
as I dreamed it would be. Mine? What does it matter? I will get
lost on a road, one of the many there are in the world. Your
trail won't be mine, you won't arrive when I do, and my rare
joys won't arrive to illuminate you, but how much I loved you!

---

*   Complete poem in Appendix I.

†   The theme of the "absent one" was also present in one of his nicknames for Albertina, "Netochka." In Dostoyevsky's first (unfinished) novel, *Netochka Nezvanova*, Netochka is a young orphaned girl with a sorrowful life. As Neruda would have known, "Netochka Nezvanova" means "nameless nobody" in Russian; Neruda would have seen Albertina as if she was someone who "weren't here now," absent—nobody but possessing all his thoughts, nameless on paper but so present. In a 1983 interview, Albertina said Netochka was her favorite nickname.

And why would this great love not be able to fill the void of this separation?

No, now I can't write you. I feel a sorrow that grasps my throat or my heart. Everything is over? Say it's not, it's not, it's not. —Pablo

"I no longer love her, it's true, but how much I loved her," he convinces himself near the end of Poem XX, which seems to spring right from the letter to Teresa. The cosmic frustration is stretched across a nocturnal landscape in which he could "write the saddest verses" (including "Love is so short, forgetting is so long"). Maybe he does still love her, he's willing to admit near the end, but he is resigned to live on without her:

> Because on nights like this I held her in my arms,
> my soul is not at peace with having lost her.
>
> Though this may be the final sorrow she causes me,
> and these the last verses I write for her.

He may have lost her, but he still has poetry, still has the power, for whatever it may serve, to write the saddest verses.

Neruda was not, however, resigned to let Albertina go. He was terribly distraught by her absence, perhaps because she had not given him a definitive answer, perhaps because he couldn't understand or simply accept that she would not be with him. His letters to her show his shattered psyche and blistering frustration:

> The only thing that makes others desperate is the hardness of the heart. Imagine how I discover that [hard heart] in you, in you who are a part of me. I want to hit my head against the wall. You think that this is injustice or evil. No, it's not that, it's desperation. You're my last hope. You must understand, it is your job to forgive me. I make it all up to you with the savage love that I feel for you. Isn't that right,

evil whore? Isn't it true that you're a bit at fault as well? Frog, snake, spider. I will pinch your nose.

He ends the letter with his customary conflation of deprecation and supplication:

> As always, ugly brat, receive a long, long kiss from your
> —Pablo.

Neruda's passion invoked a cruelty in him, as seen in these letters, a cringeful combination of scorn, despair, and tender affection. For Neruda at this time, about to turn twenty-one, love, hate, and possession intertwine: "I'll eat you up with kisses," he wrote her in April 1925. He rages against abandonment, to which he was certainly sensitized by the loss of his mother, as seen in his early poems. He also demonstrates constant neediness and extreme anxiety, perhaps results of his sickly, fragile, moody childhood. And he rages against authority figures who thwart him, like his father, Albertina's father, and the parents of other lovers in the past, as well as against the women themselves, like Albertina, whom he blames for his pain.

Albertina later said she would have married Neruda had it not been for the move and the prolonged separation that followed. Neruda, though, did little to find a way to be with her in Concepción. Her brother and his great friend, Rubén, though not in Concepción at the time, surely could have helped him to travel and stay there with mutual friends. But Neruda didn't try, perhaps because the inability to be with the "absent one," with all the seething of his nerves that accompanied it, was more fulfilling for him and his poetry than actually being confronted by her presence. As Poem XV opens with "I like it when you're quiet. It's as if you weren't here now," it moves to:

> I like it when you're quiet. It's as if you'd gone away now,
> And you'd become the keening, the butterfly's insistence,
> And you heard me from a distance and my voice didn't reach you.
> It's then that what I want is to be quiet with your silence.

Despite Neruda's alarming and often hostile passion, Albertina was still drawn to him. He now showed a good sense of humor, and he was an enigma with a brilliant mind and imagination, with growing fame and stature as the voice of their generation. Even more so by 1925, he had lost the awkward appearance and developed into a handsome young man, suave, at times even elegant, especially when dressed in a suit once the old railroad jacket and huge sombrero had grown old.

In time, Neruda was able to break through those enraging "square and rigid frames" of conservative society that restricted his potent will to love freely. His partner for this was Laura Arrué, another muse for *Twenty Love Poems*. She shimmered with an innocent radiance. With a curl to her blond hair, porcelain skin, and refined cheekbones, Diego Muñoz and others thought she resembled a young Greta Garbo. She was intelligent too, with a sharp wit.

Laura had first seen Neruda at the headquarters of the FECh during the 1921 spring fiesta, when he was crowned the top poet. She was only fourteen and had been excited by the energy and fantastic spectacle of the whole festival, including Neruda's muted eccentricity as he accepted his prize.

A couple of years later, her older sister, who was also studying at the Pedagogy Institute, brought her to one of Neruda's first big readings at the University of Chile's main hall. Two poems in particular struck chords in her young heart: "Farewell" ("deep inside you, on his knees, / a sad child, like myself, watches us"; "I love the love of sailors / who kiss, then leave") and Poem VI, about Albertina:

> I remember you as you were in that last autumn
> You were the grey beret and the heart in calm
> Deep in your eyes the twilight burned
> The dry leaves of autumn whirled in your soul.

Laura, now seventeen, thought his voice sounded like a goose's, a bit whiny, with almost a stubborn lament. Just like Albertina and her amigas, Laura would imitate it with her friends, always making them laugh. She felt that the whine in his thin reading voice must be somewhat characteristic of his personality. Still, there was something endearing about it.

Laura's father was a learned, sensitive, and popular poet who possessed an ample spirit and, as she put it, rejoiced in all of nature's manifestations. Perhaps it was from him that she acquired an enduring interest in art in all its forms. She sought out conferences, readings, concerts, and art expositions all around Santiago.

In 1923, Laura was in her third year at an experimental boarding school, the progressive Normal School (No. 1). Its founding was a breakthrough in Latin America, a model training setting that allowed women to become teachers (though without improving their stature in society). The school vigorously promoted art and literature, and invited writers, artists, and intellectuals to present and share their work and ideas.

The school decided to ask Neruda to give a reading, and it fell upon Laura and her classmate Agustina Villalobos to deliver the invitation to him on behalf of the director and the faculty. At the time, Neruda was living in a tiny room in a run-down boardinghouse at 330 Echaurren Street. He had been moving from one shabby residence to another, living on a shoestring. Laura and Agustina found him in his room, lying on a mattress atop a cheap box spring. There was an old sugar crate that served as a nightstand, and next to it was a chair with his clothes piled and hanging from it. That was all the furniture he had, as he'd sold the rest to finance the printing of *The Book of Twilights*.

When Laura and Agustina timidly entered the room, Neruda smiled, slowly putting the book he was reading atop the pile of others on the sugar crate. They handed him the invitation, along with a bouquet of white carnations. He asked their names, what grade they were in, and where they were from. Laura answered San Fernando, a tranquil town between the Andes and the coast, about ninety miles south of Santiago. San Fernando is in the province of Colchagua—Mapudungun for "valley of small lakes." The name moved Neruda. The region boasts some of the country's most fertile soils. Laura's grandparents owned a large hacienda where they grew everything from grains to onions. Laura's grandmother was adamant that their family not mix their blood with strangers'; they were supposedly of pure Spanish descent. Laura's mother, though, wanted something different for her daughters. To experience the cosmopolitan city and to attain a good education, Laura and her older sister had moved into their cousin's large house in Santiago.

Neruda might have loved to hear all of this, but the conversation that night was limited to brief remarks before the girls left, their mission completed. Neruda was immediately lured by Laura's extraordinary beauty. Due to the brevity of the encounter, he wasn't yet able to appreciate how bright and insightful she truly was. Nor did he know that even though Laura thought his style of dress somewhat pretentious, she also found him handsome.

As a result of the invitation Laura delivered, Neruda started to visit her school, in particular her history teacher, María Malvar de Leng, who lived there as well. During these visits, the teacher would call out for Laura to accompany Neruda in great shouts from the second-floor balcony that overlooked the patio. Soon Laura and Neruda began to see each other outside of school. Laura's older cousin had to chaperone. Her parents were definitely not happy about the interaction between their young daughter and this "atrocious troubadour."

It was the spring of 1923. Albertina had just left for Concepción. Little is known about the relationship between Laura and Neruda. Neruda didn't write about her later, out of respect for his friendship with Laura's future husband, Homero Arce, who would become his faithful secretary. Arce died in 1977, after agents from the dictatorship cracked his skull. Five years later, Laura opened up—to a degree—in a moving memoir: "I loved Pablito for a short and violent time."

*

On February 14, 1924, from Puerto Saavedra, Neruda wrote to his hero Carlos Sabat Ercasty: "Here I have finished my book *Twenty Love Poems and a Desperate Song,* which I think will be published in the month of April." It was finally ready, but he had yet to find a publisher. He wanted to reach a broader audience and get more recognition for this book than he had for *The Book of Twilights.* He was being amply ambitious, aiming only for established, prestigious publishers, and hoping that readers of traditional poetry would overcome their initial shock over the unconventional and explicit lines and appreciate the pure lyricism inherent in the poems.

Still, he assembled it so as to reflect his distinctive, individual, vanguard style. The aging Augusto Winter, his yellow-and-white beard overflowing, helped him type it all up in the same house and library in which Neruda had read so many books over the years, by the shores on which he first discovered the sea. Now, looking past the words themselves, Neruda insisted that they use square sheets of brown kraft wrapping paper to produce a unique look for presenting the book to publishers. Winter even gave in to Neruda's impulse to make the pages appear crimped. The elder poet used the edge of a handsaw to press the edges of the pages to create the effect.

Neruda's first efforts at convincing the more esteemed editors were not successful, and he took the rejections as personal affronts. Carlos Acuña, director and editor of *Zig-Zag,* turned him down. Neruda then sent the manuscript to Carlos George Nascimento. A Portuguese immigrant from the Azores, Nascimento had bought a bookstore in Santiago in 1917 that became a center for writers, critics, and other intellectuals to gather and discuss literary trends. Later, Nascimento expanded into publishing. He would go on to be known as one of the greatest editors in Chile's literary history, but at the time, he was still just starting out as a publisher; he turned Neruda down.

"He'll be sorry; they'll all be sorry," Neruda wrote to Pedro Prado. "Oh, bad man!" Neruda's attitude toward his work during this time is noteworthy: he was absolutely certain of its quality and was stubbornly steadfast in his determination to achieve his lofty literary aspirations. His ambition and belief in his own greatness—narcissism—would characterize and propel Neruda throughout his life. His resilience and persistence in the face of rejection are also what had allowed him to follow his calling despite his father's denigrating attempts to deter him.

Pedro Prado, now even more established as a leading poet than when Neruda first met him fresh from Temuco, lobbied Nascimento on

Neruda's behalf. Then Eduardo Barrios, one of Chile's leading novelists and a mentor to Nascimento, told him, "A very calm, modest *muchacho* who uses the pseudonym Pablo Neruda is going to talk to you. He's going to be a great poet. He's going to give them something to talk about someday. Keep your eye on him."

In the small confines of the publisher's office and bookstore, Neruda seemed very pale and skinny to Nascimento. The poet barely spoke, but still there was a fine sensibility emanating from him, and Nascimento felt it, to the point that the publisher would later admit that Neruda had convinced him without Nascimento's realizing it. Despite the fact that Neruda was so "frail and quiet; he still got his way," Nascimento reminisced years later. In person, Neruda was able not only to convince Nascimento of the inherent virtues of the collected verses, but also to convince him to publish the book in the form that he wanted: large and square, which was expensive because it was a nonstandard paper size. That square shape had recently provoked a small revolution in the design of poetry books. It stood out in bookstore windows, signaling the difference between cutting-edge poetry and regular old prose, even before a single line was read.

In June 1924, one month before Neruda turned twenty, the book was out. Nascimento's original printing was probably fewer than five hundred copies, but when Neruda first held the book in his hands fresh off the press, its ninety-two pages within a cover of thick paper, his heart palpitated triumphantly. So much of his young life had been devoted to the development of this book, whose poems had gestated over the better part of a decade, in which he had undertaken "the greatest departure from myself: creation, wanting to illuminate words." Now he had done it. And not just with a book of youthful poems published by a student press, but what he felt was a "real" book of poetry published by a press that, in the same year, was the first to publish a book in Chile by his old mentor Gabriela Mistral.[*]

---

[*]   *Desolación.* The Instituto de las Españas in New York had published a smaller version of the book in 1922.

In this book, Neruda developed a lyrical style in which he truly il-luminated words in a revolutionary way, packing them full of emo-tion and imagery. This "greatest departure" from his creative self came only when he allowed himself to give up on his writing that too closely echoed Sabat Ercasty's. He stripped that style away to reveal a new po-tency. Making that break was anguishing at the time, but instead of stagnating in his sullenness, Neruda swallowed his pride and shut those old poems in a drawer. He forged forth and triumphed.

The book generated excitement from the start. For Neruda's genera-tion, it became a monumental cultural event, breaking through the for-mal strictures that had previously defined Latin American poetry and employing a new, frank, often brutal and brutally beautiful language. The book was particularly moving to students; even engineering stu-dents were seen reading it. For many, just reading and rereading the verses wasn't enough. They had to read them out loud, at lunch with friends or at sunset all alone. Neruda's friends and many others quickly memorized a large portion of the book. People listened to recitals of the poems in theater halls and other spaces, not necessarily by Neruda but by professional readers of poetry who immediately made his *Twenty Love Poems* part of their repertoire.

It was a book that made the era and was made by it. The youth of that generation discovered themselves in the poems, recognized them-selves in them. They identified with the love they were reading. In those years, young women had started to assert themselves on the so-cial scene. The 1920s was a time of budding sexual freedom in many parts of the world, and the time was ripe for a book that spoke to the revolutionary sexual movement among Chilean youth.

Neruda's popularity soared. The potential for him to find new muses multiplied among the surging ranks of female fans captured by *Twenty Love Poems*. He had come a long way from the essay in *Claridad* about being able to have sex only with prostitutes he couldn't afford. The student activist José Santos González Vera wrote that women read Neruda's poetry and "right away wanted a memento of their own." Yet during this time period, although the poet appeared to bask in attention from women, his attention was fixed just on Albertina and Laura.

★

From the outset, Neruda had wanted *Twenty Love Poems* to appeal not only to the younger generation, but also to older readers steeped in traditional poetry. Just as publishers who catered to a broader readership rejected it, upon its release those readers met it with resistance as well. In *Zig-Zag*, whose editor had turned down the book for publication, the writer and literature professor Mariano Latorre wrote a negative review of *Twenty Love Poems*. He stated that the book "fails to convince," that "its pain, its desperation, is excessively rhetorical and cerebral." Latorre couldn't find any real fury in the book, no outburst, "no shout in which the poet lets himself go and his poetry acquires the painful and simple intimacy that marks Verlaine's."

Another critic, the Augustinian priest Alfonso Escudero, in an article on Chile's 1924 literary activity in the respected magazine *Atenea*, concluded that "emotion is absent" in Neruda's verses. Even Alone, who had financed the publication of Neruda's first book and kept up correspondence with the young poet, wasn't convinced of the new volume's merits. In his review in the newspaper *La Nación*, Alone explained that *Twenty Love Poems* was unfortunately dominated by "a certain halting, almost painful brusqueness, the result, perhaps, of an excessive ambition for novelty." While this might have worked for others, it didn't work for Alone. "Women always believe words of love directed at them are beautiful; but we find them disconcerting, disorienting and senseless." In his use of "we," he seems to separate the perspective of one generation from another, men from women. He added, "I understand that some madness is needed to speak in verse and to sing, but madness, as with everything, has its limits."

In conclusion he compares the book to a barren field. While the earth is swollen and the field well plowed, the seeds tossed by the poet's generous hands "still haven't sprouted, they lack the water of human emotion . . . Let us wait like the farmers who always defer their hope until the next year."

The contrast was stark between the established critics' rejections and the vitalized emotions so many others received from Neruda's work. Why such disparity between the critics and the public? The former simply didn't know how to respond to such work. They were disturbed by the direct mentions of sex in the poem. Yet they also failed to embrace Neruda's subliminal use of sexual wordings as a poetic tool, especially in the construction of the metaphors woven through the book. Furthermore, the fixation by critics (and many readers) on the references to the body overshadowed fundamental aspects of the book's potency. The poems are filled more with pining than professions of love. Some of the erotic language may have been strong and different, even violent in its diction—"I'm going to plow through you"—but the poems themselves are not truly seductive.

The critics and similar old-guard readers could see his imagery only as being uncomfortably direct and thus dismissed it as not being poetry of culture, as insulting and lowbrow. Traditional folklore, especially seen in the song and dance of the Chilean *cueca,* as well as in a good deal of contemporary popular art, was abundant with corporeal and sexual terms. But folklore was "low culture"; poetry was supposed to be "high culture." This separation colored most criticism of the time.

Critics like Alone and Latorre were still clinging to poetry steeped in sentimentalism, especially Chilean poets such as Manuel Magallanes Moure and Max Jara. Jara's latest book, published just two years before *Twenty Love Poems,* had swept up Alone, Latorre, and others in its melancholy. Despite the deliberately manufactured construction of that sentiment—exactly what Neruda was trying to avoid in his compositions—the critics held on to these poems as ideal representatives of Chile's high culture. They weren't sure what to do then when this "peasant" Pablo Neruda, just a kid, tried to lower, if not eliminate, the separation between the echelons, to make high-quality, serious poetry accessible to all.

While the critics seemed shocked by the raw eroticism in his lines, Neruda was not the first highly regarded South American poet to use such imagery. In the years between the turn of the century and *Twenty Love Poems'* 1924 debut, two highly successful, rather revolutionary female poets on the other side of the Andes had already written erotic verse that also visibly connected the body and the soul. The revered Uruguayan poets Delmira Agustini and Juana de Ibarbourou—the latter so popular across the continent that she'd earn the nickname Juana de América—infused such motifs into highly sexual poems. Still, to the critics (and many readers) in Santiago, these women were outside their orbit and were not seen as relevant enough to threaten the definition of poetry, as this young man from their own provinces did.

Critics and other readers also had difficulties dealing with the language Neruda constructed, not just because of its eroticism, but because the book's phrases and metaphors simply sounded so different: "Leaning into the evenings I toss my sad nets / to that sea which stirs your ocean eyes" (Poem VII), or "Thinking, trapping shadows in the profound solitude . . . Thinking, letting birds loose, undoing images, burying lamps" (Poem XVII). The forms of the poems also varied throughout the book, which was unsettling for some, captivating for others.

In his important book *The Poetry of Pablo Neruda,* René de Costa highlights other fundamental features that troubled readers while also propelling the book's potency. In *Twenty Love Poems,* the concern is with the present; in fact, it is the actual moment of pensive experience that Neruda targets. Each poem in the book sounds like a monologue in which the poet seems to be speaking to himself. He lyricizes previously unarticulated thoughts, most often aching thoughts that had been bottled up inside him. The intense concentration of this unexpressed feeling emboldens the confessional intimacy of the poet's voice. This, de Costa writes, is an underlying reason why *Twenty Love Poems* continues to be as powerful to the modern reader as it was when it was first released.

Neruda anchored these nontraditional methods of composition in basic literary devices with set meters, rhyme schemes, and internal rhyme and repetition. All his work writing alexandrines as a teenager in Temuco enabled him to form these intricate constructions, adding precision to the lyricism. They frame the poem so that when he pushes against them, the tension makes the lines spring off the page.

Neruda's poetry ventured into the same space that would be occupied by expressionist painters, as well as the monumental muralists David Alfaro Siqueiros and Diego Rivera. The poems were figurative and realist, but dimensionally epic. Neruda had great aspirations for the book, and he succeeded in his main mission, which was to communicate to a wider audience. If traditional Chilean poetry could be compared to chamber music, Neruda's book was a concert whose music resonated through a stadium. The publication of *Twenty Love Poems* was a true phenomenon.

Since the turn of the century, more and more people without a strong public education were reading poetry, and that poetry was becoming increasingly accessible. When Neruda's book came along, it reached people of diverse social origins, especially those from the lower classes and, especially, the lower-middle class, which made up a significant sector of Chilean society. The book was devoured passionately like no other book in Chile before.

Despite the fantastic reception from the general public, Neruda psychologically couldn't overcome the dismissal from established critics and academics, despite some very positive reviews by his peers. Alone's failure to grasp his work hit Neruda hard; he was frustrated and impatient.[*] Diego Muñoz tried to reason with him one night in a bar, saying that beyond the critics, the purpose of literature lies in its ability to communicate what one feels and to empower others with language to communicate what they themselves feel. With revolutionary developments, it takes time for the old guard—the Alones and Latorres—to catch up. "Your *Twenty Poems* . . . they need no explanation, no guide to explain what you wanted to say because it's clearly said."

Forget those formal critics, Muñoz urged Neruda. But the criticism had taken its toll. Neruda became depressed again and publicly defended himself in a rather audacious, if not over-the-top, open letter printed in *La Nación,* the paper that had printed Alone's negative review. Entitled "Exegesis and Solitude," it read:

> I undertook the greatest departure from myself: creation, wanting to illuminate words. Ten years of solitary labor,

---

[*] Years later, Alone admitted that his negative review derived from the fact that he was "seduced and a bit tyrannized by the French spirit." He had thought that without "clarity, simplicity, and order, there was no salvation."

exactly half of my life, have caused diverse rhythms and contrary currents to succeed one another in my expression. Tying, braiding them together, without finding anything timeless, because it doesn't exist, you have the *Twenty Love Poems and a Desperate Song* . . . I have suffered much in making them . . . I tried to add more and more emotion to my thinking and I've achieved some success: everything that's come from me I've done with sincerity and good intentions.

In fact, the jabs he received from critics were few, while the consensus of popular sentiment was positive. Carlos George Nascimento's risk had paid off. The book may, at the time, have been a succès de scandale, but it was quite a success nonetheless. And it would continue to be so: in the future, *Twenty Love Poems* would go on to become one of the most popular books of poetry in the world. By 1972, two million copies had been sold in Spanish alone, with far more sold in translation. Though global sales numbers are hard to pin down, expert estimates are around ten million copies.

The enormously influential Argentine author Julio Cortázar, while reminiscing about Neruda a year after his death, provided a poignant picture of the book's overall effect. Very few knew of Neruda when *Twenty Love Poems* first arrived in Buenos Aires. But the book

suddenly gave us back what was ours, tore us away from vague notions of European muses and mistresses to throw us into the arms of an immediate tangible woman, and teach us that a Latin American poet's love could happen *hic et nunc* [here and now] and be written that way, in the simple words of the day, with the smell of our streets, with the simplicity in which we could discover beauty without having to agree to a grand purple style and divine proportions.

That raw sexuality was key, as was the break from the traditional European tropes and the shift to a new poetic language representing a Latin America–centric voice and eroticism. The eroticism—which includes a subtle depiction of oral sex—isn't just thrown onto the page, but rather intertwines the corporeal body and the soul. The soul is painfully, intimately present and the heart is exposed. The majority of the poems are about the tragedies of love, the pining, the despair. They aren't stock phrases to try to capture or excite someone you desire.

Neruda's effectiveness in combining them is in part due to the literary devices he implements so deftly. The book begins with four stanzas of alexandrines. It also starts with a series of uncomplicated, vivid metaphors and similes—another signature trait. The first lines of Poem I are:

> Body of woman, white hills, white thighs,
> you look like the world in your attitude of giving.

Comparing women to nature was nothing new, but Neruda does it with a new richness and intensity. Diverse transcendental landscapes or nightscapes are integral components of nearly every poem of the book.

Woman is, like the world, bounteously available. Here, Neruda seems to be looking at Albertina (supposedly) right before they have sex. He's directing his attention to her straight on, as she lies in front of him in her "attitude of *entrega*." *Entrega* can be translated as a delivery, a giving of something, as well as surrender, or the giving over of one's self.

In the next lines, he penetrates her body, her world, connecting with her profoundly:

> My savage peasant body plows through you
> and makes the son surge from the depths of the earth.

His anguish relied on the hope of carnal relief:

> I went alone as a tunnel. Birds fled from me,
> I was invaded by the power of the night.
> To survive myself I forged you like a weapon,
> like an arrow in my bow, like a stone in my sling.

He shoots his phallic arrow, in retaliation for his injured heart:

> But the hour of vengeance strikes, and I love you.
> Body of skin, of moss, of ardent, constant milk.

The drama echoes his letters to Albertina: vengeance, followed by declarations of love. Here as well, Neruda portrays Albertina as absent as he engages the "chalices" of her breasts. He attempts to fill that absence and she moans:

> Ah the chalices of the breasts! Ah the eyes of absence!
> Ah the roses of the pubis! Ah your voice slow and sad!

But his orgasm does not satisfy:

> Body of my woman, I will persist in your grace.
> My thirst, my infinite anguish, my indecisive path!
> Dark riverbeds where eternal thirst follows,
> and fatigue follows, and infinite sorrow.

Despite an audience to share in his yearnings, and despite the popular acclaim for *Twenty Love Poems,* fatigue and sorrow continued to follow Neruda. As he turned twenty and embraced a life of literary success, there was another challenge that started to make itself starker, dogging him and his hopes for the future: the need to make a living.

CHAPTER SEVEN

DEAD GALLOP

Every day I have to find money to eat. I have suffered
a bit, my girl, and I have wanted to kill myself, out of
boredom and desperation.

    —Letter to Albertina Azócar, August 26, 1925

When Albertina's brother, Rubén, returned to Chile from a trip to Mexico in May 1925, he found his friend Neruda in sad shape. Despite the success of *Twenty Love Poems and a Desperate Song*, "Pablo's state of mind was anxious, disconcerted," Rubén wrote.

The frequent letters Neruda sent Albertina during this period demonstrated his disquietude. One missive is especially revealing of his mental state. It was written during a difficult visit to his parents' in Temuco, on September 24, 1924, "at night, beside the fire."

These days have been bitter, my little Albertina. Nervous breakdown or accumulation of crap. I can't bear it alone. At night: insomnia, painful, long. I become desperate, feverish. Last night I read two long novels. I already woke up and I still toss and turn in bed like an invalid . . . Why did my mother give birth to me among these stones? And as exhausted as I am I haven't the strength to take the train [back to Santiago] . . .

Rubén had noted that Neruda was suffering through a trio of problems: "money, love, and poetry."

With regard to love, Neruda was still furious at and obsessed with Albertina, who was studying in Concepción. In Temuco on summer vacation in March 1925, Neruda had written her another letter from his boyhood desk. The words he chose for the salutation were "Ugly brat." He told her that he didn't know what people were telling her about him, but that it was all meaningless, because he loved her.

Perhaps she'd heard about him sleeping with the young Laura Arrué or other girls: "You know that I like to have fun . . . [but my] heart belongs to you, my little cockroach, thread by thread, all the way down to the roots. Everything else, can it matter to you?"

He asked her what plans she had to return to Santiago. "I believe you need to do this: take advantage of the faith your father has in you, speak to him seriously, and tell him that you inevitably have to study [in Santiago], win it, conquest it." He urged her to respond, ending the letter, "Think of how I need to hear from you every day, darling bitch."

No words from Neruda could enable Albertina to challenge her father. Neruda, meanwhile, never seems to have thought to move to Concepción, even though it was home to one of the best universities outside of Santiago.

Albertina still found Neruda intriguing and compelling. While he constantly insulted her in his letters, he would wrap tender expressions of affection around his insults. He had proven his devotion by coming to her bedside every day after her surgery. He had written remarkable poems to her. He had a distinguished mind, a handsome appearance, and, of course, a prominent reputation now as a young, startling poet.

While one part of Neruda's mind was fixed on the unattainable Albertina, he was still smitten with Laura Arrué in Santiago. After she graduated from high school, they began to see each other frequently. She had a "celestial" beauty and charming disposition, according to his friends; she was bright and embarking on a successful teaching career. Their relationship seems to have been sexual from the start. In 1924, he gave her a copy of *Twenty Love Poems*. "Hide them under your mattress," he told her. "They'd better not find them because they'll tear it up."

Yet while he and Laura were engaged in their love affair, he was writing frequent letters to Albertina in Concepción. A year after the publication of *Twenty Love Poems,* his words to her continued to match its verses. "Ah," he wrote Albertina that April, "if you only knew, my dear little woman, the crazy desire to have you next to me . . . to eat you up with kisses that are greater than this absence."

Neruda faithfully accompanied Laura to the Ministry of Education as she inquired about her forthcoming teaching appointment, helping her secure the position she deserved. The job was at a little school in Peñaflor, a small town twenty miles southwest of Santiago. Despite the relatively short distance, the logistics of transportation made it difficult for Neruda to visit her. He had to take a train at eight A.M., get off in Malloco, and then take a coach pulled by four Percherons. But it was well worth it for him to surprise Laura. The *flor* in Peñaflor means "flower"; the area was famous for its abundant greenery and streams, large parks among century-old haciendas bursting with flowers. Neruda would return to Santiago before dusk, bunches of lilacs and honeysuckles in his hands, flushed and smiling.

As their romance became more intense, so did the obstacles between them. Just like with Amelia and Teresa, Laura's parents took actions to prevent their eighteen-year-old daughter from sleeping with a famed bohemian "Don Juan" poet. They called on the family in whose residence Laura stayed to watch her every move and to try to prevent contact between the lovers.

Enraged and indignant, Neruda conspired to kidnap Laura, with her consent. His partner in the operation was Eduardo Barrios, the same writer who had helped convince Carlos Nascimento to publish *Twenty Love Poems.* He owned a car—the key to the operation. The two waited until midnight, flashing the car's headlights to send off the agreed-upon signals. But Laura had lost her courage to attempt such a brazen act. While the idea had seemed thrilling and romantic at first, its potential repercussions were too severe. The writers waited and waited, but Laura never came out. Neruda returned to Santiago, sullen with disappointment.

Neruda's financial situation was as desperate as his love life. Despite

Twenty Love Poems' popularity, the number of copies actually sold was slim, the royalties a pittance. José del Carmen, having realized that his son had suspended his studies, completely cut off the allowance he had been providing.

Upon Neruda's solicitation, Nascimento hired Neruda to assemble an anthology of selected works by the Socialist French Nobel laureate Anatole France. But that money did not sustain him for long. Writing for *Claridad* couldn't keep him afloat, nor could the pieces he placed here and there in mainstream newspapers. Since he would not be graduating from the Pedagogy Institute, he could not teach in a formal setting for lack of formal credentials. He didn't teach informally either. He did receive some compensation for recitals and talks, but he was not actively marketing himself as a speaker for hire.

Though his sister, Laura, served as intermediary, delivering secret small gifts of cash from his stepmother, Neruda depended as much on his renown in the bohemian world to pay for meals and drinks as he did on his uncertain cash flow. When he returned to Santiago from Temuco at the end of March 1925, he didn't even have a room in a pension to call his own. He considered leaving Chile but didn't have the resources to do so.

Nascimento, meanwhile, was eager for more work from his star poet and gave him a tiny advance for a new book. Though it was just a minor financial contribution, it may have served as valuable encouragement during Neruda's travails to tackle new creative terrain.

Rubén had mentioned that when he returned from Mexico, Neruda was in such a state that it seemed "his soul was spinning around itself, seeking its own center . . . he wanted to renew himself in some way, to examine himself from a different dimension." The desire for self-exploration, the craving for new perspectives through which he might ground himself, was leading Neruda to experiment once again with his style—he'd revive himself through the creative process.

Facing another aesthetic crossroads, Neruda recommitted to uncharted literary adventure and experimentation. Despite the love poems' unique potency, he was restless and determined to break with their lyrical realism and with poetry's traditional forms in general. He was done with realism. He now intended to "strip poetry of all its objectiveness and to say what I have to say in the most serious form possible."

This resulted in his discovery of a unique avant-garde form. It was void of rhyme and meter, and used no punctuation or capitalization in an attempt to better replicate the raw articulation of the subconscious. He strove to bring his poetry even closer to "irreducible purity, the closest approximation to naked thought, to the intimate labor of the soul." Neruda didn't even use capital letters in the title of the book that this experiment produced: *tentativa del hombre infinito* (*venture of the infinite man*). Twenty-five years after its publication, reflecting on what the experience did for him as a writer, Neruda would call *venture* "one of the most important books of my poetry."

With *venture* he was developing a unique form of automatic writing, a technique that enabled him to successfully move forward from the realism of his earlier poetry. In fact, he expounded on this new creative process in an article in *Claridad* the very month *Twenty Love Poems* was published, June 1924. It is titled, appropriately, "A Scattered Expression":

> I write and write without being enchained by my thought, without bothering to free myself from chance associations . . . I let my feelings loose in whatever I write. Disassociated, grotesque, my writing represents my diverse and discordant depth. I build in my words a construct with free matter, and while creating I eliminate what has no existence or any palpable hold.

The approach Neruda delineates in this article is in line with many of the tenets of the surrealist movement developing in Paris. Yet "A Scattered Expression" appeared four months before André Breton published the *Surrealist Manifesto* in Paris, showing that Neruda was right there with the avant-garde, if not, in his own way, even a bit out in front of it. His writing method wasn't an appropriation; Neruda's method was very much his own.

Surrealism stems from the principle that true creative force comes from the unconscious and that art is the main vehicle for its release. As

Breton wrote in his manifesto, it is "based on the belief in the superior reality of certain forms of previously neglected associations." The "omnipotence of dream" and the "disinterested play of thought" are key.

Yet, as René de Costa highlights, while Breton and other surrealists wanted to capture the voice of the subconscious, Neruda wanted to only emulate its style. Toward this end, he didn't let the flow of spontaneous thought fall purely onto the final page. Instead, he filtered those "scattered expressions" with some review and revision, improving the composition's clarity, creating some conscious constructions and recurring themes.[*]

These measured changes gave Neruda a kind of life preserver for the poem to stay afloat above the incomprehensibility of the deep unconscious. Thus protected, Neruda moved closer toward recapturing the subconscious through his novel technique of stripping out all punctuation and capitalization, not only as a means of bringing his poetry closer to "naked thought," but as an artistic aid that loosened the flow of the poetic discourse, an uninhibited structure that mirrors the poem's dreamscape setting.[†]

That dreamscape permeates the book, which centers on the fantas-

---

[*]   There were more stylistic elements and influences in *venture* than those just behind the scattered expression initiative. The poets Neruda's eccentric French teacher Ernesto Torrealba had pushed him to read in the *liceo*, especially Mallarmé and Apollinaire, informed the book's style, substance, and vision. And *venture*'s nocturnal journey has similarities to the voyage in Rimbaud's "Le bateau ivre" ("The Drunken Boat"). Neruda was also influenced by the experimental verse of Vicente Huidobro, a Chilean writing in Paris at the time, eleven years and one literary generation his elder. *Venture* was actually a type of "poetic workshop," as Neruda once put it, in which he explored and experimented with the different styles and voices of all these different poets.

[†]   When Nascimento eventually sent him *venture*'s proofs, Neruda returned them immediately, having made no changes. "No mistakes?" the publisher asked. Neruda's response: "There are and I'm leaving them." Just as Neruda intentionally omitted capital letters and punctuation marks (though he did use accent marks), by leaving in these natural slips he felt he was better emulating the sounds of the subconscious voice.

tic nocturnal voyage of a melancholic young man who sets off on a quest to rediscover himself, to reach a state of pure consciousness. We accompany him as he embarks on a journey through time and space, through unity and disunity with the night, a lyrical narrative, played out over fifteen cantos, each uniquely composed but intimately linked. They are spread over forty-four pages, divided up and placed on each page in an inconsistent but not random fashion, creating blocks of white space that add to the book's illusory feel.

The poem's Infinite Man searches for absolute oneness, a new reality, a restored consciousness—a quest that mirrors Neruda's own search for self-discovery and expression. In fact, the book has been described as "one part quest and one part inner map." And interestingly, it is through a creative process originating in "scattered" thoughts and unconscious tone that the quest is composed. Neruda was twenty when he first started writing *venture;* at the beginning of the book we learn that the poem's subject is "a man of twenty." We see this young man with his "soul in despair," the same state in which Rubén found Neruda just before he began writing *venture,* with his soul "spinning around itself, seeking its own center."

In the opening canto, Neruda depicts an almost cinematic tapestry of the nocturnal void through which the man will travel. Soon, like Alice with her looking glass, he will shatter "my heart like a mirror in order to walk through myself." He is now enabled to travel through night, attempting to conquer it so that he can achieve that absolute oneness. In a midbook climax, he achieves physical union during a sexual experience with night, personified as a woman; he becomes one with the night:

> twisting to that side or beyond you continue being mine
> in the solitude of dusk your smile knocks
> in that instant vines climb to my window
> wind from high above lashes the hunger for your presence

Following the ecstasy of this climactic encounter with night, we no longer find him melancholic. He is enlivened:

>   ah i surprise myself i sing delirious under the big top
>   like a lovestruck tightrope walker or the first fisherman

He also now has the ability to be a poet, and he begins to meditatively seek his inner self:

>   letting the sky in deeply watching the sky i am thinking
>   sitting uncertainly on that edge
>   oh sky woven with water and paper
>   i began to speak to myself in a low voice determined not to leave

This ties in to Rubén's description of Neruda's determination to conduct his own introspective search. This desire for self-exploration and the craving for new perspectives through which he might ground himself not only led Neruda to experiment with his creative process and style, but also manifested themselves as elements of *venture*'s narrative: that meditative thinking generates the poetic narrative.

And while, by the final canto, it seems that he has achieved his quest ("i am standing in the light like midday on earth / i want to tell it all with tenderness"), off the written page, the completion of the book brought no immediate personal resolution to his trio of agitations, "love, money, and poetry." His new book failed to garner the critical and popular reception he had hoped for, outside of those few on the vanguard.* Indeed, in 1950, twenty-five years after he finished writing it, Neruda noted that *venture* was "the least read and least studied of all my work." The book has consistently been passed over primarily because of its heavy experimentalism, which, on the one hand, makes it so exceptional and rich, yet, on the other, has caused readers, critics, and publishers (and translators) to shy away from its unconventional

---

* The book was appreciated by some of the leading Latin American avant-garde poets at the time. Huidobro included it in the landmark anthology *Índice de la nueva poesía americana*, which appeared the same year *venture* came out. (It also featured a poem by Rubén Azócar.) Huidobro also published one of the cantos in an issue of the French journal *Favorables Paris poema*, which he was editing with César Vallejo.

form. It didn't help that its feeble reception was quickly overshadowed by the tremendous achievements of *Residencia en la tierra* (*Residence on Earth*), his subsequent book of poetry (achievements, as we shall see, that were in part due to his experimentation in *venture*).

One of the first mainstream reviews of *venture* came from Raúl Silva Castro, the former student leader who was the first to publish Neruda in *Claridad*. Now a critic for *El Mercurio,* he complained: "The flesh and blood we had admired so much in the author's other books are missing here . . . [A reader] might just as well begin to read from the back as from the front, or even the middle. One would understand the same, that is to say, very little." Alone, who wasn't too keen on *Twenty Love Poems,* was perplexed at this latest work. He referred to the book as "going the way of the absurd."

Venture's negative popular reception was certainly disconcerting to Neruda. But still, he had accomplished a remarkable achievement: for a poet known for his constant evolution, *venture* is one of the most striking examples of Neruda's growth as a poet. He successfully broke out of the confinements of the conventions he first trained on and found a new way to express himself freely, even inventing a way to capture the style of how language sounded inside his mind. The book may prove a bit difficult to follow, but it isn't a total spill of scattered thought. It shimmers with poetic tension and a sense of thematic purpose. Indeed, the first poems of his next book, *Residence on Earth,* drew on Neruda's unique approach to surrealism, displaying a novel use of expressive symbols and images. This is the most important result of Neruda's experimentation with *venture:* he had set forth to construct a new style and, in doing so, built the essential poetic infrastructure that served as the bridge between the blockbuster lyrics of *Twenty Love Poems* and his unprecedented, tremendously resounding, and influential *Residence on Earth.*

Neruda himself saw this work as crucial to his evolution as a poet: "I have always looked upon *venture of the infinite man* as one of the real nuclei of my poetry," he said at the age of fifty, "because working on those poems, in those now distant years, I was acquiring a consciousness that I didn't have before, and if my expressions, their clarity or mystery, are anywhere measured, it is in this extraordinarily personal little book . . . Within its smallness and minimal expression, more than most of my works . . . it claimed, it secured, the path that I had to follow."

★

Neruda's friendships were a positive note in his life, as his relationship with Rubén Azócar shows. Rubén was highly intelligent, and so diligent and passionate about his work as a teacher that his friends and students called him a *"profesor de profesores."* While he was popular in the FECh crowd, he stayed away from the vices of the bohemian lifestyle. His eyebrows were imposing, so bushy that friends called them "tree brows." Straightforward and constantly cheerful, Rubén was a steadying presence for Neruda. He was one of Neruda's closest friends, since before his first encounter with Rubén's sister Albertina.

After he returned from teaching in Mexico, Rubén received a job in the *liceo* of Ancud, the small but principal town on Chiloé, a gorgeous green island off the southern Chilean coast. Always generous, Rubén invited Neruda to join him, hoping the refreshing change of scenery from Santiago would ameliorate his friend's angst. He even offered to help Neruda financially by sharing a little of his teaching salary. Desperate for something different, Neruda accepted Rubén's offer and went with him to write on that verdant island.

Neruda and Rubén took the train to Concepción. During the few days they were there, Neruda managed to see Albertina alone. Still, she resisted his urgent pressure to join him in Chiloé, or anywhere. There was her father, but there was also her own determination to finish her degree. She wouldn't abandon her studies to go live with him on an island, especially given that neither of them had a job. Neruda left Concepción terribly frustrated, unable to persuade Albertina even face-to-face. He left for Temuco bitterly, Rubén alongside.

Concepción adjoins Talcahuano, the port city where José del Carmen had worked the dry docks and enjoyed his secret love with Aurelia Tolrá, the mother of Neruda's half sister, Laura. As Neruda's train to Temuco left Albertina behind, it followed the same rails that had taken his father from his own lover, so many years before.

It was winter, and rain covered the south, reminding Neruda of his childhood in Temuco. He was about to have another tempestuous run-in with his father. Now twenty-one, Neruda braced himself just as he had when he was a teenager. Inside their pioneer house, José del Carmen exploded at his son, yelling so loud he could be heard from the street. He demanded to know why Neruda had interrupted his studies yet again and refused to support him while he abandoned his path to a steady career and the middle class. And José certainly wasn't going to pay for him to write poetry. If Neruda insisted on being a writer, he would have to prove that he could support himself.

After a few days in Temuco, while Rubén continued on to Chiloé to begin teaching at his new school, something made Neruda turn back to Santiago. He hadn't given up on the idea of going to Chiloé entirely; in fact he wrote to Albertina from the capital of how he was imagining "the first night that we sleep together under the stars of Ancud." (At the same time, true to his nature, Neruda rekindled his relationship with Laura Arrué, even as he kept writing to Albertina.) He wrote that he'd been sick but was thinking of going to Chiloé in October or November, then begged her to go with him, admonished her for not agreeing to join him, for not even writing him. Two years had passed since the publication of Poem XV, about Albertina's silence and absence, which ends: "A word then is sufficient, or a smile, to make me happy / Happy that it seems so certain you are present." Now he concludes a letter to her, "One honest word from you, brat, and you wouldn't make me take this stupid trip."

No word came from Albertina, though, so he headed back south at the end of November. After a stop in Temuco, Neruda continued on to the town of Osorno. He'd normally be able to see the towering, active, glacier-capped Osorno volcano from town, but it was hidden by a furious rain, making it seem as displaced and dormant as so much of Neruda's inner workings. The rain covered the town in a tremendous sadness, Neruda told Albertina in a postcard he sent her the following day. On November 23, 1925, he traveled to Puerto Montt, where he took a small steamboat across the Chacao Channel to Chiloé.

The trip was a much-needed escape. His spirits started to lift while on the boat, looking out across the expanse of water in the incessant rain. This was the first time Neruda had left Chile's mainland, and it was an important break. Chiloé Island, the second largest in South America, sits off Chile's shore, just north of where Patagonia begins, snowcapped volcanoes visible in the distance. It is a fabled, myth-inspiring land of indigenous folklore, abounding with tales of forest gnomes and witches.

It was completely disconnected from Neruda's familiar terrain, especially Santiago: full of wide lakes and dense forests; tapestried with wild berries; dotted—if you could catch a glimpse of them—with tiny pudú deer, not even two feet tall; and with dolphins swimming off the coast. Chiloé is encircled by an archipelago of smaller islands. Some sixty unique wooden churches line the coast, placed like lighthouses to guide sailors home, their symmetrical tower facades and arched entrances painted in colors ranging from bright yellows to deep blues. In the towns, tiny houses painted in heart-tapping tones of blue, yellow, and red hug the shore, with the majority extending out on stilts over the free real estate of the water.

Rubén had rented a "very passable" room for the two of them in the Hotel Nilsson. It cost only about a tenth of his salary, so Rubén treated Pablo to everything and, on that first night, they ate like kings: the best lamb from Patagonia and fresh thick salmon caught right off the coast. They stayed up late smoking the best tobacco, and they sent sacks of oysters and some drinking money up to their friends in Santiago. The town took a liking to the bohemians from the capital. They made many friends and read their poetry aloud in Ancud's main plaza. In Chiloé Neruda found the enrichment, rest, diversion, and creative inspiration he needed.

After Nascimento had received the manuscript for *venture of the infinite man,* he gave Neruda a small advance to start a new project.[*] Won-

---

[*]   The interaction with Nascimento, at least when Neruda received and dismissed *venture*'s proofs, actually took place in Santiago, around the end of 1925. The school year done and the holidays coming, Rubén and Neruda had returned home for a bit. Neruda spent time with Laura Arrué, but when she left for San Fernando to spend the summer with her family, he returned to Chiloé, where his lifestyle was more affordable and conducive to writing.

dering what might become of the experiment, he asked Neruda to write a book of fiction, with the only condition that it be some type of crime story. As he started to compose this new book on Chiloé, the island's dreamscape surroundings began to inspire the novella's images and feel (to some degree, a continuation of *venture*'s oneiric atmosphere). Furthermore, the coastal geography in the story's setting mirrors the area around Puerto Saavedra, the coast of his youth.

Entitled *El habitante y su esperanza* (The Inhabitant and His Hope), it is a passionate prose adventure of love and crime in the darkness of the Chilean frontier. Neruda called it, in parentheses under the title, a "novel," but it definitely is not one. It is closer to a novella, made up of short chapters that stretch over just seventy-six pages. Nascimento published it at the end of the year, just after the author turned twenty-two. It was his fourth book. Like *venture of the infinite man,* it was received with little enthusiasm. Some found merit in it, though: Alone, in his positive review for *La Nación,* called it "a triumph."

In the book's prologue, Neruda writes:

> I've got a dramatic and romantic outlook on life; what doesn't completely enter into my awareness doesn't belong.
>
> It was very difficult for me to combine this spiritual constant with a way of expressing it that was more or less my own. In my second book, TWENTY LOVE POEMS AND A DESPERATE SONG, I already had something of a masterpiece. The levelheaded imbeciles that form part of our literary lives will never know the happiness that comes from being self-reliant.
>
> As a citizen, I am a quiet man, enemy of established laws, governments, and institutions. I am disgusted by the bourgeois and love the lives of the restless and unsatisfied, be they artists or criminals.

In *El habitante,* right after the prologue, we delve into a rich, dreamy world set in Cantalao, inspired by Puerto Saavedra, setting the sensory tone for the entire book, which is written in the first person.

Now, my house is the last one in Cantalao, facing the roaring sea, tucked in against the mountains.

Summer is sweet, languid, but winter emerges suddenly from the sea like a net of sinister fish striking the sky, piling on top of one another, jumping, spitting, and grumbling. The wind makes its sterile noises, different ones depending on whether it is whipping along, whistling through metal fences, or spinning its dark *boleadora* above the village, or coming from the ocean sweeping along in an infinite line.

Many times I have been alone in my home when a storm whips the coast. I'm calm because I don't fear or love death, but I like to watch the morning, which almost always arises clean and gleaming. It's not rare for me to sit down on a tree trunk watching the immense ocean from afar, smelling the fresh air, watching each cart crossing toward town with its merchants, Indians, workers, and travelers. A sort of waiting power has seeped into my way of living that day, a way superior to indolence, superior to my indolence precisely.

One of *El habitante*'s qualities is Neruda's juxtaposition of poetic prose against realistic narration, so that its style and imagery almost supersede the plot. As Alone put it, "It's a story and it's not a story." The story: A horse thief finds his lover dead, naked on the bed, cold like a great silver fish from the sea. She was killed by her husband, the thief's partner, after he discovered their affair. The horse thief then avenges his lover's death by murdering her husband, and then he escapes into the dark countryside of the frontier.

The "nonstory" is conjured through layers of surrealistic images. It all takes place in silence, slipping through a raging rain in the woods, with a river that collides with a crying black sea, the blackness enveloping everything. The underlying structure of Neruda's novella is based on the surrealistic idea of creating two disparate realities, and thus besides the "story," he creates an emotional power and poetic reality, which is the "nonstory," the force and the value in the book.

It was not, however, a success with the public, nor would it ever be.

Alone's review was the only notable positive one; most critics passed it over. Even Neruda's stature couldn't help sell the book. He would write several other prose books and a play, but *El habitante* would be his only published attempt at fiction.

★

In June 1926, Neruda was ready to return to Santiago from Chiloé. Always a dapper dresser, he wanted to return in style, which meant wearing oxford pants. Nobody on the isolated island knew of them, so he had to sketch out a model himself to take to the tailor. Once they were ready, a dinner was thrown for him on the evening of his departure at the Hotel Nilsson. Rubén claimed that around 150 people showed up to send Neruda off, including local dignitaries.

Just as Neruda's spirits had lifted on the ferry out to Chiloé, they sank as he took up his old life in Santiago. The new paths he had explored may have produced richness on the page, but they did not prove helpful with his mood.

Upon his return, he rented a room with two friends, Tomás Lago and Orlando Oyarzún—none of them could afford a room of his own. In that room over several months, Neruda and Lago collaborated on a small volume of twenty-one expressionistic, experimental prose pieces that would be published by Nascimento that same year, 1926. The book's title, *Anillos* (Rings), reflected the successful fusion of the pair's styles, diverse writing backgrounds, and avant-garde intentions. Their relationship was so well bonded that it is hard to tell whose story is whose, and no notations are given to convey individual authorship.

The book is heavily rooted in the landscape, weather, and seasons of the south. Along with the familiar themes of melancholy, anguish, and solitude, autumn, wind that dries out the soul, and the sea return over and over again. Produced by free association, the prose swells with potent eloquence as Neruda, with Lago, broke through to yet another poetic style. Some passages seem far out, even today:

> The southern skies keep the guards awake and move by
> great blue leaps and reveal the jewels of the sky. I will say

that I remember her; I remember her; she came barefoot
so as not to break the dawn, and the sea in her eyes still did
not retreat. The birds flew away from her death like they do
from winters and metals.

The book never received significant attention, though its publica-
tion demonstrates how prolific Neruda was. Although none of his first
books was especially lengthy, he had published five works within three
years.

★

The room Neruda, Lago, and Oyarzún shared was up a set of narrow
stairs above a small produce shop and cafeteria. Their landlords were
the Edelmiras, a humble and kindhearted couple. La señora Edelmira
served Neruda abundant plates of food and lots of coffee when Neruda
finally came down the stairs in the afternoon. Oyarzún slept on a pile
of newspapers, and Neruda and Lago shared the same wire-spring
bed—with no mattress. In Neruda's inimitable style, he hung some old
umbrellas on the wall in which he hid letters and poems.

One day Laura Arrué came to deliver the news to Pablo that she
was leaving Santiago. Her mother had shown up all of a sudden at the
"request" of her older sister, Berta. Neruda, it seemed, had gained the
reputation of being something of a Don Juan, and Berta wanted to res-
cue her little sister from the danger of the bohemian avant-garde love
poet as quickly as possible. Laura's mother was to take her back to San
Fernando. Laura had come to say good-bye.

She managed to leave Santiago without a chaperone, which allowed
Neruda to accompany her to the train station. In the waiting room, he
recited lines to her he had just composed, a good-bye letter of sorts, say-
ing how hard it would be to get used to never seeing her:

Autumn appears in the corner of town and the broken
leaves signal that it's the abandoned one's time of year. The
loneliness is sad. You are in the doorway, you, doll with
round eyes, ships of painful minerals, blue flower, daybreak

between bracelets and despairs; from afar I throw you my anxiety striped with difficult lines of fire that will surprise you when you go leave, when you go out, the girl with her mother from San Fernando . . .

The lines continue with free-associative vanguard imagery and thoughts he had been using in his recent books. It was rather strange language for a good-bye note, completely different in tone from the antagonistic, in-your-face letters to Albertina. There were no signs of desperation in his words to Laura, whom he cherished, who became yet another lover separated from him by her parents.

There was no reprieve, however, from the angry angst he expressed in his letters to Albertina. He was still writing to her, a bit manically. "I've been through so much!" he exclaimed to her in one. He had published new books, but "I've come out of all this so tired, eager to rest in you. That is the impatience, the despondency you cause in me." He later writes, "For me it's as if you didn't exist . . . It's as if you weren't here now," again right out of Poem XV. However, as he does so often in his correspondence to her, the next line completely contradicts that sentiment: "And [yet] you are an anchor, the only one in my life." That positivity is once again followed by an ugly reproach in his strange psychological game of persuasion: "Really, sometimes I would like for you to die."

Neruda was notably tired upon his return to the city from Chiloé. The publication of his works and his growing fame and stature failed to offset his despondency. "I'm bored of everything[,] I'm thinking about dying at the first opportunity," he wrote to Albertina on May 12, 1926. Lyrically, with the new voice he had been developing, Neruda dove deep into the well of his growing depression. From it came the powerful poems that would form the first volume of his landmark *Residence on Earth*.

While Neruda was troubled by the paltry attention *venture* had received, this was partly a consequence of being overshadowed by the reception of his new poem "Galope muerto" ("Dead Gallop"). The poem was an exercise by Neruda to try to tackle the dead gallop of his mental state. It was a very serious composition for him, and he aimed for perfection. It appeared in *Claridad* right after *venture* came out and is one of the most important poems in the history of Spanish literature. Professor John Felstiner of Stanford University writes that in "Dead Gallop," Neruda achieved a "sense of a new reality that included not only the world's phenomena but the mind's potential to grasp them. 'Galope muerto' is Neruda's first attempt to embody—or rather, to enact—such a reality in verse." As the mental experiences he tries to communicate are not communicable in the inherited poetic language, he invents his own, a hermetic language of strange and esoteric symbolic imagery. Just like the lyrics of a song, even if their meaning is not immediately clear, the words can still exert a powerful hold on the listener. "Dead Gallop" would be the first poem in *Residence on Earth*, published eight years later.[*]

In the poem, Neruda is trying to bring some order to his innermost feelings. He is unable to grasp the "constant swirl," the rush of life that's "so quick, so lively," where his mind is "immobile . . . like the pulley wild on itself." It is only through finding and using his poetic perspective that he is able "to perceive . . . ay, that which my pale heart can't embrace." Through poetry, which slows life down for him, he can now get to the business of making sense of it all. He can contemplate, inquire. Everything begins to fall into order. Clarity comes only through the act of creating poetry.

Neruda also expresses a rare will to remain resilient in the face of the emotional, mental, and situational stimulants that swirl around him (as described midway through the poem):

> in multitudes, in tears scarcely shed,
> and human exertions, storms,

---

[*]   Time influences the reader's appreciation of the work, especially with these early *Residence* poems. Today one can feel the greatness of a poem like "Dead Gallop." But having read the literature produced since that time, a reader now would not be as astonished as those who read it at the time it was first published. "Dead Gallop" came out in the midst of a postwar enchantment with existentialism, when readers were not accustomed to the poem's enigmatic prosody, perhaps never having read anything like it before.

black actions suddenly discovered,
like ice, vast disorder,
oceanic . . .

Instead of just expressing his helplessness in its face, he inserts himself directly into the chaos; he "enters singing / like a sword among the defenseless." His singing—his poetry—is a weapon to fight off what's subsuming him, his will to create some semblance of order.

The poem moves from negativity to positivity. The first stanza ends with:

the fragrance of the plums rolling to the ground,
which rot in time, infinitely green.

The last lines of the poem read:

Within the ring of summer
the great pumpkins . . .
[are] stretching out their poignant plants,

With this stretching out of the pumpkin plants, Neruda too decides that he will stretch out, move forward. He is like that pumpkin, now being filled with inspiration.

It is one thing to write it on paper, though, and another to endure the realities of life.

*

In order to break out of his Santiago funk, Neruda would visit Valparaíso. Beyond the port and the large plazas lined by ornate colonial buildings, customhouses, and naval facilities, the city's forty-two hills rise on curved, mounded slopes like a natural amphitheater. Laid out along narrow, winding streets free of any sense of a grid, the city's two- and three-story houses tumble over the hillsides in a patchwork of colors, each house a different-colored brushstroke—magenta, topaz, aquamarine; the rich reds of Chilean wines—a bouquet of tones like a flock of parrots. And those colors are bejeweled with glittering zinc rooftops, laundry hung from windows, and countless church spires sticking up like little masts from ships. English funiculars—little trams on cables—run up and down the steepest hills, as if in a South American San Francisco. Valparaíso, in fact, was known as the "Jewel of the Pacific," and for Neruda it was just that.

Even during his first years in Santiago, Valparaíso's "magnetic pulse" seemed to beckon to him and his friends. After spending a whole night fraternizing in Santiago, they might impulsively take a third-class train car there at the break of dawn. For this motley crew of poets and painters, activists and romantics, "Valpo" was the perfect setting to let their brimming madness expand, explode, and release down the crazy hills and out into the Pacific.

Now, more mellow and contained than in those first years of active camaraderie, Neruda made his way to Valpo alone, to escape the scene in Santiago. He stayed with some new friends he had made: Álvaro Hinojosa, his sister, Sylvia, and their mother. The Hinojosa family had extended an open invitation to Neruda, and he took them up on it for a couple of days or even a couple of months at a time, not just for the inspiration of the unique atmosphere and the salty sea breeze, but also for the friendship of the Hinojosas, especially Álvaro. In Valparaíso's offbeat culture, in the poetry of its magnificent hills, twisted streets, and alleys, in his friends' home near the ocean, Neruda sought respite from his dour mood. Despite the admiration he had earned in Santiago, despite his energetic circle of friends, he was in a haze, more depressed than before. The relief he had experienced in Chiloé was already a distant memory. It didn't help that both Laura Arrué and Albertina Azócar had been sequestered away from him by their parents. He likely had found other romantic outlets during this time, but nothing lasted.

Álvaro was also a writer, primarily of short stories and columns. He never wrote the great work to which he aspired and never published a book. But that didn't matter to Neruda. What was of great importance was Álvaro's example of discipline and commitment to writing. Every morning Neruda stayed at their house, he would see Álvaro, still in bed, glasses on the bridge of his nose, typing quickly, continuously, consuming reams of whatever paper he could get his hands on.

Álvaro was also an important literary influence on Neruda, especially in his enthused introduction of the poet to the works of James Joyce. The Irish author's aesthetic theory would become key to Neruda's artistic development as a young man, as well as to his own particular aesthetics, as it revealed itself in *Residence on Earth*.

The first time Neruda came to the Hinojosas' house, Álvaro warned everyone not to worry about conversing with him, because he simply didn't like to talk. Everybody agreed, naturally, though his mother found this to be a rather strange trait for a guest. However, one night when Neruda arrived at the house alone after an evening out, he found Señora Hinojosa still up and began talking spontaneously with her. They chatted for a long while. When Sylvia asked her later what they talked about, she answered, "About business. He's an enchanting *muchacho*."

Although his mental state was lethargic, Neruda could walk for hours. Strolling through the hills, he'd peer into the alleyways that wove horizontally across the streets, never knowing what he'd find behind the lapis lazuli or aqua-green houses. Sometimes he would just sit in one of the city's plazas with the seafolk or go down the cobblestones to look at the sea and breathe it in. He could spend the rest of the day strolling through the markets, the antique shops, the huge open plazas down on the flats with the sea breeze, seagulls, wharf fish markets, and long orange customhouses. Then he would walk back up through the hills, climbing lines and lines of steep stairs up, then back down, here and there, and taking a funicular and looking out at the view. In the late afternoon he would stand on a pier as the sun dropped down into the ocean in front of him, displaying the same colors that he had seen five years before in the pension on Maruri Street, colors that inspired *The Book of Twilights* and still absorbed him with sadness.

Nevertheless, he saw some relief and hope in the sinking of that persimmon orange down into the water every evening. At those hours the sun cast a soft haze of light onto the multicolored hills; Neruda would try to absorb some of that art as he watched the sailors from Chile's navy or those working the cargo boats, doing the same job his father had done at the dry docks in Talcahuano. With his lonely eyes, he'd watch them drink and talk among themselves, or with women, the images in front of him seemingly drawn from his first well-known poem, "Farewell," published a few years ago now:

> I love the love of sailors
> who kiss, then leave.

"The Valparaíso night!" he wrote a half century later, "a point on the planet lit up, infinitesimal, in the empty universe." With the hills glowing like a golden horseshoe above the water, Neruda went out with Álvaro and sometimes other friends to experience the nightlife of the port and the forbidden districts. When they came home, he would often write until he fell asleep. Other days, however, when his gloom overcame him, he might barely manage to move out of the house.

Years later, Neruda built his own unconventional home in the hills above the enchanted port—one of three treasured homes he would eventually own. But in the mid-1920s he was still struggling for every peso. Consequently, Neruda and Álvaro concocted at least two business schemes to come up with some cash, finally acting on Señora Hinojosa's prompting and entrepreneurial ideas. Their most successful venture was designing and printing "comic postcards" accompanied by simple rhyming lines, which they tried to sell to people in the streets, on trains, and in restaurants. Their only successful postcard had a cut-out face of an apache—gangsters of the Parisian underworld during the Belle Époque were named after the Native American tribe—that moved against the postcard thanks to a tiny metal chain. Accompanying it was the text:

> Place the card horizontally,
> Shake it or tap it lightly,
> And you'll start to laugh uncontrollably.

They managed to convince an owner of several cinemas to use the card as publicity for a film he was then showing starring Lon Chaney, and he bought two hundred. Neruda then quickly wrote to Albertina that he was "thinking about getting involved in the movie business." Predictably, nothing came of that, and no more cards were sold. He had only just managed to stay afloat ever since he first arrived in Santiago, and now his economic situation was becoming more precarious than ever. On October 8, 1926, he wrote to his sister, Laura, in Temuco, begging her to ask Papá to send money, as the cheapest pension cost a hundred pesos that he didn't have. Despite the fact that José del Carmen had been adamantly against giving him any money, Neruda implored his sister to have him send it by telegraph "because I'm eating only once a day." He also needed all kinds of clothes, "especially shirts (N.° 37) and underwear, 87 cm. [34.25 in.] waist." He asked for socks and handkerchiefs too.

As his father had warned, Neruda needed an actual job with a stable income. He also wanted to escape the tight boundaries of Chile, ideally to Paris, the cultural epicenter of the contemporary avant-garde, where he could write—and just be—in the footsteps of Rimbaud, Baudelaire, Verlaine, and Mallarmé. Novelists, philosophers, linguists, painters, musicians, sculptors, and poets from all over the world were moving to Paris's Left Bank. The great Peruvian poet César Vallejo moved there, as did the Spanish painters Pablo Picasso and Joan Miró and U.S. writers such as Gertrude Stein, William Carlos Williams, Ernest Hemingway, Hilda "H.D." Doolittle, and Ezra Pound. Where else would Neruda want to be?

If not Paris, well, anywhere other than Temuco or Santiago. Even Valparaíso, which was a good momentary escape, couldn't offer him extended mooring or occupation. His peers were coming and going from distant parts of the world: Spain, Russia, Colombia. Neruda too longed to travel. But how? Several managed to get scholarships of some sort, either domestically or abroad, as journalists or musicians, but there was nothing for Neruda as a poet. In December 1926, Neruda wrote to his sister:

Laura,

I'm writing to tell you, only you, that I'm leaving to Europe on the third of January. Why would I go to Temuco? I'm so bored of fighting with my father. And if you could see my head as it's going crazy. I have fifteen days and I only have enough money for the passage alone. What will I eat in Genoa? Smoke? Let's see if you can get a hold of some.

Your Brother

At this point, obtaining a post abroad through the Ministry of Foreign Affairs was a real possibility for Neruda. In Latin America, especially in the first half of the twentieth century, poets and intellectuals were often named to diplomatic posts, *ad honorem,* where they could live on a simple salary while working on their craft and acting as emissaries of their country's culture. Neruda realized this was his best option, his best way out of the country and his financial peril. While for the most part it was a nonpartisan nomination, it didn't hurt that Neruda was no longer acting like the young radical of previous years. There was a marked lull in his political activity at this time, as he shifted toward a self-centered focus on his own concerns. That "bonfire of my rebellion" was just smoldering now. Instead of answering the call of the poor *compañeros* on *Claridad*'s front page, he began a persistent campaign to obtain a post abroad.

Back around 1924, Neruda had had a friend speak on his behalf to a department head in the Ministry of Foreign Affairs. The department head already knew of Neruda's poetry and soon invited him to his stately office in the presidential palace, La Moneda. There, Neruda was put at ease, but he soon became frustrated by the department head, who started by saying he was fond of Neruda's poetry and that "I know of your ambitions." He invited Neruda to sit down in a comfortable armchair. He then told Neruda how lucky he was to be a young poet, complained about being in a cubbyhole, and launched into an hour-long, aimless conversation. Neruda left with a handshake and an empty promise that he'd be assigned to a post.

For nearly three years, Neruda kept visiting this department head, who, as soon as he saw Neruda coming, would arch his eyebrows and call one of his secretaries, saying, "I'm not in for anyone. The only spiritual thing in this ministry is the poet's visit. I hope to God he never abandons us." Every time, Neruda entered with the singular intention of being assigned a consular position. If he could get a meeting, the department head would just ramble on about topics from the English novel to anthropology, always leaving Neruda with the assurance that he would get his post soon.

Nothing came from the man at the ministry until April 1927, when Neruda ran into one of his friends, Manuel Bianchi. Manuel was well established in the diplomatic corps, and he knew how to work the system. "They still haven't given you your appointment yet?" he said.

"I'll have it any moment now. A high patron of the arts in the ministry assured me of it."

Bianchi smiled and said, "Let's go see the minister." He took Neruda by the arm up a marble stairway. As they walked, functionaries stepped aside out of respect to Bianchi, which surprised Neruda. After all this time, he finally saw the actual minister of foreign affairs, who hopped on top of his desk in order to compensate for how short he was. Bianchi told the minister how badly his friend wanted to leave Chile. Without missing a beat, the minister pressed a buzzer, and the department head Neruda had been visiting all this time appeared at the office door.

"What posts in the service are available?" the minister asked him.

The elegant functionary, now unable to wax poetic about Tchaikovsky or English novels, instantly rattled off all the cities scattered around the world where consuls were needed. In the rapid flow of foreign names, Neruda seemed to catch just one, Rangoon (now Yangon), which he had never heard or read about before. It was the capital of Burma (now Myanmar). After hearing the list of names, when the foreign minister asked him, "Where do you want to go, Pablo?" with no hesitation he answered: "To Rangoon."

The minister told the department head to name Neruda to the post. Rangoon certainly wasn't Paris, but it wasn't Chile either.

There was a globe in the minister's office. Neruda and Bianchi looked for the mysterious city named Rangoon. The old map had a deep dent in part of Asia and it was in this depression that they found it. "Rangoon. There's Rangoon."

CHAPTER EIGHT

AFAR

I'm alone among ruined matter,
The rain falls over me and I am like the rain,
with its absurdity, alone in the dead world,
rejected as it falls, stubborn yet nebulous.
  —"Dawn's Dim Light"

Neruda was eager to leave Chile but distraught that neither of his lovers would go with him. He pleaded with both Albertina Azócar and Laura Arrué to marry him. He went to visit Laura in her hometown in the fertile valley of Colchagua one last time before he left. Laura loved him, but it was to no avail. She was only twenty years old, and her family would not let her go. Neruda did hand her the original manuscript of *venture of the infinite man* and a portrait of him taken by the rising French photographer Georges Sauré. They weren't exactly gifts; as Laura described it, he wanted her to keep them safe while he was gone. It seemed Neruda's main intent behind this apparently heartfelt imposition was simply to keep her attention on him, that with his presence, via the manuscript and photograph, beside her, their bond wouldn't dilute too thin in his absence.

Even as he wooed Laura, Neruda wrote to Albertina again and again, begging her to go with him. He was met with the exact same problem, the same seemingly unfair obstacle of social class that had reared its head with Amelia and Teresa back in Temuco, now compounded by a bohemian life path that was even more alarming to her parents. Albertina was still living in her family home while studying in Concepción. As she tried to make Neruda understand, her father and mother were controlling, but she loved and respected them; she dreaded disappointing them. Her parents discovered their daughter's correspondence with the poet and forbade it, and though she wanted to respond to Neruda, she didn't, as she was unable to sneak out to the post office. Her ensuing silence tortured him. Her life was so restricted—how could she possibly think of escaping with him to the other side of the globe? She loved Neruda, but not nearly enough to defy her parents.

Without Laura or Albertina by his side, Neruda feared the solitude that awaited him in Burma. As much as he wanted the post, he remained timid in many ways and felt afraid of traveling abroad for the first time to such a distant destination, and one so terribly different from everything he knew. So when his eccentric friend Álvaro Hinojosa suggested that Neruda change his first-class ticket on the ocean liner for two in third class so that he could join him, Neruda immediately agreed and named Hinojosa the consulate's chancellor. The position may have sounded important, but it was an imaginary title; Neruda's own position was at the bottom of the hierarchy, too low to merit any chancellery characteristics. There would barely be enough work and money for Neruda alone. But Neruda looked up to Álvaro and was relieved by the prospect of having his companionship in this leap into the unknown.

Before he left, his band of friends gave him a spirited good-bye party, the climax of several celebrations that started as soon as the minister gave him the job. "While eating and drinking," Diego Muñoz recalled, "we would exchange information about Burma, about Rangoon, its weather, its inhabitants, of the beautiful Burmese with their Oriental garments. We painted quite an exotic picture and we all dreamed about that distant country where our friend was going to live."

On June 15, 1927, a month before Neruda's twenty-third birthday, he and Hinojosa boarded the Transandino train to Argentina. In Buenos Aires, Neruda met the great Argentine writer Jorge Luis Borges, five years his elder, whose first two books of poetry and first two books of essays had been published within the past four years. It would be the only time these titans of Latin American literature and culture would meet face-to-face. Borges already respected Neruda; a year before, he had included a piece of *venture of the infinite man* in an important anthology he had coedited. When they met, Neruda gave him a copy of the book, simply addressed, *"A Jorge Luis Borges, su compañero Pablo Neruda. Buenos Aires, 1927."*

Although Walt Whitman's influence on Neruda was still light, they talked about his importance to both of them. They also spoke of the Spanish language. Borges declared, tongue in cheek, that it was "a hopeless, clumsy language in which no one had achieved anything," referring to the sound of Spanish, with its long words and, relative to English, its rigidity for writing poetry. Smiling, they decided it was too late to start writing in English all of a sudden. They would "have to make the best of our second-rate literature," Borges said, recalling the conversation years later.

Their meeting was much more diplomatic than intimate; they would never develop a fraternal relationship. In fact, the two would become distant though relatively respectful rivals, mainly due to political differences. There was also an element of ego, as for most of the twentieth century they were considered the top two South American writers. Two years after the encounter in Buenos Aires, Neruda would write to an Argentine friend, "Borges really seems to be a ghost from an old library . . . Borges, who you've mentioned, seems too preoccupied with issues of culture and society, which don't totally interest me, as they are not human issues. I prefer good wines, love, suffering, and books as consolation for the inevitable solitude . . . I even feel a certain disdain for culture as a way to interpret things . . . In my world I see fewer ideas, always more bodies, sunlight, and sweat."

In a 1975 interview, Borges said that Neruda "wrote all those silly sentimental love poems, you know . . . When he became a Communist his poetry became very strong. I like Neruda the Communist." He may have liked Neruda the Communist poet, but he certainly did not like Neruda the Communist idealist. One of the reasons they never met again was that Borges's conservatism and Neruda's communism were incompatible.

They made special efforts to avoid further encounters. On one occasion, when Borges visited Chile, Neruda chose that time to go on vacation. It seems to have occurred to both of them that, except for the Spanish language, they had very little in common as writers.

In a 1970 interview for the *Paris Review,* Neruda was prompted by the statement: "Some people accuse you of being antagonistic toward Jorge Luis Borges."

"The antagonism toward Borges may exist in an intellectual or cultural form because of our different orientation," Neruda answered. "One can fight peacefully. But I have other enemies—not writers. For me the enemy is imperialism, and my enemies are the capitalists and those who drop napalm on Vietnam. But Borges is not my enemy . . . He understands nothing of what's going on in the contemporary world; he thinks that I understand nothing either. Therefore, we are in agreement."

*

Neruda and Hinojosa boarded the *Badén,* the boat that would take them first to Rio de Janeiro and then on to Lisbon, Portugal. "This German ship supposedly had just one class, but this 'one class' must have been the fifth," Neruda recalled. It seemed to be divided between two main groups of passengers: Portuguese and Spanish immigrants, whose meals were served together, as quickly as possible, and then a variety of others with higher social ranking, mostly Germans who were heading back from working in comfortable positions in mines and factories all over the Southern Cone.

On July 12, 1927, Neruda wrote to his sister two hours before arriving in Lisbon. It was his twenty-third birthday, though he makes no reference to it in the letter. Instead, he announces his itinerary: Portugal, Spain, and then France. While so many of his generation from around the world were in Paris long-term, he would stay for less than two weeks before heading on to Burma.

When he wrote Laura, Neruda was not thinking of the rich experiences that awaited him on the Left Bank but, rather, was focused on his anxiety:

> I'm a little scared of arriving, because here on board I've learned that life is extremely expensive there, that the cheapest boardinghouse costs $1.600 a month, and I'm going with very little money. Even more there's plague, tertian fever, fevers of all types. But what is there to do! We have to submit to life and struggle with it, thinking that nobody else will take care of you.

After a brief stay in Lisbon, they arrived in Madrid on July 16. Neruda would stay there for just three days. It was a chance to introduce himself as a poet in the land from which his mother tongue originated, but the experience was disturbing. Of the very few people he saw in the city, which in five years' time would become a beloved home, one was the critic and poet Guillermo de Torre, who happened to be Borges's brother-in-law. He had become a leading spokesperson for the Spanish avant-garde flourishing then in Europe and Latin America, especially of its experimental branch, *ultraísmo*.

There are two very different accounts of the visit. In 1950, Neruda claimed:

> When I arrived in Spain for the first time in 1927 . . . I met Guillermo de Torre, who was the literary critic with modern tendencies, and I showed him the first originals of the first volume of *Residence on Earth*. He read the first poems, and when he was done he told me, with all the frankness of a friend, "I didn't see or understand anything, and I didn't know what you proposed with them." I thought I would stay longer. But then, seeing the impermeability of this man, I took it as a bad symptom and I went to France . . . I had just turned twenty-three and it was natural that Spain in the last days of *ultraísmo* was not the place for me.

Ultraísmo favored fragmentation and surprise, a rejection of the traditional representations of reality and its "impurities," and exalted the mechanical and the scientific, everything "modern" and innovative, over the intimate, the transcendental, and the human. It was not what Neruda was about. In fact, during his return to Spain seven years later, he would write a famous essay defending his "impure poetry."

In a friendly and open letter to Neruda, Guillermo de Torre replied with his own version of their encounter, saying that they had talked cordially at a café until dawn. He didn't remember reading any of the poems from *Residence on Earth,* but "the only thing I can be certain of is that I did not pronounce the word that you perhaps hoped to hear: *genial* ['full of genius; brilliant']."

Just two weeks after their encounter in Madrid, de Torre wrote "Panoramic Sketch of Chilean Poetry." Published in the journal *La Gaceta Literaria* (which de Torre helped found), it named Neruda "the undeniable head of the lyrical advances currently occurring in Chile," the "profound star that his young colleagues followed." He admired *Twenty Love Poems,* "a point of perfection and harmony," but imperfection and instability followed, as Neruda was "unsatisfied" with that book and "tried to outdo himself." In Madrid he had given de Torre his most recently published books, such as *venture of the infinite man.* In them, de Torre wrote, Neruda leaped far forward, "banishing all coercive norms." Yet while his ambition created "an abstract, naked lyricism," he seemed to have tried too hard, this poetry not working nearly as well as when he was writing more in tune. Despite de Torre's slight reservations about the later work, the article, especially given that it appeared in a prestigious European journal, was a significant acknowledgment of Neruda's importance.

Four days after they arrived in Spain, Neruda and Hinojosa were off to Paris, the city of Neruda's dreams. All of Paris, all of France, all of Europe, seemed contained in "two hundred meters and two street corners: Montparnasse, La Rotonde, Le Dôme, La Coupole, and three or four other cafés." It was the zenith of the Montparnasse scene, and Neruda, dipping his toes in for the first time, was profoundly impressed.

He also met one significant and talented Latin American poet present at the time in the City of Light:

> During those days I met César Vallejo, the great *cholo* [indigenous]; poet of wrinkled poetry, difficult to the touch like a jungled skin, but it was magnificent poetry with superhuman power. Incidentally, we had a little run-in right after we met. It was in La Rotonde. We were introduced, and in his exquisite Peruvian accent, he greeted me by saying: "You are the greatest of all our poets. Only Rubén Darío can compare with you." "Vallejo," I said, "if you want us to be friends, don't ever say anything like that to me again. I don't know where we'd end up if we started treating each other like writers."

Neruda was also able to enjoy a particular aspect of Parisian nightlife, at least for a few hours. Alfredo Cóndon, a mediocre writer and the wealthy son of Chile's biggest shipping magnate, invited Neruda and Álvaro out for an adventurous night on the town. He was crazy but kind and well liked. He took them to a Russian nightclub whose walls were decorated with landscapes of the Caucasus. They soon found themselves surrounded by very young Russian women, or women pretending they were Russian, dressed like peasants from the mountains. They danced, as Cóndon ordered more and more champagne, until he passed out cold on the floor.

After they unloaded Cóndon at his luxurious hotel, the two Chileans turned their attention to a young woman from the bar who had accompanied them in the cab. They invited her to onion soup at dawn at Les Halles, the vibrant and immense market, always active, which dated back to the twelfth century. Neruda and Hinojosa conferred: they found the young woman neither pretty nor ugly. Her upturned nose conformed to what they thought was a Parisian style. They invited her to their seedy hotel. Neruda maintains he was so exhausted that he just went to his room and fell into his bed, while she followed Álvaro to his room. Later, though, Neruda woke to Álvaro shaking him urgently. "Something's going on," he said. "There is something exceptional, extraordinary, about this woman that I couldn't explain to you. You've got to try her right away."

Neruda wrote:

> A few minutes later, the stranger got into my bed, sleepily but indulgingly. Making love to her, I received proof of her mysterious gift. It was something indescribable that sprang from deep down inside her, something that went back to the very origins of pleasure, to the birth of a wave, to the genetic secret of Venus. Álvaro was right.
>
> The next morning he pulled me aside during breakfast and warned me in Spanish: If we don't leave this woman immediately, our trip will be a failure. We wouldn't shipwreck at sea, but in the bottomless sacrament of sex.

Neruda and Álvaro then decided to shower her with small gifts. Not only did these include flowers and chocolates, but also "half of our remaining francs." Describing this scene in his memoirs, nearly fifty years later, Neruda notes that the young woman "confessed" that she didn't work at the Russian bar, "that she had gone there the previous night for the first and only time." Then, after the soup, flowers, chocolates, and francs, "we got into a taxi with her. The driver was taking us through a nondescript neighborhood when we asked him to stop. We bid her farewell with big kisses and left her there, disoriented but smiling. We never saw her again."[*]

---

[*] The violent objectification of the woman described in this scene establishes a pattern of disturbing misogynistic behavior that would continue during Neruda's time abroad. Perhaps even more disturbing to today's reader is the fact that this description comes from what Neruda wrote in his memoirs, fifty years later. There are no archival records for this event. Therefore, it is impossible to verify this description, to fully assess whether these events took place and, if they did, whether the young woman consented to sex with Neruda purely out of her own free will. This is not the only occasion when Neruda

★

Leaving Paris behind, Neruda would never forget the train that took them to Marseilles, "loaded like a basket of exotic fruit, with a motley crowd of people, country girls and sailors, accordions and songs chorused by everyone in the coach." From Marseilles, they were off to sea again, across the Mediterranean and down through the Suez Canal. During the trip, Neruda and Hinojosa, who were carrying typewriters, passed the time composing love letters for the sailors to send to their *amants* back in Marseilles.

The poet had taken a liking to being on the road, and it was mitigating his mood, for now. Travel would become a constant refuge throughout his life. The ship sailed into the Indian Ocean, stopping at Colombo, Ceylon (now Sri Lanka); Sumatra, Dutch East Indies (now Indonesia); Singapore; and finally Rangoon, where Ricardo Neftalí Reyes, a.k.a. Pablo Neruda, assumed the position of Chilean *cónsul* in October 1927.

At that time, Rangoon was the capital and administrative center of the British colony of Burma, situated opposite India on the northeast corner of the Bay of Bengal in between Bangladesh and Thailand (known as Siam until 1949).

The British in Rangoon and throughout Burma frustrated Neruda. He saw them as imperialistic exploiters overwhelming the colony, "monotone" and ignorant. He could talk to them in his mostly self-taught English, in which he was relatively fluent by this time, but he preferred to engage as little as possible. The British tried to make others feel inferior, Neruda thought. He knew nothing of the native Burmese language, and for the most part it was prohibited throughout the colony, so many Burmese spoke English.

On October 28, shortly after he arrived, Neruda wrote to his sister that Rangoon was boring him terribly. "The women here are black," he laments, "there's nothing to worry about, I'm not going to marry." Despite the progressive class politics he had demonstrated in *Claridad*

---

self-reports such worrisome behavior in his memoirs and poems, and we are left with only his account to interpret what he wrote.

and his poetry, Neruda held the conviction of the time and place that nonwhites were beneath him. But that didn't mean they weren't sexually interesting; perhaps it made them even more so:

> a woman to love, to bed,
> silvery or black, virgin or whore,
> heavenly orange-colored carnivore,
> it mattered not.

Neruda would be more promiscuous during his time on the shores of the Bay of Bengal and later the Arabian Sea than at any other point in his life.

But aside from the thrill of the chase, Neruda was disillusioned. The tropics were sweltering for the Chilean, he knew no one, and his job was devoid of inspiration or stimulation. As Neruda explained in 1971:

> At that time, like now, Chile needed raw material to make candles. This raw material is called paraffin wax—I'll remember its name all my life—and it came from the Petroleum Harmat Oil Company, from Burma. Because of this, Chile needed someone in Burma to take care of the paperwork, to stamp documents. Later that consular invoice system was eliminated and I could go back. But nobody ever went to see me, to consult me on anything, since there were no Chileans and no connections—neither economic nor intellectual—in that country.

This may have been one reason why the Ministry of Foreign Affairs let young poets hold these outposts.

On December 7, he wrote to Yolando Pino Saavedra, a Pedagogy Institute classmate who later became a foremost researcher of Chilean folklore: "The women, indispensable material to the organism, are dark skinned; they wear their hair up, stiff with lacquer; rings in their nose, and a distinct smell. Everything is wonderful the first week. But the weeks, time, passes on!" Five days later, he wrote to the poet

Joaquín Edwards Bello, to whom he was quite close, saying that he was growing old in Burma and that tedium was setting in. "This is a beautiful country, but it smells like banishment. One quickly tires of seeing rare customs, of sleeping only with women of color."

A month later, seeking respite, Neruda and Hinojosa set off on an ambitious trip spanning from January to the end of March. It was illuminating and adventurous right from the start, in Saigon, followed by two days in Bangkok, and then the fantastic, classic eleventh-century Cambodian temples and Buddhist statues in Battambang. Before he left Chile, Neruda had been commissioned by *La Nación* to compile a series of "Reports from the Orient." In his chronicle for this trip, he paints his observations—absorptions—of these new worlds in such impressionistic imagery, it's as if everything in front of him is illusory, surrealistic:

> How difficult to leave Siam, to never lose the ethereal, murmuring night of Bangkok, the dream of its thousand-boat-covered canals, its tall enameled temples. What suffering to leave the cities of Cambodia, each with its drop of honey, its monumental Khmerian ruin in the grace of a ballerina's body. But it's even more impossible to leave Saigon, relaxed, full of enchantments.

Indochina behind, they continued to Hong Kong, followed by Shanghai and Japan. "Glittering" Hong Kong was full of surprises, alive with sounds of "mysterious exhalations, incredible whistling." In China, he marveled at how the streets of Asia were "always surprising, magnetic . . . what a bag of extravagant tricks, what a setting for exotic colors and customs, in every district." Everything seemed a strange brew "stirred by the marvelous fingers of the absurd."

Yet while these mysterious sights would be fodder for his poetry, upon his return to Rangoon the exhilarations he had experienced in the other parts of Asia soon evaporated. In a letter to his sister, Laura, on the way back from Japan, right after noting how hard it was to explain all the rare things, he complains, "Life in Rangoon is a terrible banishment," and "I wasn't born to pass my life in such a hell." "It's like living in an oven night and day," he writes. He longed to leave, to continue his studies in Europe. But his banishment was of his own design; he stayed there.

Creatively, Neruda sought inspiration via letter writing and from the letters he received in turn. His epistolary activity provided a release from the suffocation he was feeling. He began a correspondence with the writer Héctor Eandi, after the Argentine wrote a very positive article about him. On May 11, 1928, in the second of a series of raw and revealing exchanges, Neruda ended a note to him:

> Sometimes for long stretches I'm like this, so empty, so vacant, without being able to express anything or check anything inside myself, and a violent poetic disposition never stops to exist in me, each time it leads me to a more inaccessible route, so that a great part of my labor I accomplish with suffering, for the need to occupy a rather remote domain with forces that are surely too weak. I'm not talking to you about doubts, or disoriented thoughts, no, rather of an unsatisfied aspiration, of an exasperated conscience. My books are the heaping, the pile, of these anxieties without exit . . .

Upon returning from their trip, Neruda and Álvaro rented a small house on Dalhousie Street in Rangoon. Neruda was not good company. He was in a bitter mood, wanting only to read and write by himself. Álvaro was in a romantic relationship with a local woman. As he noted in a journal-like chronicle around that time:

> Our friendship with Pablo was visibly getting colder. All on the part of him. It had gotten to the point that he had converted into my declared enemy. In the things that affected both of us, he acted as if I didn't exist. One night I came back to the house and was in the mood to chat. Pablo grabbed a book, and answering me with a bad attitude, he looked for a way to end my superficial and somewhat alcoholic chat. I tried to interest him in various subjects. Nada. So I told him,

"I'm going to Calcutta tomorrow." I didn't have the slightest
inclination to make such a trip all of a sudden. But my goal
was to make him talk. His only remark was "That's crazy."
And he kept reading.

Álvaro had been intruding on the irritable poet's personal space.
Having effectively dismissed him—Álvaro did end up going to Calcutta
(now Kolkata), where he tried to make it in its film industry—Neruda
was now alone, which was what he seemed to want. Shortly, though,
he would begin to complain constantly about the solitude he felt. His
isolation was caused by his mental state, to a great degree, as much as
he would blame the culture and environment. As always, his practice
of writing poetry would serve as a balm for the utter desolation of his
mind. Neruda sieved his mental currents as he poured his soul into his
poetry. He constructed an almost unprecedented, intricate, reflective
set of symbols by giving a voice to the unconscious. This work pro-
duced the majority of the first book of *Residence on Earth*.

In August 1928, Neruda wrote to his old FECh friend José Santos
González Vera:

> I suffer, I'm so anguished with horrible discoveries, the
> weather burns me, I curse my mother and grandmother, I spend
> whole days conversing with my cockatoo, I pay an elephant in
> rent . . . my desires are influenced by storms and lemonade . . .
>
> I've already told you: great inactivity, but only on the surface;
> deep down, I was unable to stop my thoughts from churning . . .
> My scant latest works, since a year ago, have reached great
> perfection (or imperfection), but within what I strived for. It's
> to say, I have passed a literary limit that I never believed I was
> capable of surpassing, and in truth my results surprise me and
> console me. My new book will be named *Residence on Earth* and
> there'll be forty poems in verse that I hope to publish in Spain.
> It all has equal movement, equal pressure, and is developing
> in the same region of my head, like the same class of insistent
> waves.

For almost his entire life, Neruda was a tremendously prolific writer, of both poetry and prose. It wasn't a question of him consciously sacrificing quality for quantity, but that he naturally generated so much in a stretch that a superior level couldn't always be maintained. Interestingly, it was when he was in Burma, suffering through one of his most frustrating, unproductive periods, through lentitude, with his mental environment restraining the flow of his creative energy and forcing him to be more deliberate, that he wrote this book of unprecedented "great perfection." As he was forced to extract his poems from the "churning," the results were consistently of outstanding quality. Many readers and critics claim that, while they might not all be masterpieces in themselves, there are simply no "bad" or "weak" poems in *Residence on Earth* from the time he wrote in Asia. One would be hard-pressed to make that statement about any of his other books.

Returning to Burma from his trip to Saigon and Japan and the other stops in between, Neruda had written Laura, highlighting the challenge of finding language to express the fantastical elements he was observing, experiencing: "It seems difficult to tell you all about the infinite rare things that fill this side of the world; everything is distinct: the customs, the religions, the clothing, they all seem to belong to a country seen in dreams rather than in everyday reality."

Neruda, compositionally, was developing a way to interpret these "exotic colors," these "infinite rare things," these "strange brews stirred by the marvelous fingers of the absurd," as he had described them in his dispatch to *La Nación*. He was witnessing the wonders of the world in front of him, while also experiencing and interpreting them internally in his mind.

And dreams. During this period, he frequently refers to dreams, be it in his "Reports from the Orient" or when he writes, from an opium den, to a friend in Chile that he's working on a book that will be called "Nocturnal Collection"—his original title for *Residence on Earth*—and he's confident "that it will express huge swaths of my inner world."

Just as *venture of the infinite man* was a variation of surrealism and other styles that he crafted on his own to suit himself, he had now developed that further: the poems of this first volume of *Residence on Earth* redefined Spanish poetry with Neruda's individualized form of surrealism. He had created a new rhetoric distinctly his own, quickly labeled *Nerudismo,* which featured a transformational use of expressive symbols with esoteric images. With them, he was able to put a language to all the dreams, to the strange things, both external and internal and in between, in order to find a way to express them to himself, to his readers.

This new ars poetica is described in the *Residence* poem bearing that title in the new book:

> Between shadow and space, between harnesses and virgins,
> endowed with a singular heart and fatal dreams,
> impetuously pale, withered in the forehead
> and in mourning like an angry widower every day of my life,
> oh, for every drink of invisible water I swallow drowsily
> and with every sound I take in, trembling,
> I feel the same missing thirst and the same cold fever,
> an ear being born, an indirect anguish,
> as if thieves were arriving, or ghosts,
> and inside a long, deep, hollow shell,
> like a humiliated waiter, like a bell gone a bit hoarse,
> like an old mirror, like the smell of an empty house
> where the guests come back at night hopelessly drunk,
> and there's an odor of clothes thrown on the floor, and an absence
>   of flowers
> —or maybe somehow a little less melancholic—
> but the truth is, suddenly, the wind lashing my chest,
> the infinitely dense nights dropped into my bedroom,
> the noise of a day burning with sacrifice
> demand what there is in me of the prophetic, with melancholy
> and there's a banging of objects that call without being answered,
> and a restless motion, and a muddled name.

Today the book remains a powerful articulation of the poet's endeavor. The writer Jim Harrison notes in the introduction to New Directions' 2004 centennial edition of *Residence on Earth,* "In every line you trace with great difficulty the bruised consciousness that produced it because unlike most poetry it proceeds from the inner to the world outside the poet." The Pulitzer Prize–winning author Ariel Dorfman, who grew up in Chile, commented:

> Whenever I'm feeling a need to understand the turbulence, the chaos of life, how life erupts in different ways and in the everyday, I always go to *Residencia en la tierra,* and I'll go to it continually. And especially during my adolescence, my late adolescence [in the 1960s], I felt that to be very good company for me, because it is very much the way in which Neruda was referring to a reality in Latin America where everything is unsettled, where there is no center, there is no core, there is no foundation, and yet the foundation is in the words themselves.

Yet it took time to elicit such a positive reaction—or any reaction—from his contemporaries. It was a bit too avant-garde for the mainstream reader of the time. Just as he did with *Twenty Love Poems,* Neruda struggled to convince a publisher to take it on. The battle with this book would be tougher, and the response not nearly as sensational as when his first masterpiece was released.

★

Though Neruda was excited by the developments with his writing, more mundane matters required the poet's attention. In June, he sent an urgent cable to the Ministry of Foreign Affairs saying that he'd been without funds for two months. In a letter to Héctor Eandi, Neruda wrote:

> Consuls like me—"honorary"—receive a miserable salary, the lowest of the entire staff. The lack of money has

made me suffer immensely, and even now my life is full of ignoble conflicts. I receive 166 American dollars a month, and here that is about the salary of a third-rate pharmacy employee. And worse yet, this salary depends on the income of the consulate, so if there are no exports to Chile one month, there is no money for me.

Eandi worked toward finding someone to publish *Residence on Earth* in Buenos Aires, but for Neruda, Argentina "seems to me still too provincial . . . My greatest interest is to publish them in Spain." Not only did he want to get published in Spain, but he wanted to live there too, to be transferred out of his "banishment" in the Far East and obtain a post in Europe. Though he had never met him, Neruda began writing the Chilean writer-diplomat Carlos Morla Lynch, who served in a variety of positions in the Chilean embassy in Madrid. Their mutual friend Alfredo Cóndon, of the Russian bar incident, put them in touch. Neruda's letters were open and intimate from the start:

Carlos Morla, about me feeling lonely, I feel lonely. I would like to be taken to Spain. Is there any prospective consulate there? What do I have to do for the department to transfer me? Life here is so terribly dark. For years I have been dying of asphyxia, from disgust. Where's the remedy? I'd like to live in some little town in Europe, eternally, as long as my body cooperates. Is that possible? Could you and the ambassador do something for me?

The ministry heard Neruda's plea and assigned him to a post in Ceylon.

According to Neruda, that exit was expedited by a dangerous turn in a dramatic relationship he had with a Burmese woman in Rangoon a couple of months before he left. Her name was Josie Bliss. She dressed like an Englishwoman, and, in his memoirs, Neruda described her as "a species of Burmese panther" and a "love terrorist."

Josie Bliss was one of the most intriguing and exciting characters in

Neruda's life, especially as described in his memoirs. Seven or eight of his poems allude to her. She was one of six women to have an entire chapter devoted to her in a book called *Los amores de Neruda* (The Loves of Neruda), by Inés María Cardone, spanning his entire life. Yet there's a possibility that she was nothing more than an eccentric invention. Josie Bliss may not have existed at all, except in Neruda's writings and a few anecdotes he told friends later on.*

Perhaps Neruda invented her evocative name to embellish his story, or perhaps her name was of her own choosing; locals of that generation often adopted English names so they could assimilate more into the colonial economy. To this day no one knows her real name, and there is no official trace of any "Josie Bliss." She was supposedly an erratic woman, and at that time in Burma, she could have fallen through the "official" cracks. But no one has ever come forward with proof of her existence. There are no photographs. And while it is not surprising that he wouldn't mention her in any of his letters to his sister and mother, it is puzzling that someone who took up so much of his emotional time and energy didn't even once appear in all the frank correspondence he had with Héctor Eandi.

In her study "Chasing Your (Josie) Bliss: The Troubling Critical Afterlife of Pablo Neruda's Burmese Lover," Roanne Kantor writes, "Neruda and generations of critics analyzing his life and work have filled reams of paper with descriptions of Josie as exotic, passionate, animalistic and homicidally jealous. Behind all these descriptions, however, is an absolute void: we lack not just the archival evidence to corroborate this particular version of Josie, but the evidence to suggest that there was ever any Josie at all."

---

* Neruda's construction of Josie Bliss may have been partly inspired by Josephine Baker, an African-American entertainer. Beyond the similarity in names, Josephine was a mesmerizing, multi-talented performer. She rose to fame after she moved to Paris in 1925, exciting crowds with her sensational, eroticized, semi-nude dances. Josephine Baker personified a sexualized, primitive, exotic woman in ways similar to those Neruda used to portray Josie Bliss. Her fame was spreading in 1927 just as Neruda passed through France on his way to Rangoon.

Their romance was one of furious physical chemistry. Neruda's descriptions of Josie Bliss, mainly in his memoirs written decades after the encounters, stretch credulity: her obsessive jealousy and possessiveness, how she would erupt into tantrums when he received telegrams from back home and sometimes find them first and hide them without opening them, how "she glowered at the air I breathed."

> Sometimes a light would wake me up, a ghost moving behind the mosquito net. It was she, dressed in white, brandishing her long and sharpened indigenous knife. It was she, passing entire hours pacing around my bed without having decided to kill me yet or not. "When you die my fears will end," she said to me. The next day she would celebrate mysterious rites to guarantee my fidelity.

It is not impossible that there was an extremely tempestuous, young, emotionally unstable woman whom he appealed to. However, Neruda exaggerated and invented a great deal throughout his writings, throughout his life. Also, her depiction fits into problematic narratives concerning race, gender, and the Orient that developed during those years, showing fundamental aspects of how he saw himself and the world around him at the time. Josie is eccentric and exotic and of the same skin color as all the other local women he slept with, but she also has some standing, wears English clothes, and has her own place for them to live. He describes her as a true lover, someone he seriously would have considered marrying, unlike the way he perceived other native Burmese women. In other words, she embodies a fantasy, an acceptable woman on which Neruda can project all his racialized—and racist—fetishes.

George Orwell's debut novel, *Burmese Days,* published in English in 1934, is a model from which Neruda may have further developed the character in later years. Orwell's Burmese femme fatale character, Ma Hla May, closely matches Josie. Wrapped in animalistic comparisons as well, at times Ma Hla May is like a kitten; other times she's a worm. Just like Josie, who uses Western clothes to try to hide her true identity,

Ma Hla May uses white face powder. Ma Hla May is also outlandishly jealous and sometimes suicidal.

The prototypical "Oriental Woman," in a Western writer's eyes at the time, as laid out by the eminent postcolonial theorist Edward Said, was docile, graceful, and sexually pliant. Or, in the words of Kantor, Oriental women were seen as "'wise,' but paradoxically intellectually innocent to the point of naïveté or even stupidity, while animalistic in her hygiene and living arrangements, and emotionally volatile, leading to outbursts of violent, masochistic, and 'fatal' behavior." This is Josie Bliss, as Neruda portrays her, to a tee.

The prose poem "The Night of the Soldier" is the first piece thought to have a relation to Josie Bliss. The speaker approaches native "girls with your eyes and hips, beings in whose hair shines a flower yellow as lightning." As if he never had such a chance back in Chile, he uses their bodies as a classroom, a laboratory, a mirror. He wants to remove their colored necklaces "and examine, because I want to discover myself before an uninterrupted and compact body, and not to mitigate my kiss."

It does seem from his poems and other expressions that the approximately two-month period during which the supposed Josie Bliss affair took place was one of furious, raw, and uninhibited sexual activity for Neruda, with at least one woman, opening up a new level of eroticism within himself. These experiences, combined with his new environment, affected his poetry, heightening the explicitness of both its content and its imagery.

"The Young Monarch" features a clear view of the Josie Bliss character. In this short prose poem, he "wants to marry the most beautiful woman in Mandalay." (Mandalay was the capital of Burma before the British took over, the epicenter of the country's culture.) She is "a lovely girl with little feet and a big cigar." She has amber flowers in her "cylindrical" black hair. She lives dangerously; she is the daughter of the king; she is his "tiger." Yet after he kisses her coiled hair, the speaker weeps right away for his "absent one"—not this woman, but Albertina, perhaps. It is left uncertain whether the speaker ever marries his bride, or whether he really wants to.

As the narrative progressed, through the poems he wrote and later in his memoirs, by the time Neruda left Burma he was calling himself a widower. The separation from Josie Bliss is marked by the fantastical poem "Widower's Tango," where Josie is no longer the enhanced princess; now she is the "malignant"—and she hasn't actually died.

Josie Bliss would have "ended up killing me," Neruda wrote in his memoirs. When he received official notice to transfer to a new post in Ceylon, he used it as his chance to flee from her. He prepared for his departure in secret, and then, "abandoning my clothes and my books" so she wouldn't detect that something was awry, "I left the house as usual and boarded the ship that was to carry me far away."

In the literary sense, at least, the poem "Widower's Tango" acts as a letter of explanation to Josie that he never sent. After receiving his transfer from the Ministry of Foreign Affairs, before he took the boat to Ceylon, he spent "two months of life" in Calcutta, from November 1928 until the end of that year. (He reunited there with Hinojosa.) "Widower's Tango" was dated "Calcutta, 1928." It became something of a cult classic among those familiar with Neruda's work. Shortly after *Residence on Earth* was published in Madrid, Guillermo de Torre highlighted "Widower's Tango" as "profound." In 2004, Mario Vargas Llosa, Peruvian winner of the 2010 Nobel Prize in Literature, wrote that the poem sends "a shock down my spine," producing that "elated sense of disquiet and felicitous astonishment into which all absolute masterworks plunge us."

It is the potency of this poem that more than anything has perpetuated the myth of Josie Bliss, enthralling reader after reader, generation after generation. The poem is intricately structured, combining compelling sentiment with provocative imagery. It is similar to many of his letters to Albertina, in that he weaves statements of his lingering passion for her with harsh words of degradation.

The poem begins with "Oh Maligna"—the Malignant, the Evil One—

> by now you must have found the letter, you must have cried with fury,

and you must have insulted the memory of my mother,
calling her rotten bitch and mother of dogs,
you must have drunk alone, all by yourself, the twilight tea,
looking at my old shoes empty forever . . .

As the poem continues, the distance he's put between them becomes troubling. He misses the domestic life they shared: "there are no hangers in my room, no pictures of anyone on the walls." Then reflections of his projections of her as the classic masochistic, violent "fatal woman":

Buried next to the coconut tree you will later find
the knife that I hid there for fear you'd kill me . . .

Yet he longs to return to the scene:

and now suddenly I want to smell its kitchen steel . . .

Neruda cycles perceived threat, desire, and barbarity throughout the poem.

I would give this giant sea wind for your brusque breath
. . . to hear you urinate, in the darkness, in the back of the house,
as if spilling a thin, tremulous, silvery, persistent honey,
how many times would I give up this chorus of shadows that I
    possess,
and the noise of useless swords that is heard in my heart.

It was revolutionary to write a line like "to hear you urinate, in the darkness" in Spanish, a line that still sings with its provocative sound and substance. It represents the raw reality of daily life and the intimacy that can sweeten urine to honey. He almost elevates her corporal excreta to the divine. Yet there is a dark undertone: the woman in the poem is like a wild animal.

Neruda's memoirs contain a postscript to Josie Bliss. Supposedly, she discovered the location of his new post and followed him, pitching camp right in front of his house. "As she thought that rice wasn't grown anywhere but in Rangoon, she arrived with a sack of rice on her back, with our favorite Paul Robeson records, and a long, rolled-up carpet. From the front door she dedicated herself to observe and then insult and attack anybody who came to visit me." Her public disruption forced the colonial police to warn Neruda that if he didn't take her in, she'd be thrown out of the country. "I suffered for days, going back and forth between the tenderness that her unfortunate love inspired in me and the terror I had of her. I didn't dare let her set foot in my house. She was a love terrorist, capable of anything."

With a long knife (that same kitchen knife, perhaps), she supposedly attacked a sweet young Englishwoman who came to visit the consul. Neruda's neighbor eventually took her in, and then, with no explicit prompt, she finally left, vociferously begging the poet to come with her on the boat back to Rangoon. Neruda accompanied her to the dock, and as they embraced, she bathed him in tears and kisses, all the way down to his toes, "so that the chalk polish of my white shoes was smeared like flour all over her face . . . That turbulent sorrow, those terrible tears rolling down her floured face, continue to live in my memory."

Elegant writing aside, even if she did exist, Neruda has Josie appear only as an exotic tale, demonstrating how he saw himself as an exception to imperialistic culture, naive to how his own words indicate his racism. "I went so deep into the soul and the lives of those people that I fell in love with a native," he begins his story of Josie Bliss in his memoirs, a comment akin to the classic "some of my best friends are . . ." He felt he had known the Burmese culture, almost like an anthropologist, but his relationship with Josie was awash in stereotypes. He congratulates himself for his courageous, righteous interaction, for "going so deep," while propagating a racist, sexist trope. Neruda was actively promoting social equality and justice at the same time he was composing these memoirs in the 1960s. Yet his dehumanization of nonwhite women certainly undercuts his moral authority when he writes about the "downtrodden." The contradictions between Neruda's personal life and attitudes and his future political ideals were revealed glaringly during his time in Asia, and would resurface often throughout his life.[*]

---

[*] There's a natural urge to try to understand why Neruda may have conjured up Josie, but there isn't necessarily a way to know definitively whether he did. Josie is the lens through which Neruda processed his experience, and there was some benefit to him in transforming an experience, which in the actual moment we know was difficult, boring, frustrating, and disappointing, into this story, something of some lasting value. And there is a wide gap in his archives, in the testimonies of others during this period—he could take advantage of that here. Still, we can only speculate how much truth there is behind the elements of the Josie Bliss story and how much is pure fantasy. Better than speculation may be to just rest with the fact that we have a little mystery here, and leave it pretty much at that.

CHAPTER NINE

OPIUM AND MARRIAGE

I hear the dream of old friends and lovers,
dreams whose heartbeats break me open:
their carpeted floors I walk in silence,
their poppy light I bite in delirium.
 —"Nocturnal Collection"

Neruda moved to Colombo, located on the western side of the great island of Ceylon, into a bungalow outside of the city's center, near the beach. He had a dog; his mongoose, Kiria; and at least one servant, Ratnaigh. Someone took a posed photograph of him standing against a palm tree, his arms crossed over a dark vest tucked into his white trousers. His black belt sits high on his lanky torso, his legs seem disproportionately long, and his outfit is a bit formal for the occasion. He's not nearly as skinny as in his student days, though still slim, with some maturity in his face. As the photo is being taken, he stares out into the southern Arabian Sea, as if he doesn't want to be there. Beside him, Ratnaigh, dressed in white, sits crouched on the sand, his arms draped over his knees, seemingly relaxed and at ease.

The small bungalow was just outside of all the hustle and bustle of Colombo. "Have I told you about Wellawatta, the neighborhood I live in?" he wrote Eandi. "Ocean and palm trees, waters, leaves. The ocean encircles me, quickly, with fury, leaving nothing around me . . . Eandi, there is no one more alone than me."

Indeed, at first there seemed to be little difference from Rangoon. "Caught between the Englishmen dressed in dinner jackets every night and the Hindus [actually, most were Buddhists], unreachable in their fabulous immensity, I could only choose solitude, and so that time was the loneliest in my life."* It is unclear why he persistently isolated himself from others. Just as he expresses disdain for the British, he also shows entitlement and imperiousness toward the locals, as seen in his correspondence in Burma and now in his new post. "If you, my dear mother, passed by my house in Colombo, you'd hear how I yell from morning to night to the servant to pass me cigarettes, paper, lemonade, and to have ready my pants, shirts, and all the artifacts needed to live."

And he didn't isolate himself from the locals of European descent. "I never read with such pleasure and such abundance like in that suburb of Colombo," Neruda wrote in 1968, from the comforts of Isla Negra, for a magazine article. "I had a friend outside of town, Lionel Wendt, a pianist . . . Since I was so eager to read English books as I arrived in Ceylon, he took it upon himself to let me borrow his in continual succession." Every Saturday, a cyclist would bring a fresh supply in a potato sack from Wendt's house in Colombo "to my *bungalow* in Wellawatta."

The potato sacks contained the latest poems by T. S. Eliot out of London and Hemingway's newly published *A Farewell to Arms*. There were two now-classic novels published the year before (1928), both known for their shocking portrayals of relationships and sex: D. H. Lawrence's

---

* The nomenclature Neruda uses when referring to Asians—especially here in a quote from his memoirs, rather than a contemporary comment—is significant. It was conventional for Latin Americans to refer to people from the Indian subcontinent as *hindú*, regardless of their religion, to distinguish them from the indigenous *indios* of America. In Sri Lanka, the Sinhalese majority are Buddhists, and the religious difference between them and the Tamil Hindu minority is of great importance to those groups (as is the distinction among *criollo, mestizo,* and *indio* in Chile). The fact that Neruda ignored this difference speaks to his failure to recognize (or care about) the realities of the land in which he lived.

Lady Chatterley's Lover (a copy from Florence, as it was still banned in the United Kingdom) and Aldous Huxley's innovative *Point Counter Point*.[*]

He also revisited Rimbaud, Quevedo, Proust, and other classics Wendt had available.

Besides his new pianist friend, Neruda had more social interaction with Europeans than ever before. He spent time with Wendt's childhood friend George Keyt. All three were no more than four years apart in age. Wendt and Keyt were both born in Ceylon and had mixed European and Asian blood. Educated in British schools, the two were part of the colonial elite.

Yet while they may have come from and been raised in that society, they were both very unconventional members of the group. Besides being a concert pianist, Wendt was an important avant-garde art patron and an eclectic, experimental photographer.

Keyt had become a Buddhist; as a painter, his synthesis of European modernist innovations with ancient South Asian traditions would gain him world renown. Neruda even wrote a review for the *Times of Ceylon* of a 1930 art exhibition his friend was a part of: "Keyt, I think, is the living nucleus of a great painter . . . These figures take on a strange expressive grandeur, and radiate an aura of intensely profound feeling."[†]

---

[*]   The Huxley novel had actually been influenced by the Englishman's recent travels through India and the Far East. The sojourn was seen as a watershed for Huxley's intellectual development, where "idealism and mysticism had been found wanting and were rejected," and make for an interesting comparison to Neruda's experience. And as Neruda read these books amid his own insecurities and uncertainties of class and privilege, it's interesting to note too that *Point Counter Point* features a character based on Huxley's friend D. H. Lawrence, a character who acts as a spokesman for dissolving class divisions, for living life with intuitive emotions, not "British stiff-upper-lip constraint."

[†]   George Keyt's sister, Peggy, was the aunt of the highly regarded author Michael Ondaatje (known for *The English Patient,* among many others). Ondaatje was born in Sri Lanka in 1943 and left in 1954. In a memoir, he wrote, "An aunt of mine remembers [Neruda] coming to dinner and continually breaking into song, but many of his dark claustrophobic pieces in *Residence on Earth* were written here, poems that saw this landscape governed by a crowded surrealism—full of vegetable oppressiveness."

Though, as he had back home, he found camaraderie with like-minded intellectuals and artists, it didn't seem to pull him out of his mental isolation. Neruda was never an excessive drinker (though he'd always enjoy his *vino tinto* and whiskeys) except at this time, when it seemed he had nothing else better to do, other than write to Eandi: "I'm alone; every ten minutes my servant comes, Ratnaigh, he comes every ten minutes to fill my glass." He felt lonely despite this constant presence of another human being: "I feel anxious, restless, banished, moribund." After pleading for Eandi to come join him, in capital letters even—"*¡VENGA!*"—he soon returns to his compulsiveness over his particular sense of banishment, almost a self-imposed exile: "You remember those novels by José Conrads [*sic*]," he asks Eandi, "with those strange beings who've been banished, exiled, with no possible restitution? Sometimes I feel like them, just that; this is just so long." Later he wrote: "Two days ago I interrupted this letter, falling down, full of alcohol."

He had the option of returning to Chile but did nothing to change his circumstances. Instead, he wallowed in self-pity.

★

Neruda was also writing constantly to Albertina and Laura Arrué, perhaps Teresa as well.[*] There was not one response from Laura. She in fact had not received even one of the letters he had promised to write and had become disillusioned. Anticipating possible censorship by Laura's mother, Neruda had been sending her letters through his friend

---

[*] Teresa's niece Rosa León Muller, who was very close to her aunt, believes Neruda wrote to Teresa as well. Teresa kept in constant communication with Neruda's sister, Laura, during this period and, Rosa sensed, was still in love with him. She didn't marry until she was forty-five, rejecting her many suitors. She may have loved Neruda strongly, but not enough to overcome her parents' objections. Just before her wedding, Rosa, just a little girl at that point, remembers sitting next to Teresa, who was sitting next to a trunk, "taking out everything that had to do with Pablo Neruda. She took out letters; she took out clippings. She told me, 'No. I'm going to burn these things because I don't have any reason now that I'm going to get married.' She burned a lot." Any letters from Neruda when he was in Asia may have been burned then.

Homero Arce, who worked for the Chilean postal service. But Homero had fallen deeply in love with Laura; he never gave her any of Neruda's letters.

Finally, a long-awaited letter came from Albertina. She was in Paris, en route to Brussels, on a fellowship to learn a new system for teaching French to children. The poet wrote back quickly, desperately, as always, saying this would be the last chance they'd have to be together, adding, "I'm very tired from the loneliness, and if you don't come, I'll try to marry someone else." He gave her all the details of a ship that would take her from France to Colombo and told her, "Every day, and every hour of every day, I ask myself: Will she come?"

She never did. Albertina's fellowship was revoked when the school's director opened Neruda's letter to her and demanded an explanation about why she was seemingly entertaining such a proposal from Ceylon while she was there to study. Albertina refused to answer and was forced to return home. She did love him, but as she later related, "In those days, more than fifty years ago, you have to understand that things were not as they are now. I had to go back to my university, and besides that, my parents were fairly strict—I didn't dare go."

From a later letter to Héctor Eandi, written on February 27, 1930:

> A woman, whom I have loved a lot (it was for her that I wrote almost all *Twenty Poems*), she wrote me three months ago, and we worked out her coming, we were going to marry, and for a while I lived full of her arrival, arranging my bungalow, thinking in the kitchen, well, in everything. And she couldn't come, or at least not for the moment, for reasonable circumstances, perhaps, but I had a fever for a week and couldn't eat, it was like something inside me burned me up, a terrible pain . . .

At least seven of the first fifteen poems of *Residence on Earth* are about Albertina or Laura Arrué, or both. Albertina takes on the presence of a ghost, where she is the "dazzled, pale student" who "surges up from yesteryear," but she is not real, only a "phantom." In these verses

Neruda reaches a darkness only hinted at in *Twenty Love Poems*. His narrators are stuck in the past, unable to exist in the present, which in any case offers only remorse and dread:

> In the depths of the deep sea,
> in the night of long lists,
> your silent silent name
> runs past like a horse.
>
> Lodge me on your back, oh shelter me,
> appear to me in your mirror, suddenly,
> upon the solitary, nocturnal pane,
> sprouting from the dark behind you.
>
> Flower of sweet total light,
> bring your mouth of kisses to my call,
> violent from separations,
> that resolute and delicate mouth . . .
>   —"Madrigal Written in Winter"

Echoing his letters to her, Neruda accuses "Oh heartless lady" Albertina of "tyranny" over his emotions in his poetry. As we have seen before, he blames the women in his life for his psychic pain and seems impotent to do anything about it.

Sexually, meanwhile, he was comfortable in the role of aggressor—even predator—the role he played with Josie Bliss. As he wrote in his memoirs, "Female friends of various colorings visited my campaign cot, leaving no more history than the physical lightning. My body was a solitary bonfire burning night and day on that tropical coast. My friend Patsy came by a lot with some of her friends, *morena* and golden *muchachas,* girls of Boer, English, Dravidian blood. They went to bed with me sportingly with little interest."

The most beautiful woman Neruda saw in Ceylon was a Tamil of the pariah caste, an "untouchable," who cleaned out the tin box that was the bottom of his waterless toilet. "She walked solemnly toward the latrine, without so much as a side glance at me, not bothering to acknowledge my existence, and vanished with the disgusting receptacle on her head, moving away with the steps of a goddess." "She was so lovely . . . despite her humble job." For him she was not human, but an exotic "other": "Like a shy jungle animal, she belonged to another kind of existence, a different world." She wore a red-and-gold sari of the cheapest cloth, heavy bangles on her bare ankles; a tiny dot glittered on each side of her nose. He called to her, "but it was of no use."

Neruda simply couldn't get her off his mind, so "one morning, I decided to go all the way. I got a strong grip on her wrist and stared into her eyes. There was no language I could talk with her. She let me lead her, without a smile, and she was soon naked on my bed. Her skinny waist, her full hips, the brimming cups of her breasts, made her like one of the millennial sculptures from southern India. The encounter was of a man with a statue. Her eyes stayed open the whole time, impassible. She was right to despise me. The experience was not repeated."

In his and others' writings, there is no evidence that Neruda ever committed another assault of this nature, but here he describes his exercise of power and privilege with little shame. During the act of rape, he perceives her as inhuman, a piece of stone. Then he projects divinity on her, comparing her to a sublime goddess like one of the "millennial sculptures from southern India."* Perhaps he feels that he absolves himself to some degree through such exaltation.

While he may have understood class in the Marxist sense, Neruda never connected that abstraction to the institutional realities of racism, sexism, or social caste, all of which were keenly at play in this act of

---

* As appalling as the rest of the passage is, Neruda was at least not wrong on a purely *factual* basis to compare the figure of this woman to South Indian statuary. While there have been Tamil people in Sri Lanka for a very long time, ethnically they trace their lineage back to Tamil Nadu, "Land of Tamils," a region that covers southeast India, nearly touching the northwest tip of Sri Lanka. Neruda visited this area—at the time referred to by the British as Madras (after its principal city, now named Chennai)—between his stints in Burma and Ceylon. The vast majority of Tamils are Hindu (see footnote on Neruda's use of *hindús* to describe the locals on page 172).

violence. His version of events is not unrelated to his interpretation, in the same chapter, of his experiences with his "Burmese panther," Josie Bliss. The woman is not a woman, but a caricature of submissiveness and cultural inferiority that he can dominate.

Neruda's behavior, both here and throughout his time in Asia, was imperialism perpetrated on a human scale, an exact replica of the imperialism perpetrated on a geopolitical scale against which he ranted both while in Asia and while writing his memoirs. His rape of a person based on his sense of entitlement and inherent superiority was a perfect expression of the rape of one nation by another based on these same presumptions of merit and worth. In his narcissism, he could not see the connection.

His narcissism is further expressed in the way he integrates the woman's duty of cleaning his personal excrement into the story of his violation of her. It amounts to the divinization of his excrement, as it is a sublime goddess who empties his chamber pot. This goddess merits less consideration than even a prostitute, whom Neruda would at least have paid for her services. Or as the Slovenian philosopher Slavoj Žižek put it, as part of a larger study, the relationship Neruda proposes should be taken very seriously: "elevating the exotic Other into an indifferent divinity is strictly equal to treating it like shit."

Did Neruda tell the world this story in the 1960s because he consciously or unconsciously felt it had to be told? Or had he maintained the same sense of entitlement that had allowed him to commit the rape in the first place? Even later in life, he would not recognize the inhumanity of his actions. There is no true repentance, no explanation for that behavior. If perhaps he felt a twinge of regret, it passed quickly.

★

Amid speculation about a possible transfer to Singapore, Neruda expressed his excitement to Eandi for the "magical Malay Archipelago, beautiful women, beautiful rituals." "I've already been to Singapore and Bali twice and I've smoked many pipes of opium there. I'm not sure I like it, but it's different, anyhow," he wrote, placing emphasis on the word "anyhow" by writing it in English.

Yet his memoirs describe a divergent, distinctly unpleasant experience with opium. He actively used it in Ceylon, though years later, in his memoirs, he would disavow his enjoyment of it, perhaps to better reflect upon his mature career as a world-renowned poet.

"I smoked one pipe . . . It was nothing . . . The smoke was warm, gloomy, misty, and milky . . . I smoked four pipes and was sick for five days, with nauseas that came up my spinal cord, which descended from my brain.

"So much had been said, so much had been written. There had to be more to it than this."

The literature of opium has a long history, from Homer and Virgil to Shakespeare. But Neruda was most compelled by works that portrayed actual experiences with the drug, such as Samuel Taylor Coleridge's "vision in a dream" in his poem "Kubla Khan," Thomas De Quincey's *Confessions of an English Opium-Eater,* and, perhaps above all for Neruda, his hero Baudelaire's 1860 classic *Les Paradis artificiels.* Opium appeared in many works of nineteenth-century British literature,[*] especially in the English romantics' poems. Not only did they lyricize the mysteries of the Oriental drug, but they also used it heavily. As M. H. Abrams argued in *The Milk of Paradise* (1934), opium's effects caused the romantics to be "inspired to ecstasies." A nonuser could never experience the realm of dreams and sensations that led to some of the era's best writing.

There are many positive references to opium in Western literature that Neruda must have read, yet his experience was negative. Once

---

[*]   Opium appears in Latin American literature as well, perhaps most notably in Rubén Darío's 1888 story "El humo de la pipa" ("The Pipe's Smoke"), written in Valparaíso. After dinner, the host comes with a pipe for the guests, already inebriated on alcohol. "Oh, my desired Orient, for whom I've suffered the nostalgia of the unknown!!" With every puff comes a different inspired story. In one he travels to Germany, in another to Persia. Darío never names the drug, but it is obviously opium. César Vallejo wrote about it too, though it is unlikely, due to the time and place, that Neruda would have read it. Considered to be his best narrative, Vallejo's "Wax" (1923) begins, "We couldn't smoke that night. All of Lima's opium dens were closed." (Vallejo had been a heavy user himself at one point.)

again, there is a disjuncture between what he wanted from Asia and what he found in its reality. "I had to experience opium, know about opium, in order to provide my testimony . . . I smoked many pipes, until I knew . . . There are no dreams, no images, no paroxysm . . . There is a melodic debilitation, as if a smooth, infinite note lingered in the atmosphere . . . There's the fainting, a cavity within oneself . . ." He felt how the slightest movement of the body or a distant noise from the street "enter[ed] to form part of a whole." While that form was "an overflowing joy," with the experiment complete, he supposedly made the judicious decision to stop: "I did not return to the opium dens . . . I already knew . . . I had become familiar . . . I had touched something beyond reach . . . hidden deeply behind the smoke." He makes it clear that he is in command of his will.

However, there is evidence both in his correspondence and his poetry from the time that his usage may not have been as limited as he describes in his memoirs. "Pablo sleeps, pulls an opium pipe, and only wakes up to take care of his official duties," Hinojosa scribbled in a postscript to a letter Neruda wrote to Eandi. What had started out as exotic allure became an escape from his "banishment," self-medication for his incessant isolation, depression, and frustration. Opium went beyond a connection to Baudelaire and became a way to leave behind his suffering.

He describes the setting in the sixth of the twelve dispatches he wrote for *La Nación* back home. Titled "A Day in Singapore," it is dated October 1927:

> There are blacksmiths who squat to forge their metal, street vendors selling fruit and cigarettes, troubadours who make their mandolins quiver. Hair salons where the clients' heads transform into a hard castle, varnished with lacquer. There are [exotic] fish for sale [for food] inside jars; passageways and shaved ice and peanuts; puppet shows; howls of Chinese songs; opium dens with their sign on the door:
> *Smoking room.*
> Blind beggars announce their presence with clanging

bells. Snake charmers coo their cobras with their sad, in-
toxicating pharmaceutical music.

Not surprisingly, while at first seeming to form communal bonds
with the Singaporean opium users and the culture that surrounded the
drug, he'd later write about them with repulsion. In the end, the only
community he was interested in connecting with through his opium
use was the predominantly European literary community that pre-
ceded him. He never discovered the way to do that.

It's impossible to understand how Neruda's use of opium exactly
affected his writing, if at all. Yet examining a few of the poems, it
does seem, as Professor Francisco Leal puts it, that opium's "exercis-
ing effect on his body, the senses and the perception of time" is ap-
parent in some of the poems' visions—"visions at times horrible and
surprising."*

Most opiate writers craft their words once they're down from their
dream states, but lethargy and other hangover effects of the drug can
hinder the writers' ability to garner the will and energy necessary to ar-
ticulate what they experienced while under the influence of "enhance-
ments," as Coleridge described it. Nonetheless, Neruda did show that,
despite his mental withdrawal, he was motivated enough to paint those
images and sensations in a framework that holds up on the page.

---

*   In her study *Opium and the Romantic Imagination*, Alethea Hayter argues that
     "the action of opium may unbare some of the semi-conscious processes by
     which literature begins to be written." Those equipped with a creative imagi-
     nation and a tendency to *rêverie*—the ability to lose oneself in dreamy, pleas-
     ant thoughts like in a daydream—can indeed encounter "unique material"
     through the use of the drug. Opening the doors of perception, opium may
     open those individuals to "unique material for [their] poetry," "presenting ev-
     eryday images in a different light."
        "The writer," Hayter states, "can actually witness the process by which
     words and visual images arise simultaneously and in parallel in his own mind.
     He can watch, control, and subsequently use the product of the creative imag-
     ination at an earlier stage of its production than is normally accessible to the
     conscious mind." This echoes some of Neruda's discourses on how he wanted
     the "scattered expressions" and other processes of his creative mind to work.

There are five prose poems in the first volume of *Residence on Earth*. They allow Neruda the room for more narration, to relate what he sees from a distance, as opposed to the verse poems in the book that are so often based on internal observation. Three of them seem to describe experiences and settings related to opium.

In the poem "Nocturnal Collection" (which had been the working title of the book), the speaker, apparently alone in the world, has come upon the "angel of sleep." "He is the wind that shakes the months, the whistle of the train." He is "perfumed with sharp fruits," "a repetition of distances," "a wine of confused color." The angel's "substance" is "prophetic food he propagates tenaciously." In the seventh stanza, that substance is referred to as the "bland fruits of the sky." As Roanne Kantor, lecturer in comparative literature at Harvard, points out, the images "all seem to refer to a comestible substance associated with an altered state of consciousness beyond mere sleep." The substance, furthermore, is delivered to the speaker in a "black hamper," just as the black resin of opium usually comes in a dark casing. In one line we see two qualities: "he gallops in the breath [nausea] and his step is kiss-like [addictive enticement]." Toward the end, the speaker breaks from the nocturnal and emerges into the collective of other opium users, and then he turns his attention to the city he is in, far away from the embrace of the angel of sleep where he began.

"Contradicted Communications" depicts someone in an opium-induced state with corollary images and senses. The poem defines the atmosphere in which he's living now, a world opaque with opium's "milky" smoke, surrounded by a mute and motionless chorus, his bones supported by a cement armchair, subdued, where he awaits "time militarily with the foil of adventure stained with forgotten blood."

"Nocturnal Establishments" is the third prose poem that is clearly influenced by opium. The "establishments" are neither whorehouses nor bars; they are opium dens, with distinct wooden floors, no decoration, no noise. (Neruda never used the word "opium" in these poems.) "With difficulty I call to reality, like the dog, and I too howl," the poem begins, almost as an evocation, carrying his efforts to conjure up something for his mind to hold on to from "Dead Gallop" to the opium dens.

He's submerged in his own confusion and needs something to help him move forward, out of the milky haze of his mental state.

The first images are repulsive, reflecting the general atmosphere. The inhabitants of the opium joint that surround the poet-speaker are animallike and grotesque: "how many frogs accustomed to the night, whistling and snoring with throats of forty-year-old human beings." He wants to engage them, "to establish the dialogue of the nobleman and the boatman, to paint the giraffe, to describe the accordions, to celebrate my naked muse." Instead, he condemns them. There is no mention of salvation from the depths of these confusions: "Execration for so many dead who do not look, for so many wounded by alcohol or misfortune, and praise for the night watcher . . . surviving worshiper of the heavens." When his trance is broken, he tries to separate himself completely from the other users.

Opium is the subject of the poem that begins the section of poetic reflections on his time in Asia in his autobiographical *Isla Negra* (1964). The title is the site-specific "Opium in the East." This is not Coleridge and Baudelaire's European drug. The richly written poem opens with the same conceit of exploration seen in his memoirs, written later: "I wanted to know. I went in . . ." He was surprised by the silence. There was only the crackling of pipes. From their "milky smoke" came "an ecstatic joy":

> Opium was the flower of idleness,
> immobile pleasure,
> pure activity without movement.
> Everything was pure or seemed pure,
> everything sliding oily and hinged
> until it became existence alone,
> nothing burned, no one cried,
> there was no room for anguish
> and there was no fuel for anger.

But at this time of his life, turning fifty, Neruda was projecting himself to be a champion of communism, and he and his comrades condoned such drugs as an escape from reality's contradictions. From this vantage point, Neruda does not speak of how this "one single existence" became a part of his life and work while he was constantly consuming "Opium in the East" himself. His political posturing never places the onus on himself at that time, but instead lyricizes—idealizes—the notion of the "opiate for the exploited" (by the imperialists, that is):

> I looked: fallen poor,
> peons, rickshaw or plantation coolies . . .
> Here, after their wounds,
> after being not human beings but feet,
> after being not men but beasts of burden,
> after walking and walking and walking and sweating and sweating,
> after sweating blood, and no longer having a soul,
> here they were now,
> alone

With their hunger, each "had bought / an obscure right to pleasure." After "having searched for it all their lives," they finally were "in repose," "respected, at last, on a star."

In his memoirs, Neruda ends his discussion of his experiment with opium with a radical condemnation and closure: "never again" will he return to the dens or smoke this Oriental venom, for now he knows not to confuse his art with the narcotic, nor mix the poems of the singular poet with that of the junkies. It is not for him; it's for the others. Writing his reflections in the 1960s, he seems to borrow from Karl Marx's quote "Religion . . . is the opium of the people," asserting: "Opium was not the paradise of the exotic that had been painted to me, but rather an escape for the exploited."

Although Neruda would later champion the exploited people he found in the dens—"the men who pull and pull the rickshaw all day long"— when he was among them in the late 1920s, he saw nothing in them to champion. He reduced the women to sexual objects and the servants to the stroke of a ticking clock, when "every ten minutes a servant like Ratnaigh would come by to fill my glass." Just after the "escape for the exploited" remark, in the lines that follow it's as if, even three decades later, he still condemns the den dwellers for not living up to that "exotic that had been painted" to him by European literature: they were not just poor, but "poor devils." Then, in the same paragraph: "There was no embroidered cushion, not the slightest hint of even basic luxury . . . Nothing sparkled there, not even the smokers' eyes, barely open."

Neruda found a disappointing dead end in his experience with Eastern spirituality. He was a curious intellectual immersed in a Buddhist society, a new realm for him, while at the same time immersed in his own spiritual and mental depression—and one can imagine the effect of being surrounded by people working on a path toward the end of their suffering, to enlightenment, to nirvana. He began to learn about the details of the Buddha's life and philosophy. When he was in Burma, he had ventured to the striking ancient city of Pagan, where he saw perhaps the largest, densest collection of Buddhist temples and monuments in the world. In Ceylon he traveled through the jungle to five "mysterious Sinhalese [ancient Buddhist] cities," as he wrote in a *La Nación* chronicle. At Anuradhapura, with the night lit by a full moon, he was struck by the immense pagodas in shadows, "filled by kneeling Buddhists and the old orations returning to the Sinhalese lips." In a letter to Eandi, he enclosed a photograph of the "strange hungry Buddha, after those six years of senseless deprivation." "I live surrounded by thousands or millions of portraits of Gautama in ivory, alabaster, and wood"; he adds, "They accumulate in every pagoda, but none has moved me like this one of the thin penitent."

Facets of Buddhism appealed to him but challenged him at the same time. As he would tell an interviewer many years later, though his mother was devout, his father was an atheist, and this combination gave him a blend of curiosity and skepticism in approaching mystical traditions. There's a certain honesty in his approach to examining the philosophy and the practice, and it shows up in some of his writing. In

"It Means Shadows," a deep and fascinating poem, probably written in Colombo toward the end of 1929, he shows a good grasp of samsara, the Buddhist idea of a continual cycle of birth and rebirth,[*] one that would captivate many Westerners in the future.

In the poem, the speaker is enthralled to be in the cycle of reincarnation: attached to "vital, speedy wings of a new dream angel" installed on his "shoulders for perpetual security":

> in such a way that the path through the stars of death
> be a violent flight that took off many days and months and
> centuries ago . . .

It is a cycle reaching back before his birth, deep into the past, and now with the angel, heading forward, toward eternity. He wants, as he writes later, a "reservation" for his "deep place" to last eternally. However, his personalized perception of this concept is in conflict with true Buddhist thought. Buddhists, in fact, seek liberation from the condition of being trapped in the cycles, working instead toward enlightenment and nirvana.

The essence of Pablo Neruda at this time of his life was his suffering—his suffering in pursuit of his ego's desires. Buddhism advocates the release of desire in order to alleviate one's suffering. Neruda basked even in yearnings gone by—the awe he felt under the stars in Puerto Saavedra, for example, and his pining for Albertina. Embracing Buddhism was anathema for a man who clung to his desires and clung equally to his suffering, who defined himself by them. To reject them would not have meant freedom and enlightenment, as Buddhism proposes, but death. Buddhism, he realized, while fascinating, was almost antithetical to who he was.

---

* "Orient and Orient," a *La Nación* article from 1930, further displays the extent of his reading of Eastern texts and how he would articulate their thoughts. He even quotes the Upanishads, the ancient Indian text of Hindu teachings: "Never lost, yet at the same time losing itself, the being returns to the origin of its creation 'as the drop of seawater returns to the sea.'"

In "It Means Shadows," the third of the four quatrains illustrates this:

> Oh, let what I am keep on existing and ceasing to exist
> and let my obedience align itself with such iron conditions
> that the quaking of deaths and of births doesn't shake
> the deep place I want to reserve for myself eternally.

The crux of Neruda's problem, according to Buddhism, is in the last line. He asks for eternal self, while the Buddhist believes that nothing is eternal. The poem, appropriately, ends in the subjunctive, a prayer for the opposite of what Buddhism preaches. He emerges confident that he wants to continue attached to his ego. Buddhism turns worthless, like every other experience: the women, the exotic, the opium. He can't find what he needs from it and kicks it to the curb. He embraces the very cycle Buddhism seeks to release:

> Let me, then, be what I am, wherever and in whatever weather,
> rooted and certain and ardent witness,
> carefully, unstoppably, destroying and saving himself,
> openly engaged in his original obligation.

In 1964, as a strident Socialist atheist, he writes in his poem "Religion in the East" that in Rangoon he

> realized that the gods
> were every bit the enemies
> to the poor human being as was God.
> . . . .
> serpent gods coiled
> around the crime of being born,
> naked and elegant buddhas
> smiling at the cocktail party
> of empty eternity
> like Christ on his horrible cross,
> all of them capable of anything,

of imposing on us their heaven,
all of them with wounds or a pistol

. . . .

fierce gods made by men
to conceal their cowardice,

. . . .

the whole earth reeked of heaven,
of celestial commodities.

★

In 1929, nearly a year into his residence on Ceylon, Neruda was in a state of bewildering flux. "Sometimes I'm happy here, but what demonic solitude," he wrote Eandi during a monsoon.

This storm rained hard on Neruda's psyche. "Water that doesn't stop . . . an evil humidity that penetrates to the bones": it was "the saddest period in the tropics." While it rained, he read. Along with *"los Hogares,"* the Argentine magazine Eandi sent him, he read English novels borrowed from Wendt.

Solitude, Neruda wrote, was becoming:

> [A] humid room around me, it poisons me, because the small passing wounds become gaping: there's no way to stop the bleeding and they hemorrhage all the way to the soul. But what a beautiful fresh day it is, after a terrible tempest last night in which my house filled with water and two coconut trees fell in the garden, struck by lightning. Today is green and transparent: the sea is thick and detained, blue.

This last sentence suggests that the psychological bleeding may have been slowing, allowing room for optimism. He was opening further but was growing tired of his life in Ceylon, worried about getting stuck within its "inactivity of death." Fortunately, good news arrived: he would be transferred to Singapore, a much more cosmopolitan and enticing country, with jurisdiction over equally appealing Java. Animated, Neruda wrote to Eandi of stretching out his senses to finally experience and rejuvenate in the beauty of the post-monsoon mornings for the first time since he had been there. Something was "soothing him." Somehow, Neruda seemed to emerge from his doldrums just as the 1920s ended and the ensuing global depression began.

★

Wellawatta, Ceylon, February 27, 1930:

> The consul general of Calcutta has recommended that I go to Singapore and Java; it'd be good if they appoint me there.
> Yes, naturally, sometimes I'm crazy with happiness, not because of Patsy and her ilk, but rather because I've recovered my health, and my skin is still young. Stretched out in the sand, alone, in the mornings I shout with joy "EANDIIII" and anything else that occurs to me, the fishermen look at me astonished, and I help them throw out their nets.

Neruda was apparently escaping the inferno at last. He departed to Singapore with lifted spirits in early June 1930, ready to take up his new post, accompanied by his "good servant Dom Brampy," whom he referred to as "my Sinhalese boy," who at some point seemingly replaced Ratnaigh. The consul also brought his "extremely friendly" mongoose. Upon his arrival he went straight to the world-famous Raffles Hotel and checked in. He had started to do his laundry when he got the alarming news that there hadn't been a Chilean consul in Singapore for some time—there was nothing there for him. He ran back to the port, supposedly with his still-wet clothes, hoping that if the Singapore post didn't exist, the Java one did. The Dutch boat he had come on from Colombo, luckily, was still there, ready to head to the Dutch colony of Batavia (now Jakarta, the capital of Indonesia). Neruda got on board.

Batavia is located on the northwestern end of the immense yet relatively narrow island of Java.* The landscape here was unlike where Neruda had been, and was full of volcanic mountains. There were fertile swaths of rice paddies and coffee groves, making the area one of the most profitable of all the Dutch colonies. By 1930 it was also a much more cosmopolitan city than Neruda's previous posts, with shopping, entertainment, and better roads for exploring the wilder surroundings. Neruda gradually became involved with the Dutch colonial elite. Despite never having been much of a tennis player, it was at a tennis match that he met a tall, attractive blue-eyed Dutchwoman, Maria Antonia Hagenaar Vogelzang. She still lived with her parents, which was not uncommon. Neruda would call her Maruca, the Spanish version of Marietje, the name by which she went in Batavia.

Finally, in the Far East, Neruda kindled a romance with a woman who met his societal requirements. Maruca, with her European blood, was marriageable. Perhaps she felt a maternal affection for him. She did adore him at first, in an exciting, first-love, almost blind kind of way. At the tennis courts and markets and on tropical day trips, they had ample leisure time in which to develop a relationship. They shared a desire to be with someone of their own race with similar social standing. They had little else in common. The year before, Neruda had written to Eandi from Ceylon that he wanted to marry "soon, tomorrow even." That and to live in a big city were his only persistent wishes.

He would satisfy both. In a postcard marked January 31, 1931, he announced the news: "No longer alone! Dear Eandi, I got married a month ago." Their wedding took place on December 6, 1930, less than half a year after meeting at the tennis court.

A week later he wrote to his father, announcing the event and stress-

---

* The English East India Company and Dutch merchants, along with their respective governments and armed forces, clashed for nearly a decade, jockeying with Java's Prince Jayawikarta to control the trade in the area. In 1619, after having lost ground, the Dutch army took advantage of an opportunity created by the prince's rivals and attacked, burning the city of Jayakarta, as Jakarta was then known. The prince fled as the Dutch assumed power and took over the port and the area. They renamed it Batavia, and it soon became another part of the Dutch East Indies, which covered most of present-day Indonesia.

ing that his wife was from a "distinguished family" and that he had wanted to tell him earlier about his decision to marry "and wait for your consent, but due to numerous circumstances, our wedding was certified much earlier than the date we expected." Neruda placated him, writing, "From now on, you will not have to worry knowing your son is alone and far away from you, for now I have someone who will be with me forever." He added, "She brings together all the perfections and we are entirely happy." He also told his father that, as she doesn't speak Spanish and he doesn't speak Dutch, they both speak English "perfectly."

Neruda then wrote to his good friend Ángel Cruchaga Santa María (who would later marry Albertina):

> I've married. Do me the favor of publishing in good shape this portrait of my wife in *Zig-Zag*. They have a thing for me there.
>
> Why should I tell you that this is to please her. She knows you very well already . . .
>
> I beg you to send me two copies of the *Zig-Zag* in which it appears.
>
> But don't forget, if not you could disturb a home's peacefulness!
>
> > Frantically yours,
> > *Pablo*
> > *Neruda*

With the freshness of newlyweds, the couple was a handsome pair.

Ten months into the marriage, on September 5, 1931, Neruda penned details to Eandi about his life as a married man in Java. He and his Dutch wife were "extremely close," "extremely happy," he begins. Everything that follows seems to contradict that. They lived "in a house smaller than a thimble. I read; she knits. The consular life, the protocol, the meals, dinner jackets, tailcoats, formal tuxedos, uniforms, dances, cocktails, all the time: hell."

Sometimes they would get away by car, taking a thermos, cognac, and books to the mountains or the coast to look out at "the black island,

Sumatra, and the submarine volcano Krakatau. We eat sandwiches. We go back. I don't write . . . Every day is the same as the next in this land. Books. Films."

He never wrote a single love poem to Maruca. On the one page that he mentions her in his memoirs, he set her aside in parentheses, saying only, "I had met a creole, or better said a Dutch woman with drops of Malayan blood, whom I liked a lot. She was a tall and gentle woman, a total stranger to the world of arts and letters." He then, in a manner and format like nowhere else in the book, inserts the following, as if he couldn't manage to write more than just those two sentences about her in the first person:

> (Some years later, my biographer and friend Margarita Agui-
> rre would write, "Neruda returned to Chile in 1932. Two
> years before, in Batavia, he had married María Antonieta
> Hagenaar, a young Dutch woman established in Java. She
> is very proud to be the wife of a consul and has a rather
> exotic view of America. She doesn't know Spanish and is
> starting to learn it. But there is no doubt that it's not just the
> language that she doesn't know. In spite of everything, her
> sentimental adhesion to Neruda is very strong, and you al-
> ways see them together. Maruca—that's what Neruda calls
> her—is very tall, slow, formal.")

In Batavia, after sending the necessary letters announcing their mar-
riage, Neruda was eager to return to Chile with Maruca on his arm. He wouldn't have to wait long to show her off in person. The Chilean gov-
ernment drastically cut back its consular positions due to the tremen-
dous economic effect the Great Depression was having on the country. As commodity prices plunged, so did the Chilean government's trea-
sury, and as world trade dwindled, so did the amount of revenue from trade that consuls such as Neruda depended on. While Maruca's family could perhaps have arranged something for them in Batavia, he was ready to return home anyway and now had his impetus. The long-love-
scorned poet was coming home with a woman by his side.

CHAPTER TEN

AN INTERLUDE

Blood has fingers and it opens tunnels
beneath the earth.
—"Maternity"

N eruda and Maruca arrived in Chile on April 18, 1932, after a dreary
two-month journey aboard a cargo ship, the *Forafic*. The fact that
they could afford to cross the seas only on such an uncomfortable
ship, with few cabins meant for passengers and a diesel engine drasti-
cally slower than a steamship's, was a sign that marriage to Maruca
did not suddenly resolve Neruda's financial situation. This left them
with Neruda's meager consul salary, which had virtually disappeared
during his last days in Asia. The voyage was tedious, with no decks
designed for passengers, only a main deck full of open pipes, chimneys,
cables, and additional cargo. The seemingly endless isolation with his
new wife, for whom he quickly realized he had no real passion and little
patience, thwarted whatever excitement Neruda had mustered to begin
his new life in Chile. His energy evaporated, replaced by the terrible
moods he thought he had put behind him.

Throughout that passage from the Indian Ocean, across the Atlan-
tic, and up along Chile's Pacific coast, he had little else to do but write.
He wrote a brutal, haunting, hypnotic poem, "The Ghost of the Cargo
Ship." The speaker is the only passenger on board, perhaps the phan-

tom of the poem's title. The boat becomes phantasmal as well, and its engines echo the locomotive engines in "Railroad Roundhouses at Night." Here, the "tired machinery that howls and weeps" is

> pushing the prow, kicking the sides,
> mumbling low groans, swallowing and swallowing distances,
> making a noise of sour waters over the sour waters,
> moving the old ship over the old waters.

Time, notably, is "still and visible like a great disgrace." Neruda seems stuck, ghostlike, completely alone, despite his new marriage. Interestingly, in ordering the poems in *Residence on Earth*'s first volume, he placed "The Ghost of the Cargo Ship," full of his disenchantment with his white wife, right before "Widower's Tango," which expresses his desire to be with Josie Bliss again. A poem titled "Josie Bliss" closes the second volume of *Residence on Earth*.

Finally, on April 18, 1932, Neruda and Maruca disembarked in Puerto Montt, where Patagonia begins. Had they arrived at Valparaíso, the ship would have navigated through a port full of empty boats with nothing to load and nowhere to go. At the same time that the country was suffering from the repercussions of the global economic depression, Chile's critical saltpeter industry crashed as well. The Atacama Desert, which covers the northern part of the country, is the world's largest source of *salitre*—sodium nitrate, or saltpeter. It became known as "white gold" due to worldwide demand; its two principal uses were as a fertilizer, raising crop yields as the global population was surging, and as an ingredient in gunpowder, especially at the start of World War I. Export taxes on the foreign-owned mines helped fund the government, and the mines were a major source of employment. But just as the war was ending, a synthetic replacement was developed. The price of saltpeter fell by half between 1925 and 1932. International demand for Chile's copper also dropped steeply.

In its *World Economic Survey, 1932–33,* the League of Nations ranked Chile as the nation most devastated by the Depression. The signs were clear and alarming: rampant unemployment, a severe depletion of the money supply, the government's desperate efforts to bring in revenue, thousands of homeless, repression of protests, and the onset of social anarchy. The dictatorial Carlos Ibáñez was pressured into resigning, and the next elected president was toppled in a coup that created the Socialist Republic of Chile, though twelve days didn't go by until there was another coup, this one from within. Ibáñez loyalists sent the more liberal leaders off to Easter Island. Lacking support and legitimacy, the new government lasted only three months before it too was overthrown. That led to a new election in October 1932 in which Arturo Alessandri, backed by a coalition of liberals, democrats, and radicals, was elected president for the second time. (Another event that took place the year Neruda returned to Chile would have an even greater influence on the course of his life. Adolf Hitler became a German citizen in 1932, mainly so he could run in elections. He became the Führer in 1934.)

Perhaps because of the breakdown of basic services in the country, Neruda's telegram to his parents didn't arrive in time to warn them of his arrival. Laura happened to be looking out the window when she saw her half brother and new sister-in-law getting out of a car with their suitcases. José del Carmen greeted them calmly, while Doña Trinidad embraced both of them with her inherent warmth. His father went from calm to contentious quite quickly, unable to resist railing at his son about his poor choices, and now there was his daughter-in-law and perhaps grandchildren his son would have to provide for. The wintry cold and rain falling down on Temuco worsened the mood, frustrating Neruda, who had been so free from these confrontations while in the warmth of his posts; he had left those tropics and spent all those weeks on a cargo ship only to be faced with this. He took Maruca to Santiago within a week.

Neruda's old bohemian world waited in Santiago. The couple found an apartment on Catedral Street, where his friends would visit constantly. Maruca's first impression of the Chilean capital was of the grimy dark stones of the apartment building walls, the gray facades of the buildings on each side of their narrow street. Having just come from the open green landscapes of Java, this colorless scenery must have been suffocating, as her life in Chile would be.

Neruda, finally back on his own turf, assumed his place as king of "Neruda's gang," as the group would be known. Members took an immediate disliking to Maruca. "She was a hostile being," Diego Muñoz remembered. She "didn't show any interest in knowing any of Pablo's old friends." Diego thought that Maruca was a most inappropriate wife for a poet. She would close the door to Pablo's friends, so he just went out with them without her. During that first long winter, she would wait for him most evenings, watching out the window until he came home late at night. When he did, Maruca would "launch into a tirade in English, telling him off like a bucket of cold water," as Muñoz put it.

Neruda remained calm, if not indifferent, in the midst of this discord. He didn't care about the pain that was hardening her, the gulf between them growing wider. He had resigned himself to the fact that the level of elegance, education, and worldliness he had first perceived in her was not nearly enough to sustain an emotional and physical attraction, now that he'd accomplished coming home with a woman by his side and, at the same time, having escaped his alienation in Asia.

Muñoz, however, also wrote that he and his friends all found Neruda a noticeably changed man upon his return: "Now he wasn't the somber, melancholic, absent *muchacho*" they remembered. "Now he talked a lot, laughing for whatever reason." José María Souvirón, a Spanish poet who was in Santiago at the time, wrote that Pablo was at that point a rather lanky young man "with a melancholy air," yet happy with what was going on in his life. Neruda was pleasant and entertaining once he got to know you, "resolute in his likes and dislikes, skeptical but respectful, a good drinker and enjoyer of life"—even "hedonistic." His eyes, his friend insisted, were set on Spain.

His eyes were also still set on Albertina. Soon after he had returned to Chile from Asia, Neruda wrote to her in Concepción:

You know by now that I have been married since December of 1931 [*sic*, 1930]. The loneliness that you didn't want to remedy has become more and more unbearable . . .

I would love so much to kiss you softly on your forehead,

to caress your hands that I have loved so much, to give you a fraction of the friendship and affection that I still have for you in my heart.

Do not show this letter to anyone. I will not tell anyone that you write to me.

He quickly wrote to her again, overexplaining his decision to marry another woman:

My telegrams, my letters, told you that I was going to marry you when you arrived at Colombo. Albertina, I already had the marriage license, and I had asked for the necessary money. You know this, I have repeated it to you with patience in each one of my letters, in great detail.

Now my sister tells me that I asked you to come live with me, without marrying you, and that you have said this.

Never! Why do you lie? I feel a horrible bitterness, not only because you have not understood me, but also because you slander me.

I have loved you so much, Albertina, you know this, and you have behaved badly, silent when I needed you most . . .

A third letter showed he still could not reconcile himself to her silence:

My dear Albertina, I answered your letter about a month ago now, and you haven't said anything about what I asked you . . . I need so badly to talk to you, to reproach you, to tell you. I remember you every day, I thought that you would write to me every day, but you are as thankless as always.

I still cannot understand what happened to you in Europe. I still don't understand why you didn't go.

Albertina recognized his marriage as legitimate, even if he did not. She did not give in. She would, however, become friends with him again when she married his friend Ángel Cruchaga Santa María, five years later.

Neruda's attention also had returned to his inability to create a sustainable income as a poet. Through a fellow writer, he was able to get some work at the Ministry of Labor's Cultural Extension. While the pay was minimal, it was great to have any work at all as the Depression deepened in Chile. He worked on the ministry's Libraries for the People project. It was a progressive initiative that was under constant threat from conservatives, who hated these populist programs, especially during the economic crisis, which demanded austerity.

★

During this time back in Chile, works Neruda had long awaited publishing finally found their light. At the beginning of 1933, *El hondero entusiasta* (The Enthusiastic Sling-Shooter) was published, drawing on older poetry from the period when he was visibly influenced by the style of Sabat Ercasty. In his preface, Neruda admitted that Sabat's influence did indeed lead him to suppress the book for a time and that in the end it contained only a portion of the original poems. This collection, he warned, was "a document of an excessive and burning youth." The poems received minimal attention from critics and readers alike.

At the same time, Neruda had been suppressing the publication of the book that was of his greatest concern, *Residence on Earth*. Neruda was certain that this publication would be a smashing success across the Spanish-speaking world, and he pinned his literary future on it, to the point that he would not settle for it to come out anywhere other than Spain. Anywhere else, in its author's hubristic view, would be a failure in relation to all he had put in, all he felt he had achieved. Chile still seemed like a backwater country to him in the context of the great literary tradition of Europe.

But more than three years had passed since he had written to Eandi from Colombo that he had "realized yesterday that it is time to publish my long detained book of poems." "I have a publisher in Chile who would pay me and would take great care of the book, but I don't want it [to just be published there]." A few months later it seemed that while nothing was happening with the book finding a home in Spain, Eandi brought up the possibility that *Residence* could be published in Argentina, with a decent advance. But Neruda refused, insisting on Spain. He followed that proclamation with an insinuation that the poems were simply too good for any other fate: "I have been writing these poems for nearly five years . . . I feel that I have achieved that requisite essence: a style; it seems to me that each of my lines is saturated with my very self, they drip."

In the meantime, he had gotten a manuscript into the hands of Alfredo Cóndon, the aspiring Chilean writer who hosted Neruda in Paris, only to pass out on the floor of the Russian bar. What Cóndon lacked in literary talent he made up for with his personal wealth and contacts. He had already connected Neruda with Carlos Morla Lynch, the writer-diplomat based at the Chilean embassy in Madrid, where Cóndon was now a secretary. While Morla Lynch wasn't able to get Neruda transferred to Spain, he did get him to Java.

Now Cóndon came to him with the *Residence* manuscript, entreating him to find a publisher, so Morla Lynch passed the manuscript and the charge on to Rafael Alberti, a leading figure in the exciting, influential generation of young writers in Spain at the time. "From the very first reading," Alberti recalled, "those poems surprised and astonished me, so distant, as they were, from the tenor and atmosphere of our poetry." He passed the book all around Madrid, believing that "such an extraordinary book of new revelations had to come out in Spain. I proposed it to my few friends who were editors—failure. I then began a correspondence with Pablo. His replies were anguished . . . In one of his letters, he asked me for a dictionary and for my forgiveness for the grammatical errors that his letters might contain."

When Alberti arrived in Paris in 1931, he told Alejo Carpentier about this "absolutely extraordinary poet" who was serving as a consul in Java and was unknown in Europe, and that he should publish him. Carpentier had fled political repression in Cuba and was straddling the worlds of surrealism and journalism in France. He was working as the editor of a new magazine, collaborating with other stellar Latin American members of his generation residing in Paris. The endeavor was run and funded by the young writer Elvira de Alvear, another recent arrival in Montparnasse. She came from the Argentine bourgeoisie and financed the publication from income she regularly received from back home. As Carpentier recounted later, he wrote to Java, and Neruda sent him the manuscript, whose poetry amazed him. He talked to de Alvear, and they decided to first print some of the poems in the next issue of the magazine and then publish the whole book. There would even be an advance of 5,000 francs. Alberti sent a cable to Neruda with the news. But then, as a repercussion of the Depression, Argentina passed a law restricting the exportation of capital. De Alvear was forced to return home. Neruda never got the francs nor was *Residence* published in France. Everything seemed to be more of a struggle now—after having book after book come out over the past years, he no longer seemed to be infallible when it came to publishing. Even the fate of de Alvear's finances seemed like a direct reversal of the good fortune Neruda had when he ran into Alone, just after he got his stock tip money, and the critic agreed to pay off *Book of Twilights'* printer.

Neruda kept tight to his stubborn, arrogant conviction of not settling for anything "less" than having the book be published in Spain, wasting three years as he passed up opportunities for paying contracts with solid publishers in Argentina and Chile. He even had his latest (albeit much less significant) work, *El hondero entusiasta,* published by Nascimento in Santiago without a second thought. Nascimento had now published five books of Neruda's—perhaps not to the greatest sales volume, but nearly all of them worthy endeavors, and the more important ones made their way to Europe, the United States, and elsewhere.

But after three years, Neruda couldn't hold back any longer. He was still too arrogant to allow a full release outside of Spain, but he was dying to get something out there, while still holding on to his cards so that he could flush out a noble debut in Europe. He thus arranged with Nascimento to do a limited release of one hundred deluxe copies, with paper from Holland, each signed by the poet himself. For Neruda, this strategy kept the book seemingly within his control. (It was unlike Neruda's previous books: all those since *Twenty Love Poems*—*venture, El habitante, Anillos,* even the new *El hondero entusiasta*—were selling hundreds of copies each.) And most important, he would still leave open the opportunity for a Spanish publisher to print a full run of popular editions that would be considered the real first edition. These one hundred were more for friends, for the literati, for reviewers. He hoped all of their enthusiasm would create a buzz and attract a Spanish publisher.

But when Nascimento did publish the hundred copies, some critics were unenthusiastic, reacting less to the lines themselves than to Neruda's whole approach; they felt Neruda's ego had grown too big, while others were simply jealous. Some were both, such as Pablo de Rokha, one of Neruda's nemeses throughout his literary life, a poet who amassed a torrential body of work and was important enough to one day have a Santiago high school and neighborhood named after him. De Rokha had already criticized Neruda in print, and now he attacked him again in the newspaper *La Opinión,* ten days after the publication of the first *Residence,* audaciously titling the article "Epitaph to Neruda." "Neruda is the master, the owner and victim of the mask, of that 'poet's mask' that initiates and defines *Residencia,*" wrote de Rokha. The book's tone is "excessive and treacherous"; Neruda's words "hang like rags; the mask is wet, it's been rained upon inside."

He was clearly alluding to Neruda's only major poetry recital since his return, which had been at a theater staged with Asian masks, as if out of a Chinese opera. Neruda had given his reading standing behind one of the giant masks, not once showing his face, as he read the early poems of *Residence* in a "nasal twangy voice, dragging like a lament." He had started with the poem "We Together":

> How pure you are in sunlight or at nightfall,
> how boundlessly triumphant your white orbit,
> and your bosom of bread, atmospheric height,
> your crown of black trees, beloved,
> and your solitary animal's nose, a wild sheep's nose
> that smells of shadow and sudden flight.

The reading went on for over an hour, Neruda using little inflection, speaking in "a monochord deep moan," as one witness described it.

After Neruda was done, everyone waited eagerly for the poet to appear onstage. But he didn't come out to greet the mixture of applause and indifference; he remained behind the mask.

Generally, besides de Rokha, *Residence*'s first volume found favorable reviews in Chile. Despite some monotone and monotony, readers embraced this surprising poetry's high-strung intensity, an intensity spun tight by the grips of the new rhetoric, the new way to express oneself in a poem—an intensity that was a driving force through the book and into the readers' emotional receptors. Neruda had returned to the forefront. His friends considered it a precedent-breaking success. However, it was hard to find a formal nonpartisan review, the most prominent, other than de Rokha's, being written by either his friends or his devotees.* In 1935, after the second volume was printed, Alone, whose reputation as a literary critic had continued to grow through the years, gave his first full review of the work. It was positive. Alone's main point was that Neruda's ability to achieve such an earnest level of authenticity and transparency came from the fact that he had written it with true conviction. Neruda was not afraid to leave his comfort zone, he believed, and this new level of confidence is evident in the poetic forms' impenetrability. Neruda is no longer seeking clarity in order to be understood. His poetic maturity is evident; his raw evocation comes out complex and dissonant, yet completely naked.

The critical and social reception the limited edition achieved was just what Neruda had envisioned. Now he just needed to take the next step: find a publisher in Spain. And now Neruda needed to take another step as well: find a job. While he was still hoping to work in Spain, with the achievement of *Residence* under his belt, the Ministry of Foreign Affairs named him to a post in Argentina in August 1933. Four years earlier, he had written to Eandi from Ceylon; two lines after describing

---

* For example, in Santiago's main newspapers, *El Mercurio* and *La Nación*, there was a review by his friend Luis Enrique Délano in the former and a rather artificial piece by Norberto Pinilla in the latter, which more than anything defends Neruda's sad character. The rare time Pinilla has anything negative to say about a poem, he goes no further than to call it opaque and without beauty.

how life in Colombo was like death, he asked, "Buenos Aires, isn't that the name of paradise?"

★

The Chilean writer María Luisa Bombal would be a central character in Neruda's life in Buenos Aires. She had returned to Chile from Europe around the same time that Neruda came back from Asia. Twenty-three at the time, glowing, with short hair, she had become one of Chile's greatest fiction writers. While studying literature at the Sorbonne, she began experimenting with acting, taking classes at the celebrated École de l'Atelier. When word got back to her family that she had been on-stage, which they considered improper, they pressured her to return to Chile. As she disembarked, she spotted her mother and twin sisters in their winged hats and, behind them, a tall and hefty man, twenty-eight years old. This was Eulogio Sánchez Errázuriz, the wealthy grandson of a former president and a pioneer of Chilean aviation. Every move he made seemed to be full of conviction; his voice was firm. He greeted María Luisa and offered to get her luggage. Her sisters explained that he was a new friend of the family. Almost immediately, like many other women, María Luisa fell madly in love with him.

A short but intense romance began, but Sánchez soon withdrew from María Luisa's aggressiveness. She wrote him letter after letter, tried to approach him again, but it was clear to all but her that Sánchez definitively and irrevocably did not love her and would never love her. He even showed her sisters her letters and asked them to convince María Luisa to lay her passions to rest.

María Luisa was tormented by the loss. One night, trying to normalize relations, Sánchez invited her and her sister Loreto to dinner. He clearly conveyed his desire to have nothing more than a friendship with María Luisa. She left the table, went to his bedroom, searched through his drawers until she found his revolver, and then shot herself in her left shoulder. She would spend a month recovering in Santiago's Hospital del Salvador.

The Bombal twins had met Neruda shortly after his return from the Far East. One day they brought María Luisa to his house, believing the two might get along. They were right. A friend who was at the encounter said, "Pablo adored her immediately." He quickly came to feel that she was "the only woman with whom I can seriously talk about literature." Despite her suffering over Sánchez, her intelligence, culture, humor, and youth captivated Neruda. (He was also impressed by her sister Loreto. In this case, the feelings weren't platonic. According to María Luisa and others, he had fallen in love with her. And there was talk that the two had an affair that lasted until he left for Argentina.)

Having been away in Paris, and rarely in Santiago before she left, María Luisa knew little of the city's writers and intellectuals who congregated around Neruda as if he were royalty. He introduced her to his friends, who found her elegant, gracious, bright, and creative.

María Luisa also became good friends with Maruca (Maruca's only friend, other than Juanita Eandi in Argentina). As María Luisa's mental instability coincided with Neruda's new consular appointment to Buenos Aires, the poet invited her to live with them in Buenos Aires, thinking a fresh start and some distance would do her good. It did.

While his position still had the tag of consul "of choice, by election," it was beginning to look like he was establishing an actual career path within the diplomatic corps that would provide more than just small stipends. Still, when he first showed up to take his post in Buenos Aires, the *cónsul general de Chile,* Socrates Aguirre, announced, "You will be responsible for making the name of Chile shine."

"How?" Neruda asked, somewhat dubiously.

"By establishing friendly relations with writers and intellectuals. Your job is culture. Myself and another functionary will deal with all the diplomatic bureaucracy," he explained.

These new, direct relations not only would help Neruda's country to shine, but would brighten his own disposition.

The concrete experiences of fraternity that Neruda had upon his return to Chile and now in Argentina breathed new life into his sense of self and well-being. It allowed him to become an active participant in what would soon be an intense Buenos Aires social life and engage more fully in the world.

It started with Héctor Eandi, no longer just a sympathetic person on the other side of the world whom Neruda had never seen, connected only by pen or transcontinental cable; now they were face-to-face, tangible friends. Neruda was free of the disconnectedness he felt in Asia, where most of his fleeting social interactions were with people for whom he felt little more than disdain.

Two years earlier, shortly after getting married, Neruda and Maruca had sent a package of gifts to Eandi and his family from Batavia, including a pair of pajamas for his young daughter, Violna, and a Javanese hand fan for his wife, Juanita. Now all five sat in one another's company, delighted to be together, the adults conversing for hours. (However, when the conversation turned to children, and the Eandis asked the Nerudas about their plans, they answered silently, through vague smiles followed by blank faces.)

Eandi was a literary critic at heart. Neruda first became aware of him after Eandi wrote an adulatory piece on his poetry. Now he wanted to do what he could to assure that Neruda would be well received in Argentina, at least by those concerned with literature. Neruda was already a familiar name among poetry readers on the eastern side of the Andes. An edition of *Twenty Love Poems,* the first book of his to be published outside of Chile and the one that would help catapult him to international fame, had recently been released in Buenos Aires. And just upon his arrival, the legendary Argentine magazine *Poesía* published four of his *Residence* poems. Eandi promoted these publications in the Buenos Aires newspaper *La Nación* on October 8, 1933, two months after Neruda's arrival.

> Neruda's four major books, *The Book of Twilights, Twenty Love Poems, venture of the infinite man,* and *Residence* bring together works of great maturity, in which a profoundly lyrical nature is evident, served by an astonishing technique . . . His language is so deep, so rich and involved with humanity; there's a violence of passion in his words; he knows how to get to the root of emotion, that his verses powerfully create their own ambiance.

Besides Eandi's companionship, Neruda rapidly made new friends in Argentina; Maruca's and his large, modern apartment quickly became a social hub for the Buenos Aires literary world. It looked out over the "Broadway of Buenos Aires," Corrientes Street, an artery of the city's life and culture that never slept. It was a sparkling spine of the city where people forgot about the financial crisis and enjoyed themselves with abandon.

The panoramic views from their twentieth-floor apartment were fantastic, such a striking contrast to the walled gray confines around their Catedral Street apartment in Santiago. Yet even in such cheerful surroundings, despite all the advancement he had made, Neruda was still not impervious to depression. He became despondent again, his mood disordered despite the fact that he was meeting new and old friends in the cosmopolitan city, all eager to spend time with him.

Two of the renowned figures with whom Neruda, and sometimes Maruca, spent a great deal of time were the poets Norah Lange and Oliverio Girondo, a legendary couple who would eventually marry. Sara "La Rubia" (the Blonde) Tornú, an important progressive promoter of literary and artistic culture, also became a close confidante, as did José González Carbalho, lyrical poet, journalist, and principal founder of the influential magazine *Martín Fierro.*[*] Borges was in Buenos Aires during this period as well, but he was noticeably absent from Neruda's social scene.[†]

---

* Neruda was so fond of Carbalho that fifteen years later he wrote a poem dedicated to him in *Canto General,* testifying to the fraternity the two had developed in Argentina. The poem revolves around the theme of hearing the universal voice of the poet in the silence of the night. In the final stanza, Neruda tells his friend: "Brother, you're the longest river on earth / . . . faithful to the transparency of a sublime tear / faithful to mankind's besieged eternity."

† Between August 1933 and October 1934, Borges codirected and was a major contributor to *Revista multicolor de los sábados* (Multicolor Saturday Magazine), the literary supplement to *Crítica,* a newspaper with a vast circulation and notable prestige. Yet there seemed to be absolutely no contact with Neruda while he was there, with many different speculations as to why. At this time, Borges was in love with Norah Lange, who was becoming extremely close to Neruda. This could have generated jealousy and even enmity.

The first month in Buenos Aires was taxing for Neruda. One thing weighing on him was the failure of *Residence* to take off. Nearly half a year had passed since that first printing of a hundred copies in Santiago, and despite the generally good reception, despite his idea that the print run would be enough only for friends and influential readers, there turned out to be plenty of copies to spare; they just weren't really selling. That heavy negative feeling he had felt in one shape or form for so much of his life descended on him once again, just as it started to seem that he had risen above it. He couldn't pretend he'd completely escaped it. He had to have felt a sense of helplessness as he looked out from his enviable apartment with Buenos Aires throbbing at his feet, as he recalled the intimate, direct connections with such stellar new friends. This despondency is articulated in one of his true classics, "Walking Around," one of three morose poems written during the first month or so he was in Buenos Aires: "Comes a time I'm tired of being a man."

The original title for the poem was in English, not out of snobbery or affectation, but to tie it to James Joyce's *Ulysses,* in which the main character, Leopold Bloom, walks around Dublin, free-associating throughout the course of an "ordinary day" in 1904. The Irishman's influence on Neruda had grown; Neruda had read *Ulysses* in Sri Lanka and now translated some of Joyce's early poems for an Argentine magazine.

"Walking Around" shows Neruda at the height of his skills. The poem's power comes from Neruda's novel implementation of a constellation of linguistic and symbolic materials so that the poem still seems vanguard today:

> Comes a time I'm tired of being a man.
> Comes a time I check out the tailor's or the movies
> shriveled, impenetrable, like a felt swan
> launched into waters of origin and ashes.
>
> A whiff from the barber shops has me wailing.
> All I want is a break from rocks and wool,
> all I want is to see neither buildings nor gardens,
> no shopping centers, no bifocals, no elevators.

Comes a time I'm tired of my feet and my fingernails
and my hair and my shadow.
Comes a time I'm tired of being a man.[*]

*

María Luisa Bombal's presence in Buenos Aires was comforting for
Neruda, and the feeling was mutual, in a platonic way for both. Her
smooth, natural creativity and warmth helped him, as he, likewise,
helped her. She poured herself into her writing, retracing her agony
and desires of the past years in *La última niebla* (*The Final Mist*). A pre-
cursor to magical realism, it put her on the path to becoming one of the
few globally recognized female Latin American novelists. It is the first
book in Latin American literature that narrates the experience of an
orgasm from the perspective of a woman, the author herself. The novel
was published in 1935, two years after she moved in with the Nerudas.

She wrote most of it in the apartment's bright, enormous kitchen.
The floor was marble, edged in fine blue ceramic. Both the floor and the
walls were brilliant white—an ideal workspace. "What do you think?"
María Luisa would ask, reading a few sentences from her manuscript.
Neruda hesitated to give her advice, for he understood how her mind
worked. When he did make suggestions, she would consider them, but
she was clear on what she wanted to express, just as Neruda had sensed.
"Don't ever let anyone correct you," he told her. Bombal's accounts give
a rare insight into Neruda, the disinterested (and objective) friend and
editor.

Neruda came to admire her kitchen writing so much that he started
to join her there. They would work side by side, she on her novel, he
continuing on with new *Residence* poems. Such a move—to prefer to
write in another's presence instead of in isolation—signaled a change in
Neruda's disposition; his mood elevated once more, on a trend toward
greater stability.

He called María Luisa the "bee of fire," referring to the passion he
felt burning in her and the creativity by which she seemed to take

---

[*]   Complete poem in Appendix I.

flight. "We adored each other," María Luisa recalled in 1973, right after Neruda's death. "Our friendship had shades of intellectualism, but it was very emotive. We were so incredibly young and passionate. He was like a brother to me."

She described Maruca as the complete opposite of Pablo. "What would Maruca do without the daily company of María Luisa, as intelligent as she was mild, never pretending or trying to know more than she knew?" Bombal's biographer Agata Gligo asked.

To María Flora Yáñez, "Neruda's Javanese wife looked like a giant blond police officer" when they first met in the Buenos Aires apartment. María Flora was a Chilean novelist, the sister of Neruda's good friend Juan Emar, a.k.a. Pilo, though she and Neruda hadn't met in person until her recent arrival in Argentina. Neruda had gone to her hotel to greet her and invited her to a cocktail party in her honor at his "ultramodern apartment," as she described it. He wanted to introduce her to the city's greatest writers. María Flora, as accustomed as she was to being in the presence of important literary figures, was indeed struck by the depth of talent Neruda had assembled in the room. She became breathless, in fact, upon seeing the sublime Alfonsina Storni, a leading voice of modern feminism and writer of hauntingly beautiful poetry.[*] Most left early, at nine, but Neruda asked María Flora to stay, along with Storni.

María Flora wrote that when they finished eating (rather late, in accordance with Argentine custom), Neruda proposed ending the night at the underground *peña* El Signo. María Flora saw Maruca make a gesture to Neruda as she disappeared into her bedroom. He followed his wife, and soon the shouts of a heated argument filled the apartment. When they returned, Neruda seemed deflated, Maruca still convulsing with rage. "Let's go to the Signo," he ordered, and they left, without Maruca.

---

[*] Storni's poetry, erotic and almost always informed by her feminism, would have international impact. She wrote what has been called poetry of "fatal beauty that leads to an unavoidable death." A year after Neruda arrived in Argentina, she was besieged by breast cancer. Four years later, her body crushed with pain and her mind depressed and exhausted, she walked off a pier and into the ocean at Mar del Plata, where she drowned.

El Signo had just opened that year in the basement of El Hotel Castelar. At night it functioned as a *tertulia de arte,* or a salon, a gathering place to talk about the arts. It became a top place to go for many of those involved in that world. José González Carbalho and Norah Lange, among other friends who had just embraced Neruda, were the first to get it going.

Neruda began having affairs behind his wife's back. Bombal knew about them, especially because of his admiration for her sister Loreto. There were also suspicions that something more than friendship occurred between Neruda and the avant-garde Norah Lange, despite her relationship at the time with the poet Oliverio Girondo. Norah and Neruda had a lot of fun together. One night at the trendy restaurant Les Ambassadeurs, without Maruca, they made the band play "Wedding March," and the two approached the orchestra parodying the marriage ritual. Later, everyone quite drunk, they walked down the great Corrientes Street shouting and singing. At some point Norah laughed and in a loud voice said, "Pablo, tonight I'm going to sleep with you," to which Pablo, in the same tone of mirth, replied: "With pleasure." Girondo was there, just as drunk, and he also laughed, with his pipe in mouth. There were whispers, however, that it was more than just a joke.

María Luisa Bombal had her own take on Neruda's relationship with women, with whom he "always had good luck":

> And he didn't really try very hard. He let them love him, seduce him, and sometimes this resulted in tremendous relationships, very romantic and full of problems, which he loved . . . He needed to be with a woman who could tame him and spoil him. Poor Maruca was a good person, but she was so distant from Pablo's world. She didn't understand it at all. She was also cold and remote, and Pablo was so eager for affection. He always looked for a mother figure in women, and we aren't all cut out to be mothers.

And then Maruca discovered that she was pregnant. The news did not bring the couple closer together. Neruda was nervous, already feeling he had made a terrible mistake by marrying her. He continued to keep his distance and allowed himself to be swept up in events outside of the pregnancy.

One such event was his introduction, in mid-October 1933, to Federico García Lorca. The thirty-five-year-old dreamy-eyed Spanish poet, experimental playwright, and puppeteer had come to Buenos Aires for the Latin American premiere of his play *Bodas de sangre* (*Blood Wedding*). He became the talk of the town, profiled in the press. Neruda met Lorca at a reception, and so began a profound friendship. Neruda considered him to be the happiest person he had ever met, an indispensable radiance of joy. Each had a great respect for the other's writing, Lorca reading much of what Neruda wrote just after they met. Lorca inscribed a copy of his *Romancero gitano* (*Gypsy Ballads*), "For my dear Pablo, one of the few great poets I've had the good fortune to love and know." Whenever Lorca heard Neruda begin to recite his poems, he'd cover his eyes and shake his head, crying, "Stop! Stop! That's enough, don't read any more—you'll influence me!"

As for Neruda's praise of Lorca, he would one day describe his plays as if describing all of Lorca's essence: that the tragedies "reinvigorated the eternal Spanish drama, claiming a new phosphoric brilliance, love and death locked in a furious dance: love and death, masked or naked."

Lorca's verse, like his personality, was startling: often so spontaneous, often dark, often vibrant. The poet Robert Bly describes Lorca's rather magical style as "leaping poetry"—all of a sudden images leap unexpectedly, passionate to the core.

They talked nonstop, but they also listened to each other. This continued for nearly six months in Buenos Aires before Lorca returned to Spain. Neruda would remember Lorca as a torrent of motion and delight, "an effervescent child, the young channel of a powerful river . . . in his hands a prank became a work of art. I have never seen such magnetism and such constructiveness in a human being." Lorca's great appetite for life helped reinvigorate Neruda's, or perhaps invigorate it like it never had been.

In his memoirs, Neruda narrates an evening spent at the vast home of the millionaire owner of a newspaper empire, Natalio Botana, where Lorca was also present. At the party, Neruda supposedly met an "ethereal" poet who, especially as they sat across the dinner table from each other, "fixed her green eyes on me more than Lorca." Afterward, all three poets went up to a shimmering lighted swimming pool. The chemistry between Neruda and his new friend was growing. A tower rising above the pool beckoned adventure; its white lime-washed walls glowed in the nocturnal light; they climbed it. With the sound of the party's guitars and singing in the distance, Neruda "took the tall, golden girl in my arms. As I kissed her, I realized she was a carnal and compact woman, with curves in all the right places." Soon they were on the watchtower's floor, Neruda undressing her, when he realized Lorca was staring down at them, completely surprised at what he was seeing. (Lorca was homosexual.)

Neruda wrote, long after Lorca had died in Spain, that he had yelled at his friend, "Get out of here! Go and make sure no one comes up the stairs!" while he offered his "sacrifice to the starry sky and to nocturnal Aphrodite" by having sex with the female poet. Lorca ran off in such a hurry to complete his mission, Neruda wrote, that he fell in the darkness of the tower's stairwell and rolled down it. "My friend and I had to help him, with great difficulty. His limp lasted fifteen days." This story wasn't all invention at least. A young niece of two immigrants from Lorca's hometown stopped by his hotel for visits now and then. On one occasion she found him propped up in bed, his leg in bandages. "There has been an accident at a party," he explained sheepishly.

Neruda did return the favor, in a sense, helping Lorca when he was in a precarious position with women. Neruda had begun to suspect Lorca's homosexuality, though he never had an issue with it. In fact, he benefited from it: as he described it years later, Lorca told him how women—"almost always fledgling poets"—would fill his Buenos Aires hotel room, to the point that he couldn't breathe. Discovering Lorca's "panic about the feminine siege," Neruda immediately offered his services to his friend. They agreed that in moments of true alarm, Lorca would call Neruda, who'd rush over "to take charge of the agreeable mission of steering one of his admirers off elsewhere." Neruda was quite pleased with this arrangement: "With a certain degree of efficiency I reaped some unexpectedly exquisite results from my collaboration. Some of those doves, misled by Federico's light, fell into my arms."

María Luisa Bombal recalled that in those wonderful days in Buenos Aires, far removed from her suicidal thoughts:

> We were happy and carefree. Pablo would come back from the office and say, "The consul is done." And then he would ask me if we could go find Federico . . . "so that he can sing and dance for us, and make us laugh." Life with Federico was a constant party. I never met another man with a more enchanting spirit and heart. He was completely irresistible. He was always the life of the party, with his contagious smile. Pablo always liked to be the center of attention, but [with Federico] he was different; he stepped aside.
>
> His favorite thing was to play the piano for us.
>
> He would say, "María Luisa is like this," and he would play some light, buoyant notes.
>
> And he would say, "Pablo is this way," and the slow, profound chords epitomized Pablo.

Two weeks after they met, on October 28, 1933, the PEN Club of Buenos Aires held a luncheon in honor of Lorca and Neruda: "Spain and America Together." It was held on the top floor of the elegant Hotel Plaza, with more than a hundred writers in attendance. When it came time to thank their hosts, they stood up and began a tribute to Rubén Darío, who had been a leader of such transformations in Spanish poetry in the decades just before these two poets were born. While Neruda admired him, Lorca revered him—the Nicaraguan had been a major influence on his poetry. They knew that Darío had lived in Buenos Aires at one point and had even written a long "Canto a la Argentina." But the city seemed devoid of any public recognition of him—no monuments, no parks, no memory of not only one of the greatest Latin American poets, but one who had sung the country's praises in immortal verse. The two friends did not think this was right. So they decided to deliver their customary toasts, as honorees, in a manner a bit out of the ordinary (though not so extraordinary for those who knew the pair).

Lorca was passionate about bullfighting in his native Spain, and his idea was to divide the talk between himself and Neruda, as he explained to the crowd, "like bullfighting *al alimón,* in which two toreros, holding one cape between them, outwit the bull together." The talk would be on "the great poet of America and of Spain." Lorca called, "Rubén . . ." ". . . Darío!" Neruda responded.

They continued alternating, speaking antiphonally, stressing their debt to tradition as well as their generation's need to transcend it. In 2004, the legendary author Jim Harrison described the event as a "transcendent poetry slam. That evening both poets stood athwart poetry's third rail." Neruda said they spoke as if "linked by an electrical wire," as each spontaneously continued the other poet's line of thinking:

NERUDA: Where in Buenos Aires is the Rubén Darío plaza?
LORCA: Where is the statue of Rubén Darío?
NERUDA: He loved parks. Where is the Rubén Darío park?
LORCA: Where is the Rubén Darío flower shop of roses?

. . .

NERUDA: Where is the oil, the resin, the swan of Rubén Darío?
LORCA: Rubén Darío sleeps in his *natal Nicaragua* below his awful marble lion, like those lions that the rich put at the entrances to their houses.

The exchanges grew even longer and more complex, continuing to play off one another, ending in a toast in homage to Darío's glory, whose "lexical fiesta . . . crashing consonants, flights and forms," as Lorca put it, had enriched the Spanish language forever.

At literary salons in homes that opened their doors to him or which he hosted at his own apartment; at bars, restaurants, and cafés; and on sidewalks, Neruda was nourished and enlivened by the warmth of his new friends. Unlike his first three postings, this one was certainly no "banishment," literally or psychologically. In fact, it was the first time outside of Chile that he had experienced such fellowship, with such intellectual and cultured friends, such creators of new thinking and art.

Maruca's experience of Buenos Aires was considerably different. Bombal couldn't help at times overhearing the couple's arguments while they were all in the apartment. Maruca was opposed to his endless nights out in the city and was terribly bored. She had little talent for making friends, at least within Neruda's circle.

Lorca returned to Spain in March 1934. Right before he left, he was shaken by a haunting premonition of his impending death. "María Luisa, I don't want to leave. I'm going to die. I feel very strange."

A few months later, Neruda's aspirations were realized when he was transferred again to a new post, one eminently suitable for a literary man and friend to Lorca: he would be consul to Spain.

CHAPTER ELEVEN

SPAIN IN THE HEART

For me, Spain is a great wound and a great love. That
period was fundamental in my life. Therefore, almost
everything that I have done since (almost everything I
have done in my poetry and in my life) has the gravity
of my time in Spain.

—Barcelona, June 1970

The Pablo Neruda who entered Spain in the springtime of 1934 was
a different person from the Pablo Neruda who fled a bleeding Spain
in 1937. A year before he left for Spain, Neruda had written to Héctor Eandi from Santiago:

I don't feel any distress for the world at this moment.

I still feel myself reintegrating into Western life, I just want to
enjoy all the pleasures I've been denied for years.

A wave of Marxism seems to be traveling across the world;
letters from my friends urge me toward that position. Really,
politically right now you can only either be a communist or
anticommunist . . .

I still keep that anarchist's distrust of forms of the state, of
impure politics . . .

> There's an invasion of odes to Moscow here, tanks, etc. I
> continue to write about dreams . . .

Neruda's experience of the Spanish Civil War would emotionally affect him to the core; its horrors would rekindle his political engagement. Soon he too would write odes to the Soviets and Stalin.[*] Neruda would become a member of the Chilean Communist Party, joining many of his friends there. Spain ignited in him a lifetime of ardent activism for peace, justice, and the rights of the proletariat.

His three years there forged a new voice. The war compelled him to make a personal commitment to bring injustices to light. It would be some twenty years until Neruda returned to writing again "of dreams, of the leaves, of the great volcanoes of his native land." Even then, a great deal of that verse had social and political themes. After Spain, Neruda had a new sense of the poet's calling, never before having felt such a vital and immediate duty to use his poetry as a tool for social change. Spain would push Neruda toward becoming the people's poet.

Neruda prepared eagerly for his departure to Spain, where Lorca and other artists and writers awaited him, a generation that many say rivaled Spain's Golden Age. Madrid was becoming known as the new Paris. Yet he was also leaving behind the Paris of South America, Buenos Aires, and a group of friends and an experience that had shaped him as he moved into this new chapter of his life. At the farewell dinner, held at a classy restaurant in the neighborhood of La Boca, twenty of his friends posed for a cheery group photograph. Maruca, now pregnant, doesn't look directly into the camera; her gaze is almost sheepish, looking down and off to the right. It appears she is uncomfortable and does not want to be there.

The Nerudas set sail on May 5, 1934, seven years after Neruda had crossed the Atlantic en route to the Far East. Yet Neruda's move to Spain began with a bad omen: a letter from his old roommate Tomás

---

[*]   Stalin became Neruda's hero when he was the only world leader to support the Spanish Republicans after the Fascist Francisco Franco launched his military coup and initiated the civil war.

Lago with the heartrending news that their beloved friend Alberto Rojas Jiménez had just died. Rojas Jiménez and a friend had been thrown out of a bar for not having enough to pay the tab. They had walked through Santiago to his sister's house, under a cold rain, with a bottle of wine, the impoverished poet without a jacket. He caught bronchial pneumonia and died two days later. When Neruda wrote about his death to Sara Tornú in Buenos Aires, he described Rojas Jiménez as "an angel full of wine."

Neruda cried when he learned the news. He and the painter Isaías Cabezón, a friend from Chile who was in Barcelona at the time, took huge candles down to the fourteenth-century Basílica de Santa María del Mar. The church is known for its splendid stained glass, though its brilliance wasn't apparent in the darkness as they each drank a bottle of white wine, kneeling in the pews. "I didn't know how to pray," Neruda admitted to Sara Tornú, so he felt grateful for Cabezón, a Catholic, who went and "prayed at every one of the countless altars." Neruda didn't even believe in God, but there on his knees, watching their candles dance in the darkness as Cabezón performed the rituals, he felt glad that the setting of this silent ceremony drew him closer to his lost friend.

Neruda then wrote a remarkable elegy, "Alberto Rojas Jiménez Comes Flying": *viene volando* (comes flying) because one of Rojas Jiménez's games was making paper birds, often with a freshly written poem on them. The elegy would be published in the second volume of *Residence*. "It's a funeral, solemn hymn," he wrote to Tornú, "and if you read it in your house, to our friends, have Amado Villar do it, with a heartbroken voice, because that's the only way it can be done right."

> Beyond blood and bones,
> beyond bread, beyond wine,
> beyond fire,
> you come flying.
>
> Beyond vinegar and death,
> among putrefaction and violets,

with your celestial voice and your damp shoes,
you come flying.
. . . .

Oh marine poppy, oh my kinsman,
oh guitar man dressed in bees,
it can't be true how much shadow is in your hair,
you come flying.

The poem continues with this same form lyrically pounding out his pain, strophe after strophe, all twenty-four of them dramatic, ripe, and quite affecting.

★

The fellowship of intellectuals, political activists, and visual, literary, and performance artists within the progressive culture of the Second Spanish Republic would soon mitigate the pain from Rojas Jiménez's untimely death. Neruda became an integral part of that circle. Spain transformed not only his politics and poetry, but his personality as well; there he truly, finally, overcame his struggle with depression. He eventually lost all traces of melancholy; even the outbreak of the war, rather than dispiriting him, energized him to action. No more desperate letters to Albertina or other past lovers; no more desolate surrealism. Never again would he write of the acute mental anguish of his first thirty years.

From the first, Neruda simply loved being in Spain:

Spain was taut and dry, a daily
drum of opaque sound,
plains and eagle's nest, silence
of whipped inclemency.

How, until weeping, until the soul,
I love your hard earth, your poor bread,
your poor people, how until the deep site

of my being there is the lost flower of your wrinkled
villages, motionless in time,
and your mineral countrysides
extended in moon and age
and devoured by an empty god . . .
   —"What Spain Was Like"

Spain's social and political situation, however, was complicated
when Neruda arrived in 1934. In 1898, Spain had lost the vestiges of
its overseas empire after losing the Philippines and Cuba to the United
States. Using the remaining strength of the army to save the throne,
King Alfonso XIII consolidated his domestic power while renewing
military activity in Spain's last colonial battlefield, Spanish Morocco.
But he faced fierce resistance on the home front too.

In 1909, in Morocco's Rif mountains, the Spanish were vastly out-
numbered by the local tribesmen in a series of battles for territory rich
in iron ore. The army decided to call on thousands of Catalan reservists
to serve as reinforcements in Morocco; they started with working-class
Catalans. Five hundred and twenty of them had already completed their
active-duty service six years earlier, never expecting to serve again.
This was not the army's wisest move; there already was widespread,
pent-up anger against the government across Catalonia. Just a decade
earlier, at the same time women-led bread riots were breaking out, a
well-organized tax boycott started by shopkeepers and small-business
men made Barcelona seem so explosive it was put under a "state of
war." In 1901, a workers' general strike paralyzed the city; union ranks
doubled by the end of the next decade.

In July 1909, the government seemed aloof to the city's transforming
political paradigm. As the grudging reservists boarded the ship, officials
had the gall, it seemed, to greet them with patriotic addresses, even the
national anthem, "Marcha Real." Well-dressed ladies bestowed Sacred
Heart religious medals on them. And the ship that would take them to
the Rif was owned by a marquis industrialist well known for profiting
from the increased activity in Africa. On the Barcelona docks that day,
the Spanish state's "narrow social construction was on display for all to

see," notes Spanish Civil War scholar Mary Vincent. A raucous prole-
tariat crowd had assembled to protest the forced departure, cheering as
the well-dressed ladies' medals were tossed into the sea. The Catholic
oligarchy was dangerously impervious to the rise of the secular masses.

Already frustrated, and now just outraged by this latest action,
Barcelona's Socialist, anarchist, and labor leaders announced a gen-
eral strike in solidarity with the reservists. The city was already such
a tinderbox of anger against the government that the strike quickly
grew into an all-out revolt. In what became known as Barcelona's Se-
mana Trágica (Tragic Week), Republicans, communists, and anarchists
joined in taking over the city, with crowds overturning trams and
burning convents. Barcelonese soldiers refused orders to shoot at their
fellow citizens; troops from all over Spain were summoned to crush
the uprising. Over a hundred civilians were reportedly killed, and more
than seventeen hundred were indicted in military courts for "armed
rebellion." Five were executed for "moral irresponsibility."

In 1917, revolutionary labor strikes in Spain followed the overthrow
of the czar in Russia. Again, the army saved the throne. The king man-
aged to cling to power, but corruption and ineptitude grew, as did the
military's influence, weakening the monarchy. In 1929, the worldwide
economic depression made the situation even more tenuous in the al-
ready desperate country, especially for landless rural workers. When the
municipal elections of April 1931 turned decidedly anti-monarchical,
the king realized the army had given up on him. He quickly left the
country, heading for Rome. The Spanish Republic—with a government
of, by, and for the people—was proclaimed in the streets of Madrid.
"¡Viva la República!"

Formerly exiled and imprisoned Republican leaders came together
in Madrid and named a new cabinet, including Socialists as ministers of
justice and labor. A Catalan state and republic were created in Barcelona.
In the following weeks, the cabinet decreed dozens of progressive acts,
such as giving small farmers protection against mortgage foreclosures.
In its first ten months, the Republic built seven thousand schools. The
new government proclaimed full religious liberty. Although the major-
ity of world governments recognized the Republic, the Vatican and the

conservative Catholic administration in Chile did not, although they did retain a diplomatic presence there. In electing a new constitutional assembly, with suffrage extended to all those older than twenty-three, including women, a leftist coalition won a resounding majority of delegates. In honor of the French Revolution, the new assembly convened on Bastille Day, July 14, 1931. A fresh constitution ratified five months later declared Spain a "republic of workers of all categories."

The idealistic, progressive spirit of the new Republic sparked an exuberant golden age within the circle of writers and intellectuals Neruda soon joined.

★

In May 1934, shortly after he arrived in Barcelona, Neruda visited Madrid, the heart of the social and cultural scene to which he was so drawn. Lorca and other poets met him at the train station. He came out of his car, tall, with his jacket pockets stuffed with newspapers, a perfect first impression on his new friends. They immediately went to a tavern, where they talked, read poetry, and drank *vino tinto*.

Carlos Morla Lynch, who met Neruda in person for the first time that day after an extended correspondence, would describe him as follows: "He's pale, a pallor like Cinderella's, with long, narrow eyes, like black crystal almonds, that laugh at every moment, but without happiness, passive. He has very black hair as well, badly combed, gray hands. What captivates me about him is his voice, his slow voice, monotonous, nostalgic, as if it were tired, but suggestive and full of enchantment."

The next day, at a party in Neruda's honor, Lorca danced wrapped in a carpet, and Neruda read from *Residence,* his first public recital in Spain. Among those present were Rafael Alberti and Luis Cernuda, two of the most well-respected and influential members of the Generation of '27 and its social community, of which Neruda would soon become a central part.

Then, in the center of the room, Lorca followed. Lorca had "a truly extraordinary physical personality," as Neruda would one day put it, and he read with power, his eyes delivering the emotional mystery of the lines as his dark and rustic accent took command of the room. By this point Lorca was, according to his peer Pedro Salinas, an "institution" in Madrid. He was "more than a person, he was a climate." Luis Buñuel proclaimed, "Of all the human beings I've known, Federico was the finest. I don't mean his plays or poetry; I mean him personally. He was his own masterpiece . . . He was like a flame." The lines Lorca read that night were these:

> When I die,
> bury me with my guitar
> beneath the sand.
>
> When I die
> among the orange trees
> and spearmint.
>
> When I die
> bury me, if you wish,
> in a weathervane.
>
> When I die!

Neruda encountered, as he described it, "a brilliant fraternity of talents, in full knowledge of my work. And I, who had for so many years been tormented by people not understanding me, by the insults and the malicious indifference—drama of every authentic poet in our countries—I felt very happy."

When Neruda assumed his post in Spain, Chile's consul general, Tulio Maquieira, directed him: "You are a poet. Thus, dedicate yourself to being a poet. You don't have to come to this consulate. Tell me no more than where I can mail you your check each month."

This freedom easily allowed Neruda to transfer to the embassy in Madrid. Neruda and Maruca moved there on June 1, 1934. Lorca met them at the station, this time bearing flowers. Soon after, Lorca introduced Neruda at the Chilean's first public reading in Spain, at the

University of Madrid, perhaps the most admiring introduction Neruda ever received throughout his entire life:

> You are about to hear an authentic poet. One of those whose senses are trained to a world that is not ours and that few people perceive. A poet closer to death than to philosophy, closer to pain than to intellect, closer to blood than to ink . . .
>
> [This is] poetry that is not ashamed to break with tradition, that is not afraid of ridicule, and that can suddenly break out sobbing in the middle of the street . . .
>
> I would advise you to listen closely to this great poet and to let yourself be touched by him in your own way. Poetry, like any other sport, requires a long initiation, but in true poetry there is a perfume, an accent, a luminous trace that all living beings can perceive. And hopefully it will help you to nourish that grain of insanity that we all have within us, which many people kill in order to put on the hateful monocle of bookish pedantry. It would be unwise to live without it.

★

One of the central members of the cultural circle in Madrid was Delia del Carril. She was a brilliant Argentine artist, communist, and political activist, and she came from aristocratic roots, an enticing combination for Neruda. Excited for his friends to know his new amigo, Lorca often talked about "this amazing Chilean poet, Pablo Neruda," whom he met in Buenos Aires, "who's coming to be consul in Madrid in October." Delia had read some of Neruda's poems from *Residence* that had appeared in magazines before his arrival in Spain. Still, the Chilean was a mystery to her, as she was to him.

There was a magnetic feeling between the two when they first sat side by side at the bar Cervecería Correos, one of the group's main gathering places. As Delia described it, Neruda "put his arm around my shoulder, and that's how we stayed." Neither creative, nor intellectual, nor political, Maruca did not participate in Neruda's social world at all. In her last months of pregnancy, she mostly remained at home. Meanwhile, Delia's radiance was alluring, but Neruda fell in love with her primarily for her brilliant mind (which had not been the case with Maruca or Albertina). She would be central to Neruda's life for years. In Spain, they were an ideal fit. Their affair began quickly and they did little to keep it a secret.

Delia was born in 1884, into a rich and high-class family. There was nothing prim about her; she was always a rebel. She would gallop her horse through the gardens at her family's country estate. Their Buenos Aires mansion was famous for hosting some of the most celebrated intellectuals of the time. There were poetry recitals, cultural salons, art exhibitions, new dances, and long conversations about French composers. Delia and her siblings were present at the gatherings, and from there she developed an appetite for culture. She started reading French poetry as a young child.

Eight days before she turned fifteen, Delia's father, a former chief justice of Argentina's Supreme Court, shot himself in the family's garden. He had been despondent over the death of his beloved mother, who had succumbed to breast cancer exactly one year before. Delia had shared a strong bond with her father; she felt he understood her impulsive character, her outbursts, her obsession to understand everything. She never talked about her father again.

In response to the tragedy, Delia's mother took the children to Paris, dividing their lives between Europe and Buenos Aires. Delia took singing and art classes. As a debutante, she went to parties, balls, and operas. As she came of age, her gatherings with friends became increasingly intellectual in nature. Yet while she seemed to be one of the happiest and most vibrant of her circle, those who knew her well saw her searching for self-definition.

In 1921, at the age of thirty-seven, Delia ended a brief marriage to a rich poet, art critic, morphine addict, and adventurer. He had stifled her independence, and then she caught him in an affair with a famous Spanish dancer. Delia went to Argentina, where she had an intense but brief romance with the vanguard poet Oliverio Girondo. In 1929, she returned to Paris and studied painting under Fernand Léger at l'Académie Moderne. The two developed a great friendship, which was rumored to have at least sometimes been amorous. She became friends with Pablo Picasso, Rafael Alberti, and María Teresa León, as well as the French surrealist poets Louis Aragon and Paul Éluard. Here, she was introduced to Marxism and the Communist cause. It was the time of rising fascism in Europe, and in French circles, art alone wasn't enough. A political commitment had to go along with it. This new scene and its passionate ideals of equality and justice completed Delia, filling the void in her by offering the identity she had been searching for. She joined the French Communist Party and the recently formed Association of Revolutionary Writers and Artists.

While in Paris, Rafael Alberti and María Teresa León told Delia about the excitement of the new Republic in their native Spain. They were about to return, and they invited Delia to join them. Delia instantly fell into the circle of young activist intellectuals and writers in Madrid, as Neruda later would.

The youthful goatherd poet Miguel Hernández and the great filmmaker Luis Buñuel were also members of this community. Many were friends with Picasso, even though he had moved to France. The famously eccentric surrealist painter Salvador Dalí was involved too, especially in "an erotic, tragic love" with Lorca. For these young artists and intellectuals, Spain's emerging socialist, progressive culture was exhilarating. Along with Alberti, Delia became one of the political teachers of the group. With her fluency in Spanish, English, and French, Delia was indispensable as a translator for the international communists and other leftists arriving to join the creative ferment of the Republic. Neruda would receive much of his ideological training from her.

Delia was said to be tireless in her work, like an ant. Thus "la Hormiga" (the Ant) became her nickname; years after her passing, her friends still tenderly called her "la Hormiguita."

Delia was fifty when she met Neruda, who was twenty years younger than her. Inés Valenzuela, who would marry Neruda's childhood friend Diego Muñoz, and who became one of Delia's closest friends, said la

Hormiguita always looked and acted much younger than her age (Inés was thirty-six years younger than her). Carlos Morla Lynch described her in his diary as being "crazy, affectionate, and good." She'd often talk to him about communism: "It's coming."

Neruda, often with his beret, and Delia, wearing her red scarves, began to meet along with other members from the group every late afternoon at Cervecería Correos. The laughing and drinking began there. Delia would talk politics; Neruda would talk about any new poetry. If other poets were among them, perhaps some fresh verses were debuted. Later the two would head to the theater, the movies, or perhaps a party, or to the bar Satán, run by a young Cuban, or to the restaurant Granja del Henar. Or they might just walk the streets of Madrid with a bottle of wine or Chinchón anis in hand, eating calamari fried in olive oil from street vendors. As Ernest Hemingway had just written in 1932, "To go to bed at night in Madrid marks you as a little queer. For a long time your friends will be a little uncomfortable about it. Nobody goes to bed in Madrid until they have killed the night. Appointments with a friend are habitually made for after midnight at the cafe."

In Neruda's other life, with the pregnant Maruca, the couple occupied a brick apartment that Alberti had found for them. The building was located in the famous Argüelles neighborhood, brimming with vivid activity. This wasn't just the territory of poets and intellectuals but of the people of Spain. Humanity throbbed through open markets full of salty food. Neruda would linger longingly in the market, strolling around, inspecting the celery, spicy peppers, tomatoes, potatoes, and piles of fish fresh from the Mediterranean and the Atlantic, a staple of the Spanish diet.

Neruda mentions the "piles of fish" in a seminal poem he'd write, "I Explain Some Things," describing the vibrancy of the Spanish Republic, as these heaps of collective abundance and substance were a bold symbol of the "essence" of life at the time.

He would buy produce, meat, fish, cheese, bread, and more and—if he didn't head toward Cervecería Correos or a café to meet Delia and the others—would bring it all back to his new apartment. The building, part of a new block of rental apartments, was named La Casa de las

Flores, because of the geraniums that flowed down five stories of gar-
den terraces. It was a fresh, inspired, striking contrast to the traditional
bourgeois architecture of Madrid, whose houses and buildings tended
to be burdened with ostentatious facades and decorative molding. The
building, which would one day be declared a national monument, took
up a whole square block, with stores and a restaurant on the street
level, and a large enclosed garden and patio, all contributing to the so-
cial functionality of the building. Perhaps best of all, their unit was situ-
ated at the ideal angle and height for the warm glow of summer light
to illuminate everything inside. Lorca liked to compose poems there.

This was the perfect home for Neruda; its modern design, with clean
angles, matched the literary projects that would blossom there. And as
the light filled the Nerudas' fifth-floor apartment, you could look out
and see the vast, soulful, historic plains of the Castilla region, "like an
ocean of leather," as Neruda wrote in "I Explain Some Things."

Neruda tore down an interior wall to turn two rooms into one large
salon, and he filled it with books. He decorated the walls with masks
from Siam, Bali, Sumatra, the Malay Archipelago, and Bandung—
"golden, ashen, the color of tomato, with silver eyebrows, blue, infer-
nal, lost in thought," as he noted in his memoirs. Perhaps they reminded
him of Josie Bliss. Masks followed Neruda in many ways, literally and
literarily, and he treasured them; they would decorate all of his homes.

The bohemian nights with poets and friends often ended at the Ne-
rudas' apartment. The fact that Maruca was enduring the discomforts
of her final months of pregnancy didn't seem to matter. Sometimes the
parties would keep going into the next day, or the next, fueled by Ne-
ruda's powerful punch concoctions and his disregard for time. Guests
would share beds for brief naps, only to wake to find the fiesta still in
full swing.

The gatherings frequently culminated in the "inauguration" of
a public monument, a ritual invented by Lorca and Neruda, whose
friendship had deepened even more. The guests would all find their
way to a monument in Madrid, where the two poets would pose as
official government representatives. Just as they did in the Hotel Plaza
in homage to Rubén Darío, they would spontaneously deliver a poetic

speech dedicated to the subject of the monument, while their friends played the role of an imaginary ceremonial band to add more character to the event.

Just as in Santiago and Buenos Aires, Maruca did not participate. A wall had formed between the couple, and the Spanish language helped enforce the barrier. Maruca could speak it, but not quite fluently. For Neruda's new group of friends, Spanish was the essence of their communication, creation, and interest. Some of them were averse to Maruca. The Chilean diplomat Carlos Morla Lynch referred to her as "the giraffe" in his diaries.

Meanwhile, the shy, isolated Pablo Neruda with mood disorders was relegated to the past. Now, his personality blossomed and flourished in this magical Madrilenian life and fellowship; he was enthusiastic. There was also his increasing intellectual, romantic, and physical intimacy with Delia. Yet the first threat to this idyllic environment was looming on the horizon: fatherhood.

CHAPTER TWELVE

BIRTH AND DESTRUCTION

Oh child among the roses, oh press of doves,
oh presidio of fish and rosebushes,
your soul is a bottle of dried salts
and a bell filled with grapes, your skin.

Unfortunately, I've nothing to give you but fingernails
or eyelashes, or melted pianos,
or dreams that bubble up from my heart,
dusty dreams that gallop like black riders,
dreams charged with dash and disfortune.
    —"Ode with a Lament"[*]

The Nerudas' daughter was born prematurely on August 18, 1934. The baby, named Malva Marina Trinidad (in homage to Neruda's stepmother), had hydrocephaly, an enlarged head due to the accumulation of fluid in the cranium. She could not stand any light and had to be kept in a dark room. She would live for only eight years.

---

[*] "Ode with a Lament," part of *Residence,* seems uncannily as if it were written about Neruda's daughter, Malva Marina. However, it was written in Buenos Aires, before her birth.

Four weeks after her birth, Neruda wrote to his dear Buenos Aires friend Sara Tornú:

> My daughter, or at least that's what I call her, is a perfectly ridiculous creature, a semicolon species, a vamp of three kilos. Everything's okay (now) (but) everything was very bad. The girl was dying, she didn't cry, she didn't sleep. We had to give her probes, with little spoons, with injections, and we spent whole nights, the whole day, the week, without sleeping, calling the doctor, running to the abominable houses of orthopedics, where they sell terrifying baby bottles, scales, medical drinking glasses, funnels full of degrees and regulations. You can imagine how much I've suffered. The girl, the doctors tell me, was dying, and that little thing has suffered horribly, from a hemorrhage that had opened in her cerebrum at birth. But be happy, Rubia, because all goes well, the girl has started to nurse, and the doctors come around less, and she smiles and she puts on grams every day . . .

Not once in this long letter does Neruda refer to Maruca.

Vicente Aleixandre, who would win the 1977 Nobel Prize in Literature, noted Neruda's somewhat manic affection for his daughter when he came to see the child at La Casa de las Flores:

> Pablo was leaning over what seemed to be a cradle. I saw it from afar while I heard his voice. *Malva Marina, do you hear me? Come, Vicente, come. Look how marvelous. My daughter. The most beautiful in the world.* The words kept sprouting out as I came closer. He called me with his hand and looked with happiness toward the bottom of that cradle. He was full of happy smiles, with a blind sweetness in his thick voice . . . I arrived. He stood up, radiating these things, while I spied. *Look, look!* I came close to it all and then I saw what until then had been hidden within the lace. An enormous head, an implacable head . . .

Pablo, full of light and dreams, "radiated unreality." His fantasy was as firm as a stone, according to Aleixandre, marveling at the joy Neruda derived from his pride in appreciating his daughter.

While Neruda fluctuated in his gestures of both sorrow and denial, he wrote only a few disturbed poems that dealt with his daughter. One, "Maternity," was written before she was born, in Buenos Aires. In another, "Illness in My Home," he seems to complain more of the suffering he has to endure because of her than of her suffering itself. Another poem, the sublime "Ode with a Lament," appears to be a reaction to Malva's condition and his helpless inability to remedy it. However, it was also written before her birth, in Buenos Aires. "Melancholy in the Families" was written in early 1935, several months after her birth. It combines the blood of the Spanish Civil War outside the walls of their apartment with the eerie somberness within them. Again, it is narcissistically centered around his own emotions, ignoring those of his family, fixating on how:

> above all there is a terrible,
> terrible abandoned dining room
> with the cruets broken
> and the vinegar spilling beneath the chairs,
> a frozen ray of moonlight,
> something dark, and I seek
> a comparison within myself:
> perhaps it is a shop surrounded by the sea
> and torn rags dripping brine.
> It is only an abandoned dining room,
> and around it are additions,
> submerged factories, timbers
> that only I know,
> because I am sad and I travel,
> and I know the earth, and I am sad.

The one time in all his writings that he mentions her name is in a celebratory poem, in his "Ode to Federico García Lorca," written before his death. She is listed along with Maruca, Delia, Rafael Alberti, María Luisa Bombal, and fifteen others in a section envisioning the whole group coming to visit Lorca's house (even then, his wife and daughter are secondary, as he first states that "here I come with Oliverio, Norah, / Vicente Aleixandre, Delia"; it's not until the third line of names that he lists them: "Maruca, Malva Marina, María Luisa, and Larco.") Lorca had written his own mournful poem on being unable to help, "Lines on the Birth of Malva Marina Neruda." In Granada when he wrote them, he sent them to Neruda in fraternal consolation, frustrated at the hopelessness of the situation:

> Malva Marina, if only I could see you,
> dolphin of love over ancient waves,
> when the waltz of your America distills
> poison and blood of a mortal dove!
>
> To just break the dark feet
> of the night that howls through the rocks
> and stop the immense melancholy wind
> that carries away the dahlias, leaving shadows behind!

After her birth, Neruda's mentions of his daughter ebb out of his correspondence. He does not mention her once in his memoirs, as if she never existed.

Shortly after the birth and initial shock, Neruda's spirits and activity seemed to be as vibrant as ever, as if he were oblivious to the seriousness of his newborn daughter's condition. He was reluctant to be bound to Malva and the distressed Maruca by anything more than duty. His life entwined evermore with Delia's as war loomed over Europe.

*

By the beginning of 1935, Pablo and Delia were inseparable. "I adore Delia and cannot live without her," Neruda wrote in a letter. That January, Neruda wrote to Héctor Eandi again. This time he mentioned

Malva Marina, who was "growing and getting fatter," but not Maruca, while Delia was "profoundly good." He talked about his new amigos: "Like always, I'm surrounded by friends, Alberti . . . Lorca, [José] Bergamín, poets, painters, etc. No difficulty with them, they are of my blood. I, who have lived an adolescence filled with vital asperity, am convinced of the good in people, of the brotherhood of man."

Yet there was no fraternity between Neruda and two of the other most important poets from his own country, both significantly older, Pablo de Rokha and Vicente Huidobro. Tensions had been mounting among all three, de Rokha most notably taking some strong swipes at Neruda in the press. But a 1934 accusation by a disciple of Huidobro that Neruda had plagiarized one of his love poems brought about a conflagration, and a vehement and at times nasty "literary war" broke out on all sides.

At the time, Volodia Teitelboim was an eighteen-year-old member of the Chilean Communist Party and a burgeoning writer, deeply impressed by the forty-one-year-old Vicente Huidobro, the "older brother" of Chile's intelligentsia. One day at the National Library, Teitelboim was reading *The Gardener,* by the Bengalese Rabindranath Tagore. It was published in 1913, the same year Tagore was awarded the Nobel Prize for his "consummate skill" and his "profoundly sensitive, fresh and beautiful verse." When Teitelboim read *The Gardener*'s thirteenth poem, he thought immediately of Neruda's Poem XVI. From Tagore:

> You are the evening cloud floating in the sky of my dreams.
> I paint you and fashion you ever with my love longings.
> You are my own, my own, Dweller in my endless dreams!

From Neruda:

> In my sky at twilight you are like a cloud
> and your color and form are as I love them.
> You are mine, you are mine, woman with sweet lips,
> and my infinite dreams live in your life.

The rest of the poem continues to be very similar to that of Tagore, who was one of Neruda and his friends' favorite poets in their student days. After comparing the two texts, Teitelboim consulted a poet friend, and then on the front page of the cultural magazine *Pro*'s November 1934 issue, under the title "El affaire Neruda-Tagore," he printed the two poems beside each other. There was no need to accuse Neruda of plagiarism in so many words: arranged this way, it was clear how similar they were.

Pro was a project of Huidobro's; he had founded or helped lead a handful of vanguard magazines. Since no individual byline was attached to that first page, people directly attributed the charge to Huidobro, even though it was all Teitelboim. Huidobro, in Spain at the time, claimed he wasn't even aware of it.

Neruda, who had praised Huidobro's poetry in the past, especially in *Claridad,* barely reacted at all. Earlier in Neruda's life, his insecurity would have caused him to lash out in response, but now, by showing restraint, he trivialized the accusation and made his accusers appear petty.

But then Pablo de Rokha joined in the fray. He was already known for acrimonious actions against other poets—at the time the plagiarism affair came to the forefront, de Rokha was going after Huidobro, incensed that his wife had been left out of an important new anthology of Chilean poetry published under Huidobro's direction (with Teitelboim as a principal editor). De Rokha had shown animosity toward Neruda for some time, likely rooted in jealousy of the younger poet, who had surged ahead of him in public recognition. There were his negative critiques of Neruda, including the aforementioned rebuke of *Residence,* "Epitaph to Neruda." A year before that, in 1932, he wrote a nasty but eloquent newspaper column entitled "Pablo Neruda: Poeta a la moda," in which he called out Neruda for being an "opportunist" who "administers his fame prudently and patiently." Of all his works, he attacked Neruda's most popular one at length, the "trendy" *Twenty Love Poems,* as being nothing more than the "typical bible of versified mediocrity."

A month after Teitelboim published the two poems side by side, de Rokha attacked Neruda in a short article published in *La Opinión,* where he was a columnist:

> To be a plagiarist, you must be possessed of an out-of-control opportunism, a filthy and enormously objective vanity, like that of an actor or a failed buffoon, a great capacity for fraud and lying, a simultaneously miserable and egomaniacal and despicable perception . . . It has been shown and published that Pablo Neruda has plagiarized Tagore, the Indian poet.

At this point, in reaction to the public accusation, Neruda said that yes, he had borrowed from Tagore, but he insisted that it wasn't plagiarism but rather a "paraphrase" of Tagore's poem. Supposedly, several of Neruda's friends claimed that before the first edition of *Twenty Love Poems* came out, they had suggested that a note should be put in the book, explaining, or rather "putting on record," the fact that Poem XVI was a paraphrase of Tagore's *The Gardener.*

Tomás Lago and Diego Muñoz called Huidobro out for what they saw as a trifling and even treacherous act against a fellow progressive Chilean. Now Huidobro found himself forced into the controversy. The January 1935 issue of the magazine *Vital,* which he also ran and which had a much broader and more significant readership than *Pro,* appropriated the front page Teitelboim had printed in the November 1934 issue of *Pro,* noting up top that the following poems had been published without any comments. It then featured the two poems side by side once again, with "El affaire Neruda-Tagore" in large type above it.

While *Pro* contained no commentary, in the *Vital* issue Huidobro included two raw letters he wrote attacking Lago and Muñoz. In one, he stated that he knew Lago had

> lied and spouted your usual bullshit about me . . . They've already told me that you are a gossip and a busybody like an old whore. Shameless jerk. Your lies can't affect my life, the facts of which, known all over the world, speak too eloquently to be called into question. I consider you to be the

perfect idiot, an absolute cretin, and there is no greater cow-
ard than you.

In a separate piece, Huidobro also wrote an extraordinary self-
defense on the matter:

> The publication of this plagiarism has produced a curious
> phenomenon in the little circles of the friends and accom-
> plices: great indignation: (uterine) fury. Against whom?
> Against Neruda for having plagiarized? Against Tagore for
> having written a rather foolish poem ten years ago with the
> same ideas that it's going to have ten years after Pablo Ne-
> ruda? No. The indignation goes against the person who dis-
> covered the plagiarism. And that's incredible. And because
> he was right, the gang becomes infuriated with Huidobro,
> who had no art or part in the issue.

Attacks continued, especially by de Rokha, to the point that Lorca,
Alberti, Hernández, Aleixandre, Cernuda, and eleven other Spanish
poets published three recent Neruda poems in an edition entitled *Hom-
age to Pablo Neruda* in defense of their friend. Part of the prologue read:

> Chile has sent to Spain the great poet Pablo Neruda,
> whose evident creative force, in full possession of his po-
> etic destiny, is producing extremely personal work, to
> honor the Spanish language . . . We, poets and admirers of
> the young and distinguished American writer, when pub-
> lishing these unpublished poems—latest testimony of his
> magnificent creation—we do nothing more than highlight
> his extraordinary personality and his unquestionable liter-
> ary stature.

Neruda lunched at Carlos Morla Lynch's house shortly afterward.
The elder diplomat noted Neruda was delighted with the pamphlet his
friends had sent in opposition to Huidobro, his enemy. "All men are

small, when the moment demands that they be great," noted Morla Lynch.

Those opposing Neruda dismissed *Homage* as partisan praise. Eventually, the "literary war" reached such a point that in April 1935 Neruda finally entered the fray. He responded to his adversaries with a scathing poetic retort that he didn't publish, but instead let make its way hand by hand through Spain and all the way back to Chile. Everyone knew it was by him, even though he didn't sign it. The poem is defiantly entitled "I Am Here."[*]

> Bastards!
> Sons of whores!
> Neither today nor tomorrow
> never
> will you be finished with me!
> I've got my testicles full of petals,
> I've got my hair full of birds,
> I've got poetry and steam,
> cemeteries and houses,
> people who gasp,
> fires,
> in my "Twenty Poems,"
> in my weeks, in my adventures,
> and I shit on the whore who gave birth to you,
> de Rokhas, gallows,
> snaky Huidobros . . .

In the fifth edition of *Twenty Love Poems*, released in 1937, Neruda states at the beginning of the book that Poem XVI was, "for the most part, a paraphrase of Tagore's *The Gardener*." He then writes, "This has always been known publicly," adding, "Those resentful individuals who tried to take advantage of this circumstance in my absence have

---

[*]   In 1938, friends of Neruda's printed the poem on sixteen unbound pages, accompanied by illustrations by Ramón Gaya.

been punished with the obscurity they deserve and the enduring vitality of this adolescent book."

A more renowned literary rival then joined the voices criticizing Neruda. The Spanish poet Juan Ramón Jiménez, who would win the 1956 Nobel Prize in Literature, represented poetry's old guard. While Jiménez's poetry was refined, Neruda aimed to transcend formal purity. Yet it was more than just different approaches to poetic style that separated the two. Jiménez called Neruda "a great bad poet."[*] This slight seemed to come more from the fact that he was experiencing a changing of the guard in Spanish poetry. He was being left behind, while Lorca's generation—which included Neruda—was taking center stage.

After Jiménez's "great bad poet" remark, Neruda and his friends started to prank call Jiménez's house, hanging up the phone as soon as he answered. But more significantly, Neruda composed a more mature rebuttal to Jiménez's insult with his pen. The poet and printer Manuel Altolaguirre had just asked Neruda to start and edit a beautifully designed poetry review, featuring the contemporary poets, to be "the finest presentation of the best work in Spain." Neruda named the magazine *Caballo verde para la poesía* (Green Horse for Poetry). As small as they may have been, these journals helped set the cultural climate of a period of time. For the first issue, Neruda wrote a manifesto, "On Impure Poetry," proclaiming the urgent need for a new style, a direct contrast to Jiménez's beautiful but refined, "pure," distanced verse. It begins:

> It is very appropriate, at certain times of the day or night, to deeply observe objects at rest: the wheels that have covered long, dusty distances, bearing heavy loads of vegetables or minerals, sacks from the coal yards, barrels, baskets, the handles and grips of the carpenter's tool. The contact of

---

[*] As a coincidental historical note, it was Jiménez's wife, Zenobia Camprubí de Jiménez, who had translated Tagore's *The Gardener* from Hindi to Spanish, which Teitelboim read and then reprinted in *Pro* and *Vital*. Neruda would have certainly been aware of this, as she was credited below her translation in those issues.

man with the universe exudes from these things a lesson for the tormented poet. The worn surfaces, the wear that hands have inflicted on things, the often tragic and always wistful aura of these objects, lend to reality a fascination not to be taken lightly.

The confused impurity of human beings is displayed in them, the proliferation, materials used and discarded, footprints and fingerprints, the permanent mark of humanity inundating all objects from within and without. That is the kind of poetry we should strive for, worn away as if by acid from the labor of hands, impregnated with sweat and smoke, smelling of urine and lilies, and seasoned by the various professions that operate both within and outside the law.

A poetry impure as old clothes, as a body, with its food stains and shame, with wrinkles, observations, dreams, vigilance, prophecies, declarations of love and hate, beasts, blows, idylls, manifestos, denials, doubts, affirmations, taxes.

This declaration essentially rebuts Jiménez's strong advocacy for a "naked" poetry based on the nuances of language and intellect. In contrast, Neruda sought to rehumanize the poem from that form. Times were changing. Neruda's manifesto quickly influenced many of his Spanish friends and beyond, especially because of the need for turbulent poetry as an expression of the increasingly turbulent circumstances in Spain. The country was experiencing the pains of great political upheaval, bitterly polarizing and well on the road to the civil war. That war would break out just eight months after the essay was published.

The manifesto did not abandon the lyrical material that formed the first parts of *Residence*. But it did announce his new aesthetic, which was taking shape, influenced by the circumstances of his life in Spain and by the writing of his Spanish friends. He expanded the scope of his poetry to incorporate everything, from political declarations to dreams and prophecies.

Neruda described the elements of a new style of poetry grounded in human experience, an insurgent response to injustice and violence.

Neruda was surrounded by leftists doing everything they could to defend the Second Republic against its conservative, right-wing, and fascist enemies. It was against this backdrop that Neruda's "On Impure Poetry" argued for a dirty poetry, grimy from the hands of the worker, smelling of both "urine and lilies." Neruda now stressed writing about the real over the ideal, the everyday instead of the extraordinary. It was a complete departure from his poems of the Far East; there was no turning back now for Neruda.

His early 1935 poem "Statute of Wine" shows the sheer departure from any purities of the past:

> I speak of things that exist. God deliver me
> From inventing things when I'm singing!

★

While writing in Spain, inspired by Lorca and others, Neruda became deeply absorbed in reading the work of earlier master poets. He published translations of poems by William Blake and parts of Walt Whitman's epic "Song of Myself." He had started to read Whitman when he was fifteen, and at nineteen he proposed and wrote a review in *Claridad* of a new translation of the "beautiful words of the boy from Camden." Lorca had begun to idolize Whitman while living in New York six years earlier, after learning from a friend of Whitman's love for his "comrades" and of his attempt to articulate that love in *Leaves of Grass*. Lorca's exalting "Ode to Walt Whitman" is the longest (and most explicit) poem in the book that came from that trip, *Poeta en Nueva York (Poet in New York)*. But it wasn't just Whitman's homosexuality; it was his radical use of free verse, with language that surprises, and "Song of Myself" is a poem of democracy, a poem that dramatizes how one's imagination fuels creative power. All of this resonated with Neruda's mood while in Spain, as he too began to see Whitman in a heroic light.

"Song of Myself" was first published in 1855. But the outbreak of the U.S. Civil War six years later had a transformational effect on Whitman and his poetry. The tragedies surrounding him called for a more politically driven voice; his idealistic romanticism was replaced by realism, with which he directly documented what he saw through the poetry of witness, no longer of imagination. Four years after Neruda translated "Song of Myself," the outbreak of the Spanish Civil War affected Neruda in much the same way.

Neruda would have a lifelong relationship with Whitman. He was a major influence on much of Neruda's poetry written after the outbreak of the Spanish Civil War, particularly *Canto General*. In *The Western Canon*, Harold Bloom claims that Neruda "can be regarded as Whitman's truest heir. The poet of *Canto General* is a worthier rival than any other descendant of *Leaves of Grass*."[*] A few years after *Canto* came out, Neruda told a Continental Cultural Congress in Santiago how much Whitman had meant to him recently, and reprised the bard's statement from 1871: "I should demand a programme of culture, drawn out, not for a single class alone or for the parlors or lecture rooms, but with an eye to practical life, the west, the workingmen, the facts of farms and jackplanes and engineers."

> It's for an action of love to my country
> that I reclaim you, necessary brother,
> old Walt Whitman of the gray hand.
>
> so that with your extraordinary help
> verse by verse we kill Nixon, sanguinary
> president, at the root.[†]

---

[*]   Borges is the only other Latin American included among Bloom's twenty-six authors, representing Europe and all of the Americas, starting with Dante.

[†]   The original rhyme scheme is lost in translation:

> *Es por acción de amor a mi **país**
> que te reclamo, hermano **necesario**,
> viejo Walt Whitman de la mano **gris**.*
>
> *para que con tu apoyo **extraordinario**
> verso a verso matemos **de raíz**
> a Nixon, presidente **sanguinario**.*

★

Finally, in September 1935, *Residence on Earth* was published in Spain, by Cruz & Raya, who not only published the first volume, but a second containing twenty-three poems written since 1931.[*] Neruda's new poetry was enormously successful with readers. Most important, the book garnered critical acclaim outside Neruda's traditional circles. Two months after the book's publication, the Paris magazine *Le Mois* proclaimed:

> You can be sure that there is no country in Europe where poetry is as prosperous as it is in Spain and Latin America. The young stars of Spanish poetry that have gathered around the master Juan Ramón Jiménez are truly first-rate talent.
>
> However, the most important publication of the year is undeniably the combination of two volumes by the Chilean Pablo Neruda, "Residence on Earth," an admirable book, the work of a great and true poet, a poet with a powerful, courageous spirit, with a profound and broad vision.

Neruda's old mentor Gabriela Mistral was also in Madrid, serving as consul. She wrote a rave review of the book that appeared in Chile's *El Mercurio* on April 23, 1936, calling Neruda the poet who "discovers and delivers to us the most unsuspected forms of ruin, agony, death and corruption." Neruda "comes following various ripples of poetic trial runs, like a giant tidal wave that propels the very innards of the ocean onto the coast, where those before him had used nothing but weak, small strokes." Shortly after the review, Mistral—whom Morla Lynch had described as "magnificent and extraordinary"—fell from grace in Chile when a Santiago journalist published some of her private letters, which outraged Spaniards, Chileans in Spain, and the diplomatic com-

---

[*]   The poems in the 1933 Chilean edition were written between 1925 and 1931. As Neruda had hoped from the start, the book published in Spain was seen as the real first edition, the one hundred books each signed by him in Santiago just a special limited edition.

munity. In one of them, she wrote to her Chilean friends the poet María Monvel and the critic Armando Donoso:

> I still don't know whether I should tell you about the Spain I know, or let you keep your version of it. The two are so different! . . . For the past two years, I have been living in the midst of an indecipherable people, full of oppositions, absurd fraud . . . It is hungry and too inert to bring about justice; it's as illiterate as its Arab neighbors (such a sad lot). It's fractured; today it's a republic but tomorrow it may be a Philippist monarchy. All the other people look down upon it with condescension and even hate: the French, the English, the Italians, the [Latin] Americans that they call "Spanish Americans."

The Chilean Ministry of Foreign Affairs quickly sent Mistral to Portugal and promoted Neruda from cultural attaché to consul in Madrid. It was a matter of time before he too would be in trouble with the ministry, when his new political activities grew loud and controversial.

★

Even before the Spanish Civil War broke out, with Hitler and Mussolini gaining power, the rising global fascist threat was alarming progressives around the world. At the same time, the burgeoning Popular Front, the new alliance among Communists, Socialists, and others on the Left, was trying to accelerate its progress toward electoral victories, particularly in France. Toward this end, and as part of a campaign to safeguard culture "from the menace of fascism and war," the First International Congress of Writers for the Defense of Culture was held in Paris in June 1935. It was a star-studded event, with 230 delegates from thirty-eight countries. Neruda attended to represent Chile.

The diverse audience consisted of students, youth, and members of the working class. Speakers included Aldous Huxley, Anna Seghers, Louis Aragon, E. M. Forster, and Bertolt Brecht. So many people converged on the three-thousand-seat Maison de la Mutualité that for many of the sessions, loudspeakers had to be set up outside for everyone who could not get in.

Neruda was not a declared communist yet and was cautious of being partisan, as he was still an official diplomat of the conservative Chilean government. However, he was making a statement just by attending the conference as an official delegate. He made another statement at the end of the conference when he signed his name to a declaration condemning Latin American governments who were repressing intellectuals and writers.

★

On this trip, Neruda was finally part of the scene on the Left Bank. Discussions that started at the International Congress continued into the night at sidewalk cafés. He had told his travel companions to be prudent with plans and costs, trying to stretch out their stay with limited funds. This was not just for political and literary reasons; Neruda's heart was presumably pounding with pure lust. There is a long poem in the third volume of *Residence*, "The Furies and the Sorrows," a poem of romantic and erotic love, longing, and, in the end, sadness. Mystified by who the subject might be, in the 1960s scholar Hernán Loyola asked Neruda directly who the feminine figure in the poem was "in the extratextural reality." He answered, somewhat elliptically: "Carpentier's woman."

Through diligent, resourceful research, Loyola deduced that Neruda was referring to the young Parisian Eva Fréjaville. She was supposedly the illegitimate daughter of Diego Rivera and a Frenchwoman. In December 1934, she was with the influential Cuban writer Alejo Carpentier when he came to Madrid. It seems that sparks ignited between her and Neruda, despite his growing devotion to Delia and his respect for Carpentier.

Neruda knew Eva would be in Paris during the conference; perhaps it was at his insistence that Delia stayed in Madrid. While Delia was twenty years older than Neruda, Eva was quite a bit younger, just twenty-two or twenty-three. Delia was beautiful but not erotic. That was not the case with Eva. While she remained devoted to Carpentier, she loved to flirt, to test her power of seduction, not just with Neruda but with others, without committing to any of them. Neruda felt dejected, cheated of the chance to betray the lover with whom he was betraying his wife. His Parisian trip was not an uplifting experience.

★

Even with civil unrest in the air, Maruca and Malva Marina aside, Neruda's life in Madrid was idyllic. Delia was spending so much time at Neruda's apartment (while maintaining her own) that Carlos Morla Lynch once wrote that she "lives with him, his wife, and the sick baby. A drama that won't end well."

Lorca swept in and out of the city with his contagious euphoria, busy directing his theater group, La Barraca. It was made up of university students who traveled to poor villages throughout Spain to perform Cervantes and other classics. Morla Lynch remembered how one evening Lorca burst into a get-together at his house "like a strong gale," announcing his aim to bring Spanish theater "within reach of the people," his ideas on how to do it "erupting in his constantly effervescent spirit." Lorca, so vibrant at this time, was driven by the energy of the Republic and his commitment to addressing social problems through theater.* La Barraca typified the enthusiasm of the young Republic; the government made it a priority to help fund Lorca's initiative, promoting its own progressive ideals while providing important validation for the participating artists and students.

Neruda, Lorca, and other members of the gang celebrated Christmas 1935 at Delia's apartment. They decided to feast on a turkey, charging Isaías Cabezón, the Chilean painter, with buying it. He got a live one. Someone suggested they should give the bird a glass of vintage wine so the meat would be juicier. Cabezón took this seriously, or at

---

*   As Lorca explained at a "Talk on Poetry" that year, "The theater is a school of laughter and lamentation, an open tribunal where the people can introduce old and mistaken mores as evidence, and can use living examples to explain eternal norms of the heart." Lorca's devotion to this art as a social tool would inspire Neruda's new social poetry.

least acted like he did, for when he finally arrived at Delia's at ten that night, he confessed he had gone from one bar to another, serving it wine, beer, and vermouth—serving himself as well. The turkey was so big it wouldn't fit into a normal oven, so they took it to a bakery to roast. They didn't eat it until two in the morning.

A week later they spent New Year's partying in the streets. With their jacket collars up high to protect them from the bitter cold that had set in on the city, they went to the Puerta del Sol, the iconic, gracious plaza, where they ate their traditional twelve grapes, one for each month, among thousands of other jubilant Madrileños. There is no record of Maruca being present on either of these nights.

The coming year would not be as festive. Miners were killed in Asturias, a province in northwest Spain. While Alberti and María Teresa León were on a trip to Moscow, Fascists tried to destroy their house. In January 1936, the Second Spanish Republic experienced yet another governmental crisis. The previous fall, two major financial scandals, combined with internal factionalism, had discredited the administration. In the power struggle that followed, parliament was dissolved and national elections were called for February.

The left-wing parties set aside their differences and ran as the Popular Front. Right-wing propaganda labeled the Front a creation of the Soviet-headed Communist International, or Comintern, in an attempt to stir fear of an imminent Moscow-sponsored Spanish revolution. The head of Spain's Monarchist party, José Calvo Sotelo, called for military force to combat the "red hordes of communism" and warned the nation that if Spaniards did not vote for the conservative National Front, a "Red Flag" would fly over Spain.

On February 16, 1936, the Popular Front won both the popular vote and a plurality in parliament. It was a fragile victory, though; if the right-wing National Front had merged with the center, it would have obtained a slight numerical majority. Neruda and his friends celebrated the victory in a magnificent fiesta at his apartment in La Casa de las Flores.

The day following the elections, rumors of a possible military coup swept through Madrid as Francisco Franco and other generals conspired to overthrow the new government. Franco was detested by the Left for leading a brutal suppression of the miners' uprising in 1934. He often publicly praised Mussolini.

On February 19, Manuel Azaña assumed power as Spain's new prime minister. Two days later, Franco was removed from his post as chief of the general staff and ordered to Las Palmas, as commandant general of the Canary Islands. This "banishment" fueled Franco's hostility toward the new government and his ambitions to overthrow it.

In the early months of 1936, the tension between the Left and the Right in Spain intensified, both in the government and on the streets. In March, members of the Fascist group Falange started to ride ostentatiously through Madrid in squads of motorcars, wielding machine guns, sporadically firing at alleged reds in working-class neighborhoods.* After the Falange attempted the assassination of a Socialist member of parliament, Prime Minister Azaña outlawed the party and jailed much of its leadership. This created further polarization, and the violence continued. By June, many members of the Communist, Socialist, and anarchist parties were publicly promoting a revolution against the failing Republican government, while the right-wing press was instilling in the middle class a fear of a Communist state and promoting the idea that only a military coup could save Spain. The government's inability to act decisively kept the surging tempers on the Right aflame as the country fell into a state of undeclared civil war.

At the end of June, such was the state of chaos in Madrid that Neruda convinced Maruca that she and the baby would be safer in Barcelona,

---

* The Falange (the Spanish word for "phalanx," the Greek mass military formation) was a Fascist organization founded in 1934 by José Antonio Primo de Rivera, the son of General Miguel Primo de Rivera, who had run the country under King Alfonso XIII until the fall of the monarchy and the birth of the Second Republic. The Falange believed in heavy government intervention in the economy and society, but it did not believe in Bolshevism or socialism. It was Nationalist and Republican, but it did not believe in democracy. Its political objectives were very similar to those of the Italian Fascists. Franco would gather the Falange into his own brand of fascism, successfully uniting the group with the Monarchists under his Nationalist banner.

where the local Chilean consul would take care of them. With his wife and child out of the picture, Neruda and Delia lived together openly, though their time in Madrid was also running out.

On July 11, Lorca and other friends, including Fulgencio Díez Pastor, a Socialist member of parliament, dined at La Casa de las Flores. The events of that day included a group of Falangists temporarily seizing Radio Valencia and broadcasting that the Fascist revolution was on its way. Tough rumors were swirling through Madrid; everyone was on edge. At the dinner Lorca could see the extreme worry that Díez Pastor was exhibiting—and he was a member of parliament; he knew more than everyone else! Lorca was petrified and couldn't stop asking Díez Pastor question after question: *What's going to happen? What should I do? Will there be a coup?* Lorca suddenly yelled, "I'm going to Granada!" "Don't," Díez Pastor told him. "You'll be safer in Madrid." Other friends would give him similar advice over the coming days.

The next day, July 12, was Neruda's thirty-second birthday. Even that didn't bring a reprieve: Falangists assassinated the police lieutenant José Castillo, one of the leaders of the Republican Left. The next day, one of the leaders of the conservative Monarchists, José Calvo Sotelo, was kidnapped, shot twice in the back of the neck, and dumped in a cemetery on the outskirts of Madrid. That night, at dinner with friends, Delia insisted that the Fascists themselves shot Calvo Sotelo to put blame on the Republicans. In fact, Republican colleagues of Lieutenant Castillo had committed the murder, proving to many that the Republican government could no longer control its own forces. At Calvo Sotelo's funeral, his mourners raised their arms in a Fascist salute. At Lieutenant Castillo's funeral, Republican, Communist, and Socialist sympathizers raised their clenched fists into the air.

Lorca's premonition of his own death, which he had first felt when leaving Argentina, was recurring. A homosexual leftist poet who had become increasingly outspoken in his defense of the Republic, Lorca knew he would be a target of the Fascist Right. The intensity of the violence gripping Madrid was fraying his nerves. He was so frightened by it all that he rarely went out at night unless he was with friends, like Neruda or Carlos Morla Lynch. On the day of Calvo Sotelo's murder, he ran into the poet Juan Gil-Albert in a café, who later described him as being distraught, frantically asking, just as he had the other night at dinner with Díez Pastor: "What's going to happen? What's going to happen?" That evening, drinking brandy with a friend, taking drag after drag off his cigarette, Lorca warned that "these fields are going to be strewn with corpses." He left Madrid without saying good-bye and fled to his hometown of Granada, where he hoped his influential conservative family would protect him.

On July 17, General Francisco Franco led a military uprising in Spanish Morocco. He began by executing two hundred senior officers of the Spanish Foreign Legion in Africa who remained loyal to the Republican government. Meanwhile, four other generals and leading officers in Spain moved in unison to overthrow the Republican government. The Spanish Civil War had begun. Franco and his fellow insurgents took control of most of the armed forces. Mussolini and Hitler supplied him with planes and weapons. Seville fell to Franco's Nationalists the day after the uprising. The insurgents advanced quickly toward Córdoba, Granada, and Madrid. The Communist leader Dolores Ibárruri went on the radio to urge citizens to resist the rebellion. Women, she said, must prepare to fight the insurgents with knives and boiling oil. Her closing words became the Left's rallying cry: "*¡No pasarán!*" "They will not pass!"

The day after the insurgents took Seville, a rebel general led five thousand soldiers to take Barcelona. They were defeated by a coalition of forces loyal to the Republic, led by the workers' union. Franco's plans for a quick coup would not be realized; the fighting would be protracted over three years.

At the start of the war, the Marquis de Heredia Spínola and his family left Madrid to join Franco at his base in Burgos. When they abandoned their mansion, the Alliance of Anti-Fascist Intellectuals for the Defense of Culture occupied it and made it its base of operations. The alliance was a group founded by Neruda's friends who were determined to wield their intellect and creativity in support of the Republic. They used writing and theater to raise morale at home and awareness and sympathy abroad. (The group came together after members returned inspired from the International Association of Writers for the

Defense of Culture's 1935 congress in Paris. The alliance was, in effect, the Spanish chapter of the international association.)

The eccentric "Zabálburu Palace," as the marquis' mansion was known, was built from a family fortune that originated in the slave trade with New Spain. Centrally located in Madrid, it served as an ideal home for the alliance. During the war, it opened its doors to serve as an open hotel for members of the International Brigades of writers, artists, and activists who came to help the Republican cause. More than three thousand men and women came from the United States to fight, forming the Abraham Lincoln Brigade. Many of these international idealists became directly involved with the alliance's work.

The palace became even more of a center for hospitality and social activity during the Second International Congress of Writers for the Defense of Culture, which took place in 1937. Ernest Hemingway, Langston Hughes, and the photographer Robert Capa stayed there, as well as Nicolás Guillén, who was on his way to being considered the national poet of Cuba; Octavio Paz, who became the most significant Mexican poet of the century (he was named a Nobel laureate in 1990); and Louis Aragon, one of the most important French poets of the century, along with his wife, Elsa Triolet, also a prolific writer.

When Langston Hughes arrived in Madrid, with Franco battering the city almost daily, he wondered why the alliance offered him his choice of "the large and beautifully furnished front rooms on the top floor." Living quarters were very scarce, yet this room was ample and open. He soon learned its availability was due to its vulnerability to Fascist attacks.

> At night I could see the flash of enemy fire when shells poured into the city. But once I'd moved in, I stayed. Another American and I were the only tenants on the top floor. The Spanish writers, thinking that all Americans were like Ernest Hemingway, anyhow, believed we loved to live facing guns.

According to Hughes, "Guillén, much wiser, took a servant's room belowstairs." He remembered the palace as a "richly furnished house of some fifty rooms." The living room walls were covered in Goyas and El Grecos. There were real Louis XV chairs. The alliance members worked and slept surrounded by luxury. There was an entire room, as Hughes described, full of armor and suits of mail, such as those Don Quixote wore. There were trunks filled with ruffled Sevillian skirts, and others with spangled bullfighter suits. Superfluous clothing was donated to the Red Cross, though a few aristocratic get-ups were kept to wear for comic relief. The alliance members dressed in plume hats, capes, and long dresses for dinner. Hughes remembers how on some "chilly nights when we had nothing better to do, the men would all dress up in matador jackets and the women in dresses from Seville of old and have, to my jazz records, an impromptu costume ball."

In August, the Alliance of Anti-Fascist Intellectuals published its first issue of what started out as a series of leaflets and later developed into a little magazine. It was written primarily for Republican soldiers; many read it while on the front lines. Its title was *Mono azul* (Blue Overalls), the worker's uniform that was now the ad hoc uniform of soldiers on the front.* One member of a unit would often read it out loud for those who couldn't read. The list of contributors was extraordinary. It included almost all the great Spanish writers who weren't pro-Franco, including Antonio Machado, Luis Cernuda, Vicente Aleixandre, María Teresa León, and Rafael Alberti, the last two the main forces behind the publication. Vicente Huidobro contributed, as did André Malraux, the French novelist and art theorist who joined the Spanish Republican Air Force during the civil war. John Dos Passos, the great American author of *Manhattan Transfer* and the hallmark U.S.A. trilogy, also contributed, though later he would turn away from the Republican cause as his sympathies moved to the right.

At the beginning of August, the prime minister of the Spanish Republic, José Giral, asked for help from the Socialist prime minister of France, the poet Léon Blum. Blum at first had offered aid, but he was desperately trying to hold his own Popular Front alliance together.

---

* *Monos azules* were inexpensive, common, useful, and symbolic of the working class. Lorca wore them when working with his theater troupe, La Barraca.

Pressured by centrists and the Right in his own country and also by Britain's conservative prime minister, Stanley Baldwin, Blum announced France's neutrality in Spain's civil war. He even joined Baldwin in initiating the call for a European nonintervention agreement into the Spanish Civil War. Twenty-seven countries, including the Soviet Union, Germany, and Italy, signed it. The sympathies of the U.S. ambassador to Spain, Claude Bowers, lay with the Republican government, but this did not alter his support of the Roosevelt administration's strict isolationist position.[*]

Spanish Republicans were demoralized by the European and Latin American democracies that honored the nonintervention agreement and did nothing to help them. Mexico's strong support of the defense of the Republic was a notable exception, though there was little that nation could offer the cause. At least the Republicans were bolstered by the committed sacrifices of the International Brigades, which came on their own to fight for the Republic against the Fascists.

*

When Lorca had fled Madrid before the start of the war, it took a couple of days for word of his departure to spread. Neruda didn't understand why his friend had missed the wrestling match they were supposed to see together. But Lorca was in Granada, relieved to be away from the upheaval in Madrid and comforted by his family now surrounding him. He was able to relax a bit, to at least calm his anxiety enough after settling in that he began work on a new play.

Then on the night of Friday, July 17, just three days after he arrived,

---

[*] The U.S. Congress had just passed the Neutrality Act of 1935, which prevented the export of "arms, ammunition, and implements of war" from the United States to foreign nations at war. Although the act didn't apply to civil wars, the State Department dissuaded companies from selling planes to the Republic, saying to do so would be against the spirit of U.S. policy. The act didn't prohibit oil and similar resources to be sold on credit to European belligerents, as they weren't classified as "implements of war." Texaco and Standard Oil delivered about $20 million of oil to Franco, indispensable to his continued operations throughout the course of the war.

news about the uprising by army officers in Spanish Morocco reached Granada. On Monday, July 20, soldiers in the Granada garrison rose up against their Republican loyalist general. By late that afternoon, they had taken over much of the city. Lorca's brother-in-law, a Socialist physician who just ten days before had been elected mayor of Granada by the city council, was jailed. The prisons were quickly filled beyond capacity. People barred themselves inside their homes, and the city basically shut down.

Two days later Granadinos lined the streets to cheer the arrival of a general and troop reinforcements sent by Franco. Around five thousand locals enlisted in the Nationalist army. The first executions of "undesirables" took place.

Lorca's presence in the area was not a secret as neighbors ratted on neighbors, and lists were drawn up. He was staying with his family at Huerta de San Vicente, their summer home on about five acres just outside of Granada. One night he dreamed that women in black dresses and black veils approached him with crucifixes in their hands.

Members of the Fascist Falange did come out to Huerta, once to search for a shortwave radio that Lorca supposedly had and with which he was talking to Russia, another time to interrogate the property's caretaker, whose brothers had been accused of murder. They strapped the caretaker to a tree and beat him. Then they entered the Lorca residence. The Falangists threw Lorca down the stairs, hit him and called him a faggot, and demanded information about people he knew. They had lined up the whole household as if they were going to execute them, when another squad pulled up and told the first one to stop and leave.

Naively, the Lorcas didn't imagine that the danger would persist much longer. After weighing different options, they moved Federico to the house of a family friend, the internationally renowned composer Manuel de Falla, a religious Catholic who was respected by the Nationalists. But on August 15, Nationalist officers showed up at de Falla's house demanding Lorca's arrest. When Lorca's protector asked why he was being arrested, the belligerent officer in charge, Ramón Ruiz Alonso, simply responded, "His works." He took Lorca away and imprisoned him in Granada's civil government building.

Three days later, at around three A.M., Lorca was put into a car and handcuffed to a teacher who had been arrested just an hour earlier. Two guards and two members of the Falange drove them to the tiny village of Viznar, six miles from Granada. Lorca and the teacher joined two bullfighters known for their left-wing politics, who were being held in a building that had served, until that month, as a summer play place for children. Now, soldiers, guards, gravediggers, and a pair of housekeepers occupied the upper floor. Lorca was put downstairs, where a young, devout Catholic guard told him he was going to be killed, believing that it was his Christian duty to inform Lorca so he'd have a chance to make a final confession. "But I haven't done anything!" the poet cried. He tried to recite a prayer but could only weep. "My mother taught it all to me, you know? And now I've forgotten it. Will I be damned?"

Before the sun rose that morning, Lorca and the three other prisoners were shot beside a stand of olive trees. A year before, Neruda had written his "Ode to Federico García Lorca." The emotive lines now seem eerily premonitory, exuding the desperate grief Neruda would feel at his friend's death:

> If I could weep with fear in a solitary house,
> if I could take out my eyes and eat them,
> I would do it for your voice of a morning orange-tree,
> and for your poetry that comes forth shouting.

"This criminal act was the most painful in the course of a long struggle," Neruda wrote in his memoir. Alberti said that Lorca's death was his own death. "The news of his death made everyone cry," Delia reminisced years later. Besides the horror of a friend's assassination, Lorca's death represented something more. It made everybody feel vulnerable. He became a martyr because he was targeted in part for being a poet. When asked what crime Lorca could have committed, Ramón Ruiz Alonso answered, "He's done more damage with a pen than others have with a pistol." "The truth is Lorca died because he was a poet," Luis Buñuel said, echoing the thoughts of many. It felt as if the Fascists had just assassinated poetry itself.

"Death to the Intelligentsia" was a favorite wartime slogan of the Right.

Lorca's fate moved the poets to become active participants in the war, not just observers. Pablo Neruda had become a different poet; now he became a different man. There were no more surrealistic dead doves or pumpkins listening. There was the blood of children. There was Lorca's blood, and much more to follow.

Two months into the war, Spain was an open wound, bleeding. Franco and his fellow generals took over large swaths of the country as they prepared for further attacks. At the beginning of October, German Junker and Italian Caproni planes started bombing supply points and airports on the road to Madrid. European governments were aware of Hitler's and Mussolini's blatant defiance of the nonintervention agreement, yet to confront them would risk increasing tensions in a region that was already a powder keg; Spain wasn't important enough to risk causing an incendiary spark. The Soviet Union felt differently. Three months after Franco started the war, the Soviet Union began to supply military equipment to the Republicans (although sometimes at very high prices).

The Nationalist army's plan to storm the capital was based on the belief that resistance would be minimal. Yet not only were workers in Madrid being trained feverishly under the dozens of army officers who had remained loyal to the Republic, but the vast majority of the city also remained loyal, and citizens prepared "to defend every one of Madrid's cobblestones to the death," as one mantra went. Refugees fleeing the small towns that the Nationalists had seized told of the relentless brutality the rebel army inflicted as it advanced toward the capital. The stories swept through the city as it braced for the assault, but a large majority of the population believed in the essential need to defend the Republic from its enemies. The residents were ready to resist street by street and house by house.

When Neruda was asked when he would write something for *Mono azul*, he had replied vaguely. Yet suddenly one day that September, Neruda came to the *Mono azul* offices and handed Luis Enrique Délano a new poem, typewritten with some corrections in ink:

They have not died! They are there
in the gunpowder,
standing, like burning fuses.

. . . .

Mothers! They are standing in the wheat,
tall as the depth of midday

. . . .

   Sisters like the fallen
dust, hearts
shattered,
have faith in your dead!
Not only are they roots
beneath the bloodstained stones,
not only do their poor battered bones
forever work the soil,
but their mouths still bite the dry gunpowder
and attack like oceans of iron, and still
their raised fists defy death.

. . . .

Cast aside
your mourning cloaks, join together all
your tears until they become steel . . .

It was written in Neruda's new style. It was to be understood immediately, clearly, by a wide audience. Bold, repeated words and vivid images were what mattered now to serve his purpose: to send a message through verse. "Song for the Mothers of Dead Militiamen" was Neruda's first published Spanish Civil War poem, appearing in the September 24, 1936, issue of *Mono azul*. It was published unsigned, as Neruda was officially still a representative of the Chilean government.

He went on to write a total of twenty-one poems in reaction to the war, contained in his book *España en el corazón* (*Spain in the Heart*). They later formed part of *The Third Residence*. This poetry was received so enthusiastically that in 1938 the Spanish Republican Army printed it with the help of Neruda's friend, the printer and publisher of *Caballo verde para la poesía,* Manuel Altolaguirre, in the Montserrat monastery, right behind the front lines. Altolaguirre wrote later that Republican "soldiers were working in the mill on the day that the paper for Pablo's book was made. They didn't just use the raw materials provided by the Commissariat (cotton and cloth); the soldiers also threw clothing, bandages, trophies of war, an enemy flag, and the shirt of a Moorish prisoner into the pulp." (This image might be too romantic to be true; the tale is hard to believe considering the difficulties inherent in producing paper from those materials. There's also the question of whether a paper mill even existed in that area.) Wherever they got their paper from, Republican soldiers set the type, printed it, and took copies of this formidable book of poetry to the front in their backpacks. Alberti, who fought in the civil war, called them "sacred verses for us." The Commissariat of the eastern division printed the first five hundred copies, including an inscription in tribute to the author following the title page: "The great poet Pablo Neruda, who lived with us during the first months of the war."

Neruda wasn't the only poet who channeled his work into the fight to save the Spanish Republic. Others included Langston Hughes and Tristan Tzara, the Romanian French founder of Dada. The English poet W. H. Auden wrote one of the most famous poems of the war, "Spain 1937," which ends:

> The stars are dead. The animals will not look.
> We are left alone with our day, and the time is short, and
> > History to the defeated
> May say alas but cannot help or pardon

César Vallejo, Octavio Paz, and Nicolás Guillén also joined Neruda in writing for Spain. Many Spanish poets formed the center of the effort, mainly those of the Generation of '27, including Vicente Aleixandre, Miguel Hernández, Jorge Guillén, Pedro Salinas, and Rafael Alberti. Members of previous generations such as Antonio Machado and Juan Ramón Jiménez were also writing poetry against the Fascists. Their involvement was so significant that the Spanish Civil War has been called the "Poets' War,"[*] though they weren't the only ones moved by the horror of the war to create masterpieces: Pablo Picasso and Joan Miró painted their emotions onto canvases; George Orwell wrote *Homage to Catalonia,* portraying the violence, sacrifice, and inhumanity of the war.

But unlike paintings and novels, poetry was written quickly and printed immediately, sometimes on scraps of paper, making it a more effective tool during the fighting to inspire the Republican soldiers, raise morale, and bring international attention to the cause. The poets were also desperately seeking to elicit sympathy among world leaders, appealing to their governments to come to the Republic's aid as Russia did, while Germany, Italy, and Portugal steadily assisted Franco and his Nationalists.

*

Ernest Hemingway had fallen in love with Spain the decade before; he returned in 1937 as a correspondent for the North American Newspaper Alliance. He may have been the most noncommunist writer to become deeply involved in the Republican cause, and yet it could be said that no one's call for foreign help to stop the Fascists was as determined, loud, and urgent as his.

In one dispatch from the front that was published in January 1938,

---

[*]   The Spanish Civil War as a "poets' war" was unprecedented in history. Great battles had been recorded in poetry since ancient times, but those poems were read only after the moment of action. The romantics were idealistic in their desire to bring about societal change, but there were wide gaps between what they aspired to in their verses and what they achieved. An example is Percy Bysshe Shelley's response to the 1819 Peterloo Massacre, where police on horseback charged more than sixty thousand protesters: Shelley hoped his poetry would stimulate workers to rise up in further revolt. Yet nobody would publish it for over a decade, long after the moment for such a revolt had passed.

The improvement in mass communications by the 1930s made it easier and faster to receive news, allowing poets to write with more immediacy. In the wars of previous centuries, one usually had to wait for news to be delivered by horseback from a distant battle.

he reported about members of the International Brigades: "Since I had seen them last spring, they have become soldiers. The romantics have pulled out, the cowards have gone home along with the badly wounded. The dead, of course, aren't there. Those who are left are tough, with blackened matter-of-fact faces, and, after seven months, they know their trade." Hemingway's articles became increasingly propagandistic, many aimed at compelling American support for the Republic.

Hemingway also helped write, narrate, and raise funds for the propaganda film *The Spanish Earth*. The journalist Martha Gellhorn was also in Spain in 1937, covering the war for *Collier's Weekly*. She was friends with First Lady Eleanor Roosevelt and was able to arrange a screening of the film at the White House for the Roosevelts and several military advisers, with the film's director, Joris Ivens, and Hemingway also in attendance. FDR had already started out being sympathetic toward the Republic, despite concerns about leftist radicals and anarchists. And he had no illusions about the war's importance: to him it wasn't just about Spain, but an international crisis threatening to set off the greater European conflagration; in April 1936, a year before Hemingway and Gellhorn came, he had called Spain his greatest worry. After the screening, he told Ivens that he liked the film and suggested editing it to further emphasize that the "Spaniards are fighting, not merely for the right to their own government," but in particular for the right to cultivate land that the old order had forcibly left barren. Still, the film failed to budge FDR from his anti-intervention stance. (Hemingway and Gellhorn would marry three years later.)

Hemingway is most closely associated with the war through his tremendous novel *For Whom the Bell Tolls*, the story of a young American who is already in Spain before the war and joins the International Brigades after it starts. It was based on events that took place in 1936 and 1937. Some have noted that the novel was influenced and inspired by the Alliance of Anti-Fascist Intellectuals, most notably the guerrilla theater directed by Rafael Alberti and María Teresa León, which performed for the soldiers in the field. But as compelling as the book is, Hemingway didn't start writing it until 1939. He finished it in July 1940, twenty months after the Republic had fallen. Did the bell toll too late? It was published that October.

★

Neruda's most important poem of the period, one of the most outstanding of his life, was triggered by the first major attack by the Fascist forces on Madrid at the end of October 1936. It was relentless. The bombing by Junkers began on the twenty-third. Italian planes dropped leaflets warning citizens to leave the city or "the National aviation will wipe [Madrid] off the earth." A week later, Russian fighter planes were in the skies around the capital; within three days they forced all the Italian bombers to retreat, a great confidence boost for the Republicans. On November 8, twenty thousand Nationalist troops, along with German panzer tanks, attacked and began to take up positions in the city's suburbs. Later that day the first International Brigade troops arrived. The fighting continued, without pause, stretching over nearly a month. Still, citizens of Madrid and the Republican resolve continued to resist the offensive.

On November 17, spent of energy and morale, the Nationalists launched a ruthless bombardment bent on destroying the city's resistance. Two thousand shells an hour pummeled the center of Madrid. But the city held out. Franco finally relented, especially when the siege began to turn world opinion against him. He would not be able to take the city until March 1939.

Spain in the Heart's most powerful poem is arguably "I Explain Some Things." It is the second one Neruda published during the war and it builds upon the blunt realism of "Song for the Mothers of Dead Militiamen." "I Explain Some Things" appeared in *Mono azul* in January 1937 under the original title "Es así," or "It's Like This."

Neruda had reached a moment from which there was no turning back. In his youth, though he had observed the social injustices of the frontier, been influenced by his anarchist uncle in Temuco, and become involved with the radical politics of the student movement in Santiago, he'd published apolitical love poems and the metaphysical experiment *venture of the infinite man.* In the Far East, Neruda turned inward, and his poetry disengaged from politics. Now he realized that he could no longer remain focused on his internal experience. Such poetry couldn't ignore the realities of what was happening in Spain in 1936, or in Italy and Germany, or anywhere in the world.

In "I Explain Some Things," Neruda uses clear language to convey the profound change he has gone through because of the horrors he has witnessed. The experience has completely altered the orientation and purpose of his poetry. As the acclaimed author Ariel Dorfman, who grew up in Chile, paraphrases from the poem's speaker, "I can no longer write about the fragments of reality, about the fact that I'm fragmented, when the actual reality—the blood, the flesh, the children—is being fragmented by bombs."

> You will ask: And where are the lilacs?
> And the metaphysics laced with poppies?
> And the rain that often beat
> his words filling them
> with holes and birds?
>
> I'll tell you everything that's happening with me.
>
> I lived in a neighborhood
> of Madrid, with church bells,
> with clocks, with trees.
> . . . .
>   My house was called
> the house of flowers, because everywhere
> geraniums were exploding: it was
> a beautiful house
> with dogs and little kids.
> . . . .
>   Federico, you remember,
> from under the earth,

do you remember my house with balconies on which
the light of June drowned flowers in your mouth?

                              ¡Hermano, hermano!

. . . .

And one morning everything was burning

. . . .

and ever since then fire,
gunpowder ever since,
and ever since then blood.
Bandits with airplanes and with Moors,
bandits with finger-rings and duchesses,
bandits with black friars making blessings,
. . . kept coming from the sky to kill children,
and through the streets the blood of the children
ran simply, like children's blood.

. . . .

You will ask why his poetry
doesn't speak to us of dreams, of the leaves,
of the great volcanoes of his native land?

Come and see the blood in the streets,
come and see
the blood in the streets,
come and see the blood
in the streets!

CHAPTER THIRTEEN

I PICKED A ROAD

I have the same wounded hand as man,
I hold the same red cup
and equal furious amazement:
                              one day
throbbing with human
dreams, a wild
grain appeared
in my devouring night
to join my wolf's steps
to the steps of man.
                    And so, reunited,
harshly central, I seek no asylum
in the hollows of tears: I carry
the bees' bloodline: radiant bread
for the son of man: in the mystery blue prepares itself
to look upon wheat distanced from blood.
  —"Meeting Under New Flags"

As the war's violent chaos intensified, Neruda took his family out of
Spain, to Marseille. The consulate there was being used as a base
for many members of the Chilean diplomatic corps who had been
displaced by the civil war in Spain. He then took his wife and daughter

about 140 miles east to Monte Carlo, where he hoped they'd be safer. He left them there and returned to Marseille. Delia had fled Madrid as well and was now in Barcelona. On December 10, 1936, Neruda wrote to her:

> I don't want anything except for you to come, I feel lonely, this morning I washed my entire body in a hotel bidet, I have cut my fingernails for the first time alone, and in spite of the difficulties, it is so good to be without Maruca: I felt myself living again . . .
>
> I embrace you with all my heart and I love you every day, I hope and wait to see you, that's the only thing I want. Pablo.

Neruda wrote to the Ministry of Foreign Affairs, asking if he could be reassigned to Marseille, but instead he was told to return to Chile. The Spanish Civil War was creating tension within Chile's diplomatic corps, under the administration of President Arturo Alessandri, who had grown more conservative through his reliance on right-wing support. Many in the corps were pro-Franco, including Carlos Morla Lynch. When the Spanish Republic's seat in the League of Nations had come up for a vote, Chile had voted against the Republic. The Right saw Neruda as a loose cannon.

But Neruda wasn't ready to give up the fight in Europe just yet. At the beginning of 1937, he met Delia in Paris, hoping to deliver a tribute to Lorca while he was there. Neruda was conscious enough of the political sensitivities to ask for permission from his superior, Tulio Maquieira, to give the talk. From Marseille, Maquieira sent a diplomatic explanation of his disapproval:

> My dear friend:
>
> I was greatly happy to hear the good news you sent me about your little girl. I am also happy that your financial efforts are coming to fruition.
>
> . . . There are discussions of whether your poet friend is still

alive. You say the latter [that he is dead]. Fine. But in that case, García Lorca will be perceived as a victim of the belligerence that divides Spain. To make an elegy in these moments, in which passions burn red hot, will lead to a very indiscreet incitement to controversy. Even waving your illustrious name like a battle flag will give the hotheads on the other side an opportunity to damage the legacy of your friend, which you ought to keep sacred. It is useless to tell me that your talk will not be political, because in these circumstances it will have to be defined as such. No, my dear Neruda, the hour of García Lorca has not yet arrived.

Undeterred, Neruda and Delia moved into a place on the Left Bank. The bohemian neighborhood, with its famed international community of writers, artists, and intellectuals, had become a hotbed of activism against fascism and in defense of the Spanish Republic. Yet just as Neruda arrived, news broke that 10,500 Italian troops had landed in Spain. Any hope of saving the Republic seemed more tenuous than ever. Neruda became involved in the International Association of Writers for the Defense of Culture, an organization that was formed after the 1935 Paris International Congress. Delia introduced him to several literary figures, including the Communist surrealist poets Louis Aragon and Paul Éluard, who would become his close friends.

In Paris, Neruda embarked on a number of activist publishing ventures in support of the Republican cause. He collaborated with Nancy Cunard, an activist who "embodied the dazzling energy and tumultuous spirit of her age." Neruda first met Cunard in Madrid, where she reported on the war for the *Manchester Guardian* and the Associated Negro Press. Now together in Paris, they published a solidarity magazine named *Les poètes du monde défendent le peuple espagnol* (Poets of the World Defend the Spanish People). Cunard had a printing press in her house; Neruda helped set the type. The money from the sale of the magazine went to support the Republican soldiers battling Franco's troops. The funds raised were not significant, but just as with *Mono azul*, the dedicated, unabashed support from important contributors spoke volumes. Their involvement was a public pledge that boosted the morale of all those defending the Republic and helped raise international awareness and sympathy for the cause. Then on January 30, 1937, Neruda, Delia, César Vallejo, Alejo Carpentier, the Mexican muralist David Alfaro Siqueiros, and others formed the Ibero-American Committee for the Defense of the Spanish Republic. It was a strong showing of unity. Neruda became one of the editors of its weekly bulletin, *Nuestra España* (Our Spain).

In February, the first issue of Neruda and Cunard's magazine appeared in Spanish, containing one poem from each of them (Cunard's translated into Spanish by Vicente Aleixandre), as well as verse by Miguel Hernández. On the title page they announced: "Madrid will be the tomb of International Fascism—Writers: combat the assassins of Federico García Lorca in your country. We ask for money, food, clothes and arms for the Spanish Republic. *¡No pasarán!* They will not pass!"

The subsequent six issues had pieces by an array of international writers, including a previously unpublished piece by Lorca. Efforts such as these inspired solidarity efforts from writers across the globe.

Despite Maquieira's disapproval, on February 20, 1937, Neruda gave his Lorca lecture to fellow sympathizers of the Spanish Republic. Neruda first spoke at length about Lorca, and then about poets like Alberti and Hernández currently fighting in Spain. He ended the lecture:

> I have wanted to bring before you the remembrance of our great disappeared comrade. Many perhaps hoped for some tranquil poetic words from me, distanced from the earth and the war. The word "Spain" itself brings to many people an immense anguish mixed with a grave hope. I have not wanted to augment these anguishes nor disturb our hopes, but having just left Spain, I, Latin American, Spanish of race and language, could not have been able to speak except for its disgraces. I am not political, nor have I ever taken part in political arguments, and my words, which many would have liked to be neutral, have been dyed with passion. Understand me and understand that we, the poets of Spanish

America and the poets of Spain, we will never forget or
pardon the assassin of whom we consider to be the great-
est among us, the angel of this moment of our language.
And forgive me that of all the sorrows of Spain you only
remember the life and death of a poet. We will never be able
to forgive this crime or pardon it. We will never forget or
pardon it. Never.

In *Nuestra España,* Neruda had published a letter "To my American
friends":

Every day I receive solicitudes and friendly letters that say
to me: put your attitude aside, don't speak of Spain, don't
contribute to the exasperation of people's spirits, don't you
embark on favoritism, you have the high mission of being a
poet to achieve, etc. . . . I want to respond once and for all
that I have situated myself in the civil war on the side of the
Spanish people with the consciousness that the future of the
spirit and culture of our race directly depends on the result
of this fight . . .

The next day, Neruda received a letter from Tulio Maquieira saying
that he had received official word from Santiago that the minister of
foreign affairs "disapproved" of Neruda's partisan political activities.
That same month, the second edition of *Les poètes du monde défendent le
peuple espagnol* came out, this time in French, with a poem by Vicente
Aleixandre and Tristan Tzara, as well as French translations of Neru-
da's, Hernández's, and Cunard's poems from the previous issue. April's
edition had poems by Lorca and Langston Hughes. W. H. Auden had
intended to serve in the International Brigades out of a sense of obliga-
tion: "Here is something I can do as a citizen and not as a writer." Upon
his return to London, he sent "Spain 1937" to Cunard and Neruda.

Neruda and Delia joined the efforts to prepare a Second Interna-
tional Congress of Writers for the Defense of Culture, which was to be
held in Spain. Neruda worked to get Latin American writers to attend.

While he received a small salary for this, he was not fully supporting Maruca, who was still in Monte Carlo, unable to make a living. Forlorn, Maruca took her daughter to Holland. Being from Batavia, a Dutch colony, facilitated her and Malva Marina's immigration, and she had some relatives in The Hague. It was obvious at this point that the marriage would not last much longer. Neruda, it seems, may have made one trip to visit them. No matter what, his position was that the uncertainty of what awaited him in Chile and of where his new consular post could be just presented too much instability, especially given Malva Marina's condition; she and Maruca should stay in Holland. At this point it also was clear that Malva's illness was incurable.

Meanwhile, by April 1937, Franco and his generals had become frustrated with their efforts to seize control of the northern Basque country. While so much had been focused on Madrid, here there was talk of spreading terror and turning towns and cities into dust and ash, an emphatic physical statement intended to quickly destroy the people's morale and will to resist all at once. The small town of Guernica, which for centuries had held a hallowed place in Basque identity, became a target because of its significance as a symbol of regional liberties. Mondays are market days in Guernica, a time when the streets fill with people and abundant stalls, and so, on Monday, April 26, 1937, beginning at 4:40 in the afternoon, with Franco's proud approval, twenty-three warplanes in a joint operation between the Nazi Condor Legion and the Fascist Italian Royal Air Force rained bombs down onto Guernica for three straight hours. The town became engulfed in flames. The death toll was around two hundred, but the toll on the collective psyche was immeasurable. The bombing of Guernica represented the Fascists' indiscriminate incineration of innocence. Citizens trying to escape into the hills were strafed down by machine guns. Nothing like this had ever happened in Europe before. It was the first time a civilian population had been attacked by air with the apparent goal of total destruction. It was totalitarian warfare.

News of the massacre quickly sent shock waves throughout the world. Franco and his allies' goal was to wipe out morale with all those bombs. In that regard, they failed. While Guernica was a terrible blow to Neruda and his friends, it didn't devastate them. The bombing inspired some of the most impactful art of the period, especially Picasso's painting *Guernica*. They knew that the best course of action was the power of the pen or the paintbrush, and they poured themselves into creative acts to stay resilient and to shape works of resistance.

★

As the Fascists' bombs fell on Madrid, the Second International Congress of Writers for the Defense of Culture convened first in Barcelona and then in Valencia over the first weeks of July, finally ending up back in Paris. The meetings were held in different cities to show solidarity with the whole Republic. Around two hundred writers from twenty-eight countries took part in the gathering, including Ernest Hemingway, Thomas Mann, John Dos Passos, Upton Sinclair, Octavio Paz, Langston Hughes, and the Russian poet Ilya Ehrenburg. For Neruda and Delia, who were pivotal in its organization, the congress was a landmark achievement. For the struggling and bloodstained Republic, it raised some spirits.

Neruda's compatriot rival Vicente Huidobro, a militant Communist, was also in Paris at the time. The two led different delegations working toward the same cause. Huidobro's Chilean Intellectual Workers Union was a Communist organization, while Neruda's Alliance of Anti-Fascist Intellectuals' raison d'être was fighting fascism. The fact that Huidobro cofounded his union with Neruda's nemesis Pablo de Rokha only heightened concerns that tensions, however petty, could threaten solidarity among those working for the Republic.

In an effort to prevent any conflict, César Vallejo, Tristan Tzara, and nine others signed and sent a short, eloquent letter deploring the fact that "motives of discord" continued to exist between the two comrades, "both of whom struggle for the same cause." "Taking into account what each of you represent," they urged the two Chileans to "set aside any resentment and division" so that, "with increasing enthusiasm and with one united will," they could all better serve "under the flag of the victimized people for the material and moral triumph over fascism." There were no further public arguments between them.

When the congress was in Madrid, Neruda went to La Casa de las Flores, which was right on the front line of the battle for the city. The block it was on, in fact, had already changed sides several times. Miguel Hernández, in his militia uniform and carrying his rifle, had secured a van to get the books, masks, and other belongings Neruda had left behind. The apartment was in shambles from the bombings and gunfire, books strewn among the rubble on the floor. Delia recalled decades later that amid the ruins of "our" house, "our dog Flak appeared. He had knocked down a window as he sensed our presence there. Pablo rejoiced in seeing him." Neruda's consul's tailcoat and collection of Asian masks were gone, but as Neruda later wrote, the looters had left pots and pans and the sewing machine, which were more valuable than masks in wartime. "War is as whimsical as dreams, Miguel," Neruda remarked to his companion. It would be the last time the two would see each other: Hernández would die in prison five years later.

Neruda spoke publicly at the congress only once, on its penultimate day in Paris. He talked about the new unity of Latin American writers and people coming together to fight fascism. He ended his short discourse:

> Fraternity this great has never, ever situated itself so close
> to justice and life; in fact, fraternity, justice, and life stand
> together on the same battle line. All that's left for us to do
> now is spread out and fight criminal fascism in all corners of
> the world. Wherever we fight for the freedom and greatness
> of mankind, we will be fighting and struggling for Spain,
> even if we do not say her name. This will continue as long
> as Spain can continue to defend herself with a savage calm.

The final resolution of the congress urged fellow writers of the world, for the sake of culture and humanity, to not remain neutral.

Lacking a new consular appointment, Neruda arranged to return home to Chile with Delia. Before he did, he wrote a long letter to the Chilean minister of foreign affairs, defending himself against the growing criticism of his public activism. It included the line, set apart from the rest of the text: "I'm not a communist; I'm an anti-fascist."

Around the same time, he went further, answering a question by the Chilean paper *Ercilla:* "I am not a communist. Nor a socialist. Nor anything. I am, simply, a writer. A free writer who simply loves freedom. I love the people. I belong to them because I come from them. That is why I am anti-fascist. My adhesion to the people is not tainted with orthodoxy or submission."

★

Maruca wrote a letter to Trinidad, her mother-in-law or, as she put it, "my dear mother," from The Hague on September 2, 1937, announcing that "Neftalí" was traveling back to Chile. "He'll tell all." Maruca told Trinidad that she always thought of her with great affection but hadn't written in several months because "we've lived through a horrible time of wars and travels and great misery with a sick little child." She ends it by sending affection to all and a strong hug to Trinidad, from "your daughter Maruca."

Neruda and Delia had boarded the French steamship *Arica* a week earlier and arrived in Valparaíso a little over a month later. Neruda's friends and many fans were there to meet them at Santiago's Mapocho Station. Delia stepped off the train in a blue two-piece suit and a small pink hat. To the crowd, it seemed as if a famous actress had just appeared, such was her glamorous appearance. "This is la Hormiga," Neruda announced. "Say hi to her." Diego Muñoz and others immediately became friends with Delia. They had already heard many good things about her. "She was a charming, cultured woman," Muñoz wrote in his memoirs. However, Neruda looked heavier, a bit older than his thirty-three years. His experience in Spain had aged him, physically and mentally. There was a huge fiesta in their honor that night at the City Hotel. Neruda was now an important figure in his country, a poet acclaimed on the international stage.

Though he had announced that he was not a communist, his ideology and alliances were leading him in that direction. His friends, including Diego Muñoz, Tomás Lago, and Rubén Azócar, were now very active in the Communist Party, adding an intellectual and artistic component to the proletariat base. Neruda joined them in organizing Spanish solidarity events, but he would have risked expulsion from the diplomatic service if he had joined the Communist Party himself.

Neruda and his friends organized a Chilean chapter of the Alliance of Intellectuals for the Defense of Culture. In its first meeting that November, Neruda was elected president and gave a discourse entitled "Writers of Every Country, United with the People of Every Country." It was a rallying cry:

> From this moment the Alliance of Intellectuals, a group of men from different creeds and disciplines, will stand at the front of the battle for freedom and democracy, for the dignity of culture, with deeds and words, now that words are our arms, arms that can be and must be feared by the dark forces of reactionaries.

In the subsequent weeks, Neruda gave several readings of his poetry from *Spain in the Heart* in Santiago and Valparaíso. Over the months that followed, he was involved in various conferences and acts on the part of the Alliance of Intellectuals and other groups, speaking out about Spain and the threat of fascism to Chile.

At its convention in April, the Chilean Popular Front (with the Chilean Confederation of Workers added to its ranks) nominated Pedro Aguirre Cerda as its presidential candidate for the elections that October, running against the archconservative Gustavo Ross. Neruda and the Alliance of Intellectuals went to work campaigning for Aguirre Cerda.

★

Meanwhile, Neruda and Delia settled into their relationship. They rented a comfortable house in the tranquil neighborhood of Providencia, outside the city's noisy center, such a contrast to the stifling small gray apartment he had lived in with Maruca before Buenos Aires and

Spain. They opened their home to friends, as Neruda would for the rest of his years.

Fernando Sáez, executive director of the Pablo Neruda Foundation at the time of this writing, wrote in his biography on Delia that for her,

> the open house is yet another subtle way of keeping an eye on Pablo . . . La Hormiga is inflexible, and she can be tough. "No, Pablo, you are mentally retarded" is her battle cry. And he would conspire to give her a hard time, obliging some friend to tell a dirty joke or use a word with a vulgar meaning that would rattle her. But that is just one part. What you see is an affectionate, inseparable, united couple. He is much more spontaneous, loving, affectionate, and concerned. Taught in such a way as to not show her feelings, Delia seems cold, but her love is unconditional, expressed in her unrestricted support and total admiration.

Book royalties still largely nonexistent, they bought the house primarily with funds from his Ministry of Foreign Affairs pension, which he had started to accumulate when he left for Burma in 1927. It was a modest sum he had never really dipped into. Most of his housing in recent years had been paid for by the ministry, and while he'd drink and eat well, his tastes were not excessively expensive.

Shortly after their return to Chile, Delia made a trip back to Buenos Aires, primarily to attend to her financial affairs. She had been away for seven years. Her family froze her out because of her politics, effectively cutting her off from any family assets to which she may have thought she was entitled.

When Neruda's father fell ill that April, most likely from a stroke, the poet went to Temuco to be with the family. He wrote to "my dear Hormiga of my soul" that while his father had the endurance of an ox, he was still in agony. And his half sister, Laura, was "useless in this situation," so everything was falling to him. Ever since he arrived, Neruda said, his father spent hours unconscious and then, in moments of dazed wakefulness, would criticize him: "Why are you so twisted? Straighten up."

Still with his family in Temuco on May Day 1938, Neruda, representing the Alliance of Intellectuals, gave a discourse imploring workers to defend their rights. He also warned about the growth of Nazism in the south, with its large German immigrant population. May 1 was also Nazi Germany's National Day and was celebrated by many Chileans of the region. Neruda roared, "Enemies of the motherland, get out of Chile! Spies and agents of the savage carnivorous megalomaniac Hitler, get out of here! Close the Nazi schools of the frontier and south!"

★

Neruda's father died on May 7. Later in life, Neruda would speak admiringly of his father, whose rigorous objections to his son's poetry had served to strengthen his resolve. His father's personality could resemble a rock. But behind that hardness he had truly cared for his son, and Neruda knew it.

In his reflective book *Isla Negra,* Neruda remembered José del Carmen:

> My poor, hard father,
> there he was at the axis of existence,
> virile in friendship, his glass full.
> His life was a running campaign,
> and between his early risings and his traveling,
> between arriving and rushing off,
> one day, rainier than other days,
> the railwayman, José del Carmen Reyes,
> climbed aboard the train of death, and so far has not come back.
>   —"The Father"

★

For some breathing space during his time in Temuco, Neruda stayed in the house of Dr. Manuel Marín, the Reyeses' family friend and doctor. Marín noted that the night Neruda's father died, the poet shut himself in the den. The next morning the doctor found what the poet had written the night before: the first lines of the *Canto general de Chile,* which

Rosa Neftalí Basoalto Opazo, Neruda's mother, in Parral, circa 1900.

Archivo personal de Bernardo Reyes

José del Carmen Reyes Morales, Neruda's father, in Temuco, 1920s.

Archivo personal de Bernardo Reyes

Neruda, at age two, in Temuco, 1906.

Archivo personal de Bernardo Reyes

Trinidad Candia Malverde, Neruda's stepmother, whose "gentle shadow watched over my childhood." She signed the photo, "To my son Rodolfo and family, this memento of your mother . . ." It is dated Temuco, 1927.

Archivo de Marycruz Jara Urrutia, through Bernardo Reyes

Neftalí (about age fourteen) and his half sister, Laura (about age eleven), in Temuco, 1918.

Archivo de Escritor, Biblioteca Nacional de Chile

Teresa León Bettiens (around age twenty), 1925. The queen of Temuco's spring fiesta, she was a muse for *Twenty Love Poems*.

Rosa León Muller

Neruda (left) with the poet Romeo Murga, in the Calle Maruri pension house they lived in when Neruda first moved to Santiago, 1922.

Archivos de la Fundación Pablo Neruda

Cover of *Crepusculario* (1923), with illustrations by the anarchist leader Juan Gandulfo.

Colección Archivo Fotográfico, Archivo Central Andrés Bello, Universidad de Chile

Neruda in his "poet's outfit" of black cape and wide-brimmed sombrero.

Archivo personal de Bernardo Reyes

Albertina Rosa Azócar, one of the principal muses of *Twenty Love Poems,* in the 1920s.

Archivos de la Fundación Pablo Neruda

Neruda with his friend Álvaro Hinojosa, 1925. The two would travel to Burma together in 1927.

Archivo personal de Bernardo Reyes

Neruda back in Santiago, no longer the "somber, melancholic, absent *muchacho*," here with his gang of friends, including Alberto Rojas Jiménez, (top row, second from left) and Tomás Lago (top row, to the right of Neruda, fourth from left,) 1932. *Colección Museo Histórico Nacional (Chile)*

Neruda and Maria Antonia Hagenaar on their wedding day, December 6, 1930, outside their house in Batavia.

Archivo personal de Bernardo Reyes

Federico García Lorca and Carlos Morla Lynch in front of the Alahmbra of Granada, Lorca's hometown.

Editorial Renacimiento, Seville

María Luisa Bombal.

Colección Museo Histórico Nacional (Chile)

Neruda and Delia del Carril, Madrid, 1935.

Archivos de la Fundación Pablo Neruda

Neruda's daughter, Malva Marina, around age five, in Holland.

Frederik Julsing

Neruda and Delia (far left) arriving in São Paulo, July 1945. They were greeted by the renowned novelist Jorge Amado (right). Neruda, Amado, and Luís Carlos Prestes would read before a crowd of at least eighty thousand in celebration of Prestes's release from jail after ten years as a political prisoner.

Archivos personales de Bernardo Reyes

would eventually evolve into the larger *Canto general*. In these lines, Neruda took the seeds of conviction he had discovered in Spain and replanted them in his native Chile. As Spain was "in his heart," Chile, and Latin America, now took root there as never before. The poem he wrote that night was "Discoverers of Chile," depicting the violence and oppression unleashed by the conquistadores in their plunder of the New World.

While he had not yet expanded his scope to all of the Americas as he did in the larger work, in this smaller *Canto*, Neruda applied his political convictions to Chile. Here he found a new audience for his verse, not just in fellow intellectuals, but in *el pueblo*, the people. Campaigning at Santiago's great market, La Vega Central, for presidential candidate Pedro Aguirre Cerda, Neruda read almost all of *Spain in the Heart* to the workers of the porters' union. It was the first time he had taken his poetry to the streets in such a manner, and they were completely silent while he read. When he ended, many applauded, while others lowered their heads. Then a man who Neruda thought might be the leader of the union said, "*Compañero* Pablo, we are a much-forgotten people. I can tell you that we have never felt such great emotion. We want to tell you—" According to the poet, the worker then started to cry, as did others.

Neruda said that the workers' reaction made his throat feel "tied in knots by an irrepressible feeling," and that this was the most important act in his literary career until that point. While this description may seem exaggerated, it also conveys Neruda's deepening identification with the working class and the poor. He adopted a new, humble tone, saying his trade as a poet was no greater than that of the baker, the carpenter, the miner; that he was no greater than the righteous of any class.

By the time he was working on *Canto General* in 1949 and 1950, Neruda had started to write in a voice that aimed to speak for the masses. While he somewhat appointed himself to the role of advocate for the people, the "people's poet," the majority seemed to value his representation. His acclaim had earned him tremendous visibility to further his activism for workers and all those suffering from economic injustice. To some degree, his posture was manufactured, and he played up his new image as the poet of the proletariat. But there was also sincerity involved; it was a role that came naturally as part of his personal, political, and poetic trajectory since childhood. It had evolved from his life-long belief in the role of the poet, answering the poet's calling, fulfilling his obligation to share with the world and humanity the creative gifts bestowed upon him at birth, which he had worked hard to develop.

★

Neruda's stepmother died three months after the death of his father, on August 18, 1938. Her tenderness and serene strength had been essential to Neruda as a boy. Doña Trinidad Malverde's peace and equanimity had been constant through the years, a rarity in his family, in the world around him, and in himself.

Neruda had acknowledged her importance in subtle ways. The post-card considered to be his first poem was addressed only to her. While lost in Asia he wrote letters addressed just to her as well. When he wrote his father from Spain to tell him about the birth of his daughter, he explained her full name, Malva Marina Trinidad, was an homage to his stepmother, *la mamadre*.

> Dear more-mother—
> I was never able
> to say stepmother!—
> at this moment
> my mouth trembles to define you,
> for hardly
> had I begun to understand
> than I saw goodness in your poor dark clothes,
> a practical sanctity—
> goodness of water and flower,
> that's what you were . . .
>   —"The More-Mother"

At the time of Trinidad's death, Neruda's half sister, Laura, now thirty-one, was still living in Temuco. With her father and stepmother gone and never having reestablished a relationship with her own mother, she moved to Santiago in 1938 and found work in the public school administration. The bond she shared with Neruda was still firmly intact.

Neruda loved his older half brother, Rodolfo, as well, according to close comrade and biographer Volodia Teitelboim, but they were distant. Rodolfo tried his hand at a variety of entrepreneurial endeavors in Temuco, with little success. He eventually found work with the City of Santiago.

Neruda's "uncle" Orlando had left Temuco after the Ibáñez regime shut down *La Mañana,* as he related in an emotional letter to Gabriela Mistral after she won the Nobel. He eventually began working as a reporter for *La Nación.*

Meanwhile, the mother of Neruda's daughter was in The Hague, desperate for help only he could provide, but would deny her.

★

As Neruda was burying his parents, a humanitarian crisis was emerging in Europe. Just two days before Christmas 1938, Franco launched a final, decisive battle to take Barcelona and all of Catalonia, leaving the Republicans with only Madrid and its environs in the middle of the country, surrounded by the Nationalists on every side. Barcelona fell at the end of January; all of Catalonia fell shortly thereafter. As the Nationalists began to occupy Barcelona, panic swept across the region. Violence and reprisals seemed imminent.

Over a half million men, women, and children fled east into France, over the snowcapped Pyrenees, suffering pneumonia, frostbite, and hunger. French prime minister Léon Blum, intimidated by threats from the Right and having signed the nonintervention pact, did not give the refugees asylum but instead herded them into concentration camps. Many who had no family in France were sent back to Franco's Spain. Thousands died of cold, starvation, and disease in the camps. On February 27, England and France officially recognized the Nationalist government, endangering the refugees even further.

On March 4, 1939, the Chilean painter Luis Vargas Rosas wrote Neruda an urgent letter from Paris:

There are 1,600 intellectuals in the camps; only 40 have left, most of them escapees. Their situation is anguish and there is immediate need to help them . . .

If the bureaucracy is too great for them to go officially, why not collect enough to pay the passage of these comrades. In the midst of so much disgrace, Chile represents the felicity of starting life over. I know that you will do what is in your reach for humanity, solidarity, and the friendship of those who are on this list . . .

Neruda heeded the call. Pedro Aguirre Cerda had just won the election by 1 percent of the vote, 222,720 to 218,609. Neruda went to see the new president on whose campaign he had worked so hard. Aguirre Cerda received Neruda warmly and agreed to help him in his quest to support Spanish refugees.

Meanwhile, in Madrid, the Second Spanish Republic was shattered. At this point, for the Republicans, it was less a question of survival than of how to surrender with the fewest reprisals, though Franco would accept only an unconditional surrender. After holding out for so long, Madrid finally fell on March 28, 1939; Valencia, the following day. Over the next two days, all remaining Republican forces surrendered unconditionally. On April 1, the Spanish Civil War ended as General Francisco Franco declared victory, now holding power over the entire country. There would be no efforts at reconciliation. The historic idealistic energy that had created the magnificent momentary world in which Neruda and Delia had met, in which so much humanity had flourished, had been crushed by the boots of a Fascist dictator who would rule the country until his death in 1975.

Five days after Franco's victory, President Aguirre Cerda signed an order naming Neruda as consul, second class, to Paris—no longer an honorary consul, but a professional one with a real occupation (and a decent salary). He was being sent on "the noblest mission I have ever undertaken."

Delia had already been working in Santiago on projects to collect clothes and goods for the refugees. Organizers held a film festival, a book fair, and a concert. With El Comité Chileno de Ayuda a los Refugiados Españoles (Chilean Committee for Aid to the Spanish Refugees), they sold copies of "An Autograph of Pablo Neruda"—such was his stature now. In it, he claimed:

> America must take the hand of Spain in its misfortune. Thousands of Spaniards are crowded together in inhumane concentration camps, full of misery and anguish.
> We will bring them to America.
> Chile . . . opens the doors to shelter these Spanish victims of European fascism in its territory. Add your material help to this generous gesture!
> Spaniards to Chile!

Neruda and Delia arrived in France at the end of April 1939 and moved into an apartment on the Left Bank. On his arrival, Neruda realized that politics would prove a barrier to his goals. "The government and political situation in my country were now different," Neruda wrote in his memoir, referring to the new progressive president of Chile. "[But] the embassy in Paris hadn't changed. The idea of sending Spaniards to Chile infuriated our atrophied diplomats. They installed me in an office next to the kitchen, they harassed me in every way they could, even denying me writing paper."

When Aguirre Cerda gave the annual presidential address to the National Congress that May, his initial welcome to Spanish refugees had vanished. He was struggling to keep his coalition together, and he faced pressure from the Right, who feared being overrun by communists and anarchists if Chile's doors were opened. All immigration would now be controlled by Santiago and limited to industrial, mining, and agricultural laborers. Soldiers, businessmen, and people in liberal arts, humanities, or science fields were denied entry.

Neruda was not deterred. The French Communist Party had been using an old Canadian cargo ship, the *Winnipeg,* to transport arms to

the Spanish Republic. Now that the Republic had fallen, Neruda se-
cured it to evacuate refugees through the Panama Canal and down to
Valparaíso, its cargo holds converted into a cramped dormitory.

The poet was in charge of the passenger list. Refugees of every sort
wrote to him, pleading for a chance to flee the Franco regime. In the
beginning of June, the United Press reported that Neruda had compiled
a list of some two thousand refugees ready to board for South America.
This was many more than most Chileans had expected, and right-wing
politicians complained vehemently.

The minister of foreign affairs, Abraham Ortega, sent Neruda an
alarmed cable on June 17:

> Rep. de Chile   N. 2006
> MRREE
> Conchile Paris
> N. 538 – June 17/1939
>
> Information in the press informs that two thousand refugees
> will come. Committee is just formed and does not have the
> means nor the preparations to receive them. I warn you to not
> send the contingent without previous authorization [from] this
> ministry. Adhere to instructions by air.
> ORTEGA

Under further pressure from the Right, President Aguirre Cerda re-
scinded the embarkation order. As Delia recalled, Pablo "was fuming
at the ambivalence of his president. He wired the president, telling him
that if the *Winnipeg* did not sail he would shoot himself." He called Min-
ister Ortega and said he would not obey the president's countermand.
The president finally gave in.

At the start of August 1939, 2,004 refugees from concentration camps
boarded the *Winnipeg:* 1,297 males over the age of fourteen, 397 women
over the age of fourteen, and 310 children. They were farmers, fish-
ermen, cooks, bakers, blacksmiths, bricklayers, tailors, stokers, shoe-
makers, electricians, doctors, engineers, and chemists. With so many

crammed on a boat not meant for passengers, the conditions during the monthlong voyage were squalid.

The feat received international attention: newspapers across the world described the venture, with Neruda, Chile's "foremost poet," as the *New York Tribune* described him, identified as the director of the operation. With the headline "2,078 Spanish Refugees on a 93-Passenger Ship," the *New York Times* reported that the *Winnipeg* passed through the Panama Canal on August 21. The ship arrived in Valparaíso on September 3 to a grand welcome and Spanish Civil War songs. Among those who came to administer medical attention to the refugees was a young Dr. Salvador Allende.

Once in Chile, the process of finding living arrangements and jobs for the refugees went relatively smoothly. Their respectable appearance, considering what they had been through, along with their good conduct and strong work ethic garnered sympathy and support from the Chilean people. They made such a favorable impression that the Right found it difficult to disparage them and denounce their arrival, as it had planned to do. "Unexpectedly, the arrival of the *Winnipeg* didn't cause any unpleasant repercussions," President Aguirre Cerda wrote to Neruda in France, congratulating and thanking him for his successful mission.

"With marks of joy and honor they greeted us," one immigrant said to Nancy Cunard. "Praise be to Pablo Neruda," Cunard wrote, "for having exchanged for them the wretched epithet of 'refugee' against that virile word that has made the two Americas what they are, the word 'immigrant.'"

One of the immigrants remembered, "The change could not have been more striking. We, the damnable reds, the humiliated, the dangerous, the murderers, transformed into heroes of democracy, treated marvelously, praised, cheered by crowds at the Mapocho Station."

*

On the same day the *Winnipeg* landed in Valparaíso, World War II began. England and France declared war on Germany in response to the Nazi invasion of Poland. Chile was determined to remain neutral.

Neruda continued to try to get more Spanish refugees across the Atlantic, but he could not come up with the money that the Ministry of Foreign Affairs had requested for each refugee as a "guarantee" that the government would not be financially liable. On October 20, Minister Ortega cabled Neruda that the "media reports embarkment of 270 Spanish refugees. I reiterate previous instructions to absolutely suspend embarking period. Very urgent to send [refugees'] money because situation very critical."

Neruda was defying orders and trying the patience of his government, which was loath to be seen as an open port freely welcoming refugees—especially communists—not just from Spain but from anywhere in the world. Two weeks later, to create distance between Neruda and the Spanish refugees in France and rein in the rescue efforts, Ortega appointed Neruda secretary of the Chilean embassy in Mexico.

*

While he was being lauded as a humanitarian poet, Neruda, meanwhile, seemed eager to disown Maruca and his daughter. They were still in Holland, not too far away. While he brought so many people he never knew across the seas to Chile, he didn't do the same for his daughter and wife. He continued to overlook Maruca's desperate pleas for money to take care of Malva Marina. Destitute, Maruca had placed her daughter into foster care with an electrician's family in Gouda, Holland.

On November 18, 1939, she wrote a remarkable letter to Neruda (notably in English) from The Hague. It reveals her struggle with intense feelings of entrapment, longing, and despair:

My dear Pig,

It is really incredible how you are neglecting us; especially your baby. It is today the 18th of the month, I haven't received the money yet from you. On the first of this month I had to pay the board and lodging of Malva Marina for the month of October. With my salary I could only pay a part of it; now the poor people are still waiting desperately for the rest of it. What a shame really! . . . I think you are awful, awful. I can't find words for it! It can't be because you haven't got the money, as your position now is far better than ever before in Chile . . .

Well, Pig [*illegible*] dear, send me soon the money, please don't put me any more before difficulties. There is already so much sorrow in the world I'm so upset about everything that I'm losing all my hair again, the hairdresser was frightened about it, and says that nothing can be done for it . . .

Malvina sends many kisses to her daddy and love. And so do I. yours,

Pig.

CHAPTER FOURTEEN

AMÉRICA

And then on the ladder of the earth I climbed
through the atrocious thicket of the lost jungles
up to you, Macchu Picchu.
High city of scaled stones,
at last a dwelling where the terrestrial
did not hide in its sleeping clothes.
In you, like two parallel lines,
the cradle of the lightning-bolt and man
rocked together in a thorny wind.
   —"The Heights of Macchu Picchu"

Returning from France for the second time, Neruda and Delia passed through the Panama Canal, then disembarked in Lima so the poet could give a speech at a banquet. His words that night are intriguing evidence that he was now turning his focus away from Europe and back to his native continent, its people and its identity:

The people of America speak alone in a harsh, deserted world; we believe in, and yet have our doubts about, the solitude of a mysterious territory, with nothing but old sacred stones as witnesses. And we need to gain resistance and hope from this solitude, because tomorrow someone will

ask after each and every one of us, knocking on the doors
of history.

Neruda was developing a new Pan-American consciousness, rooted
in the struggles of the continent, across the centuries, from the Incan
slaves who built Machu Picchu to the injustices of his day. In Spain he
had fought fascism, and in Latin America the battle was for the rights of
indigenous and working people and against imperialism.

Neruda and Delia arrived in Chile at the end of December 1939, once
again welcomed home as celebrities, with a huge gathering at Santia-
go's Mapocho Station. The magazine *Qué hubo* reported:

> Almost never before had we seen a response as warm and
> exciting as that of Chilean intellectuals and workers, the
> people, and Spanish refugees, toward the poet and diplomat
> Pablo Neruda upon his arrival in Santiago. Writers, politi-
> cians, teachers, artists and hundreds of admirers awaited
> the poet. When Neruda got off the train, moving from hug
> to hug, you could hear passionate cries:
> "*¡Viva Pablo Neruda!*"
> "Long live the people's poet!"

For Neruda and Delia, it was a bittersweet return. Neruda yearned
to continue his work on the part of the refugees. Many of those who
remained in Europe died in the camps or were sent back to Franco's
Spain, where they lived in poverty and were often imprisoned. It was
hard for Neruda to accept his government's neutrality and toe its line.

Since he did not have to report to his new post in Mexico immedi-
ately, Neruda and Delia spent some time in Isla Negra, a tiny fishing
village about seventy-five miles from Santiago. The town was named
after an outcropping of rocks just offshore. Neruda had fallen in love
with a small house set upon a hill with a magnificent view of the Pa-
cific crashing against the boulders on the rugged beach below. The air
smelled of salt and sand, flowering trees and bushes. It was a perfect set-

ting to write his poetry. Neruda and Delia bought the house and land from the owner, a Socialist mariner.

The couple split their time between the coast and Santiago, where they had an energetic social and political life. Delia's biographer, Fernando Sáez, writes of their relationship at this time:

> Delia's role was to support the poet in his work and toward his future. But that often meant being in an unpleasant position. While she loved the conversation, the arguments and analysis of issues or events, the way things were in Chile with their circle of friends—during that permanent party, with wine flowing in excess, different secrets often came out that she would have preferred not to know and caused her to distance herself. Sometimes she had to call for order, put things in their place, take on the disagreeable role of security guard. They didn't argue about it: she just expressed her annoyance, her anger, by walking away; he would ignore it because he knew her displeasure wouldn't come to anything.

This settled domestic period was only temporary. On June 19, Neruda received a communication from President Aguirre Cerda and the new minister of foreign affairs, Cristóbal Sáenz, naming him not secretary, but rather *cónsul general de Chile* in Mexico. A month later, after send-off parties and homages, Neruda and Delia set sail once again.

On August 21, 1940, several days after they arrived in Mexico City, Neruda officially took his post of consul. The same day, in the same city, Leon Trotsky, Stalin's archrival, died after being struck with an ice pick by an assassin the afternoon before. Trotsky had appeared to be Lenin's natural successor until Stalin outmaneuvered him. He and his many supporters had been waiting for Stalin to be overthrown so that Trotsky could return as the nation's new leader. His assassination was the culmination of an extended effort by Stalin to eliminate him. Trotsky was the primary target of a wider campaign against dissidents abroad who posed ideological threats to Soviet communism during the 1930s and 1940s.

Many have since tried to connect Neruda to the assassination. Suspicion of his involvement was used during the 1960s as a reason why Neruda should not receive the Nobel Prize in Literature. In a 2004 article in the conservative *Weekly Standard,* entitled "Bad Poet, Bad Man: A Hundred Years of Pablo Neruda," Stephen Schwartz wrote that Neruda "even participated in an assassination plot." In a 2006 commentary for the *London Times,* the writer Oliver Kamm mentioned that Neruda was "so obsequious an admirer of Stalin that, as Chile's Consul-General in Mexico in 1940, he conspired in the murder of Trotsky." However, there is no evidence that might prove that the timing of Neruda's arrival in Mexico City was anything more than coincidence. When Trotsky's bodyguards ran into the room after they heard his cries, there was only one man present, a Soviet secret police agent. Neruda claimed he never saw Trotsky, "not close-up or from a distance, neither alive nor dead."[*]

However, Neruda did receive a letter from the Mexican muralist David Alfaro Siqueiros. They had first met in Buenos Aires and reconnected a few years later when Siqueiros came to Spain to join the cause against Franco, fighting on the front. After Siqueiros returned to Mexico in 1939, the KGB began putting into motion plans to kill Trotsky, who had been given asylum by Mexico's president, Lázaro Cárdenas. A Russian whom Siqueiros knew from Spain, now a KGB officer, enlisted

---

[*]   In 1944, the U.S. intelligence services intercepted and decrypted a cable from Moscow to Mexico City stating, "Pablo NERUDA is being developed [RAZ-RABOTKA]." "Development," according to the United States, consisted of being studied and/or cultivated. "Razrabotka" referred to one of the stages in recruitment, including the "assessment of the candidate and the developing of his trust in the case officer." There is absolutely no evidence that Neruda was ever "developed" to serve as an agent for the Soviets, for whatever reason.

   This information was declassified in 1995, when the CIA began to release some three thousand messages it had intercepted from Soviet intelligence as part of the Cold War–era Venona project, which included espionage around the United States' development of the atomic bomb, providing evidence against Julius Rosenberg and Alger Hiss, among others. In September 1995, a report from the NSA's policy office stated, "We have made progress on the next batch of messages to be released." It then listed seventeen names "previously indicated for redaction" that "after discussions . . . may be released." Among them: "Neruda."

him to lead one of at least two different groups ready to kill Trotsky. In May 1940, the internationally acclaimed painter's group moved first, three months before the ice pick hit its mark. Siqueiros led some twenty Mexican and Spanish Communists, almost all veterans of the civil war, in an armed assault on Trotsky's villa. It was a failure. They killed one of Trotsky's bodyguards but didn't get close to the man himself. Siqueiros was subsequently arrested. His explanation to authorities was that they were just trying to gather intelligence on Trotsky's (alleged) counter-revolutionary plots in Mexico. He was released on bail. The muralist was hiding in the hills to avoid trial, when Neruda arrived to take his post and received the note from him:

> Pablo Neruda, a fugitive of justice named Siqueiros writes you to tell you that he greatly regrets not being able to give you a welcome hug, and to plead that you will listen to something that Angélica will ask you . . .

It is unknown what Angélica Arenal, Siqueiros's second wife, had to say to Neruda. Yet the artist was arrested just a few days later. Without hesitation, Neruda eagerly assisted in his release.

While there's no factual basis to the claims that Neruda participated in Trotsky's murder, there is no denying that he was on the path to becoming a die-hard Stalinist. An enduring friendship between Siqueiros and Neruda was born from this incident, one of so many fraternal bonds between Neruda and the great artists and intellectuals of his day that were forged through Stalinism, communism, and leftist causes.

★

Neruda and Delia moved the consulate from the previous consul's house to the wide Avenida Brasil, where they set up a small Chilean library for Chilean and Mexican students. The poet-consul's reputation quickly brought him new friendships with the artists, intellectuals, and left-wing activists of Mexico. Neruda and Delia were also reacquainted with many of their old friends from Spain who had fled the war and settled in Mexico. The art deco apartment they rented on Calle Revillagigedo became a social hub. The Mexican playwright Wilberto Cantón remembered Neruda there always laughing with his wide smile and the seashell collection that littered the apartment. The only other adornments were a reproduction of an oil painting by Henri Rousseau, a portrait of the great seventeenth-century poet and playwright of the Spanish Golden Age Lope de Vega, and a portrait of Federico García Lorca.

Later they would move into a large villa in Coyoacán. Neruda was happy. Wherever they lived, there were constant fiestas. Sometimes he would dress in costume, as an owl, a fireman, an army general, a train inspector (his friend the Oaxacan novelist Andrés Henestrosa said Neruda did this to "hide his ugliness"). On one occasion he dressed up as a train conductor, cap and all, and went around the party checking everyone's ticket. The largest fiesta Delia and Neruda threw was actually to celebrate the baptism of Henestrosa's daughter, Cibeles. Four hundred guests were invited. For two days, people danced, drank, sang, and climbed the trees in Neruda's garden. It was so loud that their landlord evicted them. They then moved to an apartment next to the grand Paseo de la Reforma.

When Wilberto Cantón first heard Neruda read in public, he was struck by how "the lyrical and subterranean accent of his reading stuck in my mind: syllables that were sung in a somewhat simple and primitive melody, like a medieval priest."

Neruda was in demand to deliver both discourse and poetry readings throughout Mexico as his Pan-American-themed message became more developed and consistent. In a speech at the National Preparatory School, he assured the audience that there had never been such a close pair of seemingly dissimilar sister nations as Mexico and Chile:

> Between blue Acapulco and polar Punta Arenas there is all this land, with its different climates and races and regions . . . Mexicans and Chileans meet each other (so alone) in the roots and it is there we must look for ourselves: in the hunger and in the dissatisfaction of the roots, in the search for bread and truth, in the same needs, the same anguish, yes, in the land, in the origin, and in the terrestrial struggle

we confuse ourselves with all of our brothers, with all of the
slaves of bread, with all of the poor of the world.

The polarization between Right and Left, those for and against
fascism, was becoming more and more volatile even in Mexico. On
July 24, 1941, Neruda spoke in the National University's gorgeous
Simón Bolívar Amphitheater—where the back wall of the stage is cov-
ered by Diego Rivera's first major mural—at a tribute to Bolívar ("the
liberator of the Americas") on the 158th anniversary of his birth. After
the Spanish philosopher Joaquín Xirau spoke, Neruda walked to the po-
dium, paper in hand, and read his new, rather long "Song for Bolívar,"
delivered in his emerging emphatic voice (the poem notably starts out
describing Bolívar as "our father who art in the earth"). The audience
was silent and excited until Neruda reached the final lines:

> I came upon Bolívar, one long morning,
> in Madrid, at the entrance to the Fifth Regiment.
> Father, I said to him, are you, or are you not, or who are you?
> And, looking at the Mountain Barracks, he said:
> "I awake every hundred years when the people awake."

The audience erupted in a hail of applause until a commotion began.
Suddenly, from the upper part of the amphitheater, young Fascists be-
gan shouting, provoked by the references to Spain in Neruda's poem.
"Death to the Spanish Republic!" "Long live the Generalissimo!" They
hurled insults at the "savage" leftists who were damaging the univer-
sity's decency.

The dean, Neruda, and other guests hurried out, while those who
stayed in the audience confronted the Fascists in a battle royal. The
dean wanted to make amends to Neruda for the incident, and the uni-
versity published Neruda's poem in a special illustrated edition of five
hundred copies.[*]

---

[*]   The poem would later be included in the final section of *The Third Residence*.

*

Neruda attended to his consular obligations as well as his poetic and social duties, which seemed like a good combination for the Ministry of Foreign Affairs—at first. Testifying to his diligence, the Chilean ambassador to Mexico, Manuel Hidalgo Plaza, a Communist, registered his high satisfaction with Neruda in his annual review: "Señor Reyes is developing an interesting program of propaganda on the intellectual values of our country, and a noble and prestigious study of the commercial possibilities of our products in México."

But Neruda angered the ministry shortly thereafter, as he worked on yet another literary journal, this one entitled *Araucanía,* named after the region in southern Chile. It had a picture of a Mapuche woman smiling broadly with large teeth on the cover, and the minister of foreign affairs reprimanded him for his "bad taste" in representing Chile with such a woman, "even though," Neruda noted in his memoirs, "Don Pedro Aguirre Cerda, whose pleasant and noble face had all the features of our mixed race, was president of the republic." The journal lasted only one issue.

More serious trouble followed. In or around April 1941, Neruda learned that the Mexican government didn't want Siqueiros in a public jail. Mexico's president, Manuel Ávila Camacho, was progressive, and Siqueiros was one of the country's greatest artists. Mexican government officials hoped Neruda, as an influential consul general and friend of Siqueiros, could arrange a visa for him to go to Chile. Neruda's relationship with Siqueiros had recently become closer with both of them in Mexico City. With the aid of an officer, Neruda would take him out of jail at night for dinner. Neruda and the Mexicans came up with the idea that the visa would be issued under the pretext that Siqueiros paint a mural in a school in the town of Chillán, which had recently been devastated by an earthquake.

But on April 23, the Chilean Ministry of Foreign Affairs urged Neruda to annul the visa. The poet cabled back his refusal, defending his reasoning. The following day, Neruda received a second cable urging him to annul the visa. This time, Neruda wrote a long letter in Siqueiros's defense, maintaining that the muralist had received an invitation from the director of the Chilean National Museum of Fine

Arts. On April 30, Neruda received a cable saying that the ministry considered his actions "a grave mistake." Neruda responded by offering to renounce his position. Siqueiros and his wife, Angélica Arenal, were on their way to Chile. They were allowed a two-month stay. The ministry suspended Neruda for a month without pay.

Though the poet had already offered his resignation, he was furious that the government had reprimanded him and docked his pay. Neruda still hadn't joined the Chilean Communist Party, but these provocations drove him to become even more vocal politically. On June 8, 1941, he sent a letter to the party's secretary, Senator Carlos Contreras Labarca:

> I want to know, dear Carlos, what you think about all this, about whether I should just swallow this new provocation— which would be very difficult, considering the fact that the terms of my suspension are frankly aggressive and disrespectful to me—or whether I should put an end to this matter and return to Chile to accompany you in the struggle.

Neruda was haunted by thoughts of his comrades who had died in Spain and increasingly yearned to take a stand. He could not shake the awareness that his present position was a convenient way for the Chilean government to keep him away from the home front.

*

The insult of the suspension notwithstanding, it freed Neruda to travel. The more he saw, the more his experience of Central and South America affected his thinking, his vision, his conscience. The travels also eased his relationship with Delia, which had grown somewhat tense in Mexico City. Delia was growing tired of Neruda's constant partying and her role as disciplinarian. Neruda's infantile acts annoyed her, as did his dependence on her as both personal secretary and poetry editor. But life on the road worked well for them both.

They headed to Guatemala by car. They lived with the writer Miguel Ángel Asturias for a week, beginning a deep fraternal friendship. The dictator Jorge Ubico was ruling Guatemala at the time. Among many abuses,

freedom of speech was repressed, leading Asturias to withhold the pub-
lication of his novel *El Señor Presidente (The President)*, a book about the
evils of a despot. Eventually, it would be one of the key works that earned
him the 1967 Nobel Prize in Literature. During Neruda's trip to Guate-
mala, a group of eager, young poets asked him to give a poetry reading
(after requesting Ubico's permission by telegram). While Neruda read his
poems with enthusiasm, hoping to open a window of expression for the
students despite the oppression, the chief of police sat conspicuously in
the front row. Neruda wrote that he later learned that four machine guns
had been aimed at the audience and himself, which would have been fired
if the chief had stood up and asked for the reading to stop.

It was on this trip to Central America that Neruda witnessed first-
hand the damage that dictatorial rule can do to a country and its peo-
ple. Ubico's crimes and Guatemala's plundering by foreign companies
led directly to Neruda's lyrically searing "The United Fruit Co." Part
of its potency comes from the short lines Neruda uses, which seem in-
tended, as Robert Hass notes, "to carry a sense of contained force."

> When the trumpet sounded, everything
> on earth was prepared
> and Jehovah distributed the world
> to Coca Cola Inc., Anaconda,
> Ford Motors, and other entities:
> The Fruit Company Inc.
> reserved the juiciest for itself,
> the central coast of my land,
> the sweet waist of America.
>
> . . . .
>
> The Company disembarks
> among the bloodthirsty flies,
> brim-filling their boats that slide
> with the coffee and fruit treasure
> of our submerged lands like trays.
> Meanwhile, along the sugared-up
> abysms of the ports,

indians fall over, buried
in the morning mist:
a body rolls, a thing
without a name, a fallen number,
a bunch of dead fruit
spills into the pile of rot.

In the poem (which would be included in the *Canto General*) Neruda claims the United Fruit Co. and other imperialist interests bought their power through "unsheathing jealousy," "alienating free will," "founding a comic opera," and bestowing gifts like "crowns of Caesar." He lays out a litany of dictators, whom he refers to as "flies." First is General Rafael Leónidas Trujillo Molina—"the Dictatingest Dictator who ever Dictated," in the words of Junot Díaz's narrator in the novel *The Brief Wondrous Life of Oscar Wao*—who ruthlessly ruled the Dominican Republic from 1930 until his assassination in 1961.

Then Neruda writes of Nicaragua. "Tacho" was the nickname of the murderous Anastasio Somoza García, who brutally ruled from 1936 until he was assassinated in 1956. Franklin D. Roosevelt famously said of him, "Somoza may be a son of a bitch, but at least he's our son of a bitch." After his assassination, his two sons carried on the family's reign until the Sandinistas' 1979 revolutionary victory.

Honduras's Tiburcio Carías Andino, who ruled from 1932 to 1949, is next. Carías Andino gained the support of the banana companies by crushing strikes and the labor movement, outlawing the Communist Party of Honduras, and cracking down on the press.

Neruda continues to El Salvador: the Fascist general Maximiliano Hernández Martínez seized control of El Salvador in a 1931 coup. A year later, in response to a popular uprising, he presided over a horrific massacre that some estimate killed up to forty thousand peasants.

Last came Guatemala. Under Jorge Ubico's dictatorship from 1931 to 1944, United Fruit became the most important company there. It received enormous tracts of real estate and tax exemptions, making it the largest landowner in the country, and it also controlled the country's sole railroad, electricity production, and main Caribbean port, while, as Neruda writes, "the indigenous were collapsing in their poverty."

★

In July, his one-month suspension was over and Neruda took up his position as *cónsul general* again. He needed the money. The drama over Neruda defying orders in the Siqueiros affair had no enduring repercussions; knowing how desperate he was for it, the Ministry of Foreign Affairs even ended up reimbursing Neruda his docked salary. However, since Germany's June 22, 1941, invasion of Russia, war had broken out in earnest across Europe. For Neruda, this meant that he could no longer allow diplomacy to constrain his literary political activism.

And then the reality of the fight against fascism hit Neruda quite literally. Just after Christmas 1941, Neruda, Delia, and his consular secretary were in a park in Cuernavaca. As they toasted Roosevelt, who had just declared war on the Axis powers following the December 7 Japanese attack on Pearl Harbor; Mexico's new president, Ávila Camacho; Winston Churchill; and Stalin, a group of ten to thirteen Nazi sympathizers who had been sitting nearby suddenly attacked the festive group with fists, chairs, and bottles—"in military formation," according to Neruda—and yelled "Heil Hitler!" with their arms raised in Nazi salute. The poet suffered a four-inch wound to his head after being struck, he said, by a blackjack. The assailants fled when the police arrived.

The Associated and United Presses circulated a photograph of Neruda and his wound around the world, along with an account of the incident. (The short reports from the wire services, which appeared in the *New York Times,* the *Baltimore Sun,* and others, identified Neruda as a Chilean consul but interestingly made no mention that he was a well-recognized poet.) Neruda received hundreds of telegrams wishing him well from around the world.

His head wound didn't impede his New Year's celebrations with his friends, which had grown to include a new group of European exiles. That night they sang the Socialist and Communist anthem, "The Internationale," in Spanish, French, German, Polish, Romanian, and Czech. Many of the guests would later recall how it was at this party that they last saw the legendary Italian Communist photographer, actress, and activist Tina Modotti alive. She died five days after the fiesta, supposedly of a heart attack, though many believe she was murdered. Modotti was an inspiration to Neruda; she bore witness to fascism and other injustices through her photographs, just as Neruda was now doing through his poetry, and she often put her camera aside to do grittier work for the Communist Party, as Neruda would also do. "I cannot solve the problem of life by losing myself in the problem of art," she wrote. At her funeral, Neruda read his elegy "Tina Modotti Is Dead":

> In the old kitchens of your country, on the dusty
> roads, something is said and passes on,
> something returns to the flame of your golden people,
>   something awakes and sings.

★

It was not all peace and harmony in this social sphere, and personal discord began to arise between Neruda and others within his orbit of poets, intellectuals, and the like. One such clash erupted with Octavio Paz. At the time, Paz was the director of the literary journal *Taller* (Workshop). Neruda gave Paz a short essay to publish, in which he took some jabs at Juan Ramón Jiménez, his rival back in Spain. Through an "unforgivable error," Neruda wasn't mentioned as a contributor on the cover. In that same issue of *Taller*, Paz published poems by Rafael Alberti, which Alberti had dedicated to José Bergamín, a poet with whom Neruda had had a separate feud. Neruda became furious with Paz for publishing the dedication to his enemy: "You have been an accomplice in a plot against me." (For all the commotion this perceived slight would set off, *Taller* was a little-known publication, and Paz—though he would go on to win the 1990 Nobel Prize—was not yet an important literary figure.) Neruda was prone to paranoia regarding other artists, a problem that would continue throughout his life.

At the same time, Paz and Bergamín were editing a new anthology of modern Hispanic poetry, *Laurel*. Bergamín was in charge of selecting two Mexican and two Spanish poets to include. Neruda was further incensed when Bergamín didn't choose his friend Miguel Hernández, then jailed in one of Franco's prisons, as one of the Spaniards; in Neruda's *Canto General* poem "To Miguel Hernández, Murdered in the Prisons of Spain," he takes a swipe at Bergamín and *Laurel*, as he pays homage to his lost friend:

> And to those who denied you in their rotten laurel,
> on American soil, the space that you cover
> with your fluvial corona of bled rays,
> let me cast them scornful oblivion
> because they want to mutilate me with your absence.

Neruda refused to have his own poems included in *Laurel*. The 1,134-page anthology included his friends Alberti, Cernuda, Aleixandre, Altolaguirre (the printer of *Spain in the Heart*), and Lorca. The bottom of its last page reads: "(The authors had included the poets Pablo Neruda and Léon Felipe in this anthology. While it was at the printers, these gentlemen asked the editors that their works be excluded. Regretfully, we complied with their wishes.)"

Paz wrote years later:

> There was a change after that. He began to use the same disparaging terms for both "pure poets" and Trotskyites. [Paz was a Trotskyite himself, opposed to Stalin's leadership.] Once I dared to defend [both of] them; he looked at me with surprise, almost incredulously, and then he responded harshly. We didn't talk about the subject again, but I felt that after that, he thought of me as untrustworthy. I had fallen from his grace.

Indeed, when a banquet in honor of Neruda happened to be given just days after the publication of *Laurel*, the tensions came to a head. Neruda appeared to be uncharacteristically drunk that evening. At one point he told the others sitting with him at the table of honor, "I would like to say hello to Octavio." Paz was sitting at one of the enormous tables on the other side of the room. José Luis Martínez, who would become an illustrious leader of several Mexican cultural institutions, went to get him. But when Paz arrived to greet Neruda, he was met with a sudden dismissal: "I don't say hello to faggots," Neruda told him. "I call you a faggot because you're allied with those sons of bitches, those faggots [Bergamín and the other editors of *Laurel*]." The insult was so distasteful that it unnerved Delia, who turned to Neruda and asked, "Pablo, what are you doing?"

As he said his good-byes at the end of the night, he sarcastically complimented Paz on his shirt, saying it was "whiter than [his] conscience." He then insulted Paz's mother and grabbed Paz's shirt so strongly that he tore part of the collar. A rant on the authors of the "damned anthology" followed.

Later that night, Neruda told the Spanish poet Juan Larrea: "I don't know what you will think, Juan. But I'll tell you that to me, poetry doesn't interest me now. From now on I think I will dedicate myself to politics and seashell collection." Poetry for Neruda, however, was inescapable; it was his main outlet for political expression. But Neruda's comment to Larrea is telling of his ambition to become more active politically off the written page.

*

The second half of the third volume of *Residence on Earth* moves from Spain to the Russian front. In the summer of 1942, Hitler began a siege on the industrial city of Stalingrad. The siege was one of the most pivotal and bloodiest battles of the war. Stalin forbade civilians from fleeing on order of being shot; he put them to work barricading and setting up defenses. A major bombardment by Nazi planes caused a fierce firestorm to rage through the city; thousands died and the city was left in ash and rubble. Savage fighting continued. Tanks rolled out of factories and into battle so quickly they weren't even painted. Over half a million soldiers died in the battle, while the total casualties were near two million.

Communists and others all over the world were pleading for the

Allies to open a second front and help defend Russia. To this end, Neruda wrote a long "Song to Stalingrad":

> Russia, today you know loneliness and cold.
> When thousands of howitzers shatter your heart,
> Stalingrad, when scorpions with crime and venom
> come to gnaw on your insides,
> New York dances, London meditates, and I say *"merde,"*
> because my heart can't stand any more and our
> hearts can't stand more, they can't
> in a world that lets heroes die alone.
>
> You leave them alone? Now they'll come for you!
> You leave them alone?
> Do you want life
> to flee to the tomb, and that the smiles of men
> will be erased by the latrine and the cavalry?
> Why don't you respond? . . .

Neruda wrote this poem to raise the public's consciousness and inspire activism from the grassroots, from the proletariat to the intellectual. He first read it at the electricians' union theater in Mexico City. The workers were so inspired they made posters of the poem and put them up throughout the capital. The poem quickly spread north, to the United States and Canada, and across the ocean.

But many critics quickly came out against Neruda's political poetry, and, once again, the Ministry of Foreign Affairs was uncomfortable with his public remarks. In defiance of the criticism, Neruda wrote "New Love Song for Stalingrad":

> I wrote about the weather and about water,
> I described mourning and its bruise-colored metal,
> I wrote about the sky and the apple,
> now I write about Stalingrad.

The rhyme scheme is lost in translation; the second line always rhymes with the fourth's "Stalingrado."* The poem continues for another twenty-seven strophes, each one pounding the name "Stalingrado" into the reader's mind, reinforced by the powerful rhyme.

Reviewing the first English translations of *Residence on Earth*—all three volumes—the *New York Times* claimed that Neruda "reaches a peak of fervor in two long poems to Stalingrad. In fact, he appears to communicate his convictions most trenchantly when he is writing of the great events of his generation."[†]

★

In January 1943, after over a year of intense pressure from the United States, Chile finally ended its neutrality and broke off diplomatic relations with Germany, Japan, and Italy. Shortly after, Neruda was invited by the U.S. State Department to participate in "Night of the Americas," a program of song, dance, and music by celebrated American and Latin American artists. The Council for Pan-American Democracy was the stated organizer.

The event was hosted at the large Martin Beck Theatre (now the Al Hirschfeld Theatre), a significant Broadway venue, on February 14. Neruda had now, even in the United States, become a headliner. The ad for the event in the *New York Times* theater listings read:

---

[*]   For example:

> *Yo escribí sobre el tiempo y sobre el agua,*
> *describí el luto y su metal morado,*
> *yo escribí sobre el cielo y la manzana,*
> *ahora escribo sobre Stalingrado.*

[†]   The review appeared in 1947, the first in the *Times* on an English-language version of the book, a seminal edition by New Directions, translated by Angel Flores. *Residence on Earth: Selected Poems* was "wisely published in Spanish and English on alternate pages." It was a glowing review by Milton Bracker, one of the *Times'* top correspondents and a contributor to the *New Yorker*. "The flavor of Neruda is clearly political in the noblest sense. He is primarily a poet who combines words with a stinging originality," Bracker wrote.

NIGHT OF THE AMERICAS
Principal Speakers
Vicente **LOMBARDO TOLEDANO** * Pablo **NERUDA**
President, Confederation Latin American Workers * Great Chilean
Poet Consul General to Mexico

Langston Hughes was one of the emcees.

Neruda told the crowd about Talcahuano's coal mines, where, when the first Soviet boat came to Chile, the miners climbed up onto the hills at night and used their lanterns to cast signals out to the Soviet sailors below, a greeting of "international fraternity." He ended his speech with the conclusion that "all countries must search for each other beneath the stars to unite on the sea."

Outside of the event, talking to the press, Neruda made a push for his country to fully renew its relations with Russia, which "will definitely be in Chile's interest." His words immediately filled the papers back home. Once again, the Ministry of Foreign Affairs expressed its continued displeasure that, as consul, he would make such inappropriate public statements, especially in an international setting. Tension grew on both sides.

★

In March, Delia and Neruda headed to Washington, D.C., where Neruda was received as a celebrity poet-dignitary, with members of Washington's cultural and political elite eager to meet him. The *Washington Post* referred to Neruda as "the outstanding Spanish poet of his day." He was feted at the Chilean embassy and gave a lecture at the Pan-American Union (now the Organization of American States). Attorney General Francis Biddle invited Neruda to his home for tea; his wife, Katherine Garrison Chapin, was a poet and literary patron. He was invited to the Library of Congress by the chief librarian, the poet Archibald MacLeish, who had been picked by FDR to push a progressive agenda. Among other activities, Neruda signed the library's holding of the fifth of the five hundred copies of

Spain in the Heart printed by Manuel Altolaguirre and the Republican soldiers.[*]

On March 19, 1943, Carlos Morla Lynch, now part of the Chilean delegation in Switzerland, sent a diplomatic telegram to Santiago: "Señora Neruda advises from Holland that her little daughter died March 2nd, without suffering. She urges that her father be advised. She wants to reunite with her husband as soon as possible." There is no record of the poet demonstrating any strong emotion upon hearing the news. None of his friends remembered him talking about Malva Marina much. While he had just written a poem on Tina Modotti's death, as he had done previously for the deaths of other friends, Neruda wrote nothing upon the death of his daughter.

Nine days later, another death occurred that seemed to have a greater emotional impact on Neruda than that of his daughter. On March 28, Miguel Hernández, the young Spanish poet Neruda had urged Octavio Paz to include in *Laurel,* died of untreated tuberculosis in jail in Alicante, Spain. It was the twelfth prison he had been held in during the previous three years. Neruda, Delia, and many others had begged the Catholic Church to intervene on his behalf, to no avail. Some of Hernández's greatest poetry had been composed during his final years, his last poem scribbled next to his bed on the prison wall: "Farewell, brothers, comrades, friends: Give my good-byes to the sun and the wheat fields." Neruda and Delia were anguished by his death; they felt they should have done more to prevent it. Their grief fueled their *compromiso politico,* their personal political commitment.

Two months later, Neruda received a telegram from Morla Lynch reiterating that Maruca wanted to return to Chile and that Neruda needed to get her a Chilean passport. Neruda's response was calculated:

---

[*]   Rafael Sánchez Ventura, an "angelic poet of rebellion" and "tireless champion of absolute injustices," as Lorca put it, had been a member of the Republicans' Junta for the Preservation and Protection of Spain's Artistic Treasures. In 1940, he sent a number of Altolaguirre's works to the Library of Congress to have them preserved for posterity.

"In spite of the fact that I appreciate Ambassador Barros's interest, I lament that I must manifest that I do not want my ex-wife to return to Chile and that I'll suspend her monthly stipend if she does so."

Indeed, Neruda had already begun divorce proceedings, even before Malva's death. In his archives is a receipt from a Mexican lawyer for the sum of fifteen pesos for a certified translation of their marriage act from Dutch to Spanish. Neruda petitioned a judge near Cuernavaca for the dissolution of his marriage to Maruca. There, as in other parts of Mexico at the time, legislation had been enacted to expedite divorces, partially out of progressive ideals, partially to attract foreigners and the fees they'd pay for an easy and quick divorce.

His lawyers printed a legal notice in a small newspaper addressed to "Sra. María Antonia Hagenaar," stating that contested divorce proceedings had been "initiated against you by Neftalí Ricardo Reyes for irreconcilable differences," and that "you are summoned to respond in person to this suit within three days of this publication." If she did not respond within this time frame, she would lose her opportunity to contest the divorce. Considering that Maruca was in Nazi-occupied Holland at the time and unable to travel with her sick daughter, not to mention the probability that she never even saw the notice, it was virtually impossible for her to respond in time.

Neruda would be granted the divorce, and in the charming *pueblo* of Tetecala, in the shadows of the Xochicalco pyramid, at one o'clock on July 2, 1943, Ricardo Neftalí Reyes Basoalto married Delia del Carril Iraeta. Despite the heat and mosquitoes, they held a lunch outside for guests, and drank and sang and read poetry until nightfall. Pablo gave his new wife a necklace of Oaxacan silver. He announced that he had found in Delia that which all his friends put together could not give him.

★

A tragic incident in Brazil accelerated Neruda's involvement in politics beyond his consular role. In those years, Brazil was ruled by a right-wing dictatorship that had outlawed all leftist political activity. In 1935, Luís Carlos Prestes, the Brazilian "cavalier of hope," as Neruda called him, had been arrested and tortured. His mother, who had fled to

Spain, was now in Mexico. Neruda had been helping her to get Prestes released when she died in June 1943. Former Mexican president Lázaro Cárdenas telegraphed Brazil's dictator, Getúlio Vargas, to let Prestes out of jail to attend his mother's funeral, with a personal guarantee that he'd return to prison, but Vargas refused. The funeral turned into a mass protest, with intellectuals and workers marching side by side in the procession. Neruda read a long poem, "Harsh Elegy," which became part of *The Third Residence*. The Brazilian ambassador to Mexico was incensed by Neruda's words and complained to the Chilean government. A right-wing newspaper in Mexico City published Neruda's response:

> As the consul general of Chile (and not a diplomatic representative), my duty is to work for the strengthening of cultural and trade relations between Mexico and my country. But as a writer, my duty is to defend freedom as an absolute norm of the civil and human condition, and neither protests nor incidents of any kind will change my actions or my poetry.

It was time. Neruda decided to return to Chile and relieve himself of his consular position. His activism had made it impossible for him to serve any longer.

From the high plateaus of Mexico, from his trip to Central America, and despite the distraction of the European situation, he felt a growing urge to write explicitly against the injustices he was witnessing in an ever-broadening context. Toward the end of his stay, he began to find the lyrical forms and tools with which to reorient himself, away from his European focus, toward an expansion of his *Canto general de Chile* project. These poems marked the genesis of Neruda's embrace of using the canvas of the Americas to contextualize his concerns, a canvas he discovered when he looked out from the heights of Machu Picchu. His use of the great liberator of the Americas as the vehicle for "Song for Bolívar" is an early example.

At the beginning of the epic, he must show he is fully integrated into that canvas. He must establish that he has the impassioned heart and poetic skill to transform all that history, the geography, the people, into powerful lyrics of revelation and change. He asserts this in his poem "América, I Don't Invoke Your Name in Vain." It first appeared in the Mexican magazine *Revista América* in July 1943, and it would become a central piece in *Canto General*. In its poignant lines, he suggests that he has been called upon to assume this role, enabled by his poetic ability and progressive ideals. Neruda writes it as his personal introduction to his new calling. It is his credential, as he reports to duty, committed and empowered to lyricize and vocalize the consciousness of the continent.

> América, I don't invoke your name in vain.
> When I fix the sword to my heart,
> when I withstand the leaks in the soul,
> when your new day
> penetrates me through the windows,
> I'm of and I am in the light that produces me,
> I live in the shade that determines me,
> I sleep and awaken in your essential dawn,
> sweet like grapes and terrible,
> conductor of sugar and punishment,
> saturated in the sperm of your species,
> breast-fed on the blood of your heritage.

Neruda made use of his last weeks in Mexico to celebrate with friends and revive old feuds. He threw a parting jab at Octavio Paz: in an interview with the influential Mexican magazine *Hoy,* he said that "the agronomists and painters are the best part of Mexico," and that "there is a really impressive absolute lack of direction and moral civility in [Mexico's] poetry."

Paz responded publicly:

> Señor Pablo Neruda, Chilean consul and poet, is also a known politician, literary critic, and generous patron of certain hangers-on who call themselves "his friends." These

disparate activities cloud his vision and twist his judgment: his literature is contaminated by politics, his politics are contaminated by literature, and his critiques are often just a matter of friendly complicity . . .

The farewell party was to be thrown on August 27. Posters inviting the public were put up all around Mexico City. Ambassador Óscar Schnake wrote back to Santiago that it turned into a major tribute, with more than a thousand people in attendance:

> It was exciting, wonderful, difficult, impossible to describe. The celebration took place at the Mexico jai alai arena, because we had to choose the largest venue in Mexico. And even so, a lot of the attendees could not sit down—that was how excited everyone was at that unforgettable tribute . . . Neruda is today the purest, the human embodiment of the poet of America; the man is firm and serene, fully and generously devoted to his ideals.

The French writer Simone Téry, who knew Neruda both in Paris and Mexico, toasted the poet: "Pablo Neruda is such a boy, as down-to-earth, innocent, and mysterious as a little boy. But he is a gigantic, charismatic child, and everyone who spends time with him—soldiers, statesmen, or professors—is compelled to return to their youth."

César Martino, former president of the Mexican House of Representatives and then head of the Banco de Crédito Agrícola, addressed Neruda:

> Since you arrived in Mexico, you have echoed our country's past, in which it was unjustly exploited. You have echoed our country's present, struggling forcefully to take charge of its own destiny and stand with the free people, to bring the fires of freedom to the hearts of those who are not yet free, and look toward a better tomorrow, which will belong to everyone in splendor and justice.

On August 30, 1943, nearly two hundred people gathered at Mexico's Aeropuerto Central to bid Delia and Neruda good-bye.

*

It was not to be a hurried return home. Neruda's tour down the west side of the Americas on the way to Chile was meant "to awaken the sleeping and encourage the wakeful." He was celebrated as a folk hero, at least for the Left, throughout the continent. One of his stops was Colombia, whose leftist president, Alfonso López Pumarejo, had invited him. During their time in Colombia, Neruda and Delia visited the coffee-growing region of Caldas. There, with the Andes as a backdrop, workers joined children in a ceremony to christen a rural school "Pablo Neruda."

The reception for Neruda—his persona, his politics, and his poetry—was not always so rosy. Among his critics was the poet Pedro Rueda Martinez, who insisted in the conservative Bogotá newspaper *El Siglo* that Neruda's politics were a weakness: "He has wanted to mix his verse with the sentiment of class warfare. It's almost a fanatical proletariat who puts aside his purely emotional artistic impulse in order to foment party hatred."

The paper's founder, Laureano Gómez, also criticized Neruda, as Neruda was celebrated by the liberal government, which Gómez opposed in favor of fascism. Gómez published defamatory poems he wrote against Neruda under a pseudonym. Of course Neruda couldn't just let this go, and he responded with a tight, witty rhyme satirizing Gómez: *"Laureano never laureado."*

Delia and Neruda found themselves next in Lima, Peru, where they were given an honorary lunch by President Manuel Prado of the recently restored Peruvian democracy. In the following days, Neruda gave a lecture, "A Journey Through My Poetry," in the gorgeous Teatro Municipal. Shortly afterward he delivered a talk to Peruvian writers that he had just composed. Entitled "America, Your Lamps Must Keep Burning," it highlighted the bonds between Chile and Peru just as he had done with Mexico. Another manifestation of his evolving Pan-Americanism, the name of the talk echoes the name he'd give to the first canto of *Canto General,* which portrays the genesis of the Americas: "A Lamp on Earth."

President Prado then facilitated an expedition to Machu Picchu for Neruda and Delia. The Incan ruin was not yet the tourist spot it is today; they traveled through the Andes for three days by burro and foot. The mystical site inspired his magnificent poem "The Heights of Macchu Picchu," which became the second canto of *Canto General.* "I thought it held the umbilicus of American history there; it was the center, the apotheosis, and the origin of the entire American continent. I think that a European can admire the grandness of Machu Picchu but cannot comprehend the historical sentiment that the sight of her inspires in us."

In fact, Neruda said that the idea to expand the scope of *Canto general de Chile* into a *Canto general* for all of the Americas was born while visiting that ancient site: "The nucleus of the work emerged in my country, but after visiting Mexico, Peru, and especially Machu Picchu, I felt personally tied to American soil, to the entire continent." He needed to return and change course with the canto, to write this new projection.

One of the reasons "The Heights of Macchu Picchu" is such an extraordinary poem is that Neruda had discovered how to be politically direct without applying strict dogmatic or social realist formulas to his verse. It illuminates Pan-American history through the lens of Neruda's own process of discovery. He is able to forge a vision of the inequality in the past that still exists in the present: "I thought about a lot of things after my trip to Cuzco [the settlement near Machu Picchu]. I thought about the American man of old. I saw his old struggles as intertwined with his current ones." "The Heights of Macchu Picchu" provides a voice for generations past and present. He wrote the poem while watching the ocean at Isla Negra.

The poem's division into twelve parts resembles the Stations of the Cross, each a meditation at a stop along his pilgrimage to find his lost roots. The chronicles of the peregrination are presented almost as religious scripts, which express the continental vision he had been striving for.

The first canto begins, as Neruda put it, "with a series of autobiographic memories":

From air to air, like an empty net,
I went wandering between the streets and the atmosphere,
arriving and saying good-bye

Up until then, throughout his life, he had gone from one day to the other, "from air to air," from nothing to nothing. He felt like an empty net. From Poem VII in *Twenty Love Poems*:

Leaning into the evenings I toss my sad nets
to that sea which stirs your ocean eyes.

And from Poem XIII:

Between the lips and the voice, something goes dying.
Something with bird wings, something of anguish and oblivion
The way nets don't hold water.

The fourth section of "The Heights of Macchu Picchu" begins with his admission that "Powerful death invited me many times." But by the sixth section, he finds the resting place that allows him to see the site as sacred, to meditate on his Pan-American vision and see history and future in one continuum:

And then on the ladder of the earth I climbed
. . . .
up to you, Macchu Picchu.
High city of scaled stones,
at last a dwelling where the terrestrial
did not hide in its sleeping clothes.
In you, like two parallel lines,
the cradle of the lightning-bolt and man
rocked together in a thorny wind.

Mother of stone, spume of the condors.

High reef of the human dawn.

Shovel lost in the first sand.

He begins to find a sense of solidarity, of community, as the transform-
ing moment occurs, in which Neruda witnesses the past in the present: "I
felt the sense of community in the construction . . . as if in that construc-
tion man had left behind the truest continuation of his life."

> This was the dwelling, this is the place:
> . . . .
> Here the gold thread was fleeced off the vicuña
> to clothe the love affairs, the tombs, the mothers,
> the king, the prayers, the warriors.

The poem reaches its climax in the twelfth section, where he talks
to the slaves who built Machu Picchu:

> Rise up and be born with me, brother.
>
> From the deepest reaches of your
> disseminated sorrow, give me your hand.
> You will not return from the depths of rock.
> You will not return from subterranean time.
> It will not return, your hardened voice.
> They will not return, your drilled-out eyes.
> Look at me from the depths of the earth,
> plowman, weaver, silent shepherd:
> tender of the guardian guanacos:
> mason of the impossible scaffold:
> water-bearer of Andean tears:
> goldsmith of crushed fingers:
> farmer trembling on the seed:
> potter poured out into your clay:

bring all your old buried sorrows
to the cup of this new life.
Show me your blood and your furrow,
say to me: here I was punished
because the gem didn't shine or the earth
didn't deliver the stone or the grain on time:
. . . .
I come to speak through your dead mouth.

How did Neruda have the privilege to speak through them, to speak from them? Neruda strove to tell the history from the point of view of the people themselves, not the history told by the conquerors.

The canto ends:

Through the earth unite all
the silent and split lips
and from the depths speak to me all night long
as if we were anchored together,
tell me everything, chain by chain,
link by link and step by step,
sharpen the knives you kept,
place them in my chest and in my hand,
like a river of yellow lightning,
like a river of buried jaguars,
and let me weep, hours, days, years,
blind ages, stellar centuries.
. . . .
Come to my veins and my mouth.

Speak through my words and my blood.[*]

He sees with their eyes; they see with his. The "poet's calling" conveys a sense of vocation and, at the same time, a sense of activity: the

---

[*] Complete poem in Appendix I.

poet is simultaneously called and is calling to others, and through his voice, he gives voice to others' calls.

The Chilean Raúl Zurita, a modern master in poetry of resistance, feels this is the single greatest poem in the history of the Spanish language. For the 2014 anthology *Pinholes in the Night: Essential Poems from Latin America,* which Zurita edited (with Forrest Gander), the only selected poems by Neruda were cantos from "The Heights of Macchu Picchu." Magdalena Edwards, interviewing Zurita and Gander for the *Los Angeles Review of Books,* noted there was nothing from the *Residence*s: "How to choose in this case?"

Zurita explained that he made his selections based on "which poem makes a poet exactly who that poet is." To choose a poem from *Residence* is to choose a great work, "no doubt, one of the two or three most powerful works of 20th century poetry." But such a poem is one by an individual first named Ricardo Neftalí Reyes Basoalto, then Pablo Neruda. To choose "The Heights of Macchu Picchu," however, "is not simply to choose the most extraordinary poem in the language, it is to choose the language; that is to say, it is to choose the speech of a continent." It is attempting to wash away the crimes that came with the imposition of Spanish language on the continent through the poetic use of that very same language. For Zurita, then, choosing "Macchu Picchu" over any other poem by Neruda was to "wager on a new destiny: not for a single individual"—like the narrator of *Residence*—"but for everyone."

Neruda's poems for the Spanish Republic and the survival of Stalingrad were reactions to real-time events. "Macchu Picchu" reached far back in history. Yet unlike many of Neruda's poems to come, it is not merely Communist propaganda. Neruda's commitment to the workers who built Machu Picchu drew from a well that he had now dug and explored deeply, one of empathy and commitment that he attached to the working class on a much broader scale through a more enabled technique than he first had as a teenager with "Railroad Roundhouses at Night."

This empathy is what allowed him to audaciously appoint himself as the workers' spokesman, to say, "I've come to speak through your dead mouths," to implore, "Come to my veins and my mouth." But despite his political commitment and work, had he really earned this privilege? It was certainly a lofty assertion that few others would be bold enough to make. But Neruda's persona at this point was so great that he pulled it off, even more so because he used it so skillfully as a poetic device. It situates the poem, and the poem's speaker, so as to bring together the realities of the past and present. Regardless of his arrogance, "Macchu Picchu" succeeds and is one of the century's richest, most dynamic poems. For while Neruda proclaims that he is the one through whom the dead slaves will speak, it is in the end not about him, as Zurita emphasizes, but rather an exploration of the past as a way to create a better destiny for everyone.

And the acceptance by the general readership of Neruda as the voice of the fallen and the downtrodden further established the persona he was creating for himself, the sense of responsibility—one that he had felt ever since he began writing as a teenager. In a 1965 interview with the English critic J. M. Cohen, Neruda said, "The problem of the future in our world and in yours is man himself. In my poem 'The Heights of Macchu Picchu,' I use a vision of ancient men to understand the men of today. From the Inca to the Indian, from the Aztec to the contemporary Mexican peasant, our homeland, America, has magnificent mountains, rivers, deserts, and mines rich in minerals. Yet the inhabitants of this generous land live in great poverty. What then should be the poet's duty?"

CHAPTER FIFTEEN

SENATOR NERUDA

You, what did you do? Did your word ever come
for your brother of the deep mines,
for the pain of the betrayed,
did your syllable in flames ever come
to cry out for justice, to defend your people?
—"The Traitor"

Each time Neruda came back from abroad, whether from the Far East, Spain, or Mexico, he arrived transformed. In Lima, he told the journalist Jorge Falcón, "I am going to Chile because I have been missing it for quite some time now. I have been traveling around different countries for sixteen years, with just short trips to my country. Now, I want, I desire, to remain there, and participate more directly in its politics." He expressed his belief that a unified Left presented the strongest hope for the future of Chile, and a strong Chile would help make all of South America stronger. He would retire from the diplomatic corps.

Once in Chile, while they waited for the completion of some restorations of the new house they bought on Avenida Lynch, the Nerudas stayed at the apartment of Sylvia Thayer. Sylvia was an acclaimed actress and the sister of Neruda's pal Hinojosa, who had accompanied him to the Far East in his youth. Antonia Ramos, a young Argentine studying at the University of Chile, was also staying at the apartment. She wrote:

> Pablo was already fat then, and bald. [Delia] was thin, very refined, with magnificent manners . . . Pablo was excessively bohemian. They arrived at two A.M., woke everyone up, and stayed up talking until four or five o'clock in the morning. The house became a beehive of Spanish refugees, people from Mexico; it was impossible to imagine how she lived her life around him and his bohemian lifestyle. They had that easygoing mentality of the free; nothing at all mattered to them. But she was serious. She took care of vulgar, everyday things patiently and stylishly. She was elegance itself; he was like an *enfant terrible.*

Soon the repairs on their new home were finished, and after a tour of Chile giving lectures, they moved in. In memory of their time in Mexico, they named the house La Michoacán. Delia's family had sold a building in Argentina, and with that money the Nerudas were more stable financially; they also received help from the public employees' pension fund, now that Neruda had officially retired from the diplomatic corps. It was a medium-sized house with a small office for Pablo and a large backyard, where they built a rough amphitheater-style stage dedicated to Lorca and a studio for Delia to practice her art, in particular her printmaking. They modeled the home on the typical style of the indigenous or mestizo houses of Michoacán: thick rafters and old wood. Neruda's butterfly collection was displayed in a large frame next to the rustic dining table and chairs in front of the fireplace. He would sit outside on a stump below a huge oak tree and write his poetry.

Neruda was closely involved with the design of his houses. They were so particular, not just because he needed an environment that inspired writing, or because he derived great satisfaction from entertaining friends, but also due to his innate creativity, which resulted in environments that reflected his imagination and, in turn, sparked his imagination anew.

Out of all the objects and collections at La Michoacán, what most stood out to the Chilean writer José Donoso was a bar decorated with turn-of-the-century postcards, a great novelty then. He was always impressed by Neruda's gift "to see beyond the usual" and pick out things, either real or abstract, that only he noticed. His ability to establish a deep relationship between himself and his surroundings was, Donoso believed, essential: "He was a creator in both the poetic and the lived sense."

Neruda enjoyed sharing his homes with others. Diego Muñoz had recently begun a relationship with Inés Valenzuela, who was only eighteen at the time. Neruda and Delia invited them to share the house with them. Delia was ten years older than Inés's mother, but Inés thought of her differently. "I never thought about la Hormiga as an older person," she recalled in an interview sixty years later. Delia was "very, very young from within," and joyful. Inés felt instantly at home with her new sixty-year-old friend. Delia was "able to make everyone who came to her home—everyone she knew—feel good."

Rafael Alberti also had a lasting impression of life at La Michoacán when he visited Chile, invited by Neruda to give readings and talks. During his stay, Neruda gave a number of parties there in Alberti's honor, attended by an eclectic mix of poets, writers, politicians, painters, and complete strangers. One night, Alberti saw Neruda open the kitchen door to find a group of strange-looking gate-crashers holding glasses of wine as they fried an enormous number of eggs in a huge pan. Amused and puzzled, Neruda simply signaled to Alberti, and the two withdrew silently. "They must know what they're doing," Neruda said to Alberti. "I've no idea who they are. They've never been here before."

Neruda led Alberti away from the kitchen and other guests to a separate room, closing the door carefully behind him. He served his friend a large glass of wine and poured a generous whiskey for himself, then said, "I'm going to read you something that I think is quite important, that nobody knows about yet." As Alberti described it, "in his slow, sleepy voice," Neruda read him all of "The Heights of Macchu Picchu," which he was just finishing. When the long and secret reading was over, they returned to the party, which was in full swing.

During these parties, Neruda would sometimes go to La Vega Central himself and buy enormous pieces of cheese for the party, usually *mantecoso,* which is relatively soft, like butter on the tongue. He'd also put out several demijohns of local wine, nothing fancy. Everybody helped him- or herself to wine, bread, and those huge cheeses, as the conversation wove around the table, creating a sense of the communal.

*

While living the bohemian life at La Michoacán, Neruda ratcheted up his activism and public readings. On November 7, 1943, Neruda read "New Love Song for Stalingrad" to a gigantic crowd at the National Stadium in celebration of the twenty-sixth anniversary of the October Revolution. It was broadcast by radio throughout the country. Chile, along with many other Latin American countries, had not recognized the Soviet Union since the 1917 revolution; Neruda demanded recognition now.

And then, in December 1944, the Chilean Communist Party named its candidates for the parliamentary elections coming in March 1945. Though he was still not an official member, the party asked Neruda to be a senatorial candidate for the northern desert mining provinces of Tarapacá and Antofagasta. There were five Senate seats up for election, and this arid region was where the Communist Party had the most strength from the large working-class population. Neruda would likely be a very popular candidate there. The poet accepted the nomination.

The Atacama Desert, which covers northern Chile, is the driest desert in the world. The sand was filled with numerous valuable minerals, most importantly an abundance of copper and crucial nitrate fields. These held the ingredients that yielded sodium nitrate, or Chilean saltpeter, a superior form of gunpowder and a lucrative export to countries fighting wars around the world. Sodium nitrate was also mined as a profitable soil fertilizer (until cheaper synthetics did it in). The importance of the region's minerals was so great that in 1879, Chile started the War of the Pacific against Bolivia and Peru to take the top of the desert all for itself. (Chile emerged victorious in 1884; Bolivia lost its coastal access, and Peru, its southern territory.) Chile captured Peru's most valuable nitrate province, suddenly bringing the mines there under Chilean control. The Peruvian government had nationalized its mines by going into foreign debt, a burden the Chilean government did not want to assume. Instead, it enabled private entrepreneurs to control the resources that became the main source of revenue for the Chilean state, initiating a wave of economic expansion, while providing a bonanza to the new private mine owners.

Within the next few years, one enterprising Englishman, John Thomas North, had amassed so many holdings that he was deemed the "Nitrate King." Before the end of the 1880s, the value and expanse of the resources he controlled seemed to constitute a state within a state. And it wasn't just the nitrate fields that British capital had bought; Britons controlled the majority of Chile's means of production: the mines, the railroads, and the banks that funded the economy and reaped its rewards. The British, and then later the United States, took Spain's place in the economic exploitation of the country and its people.

Many would later criticize the government for not having kept the mines in Chilean hands, but others argued the country simply couldn't afford it and pointed toward the windfall the treasury gained from the export taxes. As then-president Domingo Santa María put it: "Let the gringos work the nitrate freely. I shall be waiting at the door."

The Chilean poor migrated in great numbers to work the mines in the north, where they were paid pitiful wages and often lived in grim company housing or shantytowns set up around the mines. As had happened throughout Latin America—in the banana industry, for example—workers were forced to rely on the company store for their provisions. The already miserable plight of the Chilean proletariat then became desperate with the virtual collapse of the economy in 1919. Not only was there a slowdown in the demand for minerals after the end of World War I, but Germany had invented a synthetic substitute for sodium nitrate, which sold at prices lower than Chile's saltpeter. Thousands of workers lost their jobs and made their way to Santiago looking for any form of employment. They lived in sprawling, filthy tenements. Many became politically active and radicalized.

The government's continual repression of the workers' movement during this time shaped the country's politics, creating tremendous tensions and divisions that lingered throughout the twentieth century. Even before the economy's collapse, the Chilean armed forces began breaking up strikes and protecting the (mostly foreign) companies. There was a massacre of fifty-eight workers (with more than three hundred injured) in Antofagasta in 1906 and another bloodbath in Iquique the following year. In the first decade of the twentieth century, Chile's tireless socialist labor leader, Luis Emilio Recabarren, was elected to the National Congress with the votes of the workers. Recabarren formed the Socialist Workers Party in 1912. Ten years later he completed his conversion to Marxism and formed the Chilean Communist Party. Neruda renders his interpretation of this history in the *Canto General* poem "Recabarren (1921)":

It is the Chilean interrupted
by unemployment and death.

It is the enduring, rugged Chilean,
survivor of the labor
or shrouded by the salt.

It was there that this captain of the people
arrived with his pamphlets.
He took the solitary offended man,
who, wrapping his broken blankets
over his hungry children,
accepted the fierce
injustices, and he told him:
"Join your voice to another voice,"
"Join your hand to another hand."
. . . .
He organized the loneliness,
he took books and songs
to the walls of terror,
he united a complaint with another complaint

and the slave without voice or mouth,
the extended suffering,
was named, it was called Pueblo,[*]
Proletariat, Union,
it took on a persona and elegance.
. . . .
and it was called Party.
Communist
Party

Workers' strikes were so rampant in 1920 that President Sanfuentes declared a state of siege in Santiago and Valparaíso. In 1925, soldiers gunned down more than twelve hundred nitrate workers at La Coruña, and some two hundred people were arrested at the Industrial Workers of the World's headquarters in Valparaíso. Workers' newspapers were banished, union headquarters ransacked, labor leaders arrested. Recabarren called for a nonviolent revolution. Over the following decades, led by the Communist Party, and granted some breathing room by less repressive administrations in Santiago, the workers in the north developed one of Latin America's most organized and influential movements.

Neruda wasn't alone as he launched his Senate campaign in this tumultuous and economically important region. He found a lieutenant in a former nitrate worker, Elías Lafertte Gaviño, a cofounder of the Socialist Workers Party and leader of its newer incarnation, the Chilean Communist Party. Lafertte was running for the other Senate seat in the north. They took their campaign to the workers in the mines, involving themselves in their daily lives, endorsing their calls for better wages, education, and working conditions.

Lafertte wrote about visiting a worker's living quarters in company housing at a nitrate mine:

---

[*]   As Alastair Reid writes, "The word *pueblo* invokes in Spanish much more than either a place or the people who inhabit it: it humanizes a place as a state of being, as a set of values and allegiances. English has nothing quite as embracing."

I enter her home and she shows me makeshift beds, some of them on the ground, a table made of boxes and only one chair for the entire house. They didn't build a kitchen for the houses . . . there's no toilet or bathroom in the camp, and since water is scarce, they sometimes have to buy it. The eczema and ulcers caused by the acids of the nitrate process are just one more problem in their fearful lives.

On February 24, 1945, Neruda and Lafertte held a huge rally at the stadium of the province's largest city, Antofagasta, presided over by the city's mayor and congressman, both Communists. Neruda read a new poem, "Salute to the North," with economical phrasing and rhymed consonants throughout, which effectively worked as a campaign speech (the rhymes are lost in translation):

North, I finally arrive at your wild
mineral silence of yesterday and today,
seeking your voice and to find my own,
and I don't bring you an empty heart:
    I bring you everything that I am.[*]

Neruda would be true to his verse; he and Lafertte were elected senators on March 4. Up and down the length of Chile, the Communist Party felt victorious, with two other senators and twenty deputies elected.

---

[*] The poem's ability to serve as effective political rhetoric revolves around the metaphor that Neruda uses throughout. He begins by presenting the image of the motherland as a svelte woman bathed in sweat, her body made of the people. From there the verse takes us to the Communist Party's founder, Recabarren, and then to Neruda's running mate, Lafertte, whose salty sweat and tears, Neruda says, remind us of saltpeter, a mineral that takes us back to the desert, the motherland itself. He not only exalts the leaders, but effectively says that they embody the country itself. Besides the metaphor, the lyrical sound (lost in translation) was key to the poem's ability to serve as a campaign speech. To raise funds, the campaign sold pamphlets with the poem printed inside and a picture of Neruda on the front.

That same month Neruda was awarded the Chilean National Prize for Literature, despite a strong political opposition within the current conservative government's self-selected jury. "This triumph over prejudice and anti-communist action," Neruda said, "with which they want to poison the world to take advantage of the leftover remnants of Nazism, is more than a personal triumph for me; it represents the hope that my homeland will achieve a more prestigious status in the world as a democratic nation." But divisive tension between communists and capitalists was brimming. The McCarthy era had begun, and anti-communist fever was being fanned in the United States and down throughout Latin America.

During his years in the Senate, Neruda demonstrated a duality in his character that many have remarked upon. Not only did he write great poetry, including political poetry, but he also proved to be an agile politician. He was much more than just a renowned figure whom the party could deploy as a candidate to capture a seat. Instead he galvanized the chamber on a variety of issues, from demanding women's suffrage—which was realized in 1949—to labor rights. His political shrewdness was such that, over the following decades, many politicians and party members would go to Isla Negra to discuss their concerns.

Neruda loved part of this new life and loathed the rest. He may have been a very effective politician, but that didn't mean he always enjoyed serving the public, as he commented in an interview in the Venezuelan newspaper *El Nacional*: "In politics, not everything can be productive, brilliant action: the strongest, most absorbing part is the everyday, routine work, the bureaucratic function of the politician that does not have an apparent objective or point, but is inevitable nonetheless."

He found the social and personal aspects—writing and answering letters, receiving and greeting people, the constant meetings, talks, bland dinner parties—to be "extremely boring and tiresome, and worse yet, it takes time that could be used to write poetry." Politics and literature were both such "overwhelming, all-consuming occupations that they are incompatible." He wrote much less during this time, but what he wrote hit its mark.

On July 8, at a ceremony in the Teatro Caupolicán, Neruda officially joined the Chilean Communist Party. Six days later, he traveled to São Paulo, Brazil, for a public celebration of Luís Carlos Prestes, the leftist leader who'd been forbidden release from prison for his mother's funeral in Mexico, setting off a firestorm. Prestes had now been let free after a decade of incarceration. Jorge Amado, one of Brazil's greatest writers and a member of the Brazilian Communist Party, received Neruda for the Prestes freedom celebration; the two would be friends for life.

Amado, Neruda, and Prestes spoke before a crowd of more than one hundred thousand enthusiastic people at the Estádio do Pacaembu. Neruda read a poem, written for the occasion, which started by him telling the crowd

> How many things I'd like to tell you today, Brazilians,
> how many stories, struggles, disappointments, victories
> harbored in my heart for many years, unexpressed thoughts
> and greetings.

The greetings he carried included words spoken to him from Chilean workers, miners, stonemasons, sailors; even the snow, cloud, and fog; and "the little girl who gave me some ears of grain":

> Their message was one. It was: Greetings to Prestes.
> Go look for him, they told me, in the jungles and rivers.
> Remove his shackles, look for his cell, call him.
> And if they don't let you talk to him, look at him until
> your eyes are tired, and tell us tomorrow what you've seen.
> —"Spoken in Pacaembú (Brazil, 1945)"

★

While Neruda was in Brazil, nitrate workers held a strike in northern Chile. Companies had broken the union's negotiated freeze on company store prices. Violence erupted between the workers and the authorities. Then the government intervened and outlawed unions in Tarapacá. Senators Lafertte and Neruda, now back in the country, tried to visit the mines but were denied entry. On January 28 the Chilean Workers Federation organized a solidarity march in Santiago. Afterward, many of the thousands of participants gathered in Plaza Bulnes, in front of the presidential palace. There was intense friction between the protesters and the police, and eventually the police fired into the crowd, killing six and wounding many more.

The poetry Neruda wrote at the time, which would fill *Canto General,* was blunt and politically charged, progressive and reactionary. He wrote not just about the history of the Americas but of current events, in such poems as "The Corpses in the Plaza (January 28, 1946, Santiago de Chile)":

> In the middle of the Plaza this crime was committed.
> The brushwood didn't hide the people's
> pure blood, nor was it swallowed by the pampa's sand.
>
> Nobody hid this crime.
>
> This crime was committed in the middle of the motherland.

In the midst of all this, Neruda once again received a cable from Carlos Morla Lynch, saying that Maruca was now in Belgium and that she still wanted to be reunited with her husband. She insisted that she hadn't received money from him in nearly six months. Neruda responded through the Ministry of Foreign Affairs that even though he was now divorced, he was still willing to send her money, and asked for her address in Belgium. That same day, August 22, Morla Lynch sent another message, saying that Señora Neruda denied that they were divorced and wanted her passage paid to Peru or Chile. Neruda stalled.

In January, Chile's president, Juan Antonio Ríos, had resigned; he was dying of cancer. As new elections were called for, the growing conservative middle class created a split in the Radical Party. One faction of the Radicals created an alliance with the Left, including the Communists. They nominated Gabriel González Videla as their presidential candidate. His exaggerated, flamboyant left-wing stance irritated the more conservative elements of the Radical Party. This was a major reason for the split.

Neruda, with his charisma and ability to bond with the people, was named the campaign's top communications official. He was to spread González Videla's image everywhere, "even into soup," according to the Chilean Communist politician and writer Volodia Teitelboim. At the kickoff to the campaign, Neruda read one of many ballads he would recite across the country, this one specifically for the candidate. The lines, the second and fourth rhyming, were sometimes stirring:[*]

> In the north the copper worker,
> in the south the railroad worker,
> from one end of the country to the other,
> the people call him "Gabriel."

Neruda campaigned all over the country, on the radio, and in the newspapers (television in Chile was still nearly a decade away). On September 4, 1946, Neruda's candidate won with 40 percent of the vote, as the Right's vote was split between two other candidates. According to the Chilean constitution at the time, however, since he didn't win a majority, González Videla had to be voted in by the National Congress. Violent altercations signaled the political polarization in the country, but González Videla was ultimately named president, after he composed a diverse cabinet and struck a secret deal with center-left Christian Democrats and some on the Right.

As soon as González Videla took office, he fulfilled his campaign promise to the Left by rescinding rural unionization restrictions. Almost immediately afterward, he made good on his secret deal with the Right, and its large constituent of landowners, and backed legislation

---

[*]   Lost in translation is the rhyme between "obrero del riel" (railroad worker) and "Gabriel."

that prohibited the new campesino unions from striking and limited their collective bargaining powers, among other restrictions.

This betrayal didn't stop the Communists from promoting unionization efforts, now more than ever. The people were responding to them, and they did have party members in the cabinet and high up in various government ministries. They took their fight to both the mines and the cities, advocating for the workers' quality of life and the right to organize. Their focus was on class struggle. The unions became the most effective tool to advance the Far Left and Communists' front, and strikes were the most practical mechanism.

Meanwhile, the economy was lagging, and González Videla switched his legislative priorities away from the social reforms he had pledged to the Left and concentrated on promoting growth through industrialization, with no provisions that would allow workers to benefit from any increase in profits. He began to blame the Communists for exacerbating the country's economic troubles.

By now, the United States had a significant influence on the Chilean economy through U.S. mining companies and the country's importation of Chilean copper. It exerted great pressure on González Videla to crack down on the unionization of the mine workers in an effort to protect its economic interests. In addition, the Cold War was gearing up; Latin America would be a major battleground of that power struggle for the rest of the century, with U.S. foreign policy strategies focused on containing the threat of communism and Soviet influence in the hemisphere. González Videla seemed to be stuck with the choice of either pleasing Washington or aligning with the Soviets. He tried to please everyone, scrambling to hold on to some semblance of support and power, juggling different parties and factions to the left and to the right, abandoning whatever ideals he may have held in the process.

The divided government had an immediate impact on Neruda in late 1946. In December, President González Videla sent the Senate his nomination of Neruda to be ambassador extraordinary and plenipotentiary before the Italian government. González Videla assumed he was still enjoying his honeymoon with the Communists and wanted to reward his campaign's chief of PR, but the marriage was about to fall apart. Members of the Liberal Party sided with the Right and voted against the poet's nomination. The result was a tie. González Videla met with leaders of the Liberal Party, asking for their support, but they refused to vote for a member of the Communist Party. The president withdrew the nomination.

As 1947 began, political tensions in the Chilean government continued to rise, inflamed by the Chilean workers' movement. On February 26, Neruda had just come back from a trip to the north, where he had visited a nitrate miners' strike. He announced in the Senate why the strikes were necessary:

> I had the opportunity to compile the necessary data: I have spent time with workers, sleeping in their dormitories, and over the past few days I have seen their work on the pampa, with the machines. Some of the jobs they do could be classified as among the hardest work done on this planet. Yet their salaries are barely enough to cover their living expenses, and naturally, they are not enough to meet any needs for cultural enrichment . . .

He went on to say that conditions were so horrendous in the mines held jointly by the Tarapacá and Antofagasta companies that there were only six showers for two thousand people and practically no latrines. "Mr. President," he pleaded, "how can we tolerate the fact that our fellow citizens are subject to this ignominious exploitation?!"

Neruda gave many lengthy speeches in the Senate throughout his short tenure about issues ranging from the dictatorship in Paraguay to an homage to Gabriela Mistral to women's suffrage. He was also active in the Communist Party's campaign for that year's municipal election. On the first Sunday of April 1947, the Communists made significant electoral gains, winning 16.5 percent of the vote. It was a substantial percentage within a system that included many parties and factions. The Communists were now the third most popular party in the country, behind the Radicals and Conservatives. Even though it was only a municipal election, it had major repercussions, setting in motion a chain of dramatic, often violent events.

The Communists were gaining ground in Chile. They held key positions in the cabinet, they had more members in other government posts up and down the length of the country, and, pivotally, they had the support of the unions. They were able to put class struggle forward as a primary political focus for the country. The other parties and the president saw this clearly. What's more, the Radical and Liberal Parties were losing traction with voters. They and the other parties had already felt the Communists were getting too much out of González Videla's presidency, and now they were further weakened while their adversaries were stronger. Unable to compete within the government, they pulled out of it, resigning their posts. Even the Socialists didn't support the Communists' power, though they wouldn't work with the Right either.

The president felt trapped; his alliance had fallen apart, and he didn't have congressional support. The day after the municipal elections, Volodia Teitelboim, the Communist Party's representative to the president, and Ricardo Fonseca, the party's secretary-general, were asked by González Videla to come to La Moneda. Teitelboim wrote:

> We thought that it would begin with a few positive words about the win. But he met us in a horrible mood. He became angry, like a blind bull. He couldn't accept that the Communists could become a grand party through the power of the ballot box. He used an expression that became popular later, asking us to "submerge" ourselves. "You need to submerge yourselves in the darkness. Be like fish, don't make noise, and stay somewhere where no one sees you. That is a condition for you to survive. Otherwise, you will succumb."

The president asked three of the Communist Party members from his cabinet to resign. They complied. González Videla replaced them with members of his Radical Party, a move that the Right welcomed.

Soon, a heightened battle between the Communists and workers and the government broke out. Incensed by the president's actions, the Left took to the streets and directly challenged the government. The winds of class warfare were blowing from the Andes to the Pacific, from the desert north to the southern coalfields.

As hard as the Left fought, the government fought back. The United States, with its vital economic interests in Chile, used its leverage to have González Videla unleash a campaign of both propaganda and policy to provoke an anti-communist backlash all over the country. Communist leaders were increasingly imprisoned. The government pointed to the party as the cause of the nation's problems. Violent confrontations continued. In June, for example, bus drivers and associated workers struck in Santiago. The government ordered the military to intervene. Four workers were killed, twenty injured, and Communist and union leaders jailed. The president declared a state of emergency in Santiago.

Then, on August 22, 1947, the National Congress approved the president's Law for the Defense of Democracy, which would have severe repercussions for years. It would effectively outlaw the Communist Party and disenfranchise its members, expelling them from the labor movement, universities, and public office. The law also gave the government more power to declare states of emergency to suppress any threat to commercial production or "national order."

On October 6, the U.S. ambassador to Chile, the writer Claude Bowers, cabled Washington: "González Videla declared war on Communism as a result of what he claims is a Communist plot to overthrow the Government and obtain control of the production (in order to deprive the United States of the use in an emergency) of strategic raw materials, namely copper and nitrates." The United States assured the Chilean president that emergency shipments of coal would be made available if the ongoing miners' strikes continued. On October 9, Ambassador Bowers cabled Washington: "Our war with Communists is on two fronts, Europe and South America." Four days later, he added, "The issue is clear as crystal—communism or democracy."

In the Senate that same day, Neruda defended the coal strikes and cited a *New York Times* editorial written two days earlier: "Are the Chilean miners well paid, well fed, well housed, with sufficient medical care and a reasonable hope of security in their old age? The answer obviously is in the negative." If the answer were reversed, "communism would have had little appeal."

The Chilean government, however, addressed none of these issues. In a bold political move, on October 21, González Videla broke diplomatic ties with the Soviet Union and Yugoslavia, justifying the move by pointing to the Chilean labor situation. The next morning, two shifts of workers at one of the largest submarine coal mines in Lota refused to return to the surface, occupying the mine from within. The workers demanded that the armed forces leave the area and that imprisoned labor leaders be set free. They were forced out by tear gas, and three hundred of them were jailed on the desolate Santa María island off of Patagonia. Meanwhile, hundreds of Communist leaders and others deemed "subversives" under the new Law for the Defense of Democracy were being held in a concentration camp in Pisagua on the country's northern coast.* The president appointed a thirty-three-year-old army captain named Augusto Pinochet to direct the camp.

González Videla continued with a litany of accusations of unpatriotic intentions against the Left, especially the labor movement. He broke off diplomatic relations with all Communist nations, claiming the Soviet Union and Czechoslovakia had infiltrated the country. The red scare now raged throughout the Americas: in Argentina, Juan Perón outlawed the Argentine Communist Party and there were plans to deny all Communists the right to vote, and the House Un-American Activities Committee investigations were at their height in the United States.

In Chile, the government's widening persecution and imprisonment of Communist labor leaders provoked precisely what those measures were intended to prevent, as mine and railway workers went on strike

---

* The Ibáñez dictatorship had first established Pisagua at the end of the 1920s to intern homosexuals.

all over the north. The military was called in to maintain order; the soldiers were far from gentle. Those arrested were sent to Pisagua, which Neruda would decry as a "Nazi-style concentration camp." On the Senate floor on October 21, Neruda raised his voice: "Now even Congress is subject to censorship. You can't even talk now!" The poet did not hold back his anger, shouting, "There have been murders in the coal-mining region!" Afterward, incensed, he told his friend Tomás Lago that González Videla was a "traitor. A despicable person of the highest order."

The government shut down the Communist newspaper *El Siglo* on November 27. With the Chilean press under such censorship, Neruda felt an "unavoidable duty, in this tragic time, to clarify the situation in Chile" for the world, and he did so through a long article for his friend Miguel Otero Silva to publish in his Caracas paper, *El Nacional*. He described it as an "intimate letter to millions," and his urgency was expressed in its title: "The Crisis of Democracy in Chile Is a Dramatic Warning for Our Continent." He began with his need to "let all my friends throughout the continent know about the despicable situation in Chile right now . . . since the North American news monopolies have surely carried out the same strategy as they have before in other areas, falsifying the truth and distorting the reality of the facts." Throughout the piece, he argued that the breakdown of democracy and basic rights that was taking place in Chile, due to the Cold War and other factors, could easily take place in any other country in the region, and more so if the situation in his country was not rectified soon.

Neruda further detailed the situation in Chile: that the Communist members of the cabinet were expelled after they courageously crusaded to make sure the government kept its promises to the Chilean people; that the "new, active, and popular style of politics" the Left was practicing "deeply offended the sensibilities of the old, feudal Chilean oligarchy, which had increasingly greater influence over the president"; and that "the agents of North American imperialism, in the form of powerful companies in Chile—all-powerful, one might say," which own "all of Chile's mineral deposits"—lost no time in wrapping their many tentacles around the recently elected president.

Neruda then explained the actions of González Videla by citing a cable that a British reporter for the *News Chronicle* had sent back to London that past June: "President González Videla thinks that the war between Russia and the USA will begin in less than three months, and current internal and external political conditions in Chile are based on that theory."

Neruda also tried to explain what the Left, in particular the Communists, was fighting for. Their ambitious agenda included distributing uncultivated land to landless campesinos, wage equality between men and women, the nationalization of major industries, the creation of a state bank like the Federal Reserve, and a national initiative to build public housing on a massive scale.

Neruda described the abuse of workers and labor leaders in his country, and warned that the repression would soon spread throughout Latin America. The United States' "puppet regimes . . . will perpetuate the cycle of sinister slavery for our countries." Such a puppet regime, he said, "will use the [conservative, anti-communist] *Reader's Digest* as his bible," combined with police tactics, to enact "torture, prison, and exile."

The article was reprinted and circulated in Chile. It was published and distributed throughout Latin America, as well as in the Soviet Union and other countries. On the Senate floor on December 10, Neruda criticized the government again for its terror tactics and censuring of the press. He lambasted the U.S. State Department for spreading anti-communist repression throughout the continent.

But his colleagues were not impressed. Under the Chilean constitution, all senators are privileged to certain protections, including immunity from legal prosecutions. On Christmas Day 1947, the Chilean government petitioned the Supreme Court "to strip Senator Neruda of his immunity for his violation of the Internal State Security Law" and for "denigrating Chile abroad and calumny and slander against the president."

But Neruda was not deterred. On December 30, he took to the Senate floor once again, to cheer the Panamanian parliament for having refused to grant the United States some of its land for military bases. Panama, he said, was an example and hope for all of Latin America, a sharp contrast to González Videla's regime. On January 5, the court of appeals ruled fifteen to one that Neruda's "false" words against the government were grounds to strip him of his immunity. Neruda and his lawyers immediately appealed.

The next day, Neruda again spoke on the Senate floor, this time in a special session. Before it started, a conservative senator asked Arturo Alessandri, the former president of the republic and current president of the Senate, to stop the session on the grounds that there were no pending issues. Rudecindo Ortega Mason, who had first showed Neruda's poems to *Claridad,* was a recently elected senator himself.* Senator Mason joined Alessandri in arguing vigorously that if they prevented Neruda from speaking, it would amount to censure. They failed to persuade the chamber, and the Senate voted in favor of closing the session, effectively censoring Neruda. Alessandri then resigned in protest and disgust of what had just occurred. His resignation wasn't accepted, though, and after much haggling, Neruda was allowed to speak.

He began his historic speech by announcing that he was returning "to occupy the Senate's attention, in these dramatic times in which our country is living," to address the "Crisis of Democracy" article, which he had written "in defense of the prestige of Chile." He then chastised González Videla, especially for his "reckless political persecution," in order to avoid "criticisms of repressive methods." "This will be the only thing in Chilean history that remains of his presidency," Neruda prophesied.

---

* Five years older than Neruda, he was the son of Charles Mason's daughter Telésfora and Orlando Mason's father, Rudecindo Ortega. He had represented Temuco as a deputy in Congress and later resigned from the Senate in protest against the Law for the Defense of Democracy; a decade later he was appointed as Chile's ambassador to the United Nations, where he served a term as president of the Security Council.

Neruda then shifted into a more sophisticated form of rhetoric:

> Speaking before the Honorable Senate on this day, an ex-
> traordinary memory comes to my mind.
>   On a January 6 like this one—January 6, 1941—a titan of
> struggles and of freedoms, a distinguished president, Frank-
> lin Delano Roosevelt, sent a message to the world of four
> freedoms, which formed the foundation of the future for
> which so many people in the world fought and bled.

He named them: "freedom of speech and expression; freedom of ev-
ery person to worship God in his own way; freedom from want; free-
dom from fear." "That was the world that Roosevelt promised," he said,
but Truman, along with Latin American dictators and the González Vi-
delas of the world, "want a different kind of world. There is no freedom
of speech in Chile; people are not free from fear. [Those] who fight to
free our country from misery are persecuted, mistreated, injured, and
condemned."

The address would later be published under the name "Yo acuso"
("I Accuse"), taken from Émile Zola's 1898 open letter in defense of the
French Jew Alfred Dreyfus, accused of selling secrets to Germany.

The threat of retaliation followed the Nerudas everywhere. Right
after Neruda gave his speech, Delia went to the hairdresser Monsieur
Paul; if they were sent to Pisagua, she wanted to be ready. Neruda had
lost over eleven pounds and was having trouble sleeping.

On January 13, the Senate debated giving the president more emer-
gency powers in certain parts of the country, which would be put under
the control of the armed forces. The president would be given a free
hand to suppress any form of "antipatriotic propaganda" and to restrict
the right to meet and assemble. Neruda continued his outspoken criti-
cism, and after debate on the emergency powers had ended, he began
to read the names of political prisoners at Pisagua, giving homage to
each one. He read more than 450 names until he was cut off by the close
of the Senate session. He continued with the remaining fifty-six names
the next day.

The Senate granted González Videla the extraordinary powers he had asked for in a vote at the end of that session, twenty-eight votes in favor, only eight against. Six days later, the country's appellate court sent the case against Neruda to the Supreme Court.

Meanwhile, the Ministry of Foreign Affairs sent a cable to its diplomatic corps in Brussels, telling them to "give every class of help to allow the legitimate wife of Señor Neruda to travel to Chile." Charges of bigamy against Neruda were coming out in the press, accusing him of still being married to Maruca. The government wanted to bring her to Chile to prove that he had two wives.

On January 21, 1948, Alessandri, still president of the Senate, granted Neruda constitutional permission to leave the country for thirty days. But while Neruda had permission to be absent from the Senate, he did not have permission from the president, who controlled the borders. Neruda asked the Mexican ambassador Pedro de Alba to help him leave Chile. De Alba had the Mexican military attaché accompany Neruda and Delia to the Argentine border in a car with diplomatic plates. But Chilean border police turned them around, claiming the documents to cross the border didn't correspond to the plates and make of their car. The Mexican attaché tried to negotiate, but the police refused. Neruda called the Mexican ambassador, who told him to return to the Mexican embassy in Santiago. Neruda was visibly anxious. He announced he would not leave the embassy because he feared for his life.

Ambassador de Alba wanted to give Neruda asylum in Mexico, but Mexico's minister of foreign affairs directed him not to, fearing an international incident. Neruda didn't want to cause problems for de Alba, so he took a taxi to the home of a friend, Carmen Cuevas, the founder of an influential folk music and dance group. The taxi driver didn't speak to or look at him during the trip. According to Neruda's friend and biographer Margarita Aguirre, when Neruda got out and asked how much the fare was, the driver responded, "You don't owe me anything, Don Pablo, and good luck."

On January 30, young members of an anti-communist organization burned a coffin symbolically marked as Neruda's in Santiago's main plaza. Three days later, Neruda and Delia once again drove to the Argentine border, but they were turned back because his documents used the name Ricardo Neftalí Reyes (he had legally changed his name to Pablo Neruda the year before). The next day, the Supreme Court, in a sixteen-to-one vote, stripped Neruda of his immunity on the grounds that he had published false and tendentious statements. The government officially ordered his arrest.

CHAPTER SIXTEEN

THE FLIGHT

To everyone, to you,
silent beings of the night
who took my hand in the darkness, to you,
lamps,
of immortal light, star lines,
bread of the living, secret brothers,
to everyone, to you,
I say: there's no thanks,
nothing could fill the glasses
of purity,
nothing can
contain all of the sun in the flags
of the invincible springtime
like your quiet dignities.
—"The Fugitive: XII"

The headline splashed across the front pages of the daily papers: "Nationwide Search for Neruda." The articles continued below the bold print: "Numerous personnel are trying to locate the fugitive Communist parliament member . . . the warrant for his arrest, search, and seizure having been issued by the summarizing minister, Mr. Gonzalez Castillo . . ." "In late breaking news we have also been informed that

300 agents were summoned to the theater of investigations to receive important instructions from high-ranking superiors." Neruda's photograph was plastered the length of the nation and rewards for his capture were offered. The radio buzzed with the latest on the Neruda case.

Neruda and Delia went into hiding immediately. For most of 1948 and through the beginning of 1949, the couple lived clandestinely in their own country, looking for a way to get across the border, while hiding out in at least eleven different houses. Agents questioned all of their friends. Police searched no fewer than sixty-three homes, sometimes so close on the trail that they arrived at a home where the couple had been just the day before. There was no warrant for Delia's arrest; as an Argentine national, the Chilean government couldn't touch her. But being close to Neruda, it was imperative she avoid being seen or questioned.

One of the homes where the couple stayed was the small apartment of the young Communists Aida Figueroa and Sergio Insunza. They had already housed a couple of labor leaders from the coal mines of Lota in the south who were fleeing persecution, but they were floored when they opened the door to find Neruda and Delia. Neruda had grown a beard and wore thick-rimmed glasses with no lenses, but the young couple recognized him immediately. Aida was so surprised to see him at her door that she lurched back and hit her head against the wall. Neruda stared at her through those fake glasses, a small Andalusian *calañés* hat perched on his large head, with its traditional conical crown and low upturned flaps, and smiled warmly. Delia was standing next to him, the legendary Hormiga, whom the couple also recognized right away, despite the hand-knitted wool balaclava covering much of her face. Behind them was the young historian and party member Álvaro Jara, directing the operation.

"Come in, come in," Aida welcomed them. The three filed in. Aida and Sergio's two-year-old daughter, Aidita, still awake despite the late hour, looked at the poet with great curiosity and asked, "Why are you wearing glasses with no lenses?" Neruda made an animated, comical face of surprise and laughed heartily.

Aida, then twenty-five years old, had never met either of them before but saw them as "monumental." She was struck by their down-to-earth nature. She offered them her and Sergio's room with a double bed, but they wouldn't accept it. "They went to sleep in the baby's bed, which was a twin-sized mattress, and they slept, according to Pablo, *como cucharitas*—like little spoons."

It was in Aida and Sergio's house that Neruda started working tenaciously on the expanded *Canto General*. He had already written "Macchu Picchu" and began working on what would be the opening section, "A Lamp on Earth," using a typewriter. The young couple were in their final year of law school and left early in the morning for classes, giving Neruda the whole day to write. The apartment was right next to the Parque Forestal, running along the canaled Mapocho River, providing the poet a soothing glimpse of stately old trees, statues, green grass, and couples sitting on benches. Often, when he was writing, Aidita climbed up and down his body as if she were scaling a friendly statue, while Neruda showed no objections or particular distraction.

In the afternoons, he would gather everybody around and read what he had written. Delia, as always, would help correct errors and make suggestions. Aida would fetch him the historical and geographic information he needed from the National Library. The four got along famously and became lifelong friends.

Neruda and Delia hid in Valparaíso for several weeks, with the idea of escaping the country by boat, but the plan never materialized. He was then sequestered again in Santiago, in the house of photographer Lola Falcon, wife of the writer Luis Enrique Délano, a very good friend of Neruda's, who was serving as Chilean consul to New York. Lola had returned to Chile at her husband's urging, as he'd come to see their own situation as precarious in light of what was happening with Chile's politics. The living situation at Lola's house, especially without her husband there, proved difficult. It lacked the carefree atmosphere of the Insunza-Figueroa household. She was nervous; there was constant tension as *La Nación* and the radio gave daily updates on the efforts to detain the fugitive Communist and claimed that his capture was imminent. Party directors visited the house for long meetings behind closed doors with their poet *compañero* and Delia, after which they stayed for a meal. Often the couple's friends would do the same.

Perhaps due to Luis Enrique's role in the New York consulate, their friends thought the Délanos were more well-to-do than they really were. Lola needed help but didn't get any monetary support from Neruda, Delia, or the party. Though she cursed about the situation under her breath, Lola was timid and she didn't complain, even when she constantly had to go out for more provisions for unexpected guests and gatherings. Delia was of little use in the kitchen, and Neruda did not volunteer, so Lola ended up cooking for everyone. She soon sent an SOS to Luis Enrique for him to send additional money.

Pablo maintained a strict work schedule while at the Délano house. He wrote in the morning, usually by hand with a fountain pen and sometimes on a typewriter. His routine was interrupted when Rubén Azócar came and informed him that the police were mounting a major search for Neruda in the neighborhood; at the very least they would certainly come close to the house. The party leadership moved him to another house within hours of what *La Nación* assured its readers was Neruda's imminent capture.

Around this time, Delia and Neruda were given refuge by Víctor Pey, a Spanish engineer who had come to Chile on the *Winnipeg*. After reading the newspapers one afternoon, he and Neruda started an ongoing debate about the situation. Pey pointed out, as many others did, that if the police did actually arrest Neruda, it would create international headlines that would reflect terribly on the government. Neruda wasn't so sure. But the blue-eyed engineer explained that politically, for Neruda and the Left, the best thing that could happen at the time was Neruda's capture. The poet stayed silent and looked at the Spaniard with incredulity. "If they get me, those guys will humiliate me. Be sure of that," Neruda insisted. "I know them. They'll submit me to all types of indignities."

Some felt that the government wasn't really serious about persecuting Neruda, fearing an international public relations scandal. However, there is evidence that the police were indeed actively looking for him during this time, including internal reports made public later. The police noted they were keeping tabs on at least sixteen different cars, but, as the chief of investigations attested in an update to the court of appeals, Neruda had numerous friends in intellectual, political, and diplomatic circles beyond his fellow party members, all of whom could easily hide him. The chief attached a list of sixty-three houses they had under surveillance.

In the last months of 1948, yearning for the camaraderie of his old literary world and wanting feedback on his new poems, Neruda invited a group of close friends over for an intimate reading of his new *Canto General* material. He was staying in Valparaíso, and great lengths were made so that no notice would be made of the gathering. Among the group were his sister, Laura; a Communist congressman; the head of the University of Chile's library; his old friends Rubén Azócar and Tomás Lago; and Lago's wife, Delia Soliman. It was the first time Lago had seen Neruda since the arrest warrant had been issued.

Starting around five o'clock, they drank whiskey and a relaxed Neruda, sitting on a divan, read from more than seventy pages of the gestating *Canto General*. Friends then took turns reading more of Neruda's new poems themselves. Neruda would watch whoever was reading with particular interest, all the while drinking his whiskey. He was so acutely focused on the reading that whenever an errant sound arose that interrupted the recital—someone clearing his throat loudly, or even just the creak of a chair—Neruda would raise his finger to whoever was reading: "Repeat. Repeat. So-and-so coughed and we couldn't hear a thing." Everyone would laugh.

The reading began to pick up a rhythm. By the end, Neruda was interjecting about historical figures or events mentioned in a poem, especially in the section "The Conquistadores." He continued drinking his whiskey, despite the protests of Delia, who was keeping count. The room was cold; there were no heaters. Around ten o'clock they ate dinner together, and by midnight everyone left, content from the brief respite in the midst of such dark times.

A few days later, Tomás Lago brought Juvencio Valle over to the Valparaíso hideout. Valle, Neruda's poet friend from growing up in Temuco, hadn't seen him in several months. He came with his dog

Kutaka, who thrilled Neruda by recognizing him immediately. Valle sat quietly as Neruda and the dog played, the fugitive's heart filling up at this simple, life-affirming pleasure.

Meanwhile, headlines kept saying that Neruda would be caught any day. The persecution of Communists continued throughout 1948. The magazine *Vea* reported:

> As of the evening of Monday, October 27, eight hundred members of the Communist Party, whether union leaders or politicians, were in jail throughout the country. This number is not official, though, because the police are keeping quiet about the extent of the offensive. But despite all the secrecy, we know that there were more than four hundred people arrested in the city of Antofagasta alone—a record.

Neruda, fearful of joining the others in jail, continued to move from one house to another, growing out his beard even fuller, now traveling under the alias Antonio Ruiz Legarreta, ornithologist. For over a year, one plan after another to flee by boat or by car failed to materialize, until Víctor Pey realized that a friend of his could help.

Jorge Bellet was a member of the party and the foreman on a ranch at the foot of the Andes, just above Patagonia. From there, Neruda could cross into Argentina on horseback through an unpatrolled pass, known to few people other than the Mapuche and smugglers. After he and Bellet formulated the plan, Pey sent a message describing it to Galo González, the main leader of the party at the time. A few days later he got the green light.

The departure was delayed for nearly a dozen weeks due to torrential rains in the austral region those winter months. When the road was finally passable, the first step was to drive some five hundred miles south to Valdivia. Pey believed it should be done in just one car, one in optimal mechanical condition. The driver needed to be a mechanic himself and to know the route perfectly. They would also get the name and addresses of reliable, long-term party members who lived in towns along the route where they could stay if anything happened.

In the end, Bellet drove the car himself, a fine-tuned cherry-red Chevrolet on loan from a party member. Getting out of Santiago was the first and most dangerous step. To this end they enlisted Dr. Raúl Bulnes, who had moved to Isla Negra just a month before Delia and Neruda first visited the coastal village and had become warm friends with them. He served as a doctor for the police force, held the rank of captain, and was able to put the green flag of the police on his car. He and Bellet would drive Neruda out of Santiago under the protection of the green and white.

When they went to the house to pick up Neruda, they found the poet, Delia, Galo González, and the Communist senators Carlos Contreras Labarca and Elías Lafertte Gaviño, who had represented the northern provinces with Neruda. Delia had been told that she wouldn't be going with Neruda, and she was irate. The party leadership said the decision was motivated by concern for her safety, though she was an equestrian and Neruda was the one who would have to learn how to ride again, not having been on a horse since childhood. But the operation was too complicated and dangerous, she was told. It would be even more complicated if a couple was involved. She shouted with frustration, but her arguments fell on deaf ears.

Dr. Bulnes's wife, Lala, urged the others to let not just Delia go, but herself as well. She was a well-trained equestrian who could help. But they refused her. "Galo was a male chauvinist," she said. "My husband [who would be part of the operation] wasn't political. I was communist to the soul."

It had been a tough year and a half of living on the run. Delia said years later, "Once Pablo and I were in a car and a policeman hitched a ride. He sat in the front and we sat in the back. We didn't say a word . . . In a sense, that period was very romantic, if you know what I mean." Others, though, have said that despite some very good times and warm bonding, the constant hardship and anxiety did put a strain on the relationship, and guarded resentments erupted with Delia's exclusion from the Andean escape. Some believed Neruda himself was opposed to her going; perhaps he didn't want to be bound to her or responsible for her safety, but he never said as much himself. Later, Delia sensed the separation would mark the beginning of a definitive distancing between them, but in that moment, no one could imagine them no longer being a couple. There were farewell hugs all around, a kiss and long embrace between Pablo and Delia.

They left in the evening, Bellet in the passenger seat, the fugitive senator in the back. Thanks to the police flag, Dr. Bulnes's car passed through a checkpoint on the edge of the city without problems. Around nine at night, at a designated site near the town of Angostura, thirty miles south of Santiago, Neruda and his car met up with Víctor Pey and the red Chevrolet. An exiled Communist congressman, Andrés Escobar, was there as well. A railroad workers' leader, he was experienced in engine mechanics and would be able to help if there were any problems with the car. Five little glasses appeared, which Neruda filled with whiskey. They toasted the mission and the end of González Videla.

Escobar, Bellet, and Neruda got in the Chevy; Pey left with Bulnes. "From this moment on," the poet said to the other two, "Pablo Neruda disappears. You must call me Antonio. I am Antonio Ruiz Legarreta, ornithologist. I'm going to the interior of Valdivia to work on the ranch you're the foreman on, Jorge. This will be our only story until I'm in the hands of our comrades in Argentina." Bellet nodded and drove in silence, all his attention on the road, the fluvial coastal town of Valdivia some five hundred miles away. From there they would turn eastward to the Andes.

They passed horse-drawn carts and carriages, then trucks. The evening air was warm and carried the scents of jasmine and manure. Neruda, who had seemed dejected and uneasy while in hiding, began to fill with hopeful, renewed spirits on the open road toward the expected escape. He broke Bellet's silence and became something of a chatterbox for most of the drive, more animated with every passing town.

In the morning hours he began to name—or try to name—the insects that splattered across the windshield, or the scientific names of trees they saw outside the windows. He talked about the agriculture of the different regions they passed through, about the pink grapes and different wines, as they made their way down and out of the Central Valley, toward where he was born and raised.

They entered what is considered Chile's south. As they were leaving the large town of Chillán, a policeman standing on the side of the road signaled with his baton for them to pull over. Bellet stopped the car. The officer approached the window and asked humbly, "If it's not a bother, can you give me a ride? I'm going about six miles up the road, to my mother's house." Bellet didn't risk making an excuse, despite the fact that Neruda's image had been shared widely in the press and in police bureaus. They dropped the officer at his mother's house without incident.

Eventually, they reached Temuco. Neruda hadn't been there in years, but he couldn't stop to see anyone. It was near noon, and nobody recognized him. He noticed how many of the main roads were now paved, but he also saw the same carts pulled by oxen, manned by the same suffering Mapuche. He felt a longing for his childhood innocence, despite the pain it brought with it. They passed a train that brought back strong memories of his father, and it inspired the poet to tell tales of his childhood to his travel companions.

Finally, they reached Valdivia and the majestic confluence of three rivers that flow along the historic town, surrounded by forests and deep green fields. They stopped only for gas, where Neruda felt the station's attendant staring at him as if he recognized the poet, though if he did, he seemed to collude with the escape, as he said nothing.

They took a boat across the massive Lake Maihue to a small landmass that separated it from another lake, on whose opposite shore sat the ranch. As Neruda would describe to Delia, the boat took them through the black night, the lake moving along a heavy swell. They drank shots of Scotch as they passed dark islands surrounded by wilderness. When they got to the next piece of land, "they lit a bonfire with burlap and wood to guide our landing, and from far away we could see the enormously tall mountain rising from the water . . . Soon we left them behind, [Bellet driving us] in a colossal tractor fast in the darkness, through huge trees, tangles of leaves, roots the size of buildings. In sum, all of my poetry."

After crossing the next lake, which felt to Neruda like approaching the end of the world, they finally reached the shore below the ranch.

A rustic log house on a hill with a roof of oak shingles and chairs fashioned out of branches would provide them shelter.

Leoné Mosalvez was fifteen years old when Neruda, a.k.a. Antonio Ruiz, stayed for a month and a half with her, her parents, and her brother on the ranch. She described him as being a bit fat, with a prominent nose. He went around dressed simply, usually in a sweater and a cap with a small visor that he never took off. He wore thick shoes made for the country. "Sometimes he wrote in some notebooks with thick covers. He went around writing, sometimes in bed, sometimes at the table. The door to his room wasn't closed. When he went out into the fields and forests, he always had a pen and a little notebook." When not with Bellet, riding horses, or writing, she said, he would often go bird-watching, most content when he saw a local woodpecker.

Soon after Neruda's arrival, José Rodríguez, the owner of the Hueinahue hacienda, made a surprise visit to the ranch. For political and economic reasons—he had made a great deal of money from Brazilian imports and land and industrial investments—Rodríguez was bound to President González Videla. But he also held his long-term foreman Bellet in great esteem. Despite Neruda's apprehensions, Bellet thought it best to come clean right away about the fugitive hiding on the property, to avoid any surprises should the owner find out later.

Fortunately, Rodríguez was a lover of poetry. When Bellet told him of Neruda's presence, Rodríguez asked to see him. Bellet drove him to the cabin where Neruda was staying, and Rodríguez got out of the jeep and walked quickly to Neruda. He hugged the poet and beamed: "You're a man I've always wanted to meet. You're the poet I most admire. Invite me to spend some time at your marvelous house, because the house that you're in will always be marvelous."

They drank whiskey and talked for hours, and Neruda read some *Canto General* poems he had just written. In a letter to Delia, Neruda described taking Rodríguez off into the woods and searching for, and naming, a whole collection of insects, just like he had done in the southern forests of his youth.

Meanwhile, Bellet had decided that Juvenal Flores and his brother Juan, ox-packers who worked at the ranch bringing down virgin timber from the heights, would guide Neruda up and through the Lilpela Pass. The Flores brothers would not be told about the escape plan until a day before they left. They weren't told who Antonio Ruiz really was, only that he wanted to learn how to ride horses.

On March 1, 1949, four days before Neruda was to meet several Argentine Communists in San Martín de los Andes on the other side of the cordillera, a serendipitous meeting occurred when Victor Bianchi arrived at the ranch. He was working as an inspector for the Interior Ministry and was an old friend of Neruda's; his brother Manuel Bianchi had helped Neruda get his first consular appointment at the Ministry of Foreign Affairs twenty-two years earlier. He was as colorful as the rest of his clan, an artist who played guitar and loved to serenade women. He also knew the land of southern Chile exceptionally well.

Bianchi had no idea that Neruda was hiding out at Hueinahue and was astonished to see him. Over sips of whiskey, Bianchi declared he'd join the expedition. Bellet wanted to clear a road all the way to the mountain, but Bianchi, who knew the area well, believed that would be a waste of time and energy and devised a more practical route. The party set off in the early morning of March 3.

Neruda carried all the pages of Canto General he had written so far in a saddlebag. Bianchi claimed that he also brought a typewriter. Neruda also brought along a huge, old illustrated volume about the birds of Chile.

The Flores brothers were armed with new pistols. They cleared the ox trail they were following with machetes. The group passed through dense wilderness, up steep inclines, and across a thin river, working slowly through the primeval forest. They came to a sunlit clearing with a gorgeous green meadow resplendent with wildflowers and a purling brook. According to Neruda, they found an ox skull that seemed to be set within a magical circle in the grass, as if it were part of a ritual. The party stopped, and the Flores brothers dismounted. They went over to the skull and put coins and food in its eye sockets, intended to help lost travelers who might find something to help them within the bones. Then they took off their hats and began a strange dance, hopping on one foot around the abandoned skull, moving in the ring of footprints left behind by the many others who had passed there before them. It was there, "alongside my inscrutable colleagues," Neruda asserted twenty-two years later in his Nobel acceptance speech, that he came to "understand in a nebulous sort of way that there existed a link between strangers, that there was an appeal, a plea, and a response in even the most distant and isolated solitudes of this world."

They ate and drank some coffee, and from the meadow they climbed and climbed some more, finally arriving at a rustic hot springs—the Cuihuío Baths—where they would rest and spend the night to prepare for the next day's push over the Lilpela Pass. At the baths, they saw what looked like broken-down stables. They entered one and saw large tree trunks burning for heat, smoke escaping through cracks in the roof. They saw mountains of local cheese and several men lying near the fire, grouped together like sacks. In his Nobel lecture, Neruda described what happened next:

> In the silence, we heard some guitar chords and the words of a song, which, out of the flames and the darkness, brought us the first human voice we had heard since beginning the trip. It was a song of love and longing, a lament of love and nostalgia to the distant spring, to the cities from which we had come, to the infinite extension of life. They did not know who we were; they did not know anything about any fugitives. They did not know my poetry or my name. Or did they? What happened was that by that fire, we sang and ate, and then we walked in the darkness to some rooms. A thermal current of volcanic water passed through them, and we submerged ourselves in this heat that came from the mountains and brought us to its breast.
>
> We swam joyously, submerging ourselves and cleaning off the weight of that long ride. At dawn, when we traveled the final kilometers of the journey that would bring me to where my country ended, we felt fresh, reborn, baptized. We left on our horses, singing, full of a new air, a breath that pushed us toward the great world journey that awaited

me. And I remember vividly: when we wanted to give the people of the mountain a few coins for their songs, their food, the water, the beds, and the roof over our heads—the unexpected shelter we had found—they refused our offering without even a gesture. They had done what they could for us, and nothing more. And in that silent "nothing more," many things were understood; perhaps acknowledgment, perhaps dreams themselves.

They started up on horseback again the next morning. The path through the valley was beautiful, surrounded by great green hills, but it was full of obstacles. They frequently had to cross fallen logs, and the forest growth was so thick it impeded their progress despite the Flores brothers' efforts to clear the way ahead of them. At one point, one of the brothers said that a curving incline ahead was particularly steep and narrow, and that it would be best if Don Antonio dismounted and went on foot for a bit. The word didn't get back in time, or perhaps it was ignored. Neruda advanced sitting poorly in the saddle, without leaning forward to help the horse as it climbed. Everything happened quickly, and Bellet saw Neruda's horse fall to the rocky ground. Neruda was fine; he had been able to break his fall somewhat by holding on to a tree as the horse fell. But according to Bianchi, the horse's face was bloodied, a piece of its tongue torn.

There was no choice but to continue on, but, as Bianchi wrote in his journal about the trip, "the wound set the poet's sentimentalism loose a bit, and soon that wilderness was witness to the most unexpected scenes of tenderness, in the midst of a fugitive's flight out of his country. Pablo caressed his horse, lavishing comforting words and promising not to ride him for the rest of the trip." This led to an absurd argument, with Bianchi and Bellet insisting that Neruda continue on horseback, and Neruda saying it would be ignoble to ride the horse. The poet finally gave in, and they rode on.

Despite sometimes struggling to breathe at the high altitude, Neruda didn't let up. They were nearing the Lilpela Pass when all of a sudden Neruda's horse lost its footing, rearing back and staggering to the edge of the path they were following. "Jump off!" Bianchi yelled, just before the horse fell on its back. Neruda managed to fall into the brush. He was tired and shaken, but unhurt. He sat on a rock and, when he finished wheezing, said, "You know, the last time I crossed the cordillera I kept complaining about how uncomfortable the Transandino train was!"

They made it through the pass and felt relief upon entering Argentina and descending into the valley of the Huahum River. The first main post on the Argentine side was at Hua Hum, next to Lake Nonthué. Bellet showed the authorities documentation for everyone in the party, including the Flores brothers, and a forged one for Antonio Ruiz, the ornithologist accompanying them. Bellet had a letter of safe passage from the Valdivian police that identified him as an administrator of an important wood farm. He explained that the trip into Argentina was for business purposes and that the Flores brothers would wait for them on the west side of the lake, taking care of the horses.

Lake Nonthué is the northern arm of long Lake Lácar. The party crossed the first few miles south by boat and then changed vessels to head due east for about fifteen miles, before they arrived at the shore of San Martín de los Andes. The stunning greenery that surrounds the lake was tinged by hues of the setting sun. They went immediately to the Hotel del Turismo a couple of miles outside of town and rested well. Bellet planned to meet the Communist *compañero* from Buenos Aires at nine o'clock the next morning.

But when Bellet went into town for the rendezvous, he found no one. So it went for the next few days. First they heard that no train had arrived. Then they heard nothing. The province's governor, the local head of the national parks, and three other local authorities, intrigued by their Chilean guests, invited them to a dinner. They even took them out to a nightclub, Antonio Ruiz using his well-developed diplomatic skills to charm them all.

Finally, the operative from Buenos Aires arrived; there had been some complications with the military. Everything was all set, and the next morning Neruda left after a festive send-off by his new San Martín friends.

The Argentine Communists drove Neruda to Buenos Aires. He borrowed the passport of his friend Miguel Ángel Asturias, who happened to be serving there as the Guatemalan consul. His face had an uncanny resemblance to Neruda's. Neruda traveled across the Río de la Plata to Montevideo, Uruguay, and then flew to France. Nearly two years had passed since the order for his arrest had been issued.

Neruda's Nobel speech provides a fitting coda to the whole sinister and exhilarating ordeal:

> I say that I do not know, after so many years, whether the lessons I learned when I crossed a daunting river, when I danced around the skull of an ox, when I bathed my body in the cleansing water from the topmost heights—I do not know whether these lessons welled forth from me in order to be imparted to many others or whether it was all a message that was sent to me by others as a demand or an accusation. I do not know whether I experienced this or created it, I do not know whether it was truth or poetry, something passing or permanent, the poems I experienced in this hour, the experiences that I later put into verse. From all this, my friends, there arises an insight that the poet must learn through other people. There is no insurmountable solitude. All paths lead to the same goal: to convey to others what we are. And we must pass through solitude and difficulty, isolation and silence, in order to reach forth to the enchanted place where we can dance our clumsy dance and sing our sorrowful song—but in this dance or in this song there are fulfilled the most ancient rites of our conscience in the awareness of being human and of believing in a common destiny.

CHAPTER SEVENTEEN

EXILE AND MATILDE

This book ends here. It was born
of fury like a live coal, like territories
of burned forests, and I hope
that it continues like a red tree
spreading its bright flame.
Yet it wasn't only rage you found
in its branches: its roots sought
sorrow but also strength,
and I am the strength of pensive stone,
the joy of joined hands.
—"I End Here (1949)"

When Neruda arrived in Paris, many illustrious leftists were in town for the First World Congress of Partisans for Peace. Pablo Picasso found him a safeguarded apartment: the home of Françoise Giroud, a journalist and leader of the French feminist movement. She had hidden Jews during the German occupation. Neruda adored the apartment—it was filled with Picasso's paintings—and sent for Delia immediately.

The World Congress had opened on April 20, 1949, with 2,895 delegates from seventy-two nations who claimed to speak for six hundred million people. (The French government barred 384 delegates because of their supposed subversive character.) A simultaneous conference convened in Prague, connecting to the action in Paris by phone and radio. There was money to cover the expenses. The goal of the World Congress was "to unite all the active forces in all countries for the defense of peace."

In Paris, the gathering was based at the splendid art deco Salle Pleyel, one of the city's largest and most celebrated concert halls. Picasso contributed his recently painted dove, which was displayed on the walls and prominently sewn into the main stage's curtain. It would become a universal symbol of peace. A banner on one wall declared: "Hitler wanted us to fight the U.S.S.R. We didn't go nor shall we go for Truman." (Many were suspicious that the military escalation by the United States and its allies was not a defensive measure, but rather a move toward initiating a war against the Soviets.)

At the conclusion of the World Congress, on April 25, Picasso stirred the crowd when he announced that he had a surprise. Timed perfectly, an apparently relaxed Neruda walked out on the stage in a pin-striped suit. It was his first public appearance since fleeing Chile, and it was in a hall filled with friends and admirers. Neruda beamed as Picasso kissed him on the cheek. The audience roared. Among them were iconic luminaries such as the artists Diego Rivera, Marc Chagall, and Henri Matisse; the Italian writer Italo Calvino; the French feminist and scientist Eugénie Cotton; and the French poets Paul Éluard and Louis Aragon. Delegates from the United States included the author of *Spartacus*, Howard Fast, who would be imprisoned a year later for refusing to testify to the House Un-American Activities Committee (HUAC); the African American activist-scholar W. E. B. Du Bois; and the singer, actor, and civil rights champion Paul Robeson. (Charlie Chaplin and Henry Miller, among many other renowned leftists, did not attend but lent their names in support of the conference.)

Du Bois noted the diversity of the crowd. There was the crucial "patent fact that the Colored World was present," not as token representatives, "but as members of a world movement in full right and with full participation." Du Bois, a veteran of such gatherings, declared that in

Paris "I have attended the greatest meeting of men ever assembled in modern times to advance the progress of all men."

On the last day, the World Congress organized "the most impressive mass demonstration" Du Bois had ever witnessed: one hundred thousand peaceful people in a stadium crying, "Peace! Peace!" "No lying, distortion and twisting of our prostituted press can conceal or erase the heartbreaking significance of this spectacle," Du Bois wrote. "None who saw it will ever forget."

The day before the rally at the stadium, Neruda began his brief speech by asking his "dear friends" to excuse him for being late to their meeting; it was "due to the difficulties I had to overcome to get here." However, the political persecution in Chile had made him "appreciate the fact that human solidarity is greater than all barriers, and more fertile than all valleys." He ended his brief remarks by reading "Song for Bolívar," the poem he had first read in front of Rivera's first mural in Mexico City in 1941.

Howard Fast reflected on the World Congress in an article printed in Spanish for the Chilean magazine *Pro arte:* "Neruda was like the conscience of the world, with a new, vital, and democratic song and new and terrible charges of the corruption of imperialism. Through Neruda, Chile had taken shape before the world."

At a break in the proceedings, Fast went to the stage and waited until he could extend his hand to the poet. Neruda seemed exhausted: "a hundred people were asking him questions all at the same time. He held Picasso's hand, as if this reality could suddenly disappear, and greeted many other people with his other hand."

HUAC had a different take on the proceedings. An excerpt from its chronicling of the World Congress:

> Paul Robeson, a Negro and a Communist, for whom America has meant fame and fortune as a concert singer, actor, and athlete, received a tremendous ovation when he declared, "It is certainly unthinkable for myself and the Negro people to go to war in the interests of those who have

oppressed us for generations" against a country (referring to Russia) "which in one generation has raised our people to the full dignity of mankind." Robeson's treasonous statements have been overwhelmingly repudiated by prominent members of his own race such as Jackie Robinson, Walter White, Lester Granger, Josh White, and many others.

These meetings were not just social gatherings; world politics was involved. HUAC stressed that the World Congress did not "tolerate any effort to disseminate the truth regarding Soviet aggression or the Communist dictatorship." There was an urge by participants to condemn media outlets, people, and organizations that, "according to Communist standards, 'disseminate propaganda for a new war.'"

Following the World Congress's after-parties, which always included some poetry reading, Neruda and Delia took the first of what would be many trips around Europe, particularly Eastern Europe. They would also go to Russia, China, and Mexico, not to escape the authorities but rather as part of a tour of political and literary actions and meetings. The pace of their activity was prodigious; they were in great demand and devoted to their cause. The Chilean government could not obstruct Neruda while he was in leftist countries, and he doubted it would anywhere else, as he was too visible on the world stage.

With great excitement, Neruda and Delia flew to Moscow on June 6. The trip was timed to coincide with the celebrations for the 150th anniversary of the birth of one of his favorite poets, Alexander Pushkin. Stalin himself received them, giving Delia an astrakhan coat, made from the pelt of a newborn Persian lamb, with red silk lining. They were in what seemed to be the promised land: their tour was tailored by officials to make sure that these prominent endorsers of the Soviets would see only the good, none of the bad. Neruda, still grateful to Stalin for his support of the Spanish Republic, did not need much convincing. Before leaving Moscow, he bought old editions of Pushkin's poetry. Pushkin's political but narrative, vernacularly lyrical voice can be seen as an influence in the conversational poetry Neruda began to write after this trip.

The festivities continued in Leningrad, where Neruda gave a rousing speech denouncing his enemies, including González Videla, while praising the father of Chile's Communist Party, Luis Emilio Recabarren. Stalingrad was next, the city to which Neruda had written two love songs. He gave a speech and read his verse. After he read his poems in Spanish, an actor followed in Russian.

Then it was off to Danzig, Poland; Budapest; and Prague. He intended to go to London next, but while in Prague, the British embassy denied him a visa. He was blocked by the walls of the Cold War, as Western governments were concerned by his rising celebrity status and vocal Communist propaganda. The United States was worried enough to keep tabs on him: after Neruda was unable to get to England, he left for a short visit to Cuba. Shortly after his arrival, the counselor at the U.S. embassy in Havana sent a confidential memo, addressed to the secretary of state, reporting how—as the missive started—"the Communist newspaper Hoy published a photograph of Pablo NERUDA, Communist poet and Senator from Chile, taken in Habana during the course of a press interview. Neruda, who, it is understood, has been in the USSR and in Paris, was refused a visa when he attempted to visit England on his return to this area." It added that "efforts are being made to obtain further information regarding the diplomatic passports used by Neruda and his wife." The embassy also noted how Neruda made statements to the press against González Videla and that "a controlled American source states that Pablo Neruda and his wife left Habana by air for Mexico on August 23." The Mexicans gladly allowed Neruda and Delia entry, on August 28, 1949, despite the Chilean government's insistence to the Mexican government that their passports weren't valid. (Neruda's close relationship with Mexico continued throughout his life.) The couple was accompanied by Paul Éluard. They were there to attend the American Continental Peace Congress in Mexico City.

Neruda delivered a momentous announcement during his speech to the peace congress: he renounced much of his early work. He told the attendees that he had just come from the World Festival of Youth and Students, held amid the ruins of Warsaw, where he had heard "a sound like bees in an infinite beehive—the sound of the pure, collective, and boundless joy of the new youth of the world." After the festival, some Hungarian translators had asked him which of his poems should be included in a new anthology. Politically invigorated by what he'd just seen, he looked through his older books to choose a selection of his poems. After he reread them, he felt that those older pages, especially *Residence*'s first two volumes, were so defeatist and despondent that they'd be detrimental to his mission to inspire socialist activism in readers around the world. He wanted positivity and at least some form of social realism, not poems full of obscure symbolism with names like "Oblivion." Everything he had written before the Spanish Civil War seemed frivolous now. As he explained his new thinking to the peace congress:

> None of those pages had the metal needed for the recon-
> struction, none of my verses brought the health and sus-
> tenance that were needed there. And I renounced them. I
> did not want old sorrows to discourage new lives. I did not
> want the reflection of a system that was able to induce such
> anguish in me to deposit the terrifying slime with which
> our enemies had darkened my own youth in the midst of
> building hope. I didn't allow a single one of those poems to
> be published in the people's democracies. And even more,
> today, having returned to these American lands of which
> I am a part, I confess that I don't want to see those poems
> printed here either.

Neruda's comments seem to have evolved from a gathering the year before, the 1948 World Congress of Intellectuals in Defense of Peace in Wrocław, Poland, where the Soviet writer Alexander Fadeyev had delivered a lengthy speech. In it, he had excoriated American culture as well as the writings of a handful of Western writers, including Henry Miller, Eugene O'Neill, and the French philosopher Jean-Paul Sartre. "If hyenas could type and jackals could use a fountain pen they would write such things," he shouted, words that brought the Eastern Bloc members to a raucous applause but horrified American and British delegates. Henry Miller, for example, was problematic for his "erotic obsessions" and Sartre for his "intellectual fornications," as one Communist put it.

The attack against O'Neill, in particular, baffled the French philosopher Julien Benda. Yes, the nature of the American's plays—often bleak, rather nihilistic, displaying hopelessness—may have been incongruent with the pure positivity of the Stalinists' social realism. But still, Benda knew O'Neill, for one, to be a leftist writer. The searing severity of the personal attack against him and the others just seemed too much to Benda. After the speech, he complained to a Soviet writer, Ilya Ehrenburg (one of Neruda's new good friends). How could Fadeyev truly compare O'Neill and others to jackals? "Is that fair or, to put it at its lowest, wise? And why do we have to clap every time Stalin's name is mentioned?" Benda affirmed that he wasn't in support of the United States' policies, but that seemed beside the point.

At the time of the 1949 peace congress, Neruda seemed sincere in the renunciation of his own poetry as well as in his condemnation of authors who were writing negative, abstract works. His premise was that writers had an obligation in the face of a war, waged by imperialist capitalists against "democracy," that threatened the entire world. His speech condemned the escapism of the existentialist literary style that had been permeating literature, illusory work that purposely elevated evasion, anguish, neurosis, and frustration and benefited the bourgeoisie and the allied governments: "In the throes of death, capitalism fills the cup of human creation with a bitter brew."

In his speech, Neruda attacked writers who fell out of the cultural doctrine just as ruthlessly as Fadeyev had. He not only invoked Fadeyev, but also took his insults a step further. He shook the Mexico City crowd, insisting that

> when Fadeyev said in his Wrocław speech that if hyenas could use a pen or typewriter, they would write like the poet T. S. Eliot or like the novelist Sartre, it seems to me he insulted the animal kingdom: I don't believe that animals, even given intelligence and expression, will come to create

an obscene religion of death squads and repugnant vices,
like these two so-called maestros of Western culture.

Neruda then turned on other writers he had once cherished, lauded,
and even translated, such as Rilke. He accused them of fomenting sad-
ness and anxiety in the population, the antithesis of what the times
demanded. There was no place for anything but optimistic, inspiring
work invested in political unity and progress. Neruda's words were
harsh and uncompromising, the first display on such a large stage of his
new bombastic, proselytizing tone. Neruda continued, detailing what
he saw as the bourgeoisie's "intense support" of these detrimental writ-
ers: "In the past years we've seen how our *snobs* [said in English] have
represented Kafka, Rilke, and all the labyrinths that don't have an exit,
all the metaphysics that have fallen like empty crates from the train of
history." The snobs, he went on, have turned into "defenders of 'spirit,'
into howling Americanists, into professional mud-makers of the pool
they splash in."

Regardless, Neruda's fans rallied behind his words. In 1950, Samuel
Sillen, a sponsor of the March 1949 Scientific and Cultural Conference
for World Peace in New York City, reaffirmed, somewhat bombasti-
cally, what Neruda had just said:

> Walt Whitman once wrote that the great poet enlisted in a
> people's cause "can make every word he speaks draw blood."
> This is true of Pablo Neruda. He is a poet-in-arms. He cre-
> ates living art in the struggle against a dying society. And
> the blood he draws is that of an imperialism which hired the
> executioners of his native Chile and which now threatens to
> plunge the entire world into a catastrophic war.
>
> As Neruda has said, before the warhawks of Wall Street
> and Washington can hurl the atom bomb they must first an-
> nihilate men morally. That is the mission of *their* poets—the
> T. S. Eliots and Ezra Pounds who degrade life and stultify
> the will to resist destruction. To this literature of decay and
> death Pablo Neruda opposes an art of moral grandeur . . .

For Sillen, among others, it was fine to dismiss the incredible poetry Neruda had written before the Spanish Civil War, when, to them, he became a "poet-in-arms."

However, as Jorge Sanhueza, who was very close to Neruda during these years, put it, "The validity of Neruda's words renouncing his earlier works, in absolute terms, only stood up for those who, from the first moment, judged those words with the goal of getting some political benefit from them." Many of Neruda's admirers virulently defended *Residence on Earth* in the face of Neruda's speech. Some started to see that at this moment Neruda, for perhaps the first time in his life, or even the only time in his life, failed to fuse his two essential components: Neruda the poet and Neruda the politician.

In 1951, within two years of his renunciation of his earlier work, the highly regarded publisher Gonzalo Losada suggested that his Buenos Aires press print a new edition of *Residence on Earth*. Neruda authorized it. (When Franco seized Spain, Losada had fled to Buenos Aires, where he started an important press and became known as the publisher of the "exiles." Losada would soon become Neruda's principal publisher, the Chilean wanting to work with him in part for their shared political sympathies, as well as for the fact that Losada's publishing house was soon more prestigious and reached a larger audience than Nascimento's.) Even at the time of the Mexico City conference, Neruda's "older" works started to emerge behind the Iron Curtain. In the Soviet Union, just five years after Neruda's speech, some of the poems from *Twenty Love Poems* as well as the disavowed poems from *Residence* were included in numerous anthologies. Elsewhere, within a decade of the renouncement, new translations of *Twenty Love Poems* came out in East Germany and Czechoslovakia, among other countries, as the book surpassed the million-copy mark.

As he and Delia traveled from stage to stage, Neruda was often gazed upon by many admiring eyes. They came to see him because he was becoming an icon, and, for the most part, he delivered moving and motivating performances. As much as he loved Delia, his eyes were always open to other women in the crowd. Delia was about to turn sixty-five and he was forty-five, though even if she were younger his eyes would probably have still wandered.

At the peace congress, his eyes caught those of a charming Chilean guitarist with an appealing mix of elegance and natural beauty. She was thirty-seven years old, living in Mexico City and working at a music school. While she held no firm political beliefs—she was certainly not a communist or an activist—when she read about Neruda and the peace congress in the newspaper, she went to one of its sessions. The poet, struck by her natural beauty, which reminded him of southern Chile, went up to her afterward and asked if she was Chilean. "You don't remember me?" she replied. Her name was Matilde Urrutia.

Supposedly he did not initially recall that they had met three summers earlier, at a concert in Santiago's Parque Forestal. Neruda's childhood friend Blanca Hauser had introduced him to her friend Matilde, who had recently returned to Chile after singing in Peru, Argentina, and Mexico. Neruda had invited both Blanca and Matilde to see his seashell collection at La Michoacán. Delia might have been there, or perhaps not.

They both participated in González Videla's 1946 run for president, Neruda as his chief of communications, Matilde as a musician singing campaign songs. They came face-to-face again at her recording of "Hymn to the Forces of the Left," which, like many of the campaign's songs, was a riff off a contemporary hit, in this case the Andrews Sisters' chart-topper "Rum and Coca-Cola."

According to Volodia Teitelboim, a friend of both, Neruda was immediately interested in this singer with the impetuous smile. They may even have had a brief affair, cut short by his busy schedule as a senator. He went to spend time with his constituents in Antofagasta and around the north, and his new friend, whose name he had trouble remembering, left to teach music in Mexico. They lost touch after that. Neruda often met people, socialized with them for a while, and then lost contact, only to reconnect later.

In his poem "Let the Rail-Splitter Awake," published in *Canto General* but dated 1948, between the time the two met at the concert and the campaign song recording, Neruda wrote:

peace for the Mississippi,
source of rivers,
peace for my brother's shirt,

. . . .

peace for the grimy
iron of Brooklyn, peace for the letter-carrier
who from house to house goes like the day,

. . . .

peace for my own right hand
that wants to write only Rosario.

Rosario was the alias Neruda would use for Matilde both to his friends and in poems up until his separation from Delia. If this indeed was written in 1948, and not added on later, it indicates that their affair began earlier.

Shortly after arriving in Mexico City, while attending the conference, Neruda's leg became severely swollen and red, radiating with pain. It was chronic thrombophlebitis, a condition that causes blood clots to form in the leg, blocking one or more veins. This time it was occurring in a deep muscle, making it even more unpleasant and prolonging the treatment. He and Delia had to remain in Mexico City, where they rented an apartment, again on the Paseo de la Reforma. The poet needed to stay immobile and take anticoagulants for at least two months, but in the end they extended their trip to nearly ten months.

Matilde came by so frequently to visit and help Delia that she effectively became Neruda's nurse. She entered their space with competitive displays of domestic abilities, helping to organize and attend to the general concerns of the house where Delia did not excel, especially as she became busier in political and literary activities outside the Mexico City house while Neruda was immobile. Matilde saw the opportunity and took advantage of it. Neruda was aroused by Matilde. She was a very attractive, nimble woman and was there almost every day helping him heal his leg. He was falling in love, the affair developing into something much deeper than a poet's fling with a pretty admirer. She became pregnant with his child.

Elena Caffarena, an emblematic leader of Chilean feminism, once remarked, "Women follow in Pablo's footsteps like flies." Yet while Neruda carries an almost legendary reputation as a love poet who engaged in innumerable affairs, this image doesn't hold true to reality. One can speculate, but other than Delia (when he was still with Maruca) and Matilde, there's little evidence that he had extramarital relationships. Only one can be fully corroborated.

According to many of those who knew him well, as close friends or from afar, as fans or skeptics, Neruda wasn't a typical womanizer. For the most part, he wasn't the one who went after women, but rather they went after him. He wasn't a great seducer and could actually be rather timid around women, especially those who were particularly attractive and bold. After leaving behind his depressed youth and lost persona in the Far East, his passion and fame as both an engaging poet and a personality drew women to him.

If Delia suspected something was happening between Neruda and Matilde in the beginning, or with others here and there, she told no one about it.

Meanwhile, González Videla's government had succeeded in bringing Maruca to Chile. The newspaper *La Última Hora* ran the headline "Neruda's First Wife Has Requested Legal Access to His Assets" on May 4, 1948. Maruca officially brought bigamy charges against him in court. Yet without Neruda in the country, and since his Mexican marriage to Delia was never legally recognized by Chile or Delia's home country, Argentina, it amounted to little more than propaganda and agitation.

The peace congress ended on September 15, three days before Chile's Independence Day. His debilitated condition wasn't going to deprive Neruda of celebrating his love for his country. Nor would it prevent him from publicly demonstrating how he was celebrating Chile, despite his being wanted by its government, and doing so amid a group of luminaries and admirers in Mexico rejoicing not just his country's independence, but the poet himself. He wanted to humiliate President

González Videla. He would not be attending the Chilean embassy's fiesta. Instead, he invited fifty people to a lunch and then some three hundred to a reception that night—according to an account, the majority of them were artists and intellectuals from a variety of countries. They included Siqueiros, Rivera, Éluard, Nicolás Guillén, the vibrant Mexican painter María Izquierdo, and Miguel Otero Silva, the Venezuelan who published the article that sent Neruda into exile.

Neruda still was rather immobile, so Delia presided over most of the festivities. As they celebrated Chile's independence, guests were given a thirty-two page pamphlet by Neruda that denounced González Videla and the rampant oppression in the country.

The United States continued to keep tabs on Neruda. The American cultural attaché in Mexico met with Neruda's supposed friend, the Mexican writer Alfonso Reyes. According to a State Department memo, Reyes "has no illusions about Neruda, whom he considers to be a Communist merely to attract attention and publicity to himself, like Diego Rivera."

Neruda was working furiously to complete a special edition of *Canto General* he had envisioned. It would include art from the Mexican muralist masters Diego Rivera and David Alfaro Siqueiros, to whom Neruda had given advance galleys. In a letter to Tomás Lago, he wrote:

> This book is agitating me more than *The Book of Twilights* ever did. I change the typefaces, send SOS messages, make corrections in bed, etc. There are lots of subscriptions, at 15 dollars each in the U.S., not one from Chile. Tell me how to send you a copy. The edition costs more than $300.000 [Chilean pesos], it's going to be wonderful.

Neruda's health was a distraction, but he was determined to push through his discomfort, as seen in a letter from Delia to his sister, Laura:

> As he still can't go down the stairs, much less walk up them, there need to be two strong men (as his weight is ever imposing) to take him by stretcher. The rest of his health,

both physical and spiritual, draws everyone's attention, especially the latter, since he's never lost patience and has endured the difficulty of forced immobility without losing his humor or ability to work for a second. Piles of subscriptions [for copies of *Canto General*] and the most enthusiastic and admiring cards come for Pablo from the United States.

There certainly seemed to be more interest from readers in the States than from other countries. Many of them saw the work as art that protested McCarthyism. They were fascinated by the South American poet whose legend had grown since he denounced González Videla and went into exile, and whose dramatic appearance when Picasso introduced him in Paris caused such a sensation. New translations were making his work more available to an English-language readership.

The production was advancing just as Neruda began to feel better, allowing him to make key public appearances to celebrate the book. On November 5, 1949, Delia wrote to Laura:

Right now his bed is next to the window and people he knows passing on the street shout hello. He is so well that he says I should treat him as if he were healthy and stop giving him the thermometer. From his bed, he continues commanding and bossing everyone around, dictating and doing several things at once. I'm running around left and right, almost flying, as I still haven't found the secret to doing many different things at once. They just brought him the first proofs (typeset).

On March 19, 1950, Diego Rivera hosted an homage to Neruda in anticipation of *Canto General*'s release at Anahuacalli, a bizarre anthropological museum Rivera had begun building in 1942. The shape of a pyramid, it was built on a lava field in Mexico City, a place for him and his wife, Frida Kahlo, to "flee" from bourgeois society and the environment of a war-torn world, and to put their roots down into the Mexican soil. It didn't open to the public until 1964, but when it did, it served as a monument to their passion for indigenous culture. Rivera's goal, not unlike Neruda's, was to return "to the people what I recover of their artistic heritage." Their relationship had developed over the years. When Neruda asked Rivera to contribute to the book, the Mexican was spending most of his time at the side of his wife, who was recuperating from one of many surgeries on her spine. Rivera took a small room next to hers in the hospital and spent most of his week there, leaving on Tuesdays to clear his mind and throw himself into painting for a day.

Since their first meeting during Neruda's time as consul, Rivera had influenced Neruda's interest in indigenous people and the history of Latin America, which then, in turn, influenced *Canto,* specifically beginning with "The Heights of Macchu Picchu." This was key to Neruda's more intimate relationship with his people and history, at least through his poetry.

Siqueiros attended the event for *Canto* at Anahuacalli. Over the past two decades Neruda had become good friends with Siqueiros, from their first meeting in Argentina to their civil war years in Spain to Neruda's embattled attempts to get Siqueiros, after his attempt to kill Trotsky, a visa to Chile in the early 1940s. There was no love lost between Siqueiros and Rivera, who, with Kahlo, had hidden Trotsky during part of his exile in Mexico. They feuded constantly over artistic, political, and personal matters. In a letter to the Russian Mexican writer Lya Kostakowsky, Delia wrote:

> I've been so absorbed in Pablo's sickness that I haven't been able to consume myself with their diatribes. Except for one by Diego that I confess made me laugh so hard I started to cry, in which he accuses David of having an "anal complex," proven by his persistence in using the color *"merde"* in his painting.

Fortunately, the muralists were on their best behavior for the eagerly awaited release party for the first edition of *Canto General.* At the party, held at the apartment of the architect Carlos Obregón on the night of April 3, 1950, Neruda, Rivera, and Siqueiros sat together and signed the books alongside a fine silver candelabra. The majority of the guests in attendance were foreigners residing in Mexico, members of European embassies, and Spanish Republicans.

Neruda considered the book to be his greatest work. *Canto General* is a Marxist and humanistic interpretation of the history of the Americas. The Argentine Chilean American writer Ariel Dorfman said in 2004, "I live, I still live, and I think many of us live inside the world Neruda discovered." In *Canto General,* Neruda "basically named Latin America in a new way, and he claimed for Latin America the possibility of being lyrically and epically in a story of resistance."

Canto General is one of the most impactful fusions of poetry driven by politics (ideals) and aesthetics ever written. In fact, from the political aesthetic point of view, it can be argued that *Canto General* has no equal. Yet while almost every poem in *Residence* is of strong merit, *Canto General* contains many verses that fall flat under the weight of sheer propaganda. "But when he hit the target in the *Canto General*," Dorfman said, "what he did was he redefined what America meant. América. Even North America, but particularly Latin America."

Awesome in scope and deeply probing, *Canto General* is considered by many to be one of the more important books in the canon of poetry. Its influence extends to readers from all walks of life. José Corriel, a construction engineer for the Santiago Metro, explained that while he had several of Neruda's books, *Canto General* was his favorite because it was *"la parte combativa de Neruda":* it revealed Neruda's combative side. "The importance of *Canto General*," he said, "is that it shows us the history of the Americas from a different point of view . . . [from] the point of view of the people themselves, not the history told by the conquerors. Yes, we could call it the 'history told by the conquered.'" *Canto General*—a title that could also, in a nuanced fashion, be translated as "Song of All."

Canto General's literary roots are the lyrics of Walt Whitman's *Leaves of Grass,* Dante's *Divine Comedy,* the Mayans' creation epic Popol Vuh, and the Bible. Especially in the beginning, it purposefully reads like a secular version of the Bible, laying out Neruda's vision of the Latin American Genesis, a pre-Columbian Eden, where all is innocent. The land and its inhabitants live in harmony until the arrival of the Spanish conquistadores and the subsequent "imperialistic" foreign powers' injustices corrupt and betray the original peoples. (González Videla's betrayal of Neruda and, in Neruda's eyes, the Chilean people and democracy is an underlying current throughout the book, informing both the past and present history.)

Neruda establishes the foundation of his utopian vision in the book's first poem, "Amor América (1400)":

> Before the wig and the dress coat
> there were rivers, arterial rivers

There were mountain ranges with "jagged waves where / the condor and the snow seemed immutable." There were jungles, there were the continent's great plains, "the planetary pampas"—all of this existed before the arrival of the Europeans. In this Eden, as Neruda described it, all was pure, so natural that "Man was earth, earthen vase."

Neruda portrays the Spanish conquest as a tragic injustice forced on "his" people, despite his own European heritage. The Europeans in his view were barbarous and ruthless, while the pre-Columbian societies are described in idealized terms. "Like a wild rose / a red drop"—the blood of the indigenous people after European colonization—"fell on the thickness / and a lamp on earth was extinguished." So ended America's Edenic first phase of history. He reaches back to when he was compelled to drink the goblet of blood from the slaughtered lamb back in Temuco, but now the blood is the tragedy of imperialism:

> My land without name, without América,
> equinoctial stamen, purple lance,
> your aroma climbed to me through my roots
> into the goblet that I drank, into the thinnest
> word still unborn in my mouth.

Neruda fails to mention the violence that many pre-Columbian so-cieties had perpetrated on the continent: the Incas' and Aztecs' aggressive war making, the Mayans' human sacrifices, or the bloody raids of the Apache. He is selective in the service of a romantic notion and a political cause.

Neruda directly identifies himself with the indigenous people. "I searched for you, my father, / young warrior of darkness and copper," he writes in "Amor América (1400)." Here, all indigenous people are his "fathers" and he is their son, despite the fact there is no evidence that he had any indigenous blood in his own heritage.

In the opening of the book, Neruda declares, "I am here to tell the story." "The story" he is telling in this case is *their* story, as the construction engineer José Corriel put it: the "story of the conquered," the people of the Americas, so as to give name to that which was "without name, without América," before the Spanish came. *Canto General* is a book of naming, of identifying, of constructing a narrative, a history, and in developing this language within a text, Neruda invites the reader to bear witness to injustice, as he attempts to give voice to the oppressed.

The epic spans the 450 years of history from the arrival of Columbus to the publication of the book. By the fifteenth and final section, the betrayals of the past are bridged to the optimism of a brighter future, as that original language has been reclaimed and restored. Through the Marxist belief that the roots of a better future grow in the hardships of the past, Neruda returns to a utopian image of Latin America and the world. This optimism, though, is dependent on continued social commitment by the masses, on collective action to sustain this new day, this better world.

Neruda and the two muralists signed a special edition of five hundred books, each 567 pages, large format (14 x 10 inches), featuring magnificent illustrations by the two painters. The publisher, Oceana, contributed some of its own money, but Neruda had for some time been working to sell advance subscriptions in order to fund the production. Three hundred books had already been sold to sponsors in Italy,

Russia, Hungary, England, France, Czechoslovakia, Spain, the United States, and all over Latin America, as well as to many Mexicans who were there that night.*

Neruda, Rivera, and Siqueiros were united by friendship, art, and their political commitment. Neruda wanted the reader to experience all of that in the book. In his memoirs, Neruda wrote that when he first came to Mexico City in 1940, Rivera, Siqueiros, and the other great revolutionary muralist José Clemente Orozco were "covering the streets of the city with history and geography, with civil uprisings, with iron-hard polemics." This directly inspired Neruda's vision and the writing for the book: their epic sweep painted on a large scale, incorporating all of history, centered on the indigenous and the proletariat; crowding the canvas with events, emboldened people, and images of struggle and victory. Just like Neruda's new poetry, they aimed their work at the common person. *Canto General* is the book-length, poetic version of their art. Neruda had also invited Orozco to participate, but he died of heart failure six months before the book's release.

One of Rivera's paintings opens the book, on the front endpapers. True to his form, Rivera's illustration/painting is titled *Pre-Hispanic America*. It is stunning. The piece is divided in two, with the left side portraying the Aztec and Mayan cultures and the right side the Inca and perhaps the Quechua in Peru. The largest subject in the painting is a strong, earthen man, with skin the color of burnt orange, sitting on top of an altar. It seems he has been sacrificed, as his blood is flowing in the shape of a

---

* Other notable subscribers included Neruda's friends Rubén Azócar; Tomás Lago; Diego Muñoz; Juvencio Valle; Gabriela Mistral; his sister, Laura Reyes; and the Partido Comunista de Chile—a total of thirty from his home country. Also on the list were the Lyceum and Lawn Tennis Club and Nicolás Guillén from Cuba, Luís Carlos Prestes from Brazil, and Miguel Otero Silva from Venezuela. There were subscribers from a total of twelve Latin American countries, as well as Picasso, Aragon, Éluard, and four others from France; twenty-eight total from the "Spanish Republic," including Luis Buñuel and Rafael Alberti; Nancy Cunard and one other from England; and people from Hungary, Italy, Poland, the Soviet Union, and Czechoslovakia.

dagger down the golden steps beneath him. Above him hangs the bottom half of a sun, sharp red rays bursting out from a gray core, suggesting that his blood perhaps went to feed Tezcatlipoca, the sun god, who needed to be nourished well enough so that he had the strength to raise the sun each morning. The sun gives light to both sides, all cultures.

The Aztec death god, Mictlantecuhtli, with his white toothy skull, stands in a pyramid to the left of the sacrificed man. He is dressed in blue, with embellishments of red, white, and yellow; his mouth is wide open, and his hands reach out to the sun. Purple and yellow hands sit atop the pyramid with their fingers pointed skyward. On the left border, away from the central image, Rivera includes a black snow-capped volcano, magenta volcanoes spewing fire, and a lithe deer being hunted. The bottom of that half of the section paints a more tranquil scene of Mayans: one is tilling a field; one is chiseling a door; there are other craftsmen working and people cooking. A fertile, Edenic scene of a serpent, a shell, and a waterfall adjoins them. A dolphin, a fish, and an alligator decorate the borders.

The Peruvian scene is simpler, with grander images, including Machu Picchu in beautiful shades of silver, white, and gray; a condor soaring over an Andean peak; and people cooking and weaving. Seashells dot the bank of the river as well.

Siqueiros's work is less mural-like, but it is powerful in its singularity: a naked, faceless, muscular man, with his long arms reaching out through what appears to be the disintegration of the world, to be sand like the *Canto General* poem "The Sand Betrayed." His body emboldened, he seems triumphant, the archetypal "new man" who will grow out of the struggles and injustices of the past once a socialist or communist society has been created.

★

In Chile, Neruda was still inspiring sedition, and the government renewed its efforts to arrest him. At the same time as the Mexican edition of *Canto General* came out, a "clandestine edition" for Chile was produced under the stamp of a fictitious printing house (Imprenta Juárez,

Reforma 75, Ciudad de México). The Communist Party was in charge of its publication. The printing was complicated and laborious, requiring endless precautions in order to avoid detection by the police. Neruda's friend José Venturelli, one of the greatest Chilean artists of the twentieth century, illustrated the book with his bold drawings. Diego Muñoz helped correct the proofs, taking the papers to one printer after another to obscure the trail. They also used obsolete linotype components so intelligence units wouldn't be able to trace the printed characters to any current printer's type. The government was still oppressing workers and the Left, and the abuses described in the book were playing out in real time. The vision of a new utopia, and of men and women arising from the sands of the Atacama Desert and the length of the country—the hope of renewal—was vital.

Higher-quality editions featuring all of Venturelli's art along with the poetry were sold to readers from "the highest class of this country" to fund the production of a more accessible edition of the book that those of lesser means could afford. For this one, they used ordinary paper, which was cheaper and did not require placing a special order to a paper company that might have aroused suspicion. All of this effort resulted in five thousand copies that included pictures and graphics, including a moving photo of Neruda and Delia, arms locked together, walking away from the camera through a rustic field in the south, just before his escape into exile.

The book was soon translated into French, Italian, German, Russian, and Chinese, among other languages. It eventually spread across the world. In 1950, the U.S. journal *Masses & Mainstream* came out with a ninety-five-page hardcover and paperback edition of poems from *Canto general* translated into English, titled *Let the Rail Splitter Awake and Other Poems.* [*] "Let the Rail-Splitter Awake" is an essential twenty-one-page poem written "from somewhere in the Americas" and addressed to the United States. It's a call for the spirit of "Lincoln [to] awake so the

---

[*]   An English translation of the entire *Canto general* would not be published until 1991, by the University of California Press, translated by Jack Schmitt.

U.S. can recover its disposition of peace and hope for all humanity," as Neruda once put it.[*] He invokes Abraham Lincoln as a North American Karl Marx:

> Let the Rail-splitter awake.
> Let Abe come with his axe
> and his wooden plate
> to eat with the farmers.
> . . . .
> Let him buy something in a drugstore
> let him take a bus to Tampa
> let him bite into a yellow apple
> and enter a moviehouse to converse
> with all the simple people.
> *Let the Rail-splitter awake.*
> . . . .
> Peace for the twilights to come,
> peace for the bridge, peace for the wine,
> peace for the stanzas which pursue me
> . . . .
> peace for the grimy
> iron of Brooklyn, peace for the letter-carrier
> who from house to house goes like the day.

Earlier he says:

> You are
> what I am, what I was, what we must
> protect, the fraternal sub-soil
> of pure America, the simple

---

[*]   Neruda described the poem as such in a 1971 interview, in the midst of his great opposition to the Vietnam War and America's subversive acts against the Allende government. "I think that these United States exist, that they will revive and shine in the coming years," he added.

men of streets and roadways.
My brother Juan sells shoes
just like your brother John,
my sister Juanita peels potatoes
just like your cousin Jane,
and my blood is of miners and sailors
like your blood, Peter.
You and I will open doors

. . . .

for beyond the land belongs to us
and no whistle of a machine-gun will be heard there,
but a song, another song, and another.

Jack Hirschman, San Francisco's poet laureate emeritus, was a student at the City College of New York when he read "Let the Rail-Splitter Awake" for the first time. "It struck me like a bomb," he recalled. It was a feeling shared by many on the Left, stemming from the pressures of the time, particularly the rabid anti-communism and the witch hunts perpetrated by Congress. "It was the first major political poem after World War II, and that it was an attack on McCarthyism, by an American poet who wrote in the Spanish language, amazed me even more. Pablo always had the guts of his poetry aimed at the contemporary moment."[*]

★

Neruda's most important work to date in terms of heft, scope, and the time he spent composing it was out, and it was a powerful success. It had been written on the run, except for "The Heights of Macchu Pic-

---

[*] Hirschman said this in the poetry room of the City Lights Bookstore in San Francisco. He turned to the legendary Lawrence Ferlinghetti, City Lights' cofounder, who was sitting next to him, and told him tenderly, "I think it was a great tribute that Allen [Ginsberg] understood also, because in the collected works of Allen, there's only one poem that's translated, and it's the poem Allen translated of Pablo Neruda, which is saying something." That one poem that Ginsberg translated was "Let the Rail-Splitter Awake."

chu" and "Canto general de Chile," composed between February 1948 and January 1949. These sections were born out of anger, as Neruda admitted, spurred by the political situation created by González Videla. Yet as he says in the poem "I End Here" and elsewhere, although the book was born from fury, he nevertheless remains positive through the end.

Though he would have liked to have been able to return to his cherished Chile, he was doing quite well in Europe and Mexico. Through his political appearances, and with *Canto General*'s celebrated release to the public, he seemed to eclipse González Videla, whom the world viewed as a petty tyrant. Neruda told an interviewer that in writing *Canto General*, "I had two immense sources of happiness: on one hand, the satisfaction of my book; on the other, its intangible elements of struggle."

However, all this satisfaction was dampened when the book's immediate reception fell far short of his expectations. After the book signing, there weren't any of the expected homages. Not one article of any significant interest was published about the book's importance in the international press. Those who did write about it at first seemed more interested in the author than the content, skirting around it, perhaps due to apprehension about being the first to critique such a monumental work. Or maybe the sheer magnitude of the book was too intimidating to take on right away, as several scholars have surmised. Even Alone never reviewed the complete *Canto General*; rather he just wrote about individual, separate parts of the epic, such as "The Heights of Macchu Picchu," as they were released, before the complete book was published. He was impressed by the poems but in the end didn't personally care for them.

Neruda was struck by this apparent indifference toward his epic work, produced with great effort, written by possibly the most famous living Latin American poet at the time. He knew it was good; his friends reassured him of it. While recognition would come later, at the time Neruda felt a disturbing emptiness that he hadn't experienced for a long time. He wanted to leave Mexico. He had recovered from the thrombosis in his leg, but his passion for Matilde had swelled in his heart and mind.

As it became time for him and Delia to return to the normality of their life-in-exile in Europe, representing the Communist Party as needed, both Neruda and Matilde felt that what had occurred between them during the previous ten months, what they felt for each other now, was quite serious. Matilde had been committed to building something real with him from the start. Neruda came to realize that his feelings for her had gone beyond simple attraction to her beauty and charm, or the fact that Delia was now sixty-six.

Delia was still either ambivalent or in denial. The three had even made a quick trip to Guatemala together as he became more mobile, just before the signing party. It would be the first of many times the trio would travel together, and despite the other two's clear romantic connection, it would be several years until Delia finally gave agency to her suspicions.

Upon their departure, Matilde installed herself in an apartment on the Paseo de la Reforma, down the street from where Neruda and Delia had lived. She made a life for herself, spending many weekends in Cuernavaca, a town she adored. Still, the man she loved and the life she wanted were in Europe.

Neruda and Delia started a surge of traveling as they returned to Europe in June 1950, a frantic international pace driven by requests for him to appear at political events from one country to the next. By planes, trains, and automobiles, the two spent time in Prague, Paris, Moscow, New Delhi, Bucharest, Warsaw, Geneva, Berlin, Beijing, and many parts of Italy.

Matilde lost the baby in Mexico, but she would not lose Neruda. It would take a year, a very long year, but Matilde eventually joined him in Paris. With the help of his friends, Neruda manipulated the levers of the Communist Parties in the various countries to act as a go-between, creating a diverse, almost nonstop itinerary of political/literary (the latter now just a stage for the former) activities of all stripes, most often with financing, which gave him more opportunities to pursue his clandestine relationship with Matilde. Their love flourished, though his poetry suffered from the constant travel and the uncertainty, not to mention his continued embrace of Stalinism and, with it, socialist realism. Regardless of the politics behind the style, it flattened his work. He did, however, manage to write one of his most beloved books of love poetry, *Los versos del capitán* (*The Captain's Verses*), to Matilde, finished right before they finally returned to Chile.

CHAPTER EIGHTEEN

MATILDE AND STALIN

Oh you, the one I love,
little one, red grain
of wheat,
the struggle will be hard,
life will be hard,
but you will come with me.
— "The Mountain and the River"

n November 1950, at the World Peace Council's Second World Congress in Warsaw, Neruda was awarded the World Peace Prize for "Let the Rail-Splitter Awake." Paul Robeson, Pablo Picasso, and others also received the award. The West always suspected the World Peace Council was a front organization formed and funded by Soviet intelligence, and Moscow did, in fact, aid it financially. The prize money, a million French francs, or around $100,000 at that time, was delivered to Neruda—in cash—in Paris.

Neruda gave the suitcase stuffed with cash to a friend, Inés Figueroa, the wife of the Chilean painter Nemesio Antúnez, and asked her to take care of it. She first hid it in her apartment and then deposited it in a bank account, despite her fears that "tax inspectors or people like that would come by someday to ask me about where it had come from."

Inés became Neruda's bookkeeper and book buyer. "He was tyrannical and adorable," she reflected later. Neruda would write or call her to ask her to buy a first edition of Arthur Rimbaud's *A Season in Hell,* Victor Hugo's *Toilers of the Sea,* and Charles Baudelaire's *The Flowers of Evil.* He had her buy a thirty-nine-volume set of the revolutionary French Enlightenment *Encyclopédie* (a book that would directly influence some of his future poetry), an edition of Shakespeare's poetry from 1630, and much more.

Inés was a scrupulous administrator who suffered interminably watching the speed with which Neruda spent his money. Her account books were meticulously detailed. He would give them a distracted glance, then ask, "But how much is left?" Inés worked to make sure Neruda was receiving royalties from the many editions of his work that were beginning to appear in different languages across Europe and Asia. This effort yielded large sums, surprising Neruda, who had earned little even from *Twenty Love Poems* for a long time.

With the new royalties added to the prize money, Neruda started to spend without restraint: old, rare books and manuscripts, seashells, antiques, plane tickets, good hotels, and pocket money for hard-up Chileans and other kindred Latin Americans traveling through Europe—"poets, students, painters, filmmakers, musicians, or whoever else—in search of art, love, and revolution." He also instructed Inés that "if this Chilean girl comes from Mexico . . . Matilde Urrutia—a very responsible person—give her 10,000 francs."

Neruda and Delia had rented a little three-story chalet at 12 rue Pierre Mille in the Fifteenth Arrondissement, right behind the Porte de Versailles. It was a popular, bohemian neighborhood that Neruda enjoyed. He roamed among mustached French workers, open markets, and cozy bistros. Each floor of the chalet was a separate apartment. Delia and Neruda lived on the first floor, which included a bedroom, living room, dining room, and kitchen.

Delia, who cared nothing about the interior design, had signed the rental agreement in her name, telling the owner that her husband, "Monsieur del Carril," was temporarily out of the country. As it already felt like an ideal art studio, Inés; her husband, Nemesio; and their young son, Pablo, took the second floor. Neruda and Delia rented the top floor for themselves as well, just so no stranger, or possible spy, could occupy it.

Neruda could not stay too long in Paris at one time, as the Chilean government was exerting a great deal of effort to convince France to expel or extradite him. France was an allied country that, as much as it respected the romantic image of Neruda, did not like his outspoken Stalinist side. As a guest of the Czech Writers' Union, Neruda took up a residency at the Dobříš Castle outside of Prague. It became his second home base from which he would travel to other countries, usually France and Italy, meeting with writer and painter friends, participating in peace assemblies, reciting poems, and speaking about Chile. At this point, all governments kept him under strict surveillance and gave him only short-term visas.

One day while Delia and Neruda were at the castle, a former Spanish Republican general told them their mutual friend Artur London, the Czech vice minister of foreign affairs, had been imprisoned. Czechoslovakia's president, Klement Gottwald, was cracking down on Communists who resisted Stalin. London and thirteen other high-ranking party members had been arrested and tortured, accused of being Titoists, Trotskyites, and Zionists; eleven of the fourteen were Jewish. After their show trials in 1952, London would be one of just three who were not hanged, but he would spend fourteen years in prison. Similar purges occurred in the new regimes in Hungary and Bulgaria. Even as his friends became victims of Stalin's repression, Neruda remained uncritical of the Soviet leader. He had wrapped himself in Stalin's flag, so committed now that it seems he lacked the courage to renounce it.

★

Nearly a year had passed since Neruda had returned to Europe from Mexico City following his phlebitis and the release of *Canto General*. Finally, the situation was right for Matilde and Neruda to reunite. On the stationery of Geneva's Hotel Cornavin, he wrote to her that they would arrange for her to travel to Europe by ship in early January 1952. "Our angel or devil continues to watch over our love and H. [la Hormiga] has accepted it fully." He ends the letter:

> Perhaps you'll have good news for me as well: that you're the same as I left you: firm, loved, sweet, brave, happy, responsible, faithful, and hugged for a lifetime by your

Captain.

Delia may have seemed "generous and full of youthful happiness," as if "she never aged," as Aida Figueroa said. But Neruda now needed more than character, intellect, companionship, political alliance, editorial help, and deep friendship. She had been an important bedrock for him for some fifteen very intense years, and she had influenced him like few other people. And yet there was no denying the fact that she was closing in on seventy, while Matilde was not yet forty. And Matilde was as Neruda hoped she would be: a vital, happy, firm, strong, attentive woman, ready to devote herself to him.

Matilde was simple, natural, and earthen, just like the rural town where she grew up in a large family with little money. She had to struggle to get by, working at a variety of jobs. While Matilde had little cultural training, she was extraordinarily intelligent, as well as spontaneous, willful, capable, and strong. For her part, Delia was extremely intelligent and cultured, with an education rooted in Paris, funded by tremendously rich parents. But she was not well versed in the mundane essentials: Delia could barely make eggs. Matilde offered domesticity. Her adoration for Neruda was warm, effusive, dedicated, and romantic. It swelled his heart and pride. When he was around Matilde, especially at first, he would beam with an almost childlike joy, even seeming to act a bit giddy at times. Though Delia still admired him, it was in a less affectionate way. And Matilde also offered something Delia could not: youth.

Many in Matilde's family were militant Communists, but she wasn't political. If anything, she seemed at this time to be conservative in comparison to Neruda and his friends; the Marxist Delia she was not. While Neruda was caught up in his promotion of Stalinism, this may have been a welcome relief, a sanctuary to escape the constant political rhetoric and show driving his life at the moment.

When Matilde first arrived in Paris, Neruda was unable to meet her; he had been in Eastern Europe, and the French had denied him reentry. He sent Matilde a welcoming telegram and told her to meet him at the Third World Festival of Youth and Students in East Berlin. At the festival, Neruda spoke out against Truman, imperialism, and the Korean War.

When Matilde arrived in Berlin, her friends told her that Pablo was at the theater at the moment and that he wanted her to meet him there immediately. As Matilde wrote in her memoir, "I was radiant. I got to the theater and there he was. His face lit up when he saw me. We embraced and he said to me, 'This is over. I never want to be separated from you again.'"

The next day, Matilde played her guitar and sang at the festival, and later that evening Neruda surprised her in her hotel room when she returned. Neruda had the boisterous Turkish poet Nazim Hikmet convince a dubious Delia that he and Neruda had to attend an urgent, nonexistent party meeting that would last until dawn and that her presence was not required. This was the first of many lies to Delia that involved fictitious party meetings as a way to be with Matilde. With Delia duped, the lovers had the whole night to themselves. As Matilde placed her head on Neruda's chest, she said, "You have the smell of tenderness."

"Be careful!" Neruda answered. "That's poetry—don't go literary on me."

When the East Berlin festival ended, Matilde received an invitation to sing on the radio in Czechoslovakia, where Neruda and Delia were traveling as well. The three of them went together by car. Two weeks later, at the end of August, they went to Bucharest, Romania. They all stayed together in one large house. Neruda and Matilde pretended that they were jovial, good friends, and Delia seemed to accept this.

One night while they were entertaining Romanian friends, Neruda slipped away. When he came back he secretly passed Matilde a piece of paper. It was a poem, "Always," the first of many he would write to her in Europe, which would form the book *The Captain's Verses*:

> In front of you,
> I'm not jealous.
>
> Come with a man
> at your back,
> come with a hundred men in your hair,
> come with a thousand men between your breasts and your feet,
> come like a river,
> full of drowned men
> that finds the furious sea,
> the eternal foam, the weather.
>
> Bring them all
> where I wait for you:
> we will always be alone,
> we will always be you and I,
> alone upon the earth
> to begin life.

The poem is curious, as Matilde was already in love with him and would never be with another man. Neruda, on the other hand, had both Delia and Maruca to contend with.

In her memoir, Matilde wrote that she wasn't jealous of Delia; instead, she "saw her like a solicitous and affectionate mother or older sister who took care of him." But living in the same house with her was difficult. The intensity of Matilde and Pablo's love, the restrictions the situation placed on it, and the confusion and discomfort caused by the secrecy became too much. Matilde broke out with a terrible case of hives. Neruda prioritized finding time to be with her then, and the two Chileans took a trip alone to Constanța on the Black Sea. Yet the vacation didn't alleviate her symptoms, despite the poetry Neruda was writ-ing for her daily and despite Delia's relative acceptance of her presence. The inability to be fully out in the open during a period of constant travel and the uncertainty of when Neruda actually might leave his wife were just all too much for her. As grounded as she could appear, her emotions were getting the best of her, living their love this way. She told Neruda, at least for leverage, that she wanted to end the affair, go back to Paris and then Mexico.

They returned to Bucharest, where Matilde would board a train to Paris and Neruda would fly to Prague and Delia. Matilde wrote that their good-bye was so emotional that afterward she turned and ran away from her lover. But before she ran, Neruda gave her a letter to read later. She opened it on the train. It was a poem, "The Potter":

> Your whole body holds
> a goblet or gentle sweetness destined for me.
>
> When I let my hand climb,
> in each place I find a dove
> that was looking for me, as if
> my love, they had made you out of clay
> for my very own potter's hands.
>
> Your knees, your breasts,
> your waist
> are missing in me, like in the hollow
> of a thirsting earth
> where they relinquished
> a form,
> and together
> we are complete like one single river,
> like one single grain of sand.

But the next poem in the letter furiously blamed Matilde for hav-ing lost their baby in Mexico. Neruda had already accused her of not taking enough care of the baby and herself. He entitled the poem "La pródiga"—the prodigal, the squanderer, the wasteful woman.

I ask you, where is my son?

Didn't he await me inside you, recognizing me,
and telling me, "Call on me to come onto the land
to continue your struggles and your songs"?

Give me back my son!

"As I read those words, I felt as if they had been addressed to a different woman," Matilde wrote after Neruda died. "Nothing had ever mattered more to me than to have his child." Still, there is no sign that she defended herself directly from his reproach in the days after reading those scathing, authoritative lines. He would actually include the poem in *The Captain's Verses*. This was cruel and narcissistic in any case, but Neruda's recent history makes it all the more galling. After having blithely abandoned his first child with hardly a glance back, now he was righteously indignant for having lost his second, callously hurling blame at the mistress he claimed to love.

★

With Matilde gone, Neruda and Delia traveled to Beijing, China, to deliver the Stalin Peace Prize to Soong Ching-ling, the widow of Sun Yat-sen, known as the "Father of the Nation." Instead of flying, Neruda wanted to see the Siberian landscapes out the window of a train.

Meanwhile, Matilde returned to Paris, back to the third floor of the rue Pierre Mille chalet. She walked around the city, dejected, but then on the day she resolved to return to Mexico, Neruda called and told her a surprise package was coming for her tomorrow. The "package" turned out to be their friend Ivette Joie, a journalist who lived in Czechoslovakia. Ivette appeared on the doorstep to deliver the news that Neruda wasn't sleeping or eating, that he didn't want to see anyone and was behaving violently. Neruda had decided that he wanted to live with Matilde somewhere in Europe where they could be free of the crowds that often accompanied him in public. Matilde took a plane to meet him in Geneva the next day.

When she saw him in a corner of the café where they were to meet, he seemed thinner, his eyes sad and lacking the luster they usually had. Immediately Matilde realized that their time apart had been worth it, because now she could feel how completely she was in love with him. She cried as he took her hands. He looked at her with great tenderness and said, "I don't ever want to see you cry again. That final sob when we left Bucharest has tortured me." He had wonderful news: he had made arrangements for them to go to Nyon, a provincial village on the shore of Lake Geneva, for a few days, just the two of them. Nobody would know where they were. Nobody in that village would know them either. Nyon was idyllic, surrounded by vineyards and rolling hills, and with a lake teeming with swans and seagulls. The couple would finally be able to be together without hiding. They could breathe and laugh and be in love freely.

They used their time in Nyon to learn about each other, swapping endless childhood stories. They both hailed from the provincial south of Chile. They both came from modest childhoods. This connection with Matilde must have been refreshing for Neruda, who had discovered in his new lover a tie to his humble roots. "You are from the poor South, from where my soul comes: / in her heaven your mother keeps washing clothes / with my mother," he would write to her in a love sonnet a few years later. "That's why I chose you, *compañera*."

He told her how it felt to have his poet's temperament as a boy, to be too sensitive for others to understand. He revealed the intimate vulnerabilities and moments of beauty of his childhood. As he shared his stories with Matilde, he prodded her to share her own. She claimed that this was the first time anyone had taken a sincere interest in her past. She had long ago set aside her personal history, having departed from the south of Chile at the age of eighteen to lead a bohemian life as a singer, dancer, and sometime actor. She reveled in recounting stories for Neruda, in making him laugh with her tales of the exploits of small-town folk. She told Neruda about how her mother, who was called Transitito, was widowed and left to raise Matilde on her own. She managed by running a boardinghouse in Chillán. They hosted several guests, among them a man called Jarita, who happened upon a discarded crystal ball one day in the town's central plaza and promptly refashioned himself as a fortune-teller. He was moderately successful in his new career, greatly helping Matilde and Transitito with his gains.

But Matilde's stories of the expansive, wild garden seemed to Neruda the most comforting. He'd repeatedly ask Matilde to tell him about that magical place where she spent so much of her childhood, helping her mother grow vegetables, fruits, and wheat. In her family's lush gardens, roses and camellias commingled with lettuce, celery stalks, and garlic's fragile spears. They shared a passion for Chile's verdant, abundant natural world. These conversations were at times wistful and made Neruda long for Chile. Through Matilde, he reconnected with his place of birth and its people. While he may have been doing well in exile, part of his heart was constantly longing for home.

Matilde quickly transformed their modest hotel room into a homey place, decorating it with paper flowers, fresh flowers, and small pieces of artwork they found in shops in the village. She set a table for them to take their meals. Her instinct for homemaking was new for Neruda; it was not something that interested Delia. Matilde's deep domestic streak was also a maternal one. She had thought she could no longer hope to be a mother; she met Neruda in Mexico City when she was thirty-seven and was now thirty-nine. Matilde didn't know it yet, but she was pregnant again.

She returned to Paris by train as Neruda went first to Prague and then to an event at the Kremlin. In the final weeks of 1951, Neruda and Delia traveled to Rome. He was growing weary from the travel, his knees were bothering him, and he wanted to rest and write. Matilde was already there, staying with Mexican friends. Forgetting his exhaustion, Neruda left Delia to tour the city with Matilde every day. Some of Neruda's friends in Europe knew of the affair, as much as Neruda tried to keep it hidden. Delia remained in denial.

On January 11, 1952, newspaper headlines around Italy announced that the Chilean government had convinced the Italian government to expel Neruda from the country. The poet had just taken a quick trip to visit friends in Naples; the news broke as he was returning to Rome by train. Hundreds swarmed the station, chanting, "Pablo! Pablo!" Years later, Matilde would write in her memoirs of her astonishment at the scene. She struggled to make her way to the platform and was able to catch Neruda's eye after he got off the train: "He smiled to me as if to say, 'Get used to it. This is my life.'" She lost him within the mass of shouting people. Soon a riot broke out, the people versus the police, the writer Elsa Morante enthusiastically wielding her umbrella in the battle. This experience was a turning point in Matilde's deepening involvement with and understanding of her lover. It was one thing to see him give speech after speech in favor of the peace and the people. Now she could really see where and how he existed in the world, the conduit he had become: "I stood there like a frightened chick who had just hatched from a shell to experience the shock of a world of life, of struggle, of people who think beyond their small lives to something bigger and better."

The outcry for Neruda was so great that, after several days of parliamentary and presidential discussions and debate, the government rescinded the order and allowed him to stay for another three months, which he extended for over five more. Edwin Cerio, the affluent Italian writer, invited him to use his house on the island of Capri to rest and write. Neruda convinced Delia to go to Chile, alone, to arrange his return. She left for Buenos Aires, and Matilde and Neruda took refuge on the gorgeous island.

The couple was able to relax there, staring out at the giant limestone rocks that rise from the sea off the coast or lying on its beaches (though they made Neruda long for the waves crashing on Isla Negra's rocks; he was not satisfied with that quiet pocket off the Mediterranean, the Tyrrhenian Sea). From the plaza lined with its open cafés to the island's remote corners, wherever they wandered they got to know the locals, who began to call Neruda "Professore."

Il professore returned to his poetry. While he never stopped writing during his exile, now he had a retreat, a residency on the island. He finished *The Captain's Verses,* a book that would soon be published

anonymously, so as not to hurt Delia. Besides the intimate love po-
etry, a couple of poems ranking among the most amorous verses he
ever wrote, and the lyrical rebuke for having a miscarriage, the book
also contains a political current. The woman he addresses in the book
is not just Matilde his lover but his comrade in arms, her potency and
sexuality symbols of their intense political commitment. In Neruda's
poem "Letter on the Road" (a twist on Whitman's classic "Song of the
Open Road") a line jumps out after the first stanza: "My adored, I am
off to my fighting." While this is the final poem of the book, 153 lines
long, it was written while they were in Nyon, unsure what awaited
their relationship after those first few days alone. He is the captain of
his women, of his ideological cause, but Matilde is the woman he'll
wait for.

> And when the sadness that I hate comes
> to knock on your door,
> tell her that I am waiting for you
> and when loneliness wants you to change
> the ring in which my name is written,
> tell loneliness to talk with me,
> that I had to go away,
> because I am a soldier,
> and that there where I am,
> under rain or under
> fire,
> my life,
> I wait for you.
> I wait for you in the harshest desert . . .

The forty-eight poems in the book were all written when he and
Matilde were first in love. Many were included in letters to her as they
crisscrossed the continents clandestinely, starting in Bucharest, in Au-
gust 1951, and then the next month, as he traveled on the Trans-Siberian
to China, on the plain between Mongolia and Siberia, followed by
Prague, Vienna, Geneva, and other cities in Europe, until Italy, where

nine or ten were written on Capri, including the illustrious "The Night on the Island."

The first edition of just forty-four copies was published in Naples. It begins with an introduction in the form of a letter from the book's publisher, explaining the source of these poems. It is signed Rosario de la Cerda—that name Rosario appearing once again: Matilde's full name was Matilde *Rosario* Urrutia *Cerda*. Her identity, the letter writer says, doesn't matter, but she is the poems' protagonist. The author of the poems came from the war in Spain, but he didn't come defeated. She never knew his real name, whether it was "Martínez, Ramírez, or Sánchez. I simply called him my Captain, and that's the name I want to keep for this book."

The letter firmly establishes the author of the poems as a heroic, idealistic captain, while Rosario portrays herself as a subservient lover. "He was a privileged man of the kind born to great destinies. I felt his force and my greatest pleasure was feeling dwarfed at his side . . . From the first moment, he felt like the owner of my body and my soul." Yet his captive powers instilled a sense of purpose in his subject: "He made me feel that everything in my life was changing, that little artist's life of mine, of comfort and ease, transformed like everything he touched." The captain is a soldier for justice but possesses the traits of a poet: as Monge did for Neftalí, he would search for "a flower, a toy, a river stone" for her, handing it over with tears flowing from his "eyes of infinite tenderness," in which she'd catch "a glimpse of a child's soul."

The forty-four copies were given to subscribers, whose names are printed in it. Most were Italian, including the writer Carlo Levi, except for a few friends from elsewhere who knew of the affair, such as Jorge Amado. Matilde and Neruda were included, as well as one "Neruda Urrutia," who, according to Matilde's memoir, represented the child the two were longing for. Soon after, the Buenos Aires publishing house Losada, which was becoming Neruda's primary publisher, released the book. Losada would print five editions without Neruda's name attached. It would be a decade after its first printing that Neruda ended the anonymity, when in 1962 *The Captain's Verses* was included in the second edition of *Obras completas* (Complete Works). The following year, Losada republished *The Captain's Verses* with Neruda fully credited as the author.[*]

At the beginning of their stay in Capri, Matilde felt that she might be pregnant again. They sent off a test to Naples. According to Matilde, when Neruda came back from the post office with the positive results, he was beaming. They kissed and danced in the plaza.

Months passed and "Pablo spoiled [Matilde] and was very loving." One day he announced, "In a few days when the moon is full, I want to get married, because we should be when the baby is born." On one beautiful spring evening, the lovers sent their maid home early, and Neruda decorated the walls of their house with flowers, branches, and "Matilde, I love you" and "I love you, Matilde" written out on pieces of paper of all colors. She cooked a duck *à l'orange* and small plates of local fish and shrimp. They walked out onto their terrace, where a brilliant full moon awaited. Neruda, very seriously, told the moon that he and Matilde couldn't get married on earth and asked her, *la luna,* the muse of so many lovestruck poets, to marry them in the sky. He took Matilde's arm and placed a ring on her finger, with an inscription that read: "Capri, May 3, 1952, Your Captain . . ."

Their time together was idyllic until Matilde started to feel sick. Knowing of her history, the doctor prescribed bed rest. At her side, Neruda would ask Matilde to tell him long stories about her childhood, about her parents, to keep her spirits up and to be engaged. They read a lot; they made fires. As they were confined to their home, their rather small dog, Nyon, named after the town where they spent those magical

---

* The edition included an explanation from Neruda for why this hadn't happened until then: his anonymity, about which "much has been said," had lasted so long "because of nothing and everything, because of this and that, because of improper pleasures and the suffering of others." He was also reluctant to expose the "private aspects of the book's birth," as that seemed "unfaithful to the fits of love and fury, the disconsolate and ardent climate of exile that had brought it forth." He concludes that "with no further explanation, I present this book as if it was mine and not mine: it's enough that it might go out into the world and grow on its own. Now that I recognize it, I hope that its furious blood will recognize me as well."

moments alone on Lake Geneva, became restless, missing and needing the long walks they used to go for. He ran away one Saturday afternoon and wasn't back that Sunday morning. They told their host, Edwin Cerio, about it, and before they knew it the island's radio started making announcements about the missing dog. Nyon returned on his own Sunday night.

But before long, "a shadow descended" on the couple, Matilde wrote, "threatening to wrap us in sadness and anxiety." She lost her child, "who already had his own copy of *The Captain's Verses*." But this time Neruda didn't hold it against her. Instead, he announced, "I'm going to give you a child. It's just been born, and its name is *Las uvas y el viento*."

The "child" does not have the haunting passion of *The Captain's Verses*. Far from the moralist realism of "The Heights of Macchu Picchu," *Las uvas y el viento* (*The Grapes and the Wind*) uses socialist realism to depict (through Stalin-colored glasses) Neruda's impressions of his travels through Eastern Europe. The book is an attempt to dazzle the reader with what lies behind the dark drapes of the Iron Curtain, as René de Costa puts it. In *Canto General*, Neruda constructed himself as the poet of the Americas; he dons the mantle of the poet of socialism. The verse, however, falls short. The only enthusiastic regard the book generated came from the Soviet Union itself, which awarded Neruda the Stalin Peace Prize for it in 1953.

As summer came, so did the tourists, who found out about the famous poet's presence on Capri and would not leave him in peace. The island quickly lost its charm, and the couple moved to the volcanic island of Ischia in the Gulf of Naples. They spent the month of June there, and then came the news: it was time to return to Chile. Neruda's political friends in Santiago had fought hard for it. The Senate itself had asked for Neruda's arrest warrant to be rescinded, and enough time had passed that the government was ready to move on. Every time he made an appearance on the international stage, officials had to defend Chile's persecution of Neruda. Additionally, high inflation, continued labor unrest, a weary and frustrated population, and the end of his presidential term had led González Videla to relax his crackdown on the Communists and left him with no political capital to continue the vendetta.

During this period, notably when the repression was at its worst, the Chilean Communist Party did not deviate from its policy of pursuing change through democracy. One faction had advocated armed struggle to achieve the party's goals, but it was expelled by the main leadership, which included Neruda's close friends. Instead, the leaders plotted a course toward a "bourgeoisie democratic revolution," where the peaceful fight for radical change would be led by the working class and the "enlightened" new bourgeoisie—capitalists with wealth and economic power who no longer wanted to exploit the workers. The road to socialism in Chile would be paved by this unity, combined with the continued industrialization of the country. Neruda supported this strategy. In his two years on the road, from 1948 to 1950, Neruda was one of the most active Communist artists in the world. He was also developing his own insights and positions that his poetry would soon illuminate.

Neruda flew to Berlin for one more political act, a special meeting of the World Peace Council. Then he met Matilde in Cannes, where they'd depart on a steamer to Uruguay. Neruda hated flying, and this voyage would give them time alone together. Neruda's friends came to give him a surprise farewell lunch in a restaurant next to the Mediterranean. Among them was Picasso, and, the weather being hot, the artist tore off his multicolored shirt. On his muscular chest was a gold Minotaur, held around his neck by a shoestring. Everyone admired it. Picasso took it off and bestowed it on Neruda.

And then, just after the large meal with flowing wine, came the news that the French government had called for Neruda's expulsion from the country. "I've been thrown out of the best places," he would say later. Though he was no longer exiled from his homeland, it still must have stung to be expelled by his beloved France.

Neruda and Matilde boarded their boat, and from somewhere off the African coast, Neruda sent a message to his country:

> The future of humanity may be endangered in the hands of a
> few evil men, but it does not belong to them. The future of man
> is ours, because we are the embodiment of hope. We Chileans
> have a lot to do. I will be working with you, among you, as just

another one of you. When I return to my homeland after such a long trip, I only say to you: "I dedicated my life to defending the honor of Chile. Now I return once again to put my life in the hands of my people."

★

On August 12, 1952, people from all over Santiago came to the airport to welcome Neruda home. He arrived alone, with Matilde traveling separately from Montevideo so as to conceal their relationship. Delia and the press went to the front of the airplane stairs. Neruda descended, a little plump, in a sports coat and a green *sombrerito*. The poet's first hug was for Delia. His first words in Chile after four years were: "I salute the noble people of Chile, to whom I owe my return. I salute my beloved homeland, and I hope that freedom, peace, and happiness will always be the law of the land here." The crowd on the terrace sang the national anthem to him.

He returned with eight suitcases stuffed with books, shells, and other objects he had collected in exile. Other possessions had been shipped separately.

Flowers lined the walk at La Michoacán from the street to the halls within, while two policemen stood outside, writing down the license plate numbers of all the guests. The crackdown on the Communists may have softened, but with the Cold War still going strong in South America, the party stayed outlawed until 1958, and the government kept tabs on its former members and other leftists.

Once in the house, Neruda gave an interview to the magazine *Ercilla*, declaring that for the upcoming elections,

> I will offer my support to Allende as the people's candidate . . . As for my future activities, I cannot add anything more at this time. Those decisions are not mine to make; they are for my party. I am a disciplined Communist militant.
>
> I want to make something clear about the rumors going around that conditions were placed upon my arrival. There

have been no such conditions, and I would not have ac-
cepted any. My arrival is the result of a triumphant struggle
that began the moment I left. I have no grudges or hatred
against anyone.

He then tried to dispel any notions that his life in exile had been
full of bourgeois indulgences, that he had become too international. He
claimed that he was just a typical Chilean, "the opposite of cosmopoli-
tan. Before, people in my generation liked living in Paris. I like living
in my land, with everything it produces. Chilean peaches and oysters
are beyond comparison." There was sincerity in those words. Neruda
could live anywhere in the world, but other than frequent short trips
and his brief time as ambassador to France in the early 1970s, from this
point on he would always live in his beloved Chile. The Uruguayan
writer Emir Rodríguez Monegal named Neruda the "Immobile Trav-
eler," with one foot always in his home country.

When he donated a vast portion of his library and seashell collection
to the University of Chile just before his fiftieth birthday, Neruda pos-
ited, "The poet isn't a lost stone. He has two sacred obligations: to leave
and to return." He added that especially in countries like Chile, geo-
graphically "isolated in the wrinkles of the planet," where the origins
of everyone from the humblest to the most distinguished are known,
"we have the fortune to be able to create our nation, to all be something
like parents to it."

The welcome party for his return from exile moved on to Plaza
Bulnes, where three or four thousand people were waiting for the re-
turning hero. There was a band dressed in yellow satin. When the poet
arrived, the crowd started chanting, "¡Neruda! ¡Neruda!" Tomás Lago
said that Neruda wept. When the speeches were done, the multitude
marched in a parade down La Alameda, Santiago's great boulevard,
to Salvador Allende's presidential campaign headquarters. The Allende
command had in fact been eagerly awaiting Neruda's return, hoping his
celebrity and energy would invigorate its campaign, which had failed
to gain much traction. But Neruda's support gained little, especially
with the Communist Party still illegal, the Socialists suffering from

internal divisions, and Allende's group lacking the resources to mount a sufficient national campaign. Allende received just 5 percent of the vote. Carlos Ibáñez, a former dictator who had run as an independent populist promising to clean up Chile, became the new president. It was Chile's first presidential election in which women could vote.

Neruda settled back into La Michoacán with Delia, where he would spend less time with her and more at his writing desk. The desk was made of blond wood and surrounded by stacks of books and photographs of Edgar Allan Poe, Walt Whitman, and Charles Baudelaire. He usually started around nine in the morning, after breakfast. He had a regimen, setting out to write one, two, sometimes three poems each day. Neruda said he had neither the time nor desire to reread his poems over and over. He always wrote in green ink, though he never specifically explained why. Many attribute Neruda's use of green to it being a symbol of hope. He rarely used a typewriter after a hand injury he had incurred. In a 1971 interview with the *Paris Review,* he explained:

> Ever since I had an accident in which I broke a finger and couldn't use the typewriter for a few months, I have followed the custom of my youth and gone back to writing by hand. I discovered when my finger was better and I could type again that my poetry when written by hand was more sensitive; its plastic forms could change more easily. In an interview, Robert Graves says that in order to think one should have as little as possible around that is not handmade. He could have added that poetry ought to be written by hand. The typewriter separated me from a deeper intimacy with poetry, and my hand brought me closer to that intimacy again.

Delia, then Matilde, or his secretaries Homero Arce and the tireless Margarita Aguirre, would type his handwritten papers. Delia often made corrections and suggestions, which he'd often take to heart and include.

Almost all of La Michoacán was made from organic materials,

like the coarse, rustic wood of Neruda and Delia's long outdoor table, which held vegetables from tender fava beans and spring onions with long green stalks to the ripest tomatoes from just outside Santiago. It might be covered with a sheet, never a more formal tablecloth. It was a stage that Neruda would set, arranging everything spontaneously. Potbellied jugs of peaches in Chilean white wine or strawberries in red wine were placed along the table, with green fluted glass goblets placed beside them.

As Aida Figueroa put it in a 2003 interview, "He was the stage designer of life. He didn't live overambitiously, but rather he lived a life filled with surprise, excitement, and exploration." Upon Neruda and Delia's return, Aida and her husband, Sergio Insunza, became close friends with the two older Communists they had hidden in their apartment before Neruda fled into exile. They came over almost every Saturday for lunch. Aida asserted that she couldn't think of a more delightful time than the hours they spent at La Michoacán between 1952 and 1955, the "years they were together before Delia knew about Matilde."

Inés Valenzuela commented on how often people came over and that Neruda "was very tender with Delia. Pablo was attached to Delia, not the other way around; she was affectionate but *tranquilla*."

Neruda the Captain was home triumphant, with wife and lover, party and friends, flourishing, beaming, fulfilled. The sickly boy from Temuco and the depressed consul in the Far East were long gone.

To visitors, life at La Michoacán was a celebration of harmony and friendship, of sharing and singing. Sometimes they put on a simple show in the garden's amphitheater, dedicated to Lorca. Neruda usually spoke little, but he was the great director of everything going on. "He made everything magical," Aida said. "And la Hormiga complemented him. That house never had a closed door. There never was a key, not to the door to the street, not to the fence, not to Pablo's room, not anywhere. It was an open house. La Hormiga kept it that way."

Neruda's poetry seemed to draw on the same sunny comforts. The poem "The Invisible Man," written in Italy just before he returned, can be seen as yet another literary manifesto. It is almost diametrically opposed to the surrealistic "Arte poética" he had written during his time in the Far East, the one he continued to shun for its abstraction and negativity in light of the battle the people were waging for justice, peace, and progress. The poem is much lighter, less dense, and while long, it signals the form of his coming odes; most of the 244 lines are short and simple, just three or four words long:

I'm not superior
to my brother,
but I smile,
because when I walk through the streets
and only I do not exist,
life runs
like all the rivers,
I am the only
invisible one,
there aren't mysterious shadows,
no mist,
the whole world speaks to me,
everyone wants to tell me things,
they talk to me about their relatives,
their miseries
and their joy . . .

Neruda had laid out this new perspective and voice in an interview with Lenka Franulic the day he returned from exile.[*] She asked if it was true that in Mexico, he publicly renounced *Twenty Love Poems* and *Residence*. Not exactly, he answered. "I've said that my first poetry is pessimistic, gloomy, and painful, that it expresses the anguish of my youth. That anguish wasn't produced by *me*, but rather by society itself, by the decomposition of life in the capitalist system. I don't want that poetry to influence the youth now. We must fight and struggle."

---

[*] Franulic is considered to be Chile's first important female journalist, at the time working for the magazine *Ercilla*.

He went on to make some of his clearest statements on realism. Because of the struggle, because of the fight, because he had "tremendous faith in Chile," because the fight must continue, he told Franulic, "I write in a different form now." His personal approach was about to become a more dynamic, subtle, natural realism, still anchored in the social, still eschewing anything complex or unclear. "When one sends people into combat, they cannot sing funeral songs. From this comes what's called new realism," he explained. "The return to realism has a double bottom: the aesthetic needs of humans and the political background. My ambition is to write like one whistles while walking down the street. I think this should be the language of absolutely straightforward, untrembling poetry."

"The Invisible Man" is his first attempt to realize this ambition. It is neither a political diatribe nor a love poem, but in it Neruda has gone from introvert to extrovert, with a language accessible to all, stripped down to the bare realities. Neruda the man, the monumental man and poet, must make himself invisible, an everyman indistinguishable in the crowd, equal to his fellow workers.

He communicates through the clarity of the language, straightforward and clean, without airs; he becomes transparent. From now on, his poetry will be transparent like never before. "There are no mysterious shadows, / there is no darkness," Neruda writes in the poem. He is still serving as a poet, but one who has come down off the pedestal to stand with the masses, with the men and women in the street. When he says, "Everyone wants to tell me things," he's showing his accessibility. They talk to him about their relatives, just as they'd talk to their friend or neighbor, and he amplifies their voices. By using the first person, the voice is grounded in a being—he is present; he is invested in it. The poem is tangible; it is not art for art's sake.

"The Invisible Man" is very reminiscent of "The Heights of Macchu Picchu." There he expressed the Incan workers' plight, their silenced language, to raise consciousness with the hope of stimulating social change. At the end of "The Invisible Man," he asks his fellow Chileans to share their concerns, their stories of suffering, in order to transmit the story of their plight as well.

"The people give me my poetry and I give my poetry to the people," Neruda proclaimed at a party fund-raiser the year the poem came out. It was a pretentious assumption, in the same vein as presuming to be the spokesperson for the ancient workers. Still, he had the perception and the motivation to create unique poetry that interpreted the social realities of "the people" in a radically different way, allowing their stories to transcend the oppressive ideologies of the upper, ruling classes. It was that reciprocity that defined his life at this stage, the role he had assumed on and off the written page, answering his calling as if it were an obligation. The poet's calling: an obligation, yet also a natural impulse; simultaneously being called while calling to others.

> give me
> the everyday
> struggles
> because they are my song,
> and that way we will walk together,
> shoulder to shoulder,
> all of humanity,
> my song unites them:
> the song of the invisible man
> who sings with humanity.

"The Invisible Man" would be the first poem, a kind of preface, for the first of four books of odes Neruda published between 1952 and 1959—a total of 216 odes.[*] In 1953, Neruda said, "On our earth, before writing was invented, before the printing press was invented, poetry flourished. That is why we know that poetry is like bread; it should be shared by all, by scholars and by peasants, by all our vast, incredible, extraordinary family of humanity." Neruda's new odes reached an extremely vast range of readers. The odes were oriented toward so-

---

[*]   This includes the book *Navegaciones y regresos* (Voyages and Homecomings), subtitled "Este libro es el cuarto volumen de las *Odas elementales*"—"this book is the fourth volume of *Elemental Odes*."

cial themes; their style was still realist, the style in which he had been writing over the past decades. Yet perhaps more than almost all the other poems written after the outbreak of the Spanish Civil War, his approach in the odes was experimental, full of the innovation and creative spontaneity with which he began his career.

Neruda's close friend Miguel Otero Silva, editor in chief of *El Nacional* in Caracas, who had published Neruda's denouncement of González Videla, asked him to contribute a weekly column of poetry. Neruda agreed but asked that the poems be printed in the main news pages rather than the arts supplement. Although only a handful of his odes appeared in the paper, through the practice he found the form for his odes.

The small columns of the newspaper obliged Neruda to make shorter lines, and the opportunity to reach all the readers of the newspaper—not just those who read the culture pages—led Neruda to make the poems seem simpler, though not simplistic, using everyday language for everyday people about everyday things. This simple, elementary form reflected the odes' relationship to the elementary objects he wanted to describe. The poems Neruda wrote for the newspaper were the drawing board for hundreds more, which would, through those four books of his, elevate the quotidian in a political act of subverting social hierarchy.

Often the ordinary subject matter—onions, tomatoes, conger eel chowder, even socks—and their free, almost prosaic voice made the odes seem less "poetic," more plainspoken. But Neruda's thoughtful, conceptual associations gave the poems a compelling, often surprising punch, so that they captured the reader's attention. Through his technique, he was able to make these everyday subjects seem sublime. As Jaime Concha, professor emeritus of Latin American literature at the University of California, San Diego, puts it: by focusing on the "fragile singularities" of these objects, individually and minute within the midst of all the universal laws of the material world, Neruda makes "the great energies of totality pulse within these minuscule grains, both symbolic and edible." One of the remarkable qualities of the odes is that he achieves all of that through complex, challenging, groundbreaking poetic work behind the scenes of the lines; he is able to place the object within a matrix of social relations and then spin a transformational poem around it without disturbing the poem's simple, elemental appearance and accessibility.

Neruda wrote odes to everything, from a chestnut fallen on the ground to poverty, from Walt Whitman to an anonymous bricklayer. Perhaps Neruda wrote too many odes, for at a certain point their efficient beauty isn't sustained. Still, this new form was among his greatest literary achievements, in particular the first two volumes. The odes are a major reason Neruda is considered to be one of the most exuberant poets of all time.

The odes are organized alphabetically, as if he set out to write an ambitious, innovative encyclopedia in line with the famous eighteenth-century French *Encyclopédie,* whose descriptions reflected the ideals of the Enlightenment thinkers who contributed to it, including Montesquieu, Rousseau, and Voltaire, with Denis Diderot as chief editor. Inspired by the thirty-nine-volume set of the *Encyclopédie* he had purchased while in exile in France, Neruda intended to describe and record everyday elements and objects that have a social function, that relate and are useful to the daily experience of humankind. He hoped to expand upon the records of the Enlightenment thinkers by adding in a higher, more developed dose of class consciousness and by elevating the ode form to deliver the essentials of each subject to the reader in a dynamic and memorable way.

In his careful, meditative examination of each subject, Neruda sometimes demonstrated social disparities. In virtually every poem he expressed a natural optimism that came from describing the reality of everyday objects, sometimes by animating them and presenting them as living beings. In a few cases the subjects were living beings, such as César Vallejo or Paul Robeson, but sometimes they were intangible, as in "Ode to Happiness," or inanimate, like in "Ode to the Chair":

> War is vast like the shadowed jungle
> Peace
> begins
> in a single
> chair.

The odes received favorable reviews, including high praise from Alone. While his conservatism never became a major factor in his literary criticism of Neruda, Alone found it hard to accept both the prosody and political bent in some of the work he wrote toward the end of his exile, heavy on social realism and Stalinist overtones, *Las uvas y el viento* in particular. This made his review of the first book of odes in the conservative newspaper *El Mercurio* more remarkable:

> Some say this clarity of expression was imposed by the Soviets so that Neruda would be able to reach the masses. If that were true, we would have to forgive the Soviets for an awful lot . . . never has the poetry of Neruda seemed more authentic . . .
>
> We would like to place a limit on this praise. It is said that no judgment is good without its reservations. But we can find none. We even forgive the poet his communism.

Alone was really impressed by the book's optimism, writing, "Neruda has never smiled as he does now." The new joy led to a new clarity in his poems, Alone believed, directly reaffirming Neruda's goals. Besides their lyrical value, many of the odes work as a political tool, using compelling verse to convey the social utility of everyday, natural objects. Because of the familiarity and accessibility of these objects, we often lose sight of their value. Neruda's goal was to help the reader to recognize their implicit virtue. "Ode to the Onion," for instance, celebrates an ordinary vegetable through elevated praise:

> the earth
> [made] you,
> onion,
> clear as a planet,
> and destined
> to shine,
> constant constellation,

round rose of water,
upon
the table
of the poor.

With "Ode to Wine" (complete poem in Appendix I) as the last poem of the first book of *Elemental Odes,* Neruda leaves his readers on a joyous note and with a renewed respect for the magic of winemaking. Neruda exalts the elixir, not as a gift from the gods of ancient times or modern religions, but as a result of man and nature's hard, collaborative work to grow the grapes and work them into the final product.

While Neruda adapted and modified the traditional ode to his own artistic purposes, he began by following Pindaric classical form, praising the poem's subject in a direct, personal address:

Wine color of day,
wine color of night,
wine with your feet of purple
or topaz blood,
wine,
starry child
of the earth

He then demonstrates that wine is for all:

you've never been contained in one glass,
in one song, in one man,
choral, you are gregarious,
and, at least, mutual

Wine is for rich and poor alike, abundantly pleasuring each and all, a salve in bad times, a celebratory toast in good. Neruda here shows the vastness of wine's spirit, its sacredness to man.

Then in a typical move, Neruda turns from the natural to the sensual:

My love, suddenly
your hip
is the curve of the wineglass
filled to the brim,
your breast is the cluster,
your hair the light of alcohol,
your nipples, the grapes
your navel pure seal
stamped on your barrel of a belly,
and your love the cascade
of unquenchable wine,
the brightness that falls on my senses,
the earthen splendor of life.

This merging of the woman's body with the celebrated object is in line with many of his odes and a nod to the work of the English romantics.

Neruda ends by ensuring that the reader appreciates the labor, especially by nature herself, that goes into creating wine and all the properties of it he has just exalted:

I love the light of a bottle
of intelligent wine
upon a table
when people are talking,
that they drink it,
that in each drop of gold
or ladle of purple,
they remember
that autumn toiled
until the barrels were full of wine,
and let the obscure man learn,
in the ceremony of his business,
to remember the earth and his duties,
to propagate the canticle of the fruit.

The poem ends with us rooted in a vision: what is most sacred about wine is the work man puts into cultivating earth's bounty. In *Canto General*, Neruda stressed how man was made from the earth. He now stresses man's duty to cultivate what the earth provides. In both cases, he reminds us that we and the earth are a single indissoluble entity and that it is through a collective, cooperative effort that this essential oneness is created.

★

Joseph Stalin died on March 5, 1953. Between 1936 and 1938, he had arrested over a million of his own party members in his Great Purge. At least six hundred thousand were killed, many from torture. He imprisoned and killed hundreds of thousands of peasants who resisted agrarian collectivization. Estimates range from five to fifty million deaths caused by the famine that resulted from Stalin's ill-conceived policies. Many believe the famine in Ukraine was an intentional act of genocide. Stalin imposed a regime of state terror all over the Soviet Union, which spread into Soviet Bloc countries as well. There were over a million and a half deportations to Siberia and Central Asia.

Still, Neruda wrote a 236-line poem, "On His Death," soon translated for communists around the world:

> To be men! This is
> the Stalinist law!
> To be a communist is difficult,
> You have to learn how to be one.
> To be communist men
> is even more difficult,
> and you have to learn from Stalin,
> his serene intensity,
> his concrete clarity,
> . . . .
> Stalin is the noon,
> the maturity of man and the peoples.
> . . . .

Stalinists. Let us bear this title with pride.
Stalinists. This is the hierarch of our times!
Stalinist workers, fishermen, musicians!
Stalinist forgers of steel, fathers of copper!
Stalinist doctors, nitrate workers, poets!
Stalinist learned men, students, campesinos!
Cheers, greetings today! The light hasn't disappeared,
the fire hasn't disappeared,
but rather the light, the bread, the fire and hope,
grow from invincible Stalinist time!

Neruda's support of Stalin, of Stalinism, is one of the most controversial aspects of his life and character, an apparent divergence from the popular image of a pacifist, humanitarian, democratic Neruda. In general, especially for American and European readers, his alignment with Stalin can be jarring.

Despite its strict belief in change through the ballot box, the Chilean Communist Party, like many Communist Parties around the world, was strictly Stalinist. It believed that defending the Soviet Union was essential to protecting the values and the people they believed in, especially in the fight against fascism. For many, this idea first grew from the political circumstances surrounding the Spanish Civil War, which pushed a vast number of people like Neruda to the left. The United States, England, and France had abandoned the Spanish Republic. France had acted indifferently toward the desperate refugees, who had nowhere else to go in their retreat from Franco's forces. So they took a side: Stalin defended their comrades and their ideals. And from that point forward they planted the flag of Stalinism, making a firm commitment that would prove hard to break later on.

Had Neruda been a U.S. or French citizen, he might have renounced Stalinism based on the realities of the Cold War and his personal convictions. He might have even renounced the Communist Party. But in Chile, the Communist Party had given Neruda a platform, a support network, and even a senatorial nomination. Neruda had become personally invested in it, to the degree that by the time Stalin's crimes came to light, it was too hard for him or other members of the party, including Delia, to break from it. Neruda had partially constructed his political identity out of the Communist Party's perspective. For him the party wasn't just a group of people who wanted to change the world, but thousands of working-class families the entire length of the country. It may have seemed impossible for Neruda to renounce his allegiance to Stalin, because in some sense he would be renouncing his family as well.

While it was one thing to defend Stalin, it was another to trample on personal friendships and practicalities in order to toe the party line. His relationship with the Polish Nobel laureate Czeslaw Milosz is one example. Milosz's anti-Soviet political views had created tensions with his Communist government, forcing him to seek political asylum in France. He had previously lived in Paris during the time Neruda was in exile, and he became friends with the Chilean, attending parties with him and his leftist friends. Milosz had even translated some of Neruda's poetry a few years earlier. But once he publicly turned away from the regimes and communism, he instantly became persona non grata. The newspaper of the French Communist Party assigned Neruda the task of writing the denunciation of Milosz, which he did, in an article entitled "The Man Who Ran Away," naming Milosz, among other slanders, "an agent of American imperialism."

Neruda was by no means the only artist, writer, or intellectual swept up by Stalinism in that period. Neruda's article isolated Milosz among French intellectuals who were all pro-Soviet in those years (except Albert Camus, who remained his friend). As Milosz explained in a 1994 *Paris Review* interview, "Anyone who was dissatisfied and who came from the East like myself was considered a madman or an agent of America."

In his classic book *Zniewolony umysł* (*The Captive Mind*), detailing the magnetism that totalitarian thought exerted on many intellectuals, Milosz mentions Neruda:

> When he describes the misery of his people, I believe him and I respect his great heart. When writing, he thinks about

his brothers and not about himself, and so to him the power of the word is given. But when he paints the joyous, radiant life of people in the Soviet Union, I stop believing him. I am inclined to believe him as long as he speaks about what he knows: I stop believing him when he starts to speak about what I know myself.

A decade and a half after Neruda wrote his denunciation of his former friend, the two saw each other at the 1966 PEN Conference in New York. Neruda saw Milosz across the room, cried, "Czeslaw!" and rushed to embrace him. Milosz turned his face away and Neruda said, "But, Czeslaw, that was politics."

Eventually, given the overwhelming evidence, Neruda would use his poetry as a means to address Stalin's abuses and the failure of the Soviet Union to achieve the ideals of socialism. He'd even criticize Stalin in public pronouncements. Though he didn't do it aloud, within the texture of his poetry, he'd even ask for absolution from his once-blind allegiance.

But in December 1953, Neruda, Delia, and Volodia Teitelboim (by then one of the highest-ranking officials of the Chilean Communist Party) traveled to Moscow for the Second Soviet Writers Congress at the Kremlin. They stayed at the luxurious Hotel Metropol, where they received intellectuals and politicians and planned great parties. The trip was cut short, as Neruda came down with the flu and decided suddenly to return home. He said he wanted to be back in Chile for Christmas. Delia couldn't understand why he would travel while so sick. She said bitterly to Teitelboim, "I don't know how he can make the trip in such conditions. It could be dangerous. Why is he in such a rush?" Teitelboim couldn't answer. Delia felt he knew more than he was letting on, which he did: Neruda had told him he was returning to see Matilde. Matilde was upset that Neruda had traveled without her, and she gave him an ultimatum: either return and be with her for the end-of-year holidays, or she would go to Mexico and leave him forever.

When he returned to Chile, Matilde made it known that she was not happy with her cramped, drab living situation. The new setting was a stark contrast to Capri, and Santiago was suffering through rolling blackouts in order to conserve energy, which added to her agitation. Gone was the light of Capri and the Mexican sun, gone was her ability to have Neruda all to herself. Having idealized Chile from afar while abroad, she wasn't prepared for its gritty realities: "What am I going to do in this piece-of-shit country?" she asked Neruda. His eyes grew wide, then he glared at her for saying this. "This piece-of-shit country is yours!" he yelled back. "No one should avoid what is ugly or difficult."

"He was right," Matilde realized. "Luckily, I started to cry, which was something Pablo could never bear." The tears worked; he apologized, adding, "I'm a total brute." They hugged and reaffirmed, according to Matilde, that "this is how it is. We live here now. We decided to be together forever."

Neruda began to take Matilde to Isla Negra instead of Delia. Meanwhile, he and his wild-haired lover searched for a home larger than her apartment. They found a piece of land in the bohemian Bellavista neighborhood, at the foot of San Cristóbal Hill. It was filled with vines and weeds on a steep slope. A stream ran across the upper edge of the property, where there was a splendid view of the city and the Andes. Matilde could buy the land and begin construction with a well-invested small inheritance. Neruda loved the idea.

And then she found out that she was pregnant again. The doctor prescribed bed rest. Neruda visited her constantly at her apartment (as the house was still being built). "He spoiled me to the extreme," she wrote. He brought her Dostoyevsky and Proust. He was hoping for a girl. When she was in her sixth month of pregnancy, the doctor said she was out of danger and could end her bed rest. Fifteen days later, she miscarried again. Matilde was forty-two at the time. She and Neruda would have no children.

On December 21, 1953, Neruda was awarded the Stalin Prize for Strengthening Peace Among the Peoples for "outstanding merit in the struggle for the conservation and consolidation of peace." It was the Soviet Union's version of the Nobel Peace Prize. Neruda had served on the prize jury in years past, and many members of the jury were his friends. "I am very moved," he said upon the news. "This is the most important honor I can have in my life." He used the prize money for the construction of the new house.

Meanwhile, Maruca appeared before a judge in Santiago to demand money from Neruda. Tomás Lago went to the courthouse to speak on Neruda's behalf. In his journal, he wrote:

> When I saw that woman there, in the crowd of people entering and exiting the second-floor offices, I had the impression that the only thing in the world left for her to do would be to get Pablo to give her enough money to live. It looks like she doesn't do anything else. She has no other activity or goal. Since she's very tall, she could be seen from afar. She was dressed in an ad hoc way, like a disgraced woman, the victim of a gutless man, wearing a fur coat that looked borrowed and a dress in a neutral color, which made it look used and cheap.

Neruda had funds to spare, but he probably viewed Maruca's lawsuit as an attempt to be part of his life once more. He ignored it, with cruel contempt, though to the public he was positioning himself as the humanitarian hero of his continent and beyond. It's not as if Maruca had slighted him—unless he still somehow held her accountable for Malva Marina's invalidity, just as he mentally manipulated Matilde for her miscarriages—it was he who had left Maruca and Malva helpless in Europe. He denied her as if to deny her existence, just as he denied the presence of Malva in his memoirs.

Neruda and Delia went to Brazil for a cultural congress organized by Jorge Amado, and Matilde was seen at some of Neruda's readings there. According to Teitelboim, who was also there, "the girls revolved around the stars, especially Neruda, with la Hormiga—in whose eyes you could see a remote sadness—constantly by his side."

Neruda moved closer to a decisive break with Delia when he convinced her to go to Paris to work on the production of a luxurious French edition of *Canto General*. With her gone, Neruda invited a handful of his close friends out to dinner with the purpose of introducing them to his new *amor*, Matilde, a.k.a. "Rosario." His friends were sitting down at the table when, as Tomás Lago wrote,

> She came dressed in white, in a moire silk suit. She was a vivacious redhead of normal height, with smiling eyes, features that were slightly hard but harmonious, and a sensual air about her. She had a head like Medusa, her hair a nest of vipers. When someone called her name, I started. Her name was Rosario. I had known it for a while . . . Her name appeared in the poem "Let the Rail-Splitter Awake," at the end: "Peace for my right hand, which only wants to write the name 'Rosario.'"
>
> During the meal, he would approach her periodically and embrace her, touch her legs and bring her close to him with true pleasure and delight. He called her *mi amor* each time . . .

Neruda seemed to hope he could orchestrate Delia's discovery of the relationship. Some days afterward, Lago was returning home with Neruda, who asked to stop off at Matilde's apartment on the way: "At one point, the two of us were left alone there, and Pablo asked me a question, looking down at his shoes. 'Well, did you tell Delia everything or not? Tell me the truth.'"

Once a little room, bathroom, and tiny kitchen had been built in Bellavista, Matilde moved in while the construction continued. The house became known as La Chascona, a Chilean word describing Matilde's wildly curly hair. Like all the houses Neruda built, it is poetically eccentric. The dining room feels like the interior of a ship. There are several pictures of Whitman in various sizes in various rooms. The letters *M* and *P* intertwine in iron in front of the windows. The house scrambles up the hill in three levels, connected by outdoor paths and stairs.

Neruda's double life was becoming very difficult to maintain. Finally, one day, when he and Matilde were at Isla Negra, the poet somehow offended the housemaid. In revenge, she told Delia about the other woman. Then the gardener at La Michoacán, after being accused by Neruda of stealing bottles of wine, told Delia how Matilde had moved in when Delia had been hospitalized briefly after a car accident. "I'm a Communist, *señora,* and Communists don't accept these things," *el jardinero* told her.

Then Neruda and Matilde got in a car accident together themselves, which made the news: a famous poet alone with a beautiful single woman. The discovery Neruda had hoped for had happened, but too publicly for his taste, and it brought no relief. Delia started to appear nervous, distracted, and panicked to her friends. Neruda slipped off during his daily siestas at La Michoacán to spend his afternoons with Matilde.

Inés Valenzuela and Diego Muñoz, who were living with Neruda and Delia at La Michoacán, decided they had to confront the issue and raised it with Neruda. He insisted that Delia would always be his *señora,* that Matilde was willing to take second stage. But Delia wanted no part of such an arrangement. A militant Communist, she took the matter to the heads of her party.

Eventually the party intervened and told Neruda that he had to decide between Matilde and Delia. With his affair gaining more gravitas, with his being a public face of the party, and with Delia being an important member as well, this could not continue. "The truth of the matter is that he didn't want to have to do without either one," recalled Inés Valenzuela. "Up until the very end, he begged Delia not to go. It was a complicated situation . . . I remember going with Delia to her room, and I said to her, 'Don't go, amiga, stay here.' And she said to me, 'Would you accept something like this?' And there you have it. So she went to Paris . . ."

Neruda sent her a telegram: "Hormiguita, come back, everything will go back to the way it was. Come home." Soon after he sent her a letter, eleven pages long, in which, according to Inés, "he begged to see her, begged her to continue being his friend. Basically he said he would never erase her from his heart, because she had been the one who had offered him the greatest friendship."

Some twenty years later, following his death, Delia said, "Since 1952 our activities sent us on divergent paths. Pablo became involved with other people. I became increasingly interested in my art. There was no animosity. There isn't much more I can say. I loved Pablo and he will always be in my heart."

At the time of the separation, Neruda was forty-eight, Matilde was forty-three, and Delia was sixty-eight.

Tomás Lago had been one of Neruda's closest friends for decades, but after the breakup with Delia, a rift occurred between the two. Lago's sympathy lay with Delia. Despite this, some months after Delia and Neruda's separation, he asked them both to be witnesses at his daughter's wedding. Neruda didn't go, apparently unable to participate alongside Delia. He just sent a gift of antique wine cruets. Lago never saw Neruda again.

Inés Valenzuela and Diego Muñoz, despite their special love for Delia, didn't take sides in front of Neruda. Shortly after the split, he invited them to a party for Chile's Independence Day, on September 18, 1955, at La Chascona, where he was now living with Matilde. Inés was reluctant to go, recovering from surgery and still upset with how Neruda had treated Delia. But Diego, Neruda's friend since grammar school, insisted. As soon as Neruda saw Inés arrive he came down. "Look, this is Matilde. I hope you can be very good friends." With so many people there celebrating, it was hard to hold a conversation. So Neruda invited them the next day for lunch, just the four of them. There, Matilde said something quite vulgar about Delia, something so inappropriate Inés refused to repeat it when recounting the story (it was a reference to her teeth). "Aside from that being a lie, it's simply slander," she told Matilde strongly. "I won't accept it, and, Matilde, I'm going to ask you that if we're going to be friends, don't even talk about la Hormiga in front of me. I don't like la Hormiga because she was Pablo's wife; I like her because she is an exceptional human being." Pablo, with a large smile, raised his glass of wine and said, "Let's drink to la Hormiga, because I love how you love her so much."

"And that was the end of that," Inés concluded.

As Neruda would write almost ten years after the breakup:

Delia is the light of the window open
to truth, to the honey-tree . . .
. . . .
Delia, among so many leaves
in the tree of life,
your presence
in the fire,
your virtue
of dew:
in the raging wind,
a dove.
   —"Loves: Delia (I)"

Delia eventually returned from Paris and lived out her life in La Michoacán, devoting all her energy to activism and her art, including a well-regarded print series of abstract horses in black, white, and silver gray. She passed away peacefully in her sleep on July 26, 1989, at the age of 104.

CHAPTER NINETEEN

FULLY EMPOWERED

I write in the clear sun, in the teeming street,
At full tide, in a place I can sing;
Only the wayward night inhibits me,
But in its interruption I recover space,
I gather shadows to last a long time.
—"Fully Empowered"

By midcentury, Neruda had lived many lives as a poet, each one with its accompanying style, constantly evolving, like a lizard shedding its skin. But there were also many Nerudas, the person with whom the poet coexisted; his personal affectations and conditions always manifested in the new styles, forms, and themes of his writing. In the late 1950s, the Neruda who settled into his poetry, into Isla Negra, into La Chascona and his now-public relationship with Matilde, was at the height of these evolutions. Neruda himself referred to this period as the "autumn" of his life, a mellow one, but like grapes in Chilean vineyards ready to transform into wine, it was a fruitful time in which he produced a cluster of outstanding, engaging books. In them, he allowed himself to be more relaxed and whimsical and personally reflective than ever before. Many of the poems are warm and affective. His social concern was still very much there, but it didn't dominate him or his poetry.

"Sometimes I'm a poet of nature, sometimes a poet of things, sometimes I'm a public poet, an angry poet, a poet of joy—but now I'm learning," Neruda noted to Alastair Reid in 1964.

In one line, Neruda rehumanizes himself as "a man rainy and happy, lively and autumn-minded." Grounded, at peace with his poetry and international success, he was perhaps at his personal apex, at the height of both his poetic and personal powers, able to use them like at no other time before or after. In the middle of this period, in September 1962, he published *Plenos poderes* (*Fully Empowered*), a small but uniquely satisfying book. A deeply personal tone sustains throughout, and it contains two of his most important political poems. In Spanish, the term *plenos poderes* most often refers to the powers given to an ambassador to take independent action on behalf of his country, but it can more generally mean powers at their peak. English has no equivalent phrase.

"Fully empowered" is translator Alastair Reid's perfect linguistic solution. It captures Neruda's personal peace, the respect he had in his country and around the world at the time, and his poetic mastery: proud to fly his own flag from the garden at Isla Negra; able to bask in the company of the love of his life; free to simply be himself, unencumbered by technicalities and bureaucrats and constant conferences as he had endured in Europe; having already put out into the world "a shelf of remarkable books, as vast and varied as the sea itself," as Reid put it. Neruda's autumn yielded fine works scribed mostly from that low bluff overlooking the Pacific, books in which he poetized his own persona, allowing himself to be more adventurous and have some fun at his own expense. Furthermore, it was during this period that he finally saw the errors of Stalinism and was emboldened enough to reject them and admit his mistakes publicly, in some cases even to take a stand. This might have been the truest sign that he was, in fact, fully empowered.

Isla Negra, the small house that Neruda and Delia had bought in 1931 in a fishing village along the rugged coast, became Neruda's sanctuary. The rocks on the beach became the cornerstones to which he would always return. It was his center, and he would transform it continuously, according to his aesthetic vision and touch. He used to say that he had a second profession, that of a rather surreal architect, a transformer of homes, and it proved true. It was from this house that he composed himself and his poetry, while sitting on a stone bench outside or in his little writing room with the infinite sea out his window. The house became his vessel with the water below him. Isla Negra was an externalization of himself.

Built on top of a small, sharp hill above a rocky beach, the house at Isla Negra spreads in various extensions to form the shape of a boat. He wanted it to have as many curves as possible, frustrated by how so many houses are just pure rectangles. He wanted his home to be impure, like the poetry he had preached. The house was furnished with his eclectic collections: ship figureheads, ships in bottles, seashells from the beaches of the world, sextants, astrolabes, ethereal rare butterflies and insects linking back to his childhood train excursions, miniature Mexican guitars, glass jugs in a spectrum of hues, beautifully carved wooden stirrups covering a wall just like in his childhood home, seventeenth-century maps of the Americas and the oceans, pictures of some of his favorite writers (Poe, Baudelaire, and Whitman) who had their place of honor wherever he lived, and first editions of their books, a giant shoe that once hung outside a cobbler's shop in Temuco. He even made a special room for the wooden horse he had fallen in love with in the saddlery shop in Temuco.

There was a chimney that looked like a cascade of lapis lazuli flowing down the tall curved wall. Among the many unique rooms was a bar with glasses of every shape and color, and inscribed on the ceiling beams were the names of his friends who had passed away. Winding paths outside, rustic gardens, and a little writer's hut on the hill completed the Isla Negra refuge. An old locomotive engine stood parked outside.

Neruda never loved being at sea. He loved the ocean, but he took ocean liners by necessity for travel and never went out in a boat. He liked to say that he was a "sailor of the land." From the shore, though, the sea was essential to him. As he once said, "To me, the sea is an element, like the air." The impact of discovering the sea in his youth, in Puerto Saavedra, never left him. The sensation that the sea was the heartbeat of the universe, as he had described it, brought him to Isla Negra and to the creation of his singular refuge there.

One single being, but there's no blood.
One single caress, death or rose.
The sea comes and reunites our lives
and attacks and divides and sings alone
in night and day and man and creature.
The essence: fire and cold: movement.
   —"The Sea"

⋆

Matilde and Neruda made frequent trips up the coast to Valparaíso, his old bohemian escape from Santiago during his student days. Soon, Neruda decided he needed his own home above the port. The Communist wanted his third house to be simpler, more modest. A Valparaíso friend, the poet Sara Vial, recalled that Neruda asked her to find him a house "neither too high nor too low, where you can't see people but where there are people, where you can't hear the buses but there are buses." It happened that a friend of Vial's had just inherited an old, eccentrically shaped house—somewhat like a tower—up on one of the city's many hills, with a very narrow staircase winding up three floors and spectacular views of the city and the sea. Neruda couldn't afford the house, so he convinced his friends Dr. Francisco Velasco and the artist María Martner (who crafted the mosaic on Isla Negra's chimney) to buy the first two floors and leave him the third.

Neruda named his new Valparaíso home La Sebastiana, in honor of the old Spaniard who had built the house, Sebastián Collado. La Sebastiana may have been Neruda's smallest home, but it had its own unique charm with its view of the city and cylindrical shape, and during the work on initial repairs, he subtly modified it to fit the Nerudian fashion. Each house was like a private stage: he would design the sets, and he always played the lead.

The house grows and speaks,
stands on its own feet,
has clothes wrapped round its skeleton,

and as from seaward the spring,
swimming like a water nymph,
kisses the sand of Valparaíso.

Now we can stop thinking. This is the house.

Now all that's missing will be blue.

All it needs now is to bloom.

And that is work for the spring.
—"To La Sebastiana"

As a mover hung up a large portrait of Whitman, he asked Neruda, "Is this your father?"

"The father of my poetry," Neruda answered.

*

Neruda's unusual book of conversational poetry, *Estravagario,* was published in August 1958. The title is a word created by Neruda. As Karl Ragnar Gierow put it in his Nobel Prize presentation to Neruda in 1971, *Estravagario* "comprises both extravagance and vagabondage, whim and errantry."

Once again, the book marked a radical change in Neruda's style. In this new, very personal prose, Neruda isn't creating poems as practical or utilitarian as the odes had been. Gone too is the overtly political poetry. Neruda had reached the point where he felt he could relax and be whimsical, with himself as the main subject. Influenced by his compatriot Nicanor Parra's *antipoesía,* Neruda had come to recognize that poetry did not have to be solemn, and, like other literary genres, it could entertain. The outlandish type and comical illustrations in *Estravagario* add to the effect. Neruda is not preaching. He is a liberated man: liberated to love Matilde, liberated from his literary past, liberating himself from Stalinism, now more interested in individual liberation rather than collectivism. His new voice is heard in "Keeping Quiet," where the narrator seems to want to take a breather from the tensions of the Cold War:

Now we will count to twelve
and we will all keep still.

For once on the face of the earth,
let's not speak in any language;
let's stop for one second,
and not move our arms so much.

It would be an exotic moment
without rush, without engines;
we would all be together
in a sudden strangeness . . .[*]

---

* Neruda (already with an honorary doctorate from Oxford) was in London with Matilde in 1967. His favorite translator, Alastair Reid, was living on a houseboat with his son; Neruda went to inspect it, fascinated. He decided to hold his birthday fiesta on the boat, during which a Ukrainian poet fell overboard and had to be rescued from the Thames mud, and then got back on board as the party continued. During that trip, as Reid accompanied Neruda through London's markets to search in vain for a ship's figurehead, Neruda conveyed his anxiousness that Reid translate all of *Estravagario*. It was evident that it was one of his favorite books, perhaps second only to "The Heights of Macchu Picchu." Neruda then gave a spectacular reading at Queen Elizabeth Hall, for which Reid served as translator onstage. Once Neruda had left London, Reid was able to closet himself "for a spell with the still photographs of the poems. I found it a relief to spend time with the moving original. I knew Neruda much better now, by way of his poems. He was always ready to answer any questions I had about them, even to talk about them, fondly, as about lost friends, but he was not much interested in the mechanics of translation. Once, in Paris, while I was explaining some liberty I had taken, he stopped me and put his hand on my shoulder: 'Alastair, don't just translate my poems. I want you to improve them.'"

Besides *Estravagario*, Reid translated *Isla Negra* and *Fully Empowered*, along with some selected poems. He found that Neruda's voice was the clue to translating his poetry, that all of Neruda's poems were "fundamentally vocative—spoken poems, poems of direct address—and that Neruda's voice was

★

Despite his more internal focus, Neruda was inspired to action by political events that disrupted his serenity. The triumph of Fidel Castro's Cuban Revolution on January 1, 1959, shook Latin America. Neruda sang exaltation to it and its leader, at first. He met Castro in Caracas soon after the victory. The Cuban was there to thank the Venezuelan people for supporting his revolution. Neruda was touring Venezuela and joined the enthusiastic multitude gathered to celebrate Castro and hear his four-hour speech.

The day after the rally, Neruda and Matilde were picnicking in a Caracas park when some motorcyclists approached with an invitation to go to the Cuban embassy for a reception that afternoon. The embassy was overflowing. Celia Sánchez, Castro's supposed lover and "the heart of the revolution," sent Neruda to a room alone, while she stayed with Matilde. Suddenly the room's door opened and Castro filled the space with his height. As Neruda wrote in his memoirs:

> He was a head taller than I. He walked toward me quickly.
> "Hello, Pablo!" he said, submerging me in a tight hug.
> Unbeknownst to me, a news photographer had entered the room and was taking pictures of us from the corner. Fidel was by his side in a second. I saw him grab the photographer by the neck; he was shaking him.

Neruda saved the photographer, who abandoned his camera and fled.

Neruda changed the focus of the book he was currently writing from the colonial situation of Puerto Rico to, now, after the Cuban Revolution, assessing the situation throughout the Caribbean. The new book

---

in a sense the instrument for which he wrote." Neruda once made a tape for him, reading pieces of different poems in different tones and rhythms. Reid would listen to it at odd moments, on buses, in the middle of the night when he was still wakeful—"so many times that I can hear it in my head at will," he wrote thirty years later.

was called *Canción de gesta,* as in the French *chanson de geste,* songs of heroic deeds. He dedicated it to "the liberators of Cuba: Fidel Castro, his *compañeros,* and the Cuban people," and continued:

> There is much for us to wash and burn in all of America.
> Many of us must build.
> Everyone contributes what they can, with sacrifice and happiness.
> Our peoples have suffered so much; us giving our all is very little
>   for them.

From Venezuela, Neruda and Matilde went for a nine-month stay in Europe. On the way back, they arrived in Havana in December 1960. Lawrence Ferlinghetti was there. His book *A Coney Island of the Mind* had just been published and was on its way to being one of the bestselling books of poetry in the United States (by the twenty-first century it would have sold over a million copies). The great Cuban writer Guillermo Cabrera Infante, thirty-one at the time (Ferlinghetti was ten years older), arranged for him to meet Neruda, who was staying at the Hotel Habana Libre—the former Habana Hilton, now controlled by the government. "Neruda sitting in plush suite with open spiral notebooks, gets up smiling, shakes hands heartily—bald with eagle eyes in round face, grave ship's-prow eyes," Ferlinghetti wrote in his journal.

Ferlinghetti was the first to publish Allen Ginsberg, and his City Lights Bookstore had become the headquarters for the West Coast Beats. Neruda had read some of their work, most recently in the literary supplement to Cuba's daily newspaper. "I love your wide-open poetry," Neruda told him.

Ferlinghetti replied, "You opened the door."

There was a large event at the capitol that night, commemorating a hero of Cuba's independence from Spain. Neruda was to give a speech and asked Ferlinghetti, "Why don't you come along?" Again from Ferlinghetti's journal:

> Down we go with his beautiful wife and get in limousine
> from Casa de la Amistad, new international "friendship

house" set up by Fidel. En route I tell him I'm staying in hotel near Capitol where there are the biggest bedbugs I ever saw. He laughs and says when he first came to Santiago de Chile from the country as a boy there were bedbugs but he didn't know what they were until they bit. Then he had Battle of Bedbugs all night, burning them up with a candle . . . says he still has candle back at hotel . . .

They arrived at the back entrance. Neruda and Matilde disappeared behind the stage; Ferlinghetti went to the main floor of the big senate chamber. It was already packed with around two thousand Fidelistas "still in their combat boots and clothes, feet up, smoking wild cigars" where "all the henchmen of the dictator had sat." The galleries were "now full to roof with *campesinos* and students." A "revolutionary euphoria filled the air"; "the whole place was just throbbing with this fantastic energy and vitality and enthusiasm." When it was his turn to come on, Neruda received an enormous ovation.

Neruda continued to give recitals in universities, libraries, and high schools, traveling all across the island and, of course, taking time to find sensational seashells to add to his collection. Casa de las Américas, a cultural institution with a Pan-American focus founded right after the revolution, published twenty-five thousand copies of *Canción de gesta*, but the book would never be published again on the island as relations between Neruda and the Cuban government deteriorated. Neruda became a cautious and critical observer of the revolution. He would never again vociferously support it as he had done with the book, which he dedicated to the revolution's triumph and the idealistic hope that came with it.

Part of Neruda's change of heart came when he met Che Guevara. Guevara was the head of the National Bank at the time, and he had set the meeting at his office there at midnight. As Neruda opened the door, Guevara didn't move his feet, which were resting in his thick boots up on his desk. Neruda was accustomed to being treated with deference. "Those aren't hours, nor manners either!" he told a friend.

Toward the end of their meeting, Neruda mentioned to Guevara that he had seen sandbags in strategic areas all around Havana. As they talked about the possibilities of the United States invading Cuba, Guevara's eyes moved slowly from Neruda's to the office's dark window. Suddenly, Guevara said: "War . . . war . . . we are always against war, but when we make war we cannot live without it. We always want to return to it."

Neruda felt Guevara was thinking out loud for his benefit, but he was disarmed and surprised. Guevara saw war as an objective, not a threat, Neruda felt, and the young revolutionary would in fact soon leave Cuba to support armed revolution in other countries. For Neruda, meanwhile, nonviolent action, whether through poetry or politics, was the route to change.

In his memoirs, Neruda wrote that it was very pleasing to hear Guevara tell him how he had often read *Canto General* to soldiers under his command when they fought in Cuba's Sierra Maestra. Guevara was captured by the Bolivian government in 1967, trying to lead a revolution there. Neruda learned that Guevara "carried two books in his backpack until the day of his death: an arithmetic textbook and my *Canto General*."[*] Neruda wrote in the 1970s, "I think about how my verses were with him when he died."

Yet when the Bolivian army executed Guevara, Neruda felt he had to publish an elegy for the fallen revolutionary, a poem entitled "Sadness on the Death of a Hero." Still, Neruda would tell a distressed Aida Figueroa not to cry for the militant Guevara, but for the pacifist founder of Chile's Communist movement, Luis Emilio Recabarren.

Neruda took a firm stand when he returned from Cuba, announcing that the Chilean Communists should not follow Castro's example. In Chile, the revolution would be peaceful and democratic. In a press conference he proclaimed, "There is hunger, misery, and backwardness in Latin America. The people can't wait any longer and are beginning to

---

[*]   In fact Guevara wasn't carrying *Canto General* with him, but rather a green notebook in which he had copied seventy-nine poems by hand. Eighteen were Neruda's, while others were by Nicolás Guillén, César Vallejo, and the Spanish Civil War veteran León Felipe.

awaken from their lethargy." While Cuba was an example, not every-where could be Cuba. "No revolution can be exported. Each country has different conditions." He reiterated a line he was very proud of and would continue to promote: "The people of Chile have chosen their path to national liberation, led by popular parties and unions. And they are keeping firm to it."

★

That year, 1959, Neruda published an apolitical work, *Cien sonetos de amor* (*One Hundred Love Sonnets*), dedicated to Matilde. Though the ti-tle has sold many copies, most of the poems are not as substantial as the love poems of Neruda's youth or *The Captain's Verses*. According to some sources, Neruda himself didn't take the book seriously. A handful of the poems, however, have become canonical, including Sonnet XVII:

> I don't love you as if you were a rose of salt, topaz,
> or arrow of carnations that propagate fire:
> I love you as one loves certain obscure things,
> secretly, between the shadow and the soul.
>
> I love you as the plant that doesn't bloom but carries
> the light of those flowers, hidden, within itself,
> and thanks to your love the tight aroma that arose
> from the earth lives dimly in my body.
>
> I love you without knowing how, or when, or from where,
> I love you directly without problems or pride:
> I love you like this because I don't know any other way to love,
> except in this form in which I am not nor are you,
> so close that your hand upon my chest is mine,
> so close that your eyes close with my dreams.

By 1961, the costs of his homes, collections, and travels drove Neruda to publish two more books in quick succession: *Las piedras de Chile* (*The Stones of Chile*) and the lyrical, but not outstanding, *Cantos ceremoniales*

(Ceremonial Songs). In the former, a rock collector praises the earthly qualities of Chile, the geology of stones and stars that form an iron clarity around their "lasting silence / beneath the Antarctic / mantle of Chile." Neruda reaches back to the essence of nature, which was starting to take a more prominent role in his poetry.

In the same year, the millionth copy of *Twenty Love Poems and a Desperate Song* was sold. Only a handful of twentieth-century individual books of poetry—such as Kahlil Gibran's *The Prophet,* Allen Ginsberg's *Howl,* and Lawrence Ferlinghetti's *A Coney Island of the Mind*—have achieved such popularity.

Still, the success of the love poems didn't alleviate Neruda's financial anxiety; all those volumes did not translate into sufficient income. His lack of cash flow is evident in a letter from his secretary Homero Arce to his good friend and publisher Gonzalo Losada, in which Arce asks for a "monetary advance, on top of the monthly payment, to finish paying the costs of the renovation of [Neruda's] house La Sebastiana in Valparaíso; this is extremely urgent."

★

That summer, done with yet another round of travel, Neruda settled back into Isla Negra with Matilde. There he worked on *Memorial de Isla Negra* and *Fully Empowered,* two of his strongest works. One of *Fully Empowered*'s poems is "Deber del poeta" ("Poet's Obligation"); *deber* can be translated as both "obligation" and "duty." At Isla Negra, likely writing on one of his outdoor benches, set beside a table made out of a carved tree trunk and overlooking the Pacific crashing below, Neruda composed the lines:

> To whoever is not listening to the sea
> this Friday morning, to whoever is cooped up
> in house or office, factory or woman
> or street or mine or harsh prison cell:
> to him I come, and, without speaking or looking,
> I arrive and open the door of his prison,
> and a vibration starts up, vague and insistent,

a great fragment of thunder sets in motion
the rumble of the planet and the foam,
the raucous rivers of the ocean flood,
the star vibrates swiftly in its corona,
and the sea is beating, dying and continuing.
. . . .
. . . through me, freedom and the sea
will make their answer to the shuttered heart.

It is an emblematic poem, and the last two lines echo his self-appointment as the lyrical spokesman to channel and change the needs and desires of others that he's asserted in "Macchu Picchu," "The Invisible Man," and a few additional works. But in "Poet's Obligation" he elevates the direct strength of his power to a transcendent level. He doesn't just speak for them, but rather his poetry becomes such a transformational portal that it can deliver the sea or assume the powers of the sea, with all its attributes. The lyricism is certainly beautiful and potently emotive, which on one hand is all that matters. On the other hand, his egotism seems to trump his empathy. This phenomenon came to the forefront even more in these later decades, emboldened by his cemented stature and fame as the people's poet. His assumption of this mantle seemed to give him a sense of empowerment, where he could self-mystify in a manner that has caused some to question the veracity of the Communist image he clung to, as well as the degree to which these declarations may have been self-serving.

★

Work and writing almost always gave way to his political responsibilities off the page. More and more, he was diverging from the party line. On September 29, 1963, at a Communist Party gathering of some three thousand people in Santiago's Parque Bustamante, Neruda attacked China. Rhetorically, he demanded to know the whereabouts of that country's best poet, his friend Ai Qing, an elderly Communist and the father of artist Ai Weiwei. He had been exiled to the Gobi Desert and forced to sign his poems using another name. Neruda confided to the audience, "I think that China's errors, and its violent internal and external policies, come from just one source: the cult of personality, internally and externally. Those of us who have visited China saw a repetition there of what happened with Stalin."

Neruda had never publicly condemned Communist authoritarian rule to such a degree as he did in this speech, a remarkable declaration after so many years of support or silence. In the poetry he was now writing, he admitted the mistakes of Stalinism and even denounced Stalin, his hero no longer, who "administered the rule of cruelty / from his ubiquitous statue":

> Everybody asked themselves: "What happened?
> . . . .
> FEAR
>
> What happened? What happened? How did it happen?
> How could it happen? But certainly
> it happened, it's very clear that it happened,
> it was true, true, the pain of *not going back.*
> Error fell in its terrible funnel,
> and out of that came his steely youth.
> And hope raised its fingers.
> Oh, the gloomy flag, that covered over
> the victorious sickle, the hammer's weight
> with a single terrifying effigy!
> . . . .
>   That dead one administered the rule of cruelty
>   from his ubiquitous statue.
> That still effigy controlled all life . . .
>   —"The Episode"

As Neruda turned sixty, *Memorial de Isla Negra* was published to a rush of general acclaim. The book is among Neruda's finest, as he had mastered a personal tone that is forthright and direct.

It's an interesting title, connoting the different layers of metaphors in this lyrical account of his life. Alastair Reid wrote that the Spanish word *memorial* should be "shaken free of association with the English word 'memorial,' for Neruda wrote not a systematic autobiography in poem form but a set of assembled meditations on the presence of the past in the present, an essential notebook." Still, Neruda seems to draw from the Latin roots of the word "memorial" to evoke a feeling of remembrance or celebration of this place, Isla Negra, this sanctuary to which he always returned, with all of its restorative and reflective powers.

A bilingual dictionary defines the Spanish word *memorial* as a "formal petition; memorial" or, in law, as a "brief."[*] Neruda used a future-oriented word for an autobiographical reflection. It implies another dynamic to the book: Neruda was asking not just his detractors (the book sometimes reads as defensive) but all his readers, present and future, to use this petition, this brief, to judge his life and his choices. It is an open book with which to sympathize and affirm his essence, as written in front of the sea, as he moved toward his final years.

*

Maruca passed away on March 27, 1965. Destitute, she was buried in a common grave in Holland. Neruda asked Delia, still living at La Michoacán, to annul their marriage, and she obliged. It was never recognized in Chile anyway, since he had never divorced Maruca. He was now free to legally marry Matilde, which he did that October.

Neruda and Matilde traveled restlessly, going by ocean liner from Montevideo to Europe and continuing via train or plane. Over the rest of 1965, they would visit Paris three times, Moscow twice, Budapest twice, East Berlin, Hamburg, England, Helsinki, Italy, and Yugoslavia.

At the same time that Matilde and Neruda were in Budapest on the invitation of the Hungarian government, Neruda's good friend, the Guatemalan novelist Miguel Ángel Asturias, was there with his wife. Fifteen years earlier, Neruda had borrowed Asturias's passport to flee to exile in Europe. Both were asked by the Hungarian government to

---

[*]   When Neruda asked him to translate the book, Alastair Reid titled the English version *Isla Negra: A Notebook*.

write something that would show off the Socialist country nearly a decade after the Soviets intervened. They decided to demonstrate the beauty and strengths of the transforming country in an ode-like manner, using its cuisine to draw out sympathy and sentiment. The result is a minor work of both prose and poetry, named *Comiendo en Hungría* (Eating in Hungary), the reader going along the Danube and out in the countryside for delicious meals and drinks, from foie gras to bruschetta, spiced with Gypsy music and old red wines.

In Yugoslavia, Neruda attended the 1965 International PEN Club meeting. There he started a warm relationship with the playwright Arthur Miller, who was then the international president of the club. The PEN Club was founded in 1921 "to promote friendship and intellectual cooperation among writers everywhere; to emphasize the role of literature in the development of mutual understanding and world culture; to fight for freedom of expression; and to act as a powerful voice on behalf of writers harassed, imprisoned and sometimes killed for their views." Miller invited Neruda to come to New York for the next year's meeting, but his visa was denied by the State Department because he was a Communist.

In March 1966, Miller wrote to Neruda from his home in Roxbury, Connecticut, that efforts to get him a visa were advancing. Another letter sent a little later stated that "private conversations with Washington indicate there will finally be no problem in your entering the country." It ended, "In short, try to come. The place is full of your friends, as you know. It is important you come. My wife speaks perfect Spanish, so that makes it more important. Your wife must come too. Here in the country we have good friends, writers, dogs, cats, birds, trout, whiskey . . ."*

The substantial pressure on the State Department from domestic and international cultural groups and individuals, led by Miller behind the scenes, eventually convinced officials to grant Neruda's visa in time for the PEN Club meeting. President Lyndon Johnson became involved

---

* The wife he refers to is the celebrated photographer Inge Morath. His marriage to Marilyn Monroe had ended five years earlier.

himself. It wasn't just Neruda's case but the whole policy that was un-
der question. Decades later Miller told a biographer that the Johnson
administration "became nervous that it would not be good to be seen
banning such a famous figure and realized that it would be wise to re-
lax the ban." The State Department even admitted that the visa policy
had "marred this country's image as a free and open society."*

On Saturday, June 11, 1966, twenty-three years after hosting him
at the Library of Congress, the poet Archibald MacLeish introduced
Neruda at the Poetry Center at the 92nd Street Y in New York: "It is
my privilege and very decidedly my honor to introduce to you a great
American poet. A great American poet in the precise and particular
sense of the word 'American.' The precise and particular sense which
includes not only the United States but Chile and not only Chile but the
United States." The words were dramatically delivered, and the audito-
rium responded with fervent applause.

MacLeish continued, stating that Neruda has "accepted for himself,
as few other poets have in the centuries of American life, the American
commitment which it imposes." He clarifies that he does not mean that
Neruda's definition of the American commitment would be the same
as his or others', nor that all U.S. citizens accept the terms in which Ne-
ruda might express it. "I merely imply—more than imply—state, that
if the American commitment is to be found anywhere, it is to be found
in Walt Whitman's love of mankind. And if it is to be found there, it is
to be found also in Neruda." Again, loud applause saturated the hall.

The reading was packed. Closed-circuit televisions were set up to
accommodate those who couldn't enter the auditorium. In attendance
was the future U.S. poet laureate Charles Simic, who was so "deeply
moved" that he "even shed a tear or two without knowing any Span-
ish." Interestingly, most of the poems Neruda read at the PEN recital

---

* The Johnson administration implemented a system to grant a group waiver
  for attendees of conferences (and sporting events) when it was in the national
  interest to not exclude anyone invited "who had at any time been associated
  with a Communist party." But this did not pertain to individuals wanting to
  enter when not attending an international event.

were from *Residence on Earth* or even earlier—beautiful but subdued choices. Missing was his vibrant political verse, here in the heart of the country that he pegged as the cause of so much global injustice.

The PEN Club had received money from the National Endowment for the Arts and other foundations to bring twenty-one other Latin American literary figures to the conference, increasing communication among the writers of the continent. Carlos Fuentes was there from Mexico, and Mario Vargas Llosa from Peru. They held a mini-congress at the Gramercy Park Hotel, a headquarters at the time of high bohemia. The one Latin American country of great writers that was not represented was, notably, Cuba. The Cubans, directed by their government, boycotted the meeting because it was being held in the United States. Whether they could have even gotten visas was also in question.

María Luisa Bombal, Neruda's "fire bee" who had shared Neruda's apartment in Buenos Aires in the early 1930s, was living in New York at the time. "They sent a messenger from the Chilean cultural attaché, to ask me to present Neruda at the recital he was going to give in New York," she remembered. But then three FBI agents came to her apartment. "They had come to *very kindly* inquire about my link to Pablo. 'It's a link between writers, Chilean writers,' I told them." Bombal was shaken, fearful for herself, a Chilean; her husband, a Frenchman; and their American daughter. In the end, while she was never threatened, she decided that she had to put her family first. She told Neruda she couldn't be involved; and he didn't take the decision well. "He saw it as a betrayal, and he could forgive anything except what he considered to be a betrayal." She felt that he never forgave her for that, which pained her. After all these years, Neruda's ego could still cause him to do great harm to those he loved. "I was no longer his 'fire bee.' He didn't want to see me again." Upon his return to Chile, he seemed to disparage and blame Bombal, telling friends like Volodia Teitelboim that he was terribly disappointed after finding her drinking in bed in her apartment. He died before they had a chance to see each other again.

After New York, Neruda visited Washington, D.C. He had been invited to give a reading at the Inter-American Development Bank, but his visit was met with protests by some of the bank's staff, calling his presence a "communist provocation." Above the protests and the sirens, the bank's president, Felipe Herrera, grabbed a bullhorn and announced the reading would take place at the landmark Mayflower Hotel.

Despite Neruda's communism, the Library of Congress asked him to come be recorded reading his poetry.[*] On June 20, 1966, Neruda delivered a wonderful reading in the tiny studio, reciting all twelve cantos of "The Heights of Macchu Picchu." It was very rare for him to read it in its entirety. Of all his work, that is what he chose then to leave as his legacy, vocalized steadily for thirty-six minutes.

As the tour wore on, Neruda visited San Francisco and read at the University of California, Berkeley, where he said that he "learned on the spot that the North American enemies of our peoples were also enemies of the North American people"—that those in the crowd were

---

[*]   Francisco Aguilera, the library's specialist in Hispanic culture, a Chilean, and a longtime friend of Neruda's, arranged a lunch in the chief librarian's office. This dignified location was a rare and notable exception to the norm; after their recordings for the Hispanic division, most writers were simply taken to the cafeteria or a nearby restaurant. Stephen Spender joined them; at the time, he was serving as the equivalent of the library's poet laureate. He and Neruda had become close in the fight for Spain, and they talked about the civil war and those years vibrantly.

Georgette Dorn, the current head of the Hispanic division, was a young reference librarian at the time of Neruda's visit. She was a lover of Latin American literature with a PhD, and Neruda was a living legend to her, a figure that towered above other great writers who came to the library. The conversation was just so "jovial and very pleasant." Neruda was "extremely gregarious," asking all about the audio archives and who had read there before. His old rival Pablo de Rokha had, and Neruda was very curious about his experience. The library was also making an LP of Gabriela Mistral at the time—she was living in New York—and he talked for a while about her, reminiscing about his childhood mentor.

They also talked about food. Dorn was born in Hungary, but she moved to Argentina when she was nine. Neruda was very disappointed that she couldn't tell him anything about her birth country's cuisine. Miguel Ángel Asturias was traveling through Hungary and had started writing *Comiendo en Hungría* just the year before. The book wasn't close to being published when Neruda was at the library; it came out in 1969.

against the U.S. government policies too. He was deeply moved when a "spontaneous roar" came from the crowd after he announced he was going to read "The United Fruit Co." The university's paper wrote that he received two standing ovations from the crowd of one thousand. Lawrence Ferlinghetti and Allen Ginsberg were among the attendees. As in New York, the overflow crowd listened in another lecture room.

From San Francisco, Neruda and Matilde traveled to Mexico and then to Peru, where Neruda lunched with the centrist president Fernando Belaúnde Terry and was decorated with the Order of the Sun, the highest honor in Peru. But trouble was brewing in the midst of these accolades.

At the time, Belaúnde Terry was battling Cuban-inspired *guerrilleros* trying to spread the revolution to Peru. Fidel Castro and the Chilean Communist Party were having a falling-out, and Neruda became a figurehead in the rift. Castro, and in particular Che Guevara, felt that Latin America was ready for a continental revolution using armed *guerrillero* force. The Chilean Communist Party and Neruda disagreed. Cuba's revolution took the course of an armed insurrection because of the repressive dictatorship controlling the country—there was no ballot box or patience for a prolonged pacifist approach. In 1965, Nicaragua, El Salvador, Panama, Paraguay, Bolivia, and Haiti were ruled by entrenched dictatorial regimes as Cuba had been. But Chile was not suffering under a repressive dictatorship. Chile's democratic tradition provided a legitimate system through which to realize a revolution.

Cuban authorities put pressure on the writer Roberto Fernández Retamar and his colleagues to denounce Neruda's visit to the United States and his meeting with Belaúnde Terry, whom the Peruvian Communist revolutionaries were fighting. Their attack on Neruda was seen as an indirect attack on the Chilean Communist Party. Just a month earlier, Fernández Retamar, a future member of Castro's cabinet, had sent Neruda an affectionate letter:

> Every once in a while, a few words written in green ink come
> to me from the deep south, which bring me happiness. But you
> need to come, you and Matilde need to come back, so that we

can be together on the island like we were six years ago . . . No
one awaits you with more friendship than your

Roberto

But suddenly, Fernández Retamar and more than 150 Cuban writers
and intellectuals, including Alejo Carpentier, Nicolás Guillén, and José
Lezama Lima, signed an open letter denouncing Neruda and his atten-
dance at the PEN Club meeting. On July 31, 1966, the letter was pub-
lished in the Cuban Communist Party's newspaper, *Granma*. Addressed
to *"Compañero* Pablo," it began by saying, "We believe it is our duty to
let you know the anxiety and uneasiness that our enemies' use of your
recent activities has caused in Cuba." "It wouldn't have occurred to us
that we would have to automatically censure your participation in the
PEN Club Congress, from which positive conclusions could have been
made, or even your visit to the United States, because this visit could
also derive positive results for our causes. But has that been the case?"
they asked. They wondered why Neruda was permitted a U.S. visa
while other Communists had been denied it for twenty years.

The letter hurt Neruda profoundly. The fact that it was published
for all to read in Cuba's main newspaper added to the pain. The letter
was even covered in the *Washington Post*. Neruda replied in an open
telegram the next day: "Dear *compañeros:* I am deeply surprised by the
unfounded concern expressed for me by a group of Cuban writers." He
stated that "it appears" they are unaware that his entry into the United
States, "as with that of Communist writers from other countries, was
achieved by breaking the prohibitions of the State Department, thanks
to the actions of left-wing intellectuals." He continued:

In the United States and the other countries I visited, I
maintained my communist ideals, my unbreakable principles,
and my revolutionary poetry. I have the right to hope and
demand that you, who know me, would not harbor or spread
inadmissible doubts about this.

In the United States and everywhere else I went, I have been listened to and respected, based firmly on who I am and who I will always be: a poet who does not hide what he thinks, who has put his life and work at the service of the freedom of our peoples . . .

Once again, I express to you, as I have done through my poetry, my passionate fidelity to the Cuban revolution.

He would never forgive his former friends who had signed the letter; they remained his enemies until death, with no movement made toward reconciliation.

CHAPTER TWENTY

TRIUMPH, DESTRUCTION, DEATH

Right, comrade, it's the hour of the garden
and the hour up in arms, each day
follows from flower or blood:
our time surrenders us to an obligation
to water the jasmines
or bleed to death in a dark street:
virtue or pain blows off
into frozen realms, into hissing embers,
and there never was a choice . . .

Ours is a lank country
and on the naked edge of her knife
our frail flag burns.
    —Untitled (1973)

On August 8, 1966, Neruda and Matilde wrote to their friend and secretary Margarita Aguirre and her husband, Rodolfo Aráoz Alfaro: "Confidential: We are getting married, Chilean style (Shhh! Quiet! Discretion! Silence!)." On a beautiful spring day at Isla Negra, October 28, they were married in a small private ceremony, Matilde in a white dress and Neruda in a dark suit, a flower in his lapel, a folded white handkerchief in his breast pocket. Neruda was now sixty-two, Matilde, fifty-four.

It was an extraordinarily fruitful time for his writing. That same year, Neruda published two more books. The first, *Arte de pájaros* (*Art of Birds*), was a private, numbered, illustrated edition. It contains poems to real and imaginary birds, including "El pájaro yo: (Pablo Insulidae Nigra)" ("The 'I' Bird: [Pablo of Isla Negra]"), where the poet is a "bird of one single feather / flyer of clear shadow," "the furious bird / of the tranquil storm."

Un casa en la arena (*A House in the Sand*) is a thin, poignant book of love to Isla Negra, thirty-eight prose poems, accompanied by photographs, all revolving around Neruda's home, the coast, and the sea: "The Pacific Ocean overflowed the map. There wasn't any place to put it. It was so large, unruly, and blue that it didn't fit anywhere. That's why they left it in front of my window." Neruda seemed to see the world as though it were made just for him.

On October 14, 1967, Neruda's play *Fulgor y muerte de Joaquín Murieta* (*The Splendor and Death of Joaquín Murieta*) premiered to an enthusiastic sold-out crowd in Santiago. The real-life bandit Murieta is usually thought to be Mexican, but due to a translation of the California gold rush story by a Chilean, many people in Chile claim him as their hero, the one who stood up and defended all Latinos.

The work unfolds like an opera, populated by "the voice of the poet"; a chorus of campesinos, miners, fishermen, and their wives; and other singers with songs often in rhyme, all the while following real figures and events from the last century. The plot begins with the righteous bandit Murieta and his friend Juan Three-Fingers following the lure of the California gold rush, sailing up from Valparaíso in 1850—as many Chileans did at that time. On the ship, Murieta marries Teresa. In California, the Chileans are shown only with Latinos, while the white rangers and hooded men are always looking over them. The hooded men quote John L. O'Sullivan of the *New York Morning News,* words that Neruda directed to be projected on a screen at the back of the set-less stage for most of the production: "It is our manifest destiny to extend ourselves until we are owners of the entire continent that providence has given us for the grand experiment in liberty."

"Only the white race!" the hooded men yell. "America for the Americans!" "We won the war" (referring to the Mexican-American War [1846–1848]). The hooded men kill Latinos and blacks, then rape and murder Teresa. Murieta then avenges the murder of his wife and all the other Latinos by killing the white oppressors. Murieta, Three-Fingers, and a gang of fellow bandits set off, taking the gold from the whites they kill and giving it to the poor. But as Murieta lays flowers at Teresa's grave, the *yanquis* find and kill him. His head is displayed at the San Francisco Fair, as it was in real life. In the play, a man charges twenty cents to see the head, while cheering, "Freedom! Freedom!" (Neruda had done research for the play across the bay from San Francisco, at the University of California, Berkeley, when he was there giving his reading the year before.)

The *New York Times* reviewed opening night, calling it "two hours of drama filled with furious hatred for the United States." The fact that the *Times* would review a play that opened in Santiago shows Neruda's high standing in the cultural world and his continuing political influence. The anti-American feeling in the play is partly anti-imperialist, partly a statement of identity politics. Murieta, whether a Chilean or Mexican, is an American, and the gold is a piece of America to which any American, whether from Valparaíso or Virginia, is entitled. The United States had stolen California from Mexico through an unjust war. The play focused more on racism, rather than just imperialism. As Neruda wrote to the editor of the *New York Times:*

> One generalization that I feel I must correct has to do with the supposed anti-Americanism of my work. This is mostly manifest in the spirit of violence, domination and racism in one historical period. By the way, I don't think that your great country has put these characteristics behind it. But by stigmatizing segregationists and violent people during the California gold rush, my work does not cover the immense majority of the American people . . .

Elsewhere, Neruda wrote that the idea of the Ku Klux Klan was undoubtedly born with the white vigilante groups that formed in California against the Latinos and blacks, "because the same wild racism that you see even today existed in those first Yankee crusaders who wanted to clean California of Latin Americans and also, logically, have a hand in their discoveries. Joaquín Murieta's wife was killed in one of these incursions."

The play was a success in Santiago, but it has seldom been performed since the opening. It was the only play Neruda wrote.

He did, however, translate Shakespeare's *Romeo and Juliet* into Spanish, on the occasion of the four hundredth anniversary of the English bard's birth. (Alastair Reid, Neruda's friend and translator, liked to say that Neruda is the most widely read poet since Shakespeare.) In a letter to his publisher Gonzalo Losada on May 12, 1964, Neruda wrote, "I've achieved a lucid translation, freeing the verse of mannerisms and pretense. It came out like crystal-clear water."

While that may be true of the literal translation of the lines, Neruda also edited his version, creating an adaptation of the original to make the play more populist, to appeal to a wider audience in Latin America. In a less direct-action, grassroots manner, Neruda's intent seems to have been to perpetuate Lorca's aim to bring Spanish theater "within reach of the people," an action that excited Neruda's idealism back in the days of the Second Republic in Madrid. Instead of playing up elements of a pertinent yet rhetorical theme like class struggle, Neruda accentuated the dramatic tension of the impossibility of Romeo and Julieta's love (and echoed the tragedies of his youth, the impossibility of love with Teresa, Maria Parodi, Albertina, and Laura due to their parents' tragic objections).

Toward this end, as Chilean poet, translator, and scholar Rodrigo Rojas points out, Neruda tried to make Romeo simpler and more romantic, so he dropped some of his dialogue, some of his words where Neruda felt he was being hesitant, doubtful, and rather lyrical, in order to make him appear more direct, less impatient, more decisive, more sure of his love for Julieta (in contrast, one could argue, to Neruda's own love life). Most of the changes were at the beginning, and they were actually rather subtle compared with many of the adaptations of the classic that are constantly staged around the world. And Neruda's changes should not be pinned to Neruda's process of translation; he could have created them had he simply been commissioned to stage a new production in English.

From 1960 to his death in 1973, Neruda never let his pen of green ink rest. He was enormously productive, despite his deteriorating health, churning out a total of twenty-six books of poetry (seven of them would be published posthumously). They were of varied quality, but many were true gems. One of the most evocative was *La barcarola,* released shortly after the premiere of *Joaquín Murieta.* It is a lengthy love song to Matilde, written in the traditional 6/8 time to reflect the rhythm of the gondolier's stroke. It is somewhat of a surrealistic departure from the straightforward personal poetry he had been writing. Aboard his imaginary boat, he tells Matilde the story of their love, their history, his love of Chile. Toward the end, the war in Vietnam fills an episode, as it often did in the books he wrote during that war. When he won the Nobel Prize in 1971, the Swedish Academy presenter called *La barcarola* his recent "masterpiece."

A year after *La barcarola* came *Las manos del día (The Hands of the Day).* In the opening poem, the speaker admits he is the "guilty one" for never having done anything physical with his hands, that he never once made a broom so he could never "gather and unite / the elements." He verges on overly apologetic, expressing an exaggerated guilt when, twenty-one poems into the book, he claims that his hands are "negative" and "useless."

> Thus forgive me for the sadness,
> of my happy mistakes,
> of my shadowed dreams,
> forgive me, everyone, for the unnecessary:
> I didn't manage to use my hands
> in a carpenter's shop or in the forest.

Once again, in *The Hands of the Day* Neruda couldn't turn his gaze away from Vietnam, where, in his universalist view that all men are brothers, he urged readers to look for their own bones and blood in the mud among those of so many others:

> now, all burned, they aren't anyone's,
> they are everyone's,
> they are our bones, seek
> your death in that death,
> because those same people are stalking you
> and they intend for you to enter that same mud.
> —"In Vietnam"

Neruda's next book, *Aún* (published in English as *Still Another Day*), is from the earth and of the earth, which nurtures but also takes away:

> Forgive me, if when I want
> to recount my life
> it is the earth of that I talk.
> This is the earth.
> It grows in your blood
> and you grow.
> If it's extinguished in your blood,
> you are extinguished.

As seen in his verse, Neruda was now moving from the autumn of his life into a more focused meditation on mortality. The lines above presage his coming illness. Neruda was now sixty-five and clearly reflecting on the course of his life, though he still maintained his humanitarian duties to which he was called, as a poet and as a person.

★

Political tumult around the world contributed to Neruda's reflections on his life choices—his acts of omission and commission, his choices of heroes and villains. In 1968, the Czechoslovak Socialist Republic bowed to the winds of change in what became known as the Prague Spring, a period in which newly elected leaders there enacted brave new reforms to liberalize their economy and give citizens more rights, including a ten-year plan to establish democratic socialism. The Soviet ruler, Leonid Brezhnev, threatened to use military force if needed to stop any of Russia's satellite states from compromising the rest of the Eastern Bloc's national interests and cohesion. He was particularly fearful Czechoslovakia would leave the bloc, weakening it and opening up the possibility of more defections.

On August 20, 1968, Russia and the Warsaw Pact countries of East Germany, Poland, Bulgaria, and Hungary (all of which had been similarly invaded in 1956) attacked Czechoslovakia with a half million troops. The hope and progress that had developed that spring were quickly destroyed. Reformists and liberals were arrested; a student set himself on fire in a Prague square protesting the repression. A Moscow-friendly government was installed.

Jorge Edwards, among other friends, was at Isla Negra with Neruda the day after the invasion of Czechoslovakia. As Edwards wrote in his memoir, *Adiós, poeta . . .* :

> Books and authors were discussed; we commented on people we considered friends and those we didn't; we told repetitive, hackneyed jokes in an atmosphere of naturalness or relaxation that was rather fake. And not a word was spoken, *not one,* about the events in Czechoslovakia. Upon leaving, as we were sharing—under the fresh night air—one of those prolonged good-byes so typical of Chileans, I asked Pablo when he was leaving for Europe. "I don't think I'll travel after all," he responded pensively, worried, upset: "It seems to me the situation is too Czechoslovakian."

When asked what he thought about the Prague Spring a month later while in Brazil, Neruda first tried to evade the question and then couldn't commit to a side publicly:

I am a friend of Czechoslovakia, the country that gave me
asylum when I needed it, and I am also a friend of the Soviet
Union. For that reason, when you ask me what side I am on,
I feel like a child who is being asked if he is with his father or
with his mother. I am with both.

He then admitted, "I suffered a lot from the events. But now things
are normalizing and I hope that the process of democracy continues in
that country."

A year later, Neruda published *Fin del mundo* (*World's End*). The fol-
lowing poem, "1968," is emblematic of the book:

The hour of Prague fell
on my head like a stone,
my destiny was unsteady,
a moment of darkness
as in a tunnel on a journey
and now, by trying to understand
I do not understand anything:
when we should be singing
instead we must knock upon a sarcophagus
and how awful it is that they hear you
and that the coffin invites you.

Throughout the book, Neruda purges his allegiance to Stalin in par-
ticular, as well as Soviet stances that followed in his wake. In "1968" he
appeals "to the coming age / to judge my affliction / the company I
kept / despite so many mistakes." In these poems of repentance, it may
seem that Neruda wants to be absolved too easily. In the second of two
poems in the book aptly titled "The Worship," he postulates,

I was unaware of that which we were unaware.
And that madness, so long lasting,
was blind and buried
in a demented grandeur.

But he had been aware and admitted as much. Aida Figueroa and her husband, Sergio Insunza, traveled with Salvador Allende to the Soviet Union in 1954, a year after Stalin's death. "When we made that trip Pablo had already warned us of the excesses of Stalinism, verbally," Aida explained in 2005. "Twenty million people had died, and he said so in conversations." Yet he seemed to have said that only after Stalin died.

He was not "unaware," but he had indeed turned a blind eye: in the poem "1968" he pleads, "I beg forgiveness for this blind man / who saw [the crimes of Stalin and the Soviets] and who didn't see." For a political poet so in tune with the metaphor of his eyes as his poetic vision ever since his adolescent poetry, this is a critical admission of change. Still, one must take all his remorse with a grain of salt.

In a literal example of how his former idealism had now turned into a sense of hopelessness, in a 1947 prose piece he had written, "Tyranny cuts off the singer's head, but the voice from the bottom of the well returns to the secret springs of the earth and rises out of nowhere through the mouths of the people." Now, he ends his poem about the Prague Spring:

> The doors of the century close
> on those left unburied
> and again they will call in vain
> and we will leave without hearing,
> pondering the grandest tree,
> the space of our happiness.

He is resigned, if not cynical. In another poem in the book, "Death of a Journalist," also about the Soviet invasion of Czechoslovakia, he writes, "Let us prepare to die / in the jaws of machinery." Neruda had always fought against the machinery of materialism, unbridled capitalism, and fascism. Now he could find no escape.

The title of the intense book, *World's End*, says it all. In it, Neruda critiques the fact that socialism—in Cuba, China, the Soviet Union, and elsewhere—had failed to create a truly fair society. By the end of the book, it seems he has given up his ardent faith that socialism would be successful. He is ready for the century to end, a century full of horrific war, which he labels the century of destruction.

★

Soon after Neruda's sixty-fifth birthday party, in 1969, he went to the doctor complaining of irritation during urination. A biopsy discovered the cause: prostate cancer. He had a mass that would continue to spread until it metastasized to his bladder. He would go to the best French surgeons, the best Russian surgeons in the Soviet Union, but there was nothing anyone could do. Chemotherapy was not yet widely available as a treatment for cancer.

Despite his illness, Neruda would not give up his political obligations. The 1970 Chilean presidential elections were coming, and the Far Left did not yet have a clear candidate. There was Salvador Allende, but many thought that he was damaged goods after having already lost three presidential races, in 1952, 1958, and 1964. Neruda himself seemed ambivalent; perhaps he believed that Allende had aligned himself too much with Fidel Castro and would try to bring Castroism into Chilean politics.

The Left failed to find a consensus candidate to rally behind, so each party would, for now, run its own candidate in what would amount to a primary contest within the Unidad Popular (Popular Unity, or UP) coalition. The Socialists ran Allende. The Communists at first didn't have a candidate, but as Sergio Insunza, who would be Allende's justice minister, explained,

> There was disagreement there about which candidate to choose . . . And then a voice: "Why not Pablo Neruda? Why not Pablo Neruda as the Communist Party candidate for the presidency?" And, curiously, it was a candidacy that began as a joke, without any expectations, naturally, that he would win. But it gathered quite a bit of steam, and even he got enthusiastic about it.

Neruda agreed to run, but only with the understanding that once the parties of the UP coalition came to an agreement, he would retire his candidacy. He ran an enthusiastic campaign regardless, touring the country, making proclamations, meeting with unions and organizations, speaking to crowds of all sizes in barns in the countryside and in town plazas. While he dispensed the ritual campaign rhetoric, the heart of his appearances was the recital of his own verse. Sometimes there was no stump speech at all, just poetry.

If he did make a speech, he would close it by saying, "I'll just read you a poem, okay?" And then he continued to read poems for hours. People would say, "Read that one!" and he would reply, "If you've got it." Inevitably, someone would hand him the poem or recite a few lines from memory. He read them, and often the crowd read along, out loud, reciting in unison with him.

Young Communists armed with guitars and art set out to spread propaganda. His friends saw Neruda quickly revived, acquiring a dynamism that actually surpassed the party's own ambitions for his candidacy.

The people's love for the poet took over Santiago on October 9, 1969, when four marches of Communists from different parts of the city rallying for Neruda converged in the working-class Barrancas neighborhood, where fireworks were set off above the multitude that crammed the streets. The crowd roared, *"¡Neruda, Neruda, Barrancas te saluda!"* "Neruda, Neruda, Barrancas salutes you!" "Viva the future president of Chile!" The poet gave a speech, ending with:

> Victory depends on us, all of us together, on our ability to spend time together, argue and change minds, in order to change the historical panorama of our homeland, alter the course of history and bring about a people's government, so that we can be proud of who we are as Chileans . . .

Neruda's campaign fired up and mobilized the Communist and Socialist voting base. Once it was evident that he wouldn't win, he (at least publicly) threw his weight behind Allende. Neruda's energy and strategy helped to open the road for UP's success in the general election.

★

Done with the campaign trail, the Nerudas began to travel again out-side Chile, despite Pablo's worsening illness. They went to Paris, Moscow, London, and Milan (for a performance of *The Splendor and Death of Joaquín Murieta*), with a stopover in Barcelona, an emotional visit for Neruda to Franco's Spain. There he spent the day with Gabriel García Márquez, who would write a fictionalized account of the afternoon in his short story "Me alquilo para soñar" (perhaps translated best as "Dreamer for Rent"), published in *Doce cuentos peregrinos* (*Twelve Pilgrim Stories*). García Márquez caricatured his good friend Neruda roaming through bookstores on a "major hunt," moving among the people "like a crippled elephant, with an infantile interest in the internal mechanism of everything—to him, the world seemed like an immense string toy in which he invented life." When it was time to eat, he was "gluttonous and refined." García Márquez writes that he ate three whole lobsters, all the while talking about other culinary delights, especially the "prehistoric shellfish of Chile."

★

On their return from Europe by boat, Neruda and Matilde stopped first in Venezuela, where an elaborate afternoon banquet was held in his honor at *El Nacional* editor in chief Miguel Otero Silva's contemporary mansion.

A twenty-two-year-old Columbia University graduate student, Suzanne Jill Levine, now an esteemed translator of Latin American literature, was at the party. She was traveling with the "wonderfully wry" Uruguayan critic Emir Rodríguez Monegal, who was teaching at Yale. The expansive, modern home was marvelously designed, built into a hillside, with three levels projecting outward, each with its own garden. Levine recalls standing in one of the gardens, admiring Henry Moore's large sculpture of a reclining nude—a private possession of the Communist writer. When it was time for the banquet to be served, around three P.M., she was further impressed by the uniformed waiter who brought a lavishly adorned silver tray to serve to each guest. It was then that she learned the term "Champagne Communist," a term that could often have been ascribed to Neruda—especially in his later years.

Neruda's next stop on the trip back home was Lima, where Jorge Edwards was serving as the concierge of the Chilean embassy. Neruda gave a benefit reading for the victims of a recent earthquake in northern Peru, and the event was attended by an overflow crowd.

The Nerudas stayed at Edwards's house, and he described the complex process of making things just right for the poet, including ensuring that expensive whiskeys and fine wines were always on hand: little luxuries, among others, that Neruda had come to expect wherever he went.

The exorbitant tastes and possessions of these literary Champagne Communists, especially at this point in the century, in their careers, and in their lives, led to much criticism. There was, however, theoretical justification that both Jill Levine, then and now, and Edwards could appreciate. As the latter put it: "No one was seeking absolute egalitarianism—which had been discredited in the early years of the revolution—but rather equality of possibilities. Among other things, socialism had been formulated precisely in order for poets and creators to consume a magnum bottle of Dom Pérignon once in a while. It wasn't just for the empty-headed children of multimillionaires!" Neruda certainly held himself to this standard rather than a more modest lifestyle. Even his Nobel winnings would go toward acquiring another large home.[*]

---

[*] Levine—on this first of the three times she would meet Neruda—could see how his poetry still came to him naturally. Perhaps because she was the youngest person at a long table of some twenty guests and an unknown American female, she wound up seated next to Neruda. When the waiter came to her with the platter of exquisitely prepared fish—presented in full, eye and all—she struggled to transfer it to her plate, an embarrassing undertaking right next to the legendary poet. However, the "challenge par excellence" for her was dessert: a whole mango served with a single small knife, in a time when the tropical fruit was not nearly as familiar in the States as it is today. When Neruda saw her pained hesitation to attempt to take the knife to it, he came to her rescue: "Jill"—pronouncing the soft g correctly, uncommon for Spanish speakers—"I'll cut it for you." He proceeded to methodically cut her

Many of Neruda's friends and peers, however, took issue with what they saw as a gulf between his words and actions. Stephen Spender, for instance, who worked with him supporting the Spanish Republic and championed his poetry in the English-speaking world, said, "I cannot really consider Pablo Neruda a communist at all. His kind of communism was almost entirely rhetorical; he was a sort of highly privileged propagandist."

Even Matilde, who was so far from being a communist, played both sides. During the Allende years, Neruda helped in every way he could, giving readings, fund-raising, and making appearances. Matilde complained: "Listen, dammit, you know the Communists are screwing you over." "Sure," he answered, "but don't you like it when you go to the Soviet Union and they treat you like a queen?"

*

The UP's electoral agenda called for revolutionary changes in Chile's political, economic, and social structures in order to overcome the misery imposed upon the working class by capitalism, exploitation, and class privilege. Allende promised a peaceful transition to socialism. The centrist Christian Democrats' Radomiro Tomic was considered to be an uncompromising leftist by the Chilean Right, and the two groups were unable to form an alliance. The Right thus supported the Nationalist Party's Jorge Alessandri (son of previous progressive president Arturo Alessandri). The Chilean vote was divided once again into thirds.

President Richard Nixon felt that "if Allende should win the election in Chile, and then you have Castro in Cuba, what you'll in effect have in Latin America is a red sandwich, and eventually, it will all be

---

mango into delicate pieces. As she reflected later, "To me this act of chivalry, a veritable ode to the mango, seemed like the attentions of a lover; I felt both honored and tongue-tied, and, blushing deep red again, managed to thank him. As the coffee was brought in, Matilde announced that Pablo was going to take a siesta, and so the great bearlike man beside me got up and swiftly, as by the wave of a wand, vanished into the intimate labyrinth of that luxuriant home."

red."[*] The CIA had intervened in past elections, but not to the extent that it was doing so now. In fact, in the run-up to the 1964 presidential campaign, the CIA had spent an astounding $3 million on anti-Allende propaganda. It comprised the extensive use of the press, radio, even direct mailings, relying heavily on images of Soviet tanks and Cuban firing squads and targeting especially women.

With the centrist Christian Democrat Eduardo Frei's victory in that election, President Johnson's administration moved to support the government, trying to appease the Chilean people enough to prevent them from turning to the Left and Allende's UP coalition. Suddenly, Chile was receiving more aid per capita than any other country in the hemisphere. Though Chile faced few, if any, security threats, the United States also upped its military aid, totaling $91 million from 1962 to 1970, trying to establish good relations with the highest generals. Meanwhile, the CIA continued to infiltrate Chile, spending over $2 million on propping up the Christian Democrats and diminishing support for the UP. It also now appears that the KGB spent hundreds of thousands of dollars in Chile leading up to the election, supporting Allende's campaign.

Leading up to the 1970 election, with Allende appearing so strong, the CIA stepped up its game. But still its efforts failed, despite nearly a decade of experience in covert action against Allende.

Salvador Allende received the most votes on September 4, with 36.3 percent, just 1.4 percent more than the Right's Jorge Alessandri. With almost three million votes cast, the margin between the two was just under forty thousand. Tomic came in a close third, with a strong

---

[*]   It wasn't just global politics Nixon was worried about. Henry Kissinger ordered the CIA and the State and Defense Departments to study the implications for the United States in the event of an Allende win. The report concluded that there would be "tangible economic losses." "The world military balance of power would not be significantly altered by an Allende government," but it would threaten hemispheric cohesion. "We do not see, however, any likely threat to the peace of the region." Yet the victory would have "considerable political and psychological costs": "a definite psychological setback to the U.S. and a definite psychological advance for the Marxist idea."

27.8 percent, reflecting just how divided the country was. According to the Chilean constitution at the time, if no candidate was elected with a 50 percent majority, the National Congress chose who would be president between the top two in the popular vote. In the three times this had occurred since 1932, Congress had always confirmed the candidate who earned the most votes in the popular election. The confirmation vote would take place on October 24.

Following Allende's victory, in a meeting with Secretary of State Henry Kissinger, CIA director Richard Helms, and Attorney General John Mitchell, Nixon issued explicit orders to foment a coup to prevent Allende's inauguration or, failing that, to destroy his subsequent administration. The CIA took down Nixon's directives in handwritten notes. They constitute the first record of a U.S. president ordering the overthrow of a democratically elected government.

Nixon ordered the CIA to "make the [Chilean] economy scream" to "prevent Allende from coming to power or to unseat him." Helms cabled Kissinger, asserting that a "suddenly disastrous economic situation would be the most logical pretext for a military move." The "only practical way to create the tense atmosphere in which Frei [still in power] could muster the courage to act is to see to it that the Chilean economy, precarious enough since the election, takes a drastic turn for the worse . . . At least a mini-crisis is required." They conspired with right-wing groups and economic players, which above all included the International Telephone and Telegraph Co. ITT had holdings of $153 million in Chile, owning the phone company, two Sheraton hotels, and Standard Electric, among other entities. The firm collaborated with the CIA in an attempt to destabilize the economy through various means, including cancellations of loans and credits and stirring up panic among Chile's private businesses. U.S. interests also schemed to covertly bankrupt savings banks and induce unemployment.

As the Church Committee report affirms, "at the express request of the President . . . The CIA attempted, directly, to foment a military coup in Chile." The CIA funneled weapons to a group of Chilean officers who plotted a takeover, which was to begin with the kidnapping of René Schneider, the commander in chief of the Chilean army and a constitutionalist who had publicly stated he would support the proper transfer of power. U.S. ambassador Edward Korry had identified a retired general as a military figure who could move against Allende with Schneider out of the way. But two days before the congressional vote, a different group of right-wing extremists, not known to be tied to the CIA, tried to kidnap Schneider. General Schneider tried to defend himself and was mortally wounded in the exchange of gunfire.[*]

Nixon's policies did not succeed in diminishing Allende's popular support. Furthermore, the assassination so close to the congressional vote drew sympathy away from the Right. The Christian Democrats in Congress were already siding with Allende, aligning themselves with UP rather than the Right, thus maintaining Chile's democratic precedent of confirming the candidate who won the most popular votes, no matter how slight the victory. First, though, they demanded and received a package of guarantees: UP would keep the multiparty system, would maintain civil liberties and freedom of the press, and would protect the armed forces from political purges. Allende wholeheartedly accepted the measures and was confirmed.

Among many on the Chilean Left, perhaps especially among the younger generation, Allende's triumph brought the sense of a historic shift. The victory also reverberated throughout Latin America, where all eyes were turned toward Chile. This was the world's first democratic election of a "Socialist parliamentarian," as Allende described himself, who also held some Marxist ideas. The old orthodoxy of socialism and communism at that point maintained that the only way to create a new society was to take over the state, and the only way to do that was through armed revolution, as in Cuba. In order to establish a government that could implement socialism or communism, it was believed that it was necessary to impose terror on anyone who obstructed

---

[*]   In a phone call with his press secretary, Nixon acknowledged that the U.S. ambassador in Chile had been instructed to "do all possible short of a Dominican Republic–style action"—assassination—to keep Allende from assuming office. The March 1972 conversation was captured on his secret Oval Office taping system: "But he just failed, the son of a bitch. That was his main problem. He should have kept Allende from getting in."

the necessary changes. Allende, and those who supported him, suggested and believed that democracy was another means to the same end, without violence.

After Allende's inauguration, the UP government tried to establish socialism within a bourgeois state where the center and the Right controlled the judiciary and legislature. The UP's strategy was to use the executive branch's considerable strength to carry out some immediate economic reforms that would snap the economy out of the recession that Allende inherited. This included the nationalization of large industries, redistribution of income, and state hiring of the unemployed. The subsequent economic pickup was intended to be accompanied by mass political mobilizations, leading to a parliamentary electoral majority for the UP.

The CIA, as confirmed by a 1975 U.S. congressional investigation, covertly spent $8 million in the three years between 1970 and the coup in September 1973, sabotaging Allende's government. Nixon blocked copper exports to the United States, which had been a staple of the Chilean economy. Meanwhile, those to the UP's left, including organized Mapuche and the Marxist Movement of the Revolutionary Left (Movimiento de Izquierda Revolucionaria, or MIR), were wreaking havoc with acts of political terrorism. The UP itself was a precarious coalition with little cohesion or agreement regarding the pace and character of change the government was to implement. Allende lacked a mandate while working within a democracy; unlike Castro, he wasn't relying on a revolutionary army. The result was chaos and extreme political polarization.

Allende's initial success with government programs ironically helped bring about their demise. Early efforts at redistribution of income through wage and salary adjustments, as well as increased government spending, boosted the stagnant economy. The adjustments were meant to eliminate a wide income gap, while also giving a stimulus to the middle class. But Chilean businesses, manipulated by rampant anti-communist propaganda and fearing what Allende might bring, didn't reinvest their gains; instead, they sold off their inventory at speculative prices. They invested in dollars and other hard currencies instead of the Chilean peso, which, combined with hoarding and black market trade, consequently created severe shortages of basics: flour, cooking oil, soap, common car and television parts, bedsheets, toilet paper, comfort foods, and, perhaps most aggravating for those dependent on them, cigarettes. Discontent rose along with prices. The U.S. campaign against Allende didn't help the situation. Upon Allende's election, Ambassador Korry proposed a series of actions to destabilize the economy, including having U.S. companies in Chile "foot-drag to maximum possible" and "hold off on orders, on deliveries of spare parts." Starting rumors of imminent rationing created a "run on food stocks." He also suggested asking U.S. banks to suddenly halt renewal of credit to Chile, saying, "Not a nut or bolt will be allowed to reach Chile under Allende. We shall do all within our power to condemn Chile and the Chilean to utmost deprivation and poverty."

Inflation skyrocketed. By mid-1973, the annual inflation rate had risen to over 300 percent.

The UP's land-reform program also lacked a clear vision and resulted in the disorganization of the agricultural economy. Production dropped so sharply that the government was forced to import food to meet the increased demand brought on by the higher incomes of workers. At the same time, sparked on by the MIR and radical Mapuche, campesinos temporarily or permanently occupied some seventeen hundred rural properties. The owners of these properties were terrified, and this helped fuel the opposition against Allende. Many think it was the Ultra-Left's intimidation of centrists and landowners that sealed the fate of the UP.

★

Even before Allende's victory, Neruda had had concerns about Chile. According to Jorge Edwards, Neruda feared the situation in Chile might be difficult: "He wasn't optimistic at all; he held no illusions about it . . . If Allende won, as his party quite realistically supposed, he was afraid that things would end badly."

Nevertheless, Neruda was tremendously proud of what his country had done. After all, he had played a role in its success, both on and off the page.

His sentiments could be heard in his reading at the Royal Festival Hall in London in April 1972. With his earnest, at times dramatic voice carrying a twinge of sweetness, he began by telling the audience, in English:

> Last time I read some of my poems before you [pauses, breathes out] but this time I am a different person, I am two persons, you see I was a [pauses] roving poet in that moment when I was here, but something happened to my country in Chile. After one hundred years of struggles of the humiliated and the trashed and the working class, we had [raises his voice just enough, with a dramatic pause] a great victory. [Applause.] We had at last a good and great victory and I am not only a roaming poet now, I am also the proud representative of the first popular government after centuries in my country, Chile. [Long, raucous applause.]

He was not without his detractors, though. Someone jeered at Neruda during his opening remarks but was quickly drowned out by loud noise in favor of the poet. The writer Jay Parini, then a graduate student, was at that London reading, sitting toward the back. He recalled how there had been a great deal of muttering in the audience, people talking over each other. At one point, "a bald-headed man in front of me was shouting something in Spanish—I couldn't really understand it, but it seemed offensive." Several people were telling him to shut up when "a well-dressed woman sitting next to me took off one shoe and brought a stiletto heel down hard on the man's scalp, producing shrieks and a good deal of blood. A policeman dragged off the man, with the woman chasing after him, hitting him more times. The audience was in pandemonium, until Neruda—a large, impressive-looking man—raised a big hand and, like Moses parting the Red Sea, made a way for his poem, reading his masterpiece 'The Heights of Macchu Picchu.'"

Neruda was accompanied on the stage by Alastair Reid, his Scottish-born English translator and dear friend. Reid read the English first, followed by Neruda reading the Spanish, in sections, so that the "sense comes first and the sound follows," as Reid put it. If four decades earlier Neruda's reading voice had been nasal and monotone, now it resounded, especially pronounced by the crisscross rhythm between the Spanish and the English, alternating long strands or stanzas or just couplets back and forth, the poems broken up as if into meter, creating varying speeds and tension and song. Reid had heard Neruda read many times, but on that night he sensed something truly special: the Chilean's voice was "spreading itself like a balm over the English audience." It was "a magical sound."

Fueled by the energy of the crowd, Neruda's voice reached a climax while reading "Macchu Picchu." The pace of the poem was growing with force as he struck the lectern loudly with his fist while speaking the final line, *"Hablar por mis palabras y mi sangre."* "Speak through my words and my blood." The dramatic, emotional flair of his voice was both inspiring and chilling. With his country's revolution as a backdrop, Neruda's words resonated with authority and power. The audience erupted into a thunderous, jubilant applause.[*]

★

Neruda's domestic life was once again in turmoil in 1970. Matilde's niece Alicia had found out that her husband, the father of her child, was already married to another woman. As Alicia struggled to recover, Matilde invited her to live at Isla Negra in exchange for occasional domestic work, including as a dressmaker. Alicia was in her early thirties, exuberant and light skinned. Very quickly, she and Neruda became intimate. The affair was evident to visitors who had known Neruda through his relationships with Delia and Matilde. Aida Figueroa reported that Neruda summoned Alicia frequently and that his attachment struck her as profoundly sad, his "one last senile love." Neruda never wanted to be disturbed during his daily siestas, so it was at this time that Matilde would take a long walk on the beach. And it was also then that Alicia and Neruda were alone together. Neruda wrote and published a book of poetry for and about her.

---

[*]   While in London, Parini had dinner with Reid and Neruda, "and it was wonderful: he was so sweet and affecting, and when Alastair told him I was a poet, he gave me a lovely kiss on the forehead: almost a benediction."

There is a consensus among those who knew Neruda that the book, the phallically titled *La espada encendida* (The Flaming Sword), was intended as a mythological work in which a new Adam (Neruda) and Eve (Alicia) find each other in the destruction after nuclear war. Together, they set off to found a utopia.

Long before the book was published, Matilde became suspicious. One day when Alicia had gone to Santiago, Neruda made up a trip, saying he didn't want Matilde to come along. He left alone with the chauffeur. Matilde followed him and caught them in a tryst. "I'll tell you that your friend is not a healthy man," Matilde told Neruda's comrade Volodia Teitelboim. "He has gotten mixed up with dirty women, and now he's sick in the part where he was doing that. And he's not getting better. Where your sins are, you pay."

Alicia was dismissed from Isla Negra, and Matilde told Neruda that they had to leave Chile. The party, helpfully, asked Allende to nominate Neruda as ambassador to France. On January 21, 1971, in a Senate session to confirm new nominations by Allende, the senators of the Right voted against Neruda, and the Christian Democrats abstained. He did get enough votes from UP senators, but the fact that the Christian Democrats abstained was an indication of their extreme dissatisfaction with the Communists and the Allende administration.

By serving in France, Neruda was fulfilling his youthful diplomatic dream. But all was not well. He was visibly agitated and anxious. Teitelboim remembers the day the poet left for Paris: "There is a part of the night that accompanies man even in daytime, especially when he has an ear finely tuned enough to hear the thunder before seeing the lightning. As if he had a covenant with something that was still hidden, Neruda did not seem happy when we bade him farewell at the airport, even though things were going well at that time."

Despite his departure for Paris, the passion between Neruda and Alicia remained. They corresponded via Jorge Edwards, whom Neruda insisted on having as his chancellor at the embassy. Neruda would send gifts to Alicia and her daughter with friends returning to Chile. For his sixty-seventh birthday, she wrote him: "I kiss you and I caress your entire beloved body, my beloved love, love, my love, love . . ."

CHAPTER TWENTY-ONE

THE FLOWERS THAT SLEEP

> Wrapped in the sky, I return to the sea:
> the silence between one wave and the next
> creates a dangerous suspense:
> life ebbs out, the blood slows down
> until a new movement crashes
> and the voice of infinity resounds.
> —"Autumn"

Neruda arrived in Paris at the end of March 1971. When he was asked about his new position by a Swedish television station, Neruda had a righteous-sounding cover for the affair that had hastened his and Matilde's departure:

> My country is experiencing a peaceful revolution: We are changing our feudal system, we are fighting against the foreign domination of our economy, we are rescuing our natural riches, we are giving greater dignity to the life of the Chilean people. I could not have turned down this job. That's it. I have come here because it is my duty.

As soon as they arrived in Paris, he and Matilde went immediately to a well-known urologist. A tube was placed into his bladder to ease his discomfort and ward off urinary tract infections. He couldn't bear the hospital regimen and asked to be discharged as early as possible.

By July, Neruda's prostate cancer symptoms were taking their toll on his tired body. His enthusiasm for all the cultural events he had imagined attending as ambassador would be put aside—soon, everything would be put aside. He wrote to Volodia Teitelboim on July 11:

> Everything is the same here inside this catacomb. I have not seen friends or been to museums. Every once in a while, we go to the movies, with great effort, as if we were traveling from Isla Negra to Valparaíso. I am not going to talk to you about my poetry, because I have not taken it up again . . . If I keep dictating it to Matilde, she will catch my fever.

October brought a great affirmation of Neruda's life in letters. His old friend Artur Lundkvist came from Stockholm to tell him he had won the Nobel Prize in Literature. His admirers had long campaigned for this. The Chilean Ministry of Foreign Affairs had even tried to set up a bibliographic exhibition of Neruda's works in Stockholm in 1966 to influence the judges. Many believe he didn't receive the prize earlier because of pressure not to award it to such a prominent Communist. Following the public announcement of the prize, Neruda gave a press conference, and Allende called in the middle of it. Gabriel García Márquez, David Alfaro Siqueiros, Julio Cortázar, and other artists traveled to attend the party that night at the embassy. Telegrams came from all over the world, and Allende said, "Neruda is Chile."

Immediately after Neruda heard the news, he asked Edwards to help him find a house in Normandy. The Chilean ambassador's residence was part of the embassy complex; the poet wanted privacy and refuge, and access to nature.

That very morning, they found what they were looking for in Condé-sur-Iton. Near an old sawmill, on expansive land, was a chateau from the Renaissance era. Because of its low elevation, it couldn't be seen from town. As per his custom, Neruda made the decision to buy it immediately. Matilde's input, if any, had little effect on the decision. He instantly started to plan his life around the new property, as if, Edwards felt, "the house grew within him from that very instant." He named his new house El Manquel, which is the Mapuche's Mapudungun word for "eagle."

The Chilean Right attacked him in the press for what it characterized as hypocrisy, a Communist making such an extravagant purchase. Neruda paid $85,000 for the home, taken from the $450,000 of his Nobel Prize.

The prize ceremony was held on December 11, 1971. In his presentation speech, Karl Ragnar Gierow of the Swedish Academy proclaimed, "His work benefits mankind precisely because of its direction . . . What Neruda has achieved in his writing is community with existence . . . In his work a continent awakens to consciousness."

The sick poet's voice was not weak when he accepted the prize and gave his lecture. He sounded clear but tired. As he spoke, Neruda hit his rhythm, and his words resonated.

> The poet is not a "little god." No, he is not a "little god." He is not assigned a superior mystical destiny over those who pursue other crafts and careers. I have often said that the best poet is the one who gives us our daily bread: the local baker who does not feign godliness . . .
>
> Exactly one hundred years ago today, a poor and magnificent poet, the most tremendous of all woeful souls, wrote this prophecy: *"À l'aurore, armés d'une ardente patience, nous entrerons aux splendides villes."* "At dawn, armed with a burning patience, we will enter the splendid cities."
>
> I believe in the prophecy of Rimbaud, the Visionary. I come from a dark province, a country separated from all others by a sharp geography. I was once the most dejected of poets and my poetry was provincial, painful, and rainy. But I always had faith in humanity. I never lost hope. That is why perhaps I have made it this far, arriving here with my poetry and also my flag.
>
> In closing, I must say to the goodhearted people, to the

workers, to the poets, that the future's entirety is expressed in Rimbaud's lines: only with a burning patience will we triumph in the splendid city, the city that will give light, justice, and dignity to us all.

★

Meanwhile, Neruda had serious diplomatic duties to attend to. In November 1971, due to the depleted treasury, Allende was forced to announce a moratorium on paying back foreign debt. He hoped the creditor nations would reschedule and restructure Chile's nearly $2 billion owed to eleven countries. This was done through the Paris Club, an informal assembly of representatives of the world's major creditor nations. With the meetings being held in Paris, Neruda as ambassador led the negotiations for his country. Nearly two-thirds of the debt, though, was owed to the United States, who wanted any refinancing to be tied to compensation for the expropriation of copper companies. Neruda helped to secure what was perceived as a favorable deal. He also worked to persuade the French to dismiss the pressure of expropriated American companies to put an embargo on Chilean copper exports.

★

Neruda's health continued to deteriorate, but this did not prevent him from traveling to New York City, in early April 1972, to deliver the opening speech at the PEN American Center's fiftieth anniversary celebration. There were no visa issues now, even though Neruda had been writing fervently about Vietnam, and even though he was an ambassador of a government Washington was trying to destroy. Nixon had denied entry to other artists, but Neruda's star, especially after the Nobel Prize, shone too bright now. Even Nixon understood what Johnson surmised: that to censure his voice, prevent his presence, would do much more damage than good.

The evening began with the president of PEN America reading a greeting from Nixon, to which the seven hundred or so guests who filled the grand ballroom "hissed, laughed and booed," according to the *New York Times*. Arthur Miller then introduced Neruda as the "father of

Delivering his "Yo Acuso" ("I Accuse") speech on the Senate floor, 1948.

Archivos de la Fundación Pablo Neruda

Just before crossing the Andes into exile with Jorge Bellet and Victor Bianchi.

Colección Archivo Fotográfico, Archivo Central Andrés Bello, Universidad de Chile

Neruda and Matilde in Nyon, on the shore of Lake Geneva, where they spent a few days alone for the first time, 1951.

Archivos de la Fundación Pablo Neruda

On April 25, 1949, at the end of the First World Congress of Partisans for Peace in Paris, Pablo Picasso announced he had a surprise and revealed Neruda, who had just fled Chile into exile.

Associated Press

Neruda's bedroom, Isla Negra, 2015.

Danielle Villasana

Neruda's house in Isla Negra, spreading across the hill like a ship above the water, 1999. *Macduff Everton*

"Neruda for President" rally in Santiago's working-class Barrancas neighborhood, October 1969.

Colección Archivo Fotográfico, Archivo Central Andrés Bello, Universidad de Chile

The bar inside Isla Negra, with rafters carved with names of friends who had died, 1967.

Milton Rogovin/Courtesy Center for Creative Photography, University of Arizona Foundation

Neruda campaigning for Salvador Allende.

Archivos de la Fundación Pablo Neruda

Matilde hugging Neruda after hearing the announcement that he had won
the Nobel Prize, October 21, 1971.

Bridgeman Images

Neruda's funeral, September 25, 1973.

Marcelo Montecino

Soldier flanking the funeral procession.

David Burnett/Contact Press Images

Matilde Urrutia walking behind her husband's coffin.

David Burnett/Contact Press Images

contemporary Latin-American literature." Onstage, Neruda "humbly" asked for forgiveness as he broke away from the literary discourse for a moment to "return to the concerns of my country," in particular debt relief. "The entire world knows that Chile is undergoing a revolutionary transformation, within the dignity and severity of its laws. That is why there are a lot of people who feel offended."

While just a few years ago he would have been animated by such attention, now, besieged by an admiring crowd after the conference, Neruda's dear friend Fernando Alegría saw him turn gray. The press and the fans cornered him, and "there [were] already ashes clinging to his dark suit." Next, gathered with an intimate group at an elegant salon, his friends offered him breathing room and flutes of champagne. He was fatigued and headed back toward the bathroom with "slow, tired steps," in Alegría's words. "He says in passing that he isn't well, that he will return to Chile in November and that no one must know. But everyone did."

The endless questions he faced in public seized upon him in his final act in New York, a symposium at Columbia University, where the Q&A became contentious with sharp inquiries into his opinion on international politics, with little attention to poetics. He was done with all this.

He and Matilde quickly took off for Moscow, on April 24, where he got another prognosis. On their flight to Russia, he wrote to Francisco Velasco and María Martner, their La Sebastiana housemates: "We are sick ones but still fighting." The doctors confirmed what Neruda had been told before: there was nothing to be done. It was his final visit to the Soviet capital, and he wrote a book to it, *Elegía* (*Elegy*), poems celebrating his friends and the city, while also denouncing social realism and the former hero he now called "Stalin the terrible." The book would be published posthumously.

Neruda celebrated his sixty-eighth birthday in warm company at his Normandy country house, along with Julio Cortázar, Gabriel García Márquez, Carlos Fuentes, and Mario Vargas Llosa, arguably four of the five most important Latin American prose writers at the time (Neruda's quiet rival Jorge Luis Borges being the fifth).

Shortly thereafter, Neruda realized he was too tired to continue as ambassador. He was ready to retire to Isla Negra. He handed over the reins of the embassy to Edwards, but before he left, he met with French president Georges Pompidou in the Palais de l'Élysée. The poet gave him a signed copy of the just-published French translation of García Márquez's *One Hundred Years of Solitude*. They conversed about literature; Pompidou had been a teacher of literature and had edited an anthology of French poetry in his youth. Neruda then put in his word for the nationalization of French interests in Chilean copper, but Pompidou said that was a matter of the courts, not the executive.

When the Velascos met Neruda and Matilde at the airport on their return from France, Neruda told Francisco he wanted to go straight to Isla Negra; he refused to greet anyone in the official committee that awaited him. He got into his friend's old Citroën with great difficulty. "I realized he was very bad," wrote Velasco. Neruda was struggling with his breath—he had dyspnea, set off with the slightest effort. Gone was his heavy set; he was remarkably thinner, with "a jaundiced pallor" and, "above all, a sadness unlike I've ever seen."

★

The Chile of October 1972 was a place of upheaval and civil unrest. A conflict that began in a remote region of Patagonia set off a spark, igniting a conflagration of tension that consumed the country that month. Local truckers had protested the Allende administration's plan to create a state-owned trucking enterprise in Aysén, the country's least populated area. The government felt the private trucking system was inadequate, while the truckers blamed the government's inability to secure replacement parts and other supplies to keep them efficient. They announced a strike, and the National Truckers Confederation joined them, forty thousand members staying off the road. Telling of the tension that was gripping the country, the shopkeepers' and merchants' organizations joined the now-national strike, adding their own specific demands. They were followed by the Engineers Association, then bank clerks, gas workers, lawyers, architects, and taxi and bus drivers—a national strike that strove to paralyze the economy to leave the government no other choice than to make transformative changes. Patience had simply worn out. Moderate groups like the Christian Democratic Party supported the strike, which had wide consequences: influenced by Christian Democratic union leaders, for instance, one hundred thousand campesinos joined the strike as well.

Allende declared a partial state of emergency. The military, for the moment loyal to the government, was called in to maintain order and, in effect, help shore up the UP's fragile position. Enough factories were still producing, and there were enough loyal supporters of the government that the economy held and the country wasn't completely paralyzed, but the strike wore on.

On November 2, Allende shook up his cabinet in hopes of stemming the assaults on his administration and even ending the strike. He invited the army's commander in chief, Carlos Prats, to serve as minister of the interior while still maintaining his military post. The moves worked. Twenty-five days after they started the strike, the National Truckers Confederation declared their full confidence in General Prats and negotiated an agreement. The government survived, but the strike had made the military the arbiter of the country's political conflicts.

A year earlier, Neruda had written an article for *Le Monde* praising Prats, highlighting that, in Chile, the military was loyal to the country's constitution. Prats, who would remain loyal to Allende, wrote a letter thanking the poet. On December 6, 1972, General Prats was the one to welcome the poet back from France at the National Stadium, in a great celebration for both his homecoming and winning the Nobel Prize. Neruda was very ill, but he mustered his strength for this great homage, complete with a balloon launch and a parade around the stadium's track of young Communists, workers, horses, and a float dedicated to Luis Emilio Recabarren.

President Salvador Allende and First Lady Hortensia Bussi Soto took a helicopter to Isla Negra to visit the sick poet and officially receive his resignation as ambassador in person. Neruda read from his new book, *Incitement to Nixoncide and Praise for the Chilean Revolution*. When Neruda became bedridden and no longer made public appearances, his friends brought the outside world to his bedside. Julio Cortázar visited him that February. As he and his wife entered Neruda's bedroom, the sea breaking directly outside the enormous window that took up a whole wall, it seemed to Cortázar that the poet was still "carrying on his perpetual dialogue with the sea, with those waves that he had always seen as great eyelids." He went on:

> In the evening, although we insisted on leaving so that he could rest, Pablo made us stay with him to watch a dreadful melodrama about vampires on television, which fascinated and amused him at the same time, as he gave himself up to a ghostly present that was more real to him than a future he knew to be closed to him. On my first visit, which had taken place in France two years before, he had embraced me with a "See you soon." Now, he looked at us for a moment, his hands in mine, and said, "Better not to say good-bye, right?" his tired eyes already far away.

Though he appeared tired to his friends, Neruda still found energy to pursue Alicia, Matilde's niece. Their separation had put the affair on hold, but their emotions had not faded, and they had maintained a correspondence. Believing her ailing husband was in good hands, Matilde had returned to Europe to settle various affairs, including selling their house in Normandy. On April 29, 1973, Neruda wrote to her, first describing the ten or so people who had come to lunch the day before. Then, showing the state of his health and the difficulties of obtaining even basic medicine in Chile at the time, partly due to economic blockades, Neruda asked Matilde to send or "bring back phenindione [an anticoagulant] for the veins. And Cortancyl (Prednisone) [cortisone, a steroid]."

He ends the letter: "I'm angry because you don't write, dammit! I forgive you for today. I love you, I kiss you, but enjoy your trip." He closes it, addressing her as "Perro-tita [little dog], *hasta luego*, your"— and then draws in a small picture of a dog for himself.

In her absence, when he went to Valparaíso for cancer treatments, he and Alicia reunited at the city's iconic Hotel Miramar, overlooking the sea. These rendezvous occurred with some frequency, always in the same hotel. She would also accompany him at the hospital. It seems Matilde never knew anything of the post-France affair between her husband and niece. It's possible that the two also saw each other behind Matilde's back when she was in Chile, when Neruda dissuaded her from making the trips to Valparaíso for treatment.

Alicia was struck by how thin he was becoming. Sometimes he was so sick a doctor had to come to the hotel. She found him in great pain, walking with difficulty, but trying to hide the extent of his suffering. Alicia begged him to take better care of himself.

But little, if anything, could be done at this point. Dr. Velasco remembers how the cancerous metastasis in his hips provoked so much pain that he could barely walk. On his last visit to La Sebastiana in Valparaíso, Velasco had to put one of his old friend's arms over his shoulders and help him with his cane as they walked down the long alley to the iconic house they had shared. On one of Velasco and María's last trips to Isla Negra, he saw Neruda trying to write his memoirs in bed, with great difficulty. At one point the pen fell out of his hand as he fell into a state of semiconsciousness from which he recovered rather quickly. His body was failing him, but he persevered.

*

On February 27, Dr. John R. G. Turner of the State University of New York at Stony Brook wrote Neruda a letter that lifted his spirits and expanded his legacy in a romantic, nostalgic way. Turner explained (in Spanish) that a new subgenus of South American butterflies of the genus *Heliconius* needed a name. With Mount Helicon being a setting in Greek mythology where inspirational muses dwelled, the custom of the past century was to name a new subgenus after a muse, such Melpomene, the muse of tragedy, whom one evokes to stimulate poetry, or Erato, the muse of erotic poetry. "The era of those classical names has come and gone, but we still think it appropriate to name the new subgenus after a poet of our time, and since said butterflies are from South America, we were thinking about a Hispano-American poet": Pablo Neruda. (No other *Heliconius* subgenus has been named after a modern writer.)

The butterfly Neruda is found in Peru, Ecuador, and French Guiana. It is beautiful, dark with orange stripes and white splotches. Neruda, a collector of butterflies since his youth, was thrilled. Neruda wrote a brief and charming note back to Turner: "I've never been given such a great honor as the one you propose. I am deeply moved to accept the tribute and will be delighted to think of those butterflies flying in some corner of our continent with my name on their wings." The name Neruda has remained in use, and it was even elevated to the level of genus by one of Turner's colleagues, meaning that butterflies have been flying around with names like *Neruda aoede* and *Neruda metharme* on their wings.

Another respectful acknowledgment of Neruda's significance came when the Cuban publisher Casa de las Américas published an anthology of Neruda's poetry with a prologue by Roberto Fernández Retamar. But the Chilean still held great animosity for the man who had signed the 1964 letter of attack against him. Neruda wrote to the publisher:

> Unfortunately, I must seriously protest against a part of the new edition that you have done. It has to do with the name, and prologue, of Señor Fernández Retamal [Neruda played on Retamar's name, changing the final *r* to *l*, making it "Reta-bad"].
>
> A while back, a defamatory and calumnious letter was widely distributed around the world. Señor Fernández was the main author of that erroneous, monstrous, and unjustifiable letter . . .

His body may have been failing him, but his defiance could still flare, and his ego could still inflate.

★

Throughout this time, the democratic Chilean revolution was in tatters. Allende hoped that General Prats would anchor his administration amid rampant inflation, constant political and economic crises, and the rising pitch of rhetoric between the government and its opposition. However, Prats was losing his popularity with the public. His support among fellow officers was eroding because he remained an Allende loyalist, with his own personal political ambitions becoming more evident. Additionally, he made the mistake of threatening a woman driver with death after she reportedly stuck out her tongue at him, an embarrassing, if not fateful, public relations disaster.

The streets of Santiago became violent with terrorist acts from both the Far Right and the Far Left. Chile was in chaos. Many felt the situation was moving toward civil war.

On May 26, from Isla Negra, Neruda gave an interview that was broadcast on national television, in which he spoke of the danger of fascist takeover and, alluding to his experiences in Spain, urged the people to realize what a civil war would really mean in terms of human suffering.

In the words of Joan Jara, wife of the activist folk singer Victor Jara:

> The whole cultural movement responded to Neruda's call. Exhibitions and television programmes were organised; a cultural open-air marathon [of activity] took place in the Plaza de la Constitución. It lasted several days and hundreds of artists, poets, theatre and dance groups, musicians and song groups took part. It was a great anti-fascist event to which thousands came, and there were similar events all over the country. Victor's contribution, apart from performing as a singer, was to direct a series of programmes for the National Television Channel with a common theme: a warning, relating documentary material about Nazi Germany and the Spanish Civil War to the situation in Chile, to make people aware of the real dangers of the same things happening here and now. Victor had put to music one of Neruda's latest poems which had the refrain "I don't want my country divided . . . ," and he sang it as the opening theme for each programme.

Yet while Neruda appealed to everyone to join in to stop this confrontation among brothers, many already thought the collapse of the Allende experiment was inevitable and readied themselves for the transition.

In Congress, the opposition (the center-left to the right wing) called for the military to intervene to guarantee institutional stability, civil peace, and development. At the same time, hundreds of military officers' wives protested in front of General Prats's home, demanding that he resign. He subsequently did so, and two other generals followed suit. Allende was now at the mercy of General Augusto Pinochet.

On August 31, 1973, Neruda wrote a letter to Prats, telling him that the great majority of Chileans would continue to consider him their "chief general and an exemplary citizen . . . It would be impossible to look without anguish upon the blind insistence of those who want to drive us into the misfortune of a war pitting brother against brother."

The general wrote back, thanking Neruda and stating that it had been edifying to be the one to welcome him upon his return from France at the National Stadium, adding:

> I send my best wishes for the quick restoration of your health, because Chile—on the brink as it is of political entrenchment—needs the important intellectual values that you symbolize so that reason and common sense can once again prevail in this beautiful country, so that its people can achieve the social justice that they so deserve . . .

The Pinochet regime would later assassinate Prats in Argentina, where he lived in exile after the coup.

At 7:55 A.M. on the morning of September 11, 1973, on a phone connected to Radio Corporación, Salvador Allende addressed his country:

> This is the president of the republic speaking from El Palacio de la Moneda. Reports confirm that a sector of the navy has set siege to Valparaíso and that the city is occupied, signifying an uprising against the government, the legitimate, constituted government, the government that is supported by the law and the will of the citizens.
>
> In these circumstances, I call on all workers: Stay in your workplaces, go to the factories, stay calm, keep calm . . .

After two other broadcasts, at 9:03 the president again spoke on the radio:

> Planes are flying over us right now. They may riddle us with fire. But let them know that here we stand, at least with our example that in this country there are men who know they must fulfill the obligation they have. I will follow the orders of the people and the orders of the conscience of a president who has the dignity of his post given to him by his people in free and democratic elections . . .
>
> I will pay with my life to defend the principles this country holds dear. Shame will fall upon those who have betrayed their commitments, broken their words . . . broken the doctrine of the armed forces . . .

Gunshots were heard in the background. An air force plane bombed La Moneda. Six minutes later, Allende sat in his armchair and spoke into his telephone, which was connected now to only Radio Magallanes:

> This will surely be the last opportunity for me to address you. The air force has bombed the towers of Radio Postales and Radio Corporación . . .
>
> Workers of my homeland! I have faith in Chile and its destiny. Other men will overcome this dark and bitter moment when treason seeks to prevail. Keep in mind that, much sooner than later, the great avenues will again be opened, through which the free man will pass to construct a better society . . .
>
> Long live Chile! Long live *el pueblo*! Long live the workers! These are my last words. I am sure that my sacrifice will not be in vain . . .

Then the tanks started making their approach on La Moneda. The air force's jets screamed in and dropped their bombs. Eventually,

Allende shot himself in order to evade certain imprisonment and likely torture and murder by the coup regime.

Pinochet seized control of the country.

The general always seemed much more interested in power than ideology. He was not known for his intelligence, but his methodical maneuvers always seemed to work out, just as he managed to take sole control of the junta, which was supposed to have been a rotating presidency. With the army behind him, he secured the title of "President of the Republic" for nearly two decades. U.S. intelligence was caught off guard by his brutality and ruthlessness. After the coup, a Defense Intelligence Agency report described him as "quiet; mild-mannered; very businesslike. Very honest . . . A devoted, tolerant husband and father; lives very modestly." Yet by late October, a fact sheet prepared for Kissinger on "post-coup repression" showed that in Pinochet's first six weeks in power, the military had massacred approximately 1,500 civilians, with more than 300 being summarily executed, and more than 13,500 already arrested. The enigmatic folk hero Victor Jara, for example, had been kept in depraved conditions in the National Stadium. His body was later found in a canal, with his guitar-playing hands mutilated and forty-four bullet holes in his body.

★

Neruda had listened to the day's news at Isla Negra, feverishly changing the radio dial from one report to another. Matilde felt that Neruda was reacting in a manner uncharacteristic of the fighter she had always seen in him. Instead, he seemed broken inside; there was "an empty gleam of unconscious desperation in his eyes and his attitude." Neruda could barely walk. He had developed a high fever as they watched the television broadcasts of La Moneda on fire, tanks passing through Santiago, and people being arrested all around the city. Once again—now in his own country—fascism, the enemy he had spent so much of his life battling, was killing his friends.

Three days later, the military came to search the house at Isla Negra. Neruda was still in bed when they entered his room, looking for arms or *guerrilleros*, but really just trying to intimidate Neruda and his family.

"Look all you want," Neruda is said to have told the captain. "There's only one thing here that's dangerous to you."

"What's that?" the officer asked, his hand on his holster.

"Poetry!"

The young folk singers Hugo Arévalo and Charo Cofré, friends of Neruda's, were in Santiago. By September 18, Chile's Independence Day, rumors were rampant that Neruda was dead, perhaps even assassinated. Arévalo and Cofré drove to Isla Negra, despite the risk of being stopped by the police. As Arévalo recalled the visit, they went up to Neruda's room and he was delighted to see them, and then "he started asking us how we had survived the coup in Santiago; who, of the people we saw, was still alive; whether or not we knew of anyone who had died or had been arrested."

Around two that afternoon, it being Chile's Independence Day, Neruda declared that they must celebrate it as always, even though they didn't consider Chile an independent country since the coup. "So we toasted to the eighteenth of September, in parentheses."

Every Independence Day, the Catholic Church holds a special Mass, the ceremonies of Te Deum. They watched the event on TV. Ex-presidents attended, and this year they saw Jorge Alessandri, Gabriel González Videla, and Eduardo Frei. The turning point in the day came when Neruda saw González Videla, who had called him a traitor and sought his arrest. Neruda became very distressed, like a wild animal. "I think that this was the culmination of his nightmare," Arévalo said, "and that it led to his end."

Neruda's condition started to visibly worsen. Around eleven o'clock that night, as they were watching the news on TV, his hands started to shake. He asked Matilde to take Arévalo and Cofré to their bedroom, where they would hardly sleep. Matilde knocked on their door at five in the morning, saying that Neruda was very ill and that an ambulance was on its way.

On the way to Santiago, the ambulance was stopped at several checkpoints. The military searched it, including underneath the stretcher where Neruda lay. He was taken to the Clínica Santa María. Doctors came in and out of his hospital room, prescribing medicines, some of them distraught themselves. The poet was suffering intense pain. On September 20, the Mexican embassy told Neruda that President Luis Echeverría Álvarez had offered him asylum and a flight to Mexico in a private plane. Neruda thanked the ambassador but said he would stay in Chile because he could never live anywhere else.

On September 21, Matilde found out that the military had ransacked their Santiago home, La Chascona, and flooded it by diverting the canal that ran at the top of the hill. Matilde pleaded that they go to Mexico, at least for a couple of months until order was restored in Chile. Neruda was silent for hours and then said, "Yes, we'll go." Matilde went back to Isla Negra to get some more clothes. She had kept Neruda's friends at arm's length, not wanting him to hear about what Pinochet was doing, but when she left, they came to the hospital and told him who had been arrested, who was being tortured, who had been killed.

According to Matilde, when she returned that night she found Neruda in a state of madness, very sick and disturbed. He reproached his wife for not having told him the reality of what was happening to his friends, the atrocities that were occurring daily; that the junta was murdering people. She told him that it wasn't true, that his friends were exaggerating, that "one should only believe a part of what one hears."

As Matilde wrote in her memoir, that evening, Neruda began talking to her about their honeymoon, sweetly, more sweetly than he ever had. Then a tremendous despair passed over him again as he slipped into delirium. "They're shooting them!" he yelled over and over. A nurse gave him an injection to relax. He fell asleep and then into a coma. Pablo Neruda died on September 23, 1973.

Matilde had to face his death along with the reality of the coup. In La Chascona, furniture was overturned, the telephone line cut, books tossed up and down the hill, and flood damage setting in. Everything was in chaos.

They eventually got the coffin to the living room, which was filled with shattered glass. Homero Arce asked Inés Valenzuela, "Inésita, don't you think it would be best to sweep up some of this?"

"No, under no circumstances" was her proud reply. "Let the ambassadors come and see how all of this is."

Within a few hours, the Swedish ambassador arrived, carrying with him an immense crown that he placed at Neruda's feet. Other diplomats came, as well as a camera crew from an East German news television program, who hid from the military under the cover of being from West Germany.

Matilde, Inés, and their friends decided to make the funeral a public event, to march out of the house and take the body to the Santiago cemetery in a procession. "We knew what we could do," Inés recounts.

Matilde had the procession start at La Chascona on the twenty-sixth so the press would show the world what the military had done to the house. The military junta, realizing Neruda's international popularity, retroactively declared three official days of mourning for Chile's great poet, starting on the twenty-third, the day he died, and ending the day of the funeral. Neruda's friends, as well as some students and workers—people from all walks of life—came to the house where Neruda lay in rest.

And then, in the first open act of resistance by the Left since the coup, Neruda's *pueblo* came from all over Santiago. As his coffin was taken from La Chascona, they marched to the Cementerio General de Santiago, with people joining in from all corners of the city, as defiance overcame their fear. They marched in front of soldiers who held their guns at the ready but did nothing, because this was Pablo Neruda; the world was watching.

"We were afraid but we were also defiant, because we were going to have that funeral," recalled the painter Roser Bru, who as a five-year-old Spanish Civil War refugee escaped Europe on the *Winnipeg,* thanks to Neruda's efforts. "This was a way of making our presence felt."

The marchers were mourning the death of their poet, the deaths of so many *compañeros* taken by the regime, the death of their democracy. It was terribly cathartic. They tossed red carnations on Neruda's coffin as it passed through the streets. They solemnly sang the Socialist anthem, "The Internationale." Then over the tears came the chants.

Someone called out, *"¡Compañero Pablo Neruda!"* and the whole procession answered, *"¡Presente!"* "Here, now!"

"Compañero Pablo Neruda!"
"¡Presente!"
"Compañero Salvador Allende!"
"¡Presente!"
"Compañero Victor Jara!"
"¡Presente!"
"Compañero Pablo Neruda!"
"¡Presente!"

Other shouts rang out from the crowd, drowning out the other chants: "He hasn't died! He hasn't died! He has only fallen asleep. Like the flowers that sleep when the sun has set."

EPILOGUE

Eight small books of poetry sat on Neruda's desk when he died, eight books he was waiting to publish the following year on his seventieth birthday. They are a collection of books written by a man who knew his life was at its end and had accepted it. The poetry is simple, as had been his style. Love and politics are present, as always—his observations of the impending downfall of the Allende government are notable—but these are not the dominant subjects or themes. Instead, in these books the reader most often finds Neruda by himself, contemplating. The poetry is deeply personal, penetrating, and meditative, set in and borne by nature.

The books are also at times playful, especially in *Libro de las preguntas* (*The Book of Questions*), a collection of whimsical rhetorical questions, which, in the words of William O'Daly, who translated these final books into English, "coalesce in the realm of paradox." In the work, Neruda did not let his rational mind restrain his whim.

> If all rivers are sweet
> where does the sea get its salt?
>
> Which yellow bird
> fills its nest with lemons?

The book also contains many questions addressing political and social concerns. He could not avoid them. Neruda questions Hitler's and Nixon's fates and shows his increasing fear for his own country's destiny, as the drama among factions between 1971 and 1973 became starker:

> Is it true that a black condor
> flies by night over my country?

These books contain the poetry of a man who knows he is dying. They are his homecoming, as seen in a poem from *El mar y las campanas* (*The Sea and the Bells*):

> One returns to the self as if to an old house
> with nails and slots, so that
> a person tired of himself
> as of a suit full of holes,
> tries to walk naked in the rain,
> wants to drench himself in pure water,
> in elemental wind, and he cannot
> but return to the well of himself,
> to the least worry
> over whether he existed, where he knew how to speak his mind
> or to pay or to owe or to discover,
> as if I were so important
> that it must accept or not accept me,
> the earth with its leafy name,
> in its theater of black walls.
>   —"Returning"

Before the final silence of death, there is spiritual renewal, in which nature becomes the vehicle for reflection and connection to the larger world. This occurs in "Winter Garden":

> Winter arrives. Shining dictation
> the wet leaves give me,
> dressed in silence and yellow.

I am a book of snow,
a spacious hand, an open meadow,
a circle that waits,
I belong to the earth and its winter.

Earth's rumor grew in the leaves,
soon the wheat flared up
punctuated by red flowers like burns,
then autumn arrived to set down
the wine's scripture:
everything passed, the goblet of summer
was a fleeting sky,
the navigating cloud burned out.

I stood on the balcony dark with mourning,
like yesterday with the ivies of my childhood,
hoping the earth would spread its wings
in my uninhabited love.

I knew the rose would fall
and the pit of the passing peach
would sleep and germinate once more,
and I got drunk on the air
until the whole sea became the night
and the red sky turned to ash.

Now the earth lives
numbing its oldest questions,
the skin of its silence stretched out.
Once more I am the silent one
who came out of the distance
wrapped in cold rain and bells:
I owe to earth's pure death
the will to sprout.

★

Alastair Reid translated *Isla Negra, Extravagaria,* and *Fully Empowered,* along with many other individual poems. They first met at Isla Negra in 1964 as Neruda was turning sixty; Alastair was thirty-eight. Over the next decade, the two listened to each other and heard each other, sharing a friendship that was profound for them both. Shortly following Neruda's death, Alastair wrote this:

Translator to Poet

There are only the words left now. They lie like tombstones
or the stone Andes where the green scrub ends.
I do not have the heart to chip away
at your long lists of joy, which alternate
their iron and velvet, all the vegetation
and whalebone of your chosen stormy coast.
So much was written hope, with every line
extending life by saying, every meeting
ending in expectation of the next.
It was your slow intoning voice which counted,
bringing a living Chile into being
where poetry was bread, where books were banquets.
Now they are silent, stony on the shelf.
I cannot read them for the thunderous silence,
the grief of Chile's dying and your own,
death being the one definitive translation.

★

The dictatorship tried to proscribe Neruda from the country in which he was so ingrained. It vaulted the virtuous Gabriela Mistral into his place as the country's main cultural figure, enshrining her as "the mother of the nation." Still, like those cries of *"¡Neruda!" "¡Presente!"* at his funeral, Neruda remained present throughout those fifteen dark years, as the dark condor he had written about gripped his country.

In 2004, Ariel Dorfman, Duke University's distinguished professor of literature and Latin American studies, reminisced:

> When I went back to Chile after ten years of exile, I went to see Neruda's house in Isla Negra. I knew it was boarded up, and what I found there on that extraordinary fence—I found it full of graffiti. And I had not till then understood to what point Neruda was a saint for the people of Chile. Of course there were a lot of anti-dictatorial messages, but most of the messages were "Pablo, I brought my son here, you're alive." "Pablo, thanks for having helped me in such a way." . . . It was full of little messages to him, directly . . . And what's wonderful about that is that the fence had become symbolic of the way we had gotten rid of the dictatorship . . . in the sense of taking over the public space. Okay, they've shut down Neruda's house, we can't go to this house—you know what, they can't stop us writing on the walls. And when they whitewash it, tomorrow we'll write on it again.

★

Chile's nightmare finally ended in 1988. At the beginning of that decade, Pinochet and the regime felt invincible, strong enough to legitimize their rule and regularize their reforms in a new "constitution of liberty." They put it to a national plebiscite, which may have seemed bold, but with no safeguards for the opposition and balloting, and with human rights violations still occurring, no one pretended it would be a clean election. The government claimed it received 67 percent of the vote, and, with it, Pinochet was granted an eight-year term as president. Another plebiscite would be held at the end of that term. If the people voted in his favor, then he'd have an additional eight years in office. If not, democracy would return. Pinochet always believed he would rule for life.

But the tide began to turn against the dictatorship. The strong economy, a source of great pride and a bulwark of Pinochet's power, collapsed in 1982. The recession allowed widespread protests to break out, protests that opened up space for a broader section of the population to voice their opposition. Meanwhile, by 1987, Pinochet was the only dictator left standing in the region: Brazil, Bolivia, Paraguay, Argentina, and Uruguay had returned to democracy after suffering through their own military dictatorships. Mikhail Gorbachev was introducing democratic reforms in the Soviet Union. Western Europe and even the United States pressured Pinochet to restrain himself.[*]

Pope John Paul II's 1987 visit to Chile was a tipping point. He said the Catholic Church must work to bring democracy back to the Chilean people and accused the "dictatorial" government of trampling on human rights and using torture against its opponents. This pronouncement electrified the opposition, as it stripped away the false Chile that the regime tried to present. On one day of his visit, students chanted, "John Paul, brother, take the tyrant with you!" outside a cathedral where he was delivering a homily, until the police's tear gas, batons, and dogs forced them to run.

The pope reportedly advised Pinochet to resign when they met privately.

The 1988 plebiscite was a yes-or-no vote for one single candidate, General Augusto Pinochet. Under his dictatorship, the Chilean military had been responsible for the murder, disappearance, and death by torture of some 3,197 citizens, with thousands upon thousands more brutally tortured, arbitrarily imprisoned, forced into exile, or subjugated to other forms of state-sponsored terror. Beginning in 1980, seventeen different political parties had revived and formed a rather unified opposition. Ruptures that had once helped open the doors for Pinochet, namely between the Socialists and Christian Democrats, now healed. Their vast grassroots voter registration drive, starting several years before, was vital. Despite worries of violence or fraud, more than 7.5 million Chileans registered to vote. The "NO" campaign was

---

[*]   Reagan disfavored Pinochet for marginalizing the Chilean center. The U.S. ambassador to Chile, Harry Barnes, actually helped Chilean organizations work toward rejecting Pinochet in the 1988 plebiscite; the pro-Pinochet press started calling him "Dirty Harry."

based around their "Happiness Is Coming" slogan—broadcast during slotted TV times in the two weeks leading up to the vote, in ads, in posters and flyers hung up and down the country—accompanied by a graphic of a rainbow.

On October 5, 1988, 97 percent of registered voters participated in the election, a rate that ensured the historic validity of this democratic choice by the Chilean people. It was a relatively orderly process, with few disturbances or complaints. In the end, 54.7 percent voted "no" to Pinochet staying in power, 43 percent "yes." Spontaneous rallies and celebrations broke out the length of that long, thin petal of a country.

When they realized what had just happened, "there was a sense that a great weight had been taken off our shoulders. I guess it was fear," explains the poet Rodrigo Rojas, who was seventeen at the time. "We had grown so accustomed to fear without even knowing that it was there. Since the campaign for the 'no' was based on the phrase 'Happiness Is Coming,' in a way we truly believed in the phrase. Suddenly with this vote we all felt a little bit lighter, much lighter."*

With the return of democracy came the return of Neruda. The doors of Isla Negra opened again, now to the public, to the world. The Pablo Neruda Foundation took charge of his estate. It was the legal entity Matilde had put in place to protect and organize everything, from their property to his copyrights, as there were no specific heirs to their estate, and she was growing sick. In the years after Neruda's death, Matilde had championed the preservation of her husband's legacy as the regime tried to diminish it. Matilde was boldly outspoken against the regime. She died of cancer in 1985 at the age of seventy. Bedridden in La Chascona during her final days, Matilde told her friends that she was happy, eager to return to her Pablo. She was buried next to him in the Santiago cemetery.

---

* There were fears and doubts about how the dictatorship would handle the results. The CIA, for instance, had discovered "a clear sense of Pinochet's determination to use violence on whatever scale is necessary to retain power." U.S. officials were to warn regime officials that "such a plan would seriously damage relations" and "utterly destroy Chile's reputation in the world."

Isla Negra had suffered some damage from a small earthquake, flooding, and years of neglect during the dictatorship. By April 1990, all the repairs and transformations had been made for it to be opened to the public as a museum, a *casa-museo,* as all three of his houses would be. Gabriel García Márquez was one of the many major cultural and political figures who came to the event. Swiss and German diplomats were praised for their countries' financial contributions to the restoration. The opening of Isla Negra was seen by many as one of the most important, iconic milestones in the transition back to a free Chile.

Today, Isla Negra is treated by many as holy ground. Some visitors experience all his collections as kitsch. But in these spaces, just like in Neruda's poems, there is room for everyone, from literary pilgrims to those who come as part of a package tour to nearby wineries. As for La Chascona, the house is now one of Santiago's most popular tourist attractions.

> *Compañeros,* bury me at Isla Negra,
> in front of the sea I know, to each wrinkled area of stones
> and to the waves that my lost eyes
> won't go back to see.

Nearly twenty years after Neruda's death, the wish he had expressed fifty years earlier in that *Canto General* poem was finally fulfilled. Due to legal and administrative hurdles, though, it took over a year after Isla Negra was opened for Neruda to make his final homecoming. One impediment was that Chile has strict sanitary laws regarding burials; even cemeteries have to pass strict requisites. A legal ruling had to be made in order to authorize an exception to allow the burial of a body on private land. In 1991, Law Number 19.072 was passed: "In recognition of his literary work and so that his work receives fair recognition of the present generations and serves as an example to future generations," it awarded "the right for his mortal remains and those of his wife, Matilde Urrutia Cerda, to rest in the building that today houses the Pablo Neruda Museum."

On December 12, 1991, three years after the "no" vote won, Neruda's and Matilde's coffins were taken out of the Santiago cemetery. Before their procession to Isla Negra, they were brought to the beautiful hall of honor at the Ministry of Foreign Affairs. The coffins were draped in Chilean flags, as if lying in state. A crowd surrounded them, though the Chilean Right was notably absent. Dignitaries spoke; a telegram from Rafael Alberti was read.

Neruda's old *compañero* Volodia Teitelboim, now the president of the Communist Party, gave the closing remarks. The return of Neruda to Isla Negra, he announced, represented "the victory of poetry against wind and tide, against Pinochet and the anti-Chile, anti-culture dominion. It's a great achievement for all of us who believe in human rights."

Dr. Francisco Velasco, who had shared the La Sebastiana house with his dear friend Neruda, missed the poet's funeral following the coup because he had been arrested and imprisoned on one of the regime's boats, anchored in Valparaíso's harbor. But he was present for this second funeral. "It was very moving, very moving . . . We were there with a ton of people. Down at the beach there were more people—because they didn't all fit up here—so all these people were on the beach. And Pablo arrives and they ring the bell: 'Don Pablo has arrived,' they were saying, and then it felt like he was going to arrive alive. Whenever we went to see him the bell sounded and [someone from the house] would yell, 'Don Pablo has arrived.' The man who brought him said the same, 'Don Pablo has arrived.' And then they buried him there."

★

Twenty-one years later, in April 2013, Neruda's body was brought back out of Isla Negra's humid soil. Someone claimed that the poet had been poisoned by the Pinochet regime, supposedly to prevent him from leaving for Mexico and using his exile to become a leading voice of the resistance. With this assertion, the circumstances surrounding his death suddenly took on a life of their own in the press, while they were discussed with furious passion by many on both sides of the argument.

There has never been enough factual evidence to convincingly show that the possibility of Neruda's murder is anything more than just that, a possibility. The theory is backed only by presumptions. Still, the degree to which the story was covered and sensationalized around the world warrants a review of the phenomenon's history.

In December 1972, Manuel Araya, a young member of the Communist Party, was hired to be Neruda's new chauffeur. Skip to nearly a year later, when Neruda, in the hospital, finally agreed to take Mexico's offer of asylum (and stay at its National Cancer Institute, as his cancer was so severe). Neruda asked Araya and Matilde to go to Isla Negra and get some of his belongings to take with them. Upon their return, Araya says, "Neruda was feverish and flushed. He said they had stuck him in the gut." There was a red mark on his belly. That injection was, Araya maintains, the "evil ordered by the dictator Pinochet." Neruda died that night, September 23.

Pinochet's rule ended in 1989. For whatever reason, it wasn't until 2004—Neruda's centennial—that Araya told his story assertively enough that his claim was published, though only in his tiny hometown newspaper. It received little coverage and was quickly dismissed. Yet, in 2011, one of Araya's Communist *compañeros* enticed a major left-wing Mexican newsmagazine, *Proceso,* to hear him out. This time, it became a big deal. The headline "Neruda Was Assassinated," followed by Araya's testimony, quickly captured the world's imagination. The story had a romantic ring: Pablo Neruda, the heroic and globally beloved poet, had purportedly been murdered because he was the people's poet, the poet of love, the poet of human dignity.

Many, from all parts, believed that Neruda might have been poisoned, but the story relied on inconclusive narratives. With everybody excited, the Chilean Communist Party; Rodolfo Reyes, the son of Neruda's half brother; and even the Interior Ministry's Human Rights Program spearheaded a formal complaint. There were assumptions, some discussed below, that could point to the possibility of a homicide. A judge opened a formal investigation.[*]

---

[*]   See endnotes for additional details on this history.

Those supporting the assassination theory were emboldened by discoveries in the case of former president Eduardo Frei's death following a 1982 hernia operation, performed in the same hospital where Neruda had been. Frei had supported the coup but, like other members of his Christian Democratic Party, had turned against Pinochet when the dictator's absolute nature and intentions became clear. He had begun to influentially organize resistance to the dictatorship. His daughter insisted that he could not have died of natural causes. Though her claims were initially met with skepticism, in 2009, six members of the regime's intelligence unit were arrested for lethally mixing thallium and mustard gas into his medication. However, it has been found and reported on that the regime did not begin to carry out such lethal injections until 1976, ruling out the possibility that such an injection was used on Neruda just after Pinochet took over in 1973.

Nonetheless, while not debunking that red herring themselves but having other assumptions to fuel the story, the press and others ran with it, sensationalizing the poet's death the world over. "Pablo Neruda May Have Been Killed by a CIA Double Agent" announced an ABC News/Univision web article as the investigation started. Neruda's nephew Rodolfo Reyes told a magazine that Neruda's case was "worthy of crime fiction."

Neruda's body was exhumed and his well-preserved bones sent to labs in Chile, in Spain, and at the University of North Carolina. Five thousand X-rays and further microscopic examinations revealed widespread evidence of metastatic prostate cancer in his bones. The remains were checked for more than two thousand chemicals. Nothing was found. In 2013, the panel of examining teams announced that their "results mean that there is no forensic evidence of any unnatural cause of death."

Still, Neruda's nephew and the Communist Party demanded more testing, this time for any protein damage caused by chemical agents. The Human Rights Program was of similar sentiment and sent a confidential report to the judge, pressing him to continue the investigation, insisting that "it is clearly possible and highly probable" that Neruda's death "was caused by third-party intervention."

The document, though, just consists of presumptions that are not based on fact. As with much of the argument on behalf of the assassination theory, this text describes a true fact and then extrapolates from it, taking cognitive leaps toward one particular possible outcome, namely that Neruda was murdered, while downplaying the ways that same fact could reasonably be construed in other scenarios in which no murder took place.

An example of this is one of the eight "antecedents that seem to indicate a third party was involved in Neruda's death": the fact that La Chascona was ransacked by the military following the coup. The raid, which took place while Neruda was at Isla Negra, did show that the regime hated him, that he was an enemy of the state, for which he might be murdered. Many enemies of the state were being murdered. But it is also possible that they hated him, they raided his house, and yet, for various reasons, or no reason at all, they didn't kill him. In other words, a range of conclusions could be drawn from the facts at hand.

Another example of the reasoning the Human Rights Program and others used to base their claim is that, as the report states, since the forensic tests were done four decades after Neruda died, the fact that the tests came back negative does not "prove or disprove the possibility that hours before the death of the patient he could have been injected with a chemical agent." And while the report concludes that "if there would have been a third-party intervention, it would have consisted in [an] inoculation, through an injection in the abdomen of the Poet," it admits, "We don't know who gave him the injection, what it contained, whether or not it was noted in the medical file."

Still, the judge agreed to order tests, and the Human Rights Program assembled a panel of experts. Again, the results showed no conclusive evidence of anything that would support the assassination theory. "No Foul Play in Death of Chilean Poet Neruda, Researchers Say," Reuters reported.

As of this writing, genomics experts in Canada and Denmark have been contracted to examine one last pathogen, and if plausible, to sequence and interpret its genome. But as the lead investigator from Canada's McMaster University put it, "I have no doubt that if it's there, we'll find it. But then the next question becomes 'Was it deliberately put there?'"

No matter the result of this last investigation, perhaps the most ironic aspect of this drama is that, even if we could imagine for a moment that Neruda had been assassinated in order to be silenced, his death had the opposite effect. Far from erasing his presence, Neruda's death inflamed the resistance and gave it voice, on the day of his funeral and beyond.*

---

* The second international panel of experts investigating Neruda's death convened in Santiago over the week of October 15, 2017. Their announcements generated headlines like "Researchers Raise Doubts Over Cause of Chilean Poet Neruda's Death" (as seen in the *New York Times*). This has just occurred while this book is in its final stages of production. There is time to add these notes about the panels' findings, though the full official report has not yet been released:

While the panel still could not "rule out or prove the nature, natural or violent" of Neruda's death, they determined that prostate cancer was not the direct cause. They could not rule out that it was a natural death indirectly caused by the cancer—his body may have been so weak and immunocompromised by the cancer that it simply could not overcome an infection, for instance. The panel is in "100% agreement" that Neruda's official death certificate was "invalid." "Cachexia, cancer" was listed as the immediate cause. Cachexia is a weakness and wasting of the body due to a chronic illness, a state he was clearly not in, they determined.

The other focus was on the recovery of bacteria from Neruda's remains. Based on their testing, they do not believe he died from the *Staphylococcus aureus*. The undamaged nature of the bacteria indicates that it was from a modern source of contamination. Even if it was present in 1973, the level found in their samples is so "extremely low" that it was highly unlikely to have caused a mortal infection.

There are, though, thousands of different bacteria present in Neruda's remains. While looking through all the data, the team at Canada's McMaster University came upon something "of interest" in the samples. This bacteria has "a long history of use as a biological agent, and it does produce a very lethal toxin," explained Debi Poinar, a fellow research associate at their Ancient DNA Centre. It appears the Danish team has found similar results using different samples. (The name of the bacteria is being withheld during the investigation.)

The next step for both labs is to reconstruct the genome through computer analysis so they can identify the bacteria's strain. This will "enable us to rule in, or, just as importantly, rule out the presence of an important pathogen."

★

In the twenty-first century, Neruda's works and legacy continue to live and breathe throughout the world. He transcends class and political connotations: he is the public poet, a people's poet, appearing with increasing frequency in popular culture. We see his presence in art from the streets to the opera stage: Taylor Swift cites Neruda's Poem XX as the inspiration behind her quadruple-platinum album *Red;* in an episode of *The Simpsons,* Lisa tells Bart, "Pablo Neruda said, 'Laughter is the language of the soul.'"

The wrenchingly beautiful film *Il postino (The Postman)*, based on the 1985 novel by the Chilean writer Antonio Skármeta, is a fictional portrait of the relationship between Neruda, in exile on an Italian island, and Mario, a sensitive young mail carrier. Neruda's role as the people's poet is displayed, as the film illustrates him writing for the common person, enabling a poorly educated postman to enjoy the wonders of poetic language. Politics are treated vaguely here, offering what has been called a "safe" version for the mainstream viewer. We know Neruda is a Communist, but we don't know why he's in exile. Neruda talks to Mario about politics directly only when he discusses *Canto General* and, in another scene, asks if there are protests when the island has no running water. In the end, though, after Neruda has left the island, Mario has been so inspired that he reads a poem at a leftist gathering.

Neruda has also shown his aliveness in the halls of "high" culture. In 2010, the renowned Plácido Domingo played Neruda in the Los Angeles Opera's version of *Il postino* (Domingo has said that he has "known Neruda's poetry since childhood"). It is based on a libretto that revived some of the political and sexual intensity of Skármeta's original novel.

These examples illustrate the enduring reach and resonance of Ne-

---

As they presented their findings to the other members of the panel, the scientists asked for more time to finish this (mostly pro-bono) work. Judge Carroza has asked them to continue. Assuming the DNA from the bacteria is not too degraded, preventing the reconstruction of the entire genome and reaching those conclusive answers, results are expected within a year, hopefully much less.

ruda's work. Some of these instances might take the work out of context or less than fully represent the poet as a whole. However, Neruda himself would surely have gotten a kick out of these manifestations, not only as a tickling of his ego, but also because the phenomenon is fully aligned with his vision of being a poet for the people, not just the people of the lower or working classes, or leftist activists.

And while our cultural engines sometimes depoliticize and commercialize Neruda, decaffeinating and reducing him for easy consumption into a "Neruda lite," his popularity resonates with his fundamental simile that poetry is like bread—that it is about sharing, cooperation, and community. In his Nobel lecture, Neruda maintained that when poets prepare and hand over "our daily bread," they are answering their call to the "duty of fellowship." When poetry and bread are shared, there is a sense of communion, and we are all the more whole.

It is no wonder then that new editions of Neruda's poetry continue to be released in the United States and around the world, from individual volumes to edited collections, from multiple retranslations to discoveries of new text. His poetry's fusion of raw sexual longing with the potency of nature restores an essential connection between human beings and the natural world. His expressions of the endless facets of love and longing are timeless.

Neruda's social poetry and personal history are certainly still vital today as well. Since the election of Donald Trump as the forty-fifth president of the United States, questions of the relationship between cultural production and social movements have become more relevant than ever. The legacy of last century's consummate "people's poet" resonates strongly with the surge of resistance movements in the United States and beyond, and has much to offer to present-day artists and activists alike as they navigate the tides of a rapidly changing world.

Neruda's poems have long been used to evoke the power of solidarity and to ignite social change, a trend that is bound to continue. In San Francisco, California, in the tense political climate of 2003 during the lead-up to the invasion of Iraq, his verses were draped on banners over the streets, social slogans as urgent then as when he first wrote them. Nearly a decade later, Egyptian art historian Bahia Shehab spray-painted Neruda's words on the streets of Cairo during the Arab Spring: "You can crush the flowers, but you can't delay spring."* Bahia emotionally recounted this story in a 2012 TED Talk.

Five years later, during the January 21, 2017, Women's March—perhaps the largest protest in U.S. history—those same words of Neruda's that had appeared in Cairo would grace at least one poster, seen in Oakland, California, bearing the original Spanish: *"Podrán cortar todas las flores, pero no podrán detener la primavera."*

★

Meanwhile, as Neruda's legacy persists on the world's stage in so many forms, how does today's generation of young Chileans feel about him, about his poetry?

They are a post-Neruda generation. Many consider him a great poet, part of Chile's identity, but also a relic of the past. They don't want to be held down by him. Many love him as much as anyone who reads his lines, but many others, especially those closely involved with literature, see beyond his iconic status, questioning the hypocrisies and misogyny they perceive in Neruda's work and life.

That shift might be attributed to the decades that have passed between his life and theirs, except that, curiously, when asked which poets they most admire, these young Chileans often first point to Neruda's contemporaries, rather than to more recent voices; they cite Mistral, Huidobro, de Rokha, Parra.

An attempt to grasp how a whole generation feels about a poet, and to explore the reasons for the phenomenon, invites the danger of overgeneralization. Yet, to provide some perspective, the following testimonies do provide some insight.

Clearly, Neruda's poetry still has the power to affect the youth of his

---

* Surprisingly, perhaps disappointingly so, this quote is actually apocryphal. Despite its popular use and consistent attribution to Neruda, there's no record of Neruda ever saying or writing it. It has actually been attributed to Ernesto "Che" Guevara.

country. In 2003, I talked to Jorge Rodríguez, an anthropology student. He said that he enjoys Neruda's poems "because they hit you"—above all, perhaps, the poem "Walking Around," with its line "I'm tired of being a man." There comes a time, Jorge said, when you feel as though you can't take any more. But then "the poetry gives you strength to go on, thinking and creating and feeling it. So, Neruda, I don't know, it's like he's got that strength."

Later, in 2014, I wanted to get a sense of how millennials, specifically those concerned with poetry, felt about Neruda, a decade after his centennial. I posed this question to a few literature students at the Universidad Diego Portales in Santiago. The following are their responses:

María Lucía Miranda, twenty-three years old:

> Poetry that idealizes the feminine image, highlighting only its physical attributes from a male perspective, doesn't work as well in the twenty-first century as it did before, at least for me and other friends. So I don't think Neruda's poetry is all that relevant these days.

Aníbal Gatica, twenty-five:

> Neruda seems to be loaded with a basic machismo, good bourgeois taste with the Communist flag in hand, and a pompous heroism that seems very far away from us. Still, few can escape the seduction of "white breasts [white hills, white thighs]."

Loreley Saavedra, twenty-one:

> In my opinion, Pablo Neruda serves as an ideal example of

what is happening today with the "authority figure" in diverse subjects, like politics and religion. In the realm of literature, Neruda is the figure of a poet fallen from the heavens, a fallen angel, as certain truths about him have come to light and knocked him from his pedestal—far from exemplary acts, now known, that merit scrutiny—like how he abandoned his daughter, who was born with hydrocephaly. New ethical-moral visions have changed how we perceive public figures: Neruda's consecration as a poet is not enough in our culture now; his failings as a human being must also be acknowledged.

★

On July 12, 2004, Pablo Neruda's centennial was celebrated with a wide range of events throughout the world, most poignantly in Chile. Isla Negra's narrow dirt roads swelled with more than seven thousand fans, who flocked to their beloved Pablo's house and resting place. The festivities continued well past midnight, fireworks shooting out over the beach.

The Chilean government, led then by President Ricardo Lagos of the Socialist Party, had formed an official commission for the centennial two years in advance. According to Lagos, Neruda's work is part of Chile's foundation, its essence, "a component of our nationality, an obligatory and joyful point of reference every time we want to know who we are, where we come from, or which direction we should take in order to continue the construction of this proud residence on earth that's called Chile."

In one of the many quotes supplied for the government's official book for the centennial, the Peruvian Nobel laureate Mario Vargas Llosa hit on a vital point, stressing how Neruda's poetry "has touched so many different worlds and nourished so many varied and contradictory callings and talents." (This broad spectrum may have been particularly salient to Vargas Llosa, who turned away from the leftism of his early years and eventually ran for president of Peru as a conservative.)

In the United States, an important event was held at the John F. Kennedy Center for the Performing Arts in Washington, D.C., featuring Neruda's friends Volodia Teitelboim, Alastair Reid, and Antonio Skármeta, author of *Il postino,* among other writers, poets, actors, and singers. It took place in March, just three days after the terrorist attacks in Madrid that killed nearly two hundred and injured some eighteen hundred. Ariel Dorfman was a participant at the event. Even before the train bombings, he had planned to recite and talk about Neruda's "I Explain Some Things," about the bombing of civilians in Madrid a half century before. Dorfman just happened to be reading the poem over and over in preparation for the event when he heard about the attacks.

Dorfman saw it as a "sign in some sense." In fact, he had originally chosen to recite that specific poem

> because I felt it was a way of allowing Neruda to condemn the invasion and occupation of Iraq, the bombs falling upon the innocent, the blood of children that runs, today as yesterday, "simply like blood of children." And I also wanted Neruda's verses to howl against the destruction of so many other cities and lives . . .
>
> The poem ended up being more relevant than I had planned. When I finally read it at the Kennedy Center, I understood, as did the audience, that Neruda had captured my mouth, stolen my throat, in order to whisper something far more urgent.

But while many still use Neruda's voice and example to speak out against contemporary forms of injustice, some believe that his Stalinism disqualifies him, making him inappropriate, if not hypocritical, for such a role. An article in the *National Review* announced, "You would have no idea reading Dorfman's piece [in the *L.A. Times*] that Neruda was such a hard-line true believer that he was awarded the International Stalin Prize and the Lenin Peace Prize." Then the author quoted his poem on Stalin's death: "We must learn from Stalin / His sincere intensity / His concrete clarity . . ." This was followed by a quote from a *National Review* contributor who had emigrated from Russia in 1991, at the age of nineteen: "Neruda was not even a sympathizer—he was an active agent. We have no idea how much blood is on his hands in Spain, and I don't mean just fascist blood we don't care for."

★

Neruda would have turned a hundred years old on July 12, 2004. As he was celebrated across the world, my day began being interviewed by Renee Montagne on NPR's *Morning Edition*. It felt like the culmination of a long journey for me, from my early forays in Chile to now launching *The Essential Neruda* and sharing his work with some ten million people on the airwaves, striving to help spread Neruda's poetry, its power to evoke emotion, to perhaps foster consciousness.

That night we threw our own birthday party for Pablo at the Project Artaud theater in San Francisco. It opened with a lively poetry reading, featuring Lawrence Ferlinghetti, Robert Hass, Jack Hirschman, and Stephen Kessler. Then the musical group Quijeremá performed a riveting set of South American–infused jazz, led by Quique Cruz, who had grown up a few coastal towns away from Isla Negra and who had been tortured by the regime before being exiled. He recounted that Neruda had come to his school to read his poetry; Cruz was twelve then, and deeply moved. The composition his band played for us was the score for the documentary on Neruda we had rushed to finish that very morning.

The evening was sold out, the 350-person theater filled, and an energetic crowd filled the expansive lobby, hoping to get in too. The house crew set up extra loudspeakers so everyone could at least hear the performances. I thought of Neruda's fabled appearance at the 92nd Street Y in New York, in 1966, the poet–rock star's reading so packed organizers set up closed-circuit televisions for those who couldn't get into the auditorium. Now, half a century later, a full century after his birth, in a theater in San Francisco, it was happening again, a testament to the enduring potency of Neruda's poetry, of its continued resonance.

Lawrence Ferlinghetti took the stage. He spoke of Neruda's legacy, of his "hundred years of beatitudes." He read his own 1960 poem, written while on Machu Picchu, titled "Hidden Door," which he had dedicated to Neruda. Watching the audience from behind the stage, I could sense Neruda's presence filling that hall in all his enduring complexity: the love poet, the political poet, the experimental poet; Neruda the Communist, Neruda the womanizer, Neruda the sailor on earth. We were there that night to celebrate Neruda: not just the idealized poet, but the whole man, the multifaceted human being.

After the readings, we screened the documentary. It opened with Isabel Allende's narration, recounting her tale of taking Neruda's book of odes with her into exile, as Neruda appeared on-screen, wearing a poncho and gray beret, walking along the coast at Isla Negra. The foam crests behind him as he looks out, then points to the sea, that sea that was such a part of him, a dominant metaphor. "In some magnetic way," he once wrote, "I move in the university of the waves."

The sea, wide and vast, was like all the multitudes he contained and poured forth. Wide and vast like the plenitude of his soul as well as the plenitude of his ego. And like that sea that seemed a part of him, Neruda was so complex and yet at times so simple. With all the different aspects of Neruda, and all their contradictions, at his core he is one great body, still, in all its fullness, stretching across the world, to all its famous and hidden corners.

There, on the screen, Neruda watches the same waves that crash on Isla Negra's rocks today. The folk singer Hugo Arévalo, who now lives in Isla Negra himself, had told me that one of the things that had brought Neruda to live there was the ability to see the line between land and sea moving constantly, never fixed. "I think that movement had a meaning in his poetry," he said. And as I myself saw it, that motion also had a role in the nuances of his life, in the balance between self-mystification and truth, in the need to adapt to shifting realities while always keeping his edge.

That shore reflects all the changes he went through, all the battles, all the triumphs, all the tragedies—of anyone's life, but certainly heightened in his—before coming back to the core:

> Let us look for secret things
> somewhere in the world,
> on the blue shore of silence
> or where the storm has passed,
> rampaging like a train.
> —"Forget About Me"

Neruda, mysterious as the sea: as much as we think we know him, as much as we could describe him that night in the reading and the film and music, as much as I try to in this book, we'll never know everything, because he wasn't only a figurehead, nor merely an icon; he was also, simply, a human being.

As the audience watched those waves crashing over the black rocks of Isla Negra, they heard an actor read part of Neruda's poem "Lazybones." Working on the movie, I had heard the poem so many times that it had begun to lose its effect on me. But as I listened to it in that packed theater, the words struck me with renewed emotion. Neruda composed the poem overlooking the waves at Isla Negra, not long after the space race had begun. The "metal objects" he refers to are the new satellites circling above in the night sky. While the possibilities they represent may catch his attention, the poet is still consumed by the beauty right here on earth:

> Metal objects will still
> journey among the stars,
> weary men will still go up
> to assault the gentle moon
> and install their pharmacies.

> In this season of swollen grapes
> wine begins its life
> between the sea and the mountains.

In Chile the cherries dance,
dusky girls sing
and the water gleams from guitars.

The sun knocks on every door
and works miracles with wheat.

The first wine is pink,
sweet as a tender child,
the second wine is robust
like the voice of a sailor
and the third wine is a topaz,
a poppy and a fiery blaze.

My house has the sea and the earth,
my woman has majestic eyes
the color of wild hazelnuts,
when night falls the sea
adorns itself in white and green
and then the moon in seafoam
dreams like a maritime bride.

I do not want any other planet.

The poem's melody of innocent thoughts and imagery conveys that Neruda's work doesn't always have to be raw with politics or love; that, at the heart of it all, his poetry is about the wonder of being human. This is what keeps people coming back to Neruda, the essential poetic expression of what we are at our core, the elementary within the complex, the ordinary and the infinite, the true and the unknowable.

Selected Poems in Their Full Length

Where Can Guillermina Be?

Where can Guillermina be?

When my sister invited her
and I went out to open the door,
the sun came in, the stars came in,
two tresses of wheat came in
and two inexhaustible eyes.

I was fourteen years old,
brooding, and proud of it,
slim, lithe, and frowning,
funereal and formal.
I lived among the spiders,
dank from the forest,
the beetles knew me
and the three-coloured bees,
I slept among the partridges
hidden under the mint.

Then Guillermina entered
with her blue lightning eyes
which swept across my hair
and pinned me like swords
against the walls of winter.
That happened in Temuco.
there in the South, on the frontier.

The years have passed slowly,
pacing like pachyderms,
barking like crazy foxes,
The soiled years have passed,
waxing, worn, funeral,
and I walked from cloud to cloud,
from land to land, from eye to eye,
while the rain on the frontier
fell in its same grey shape.

My heart has travelled
in the same pair of shoes,
and I have digested the thorns.
I had no rest where I was:
where I hit out, I was struck,
where they murdered me I fell;
and I revived, as fresh as ever,
and then and then and then and then—
it all takes so long to tell.

I have nothing more to add.

I came to live in this world.

Where can Guillermina be?

—From *Estravagario* (1958). Translated by Alastair Reid in *Extravagaria*,
Farrar, Straus & Giroux, 1974.

———

Poem XV

I like it when you're quiet. It's as if you weren't here now,
and you heard me from a distance, and my voice couldn't reach you.
It's as if your eyes had flown away from you, and as if
your mouth were closed because I leaned to kiss you.

Just as all living things are filled with my soul,
you emerge from all living things filled with the soul of me.

It's as if, a butterfly in dreams, you were my soul,
and as if you were the soul's word, melancholy.

I like it when you're quiet. It's as if you'd gone away now,
And you'd become the keening, the butterfly's insistence.
And you heard me from a distance and my voice didn't reach you:
it's then that what I want is to be quiet with your silence.

It's then that what I want is to speak to your silence
in a speech as clear as lamplight, as plain as a gold ring.
You are quiet like the night, and like the night you're star-lit.
Your silences are star-like, they're a distant and a simple thing.

I like it when you're quiet. It's as if you weren't here now.
As if you were dead now, and sorrowful, and distant.
A word then is sufficient, or a smile, to make me happy,
Happy that it seems so certain that you're present.

—From *Veinte poemas de amor y una canción desesperada* (1924). Translated by Robert Hass in *The Essential Neruda: Selected Poems,* City Lights Books, 2004.

A note on this translation and the art of translation in general: The literal translation into English of the first line of the opening and closing stanzas of Poem XV, *"Me gustas cuando callas porque estás como ausente,"* becomes "I like it when you become quiet because it's as if you were absent." But in the version above, Pulitzer Prize winner and U.S. poet laureate emeritus Robert Hass varies his translation from the traditional. His starts, "I like it when you're quiet. It's as if you weren't here now." "I was reading XV out loud to myself and it struck me that the alexandrines sounded exactly like an old Leonard Cohen lyric—'Suzanne'—so I tried to render that rhythm," he told me. He tried—and succeeded—to translate not just the meaning of the words but also the inherent poetry of the original. His decision was guided by "sound, which may or may not be a good reason. I was trying to imitate the meter, which 'as if you weren't here now' fit and which the more abrupt 'as if you were absent' didn't. 'As if you weren't here now' sounded more like *'porque estás como ausente,'* especially if the vowels are elided in *'com'ausente.'"*

Poem XX

I can write the saddest verses tonight.

Write, for example, "The night is filled with stars,
twinkling blue, in the distance."

The night wind spins in the sky and sings.

I can write the saddest verses tonight.
I loved her, and sometimes she loved me too.

On nights like this I held her in my arms.
I kissed her so many times beneath the infinite sky.

She loved me, at times I loved her too.
How not to have loved her great still eyes.

I can write the saddest verses tonight.
To think that I don't have her. To feel that I have lost her.

To hear the immense night, more immense without her.
And the verse falls onto my soul like dew onto grass.

What difference does it make if my love could not keep her.
The night is full of stars, and she is not with me.

That's all. In the distance, someone sings. In the distance.
My soul is not at peace with having lost her.

As if to bring her closer, my gaze searches for her.
My heart searches for her, and she is not with me.

The same night that whitens the same trees.
We, of then, now are no longer the same.

I no longer love her, it's true, but how much I loved her.
My voice searched for the wind which would touch her ear.

Another's. She will be another's. As before my kisses.
Her voice, her bright body. Her infinite eyes.

I no longer love her, it's true, but maybe I love her.
Love is so short, and forgetting is so long.

Because on nights like this I held her in my arms,
my soul is not at peace with having lost her.

Though this may be the final sorrow she causes me,
and these the last verses I write for her.

—From *Veinte poemas de amor y una canción desesperada* (1924). Translated by Mark Eisner in *The Essential Neruda: Selected Poems,* City Lights Books, 2004.

Walking Around

Comes a time I'm tired of being a man.
Comes a time I check out the tailor's or the movies
shriveled, impenetrable, like a felt swan
launched into waters of origin and ashes.

A whiff from the barber shops has me wailing.
All I want is a break from rocks and wool,
all I want is to see neither buildings nor gardens,
no shopping centers, no bifocals, no elevators.

Comes a time I'm tired of my feet and my fingernails
and my hair and my shadow.
Comes a time I'm tired of being a man.

Yet how delicious it would be
to shock a notary with a cut lily
or to kill off a nun with a blow to the ear.
How beautiful
to run through the streets with a green knife,
howling until I died of cold.

I don't want to go on like a root in the shadows,
hesitating, feeling forward, trembling with dream,

down down into the dank guts of the earth,
soaking it up and thinking, eating every day.

I don't want for myself so many misfortunes.
I don't want to keep on as root and tomb,
alone, subterranean, in a vault stuffed with corpses,
frozen stiff, dying of shame.

That's why Monday burns like kerosene
when it sees me show up with my mugshot face,
and it shrieks on its way like a wounded wheel,
trailing hot bloody footprints into the night.

And it shoves me into certain corners, certain damp houses,
into hospitals where bones sail out the window,
into certain shoe stores reeking of vinegar,
into streets godawful as crevices.

There are sulfur-colored birds and horrific intestines
adorning the doors of houses I hate,
there are dentures dropped in a coffeepot,
mirrors
that must have bawled with shame and terror,
there are umbrellas everywhere, poisons and belly buttons.

I pass by peaceably, with eyes, with shoes,
with fury and forgetting,
I cruise the offices and orthopedic stores,
and patios where clothes hang from a wire,
where underwear, towels and blouses cry drawn out, obscene tears.

—From *Residencia en la tierra II* (1933). Translated by Forrest Gander in
The Essential Neruda: Selected Poems, City Lights Books, 2004.

The Heights of Macchu Picchu: XII

Rise up and be born with me, brother.

From the deepest reaches of your

disseminated sorrow, give me your hand.
You will not return from the depths of rock.
You will not return from subterranean time.
It will not return, your hardened voice.
They will not return, your drilled-out eyes.
Look at me from the depths of the earth,
plowman, weaver, silent shepherd:
tender of the guardian guanacos:
mason of the impossible scaffold:
water-bearer of Andean tears:
goldsmith of crushed fingers:
farmer trembling on the seed:
potter poured out into your clay:
bring all your old buried sorrows
to the cup of this new life.
Show me your blood and your furrow,
say to me: here I was punished
because the gem didn't shine or the earth
didn't deliver the stone or the grain on time:
point out to me the rock on which you fell
and the wood on which they crucified you,
burn the ancient flints bright for me,
the ancient lamps, the lashing whips
stuck for centuries to your wounds
and the axes brilliant with bloodstain.
I come to speak through your dead mouth.
Through the earth unite all
the silent and split lips
and from the depths speak to me all night long
as if we were anchored together,
tell me everything, chain by chain,
link by link and step by step,
sharpen the knives you kept,
place them in my chest and in my hand,
like a river of yellow lightning,
like a river of buried jaguars,
and let me weep, hours, days, years,
blind ages, stellar centuries.

Give me silence, water, hope.

Give me struggle, iron, volcanoes.

Fasten your bodies to mine like magnets.

Come to my veins and my mouth.

Speak through my words and my blood.

—From *Canto general* (1950). Translated by Mark Eisner in collaboration with John Felstiner and Stephen Kessler in *The Essential Neruda: Selected Poems,* City Lights Books, 2004.

Ode to Wine

Wine color of day,
wine color of night,
wine with your feet of purple
or topaz blood,
wine,
starry child
of the earth,
wine, smooth
as a golden sword,
soft
as ruffled velvet,
wine spiral-shelled
and suspended,
loving,
marine,
you've never been contained in one glass,
in one song, in one man,
choral, you are gregarious,
and, at least, mutual.
Sometimes
you feed on mortal
memories,
on your wave
we go from tomb to tomb,
stonecutter of icy graves,
and we weep
transitory tears,

but
your beautiful
spring suit
is different,
the heart climbs to the branches,
the wind moves the day,
nothing remains
in your motionless soul.
Wine
stirs the Spring,
joy grows like a plant,
walls, boulders,
fall,
abysses close up,
song is born.
Oh thou, jug of wine, in the desert
with the delightful woman I love,
said the old poet.
Let the pitcher of wine
add its kiss to the kiss of love.

My love, suddenly
your hip
is the curve of the wineglass
filled to the brim,
your breast is the cluster,
your hair the light of alcohol,
your nipples, the grapes
your navel pure seal
stamped on your barrel of a belly,
and your love the cascade
of unquenchable wine,
the brightness that falls on my senses,
the earthen splendor of life.

But not only love,
burning kiss,
or ignited heart—
you are, wine of life,
also
fellowship, transparency,

chorus of discipline,
abundance of flowers.
I love the light of a bottle
of intelligent wine
upon a table
when people are talking,
that they drink it,
that in each drop of gold
or ladle of purple,
they remember
that autumn toiled
until the barrels were full of wine,
and let the obscure man learn,
in the ceremony of his business,
to remember the earth and his duties,
to propagate the canticle of the fruit.

—From *Odas elementales* (1954). Translated by Mark Eisner in *The Essential Neruda: Selected Poems,* City Lights Books, 2004.

On the Importance of Poetry in Chile

Poetry has been woven into the cultural history of Chile for centuries, giving Neruda a unique and advantageous foundation as a writer. The quality of his mentors, including teachers in his school; the opportunities to publish; the competitions in distant towns—all were products of this environment, and poetry's stature in Chilean culture continued to provide momentum throughout his development. When he moved to Santiago at age sixteen, the importance of literature among the activists and bohemians who took him in fomented the completion, publication, and wide reception of his first books, launching his career.

While it is impossible to provide hard proof of the theories as to why these conditions arose, there are certain historic truths that lend some solid insight and help us understand the cultural nutrients that fertilized the land from which grew not only Neruda's poetry, but the verse of a slew of superior lyricists, all from the same soil of such a small country.

Chile has long produced a wealth of luminary poets, from the sixteenth-century epic poetry of Alonso de Ercilla, to early twentieth-century voices such as the Nobel Prize–winning Gabriela Mistral and Vicente Huidobro, to the many important contemporary voices of this day. These include the Mapuche Elicura Chihuailaf; Raúl Zurita, a modern master in the poetry of resistance; and Nicanor Parra, who pushed the limits of Chilean poetry as much as Neruda may have defined them. There are also two legendary singer-songwriters, Violeta Parra (Nicanor's sister) and Victor Jara. For centuries, Chileans have lived with poetry, reading and reciting and absorbing themselves in it. This tradition traces back to the people who inhabited the land before colonization, especially in Neruda's south. The culture and oral traditions of the indigenous Mapuche people were steeped in lyric verse through their unwritten language, Mapudungun. The manner in which they elected their leaders exemplifies this. For the position of strategic leader, a candidate must prove he is a sage: that he is wise, prudent, and patient. He also must demonstrate his command of the language. Toward this end, one of the tests was a trial of rhetoric in a ritual exercised through poetry. The candidates recited, they sang, they engaged their audience with poems they created spontaneously, odes to everything that surrounded them (as Neruda did in his four books of odes). Through language they had to connect the tribe to its ancestors (as Neruda did in *Canto General*).[*] The most legendary strategic leader in Mapuche history was named Lautaro. The house in which Neruda grew up, in Temuco, was located at 1436 Lautaro Street.

This is how deeply poetry is ingrained in the Mapuche culture, the Mapuche who constituted Chile before the conquistadores. There were other indigenous people in the north with cultural ties to the Inca and the Aymara and Quechua peoples and languages. The claims are uncertain, but these small nation groups seem to also have influenced the importance of poetry in Chilean society. They had their own oral poetic tradition, and some contemporary Chile-specific vocabulary derives from them. Music has always been crucial to the Aymaran culture, with *copla*, rhymed verse composed by special techniques, playing a central role.[†]

As a child in Temuco, Neftalí's worldview was influenced by the Mapuche but not necessarily by their language. At the time it was still a secret language, as missionaries and colonists still repressed the Mapuche when they spoke Mapudungun. He would have rarely heard it and definitely not

---

[*]   Chronicles written by priests and some conquistador generals describe their awe of the Mapuche's relationship with language, especially seen in the *parlimentos,* the peace negotiations after each major battle. They were exhausting negotiations that could last ten days, and a speaker for the Mapuche nation might speak for forty-eight hours in a row. As he spoke, he would sometimes improvise poetry about a subject to clarify it. He might also refer to all the spiritual implications of his talking points. Much of this rhetorical rapture was lost on the Europeans, however, as their translators couldn't keep up during the long sessions or convey the language accurately.

[†]   In the twenty-first century, Aymaran music is still played straight through the four days and nights of their carnival, celebrating the end of harvest. In gatherings in little towns in Chile's high plains, to the accompaniment of flutes and sixteen-string guitars, everyone present sings the *coplas* together. Sometimes there's a competition to see which of the two parts of town produces the best singer and who can chant the rhymed verse the longest and loudest. The *coplas* are made up of quatrains, each line eight syllables long, rhyming *abcb*. Often a product of pure improvisation, they go on and on, themes linking from one to another.

understood it. If anything, over the years he might have picked up on some of the syllables and sounds.*

The importance of language, especially poetic language and structure, to Chilean indigenous peoples created a foundation upon which conquering Europeans would build. The colonists established a special lyrical culture specific to Chile from their arrival, specifically in the person of Alonso de Ercilla, a member of the Spanish troops. In a 1970 interview for the *Paris Review,* Neruda said,

> Chile has an extraordinary history. Not because of monuments or ancient sculptures, which don't exist here, but rather because Chile was invented by a poet, Don Alonso de Ercilla y Zúñiga . . . a Basque aristocrat who arrived with the conquistadores—quite unusual, since most of the people sent to Chile came out of the dungeons.

De Ercilla, "the young humanist," wrote *La Araucana* on scraps of paper as the Spanish troops pursued the native people in the forests and towns around Temuco, the region from which the poem's name derives. Neruda

---

* In some of Neruda's adult poems he began to explore how the Mapuche words relate to colors, to landscapes, and to circles in cycles, the poetry drawing from their vision and worldview. He also described some of their rituals, in particular one where they dance and bend the fruit and other trees in order to wake them up for springtime. His affiliation with Mapuche imagery and poetics stands out in one set of lines in particular, in a poem depicting the ritual around the area of Angol (located between Temuco and Talcahuano), which is filled with the song of the naked ax that strikes the oaks.

> Angol, Angol, Angol
> deep ax,
> song
> of pure stone
> in the mountain

The beauty and the resemblance to the Mapuche sounds are lost in translation from the Spanish original of *"canto / de piedra pura / en la montaña."*

Neruda particularly esteemed the profoundness of the Mapuche's culture of poetry, its deep roots in the development of Chilean culture and literature. While he had no known indigenous blood, he refers to the Mapuche people as his "father" while describing Chile's genesis in *Canto general.* (He describes and relates to them with considerable tenderness in the book.)

described the poem as "the longest epic in Castilian literature, in which he honored the unknown tribes of Araucania—anonymous heroes to whom he gave a name for the first time—more than his compatriots, the Castilian soldiers."

Published in full in 1589 and then translated throughout Europe, it is still considered one of the great masterpieces of the Spanish Golden Age, one of the most significant epics of the Spanish canon. It is also the first Spanish American poem where nature emerges as part of the actual narrative story, an element in the heroic quest itself. That was especially important to Neruda, as it is set in the wilderness around Temuco. The forests described in the lines were some of those that he explored; the deluging rains were the same that he endured; he walked the great rivers whose banks became literary and logical obstacles to the conquistadores' advances. The use of nature as the protagonist in such a fundamental text heavily influenced the poetry of many of the great Chilean poets, Raúl Zurita believes.

The first Spanish who came to Chile gave birth to a creole and mestizo class, who in turn used popular lyric poetry to protest the Spanish rule, which became part of the country's culture leading to Chile's independence.

These are the anthropological explanations that help explain the uniqueness of poetry in Chile. But there are social factors that were also of great importance. Chile's poetry is rooted in the remarkable oral storytelling tradition of the Chilean campesino, the mine worker, the factory worker, the proletariat of the country. Stories told through verse were passed down in front of a fire, from one generation to another. At the turn of the twentieth century, northern miners would break into poetry readings at social gatherings.

In the early twentieth century, coinciding with Neftalí's coming of age, poetry in Chile served as an art that was accessible to people who were poorly educated. They were the principal audience for the poets, more so than those in the high-society literary salons. Poetry was not perceived as elitist but as an art form with wide appeal. Indeed, this is partly why Neruda's *Twenty Love Poems* became so popular at the time.

Rodrigo Rojas, a poet and professor at Chile's Universidad Diego Portales, says that to this day he encounters many kids who come from "very humble origins who see poetry as a very complex art that they can have access to. It's not something that is reserved exclusively for very rich or very well-educated people, although it still remains very difficult. But you don't need a huge education for that."

Chile has an extraordinary concentration of poets, of all levels of brilliance, per capita. Raúl Zurita provides yet another reason this has happened, why other countries may have somewhat similar social and anthropological histories, but Chile is still unique as a "nation of poets": geography may have played a role in the flourishing of the art form. Zurita illuminates the circumstances, explaining that while Chileans were not blessed with an Italian Renaissance so that one can walk around the city and say, "There's the Sistine Chapel!" or "Michelangelo made that sculpture," Chile does have a huge landscape, a varied landscape. Chile's Sistine Chapel is the Cordillera de los Andes and its Italian Renaissance painters are its poets. Out of this geographical landscape, the social landscape was molded by their words. That's Chile's cultural background, Zurita and others attest. Within such a small country, rugged and sparsely populated, isolated in many ways from the rest of the world, especially before modern communications and transportation, and surrounded by such an overpowering, dominant, impressive landscape, what do you do with it? Do you fight off the situation, or do you celebrate it with language? Chileans have done the latter.

Basic Chronology

July 12, 1904—Ricardo Eliecer Neftalí Reyes Basoalto (Pablo Neruda) is born in Parral, Chile.

1915—Neruda writes his first poem.

1918–20—Nearly thirty of Neruda's poems are published in a variety of different journals, magazines, and newspapers throughout Chile.

1920—Neftalí begins to sign his poems as Neruda. He wins first place at the Temuco spring festival and graduates from high school.

1921—Neruda moves to Santiago and enters the University of Chile to study French pedagogy; he wins first prize in the Federación de Estudiantes de la Universidad de Chile poetry competition.

1923—First book, *The Book of Twilights*, is published.

1924—*Twenty Love Poems and a Desperate Song* is published.

1927—Neruda assumes the position of Chilean *cónsul* in Rangoon, Burma (now Yangon, Myanmar).

1928—Consul in Colombo, Ceylon (now Sri Lanka).

1930—Consul in Holland's colony of Batavia (now Jakarta, Indonesia). He marries Maria Antonia Hagenaar Vogelzang ("Maruca").

1932—Neruda and Maruca return to Chile.

1933—Neruda publishes the first of three volumes of *Residence on Earth*. He is named consul to Argentina, where he meets Federico García Lorca in Buenos Aires.

April 1934—Neruda is named consul to Barcelona, then Madrid.

August 1934—Neruda and Maruca's daughter, Malva Marina, is born prematurely with hydrocephaly.

July 1936—General Francisco Franco leads an uprising in Morocco, starting the Spanish Civil War. Lorca is killed by firing squad in August.

January 1937—Neruda abandons Maruca and Malva Marina to be with Delia del Carril.

1938—The Spanish Republican Army prints Neruda's *Spain in the Heart* on the front lines of the war.

April 1939—Franco declares victory.

August 1939—Neruda organizes the immigration of more than two thousand Spanish Civil War refugees to Chile aboard the *Winnipeg.*

1940—Neruda named *cónsul general de Chile* in Mexico.

1943—Malva Marina dies at age eight.

1945—Neruda is elected senator as a member of the Chilean Communist Party.

1947–49—As senator, Neruda denounces President Gabriel González Videla's oppression of workers and Communists. His arrest is ordered and he escapes over the Andes into exile in March 1949.

September 1949—Neruda begins his affair with Matilde Urrutia.

April 1950—Neruda holds a signing party with Diego Rivera and David Alfaro Siqueiros for *Canto general.*

1952—Delia returns to Chile and Neruda and Matilde stay in Capri. *The Captain's Verses* is published anonymously.

March 1953—Joseph Stalin dies; Neruda writes "On His Death" in his honor.

1954—First book of odes, *Elemental Odes,* is published; Neruda officially chooses Matilde over Delia.

1958—*Estravagario* is published.

1959—*One Hundred Love Sonnets* is published.

1961—The millionth copy of *Twenty Love Poems and a Desperate Song* is sold.

1962—*Fully Empowered* is published.

1964—*Memorial de Isla Negra* is published.

1966—Neruda travels to the United States on the invitation of Arthur Miller and the PEN Club.

1967—Neruda's only play, *The Splendor and Death of Joaquín Murieta*, premiers in Santiago.

1970—Salvador Allende is elected president of Chile.

March 1971—Neruda arrives in Paris as the Chilean ambassador to France.

October 1971—Neruda wins the Nobel Prize in Literature.

April 1972—Neruda travels to New York City to deliver the opening speech at the PEN American Center's fiftieth anniversary celebration.

December 1972—Neruda, too sick from cancer to continue as ambassador, returns to Chile.

September 11, 1973—Augusto Pinochet stages a military coup. President Allende dies, and a seventeen-year-long dictatorship begins.

September 23, 1973—Neruda dies of prostate cancer. His public funeral two days later becomes the first act of resistance against the dictatorship.

Books by Pablo Neruda and Their Selected In-Print
English Translations

In-print English versions, when available, listed with translator name, publisher, and year of first edition.

Crepusculario [*The Book of Twilights*]. Santiago: Ediciones Claridad, 1923. (William O'Daly, Copper Canyon Press, 2017.)

Veinte poemas de amor y una canción desesperada [*Twenty Love Songs and a Desperate Song*]. Santiago: Nascimento, 1924. (Most popular English version is by W. S. Merwin, *Twenty Love Songs and a Song of Despair*, Jonathan Cape, 1969; Penguin, 2006 [with an introduction by Cristina García].)

tentativa del hombre infinito [*venture of the infinite man*]. Santiago: Nascimento, 1926. (Jessica Powell, City Lights Books, 2017 [with an introduction by Mark Eisner].)

El habitante y su esperanza [The Inhabitant and His Hope]. Santiago: Nascimento, 1926.

Anillos [Rings], with Tomás Lago. Santiago: Nascimento, 1926.

El hondero entusiasta [The Enthusiastic Sling-Shooter]. Santiago: Empresa Letras, 1933.

Residencia en la tierra [*Residence on Earth*]. First volume published by Nascimento (Santiago), 1933; volumes 1 and 2 then published by Ediciones Cruz y Raya (Madrid), 1935. All three volumes together published by Editorial Losada (Buenos Aires), 1947. (Donald Walsh, New Directions, 2004 [with an introduction by Jim Harrison].)

España en el corazón [*Spain in the Heart*]. Twenty-three poems dealing with the Spanish Civil War, most also a part of *Residencia III,* first published during the war under the direction of Manuel Altolaguirre, in Catalonia, in November 1938 (500 copies) and reprinted in January 1939 (1,500 copies). (Donald Walsh, New Directions, 2006.)

Canto general. Mexico City: Talleres Gráficos de la Nación, 1950. (Jack Schmitt, University of California Press, 1993 [with an introduction by Roberto González Echevarría].)

Los versos del capitán [*The Captain's Verses*]. Naples, Italy: L'Arte Tipografica, 1952. (Donald Walsh, New Directions, 1972.)

Las uvas y el viento [The Grapes and the Wind]. Santiago: Nascimento, 1954.

Odas elementales [*Elemental Odes*]. Buenos Aires: Losada, 1954. (None of the books of odes has been translated individually in English [Margaret Sayers Peden's translation of *Elemental Odes* was published in 1991 by Libris, but it remains out of print and very hard to find]. Among other collections, there are the *Selected Odes of Pablo Neruda,* translated by Peden [University of California Press, 1990], and the anthology *All the Odes,* edited by Ilan Stavans [Farrar, Straus & Giroux, 2013]. Little, Brown published two slender volumes ideally illustrated by Ferris Cook, with translations by Ken Krabbenhoft: *Odes to Common Things* [1994] and *Odes to Opposites* [1995].)

Viajes [Voyages]. Santiago: Nascimento, 1955. (Prose essays.)

Nuevas odas elementales [New Elemental Odes]. Buenos Aires: Losada, 1956.

Tercer libro de las odas [The Third Book of Odes]. Buenos Aires: Losada, 1957.

Estravagario [*Extravagaria*]. Buenos Aires: Losada, 1958. (Alastair Reid, Jonathan Cape, 1972; Farrar, Straus & Giroux, 1974.)

Navegaciones y regresos [Navigations and Returns]. Buenos Aires: Losada, 1959.

Cien sonetos de amor [*One Hundred Love Sonnets*]. Santiago: Editorial Universitaria, 1959. (Stephen Tapscott, University of Texas Press, 2015.)

Canción de gesta [*Chanson de Geste*]. Havana: Casa de las Américas, 1960.

Las piedras de Chile [*The Stones of Chile*]. Buenos Aires: Losada, 1961. (Dennis Maloney, White Pine Press, 1986.)

Cantos ceremoniales [*Ceremonial Songs*]. Buenos Aires: Losada, 1961. (Maria Jacketti, Latin American Literary Review Press, 1996.)

Plenos poderes [*Fully Empowered*]. Buenos Aires: Losada, 1962. (Alastair Reid, Farrar, Straus & Giroux, 1975.)

Memorial de Isla Negra. Buenos Aires: Losada, 1964. (Alastair Reid, *Isla Negra: A Notebook,* Farrar, Straus & Giroux, 1981 [with an afterword by Enrico Mario Santí].)

Arte de pájaros [*The Art of Birds*]. Santiago: Sociedad de Amigos del Arte Contemporáneo, 1966. (Jack Schmitt, University of Texas Press, 1985 [currently out of print].)

Una casa en la arena [*A House in the Sand*]. Barcelona: Lumen, 1966. (Poetry and prose.) (Dennis Maloney and Clark Zlotchew, Milkweed Editions, 1990; White Pine Press, 2004.)

Fulgor y muerte de Joaquín Murieta [*The Splendor and Death of Joaquín Murieta*]. Santiago: Zig-Zag, 1967.

La barcarola [The Barcarole]. Buenos Aires: Losada, 1967.

Las manos del día [*The Hands of the Day*]. Buenos Aires: Losada, 1968. (William O'Daly, Copper Canyon Press, 2008.)

Comiendo en Hungría [Eating in Hungary], with Miguel Ángel Asturias. Barcelona: Lumen, 1969.

Fin de mundo [*World's End*]. Santiago: Sociedad de Arte Contemporáneo, 1969. (William O'Daly, Copper Canyon Press, 2009.)

Aún [*Still*]. Santiago: Nascimento, 1969. (William O'Daly, *Still Another Day*, Copper Canyon Press, 1983.)

Maremoto [*Seaquake*]. Santiago: Sociedad de Arte Contemporáneo, 1970. (Maria Jacketti and Dennis Maloney, White Pine Press, 1993.)

La espada encendida [The Flaming Sword]. Buenos Aires: Losada, 1970.

Las piedras del cielo [*The Stones of the Sky*]. Buenos Aires: Losada, 1970. (James Nolan, Copper Canyon Press, 1987.)

Geografía infructuosa [Fruitless Geography]. Buenos Aires: Losada, 1972.

La rosa separada [*The Separate Rose*]. Paris: Éditions du Dragon, 1972; Buenos Aires: Losada, 1973. (William O'Daly, Copper Canyon Press, 1985.)

Incitación al Nixonicidio y alabanza de la revolución chilena [*Incitement of Nixoncide and Praise of the Chilean Revolution*]. Buenos Aires: Losada, 1973. (Teresa Anderson, West End Press, 1980.)

POSTHUMOUS PUBLICATIONS

El mar y las campanas [*The Sea and the Bells*]. Buenos Aires: Losada, 1973. (William O'Daly, Copper Canyon Press, 1988.)

Jardín de invierno [*Winter's Garden*]. Buenos Aires: Losada, 1974. (William O'Daly, Copper Canyon Press, 1986.)

El corazón amarillo [*The Yellow Heart*]. Buenos Aires: Losada, 1974. (William O'Daly, Copper Canyon Press, 1990.)

Libro de las preguntas [*The Book of Questions*]. Buenos Aires: Losada, 1974. (William O'Daly, Copper Canyon Press, 1991.)

2000. Buenos Aires: Losada, 1974.

Elegía [*Elegy*]. Buenos Aires: Losada, 1974. (Jack Hirschman, David Books, 1983.)

Defectos escogidos [Selected Defects]. Buenos Aires: Losada, 1974.

Confieso que he vivido [*I Confess That I Have Lived*], edited by Matilde Urrutia and Miguel Otero Silva. Barcelona: Seix Barral, 1974. (Memoir.) (Hardie St. Martin, *Memoirs,* Farrar, Straus & Giroux, 1977. In 2017, an expanded edition was published with newly discovered texts from Neruda's archives, some that Neruda had destined for his memoirs, which he didn't complete before he died [edited by Darío Oses, Seix Barral].)

Para nacer he nacido [*I Was Born to Be Born*], edited by Miguel Otero Silva and Matilde Urrutia. Barcelona: Seix Barral, 1978. (Collected prose texts.) (Margaret Sayers Peden, *Passions and Impressions,* Farrar, Straus & Giroux, 1983.)

El río invisible [The Invisible River]. Barcelona: Seix Barral, 1980. (Poetry of his youth.)

Cuadernos de Temuco [Temuco Notebooks]. Buenos Aires: Seix Barral, 1996. (His earliest poetry.)

Obras completas [Complete Works], edited by Hernán Loyola. 5 vols. Barcelona: Galaxia Gutenberg:

Obras completas I: De Crepusculario *a* Las uvas y el viento, *1923–1954* (1999).

Obras completas II: De Odas elementales *a* Memorial de Isla Negra, *1954–1964* (1999).

Obras completas III: De Arte de pájaros *a* El mar y las campanas, *1966–1973* (2000).

Obras completas IV: Nerudiana dispersa I, 1915–1964 (2001). (Contains the unpublished poems of his youth, various interviews, and texts and speeches up to 1964.)

Obras completas V: Nerudiana dispersa II, 1922–1973 (2002). (Contains his memoir, translations of other writers' works, correspondence, and various texts from 1964 to 1973.)

There are quite a few collections of selected works in English translation, including *The Essential Neruda: Selected Poems,* edited by Mark Eisner, foreword by Lawrence Ferlinghetti, with translations by Eisner, John Felstiner, Forrest Gander, Robert Hass, Jack Hirschman, Stephen Kessler, Stephen Mitchell, and Alastair Reid (City Lights Books, 2004).

Stephen Mitchell's collection *Full Woman, Fleshly Apple, Hot Moon: Selected Poems of Pablo Neruda* (Harper, 1997) provides wonderful translations of a selection of Neruda's lighter poems.

The Poetry of Pablo Neruda, edited and with an introduction by Ilan Stavans (Farrar, Straus & Giroux, 2003) is the most extensive anthology.

Then Come Back: The Lost Poems, translated by Forrest Gander, introduction by Darío Oses (Copper Canyon Press, 2016), is a collection of poems recently discovered in Neruda's archives, never known of before. Some are true gems.

Two stirring, poetically painted books by Mary Heebner, with translations by Alastair Reid, are *On the Blue Shore of Silence: Poems of the Sea* (Rayo, 2003) and *Intimacies: Poems of Love* (Harper, 2008).

For those seeking a more extensive bibliography of Neruda's books, the Poetry Foundation lists all of his minor works and omnibus editions not included here: https://www.poetryfoundation.org/bio/pablo-neruda.

Selected Bibliography of Secondary Sources

This list contains secondary sources cited in this book and used in research that could be useful to the reader for further study. It excludes less significant articles, speeches, and the like that are referenced in the endnotes, where bibliographic information for all cited work is listed. The most comprehensive bibliography of secondary sources is Hensley Woodbridge and David Zubatsky's 629-page *Pablo Neruda: An Annotated Bibliography of Biographical and Critical Studies*. It came out in 1988, though, thus it lacks pertinent material published since then. Furthermore, many of the listings are newspaper or magazine articles. The Centro Virtual Cervantes has a very fine up-to-date bibliography of Neruda studies (http://cvc.cervantes.es/literatura/es critores/neruda/bibliografia/estudios.htm). Jason Wilson's *A Companion to Pablo Neruda: Evaluating Neruda's Poetry* contains its own well-selected listing of books by other writers that help inform Neruda's work and life. Mario Amorós's *Neruda: El príncipe de los poetas* contains a thorough list of historical books relevant to Neruda's life.

Agosín, Marjorie. *Pablo Neruda*, trans. Lorraine Roses. Boston: Twayne, 1986.

Aguirre, Margarita. *Genio y figura de Pablo Neruda*, 3rd ed. Buenos Aires: Eudeba, 1997.

———. *Las vidas de Pablo Neruda*. Santiago: Zig-Zag, 1967.

Alazraki, Jaime. *Poética y poesía de Pablo Neruda*. New York: Las Américas, 1965.

Alberti, Rafael. *La arboleda perdida*. Barcelona: Seix Barral, 1971.

Alegría, Fernando. *Las fronteras del realismo: Literatura chilena del siglo XX*. Santiago: Zig-Zag, 1962.

———. *Walt Whitman en Hispanoamérica*. Mexico City: Studium, 1954.

Alone (Hernán Díaz Arrieta). *Los cuatro grandes de la literatura chilena durante el siglo XX: Augusto d'Halmar, Pedro Prado, Gabriela Mistral, Pablo Neruda*. Santiago: Zig-Zag, 1963.

Amado, Alonso. *Poesía y estilo de Pablo Neruda: Interpretación de una poesía hermética*. Madrid: Gredos, 1997.

Arrué, Laura. *Ventana del recuerdo.* Santiago: Nascimento, 1982.

Azócar, Rubén, et al. "Testimonio," *Aurora,* nos. 3–4 (July–December 1964), 203–249.

Bizzarro, Salvatore. *Pablo Neruda: All Poets the Poet.* Metuchen, NJ: Scarecrow Press, 1979.

Bloom, Harold. *The Western Canon: The Books and School of the Ages.* New York: Harcourt Brace, 1994.

Breton, André. *Manifestoes of Surrealism,* trans. Richard Seaver and Helen R. Lane. Ann Arbor: University of Michigan Press, 1969 [1924].

Brotherston, Gordon. *Latin American Poetry: Origins and Presence.* Cambridge, UK: Cambridge University Press, 1975.

Carcedo, Diego. *Neruda y el barco de la esperanza: La historia del salvamento de miles de exiliados españoles de la guerra civil.* Madrid: Temas de Hoy, 2006.

Cardona Peña, Alfredo. *Pablo Neruda y otros ensayos.* Mexico City: Ediciones de Andrea, 1955.

Cardone, Inés M. *Los amores de Neruda.* Santiago: Plaza Janés, 2005.

Collier, Simon, and William F. Sater. *A History of Chile, 1808–1994,* 2nd ed. Cambridge, UK: Cambridge University Press, 2004.

Colón, Daniel. "Orlando Mason y las raíces del pensamiento social de Pablo Neruda," *Revista chilena de literatura* 79 (September 2011): 23–45.

Concha, Jaime. *Neruda (1904–1936).* Santiago: Editorial Universitaria, 1972.

———. *Tres ensayos sobre Pablo Neruda.* Columbia: University of South Carolina, 1974.

Craib, Raymond B. "Students, Anarchists and Categories of Persecution in Chile, 1920," *A Contracorriente* 8, no. 1 (Fall 2010): 22–60.

———. *The Cry of the Renegade: Politics in Interwar Chile.* New York: Oxford University Press, 2016.

Cruchaga Azócar, Francisco, ed. *Para Albertina Rosa,* by Pablo Neruda. Santiago: Dolmen Ediciones, 1997.

Dawes, Greg. *Multiforme y comprometido: Neruda después de 1956.* Santiago: RIL, 2014.

———. *Verses Against the Darkness: Pablo Neruda's Poetry and Politics.* Lewisburg, PA: Bucknell University Press, 2006.

De Costa, René. *The Poetry of Pablo Neruda.* Cambridge, MA: Harvard University Press, 1979.

Durán, Manuel, and Margery Safir. *Earth Tones: The Poetry of Pablo Neruda.* Bloomington: Indiana University Press, 1981.

Edwards, Jorge. *Adiós, poeta . . .* Barcelona: Tusquets, 2000.

Escobar, Alejandro Jiménez, ed. *Pablo Neruda en O cruzeiro internacional.* Santiago: Puerto de Palos, 2004.

Feinstein, Adam. *Pablo Neruda: A Passion for Life.* London: Bloomsbury, 2004.

Felstiner, John. *Translating Neruda: The Way to Macchu Picchu*. Stanford, CA: Stanford University Press, 1980.

Flores, Angel. *Nuevas aproximaciones a Pablo Neruda*. Mexico City: Fondo de Cultura Económica, 1987.

Foster, David W., and Daniel Altamiranda, eds. *Twentieth-Century Spanish American Literature to 1960*. New York: Garland, 1997.

Furci, Carmelo. *The Chilean Communist Party and the Road to Socialism*. London: Zed Books, 1984.

Gligo, Agata. *María Luisa: Sobre la vida de María Luisa Bombal*, 2nd ed. Santiago: Editorial Andrés Bello, 1985.

González Echevarría, Roberto. Introduction. *Canto general*, by Pablo Neruda. Berkeley: University of California Press, 1991.

———, ed. *Los poetas del mundo defienden al pueblo español (París, 1937)*, by Pablo Neruda and Nancy Cunard. Seville, Spain: Renacimiento, 2002.

González Vera, José Santos. *Cuando era muchacho*. Santiago: Nascimento, 1951.

Guibert, Rita. "Pablo Neruda." In *Writers at Work: The* Paris Review *Interviews: Fifth Series*, ed. George Plimpton. New York: Viking, 1981.

Harrison, Jim. Introduction. *Residence on Earth*, by Pablo Neruda. New York: New Directions, 2004.

Jackson, Gabriel. *The Spanish Republic and the Civil War, 1931–1939*. Princeton, NJ: Princeton University Press, 1965.

Jaksić, Iván. *Academic Rebels in Chile: The Role of Philosophy in Higher Education and Politics*. Albany: State University of New York Press, 1989.

———. *Rebeldes académicos: La filosofía chilena desde la independencia hasta 1989*. Santiago: Universidad Diego Portales, 2013.

Jofre, Manuel. *Pablo Neruda: Residencia en la tierra*. Ottawa, Canada: Girol Books, 1987.

Lago, Tomás. *Ojos y oídos: Cerca de Neruda*. Santiago: LOM Ediciones, 1999.

Larrea, Juan. *Del surrealismo a Machu Picchu*. Mexico City: Joaquín Mortiz, 1967.

León, María Teresa. *Memoria de la melancolia*. Barcelona: Bruguera, 1982.

Loveman, Brian. *Chile: The Legacy of Hispanic Capitalism*, 3rd ed. New York: Oxford University Press, 2001.

Loyola, Hernán. *El joven Neruda*. Barcelona: Lumen, 2014.

———. *Neruda: La biografía literaria*. Santiago: Seix Barral, 2006.

———. *Ser y morir en Pablo Neruda 1918–1945*. Santiago: Editorial Santiago, 1967.

Macías, Sergio. *El Madrid de Pablo Neruda*. Madrid: Tabla Rasa, 2004.

Montes, Hugo. *Para leer a Neruda*. Buenos Aires: Editorial Francisco de Aguirre, 1974.

Moran, Dominic. *Pablo Neruda*. London: Reaktion Books, 2009.

Morla Lynch, Carlos. *En España con Federico García Lorca: Páginas de un diario íntimo, 1928–1936*. Seville, Spain: Renacimiento, 2008.

Muñoz, Diego. *Memorias: Recuerdos de la bohemia Nerudiana*. Santiago: Mosquito Comunicaciones, 1999.

Olivares Briones, Edmundo. *Pablo Neruda: Los caminos de América*. Santiago: LOM Ediciones, 2004.

———. *Pablo Neruda: Los caminos del mundo*. Santiago: LOM Ediciones, 2001.

———. *Pablo Neruda: Los caminos de Oriente*. Santiago: LOM Ediciones, 2000.

Oses, Darío, ed. *Cartas de amor: Cartas a Matilde Urrutia (1950–1973)*, by Pablo Neruda. Barcelona: Seix Barral, 2010.

Perriam, Christopher. *The Late Poetry of Pablo Neruda*. Oxford: Dolphin Book Co. Ltd., 1989.

Poirot, Luis. *Pablo Neruda: Absence and Presence*, trans. Alastair Reid. New York: W. W. Norton, 1990.

Quezada, Jaime, ed. *Neruda–García Lorca*. Santiago: Fundación Pablo Neruda, 1998.

Quezada Vergara, Abraham, ed. *Cartas a Gabriela: Correspondencia escogida de Pablo Neruda y Delia del Carril a Gabriela Mistral (1934–1955)*. Santiago: RIL Editores, 2009.

———. *Correspondencia entre Pablo Neruda y Jorge Edwards: Cartas que romperemos de inmediato y recordaremos siempre*. Santiago: Alfaguara Chile, 2007.

———. *Epistolario viajero: 1927–1973*, by Pablo Neruda. Santiago: RIL Editores, 2004.

———. *Pablo Neruda–Claudio Véliz, correspondencia en el camino al Premio Nóbel, 1963–1970*. Santiago: Dirección de Bibliotecas, Archivos y Museos, 2011.

———. *Pablo Neruda y Salvador Allende: Una amistad, una historia*. Santiago: RIL Editores, 2014.

Reid, Alastair. "Neruda and Borges," *New Yorker*, June 24, 1996.

Reyes, Bernardo. *El enigma de Malva Marina: La hija de Pablo Neruda*. Santiago: RIL Editores, 2007.

———. *Neruda: Retrato de familia, 1904–1920*, 3rd ed. Santiago: RIL Editores, 2003.

———. *Viaje a la poesía de Neruda: Residencias, calles y ciudades olvidadas*. Santiago: RIL Editores, 2004.

Reyes, Felipe. *Nascimento: El editor de los chilenos*, 2nd ed. Santiago: Minimocomun Ediciones, 2014.

Rodríguez Monegal, Emir. *Neruda: El viajero inmóvil*. Barcelona: Editorial Laia, 1985.

Sáez, Fernando. *La Hormiga: Biografía de Delia del Carril, mujer de Pablo Neruda*. Santiago: Catalonia, 2004.

———. *Todo debe ser demasiado: Biografía de Delia del Carril, la Hormiga.* Santiago: Editorial Sudamericana, 1997.

Santí, Enrico Mario. *Pablo Neruda: The Poetics of Prophecy.* Ithaca, NY; London: Cornell University Press, 1982.

Schidlowsky, David. *Las furias y las penas: Pablo Neruda y su tiempo,* 2 vols. Providencia, Santiago: RIL Editores, 2008.

Schopf, Federico. *Del vanguardismo a la antipoesía: Ensayos sobre la poesía en Chile.* Santiago: LOM Ediciones, 2000.

———. *Neruda comentado.* Santiago: Editorial Sudamericana, 2003.

Sicard, Alain. *El pensamiento poético de Pablo Neruda,* trans. Pilar Ruiz. Madrid: Gredos, 1981.

Silva Castro, Raúl. *Pablo Neruda.* Santiago: Editorial Universitaria, 1964.

Stainton, Leslie. *Lorca: A Dream of Life.* New York: Farrar, Straus & Giroux, 1999.

Suárez, Eulogio. *Neruda total.* Bogotá: Cooperativa Editorial Magisterio, 1988.

Teitelboim, Volodia. *Neruda: La biografía.* Santiago: Editorial Sudamericana, 2004.

Urrutia, Matilde. *Mi vida junto a Pablo Neruda.* Barcelona: Seix Barral, 1986.

———. *My Life with Pablo Neruda,* trans. Alexandria Giardino. Stanford, CA: Stanford University Press, 2004.

Varas, José Miguel. *Aquellos anchos días: Neruda, el oriental.* Montevideo: Monte Sexto, 1991.

———. *Neruda clandestino.* Santiago: Alfaguara, 2003.

———. *Nerudario.* Santiago: Planeta Chilena, 1999.

Velasco, Francisco. *Neruda: El gran amigo.* Santiago: Galinost-Andante, 1987.

Vial, Sara. *Neruda vuelve a Valparaíso.* Valparaíso, Chile: Ediciones Universitaria de Valparaíso, 2004.

Wilson, Jason. *A Companion to Pablo Neruda: Evaluating Neruda's Poetry.* Woodbridge, Suffolk, UK: Tamesis, 2008.

Zerán, Faride. *La guerrilla literaria: Pablo de Rokha, Vicente Huidobro, Pablo Neruda.* Santiago: Ediciones Bat, 1992.

Acknowledgments

It is as if there were a *Canto General* that orchestrated this book's creation and delivery into the world. I am so grateful to all those who, in one way or another, contributed their voice, from those who have been with me throughout the entire history of this project to those who spontaneously crossed my path in a market, a construction site, or a Valparaíso bar, appearing right on cue, as if Pablo had sprinkled his poetic pixie dust on this venture; an impossibility that seemed impossibly to happen over and over, and at just the right moment. Buoyed by this presence, I borrow his line and say thank you, *to everyone, to you . . .*

At the genesis were my parents, Gilbert and Rona Eisner, and their love, their example, their belief and support. From there, I have had the greatest fortune to have encountered what Pablo would call *Lamp(s) on Earth,* such kindred exceptional souls who have chosen to illuminate, accompany, and guide me on this path: *numero uno,* Abram Brosseit, whose brotherhood, teaching, and unwavering belief in me have made me realize literature, writing, my dreams, this book, myself. Thomas Kohnstamm's writing *compañeroismo,* his concern and consideration, have been so considerable. I first met Liza Baskind in 1994, the first week I stepped foot in Latin America. She became like a sister to me as the land, that experience, imprinted itself into us. Five years later, I visited her on my first-ever trip to San Francisco. On that very first morning, she led me to another important first step: into City Lights Books. Liza's part in that connection makes my connection between those two worlds even more special—yet nothing near as special as that cherished friendship I share with her and her husband, Brian Steele. Lucho Vasquez, from passing Abram and me copies of Kenneth Patchen and other writers in our first year at Michigan, has continued to be a teacher, an inspiration, the most solid friend. I am also very appreciative of my brother Eric Eisner, of his exceptional intelligence and truly sweet nature.

To the Meta-Metcalves, with a particular nod to Aly's ability to artfully put words to colors, words that help paint this book. As if their friendship and motivation, their examples of how to live a life and be a human, were not enough, it was Aly who introduced me to Jessica Powell. Witnessing her creative brilliance, I asked Jessica to translate Neruda's book *venture of the infinite man*, a project I had brought to City Lights. The world is richer for her talent. She has also been a major help to this book, never flinching to lend her time to help with a passage or two, a page or two, or more. The growth of our friendship through this process has been the most rewarding outcome of it all.

I am thankful for those friends whose particular knowledge nourished this book: Soledad Chavez, linguistic professor at the University of Chile; Tina Escaja, dynamic Spanish poet, visual artist, and scholar; Rodrigo Rojas, professor and poet (whom I first met, by chance, at a reading at Neruda's Santiago house, circa 2001).

Federico Willoughby Macdonald's generosity and guidance opened Chile up to me. My gratitude to him is profound. He invited me to live on the ranch where the idea for *The Essential Neruda: Selected Poems* was born. Forrest Gander, Robert Hass, Jack Hirschman, Stephen Kessler, and Stephen Mitchell's poetry, generosity, and belief in a very young me all enabled that book to take form. Alastair Reid, a contributor as well, was a special kindred angel on this path. These friendships have continued, their wisdom and support informing this book. With them aboard, Elaine Katzenberger at City Lights took on *The Essential* and published it. How my life has changed because she recognized something in it. And at holy City Lights, my continued appreciation for Stacey Lewis, Robert Sharrard, Chris Carosi, and, of course, Lawrence Ferlinghetti, who has been a hero of mine since college, since I first set out on this literary *camino*.

Those early days at the University of Michigan were formative in so many ways. I am deeply thankful for all Michigan gave me, but here in particular I can't express warmly enough my appreciation for its creative writing undergraduate program. With their huge hearts and gifted prose, Eileen Pollack and Alyson Hagy both saw me for who I was, recognized the writing I had to do, and helped to launch me on this path. They've both been alongside ever since, which means so much to me and my writing. More recently, Jeremy Chamberlin, currently the associate director of the writing program, helped give me the tools to reimagine the narration at a time I felt the whole book was stuck.

At Stanford, I am grateful to Katherine Morrison, Jim Fox, Terry Karl, and the Center for Latin American Studies; Yvone Yarbo-Bejarano and the Department of Spanish and Portuguese; and Tobias Wolff and the Creative Writing Program for grants that enabled me to do some of the initial work toward what would eventually become this book. A special shout-out to Terry, my thesis adviser, for her teaching and understanding. Stanford's Bing Overseas Studies Program funded a crucial 2002 trip to work out of its center in Santiago. In 2015, Iván Jaksić, the Santiago center's current director, opened its doors to me again. And his warmhearted help on early twentieth-century Chilean thought proved invaluable.

It was on that 2002 trip that the Pablo Neruda Foundation welcomed me in, leading to some wonderful, important relationships. In particular for this biography, I had the opportunity to spend days in the library and archives, where Darío Oses, a saint, afforded me so many hours, helping me research the treasures of archival documents, answering my questions, and engaging in probing conversations, all the while looking out over La Chascona's patio and the mountains beyond. In addition, much gratitude to Carmen Morales, executive director Fernando Sáez (whose excellent biography of Delia del Carril was very helpful to me), Adriana Valenzuela with the library, and the so *cariñosa* Carolina Briones, among many others. And for their dedicated and gracious help in granting the permission to use much of the original material used in this biography, *gracias a* Carina Pons, Ana Paz, and the late Carmen Balcells at the latter's famed agency, who represented Neruda and now the foundation.

My first tentative interaction with the foundation was in 1999, through Verónica, the student I described meeting at La Chascona in the introduction to this book. She of course has my sincere thanks for being such a kind, brilliant catalyst. One of the first people she introduced me to was Federico Schopf, poet and professor at the Universidad de Chile. Federico's initial encouragement was foundational, and the wisdom and knowledge he shared through long discussions over bottles of *vino tinto* served as the initial bedrock of what came forth. Federico introduced me to Jaime Concha, a Chilean teaching at the University of California, San Diego. His writing, insights, and gentle soul have made a significant impression on me. And perhaps even more key to my journey, Jaime introduced me to his dear friend Michael Predmore, who became my mentor at Stanford, where he was a professor of Spanish. I am indebted to Michael, not only as a teacher but as an inspiration. He deserves a whole paragraph here. John Felstiner, also at Stanford, was affable and helpful. The Chilean author and scholar Marjorie Agosín was also one of the first to endorse, and then help enrich, my work.

René de Costa's insight lines this biography (somewhat separately, it was his call for a reappraisal of *venture of the infinite man* that catalyzed me to propose the project to City Lights). A coda to our Nerudian relationship occurred recently during a long afternoon spent with him in Barcelona, where he is now retired, just after I delivered this book to Ecco from its Catalan shores. The richness of the conversation we sustained recalled the time I first visited him at the University of Chicago in 2004. We had been participants together in events celebrating Neruda's centennial that year. At the same time, René was preparing his office for that move to Spain. And at one point he reached up and plucked a woodprint from where it hung on the wall above his desk. It was the artwork from the cover of his seminal book *The Poetry of Pablo Neruda*. He handed it to me, saying something along the lines that I should have it. It's a gesture that still humbles me, one that has fortified me through the fight to finish this book.

Along with what I have gained from these kindred scholars, my research is built upon the monumental work of some truly fastidious, impassioned erudites. Many of their names are signaled in the bibliography, but some merit extra recognition: the endnotes should testify to how important Dr. David Schidlowsky's incredibly relentless research effort has been. The emotion we shared in our correspondence made all that information even more significant. I so appreciate the blessing he has given my venture. This book owes so much to him, as it does to Hernán Loyola and his tremendous, noble Nerudian work across the decades, from the many manifestations of his analysis to his scrupulous compilation of the *Obras completas*. Edmundo Olivares's trilogy on Neruda's experience abroad was broadening. Besides the value of his writings, Peter Wilson took the time to answer my doubts via email. Ever since our first *café* next to Chile's Biblioteca Nacional, Raymond Craib has awed me with his insight. Fortunately his scholarship on the Chilean student movement is available for all to read through his writings. I met Federico Leal at a Nicanor Parra talk, where he turned me on to his exclusive look at Neruda's relationship with opium and other facets of his time in the Far East. I appreciate his spirit and his willingness to share early drafts of his work with me. Roanne Kantor's intuitiveness brought up groundbreaking questions about the Far East periods as well, most significantly around Josie Bliss. I am moved to laughter again recalling our conversations and the dynamism of Roanne's genius. It was Megan Coxe who introduced me to Roanne; the two studied at Austin together. While Megan's contribution to the seemingly ceaseless translation of original material was valuable, her friendship and grounding concern, particularly about this project, has been a warmth and a comfort.

Throughout the years, through his books and emails, the so *cariñoso* Bernardo Reyes, grandson of Neruda's half brother, Rodolfo, provided many answers for me, especially with regard to his great-uncle's childhood. He also generously allowed me to use photos from his precious collection. I also had the great fortune to have the help of the brilliant Patricio Mason, great-great-grandson of Charles Mason, head of the Temuco Mason clan.

I received invaluable research assistance in Santiago from a trio of young freshly graduated literary students. It started with Jimena Cruz's diligent help, particularly obtaining articles from the National Library when little was digitalized yet. Later, Francisca Torres and Tania Urrutia provided consistently ingenious assistance. And on the other side of the Andes, Natalie Prieto was essential in educating me and aiding my research concerning Neruda's time in Argentina. Above all, the friendship, the laughs, the learning.

Isabel Allende's writing brought me to Chile before I set foot there. Upon my return, she doubled her influential effect, providing her time and thoughtfulness as she shared her personal connection to both poet and country with me directly.

So many have opened their doors to me throughout this journey, and a humble *gracias* to all those who invited me into their homes and their personal Nerudian worlds (or gave me time on the street): there are too many to list here without leaving some equally deserved mention out, but all their names, whether or not they appear on a page, are imprinted within. In memoriam, though: José Miguel Varas, Sergio Insunza, Sara Vial, Francisco Velasco, Marie Mariner. Lily Gálvez, who embodies humanitarian warmth, helped introduce me to many of Neruda's friends in Santiago.

In 2015 I was invited into the home of Rosa Ermilla León Muller, the niece of Teresa León Bettiens, Neruda's Temuco muse. The enchantment Teresa realized continues down the generations. Rosa, her children and grandchildren, and the laugher that afternoon just filled up my tank. Our continued long-distance communication has sustained the life-affirming fulfillment their spirit provides.

In Puerto Saavedra, where Pablo and Teresa's romance played out along the shore, I was welcomed by the lively Eugenia Vivanca, head of the town's library, which is a continuation of Augusto Winter's, in which Neruda spent so many afternoons. She took me to the lost red poppy gardens and the specific hills sloping to the sea on which Neruda's poetry and personality developed across so many crucial summers.

To the east of Puerto Saavedra and Temuco, in Pucón, up against the Andes, surrounded by snowcapped volcanoes, the *hospedaje* and eco-conservation base ¡Ecolé! often served as a home away from home during the writing of the book, and I am grateful to all those involved, especially Marta Barra. Following in that stream is Patrick Lynch, a persistently determined environmental lawyer, working to keep Patagonia's rivers running wild. His insight, introductions, motivation, and friendship helped sustain the flow of this book.

From southern Chile to Northern California, where Cannon Thomas's cognitive guidance and inspiration have helped empower me to have all that I hold essential in my heart breathe fully. Without that help, I highly doubt this book would have ever been finished. In San Francisco's Mission district, thanks to Todd Brown and the Red Poppy Art House for the dynamic buttress. In Marin, Alexandria Giardino, champion and translator of Matilde Urrutia, has been such a champion supporter of all my work, and a champion of a friend. In Oakland, the novelist Carolina de Robertis and her beautiful heart provided strong, gemlike gleams to some sections of the text as well as thoughtful overarching insight and guidance. Raised in Oakland, Zafra Miriam was named for the sugarcane harvest in Cuba. When this manuscript was a wild field, she helped cut away the excess, creating the sweet. Stephanie Gorton Murphy, a talented wordsmith, also provided crucial help through a thorough, transformative edit. Carl Fischer and Teresa Delfin, both of whom I met in Palo Alto before they earned their PhDs, provided astute insight into linguistics and literature.

Moving south to Santa Barbara, where Aly Metcalfe introduced me to Mary Heebner (who pairs her paintings with Neruda's poetry in sublime artist's books) and her husband, the photographer Macduff Everton (whose breathtaking picture of Isla Negra is in this book). This joyous connection and our conversations of reverence for our mutual friend Alastair Reid, of Pablo, of traveling through Latin America, have filled me with beauty.

Out East, my thanks to the amazingly creative Ram Devenini's constant encouragement and insight, and the AE Venture Foundation, which provided me with a generous grant to support the completion of this work. Leslie Stainton for her early encouragement, her ability to animate Lorca and Spain in her beautiful biography *Lorca: A Dream of Life,* and the insightful answers about those subjects she kept affording me. *Unas gracias al poeta y profe* Martín Espada. Keila Hand, *obrigado,* warmest heart from the depths of Brazil's rain forests, who set forth to help sustain the forests of the world, who with her friendship helped sustain me through the completion of this book. Jonathan Denbo has always had my back and helped me keep my head up. Pedro Billig, *camino* sage, *buena onda* shepherd; and Dan Long too, their long unwavering run of *respaldo* and friendship since I met them in the fourth grade.

Washington: Shortly after I arrived, I was surprised by an email from Marie Arana, a golden-hearted literary powerhouse whose books I've adored. She wanted to use clips from my documentary as part of a Kennedy Center event on the "Tres Pablos"—Picasso, Neruda, and Pau Cassal. Ever since, her fervent support and guidance have continued to be crucial. John Dinges, who recently was awarded the Chilean government's highest honor to foreigners for his journalistic work on the atrocities during the Pinochet regime, has given me hours of his time in various D.C. bars helping me wrap my head around all that history, most especially the phenomenon of the assassination presumptions. My thanks to the writer Roberto Brodsky, currently Chile's cultural attaché, for his perspective and the doors he has opened.

Renata Gorzynska was engaging in her help around Czeslaw Milosz's interactions with Neruda and other leftists. At the Library of Congress—truly a world treasure—many have been incredibly helpful; above all, those in the Hispanic Division under the leadership of the amazing Georgette Dorn. Not only did they provide great assistance, but they made me feel so at home in their reading room. An additional thank-you to Cheryl Fox, head of the Manuscript Division. I'd also like to thank the Textual Records Division of the National Archives, in particular David Langbart.

As I finished the book in Washington, three friendships in particular have meant so much to me: Anna Deeny Morales, Gwen Kirkpatrick, and Vivaldo Santos. Each holds a beautiful mix of character and brilliance. All three are professors at Georgetown University, and I appreciate their intellectual contribution to this work. However, it is their emotional contribution to my well-being that has been so vital.

Quickly then, to across the pond: A flurry of excitement came over me when I first found Dr. John R. G. Turner's letter in Neruda's archives, announcing they wanted to name a butterfly after him. That joy has sustained: in between Dr. Turner's long stints researching winged insects "in the wilds of Scotland," we've begun our own correspondence, through the course of which in addition to sharing with me Neruda's reply to his letter we've discussed a kaleidoscope of intriguing thoughts prompted by poetry and butterflies. Dr. Turner is not only an essential evolutionary biologist, but an award-winning translator of Verlaine. I appreciate him greatly.

In the home stretch, thanks to the journalist Mike Ruby for his benevolence in helping this manuscript find a home. He got it into the hands of Amy and Peter Bernstein, agents who time and time again have proven their warmth, and intelligence, and dedication to this project. I could not be more grateful for their trust. With thanks to Dan Halpern at Ecco, a publisher I've always considered to be the City Lights of New York, for the enthusiasm he's displayed for the project. I could not have imagined a better outcome. At Ecco, among many, my sincere thanks to Bridget Read for enabling this book to reach its finest form, to Gabriella Doob for bringing it all together, to Nancy Tan for her astonishing copyedit, to Alison Law, who similarly blew me away with her proofread, to David Palmer and others in production for their patience and diligence, and to Miriam Parker, Meghan Deans, and Martin Wilson, for getting it out into the world. Finally, a deep sigh of awe and gratitude to Jillian Tamaki for the cover and Michelle Crowe for the design; a deep sigh of awe and gratitude to all who have joined this collective song.

Notes

Due to multiple editions throughout the years of his books of poetry, page numbers are not listed with the citation of a poem, assuming the reader can easily find the poem armed with the book's and poem's titles, and any extra information that might be needed. If not listed in the citation, the English translation of a book's title can be found in the list of Neruda's works on page 527.

Abbreviations

OC = *Obras completas* (Complete Works), edited by Hernán Loyola. The volume number and page number follow. Bibliographic details of this series are on page 530 in the list of Neruda's works.

APNF = Material (generally correspondence) located in the archives of the Pablo Neruda Foundation, Santiago, Chile. Some of these letters are also found in *Obras completas,* volume 5.

CHV = Neruda's memoir, *Confieso que he vivido.* Because of the numerous editions, page numbers here correspond to the text in *Obras completas,* volume 5.

INTRODUCTION

1   "The Word": "La palabra," *Plenos poderes,* in Neruda, Pablo. *Fully Empowered,* trans. Alastair Reid (New York: Farrar, Straus & Giroux, 1975).

11 the first time the art form had been featured: The Academy of American Poets looked at the *New York Times* archives and only identified front-page pieces about poets on their deaths, as related to author by executive director Jennifer Benka, August 24, 2017.

11 "American Poets": Alter, Alexandra. "American Poets, Refusing to Go Gentle, Rage Against the Right," *New York Times,* April 21, 2017.

CHAPTER ONE: TO TEMUCO

13   "The Birth": "Nacimiento" (1964), *Memorial de Isla Negra,* in Neruda, Pablo. *Isla Negra: A Notebook,* trans. Alastair Reid (New York: Farrar, Straus & Giroux, 1981).

14   Their property had a little more: Loyola, Hernán. *Neruda: La biografía literaria* (Santiago: Seix Barral, 2006), 18.

14   As José del Carmen grew: The background information on this period of José del Carmen's life comes primarily from two living relatives, both of whom have been so helpful to me: The first is Bernardo Reyes, grandson of Neruda's half brother, Rodolfo Reyes Candia, who was generous in our correspondences and who also wrote a book, *Neruda: Retrato de familia, 1904–1920,* 3rd ed. (Santiago: RIL Editores, 2003). I have also used material from the first two chapters of his *Viaje a la poesía de Neruda: Residencias, calles y ciudades olvidadas* (Santiago: RIL Editores, 2004). The second is Patricio Mason, great-great-grandson of Charles "Carlos" Mason, who generously shared with me crucial facts and insights into the history of his fascinating family, via correspondence. He also took upon himself the inspired noble mission of constructing a complete extended family tree for the Mason family from 1634 to 2016, viewable at http://www.ics.cl/Familia_Mason/index.html.

15   allowing him to find: Loyola, *Neruda: La biografía literaria,* 19.

15   fundamental role in Neruda's life: Espinoza, Miguel. "Mason, 'el constructor,'" *Neruda in Temuco* (blog), February 21, 2010, http://neru daentemuco.blogspot.com.es/2010/02/neruda-en-temuco-mason -el-constructor.html.

16   In 1888: Mason, Patricio. "History of the Mason Family in Chile and Their Relatives by Marriage, 1634–2016," http://www.ics.cl/Familia _Mason/persons/person137.html.

16   he quickly ascended to the top: Espinoza, "Mason, 'el constructor.'"

16   on land he had managed to obtain: Ibid., and author correspondence with Patricio Mason, 2017.

16   The hotel allowed Mason to: Espinoza, "Mason, 'el constructor.'"

18   "an enormous cooking pot": *CHV,* 401.

20   Far along in her pregnancy: Author correspondence with Patricio Mason, 2017.

20   The baby was handed off: Ibid.

22   He may have been harboring: Ibid.

22   At 7:30 on the evening: Ibid.

22   It belonged to Trinidad: Ibid.

22   he wasn't nearly as involved: Patricio Mason discovered nearly eighty

legal documents from Chile's National Archives showing all manner of transactions between Charles Mason and his Candia in-laws and his sons-in-law, but absolutely none involving José del Carmen. The sole historical document kept at the National Archives involving José del Carmen shows him, in 1894, buying at auction a piece of property on behalf of José Rudecindo Ortega.

23 the barefoot, semiwild son: As described by Bernardo Reyes, Rodolfo's own grandson, in *Neruda: Retrato de familia.*

24 He brought his son Neftalí: Loyola, Hernán. *El joven Neruda* (Barcelona: Lumen, 2014), 30.

25 Trinidad had a certain equanimity: Neruda, Pablo. "Infancia y poesía," Salón de Honor of the University of Chile, January 1, 1954. Available in *OC,* 4:918.

CHAPTER TWO: WHERE THE RAIN WAS BORN

27 "The Frontier (1904)": "La frontera (1904)" (1950), *Canto general.*

27 "guardian angel": *CHV,* 405.

27 "gentle shadow": *CHV,* 416.

28 "tools or books": *CHV,* 401–408.

28 all lived on the same block: Author correspondence with Patricio Mason, 2017.

28 six children: Ibid., and Mason, "History of the Mason Family in Chile." Charles Mason also had a son with a Peruvian woman before he met and married Micaela Candia. This son, the eldest of the Mason siblings, also settled in Temuco.

28 Rudecindo Ortega, who had fathered: Author correspondence with Patricio Mason, 2017.

28 Incomplete staircases led to floors: "Infancia y poesía," *OC,* 4:917.

30 "Below the volcanoes": *CHV,* 399.

30 "The essential Neruda was a human being": Author interview with Alastair Reid, 2004.

31 "terrestrial core": Neruda, Pablo. "El joven provinciano," Las vidas del poeta. Memorias y recuerdos, *O cruzeiro internacional* (Rio de Janeiro), January 16, 1962. Quoted in Escobar, Alejandro Jiménez, ed. *Pablo Neruda en* O cruzeiro internacional (Santiago: Puerto de Palos, 2004), 28. Most of the rest of the details of the trips into the forests with his father are from *CHV,* 402–403.

31 "in the middle of green": Neruda, "El joven provinciano," in Escobar, *Pablo Neruda en* O cruzeiro internacional, 27–29.

31 as Neruda would later lyricize: "Las cicadas," *Las uvas y el viento.*

32   "La Casa": *Canto general.*

32   By the time he was ten years old: *CHV,* 402–404.

33   "I lived with the spiders": From "Where Can Guillermina Be?" in Neruda, Pablo. *Extravagaria,* trans. Alastair Reid (New York: Farrar, Straus & Giroux, 1974).

33   Neftalí's explorations piqued: From the poem "Las cicadas," *Las uvas y el viento;* words from "Infancia y poesía," *OC,* 4:917–918; and a talk given at the University of Chile around his fiftieth birthday. Much of the text would find its way into his memoirs.

33   "Along endless beaches": *CHV,* 413.

34   "just a sack of bones": *CHV,* 403.

34   They had a cook: Neruda mentions the presence of a cook in *CHV,* 409. As Patricio Mason explained, "Having a local lady come in to prepare meals was certainly a service a railroad conductor could afford" (author correspondence, January 2017).

34   it had a dignifying presence: Neruda, Pablo. "Viaje por las costas del mundo," lecture, 1942. Available in *OC,* 4:505.

35   One evening when Neftalí: "La copa de sangre," *OC,* 4:417.

35   "like a man in mourning": "Infancia y poesía," *OC,* 4:922.

35   The blood fell into a basin: "La copa de sangre," *OC,* 4:417–418, and "Infancia y poesía," *OC,* 4:922.

35   "The Heights of Macchu Picchu": Canto XII, *Canto general.* My translation builds upon earlier versions by John Felstiner and Stephen Kessler.

36   "where the rain was born": *CHV,* 400.

36   Neftalí was always the last: Author interview with Inés Valenzuela, widow of Neruda's childhood friend Diego Muñoz, July 2003. She and Neruda instantly formed a strong friendship upon Diego's introduction.

37   "He wanted to give me his cup": Valle, Juvencio. "Testimonio," *Aurora,* nos. 3–4 (July–December 1964): 248.

37   When he was confined to his bed: From an interview with Neruda's sister, Laura, in a compilation of his letters to her: *Cartas a Laura,* ed. Hugo Montes (1978; Santiago: Andres Bello, 1991), 12–13.

37   "an imperceptible vibration": Valle, "Testimonio," 247–248.

38   They took "refuge": Ibid., 249.

38   "Poetry": *Memorial de Isla Negra,* in Neruda, *Isla Negra.*

38   "a kind of anguish and sadness": *CHV,* 416.

39   The original Spanish: Jofré, Manuel. *Pablo Neruda: De los mitos y el ser Americano* (Santo Domingo, Dominican Republic: Ediciones Ferilibro, 2004).

40   the beginnings of a cosmic vision: From the text of the poem "Poetry," *Memorial de Isla Negra*, Neruda, *Isla Negra*.

CHAPTER THREE: AWKWARD ADOLESCENCE

41   "Where Can Guillermina Be?": Neruda, *Extravagaria*. Translations of poem in this chapter by author; translation in appendix by Alistair Reid, as noted.

41   "Desperation": Collected in a text entitled *Los cuadernos de Neftalí Reyes*, available in *OC*, 4:65.

43   it was precious: From an expanded edition of Neruda's memoir *Confieso que he vivido*, ed. Darío Oses (Barcelona: Seix Barral, 2017), 44.

43   When he grew bold enough: Ibid., 45.

43   his detour to touch it: Ibid., Neruda mentions the frequency. Gloria Urgelles writes that he stopped to pet its nose on his way to school on a daily basis in "Las casas de Pablo Neruda," *El Mercurio* (Santiago), September 15, 1991. Available at http://www.emol.com/especiales /neruda/19910915.htm.

43   Orlando was young and unruly: Particular credit goes to Bernardo Reyes for his description of Orlando throughout *Neruda: Retrato de familia*.

43   "Orlando Mason protested": "Infancia y poesía," *OC*, 4:923–924.

44   between eight and sixteen years old: Danús Vásquez, Hernán, and Susana Vera Iturra. *Carbón: Protagonista del pasado, presente y futuro* (Santiago: RIL Editores, 2010), 95.

44   "With a glance, the penetrating eyes": Lillo, Baldomero. *Sub-Terra: Cuadros mineros* (Santiago: Imprenta moderna, 1904), 21–22.

46   "A deplorable neglect continues": Venegas, Alejandro. *Sinceridad: Chile íntimo en 1910* (1910; repr., Santiago: CESOC Ed., 1998), 250–251.

47   "These two are the factors": Neruda, Pablo. "Entusiasmo y perseverancia," *La Mañana*, July 18, 1917. Available in *OC*, 4:49–50.

47   Neftalí was reflecting on: Victor Farías notes the sense of responsibility for what Neruda witnessed in the prologue to Neruda, Pablo. *Cuadernos de Temuco: 1919–1920* (Buenos Aires: Seix Barral, 1996), 19.

47   In broad, abstract terms: Colón, Daniel. "Orlando Mason y las raíces del pensamiento social de Pablo Neruda," *Revista chilena de literatura* 79 (September 2011): 23–45.

48   "a very beautiful woman, dark skinned": Author interview with Inés Valenzuela, July 2003.

48   verses of Garcilaso de la Vega: Author correspondence with Tina Escaja, poet and director of gender, sexuality, and women's studies at the University of Vermont, 2011.

48 "historical cadences" of Francisco de Quevedo's: Ibid., Much of this information and analysis, including the "historical cadences" wording.

49 "the way the poem embodies": Hass, Robert. *A Little Book on Form: An Exploration into the Formal Imagination of Poetry* (New York: Ecco, 2017), 3.

49 an additional, purposeful effect: Ibid.

49 As author René de Costa: De Costa, René. *The Poetry of Pablo Neruda* (Cambridge, MA: Harvard University Press, 1979), 35.

50 "My Eyes": *Los cuadernos de Neftalí Reyes, OC,* 4:55.

51 nearly thirty poems: Schidlowsky, David. *Las furias y las penas: Pablo Neruda y su tiempo,* vol. 1 (Providencia, Santiago: RIL Editores, 2008), 51.

CHAPTER FOUR: THE YOUNG POET

53 Teresa León Bettiens won the title: After her mother remarried, Teresa León Bettiens went by Teresa Vasquez. For clarity, her original last name is used throughout this book.

54 On the first day of vacation: *CHV,* 408–409.

54 the heartbeat of the universe: *CHV,* 410.

55 "but that cry of all": "Chucao tapaculo," *Canto general.*

55 a masculine model: Loyola, *Neruda: La biografía literaria,* 64–65.

55 "Hate": "Odio" (October 11, 1919), *Los cuadernos de Neftalí Reyes, OC,* 4:110.

55 "Puerto Saavedra had the smell": Neruda, Pablo. "65," *Ercilla,* July 16, 1969. Available in *OC,* 5:234–235.

56 "they'd both starve": Author interview with Rosa León Muller, Teresa León Bettiens's niece, 2014.

57 "black and sudden eyes": "65," *OC,* 5:234–235.

57 "condemned to read": Ibid.

57 "Have you read this one yet?": *CHV,* 416.

58 Neruda once noted: Cardona Peña, Alfredo. *Pablo Neruda y otros ensayos* (Mexico City: Ediciones de Andrea, 1955), 25.

59 "I have fixed myself up": Teitelboim, Volodia. *Neruda: La biografía* (1996; Santiago: Editorial Sudamericana, 2004), 39.

59 "terrible vision": *CHV,* 418.

60 He was a flamboyant man: Lago, Tomás. *Ojos y oídos: Cerca de Neruda* (Santiago: LOM Ediciones, 1999), 24.

60 "in Chemistry class": At bottom of the poem, *OC,* 4:82.

61 "Damn slackers": Reyes, *Neruda: Retrato de familia,* 89–91.

61 Neftalí was crestfallen: Ibid., 106–107.

62   "Sensación autobiográfica": *Los cuadernos de Neftalí Reyes*, *OC*, 4:132–135.

62   It showcases how Neftalí: Loyola, Hernán. "Los modos de autorreferencia en la obra de Pablo Neruda," *Aurora*, nos. 3–4 (July–December 1964). Available at http://www.neruda.uchile.cl/critica/hloyolamodos.html.

63   "¡El liceo! ¡El liceo!": *Los cuadernos de Neftalí Reyes*, *OC*, 4:159–161.

63   Through most of his life: Guibert, Rita. "Pablo Neruda," *Writers at Work: The* Paris Review *Interviews, Fifth Series*, ed. George Plimpton (New York: Viking, 1981).

63   "completely off the scent": *CHV*, 571.

63   "No one until now": Lispector, Clarice, interview with Pablo Neruda, *Jornal do Brasil*, April 19, 1969. Quoted in Lispector, Clarice. *A descoberta do mundo* (Rio de Janeiro: Nova Fronteira, 1984), 278.

64   "The Flesh Is Sad, Alas!": *Los cuadernos de Neftalí Reyes*, *OC*, 4:164–165.

65   Latin America's very first: Ramirez, Felipe. "Los 110 años de la Federación de Estudiantes de la U. de Chile," Universidad de Chile, October 21,2016,http://www.uchile.cl/noticias/127751/los-110-anos-de -la-federacion-de-estudiantes-de-la-u-de-chile.

65   born of a hatred of war: Racine, Nicole. "The Clarté Movement in France, 1919–21," *Journal of Contemporary History* 2, no. 2 (April 1967): 195.

65   internationalism, pacifism, and political action: Ibid., 203.

65   "radicals, masons, anarchists": González Vera, José Santos. "Estudiantes del año veinte," *Babel* 28 (July–August 1945): 35.

66   One of them vomited: Craib, Raymond B. *The Cry of the Renegade: Politics and Poetry in Interwar Chile* (New York: Oxford University Press, 2016), Kindle location 1091.

67   "respectable persons": Ibid., Kindle location 1615–1616.

67   In fact, after the assault: Accounts of the attack from various sources but principally Craib, *Cry of the Renegade*, and Craib, Raymond B. "Students, Anarchists and Categories of Persecution in Chile, 1920," *A Contracorriente* 8, no. 1 (Fall 2010): 22–60. *A Contracorriente* is a great online journal run by Greg Dawes at North Carolina State University. José Santos González Vera's accounts were also illustrative, especially "Estudiantes del año veinte," 34–44.

67   "that aspired to give": Schweitzer, Daniel. "Juan Gandulfo," *Babel* 28 (July–August 1945): 20.

67   Under harsh prison conditions: Author correspondence with Raymond B. Craib, 2015.

68   "Within the national context": *CHV*, 435.

68   "aggressive, combative, destined": Silva Castro, Raúl. *Pablo Neruda* (Santiago: Editorial Universitaria, 1964), 29.

69 "Through these verses": Ibid., 31.

69 Silva Castro quite astutely: Ibid.

69 one of the most emotionally effective: Author correspondence with Jaime Concha, professor emeritus of Latin American literature at the University of California, San Diego, 2001, among other sources.

70 He seamlessly illustrates: Analysis influenced by Victor Farías's prologue to Neruda, *Cuadernos de Temuco*, 22.

70 San Gregorio massacre: Details of massacre from Recabarren, Floreal. *La matanza de San Gregorio, 1921: Crisis y tragedia*, 2nd ed. (Santiago: LOM Ediciones, 2003). Observation of timing between the publication and event from Schidlowsky, *Las furias y las penas* (2008), 1:54.

71 Serani ended up having: Aguirre, Margarita. *Genio y figura de Pablo Neruda*, 3rd ed. (Buenos Aires: Eudeba, 1997), 81–82.

71 "I waited for him": González Vera, José Santos. *Cuando era muchacho* (Santiago: Nascimento, 1951), 270.

72 "Moon": "Luna," *Los cuadernos de Neftalí Reyes, OC*, 4:204–205.

72 The poem was in a newly: Loyola, *El joven Neruda*, 98.

72 it would serve as a calling card: *OC*, 4:1239.

CHAPTER FIVE: BOHEMIAN TWILIGHTS

73 "Night Train": "El tren nocturno," *Memorial de Isla Negra*, in Neruda, *Isla Negra*.

73 "the indispensable black suit": *CHV*, 427.

74 "thousands of buildings housing": *CHV*, 436.

74 impressed by new sights: Lago, *Ojos y oídos*, 18.

74 "her enormous womb": Neruda, Pablo. Lecture, Facultad de Arquitectura y Urbanismo de la Universidad de Chile, April 23, 1969. Quoted in Reyes, *Viaje a la poesía*, 7.

74 The odor of gas fumes: *CHV*, 436.

74 the barks of old dogs: Reyes, *Viaje a la poesía*, 26.

74 "magnificent sheaves of colors": *CHV*, 428.

75 "The Pension House on Calle Maruri": "La pension de la calle Maruri" (1962), *Memorial de Isla Negra*, in Neruda, *Isla Negra*.

76 He continued to feel: Concha, Jaime. "Proyección de *Crepusculario*," *Atenea*, no. 408 (April–June 1965). Available in Concha, Jaime. *Tres ensayos sobre Pablo Neruda* (Columbia: University of South Carolina, 1974), 13–19.

76 "Neighborhood Without Light": "Barrio sin luz," *The Book of Twilights*.

77 Murga was seen as: Tellier, Jorge. "Romeo Murga, poeta adolescente," *Atenea*, no. 395 (January–February 1962): 151–171. Available at http://www.uchile.cl/cultura/teillier/artyentrev/16.html.

78   "What she had hoped": Lagerlöf, Selma. *The Saga of Gösta Berling*, trans. Paul Norlén (New York: Penguin, 2009), 141.

79   These incorrigible bohemians: Author interview with José Miguel Varas, Chilean author and friend of Neruda's, 2003.

79   "semi-mute" childhood: Author interview with Aida Figueroa, attorney and wife of Minister of Justice Sergio Insunza, 2003.

80   "Carlos Sabat is a great river": Neruda, Pablo. *Claridad*, December 5, 1923. Available in *OC*, 4:311.

80   "Carlos Sabat. From the first": *OC*, 5:923–933.

81   "the eccentricity of a storybook prince": *CHV*, 437.

82   "in the midst of so much despicable": Descriptions of the Grand Bacchanalia from Muñoz, Diego. *Memorias: Recuerdos de la bohemia Nerudiana* (Santiago: Mosquito Comunicaciones, 1999), 105–109.

82   twenty-five or so other poets: González Vera, *Cuando era muchacho*, 222.

82   "Song of the Fiesta": "La canción de la fiesta," *OC*, 4:227.

82   *"La juventud tenía"*: Teitelboim, *Neruda: La biografía*, 56.

82   Neruda was asked to read: González Vera, *Cuando era muchacho*, 222.

83   "1921": *Memorial de Isla Negra*. Translated by Jessica Powell.

83   "You don't know that": Neruda, Pablo. "Empleado," *Claridad*, August 13, 1921. Available in *OC*, 4:253.

84   In a 1922 editorial: Neruda, Pablo. *Claridad*, May 20, 1922. Available in *OC*, 4:262–263. Pointed out in Craib, *Cry of the Renegade*, 176, 177i.

85   His friends at *Claridad*: *CHV*, 449.

85   As Alone wrote in a book: Alone (Hernán Díaz Arrieta). *Los cuatro grandes de la literatura Chilena durante el siglo XX: Augusto d'Halmar, Pedro Prado, Gabriela Mistral, Pablo Neruda* (Santiago: Zig-Zag, 1963), 175–176.

85   Alone had just cashed in: Alone (Hernán Díaz Arrieta). "Pablo Neruda, Premio Nobel de Literatura," *El Mercurio* (Santiago), October 24, 1971. Quoted in Salerno, Nicolás. "Alone y Neruda," *Estudios públicos* 94 (Fall 2004): 297–389.

85   "That moment when the first book appears": *CHV*, 450.

86   The book itself marks: Concha, Jaime. *Neruda (1904–1936)* (Santiago: Editorial Universitaria, 1972), 84.

86   "The dizzying array": Craib, *Cry of the Renegade*, 89.

86   T. S. Eliot's "The Waste Land": Author correspondence with Raymond B. Craib, July 1, 2015.

87   Thus *The Book of Twilights* wasn't: Most of this analysis comes from Concha, *Tres ensayos*, 13–18.

87   "We are wretched": Neruda, Pablo. "Miserables!" *Claridad*, September 1, 1923. Available in *OC*, 4:317.

88 Within them he employed: Drawn from Montes, Hugo. *Para leer a Neruda* (Buenos Aires: Editorial Francisco de Aguirre, 1974), 10.

88 Neruda acutely feels: Concha, "Proyección de *Crepusculario*," in *Tres ensayos*, 18.

88 And the poems' speaker: Montes, *Para leer a Neruda*, 10.

88 We see the purity: Concha, *Neruda (1904–1936)*, 84.

88 "I'm Scared": "Tengo miedo," *The Book of Twilights*.

88 The scream stays paralyzed: Concha, *Tres ensayos*, 5–24.

89 "Overall, the work seems": Concha, *Neruda (1904–1936)*, 138.

89 "My Soul": "Mi alma," *The Book of Twilights*.

90 Diego Muñoz wrote that shortly: Muñoz, *Memorias*, 105–109.

91 prescreened these disciples' verses: Ibid., 47.

92 Early in 1924, Neruda: Alazraki, Jaime. *Poética y poesía de Pablo Neruda* (New York: Las Américas, 1965).

92 "All of you, everyone": Neruda, "Miserables!" in *OC*, 4:317–318.

93 He was now fixed: Neruda, Pablo. "Algunas reflexiones improvisadas sobre mis trabajos," *Mapocho* (Santiago) 2, no. 3 (1964). Available in *OC*, 4:1201–1202.

93 "curious experience": *CHV*, 451.

93 As if possessed by some: Neruda, "Algunas reflexiones," in *OC*, 4:1201–1202.

93 Neruda felt he had discovered: Ibid.

94 "Are you sure those lines": *CHV*, 451.

94 "Read this poem": *OC*, 5:934.

94 "Seldom have I read": *CHV*, 451.

94 "Sabat Ercasty's letter ended": *CHV*, 452.

CHAPTER SIX: DESPERATE SONGS

95 Poem V: Neruda, Pablo. *Veinte poemas de amor y una canción desesperada* [*Twenty Love Poems and a Desperate Song*] (Santiago: Editorial Nascimento, 1924).

95 Albertina knew of his intelligence: Neruda, Pablo. *Para Albertina Rosa: Epistolario*, ed. Francisco Cruchaga Azócar (Santiago: Dolmen Ediciones, 1997), 9–15.

95 Ninety-six female: Reyes, *Viaje a la poesía*, 25.

95 She ignited romantic: Loyola, *El joven Neruda*, 79. Physical appeal and other attributes from author's interviews with others and various readings.

95 They saw each other at: Information on Albertina in this paragraph from Poirot, Luis. *Pablo Neruda: Absence and Presence*, trans. Alastair Reid (New York: W. W. Norton, 1990), 144.

96 "He was so young": Neruda, Pablo. *Cartas de amor de Pablo Neruda*, ed. Sergio Fernández Larraín (Madrid: Ediciones Rodas, 1974); and Loyola, *Neruda: La biografía literaria*, 144.

96 April 18, 1921: Various sources indicate that this is the probable date, including Teitelboim, *Neruda: La biografía*, 96, and Neruda, *Para Albertina Rosa*, 9.

96 He continued to walk: Poirot, *Pablo Neruda*, 144.

96 Albertina was smart: Author interviews with Inés Valenzuela, 2003 and 2008; Aida Figueroa, 2003; and José Miguel Varas, 2003.

97 Albertina's significance for Neruda: Teitelboim, *Neruda: La biografía*, 86, and Loyola, *Neruda: La biografía literaria*, 115.

97 At first, their relationship: Loyola, *El joven Neruda*, 79.

98 "Sex": Neruda, Pablo. *Claridad*, July 2, 1921. Available in *OC*, 4:225.

98 A piece Neruda wrote in his sixties: *CHV*, 304.

99 That would be a pivotal: As Loyola titles three of the subsections in this part of his book *Neruda: La biografía literaria*, "1923: El año de la encrucijada," 141–148.

99 "And as you know": Translated by Megan Coxe. *OC*, 5:847.

100 "It rained yesterday": Coxe, trans., *OC*, 5:848.

100 "I confess to you": Coxe, trans., *OC*, 5:850.

100 "The sole center of my existence": *OC*, 4:285.

102 "spread out on the moist grass": *OC*, 5:862.

102 Poem VI: Rexroth, Kenneth, ed. and trans. *Thirty Spanish Poems of Love and Exile* (San Francisco, CA: City Lights Books, 1968).

102 "Little One": *OC*, 5:862.

103 "This lullaby is for you": "Poema de la ausente," *OC*, 5:291.

103 "Did you like it": Letter dated January 25, 1922/3, *OC*, 5:855.

103 "Almost always I feel": Ibid.

103 Poem XV: Translation of second and third lines by Robert Hass (see Appendix I); "sealed" from W. S. Merwin.

104 "when we went for walks": Poirot, *Pablo Neruda*, 144.

104 Albertina herself said: Cardone, Inés M. *Los amores de Neruda* (Santiago: Plaza Janés, 2005), 50.

104 "Your life, God, if he exists": *OC*, 5:851.

105 "The only thing that makes": Letter dated September 1925, *OC*, 5:900.

106 "I'll eat you up with kisses": *OC*, 5:887.

107 "square and rigid frames": In the *Claridad* article "Sex," he describes a "wave of rage" against those who make him fit his life into "square and rigid frames." *OC*, 4:225.

107 a young Greta Garbo: Muñoz, Diego. Prologue to *Ventana del recuerdo*, by Laura Arrué (Santiago: Nascimento, 1982), 8.

107 A couple of years later, her older sister: Arrué, *Ventana del recuerdo,* 53.

107 Laura, now seventeen, thought: Ibid., 52.

108 Laura's father was a learned: Ibid., 12.

108 Perhaps it was from him: Ibid.

108 Laura and Agustina found him: Ibid., 54.

108 an old sugar crate: Teitelboim, *Neruda: La biografía,* 115–116.

108 Laura's grandparents owned: Arrué, *Ventana del recuerdo,* 14–16.

109 "atrocious troubadour": Cardone, *Los amores de Neruda,* 75.

109 "I loved Pablito": As quoted by her niece, Susan Sanchez, in Cardone, *Los amores de Neruda,* 85. The quote itself does not appear in the memoir *Ventana del recuerdo,* used throughout the paragraphs above.

109 "Here I have finished": *OC,* 5:934–935.

110 overcome their initial shock: De Costa, *Poetry of Pablo Neruda,* 19–25.

110 The aging Augusto Winter: From Neruda's introduction to the seventh edition of *Twenty Love Poems,* commemorating a million copies in print: Neruda, Pablo. "Pequeña Historia," *Veinte poemas de amor y una canción desesperada* [*Twenty Love Poems and a Desperate Song*], 7th ed. (Buenos Aires: Losada, 1961).

110 "He'll be sorry": *OC,* 5:1024.

110 Neruda's attitude toward his work: De Costa, *Poetry of Pablo Neruda,* 20.

111 "A very calm, modest *muchacho*": Reyes, Felipe. *Nascimento: El editor de los Chilenos,* 2nd ed. (Santiago: Minimocomun Ediciones, 2014), 119–120.

111 "frail and quiet": Ibid., 120.

111 In person, Neruda was: Testimony of Nascimento from *El Siglo* (Bogotá), July 11, 1954, quoted in Reyes, *Nascimento,* 120; and author correspondence with Felipe Reyes.

111 That square shape: Neruda, "Pequeña historia," *Veinte poemas* (1961).

111 "the greatest departure from myself": Neruda, Pablo. "Exégesis y soledad," *La Nación,* August 20, 1924. Available in *OC,* 1:323–324.

112 It was a book that made: Author interview with Federico Schopf, poet and professor of literature at the University of Chile, 2003.

112 "right away wanted a memento": González Vera, *Cuando era muchacho,* 222.

113 "fails to convince": Latorre, Mariano. "Los Libros," *Zig-Zag,* August 16, 1924. Quoted in Schopf, Federico. *Neruda comentado* (Santiago: Editorial Sudamericana, 2003), 84.

113 "emotion is absent": Escudero, Alfonso. "La actividad literaria en 1924," *Atenea,* February 31, 1925. Quoted in Schopf, *Neruda comentado,* 85.

113 "a certain halting": Alone (Hernán Díaz Arrieta). "Crónica literaria:

Veinte poemas de amor y una canción desesperada, Editorial Nacimiento,"
La Nación, August 3, 1924.

113   "still haven't sprouted": Ibid.

114   The critics and similar old-guard readers: Much of the discussion in this
and the following paragraphs on the differences between *Twenty Love
Poems* and the poetry of Max Jara and others is drawn from conversa-
tions between the author and Chilean poet and scholar Rodrigo Rojas,
particularly in April and June 2005.

115   In his important book: De Costa, *Poetry of Pablo Neruda,* 32–33.

116   Diego Muñoz tried to reason: Muñoz, *Memorias,* 39.

116   "I undertook the greatest": Neruda, "Exégesis y soledad," in *OC,*
1:323–324.

116   Years later, Alone admitted: Alone, *Los cuatro grandes,* 196.

117   a succès de scandale: De Costa, *Poetry of Pablo Neruda,* 25.

117   By 1972, two million copies: *OC,* 1:1149. A commemorative edition for
reaching two million copies was published by Losada in December
1972.

117   Though global sales numbers: Hernán Loyola, for example, states that
more than ten million copies had been sold by 2004, as referenced in the
Santiago newspaper *La Opinión,* "Celebran los 100 de Neruda," July 12,
2004. Also as reported by the Spanish international news agency
Agencia EFE. For example, Wolter, Matilde. "Neruda sigue siendo el
poeta más leído," Agencia EFE, December 7, 2004. Available at http://
www.elperiodicomediterraneo.com/noticias/sociedad/neruda
-sigue-siendo-poeta-mas-leido_114767.html.

117   "suddenly gave us back": Cortázar, Julio. "Neruda entre nosotros," *Plural*
(Mexico City) 30 (March 1974): 39. Quoted in Felstiner, John. *Translat-
ing Neruda: The Way to Macchu Picchu* (Stanford, CA: Stanford Univer-
sity Press, 1980).

CHAPTER SEVEN: DEAD GALLOP

121   "Every day I have to find": *OC,* 5:899.

121   "Pablo's state of mind": Azócar, Rubén. "Testimonio," *Aurora,* nos. 3–4
(July–December 1964): 215.

121   "These days have been bitter": Neruda, *Cartas de amor de Pablo Neruda,*
228–229.

122   "money, love, and poetry": Azócar, "Testimonio," 215.

122   "You know that I like": *OC,* 5:884–885.

122   "Hide them under your mattress": Arrué, *Ventana del recuerdo,* 62.

123   "Ah," he wrote Albertina: *OC,* 5:887.

123 Neruda conspired to kidnap Laura: Cardone, *Los amores de Neruda*, 75–76. Cardone points out that it was Loyola who identified, through direct conversations with Arrué, that Neruda's companion for the kidnapping was indeed Barrios.

124 "his soul was spinning": Azócar, "Testimonio," 215.

125 "strip poetry of all": Silva Castro, Raúl. "Una hora de charla con Pablo Neruda," *El Mercurio*, October 10, 1926.

125 "irreducible purity": Neruda, Pablo. "Erratas y erratones," *Ercilla*, August 27, 1969. Available in *OC*, 5:237.

125 "one of the most important books": Neruda in conversation with Cardona Peña: Cardona Peña, Alfredo. "Pablo Neruda: Breve historia de sus libros," *Cuadernos americanos* 54, no. 6 (November–December 1950): 265.

125 "A Scattered Expression": Cited and contextualized in de Costa, *Poetry of Pablo Neruda*, 43–44. Full text in *OC*, 4:322.

125 As Breton wrote: Quotes from Breton, André. *Manifestoes of Surrealism*, trans. Richard Seaver and Helen R. Lane (1924; Ann Arbor: University of Michigan Press, 1969), 26.

126 These measured changes: De Costa, René. *Pablo Neruda's* tentativa del hombre infinito: *Notes for a Reappraisal* (Chicago: University of Chicago, 1975); originally published in *Modern Philology* 73, no. 2 (November 1975): 141–142.

126 The poets Neruda's eccentric: Wilson, Jason. *A Companion to Pablo Neruda: Evaluating Neruda's Poetry* (Woodbridge, Suffolk, UK: Tamesis, 2008), 82.

126 "poetic workshop": From a speech given with Nicanor Parra at the University of Chile, March 1962, published as Nicanor, Parra, and Pablo Neruda. *Discursos* (Santiago: Editorial Nascimento, 1962). Pointed out for this context in Wilson, *Companion to Pablo Neruda*, 81.

126 When Nascimento eventually sent: According to Neruda, "Erratas y erratones," in *OC*, 5:237–238.

127 "one part quest": Author Tomás Q. Morín's blurb for Neruda, Pablo. *venture of the infinite man*, trans. Jessica Powell (San Francisco, CA: City Lights Books, 2017). Excerpts of *venture of the infinite man* are from Powell's translation.

127 like Alice with her looking glass: Wilson, *Companion to Pablo Neruda*, 85.

127 In a midbook climax: René de Costa explains how this "sexual act becomes a metaphor for ultimate oneness" in *Poetry of Pablo Neruda*, 53.

127 "twisting to that side": *venture of the infinite man*, trans. Jessica Powell (all passages quoted herein).

128   meditative thinking generates: Wilson, *Companion to Pablo Neruda*, 85.

128   "the least read": Cardona Peña, "Pablo Neruda: Breve historia," 265.

129   "The flesh and blood": Quoted in de Costa, *Poetry of Pablo Neruda*, 45.

129   "going the way of the absurd": Ibid., 42.

129   It shimmers with poetic tension: De Costa, *Pablo Neruda's tentativa del hombre infinito*, 146–147.

129   "I have always looked": Neruda, "Algunas reflexiones," in *OC*, 4:1204.

130   "*profesor de profesores*": Arrué, *Ventana del recuerdo*, 46.

130   Neruda managed to see Albertina: Varas, José Miguel. "El cara de hombre," *Mapocho* 33 (First Semester 1993): 14.

131   He was about to have: Azócar, "Testimonio," 215.

131   After a few days in Temuco: Loyola, *Neruda: La biografía literaria*, 206.

131   "the first night that we": Letter dated September 15, 1926, *OC*, 5:901.

131   Neruda rekindled his relationship: Loyola, *Neruda: La biografía literaria*, 207.

131   "One honest word from you": Letter dated November 1925, *OC*, 5:908.

131   The rain covered the town: *OC*, 5:909.

132   Rubén had rented: Azócar, "Testimonio," 216.

133   "a triumph": *La Nación*, September 26, 1926. Quoted in Alone, *Los cuatro grandes*, 186.

133   "I've got a dramatic": Translated by Megan Coxe. *OC*, 1:217.

134   "Now, my house is the last one in Cantalao": Coxe, trans., *OC*, 1:219.

134   "It's a story": *La Nación*, September 26, 1926. Quoted in Alone, *Los cuatro grandes*, 186.

135   a dinner was thrown: Azócar, "Testimonio," 217.

135   "The southern skies": "Tristeza," *Anillos*.

136   The room Neruda, Lago, and Oyarzún shared: Arrué, *Ventana de recuerdo*, 60.

136   One day Laura Arrué came: Ibid., 61.

136   "Autumn appears in the corner": Ibid., 112.

137   "I've been through so much!": Letter dated January 9, 1927, *OC*, 5:915.

137   "I'm bored of everything": *OC*, 5:912–914.

138   It was a very serious composition: Letter to the Argentine writer Héctor Eandi, July 2, 1930, *OC*, 5:959. All correspondence between Eandi and Neruda cited in this book is found in *OC*, 5:936–975, identifiable by date.

138   "sense of a new reality": Felstiner, *Translating Neruda*, 67.

138   Clarity comes only through: Part of this analysis comes from my work with Professor Michael Predmore at Stanford University, influenced by his analysis and lectures.

139   His singing—his poetry: Concha, *Neruda (1904–1936)*, 262.

139 He is like that pumpkin: Wilson, *Companion to Pablo Neruda*, 127.

140 Valparaíso's "magnetic pulse": *CHV*, 456–459.

140 Álvaro's example of discipline: *CHV*, 478.

141 Álvaro was also an important: *CHV*, 478.

141 The first time Neruda came: Thayer, Sylvia. "Testimonio," *Aurora*, nos. 3–4 (July–December 1964): 241.

141 Neruda could walk for hours: Ibid.

142 "The Valparaíso night!": *CHV*, 463.

143 "thinking about getting involved": Loyola, *El joven Neruda*, 141.

143 On October 8, 1926, he wrote: *OC*, 5:797.

144 "Laura, I'm writing to tell you": *OC*, 5:799.

145 Neruda kept visiting this department head: *CHV*, 467.

145 one of his friends, Manuel Bianchi: Schidlowsky, *Las furias y las penas* (2008), 1:120–121.

146 "Rangoon. There's Rangoon": *CHV*, 468.

CHAPTER EIGHT: AFAR

147 "Dawn's Dim Light": "Débil del alba," *Residence on Earth I* (1933). Written probably in 1926, most likely just before or after he arrived in the Far East.

148 "While eating and drinking": Muñoz, *Memorias*, 146.

149 Neruda gave him a copy of the book: Yates, Donald. "Neruda and Borges," *Simposio Pablo Neruda: Actas*, ed. Juan Loveluck and Issac Jack Lévy (Columbia: University of South Carolina, 1975), 240. Quoted in Wilson, *Companion to Pablo Neruda*, 109.

149 "a hopeless, clumsy language": Chiappini, Julio O. *Borges: La persona, el personaje, sus personajes, sus detractores* (Rosario, Argentina: FAS, 2005), 241.

149 "Borges really seems to be a ghost": Letter to Héctor Eandi, April 24, 1929, *OC*, 5:942–943.

149 In a 1975 interview: Borges, Jorge L. *Jorge Luis Borges: Conversations*, ed. Richard Burgin (Jackson: University Press of Mississippi, 1998), 139.

150 "Some people accuse you": Guibert, "Pablo Neruda," 67–68.

150 "This German ship": *CHV*, 468.

151 "I'm a little scared of arriving": *OC*, 5:803.

151 "When I arrived in Spain": Cardona Peña, "Pablo Neruda: Breve historia," 273.

152 Guillermo de Torre replied: De Torre, Guillermo. "Carta abierta a Pablo Neruda," *Cuadernos americanos* 57, no. 3 (May–June 1951): 277–282.

152 "Panoramic Sketch of Chilean Poetry": De Torre, Guillermo. "Es-

quema panorámico de la nueva poesía Chilena," *Gaceta literaria* 15, no. 1 (August 1927): 3.

152   "two hundred meters": *CHV,* 469–471.

152   profoundly impressed: Camp, André, and Ramón Luis Chao. "Neruda por Neruda," *Triunfo* (Madrid), November 13, 1971.

153   "During those days I met": *CHV,* 470.

153   He was crazy but kind: Diary entry after Cóndon's death, October 22, 1934, in Morla Lynch, Carlos. *En España con Federico García Lorca: Páginas de un diario íntimo, 1929–1936* (Seville: Renacimiento, 2008), 430–442.

153   After they unloaded Cóndon: *CHV,* 473.

155   "loaded like a basket": *CHV,* 473.

155   composing love letters: *CHV,* 474.

155   imperialistic exploiters: Author interview with Aida Figueroa, 2003, among other sources.

155   "The women here are black": Letter dated October 28, 1927, *OC,* 5:804.

156   "a woman to love, to bed": "Rangoon, 1927," *Memorial de Isla Negra,* in Neruda, *Isla Negra.*

156   "At that time, like now": *Triunfo,* November 13, 1973.

156   "The women, indispensable material": Letter dated December 7, 1927, in Neruda, Pablo. *Epistolario viajero: 1927–1973,* ed. Abraham Quezada Vergara (Santiago: RIL Editores, 2004), 49.

157   "This is a beautiful country": Letter dated December 12, 1927, Archivo del Escritor, Biblioteca Nacional de Chile. (My understanding was later supplemented by Abraham Quezada Vergara's annotations in Neruda, *Epistolario Viajero,* 51.)

157   "How difficult to leave Siam": Written in February 1928; appeared in *La Nación,* April 8, 1928. Available in *OC,* 4:349–352.

157   "Life in Rangoon": Letter dated February 22, 1928, *OC,* 5:806.

158   "Sometimes for long stretches": *OC,* 5:937.

159   "Our friendship with Pablo": Olivares Briones, Edmundo. *Pablo Neruda: Los caminos de Oriente* (Santiago: LOM Ediciones, 2000), 152.

159   "I suffer, I'm so anguished": *OC,* 5:1026–1027.

160   "It seems difficult to tell": Letter dated February 22, 1928, *OC,* 5:806.

160   "that it will express": Letter dated December 7, 1927, in Neruda, *Epistolario viajero,* 50.

161   He had created a new rhetoric: Schopf, Federico. "Recepción y contexto de la poesía de Pablo Neruda," *Del vanguardismo a la antipoesía: Ensayos sobre la poesía en Chile* (Santiago: LOM Ediciones, 2000), 88. Schopf did not specifically mention that it was "quickly labeled."

161   "Between shadow and space": "Arte poética," *Residence on Earth I.* Trans-

lated by Stephen Kessler in Neruda, Pablo. *The Essential Neruda,* ed. Mark Eisner (San Francisco, CA: City Lights Books, 2004).

162 The writer Jim Harrison: Harrison, Jim. Introduction to *Residence on Earth,* by Pablo Neruda (New York: New Directions, 2004), xiv.

162 "Whenever I'm feeling": Author interview with Ariel Dorfman, 2004.

162 In June, he sent: Again, from Schidlowsky's pioneering archival research in *Las furias y las penas* (2008), 1:140.

163 "Consuls like me": Letter started on October 5, 1929, in *OC,* 5:945.

163 "seems to me still too provincial": Letter started on October 5, 1929, this part from a section he wrote on October 24. He continued writing the letter into November before sending it, occasionally marking the date of new entries. *OC,* 5:946–947.

163 Their mutual friend Alfredo Cóndon: Morla Lynch, *En España con Federico García Lorca,* 430.

163 "Carlos Morla, about me feeling lonely": Letter dated November 8, 1930, a photocopy of which appears in Macías, Sergio. *El Madrid de Pablo Neruda* (Madrid: Tabla Rasa, 2004), 24.

164 In her study "Chasing Your (Josie) Bliss": Author interview with Roanne Kantor, 2015 and 2017, as well as from her article "Chasing Your (Josie) Bliss: The Troubling Critical Afterlife of Pablo Neruda's Burmese Lover," *Transmodernity* 3, no. 2 (Spring 2014): 59–82. Available at https://escholarship.org/uc/item/5dv9d4jq.

165 "she glowered at the air": *CHV,* 491.

166 The prototypical "Oriental Woman": Said, Edward W. *Orientalism* (New York: Pantheon Books, 1978), 180–190.

166 Or, in the words of Kantor: Published under her maiden name as Sharp, Roanne Leah. "Neruda in Asia/Asia in Neruda: Enduring Traces of South Asia in the Journey Through *Residencia en la tierra,*" master's thesis, University of Texas at Austin, 2011.

166 "The Night of the Soldier": "La noche del soldado," *Residence on Earth I.*

166 "The Young Monarch": "El joven monarca," *Residence on Earth I.*

167 "ended up killing me": *CHV,* 491.

167 "two months of life": Letter to Héctor Eandi, January 16, 1929, *OC,* 5:939.

167 "Calcutta, 1928": *OC,* 1:1182.

167 "a shock down my spine": Vargas Llosa, Mario. "Neruda cumple cien años," *El País* (Madrid), June 27, 2004.

168 "Oh Maligna": "Tango del viudo," *Residence on Earth I.*

169 "As she thought that rice": *CHV,* 501.

170 There's a natural urge: Discussed as part of author interview with Roanne Kantor, 2017.

CHAPTER NINE: OPIUM AND MARRIAGE

171   "Nocturnal Collection": "Colección nocturna," translated by Jessica Powell. Loyola dates this as the first poem in *Residence on Earth* written outside of Chile, begun in 1927, if not 1928, and revised in 1929 to be part of *Residence on Earth (1925–1931)*, first published in 1933 (*El joven Neruda*, 163).

171   Someone took a posed: Among other places, this photo can be seen in Olivares, Edmundo, ed. *Itinerario de una amistad: Pablo Neruda–Héctor Eandi: Epistolario 1927–1943* (Buenos Aires: Corregidor, 2008), 87.

171   "Have I told you about Wellawatta": Letter dated April 24, 1929, *OC*, 5:942.

172   "Caught between the Englishmen": *CHV*, 493.

172   "If you, my dear mother": Letter dated March 14, 1929, *OC*, 5:811.

172   "I never read": "Sonata con recuerdos," *OC*, 5:162.

172   The potato sacks contained: *OC*, 5:162.

173   synthesis of European modernist innovations: "George Keyt," artist bio, Christie's, http://artist.christies.com/George-Keyt-29852-bio.aspx.

173   wrote a review: *George Keyt, a Centennial Anthology* (Colombo: George Keyt Foundation, 2001), 4.

173   "idealism and mysticism": Bradshaw, David. "The Best of Companions: J. W. N. Sullivan, Aldous Huxley, and the New Physics," *Review of English Studies* 47, no. 186 (May 1996): 188–206. Quoted in Sexton, James. "Aldous Huxley's Three Plays, 1931–1948," in *Aldous Huxley Between East and West*, ed. C. C. Barfoot (Amsterdam; New York: Rodopi, 2001), 65.

173   "An aunt of mine remembers": Ondaatje, Michael. *Running in the Family* (New York: W. W. Norton, 1982), 79.

174   "I'm alone": Letter dated April 24, 1929, *OC*, 5:942.

174   "taking out everything": Author interview with Rosa León Muller, 2014.

175   "I'm very tired from": Letter dated December 17, 1929, *OC*, 5:916–917.

175   "In those days, more than": Quoted in Poirot, *Pablo Neruda*, 144.

176   "Madrigal Written in Winter": "Madrigal escrito en invierno," *Residence on Earth I*.

176   "Oh heartless lady": From the poem "Tiranía" ["Tyranny"], *Residence on Earth I*.

176   "Female friends of various colorings": *CHV*, 504.

176   "She walked solemnly": *CHV*, 505.

178   "elevating the exotic Other": Žižek, Slavoj. *Living in the End Times* (London; New York: Verso, 2011), 25.

178   "magical Malay Archipelago": Letter dated February 1, 1930, *OC*, 5:950.

179 "I smoked one pipe": *CHV,* 492.

179 "inspired to ecstasies": Abrams, M. H. *The Milk of Paradise: The Effect of Opium Visions on the Works of De Quincey, Crabbe, Francis Thompson, and Coleridge* (Cambridge, MA: Harvard University Press, 1934), 3.

180 there is a disjuncture: Sharp (Kantor),"Neruda in Asia/Asia in Neruda."

180 "I had to experience opium": *CHV,* 492–493.

180 "Pablo sleeps, pulls": Hinojosa's postscript is contained and transcribed in Olivares, ed., *Itinerario de una amistad,* 45. The letter seems to have been written as they crossed the Bay of Bengal from Calcutta to Ceylon.

180 "A Day in Singapore": Published in *La Nación,* February 5, 1928. Available in *OC,* 4:341.

181 In the end, the only community: Much of this discussion of Neruda's relationship with opium was informed by Chilean professor Francisco Leal at Colorado State University, through correspondence and conversations during the spring and summer of 2015, in addition to his work "Pablo Neruda y el opio (del pueblo). Reflexiones en torno a la 'metafísica cubierta de amapolas' de *Residencia en la tierra*" (unpublished manuscript, 2013). Discussions with Roanne Kantor and her work "Neruda in Asia/Asia in Neruda" helped to inform this area as well.

181 opium's "exercising effect": Leal, "Pablo Neruda y el opio."

181 "the action of opium": Hayter, Alethea. *Opium and the Romantic Imagination* (London: Faber and Faber, 1968), 334.

182 "Nocturnal Collection": "Colección nocturna," *Residence on Earth I.*

182 As Roanne Kantor: Sharp (Kantor), "Neruda in Asia/Asia in Neruda," 14–15.

182 "Contradicted Communications": "Communicaciones desmentidas," *Residence on Earth I.*

182 "Nocturnal Establishments": "Establecimientos nocturnos," *Residence on Earth I.* Analysis of the poem guided by the insightful points in Leal, Francisco. "'Quise entonces fumar': El opio en César Vallejo y Pablo Neruda, rutas asiáticas de experimentación" (unpublished manuscript, 2013).

183 "Opium in the East": "El opio en el Este," *Memorial de Isla Negra.* Translated by the author and Jessica Powell.

184 "opiate for the exploited": The idea from Leal, "'Quise entonces fumar,'" among others.

184 "never again": *CHV,* 492.

185 city of Pagan: Teitelboim mentions that Neruda visited Pagan while in Burma in *Neruda: La biografía,* 153.

185 "mysterious Sinhalese": Neruda, Pablo. "Ceylon espeso," *La Nación*, November 17, 1929. Available in *OC*, 4:354-356.

185 "strange hungry Buddha": Letter dated September 8, 1928, *OC*, 5:939.

185 blend of curiosity and skepticism: *Triunfo*, November 13, 1971, 18.

186 toward the end of 1929: *OC*, 1:1183.

186 "vital, speedy wings": "Significa sombras" ["It Means Shadows"], *Residence on Earth I*. Translated by Stephen Kessler in Neruda, *The Essential Neruda*.

186 "Never lost": Neruda, Pablo. "Orient and Orient," *La Nación*, August 3, 1930. Available in *OC*, 4:356–357.

187 The crux of Neruda's problem: Author interview with Roanne Kantor, 2015.

187 "Religion in the East": "Religión en el este," *Memorial de Isla Negra*.

188 "Sometimes I'm happy here": From entries dated October 31 and November 21 as part of a letter he started on October 5, 1929. He continued writing the letter into November before sending it, occasionally marking the date of new entries. *OC*, 5:947–949.

189 "good servant Dom Brampy": Letter to Héctor Eandi dated April 23, 1930, *OC*, 5:956.

189 "my Sinhalese boy": "Boy" was written in English. *CHV*, 506.

189 "extremely friendly": Letter to Héctor Eandi dated April 23, 1930, *OC*, 5:956.

190 She did adore him at first: As seen in a letter to Neruda from The Hague, November 18, 1938, APNF.

190 "soon, tomorrow even": Letter dated October 5, 1929, *OC*, 5:946.

190 A week later he wrote: *OC*, 5:817–818.

191 "I've married": *OC*, 5:1028.

191 "extremely close": *OC*, 5:959–960.

192 "Some years later, my biographer": *CHV*, 515.

CHAPTER TEN: AN INTERLUDE

193 "Maternity": "Maternidad," *Residence on Earth II*. Written in 1934, though not published until 1938, this poem is unique because there was an unusual amount of time between the year of composition and when the book was published, and also because so much had changed in his life and the world during those years.

193 "The Ghost of the Cargo Ship": "El fantasma del buque de carga," *Residence on Earth I*. Translated by Stephen Kessler, using the title "The Phantom of the Cargo Ship," in Neruda, *The Essential Neruda*.

194 Finally, on April 18, 1932: Loyola, *El joven Neruda*, 254.

195 Neruda's telegram to his parents: Teitelboim, *Neruda: La biografía*, 67.

196 "She was a hostile being": Muñoz, *Memorias*, 182.

196 Neruda remained calm: Ibid.

196 "Now he wasn't the somber": Ibid., 180.

196 "with a melancholy air": Souvirón, José María. "Pablo Neruda," *ABC* (Madrid), December 4, 1962. Quoted in Schidlowsky, *Las furias y las penas* (2008), 1:205.

196 "You know by now": Letter dated May 1932, *OC*, 5:924–925.

197 "My telegrams, my letters": Letter dated May 15, 1932, *OC*, 5:925.

197 "My dear Albertina": Letter dated July 11, 1932, *OC*, 5:925.

198 Through a fellow writer: Olivares Briones, *Pablo Neruda: Los caminos de Oriente*, 430–431.

198 "a document of an excessive": Neruda, Pablo. "Advertencia del autor," *El hondero entusiasta* (Santiago: Empresa Letras, 1933). Available in *OC*, 1:159.

198 "realized yesterday that it is time": Letter dated April 24, 1929, *OC*, 5:944.

199 "I have been writing": Entry marked October 24, part of a letter started on October 5, 1929, *OC*, 5:946–947.

199 "From the very first reading": Alberti, Rafael. *La arboleda perdida* (Madrid: Alianza, 1998), 324.

199 "absolutely extraordinary poet": Carpentier, Alejo. "Presencia de Pablo Neruda," *Pablo Neruda*, ed. Emir Rodríguez Monegal and Enrico Mario Santí (Madrid: Taurus, 1980), 57.

200 whose poetry amazed him: Carpentier, "Presencia de Pablo Neruda," 58.

200 Alberti sent a cable: Vasquez, Carmen. "Alejo Carpentier en París (1928–1939)," in *Escritores de América Latina en París: Sesión: "Vida y obra de escritores latinoamericanos en París,"* *Conferencia inaugura I*, ed. Milagros Palma and Michèle Ramond (Paris: Indigo & Côté-femmes, 2006), 109.

201 He hoped all of their enthusiasm: De Costa, *Poetry of Pablo Neruda*, 8.

201 a torrential body of work: Handal, Nathalie. "Paradise in Zurita: An Interview with Raúl Zurita," *Prairie Schooner*, n.d., http://prairie schooner.unl.edu/excerpt/paradise-zurita-interview-raul-zurita.

201 "Epitaph to Neruda": De Rokha, Pablo. "Epitafío a Neruda," *La Opinión*, May 22, 1933. Full article in Zerán, Faride. *La guerrilla literaria: Pablo de Rokha, Vicente Huidobro, Pablo Neruda* (Santiago: Ediciones Bat, 1992), 175–178.

201 "We Together": "Juntos nosotros," *Residence on Earth I*. Translated by Jessica Powell.

201 "a monochord deep moan": Teitelboim, *Neruda: La biografía*, 168. Teitelboim would later become a close comrade of Neruda's and write a

biography of him. He had just moved to Santiago before the reading. This was the first time he had ever seen Neruda in person.

202 readers embraced this: Schopf, "Recepción y contexto," 84.

202 Alone's main point was: Alone (Hernán Díaz Arrieta). *"Residencia en la tierra, de Pablo Neruda," La Nación,* November 24, 1935.

203 "Buenos Aires, isn't that": Letter dated April 24, 1929, *OC,* 5:942.

203 A short but intense romance began: Gligo, Agata. *María Luisa: Sobre la vida de María Luisa Bombal,* 2nd ed. (Santiago: Editorial Andrés Bello, 1985), 61–62.

204 "Pablo adored her": The friend was Porfirio Ramírez, who was in love with Loreto (Gligo, *María Luisa,* 52).

204 "the only woman with whom": Gligo, *María Luisa,* 54.

204 her intelligence, culture: Ibid., 53.

204 fallen in love with her: Vial, Sara. *Neruda vuelve a Valparaíso* (Valparaíso, Chile: Ediciones Universitaria de Valparaíso, 2004), 245; Teitelboim, *Neruda: La biografía,* 174.

204 the two had an affair: Reyes, Bernardo. *Enigma de Malva Marina: La hija de Pablo Neruda* (Santiago: RIL Editores, 2007), 85–86.

204 "You will be responsible": Varas, José Miguel. "Margarita Aguirre," *Anaquel Austral,* January 22, 2005, http://virginia-vidal.com/cgi-bin /revista/exec/view.cgi/1/17.

205 However, when the conversation: Olivares Briones, Edmundo. *Pablo Neruda: Los caminos del mundo* (Santiago: LOM Ediciones, 2001), 21.

205 recently been released in Buenos Aires: A celebrated and important pirated edition (from publishers Tor)—reprinted in 1934, 1938, and 1940—that catapulted *Twenty Love Poems* to international fame, as Loyola notes in *OC,* 1:1147.

205 "Neruda's four major books": Olivares, ed., *Itinerario de una amistad,* 165.

207 during the first month or so: Dates from Loyola in *OC,* 1:1184.

207 The Irishman's influence: This and the following paragraph draw from Wilson, *Companion to Pablo Neruda,* 145, and Loyola, Hernán. "Lorca y Neruda en Buenos Aires (1933–1934)," *A Contracorriente* 8, no. 3 (Spring 2011): 1–22. Available at https://acontracorriente.chass.ncsu .edu/index.php/acontracorriente/article/view/9/32.

207 "Walking Around": *Residence on Earth II.* Translated by Forrest Gander in Neruda, *The Essential Neruda.*

208 She wrote most of it: Gligo, *María Luisa,* 69.

208 "bee of fire": Ibid., 75.

209 "We adored each other": Vial, *Neruda vuelve a Valparaíso,* 246.

209 "What would Maruca do": Gligo, *María Luisa,* 69.

209 "Neruda's Javanese wife": More precisely, María Flora compared

Maruca to a gendarme. Yáñez, María Flora. *Historia de mi vida: Fragmentos* (Santiago: Nascimento, 1980), 210.

209   María Flora wrote that: Yáñez, *Historia de mi vida*, 210.

209   "fatal beauty": Gonzalez, Ray. "Alfonsina Storni: *Selected Poems*," *The Bloomsbury Review*, no. 8 (July/August 1988), 31.

210   Bombal knew about them: Vial, *Neruda vuelve a Valparaíso*.

210   One night at the trendy restaurant: De Miguel, María Esther. *Norah Lange: Una biografía* (Buenos Aires: Planeta, 1991), 158.

210   "always had good luck": Vial, *Neruda vuelve a Valparaíso*, 246.

211   He became the talk of the town: Gibson, Ian. *Federico García Lorca: A Life* (New York: Pantheon Books, 1989), 365.

211   Neruda considered him to be: Teitelboim, *Neruda: La biografía*, 174.

211   "Stop! Stop!": Stainton, Leslie. *Lorca: A Dream of Life* (New York: Farrar, Straus & Giroux, 1999), 336.

211   "reinvigorated the eternal": *OC*, 4:390–391.

211   "leaping poetry": Bly, Robert. *Leaping Poetry: An Idea with Poems and Translations* (Pittsburgh: University of Pittsburgh Press, 2008), 40–42.

211   "an effervescent child": From a speech delivered during the dedication of a new monument to Lorca in São Paulo, Brazil, 1968, "Un monumento a Federico," *OC*, 5:150–152.

211   In his memoirs, Neruda narrates: *CHV*, 521.

212   "There has been an accident": Gibson, *Federico García Lorca*, 370.

212   "Neruda had begun to suspect": Neruda, *Confieso que he vivido* (2017), 143.

212   "almost always fledgling poets": Ibid., 143–144.

213   "We were happy and carefree": Vial, *Neruda vuelve a Valparaíso*, 247.

213   Lorca revered him: Backstory about Darío in Gibson, *Federico García Lorca*, 370.

214   They continued alternating: De Costa, *Poetry of Pablo Neruda*, 73.

214   "transcendent poetry slam": Harrison, introduction to Neruda, *Residence on Earth*, xi.

214   "Where in Buenos Aires is": Full text of the discourse is in *OC*, 4:369–371. With her permission, I take from Leslie Stainton's translation the "lexical fiesta" line, from her book *Lorca*, 336.

215   Bombal couldn't help: Gligo, *María Luisa*, 75.

215   "María Luisa, I don't want": Vial, *Neruda vuelve a Valparaíso*, 247.

CHAPTER ELEVEN: SPAIN IN THE HEART

217   "For me, Spain is a great wound": Quoted in Gálvez Barraza, Julio. *Neruda y España* (Santiago: RIL, 2003), 15.

217   "I don't feel any distress": Letter dated February 17, 1933, *OC*, 5:966–976.

218   "of dreams, of the leaves": "Explico algunas cosas" ["I Explain Some Things"], *Third Residence*.

218   a cheery group photograph: Picture in Aguirre, Margarita, ed. *Pablo Neruda, Héctor Eandi: Correspondencia durante* Residencia en la tierra (Buenos Aires: Editorial Sudamericana, 1980). Insight on Maruca's line of vision in Olivares Briones, *Pablo Neruda: Los caminos de Oriente*, 89.

218   a letter from his old roommate: The author Luis Enrique Délano discovered this information from Lago's article "La dura muerte" in *El Siglo*, October 14, 1968. Quoted in Plath, Oreste, ed. *Alberto Rojas Jiménez se paseaba por el alba* (Santiago: Dirección de Bibliotecas, Archivos y Museos, 1994), 246.

219   "an angel full of wine": Letter dated September 19, 1934, APNF, and *OC*, 5:1030.

219   "I didn't know how to pray": APNF, and *OC*, 5:1031.

219   "It's a funeral, solemn hymn": APNF, and *OC*, 5:1031.

219   "Beyond blood and bones": "Alberto Rojas Jiménez viene volando," *Residence on Earth II*.

221   "What Spain Was Like": "Como era España," *Third Residence*.

221   they started with working-class Catalans: Herr, Richard. *An Historical Essay on Modern Spain* (Berkeley: University of California Press, 1974), 130.

221   there already was widespread: Ibid.

221   "state of war": Vincent, Mary. *Spain, 1833–2002: People and State* (Oxford: Oxford University Press, 2007), 99.

221   "narrow social construction": Ibid., 103.

223   Lorca and other poets met: Stainton, *Lorca*, 358.

223   "He's pale, a pallor": Morla Lynch, *En España con Federico García Lorca*, 392.

223   "a truly extraordinary": *Triunfo*, November 13, 1971.

223   he read with power: Stainton, *Lorca*, 119.

224   an "institution" in Madrid: From Salinas, Pedro. "Federico García Lorca" (unpublished manuscript), in his papers at Houghton Library, Harvard University. Also quoted in Stainton, *Lorca*, 375.

224   "Of all the human beings": Buñuel, Luis. *My Last Sigh: The Autobiography of Luis Buñuel*, trans. Abigail Israel (New York: Knopf, 1984), 158.

224   "When I die, / bury me with my guitar": Lorca, Federico García. "Memento," *Poema del cante jondo [Poem of the Deep Song]* (Madrid : Ediciones Ulises, 1931). Most of the poem was written by 1921.

224   "a brilliant fraternity of talents": Cardona Peña, *Pablo Neruda y otros ensayos*, 31; and Cardona Peña, "Pablo Neruda: Breve historia," 274.

224   "You are a poet": Edwards, Jorge. *Adiós, poeta* ... (Barcelona: Tusquets, 2000), 81.

225   "You are about to hear": Lorca, Federico García. "Presentación de Pablo Neruda," Madrid, December 6, 1934. Quoted in Quezada, Jaime, ed. *Neruda–García Lorca* (Santiago: Fundación Pablo Neruda, 1998); and Neruda, Pablo. *Selección,* comp. Arturo Aldunate Phillips (Santiago: Nascimento, 1943), 305–306.

225   "this amazing Chilean poet": As recounted by Vicente Aleixandre in his piece "Con Pablo Neruda," *Prosas recobradas,* ed. Alejandro Duque Amusco (Barcelona: Plaza & Janés, 1987), 24.

225   "put his arm around": Sáez, Fernando. *La Hormiga: Biografía de Delia del Carril, mujer de Pablo Neruda* (Santiago: Catalonia, 2004), 89.

226   Eight days before she turned: Ibid., 25–26.

227   A political commitment: Ibid., 79.

227   "an erotic, tragic love": As put by Dalí in a January 30, 1986, letter to the Madrid newspaper *El País.* Quoted in Dalí, Salvador, and Federico García Lorca. *Querido Salvador, Querido Lorquito: Epistolario 1925–1936,* ed. Víctor Fernández and Rafael Santos Torroella (Barcelona: Elba, 2013), 157.

228   "crazy, affectionate, and good": Diary entry dated March 24, 1936, in Morla Lynch, *En España con Federico García Lorca,* 519.

228   Neruda, often with his beret: Ibid.

228   Chinchón anis: Sáez, *La Hormiga,* 93.

228   "To go to bed at night": Hemingway, Ernest. *Death in the Afternoon* (New York: Scribner's, 1960), 48.

229   It was a fresh: Macías, *El Madrid de Pablo Neruda,* 55–61.

229   Lorca liked to compose: Gibson, *Federico García Lorca,* 396.

229   "golden, ashen": *CHV,* 542.

229   fueled by Neruda's powerful punch: I'm grateful to Leslie Stainton for permission to adopt some of her language from her researched description in *Lorca,* 359.

229   "inauguration" of a public monument: Ibid.

229   whose friendship had deepened: Gibson, *Federico García Lorca,* 403.

CHAPTER TWELVE: BIRTH AND DESTRUCTION

231   "Ode with a Lament": "Oda con un lamento," *Residence on Earth II.* Translated by Forrest Gander in Neruda, *The Essential Neruda.*

232   "My daughter, or at least": APNF, and *OC,* 5:1029–1031.

233   "Pablo was leaning over": Aleixandre, "Con Pablo Neruda," 27–28.

233   "Melancholy in the Families": "Melancolía en las familias," *Residence on Earth II.* Translated by Jessica Powell.

234 "Lines on the Birth of Malva Marina Neruda": Lorca, Federico García. Undated poem first published in the Madrid newspaper *ABC*, July 12, 1984. Among other sources, quoted in: Reyes, *Enigma de Malva Marina*, 111, collected in Lorca, Federico García, *Poesía completa*, ed. Miguel García Posada (New York: Vintage Español, 2012), 581–582.

234 "I adore Delia": Letter to Adelina, Delia's sister. Quoted in Sáez, *La Hormiga*, 98.

234 That January, Neruda wrote: *OC*, 5:971–972.

235 One day at the National Library: Teitelboim, Volodia. *Huidobro: La marcha infinita* (Santiago: Ediciones BAT, 1993), 184. Also see Loyola, Hernán. "Volodia y Pablo: El comienzo de una larga amistad," *Nerudiana*, no. 5 (August 2008): 4.

236 people directly attributed the charge: De Costa, René. "Sobre Huidobro y Neruda," *Revista iberoamericana* 45, nos. 106–107 (1979): 379.

236 He was already known for: Ibid.

236 "Pablo Neruda: Poeta a la moda": The article appeared in *La Opinión*, November 11, 1932, available at Archivo Chile, http://www.archivo chile.com/Ideas_Autores/rokhap/o/rokhaobra0014.pdf.

237 "To be a plagiarist": De Rokha, Pablo. "Esquema del plagiario," *La Opinión*, December 6, 1934. Available in Zerán, *La guerrilla literaria*, 179.

237 several of Neruda's friends claimed: Teitelboim, *Neruda: La biografía*, 205.

238 "The publication of this plagiarism": Huidobro, Vicente. "Carta a Tomas Lago" and "El otro," *Vital* (January 1935): 3–4, available via the Chilean National Library at http://www.memoriachilena.cl/ar chivos2/pdfs/MC0002197.pdf.

238 "Chile has sent to Spain": Among other sources, quoted in Quezada, ed., *Neruda–García Lorca*, 157.

238 "All men are small": Morla Lynch, *En España con Federico García Lorca*, 519.

239 "I Am Here": "Aquí estoy," *OC*, 4:374.

240 "great bad poet": Juan Ramón Jiménez originally wrote this in an article entitled "A Great Bad Poet" in the Paris magazine *Cuadernos*, May–June 1958. Among other sources, quoted in Schidlowsky, *Las furias y las penas* (2008), 1:986.

240 Neruda and his friends started: Prank calling noted in author interview with Michael Predmore, 2001. The Spanish critic Ricardo Gullón infers insults may have even been made; see Peñuelas, Marcelino C. "Review: Conversaciones con Ramón I. Sender," *Hispanic Review* 54, no. 3 (1971): 334–337.

240 "the finest presentation": *CHV*, 527.

240 these journals helped set: De la Nuez, Sebastián. "La poesía de la revista *Caballo Verde*, de Neruda," *Anales de literatura hispanoamericana 7* (1978): 205–257, https://revistas.ucm.es/index.php/ALHI/issue/view/ALHI787811.

240 "On Impure Poetry": *OC*, 5:381.

242 "Statute of Wine": "Estatuto del vino," *Residence on Earth II*. De Costa points this example out in *Poetry of Neruda*, 81. This translation is his.

242 He had started to read Whitman: Neruda, Pablo. "Walt Whitman según torres rioseco," *Claridad*, May 5, 1923.

242 Lorca had begun to idolize: Stainton, *Lorca*, 239.

242 a poem that dramatizes how: Hass, Robert. Introduction to Whitman, Walt. *Song of Myself, and Other Poems* (Berkeley, CA: Counterpoint, 2010), 5.

243 In *The Western Canon*: Bloom, Harold. *The Western Canon: The Books and School of the Ages* (New York: Harcourt Brace, 1994), 478.

243 Neruda told a Continental Cultural Congress: Santiago, May 26, 1953, *OC*, 4:891.

243 "I should demand": from Whitman, Walt. *Democratic Vistas*, available in *The Project Gutenberg EBook of Complete Prose Works by Walt Whitman*, https://www.gutenberg.org/files/8813/8813-h/8813-h.htm#link2H_4_0005.

243 "It's for an action": "Comienzo por invocar a Walt Whitman," *Incitación al Nixonicidio y alabanza de la revolución chilena*.

244 "You can be sure": *Les Mois*, November 1935. Quoted in Aldunate Phillips, Arturo. *El nuevo arte poético y Pablo Neruda* (Santiago: Nascimento, 1936), 28.

244 She wrote a rave review: The article, entitled "Recado sobre Pablo Neruda," is quoted in Schopf, *Neruda comentado*, 179–184.

244 "magnificent and extraordinary": Morla Lynch, *En España con Federico García Lorca*, 362.

245 "I still don't know whether": Written before and after October 2, 1935, quoted in Vargas Saavedra, Luis. "Hispanismo y antihispanismo en Gabriela Mistral," *Mapocho* 22 (Winter 1970): 5–7, available via the Chilean National Library at http://www.memoriachilena.cl/602/w3-article-76656.html.

245 "from the menace of fascism and war": Aaron, Daniel. *Writers on the Left: Episodes in American Literary Communism* (New York: Columbia University Press, 1992), 305.

245 The diverse audience: Lottman, Herbert R. *The Left Bank: Writers, Art-*

ists, and Politics from the Popular Front to the Cold War (Chicago: University of Chicago Press, 1998), 83–99.

246 "in the extratextural reality": Loyola, *El joven Neruda*, 440–456.

247 Neruda felt dejected: Ibid., 455–456.

247 "lives with him, his wife": Diary entry dated June 19, 1935, in Morla Lynch, *En España con Federico García Lorca*, 485.

247 Lorca swept in and out: Diary entry dated November 3, 1931, ibid., 147.

247 Morla Lynch remembered how one: Ibid.

247 Lorca, so vibrant at this time: Maurer, Christopher. "Poetry," in *A Companion to Federico García Lorca,* ed. Federico Bonaddio (Woodbridge, Suffolk, UK: Tamesis, 2007), 34.

247 They decided to feast: Délano, Luis Enrique. *Sobre todo Madrid* (Santiago: Universitaria, 1970), 88.

247 As Lorca explained: Lorca, Federico García. *Deep Song and Other Prose,* ed. and trans. Christopher Maurer (New York: New Directions, 1980), 124.

248 they spent New Year's: Sáez, Fernando. *Todo debe ser demasiado: Biografía de Delia Del Carril: La Hormiga.* Santiago: Editorial Sudaméricana, 1997.

248 With their jacket collars up high: Délano, *Sobre todo Madrid,* 88.

248 "red hordes of communism": Bullón de Mendoza, Alfonso. *José Calvo Sotelo* (Barcelona: Ariel, 2004), 558–561.

248 "Red Flag": Thomas, Hugh. *The Spanish Civil War* (London: Eyre & Spottiswoode, 1961), 92.

249 In March, members of the Fascist: Stainton, *Lorca,* 427, including, with permission, borrowing the word "ostentatiously."

250 Lorca was petrified: Gibson, *Federico García Lorca,* 442.

250 Delia insisted that the Fascists: Sáez, *La Hormiga,* 107.

251 "What's going to happen?": Stainton, *Lorca,* 437–438.

252 When Langston Hughes arrived: Hughes, Langston, and Arnold Rampersad. *I Wonder as I Wander: An Autobiographical Journey,* 2nd ed. (New York: Hill and Wang, 1995), 333.

253 The alliance members dressed: Sáez, *La Hormiga,* 108.

253 "chilly nights when we": Hughes and Rampersad, *I Wonder as I Wander,* 334.

254 The sympathies of the U.S. ambassador: Jackson, Gabriel. *The Spanish Republic and the Civil War, 1931–1939* (Princeton, NJ: Princeton University Press, 1965), 256.

254 The U.S. Congress had just passed: Ibid.

254 The act didn't prohibit oil: Anderson, James. *The Spanish Civil War: A History and Reference Guide* (Westport, CT: Greenwood Press, 2003), 93.

255 Lorca's brother-in-law: Stainton, *Lorca,* 444–445.

255 One night he dreamed: Ibid., 448.

256 a young, devout Catholic guard: Testimony of the guard, José Jover Tripaldi, among other sources in Gibson, Ian. *El asesinato de García Lorca* (Barcelona: Plaza & Janés, 1997), 243.

256 "But I haven't done anything!": Stainton, *Lorca*, 454.

256 Before the sun rose: Ibid.

256 "Ode to Federico García Lorca": "Oda a Federico García Lorca," *Residence on Earth II*.

256 "This criminal act": *CHV*, 532.

256 "The news of his death": Bizzarro, Salvatore. *Pablo Neruda: All Poets the Poet* (Metuchen, NJ: Scarecrow Press, 1979), 142.

256 "He's done more damage with a pen": Stainton, *Lorca*, 452.

256 "The truth is Lorca": Buñuel, *My Last Sigh*, 158.

257 European governments were aware: Anderson, *Spanish Civil War*, 85.

257 The Nationalist army's plan: López Fernández, Antonio. *Defensa de Madrid* (Mexico: A. P. Marquez, 1945), 134–135. "Street by street and house by house" phrasing taken from Jackson, *Spanish Republic and the Civil War*, 322.

258 "They have not died!": "Canto a las madres de los milicanos muertos" ["Song for the Mothers of Dead Militiamen"], *Mono azul*, September 24, 1936, later included in *Spain in the Heart* and *Third Residence*. Translated by Jessica Powell.

259 "soldiers were working": Letter from Manuel Altolaguirre to José Antonio, November 1941, on the "occasion of the third printing of *España en el corazón.*" Available in Neruda, *Selección*, 321–322.

259 This image might be too romantic: Moran, Dominic. *Pablo Neruda* (London: Reaktion Books, 2009), 85.

259 "sacred verses for us": Alberti, Rafael. "Testimonios sobre Neruda," *Aurora*, nos. 3–4 (July–December 1964).

260 no one's call for foreign help: Sanders, David. "Ernest Hemingway's Spanish Civil War Experience," *American Quarterly* 12, no. 2 (Summer 1960): 133.

261 "Since I had seen them last": Hemingway, Ernest. "Hemingway Reports Spain," *New Republic*, January 11, 1938. Accessed at http://www.newrepublic.com/article/95915/hemingway-reports-spain.

261 Hemingway's articles became: Sanders, "Ernest Hemingway's Spanish Civil War Experience," 139.

261 After the screening: Tierney, Dominic. *FDR and the Spanish Civil War: Neutrality and Commitment in the Struggle That Divided America* (Durham, NC: Duke University Press, 2007), 34–35.

261 Some have noted that the novel: LaPrade, Douglas Edward. *Hemingway and Franco* (Valencia, Spain: Universitat de València, 2007), 181.

262   The bombing by Junkers: Jackson, *Spanish Republic and the Civil War*, 320.

262   On November 17: Gibson, *Federico García Lorca*, 310–332.

263   "I can no longer write": Author interview with Ariel Dorfman, 2004.

CHAPTER THIRTEEN: I PICKED A ROAD

265   "Meeting Under New Flags": "Reunión bajo las nuevas banderas," *OC*, 1:1198. Translated by Jessica Powell. The poem was written in 1940, seven years before *Third Residence* was published, placing it out of the context in which it was written.

266   "I don't want anything except": APNF, and *OC*, 5:976–977.

266   Neruda wrote to the Ministry: Letter dated December 23, 1936, APNF.

266   "My dear friend": Letter dated January 31, 1937, APNF.

267   "embodied the dazzling energy": Inside-cover flap copy for Gordon, Lois. *Nancy Cunard: Heiress, Muse, Political Idealist* (New York: Columbia University Press, 2007).

268   "I have wanted to bring": Speech entitled "Federico García Lorca," *OC*, 4:393.

269   "To my American friends": Neruda, Pablo. "To My American Friends," *Nuestra España* (Paris), March 9, 1937. Quoted in Schidlowsky, *Las furias y las penas* (Berlin: Wissenschaftlicher Verlag, 2003), 1:280–281.

269   The next day, Neruda received: Letter dated March 10, 1937, APNF.

269   "Here is something I can do": Sharpe, Tony. *W. H. Auden in Context* (Cambridge, UK; New York: Cambridge University Press, 2013), 4.

270   Neruda, it seems, may have: Reyes, *Enigma de Malva Marina*, 152. No documents exist that can attest to whether he did visit them.

270   No matter what, his position: Ibid.

270   spreading terror: Preston, Paul. *The Destruction of Guernica* (London: HarperPress, 2012), Kindle location 12.

270   cities into dust and ash: Ibid., Kindle location 161. According to Preston, citing German lieutenant colonel Wolfram von Richthofen's diary, rebel and German leaders were sufficiently frustrated by the slowness of the advance to talk again of reducing Bilbao to "debris and ash."

270   Mondays are market days: Jackson, *Spanish Republic and the Civil War*, 380.

270   on Monday, April 26, 1937: Preston, *Destruction of Guernica*, Kindle location 184–237.

271   Chilean Intellectual Workers Union: The full name of the union was Sindicato Profesional de Trabajadores Intelectuales de Chile.

271 The fact that Huidobro cofounded: De Costa, "Sobre Huidobro y Neruda," 381.

271 "motives of discord": Ibid., 381–382.

272 "our dog Flak appeared": Bizzarro, *Pablo Neruda*, 144.

272 "War is as whimsical": *CHV*, 542.

272 "Fraternity this great": Aznar Soler, Manuel, and Luis Mario Schneider. *II Congreso Internacional de Escritores para la Defensa de la Cultura: Valencia-Madrid-Barcelona-Paris, 1937*, vol. 3 (Valencia, Spain: Generalitat Valenciana, Conselleria de Cultura, Educació i Ciència, 1987), 262.

273 "I'm not a communist; I'm an anti-fascist": Letter dated August 3, 1937, APNF.

273 "I am not a communist. Nor a socialist": Morales Alvarez, Raúl. "Habla Neruda: El arte de mañana será un quemante reportaje hecho a la actualidad," *Ercilla*, November 12, 1937. Quoted in Carson, Morris E. *Pablo Neruda: Regresó el caminante (Aspectos sobresalientes en la obra y la vida de Pablo Neruda)* (Madrid: Plaza Mayor, 1971), 87.

273 Maruca wrote a letter to Trinidad: Reyes, *Enigma de Malva Marina*, 153.

273 "This is la Hormiga": Sáez, *La Hormiga*, 123.

273 "She was a charming, cultured woman": Muñoz, *Memorias*, 216.

274 he would have risked expulsion: Author correspondence with José Miguel Varas, March 13, 2006.

274 "Writers of Every Country": *Frente Popular* (Santiago), November 9, 1937. Quoted in Schidlowsky, *Las furias y las penas* (2008), 1:356.

275 "the open house is yet": Sáez, *La Hormiga*, 125.

275 they bought the house: Vidal, Virginia. *Hormiga pinta caballos: Delia del Carril y su mundo (1885–1989)* (Santiago: RIL Editores, 2006), 69.

275 Shortly after their return to Chile: Sáez, *La Hormiga*, 127.

275 "my dear Hormiga of my soul": Undated letter, APNF.

275 "Why are you so twisted?": Aguirre, Margarita. *Las vidas de Pablo Neruda* (Santiago: Zig-Zag, 1967), 44.

276 "Enemies of the motherland": Neruda, Pablo. "Pablo Neruda el 1. de mayo del presente año en la casa del pueblo, de nuestra ciudad, dijo," *La voz radical* (Temuco), July 2, 1938. Quoted in Schidlowsky, *Las furias y las penas* (2008), 1:375.

276 "The Father": "El padre," *Memorial de Isla Negra*.

276 Marín noted that the night: Aguirre, *Las vidas de Pablo Neruda*, 43.

277 "tied in knots": Neruda, Pablo. "Algo sobre mi poesía y mi vida," *Aurora*, no. 1 (July 1954). Available in *OC*, 4:930–931.

277 He adopted a new, humble tone: Moran, *Pablo Neruda*, 85, including highlighting the roles of baker, carpenter, and miner.

278   "The More-Mother": "La mamadre," *Memorial de Isla Negra.*

279   Neruda's "uncle" Orlando: Letter dated November 16, 1945; from author's correspondence with Patricio Mason, 2017; and Mason, "History of the Mason Family in Chile."

279   Franco launched a final: Jackson, *Spanish Republic and the Civil War,* 463.

280   "There are 1,600 intellectuals": APNF.

280   Aguirre Cerda received Neruda warmly: *CHV,* 550.

280   President Aguirre Cerda signed: The order is in document #18, 1939, APNF.

280   "the noblest mission": *CHV, 550.*

281   Delia had already been working: Sáez, *La Hormiga,* 132.

281   "An Autograph of Pablo Neruda": Neruda, Pablo. "Un autógrafo de Pablo Neruda," *Aurora de Chile,* July 4, 1939.

281   Neruda and Delia arrived in France: Sáez, *La Hormiga,* 131.

281   "The government and political situation": *CHV,* 550–551.

281   When Aguirre Cerda gave: Schidlowsky, *Las furias y las penas* (2003), 1:372–379.

281   The French Communist Party: Among other sources, ibid., 1:374.

282   In the beginning of June: Neruda, Pablo. "Se estarían haciendo gestiones para la traída a Chile de miles de refugiados españoles," *La Hora,* June 8, 1939. Quoted in Schidlowsky, *Las furias y las penas,* 1:428.

282   "Information in the press informs": Ministerio de Relaciones Exteriores de Chile, Archivo General Histórico. Quoted in Schidlowsky, *Las furias y las penas,* 1:375. Like other diplomatic communications, this was uncovered by the meticulous scholar Dr. David Schidlowsky in the previously classified archives of the ministry.

282   "was fuming at": Bizzarro, *Pablo Neruda,* 144.

282   1,297 males: "Clasificación de los españoles que trae a bordo el 'Winnipeg,'" *La Hora,* August 17, 1939. Quoted in Schidlowsky, *Las furias y las penas* (2008), 1:438.

283   Chile's "foremost poet": "1,600 Refugee Spaniards Due in Chilean Haven This Month," *New York Tribune,* August 6, 1939.

283   "2,078 Spanish Refugees": "2,078 Spanish Refugees on a 93-Passenger Ship," *New York Times,* August 22, 1939.

283   "Unexpectedly, the arrival": Letter dated October 2, 1939, APNF.

283   "With marks of joy": "To Live Again," APNF. From Cunard, Nancy. "To Live Again," March 26, 1940.

283   "The change could not have been": Sáez, *La Hormiga,* 133.

284   "media reports embarkment": Ministerio de Relaciones Exteriores de Chile, Archivo General Histórico. Quoted in Schidlowsky, *Las furias y las penas* (2003), 1:389.

284   Destitute, Maruca had placed: Feinstein, Adam. *Pablo Neruda: A Passion for Life* (London: Bloomsbury, 2004), 165.

285   "My dear Pig": APNF.

CHAPTER FOURTEEN: AMÉRICA

287   "The Heights of Macchu Picchu": Canto XI, *Canto General*. My translation builds upon earlier versions by John Felstiner and Stephen Kessler.

287   "The people of America": "Llena de Grandeza es la página más reciente de Neruda," *Qué hubo*, January 2, 1940. Quoted in Schidlowsky, *Las furias y las penas* (2003), 1: 392–393, and Olivares Briones, Edmundo. *Pablo Neruda: Los caminos de América* (Santiago: LOM Ediciones, 2004), 23.

288   "Almost never before had we": Ibid.

289   "Delia's role was to support": Sáez, *La Hormiga*, 135.

289   On June 19, Neruda received: APNF.

289   On August 21, 1940: According to a Ministry of Foreign Affairs communication by Neruda, document #176. Available in Schidlowsky, *Las furias y las penas* (2003), 1:408.

289   His assassination was the culmination: Haynes, John E., and Harvey Klehr. *Venona: Decoding Soviet Espionage in America* (New Haven, CT; London: Yale University Press, 2000), 250.

290   In a 2004 article: Schwartz, Stephen. "Bad Poet, Bad Man: A Hundred Years of Pablo Neruda," *Weekly Standard*, July 26, 2004.

290   In a 2006 commentary: Kamm, Oliver. "Why Grass Deserves to Have His Writing Hurled Back in His Face," *London Times*, August 19, 2006.

290   Neruda claimed he never saw: Interview in *Marcha* (Montevideo), September 17, 1971. Available in *OC*, 5:1201.

290   In 1944, the U.S. intelligence: Memo ref. no. 3/NBF/T800, December 7, 1956, Venona Project, NSA. Available at https://www.nsa.gov/news-features/declassified-documents/venona/dated/1944/assets/files/11may_neruda.pdf.

291   His explanation to authorities: Haynes and Klehr, *Venona*, 277.

291   "Pablo Neruda, a fugitive": Letter dated September 25, 1940, APNF.

291   where they set up a small: Letter from Neruda to Minister of Foreign Affairs Ernesto Barros Jarpa, April 22, 1942, APNF. Quoted in Neruda, *Epistolario viajero*, 175.

292   Sometimes he would dress: Toledo, Víctor. *El águila en las venas: Neruda en México, México en Neruda*, 2nd ed. (Puebla, Mexico: BUAP-Dirección de Fomento Editorial, 2005), 74.

292   The largest fiesta: Sáez, *La Hormiga*, 138.

292 "the lyrical and subterranean accent": Cantón, Wilberto. *Posiciones* (México: Imprenta Universitaria, 1950), 91.

292 "Between blue Acapulco": Ibid., 96–97.

294 "Señor Reyes is developing": Quoted by Neruda in his letter to Ernesto Barros Jarpa, April 22, 1942, APNF, and in Neruda, *Epistolario viajero*, 175.

294 "bad taste": *CHV*, 576.

294 In or around April: From Delia del Carril's testimony in Bizzarro, *Pablo Neruda*, 144.

295 "I want to know, dear Carlos": APNF.

295 The travels also eased his relationship: Sáez, *La Hormiga*, 138.

296 "The United Fruit Co.": "La United Fruit Co.," translated by Jack Hirschman in Neruda, *The Essential Neruda*.

296 "to carry a sense": Hass, *Little Book on Form*, 331.

298 knowing how desperate he was: Schidlowsky, *Las furias y las penas* (2003), 1:436.

298 The short reports from: "Chilean's 'Viva Roosevelt' Stirs Nazi Riot in Mexico" (United Press), *New York Times*, December 29, 1941; "Pro-Nazi Attack Case Probed in Mexico City" (AP), *Baltimore Sun*, December 30, 1941.

298 Neruda received hundreds of telegrams: Letter dated December 31, 1941, APNF.

298 That night they sang: Schidlowsky, *Las furias y las penas* (2003), 1:452.

299 "I cannot solve the problem": Hooks, Margaret. *Tina Modotti: Photographer and Revolutionary* (New York: Da Capo Press, 2000), 104. (As written in a letter to her partner Edward Weston: "I cannot—as you once proposed to me—'solve the problem of life by losing myself in the problem of art.'"

299 "Tina Modotti Is Dead": "Tina Modotti ha muerto," *Third Residence*.

299 "unforgivable error": Contreras, Jaime Perales. "Clash of Literary Titans," *Americas*, July–August 2008.

299 "You have been an accomplice": Paz, Octavio. Epilogue to *Laurel: Antología de la poesía moderna en lengua española*, comp. Emilio Prados, Xavier Villaurrutia, Juan Gil-Albert, and Octavio Paz, 2nd ed. (Mexico: Editorial Trillas, 1986), 489.

299 not yet an important literary figure: As told by Mexican poet Homero Aridjis in conversation with author, 2017.

300 "To Miguel Hernández": "A Miguel Hernández, asesinado en los presidios de España," *Canto general*.

300 he takes a swipe at Bergamín: Pointed out in Contreras, "Clash of Literary Titans."

300 "The authors had included": Prados, Emilio, Xavier Villaurrutia, Juan

Gil-Albert, and Octavio Paz, comps. *Laurel: Antología de la poesía moderna en lengua español* (Mexico: Editorial Seneca, 1941), 1134.

300   "There was a change after that": This epilogue was not printed in the original 1941 edition. Paz, epilogue to *Laurel* (1986), 488.

300   uncharacteristically drunk: Contreras, "Clash of Literary Titans."

300   At one point: As the Mexican poet Alí Chumacero recounted to his fellow poet Homero Aridjis, who recounted the tale (up until Delia's reaction) to author in correspondence, 2017.

301   As he said his good-byes: Contreras, "Clash of Literary Titans."

301   "I don't know what": Larrea, Juan. *Del surrealismo a Machu Picchu* (Mexico: Joaquín Mortiz, 1967), 114.

302   "Song to Stalingrad": "Canto a Stalingrado," *Third Residence.*

302   "New Love Song for Stalingrad": "Nuevo canto de amor a Stalingrado," *Third Residence.*

303   Reviewing the first English: Bracker, Milton. Book review of *Residence on Earth*, by Pablo Neruda, *New York Times,* January 26, 1947.

303   The ad for the event: *New York Times,* February 12, 1943.

303   "wisely published in Spanish and English": Ibid.

304   "international fraternity": Zegri, Armando. "Pablo Neruda debuta en Nueva York," *La Hora,* March 15, 1943.

304   "will definitely be in Chile's interest": "Ahora será possible establecer relaciones con la URSS, dice Neruda: Declaraciones a la prensa EE.UU.," *El Siglo,* February 15, 1943. Quoted in Schidlowsky, *Las furias y las penas* (2008), 1:546.

304   "the outstanding Spanish poet": "Tea Honors Two Writers from Chile," *Washington Post,* March 4, 1943.

305   "Señora Neruda advises": Schidlowsky, *Las furias y las penas* (2003), 1:578.

305   Two months later, Neruda received: Ibid.

305   "angelic poet of rebellion": Written in a picture Lorca drew of Sánchez Ventura, quoted in "Rafael Sánchez Ventura," Fundación Ramón y Katia Acín, http://www.fundacionacin.org/index.php/ramon/detalle_personaje/29/. A section of Lorca's book *Poet in New York,* "Introduction to Death: Poems of Solitude in Vermont," is dedicated to Sánchez Ventura.

305   In 1940, he sent: Fisher, Bill. "Pablo Neruda in the Heart of the Library of Congress," video, 52 minutes. Available at http://www.loc.gov/today/cyberlc/feature_wdesc.php?rec=7046.

306   "In spite of the fact that I": Letter dated May 26, 1943, APNF.

306   His lawyers printed a legal notice: *Periodico oficial* (Cuernavaca, Morelos), May 3, 1942. Quoted in Schidlowsky, *Las furias y las penas* (2008), 1:532.

306   in the charming *pueblo* of Tetecala: Sáez, *La Hormiga,* 140.

306   He announced that he had found: Bizzarro, *Pablo Neruda,* 138.

307   "As the consul general of Chile": "Neruda dice que no acostumbra re-
       tracarse de sus actos," *Excelsior* (Mexico City), June 22, 1943. Quoted in
       Cantón, *Posiciones,* 101.

307   From the high plateaus: Some terminology from de Costa, *Poetry of
       Pablo Neruda,* 114.

308   At the beginning of the epic: Ibid.

308   "América, I Don't Invoke Your Name in Vain": "América, no invoco tu
       nombre en vano," *Canto general.*

308   "the agronomists and painters": Quoted in Cantón, *Posiciones,* 103–104.

308   "Señor Pablo Neruda, Chilean": Paz, Octavio. "Respuesta a un cónsul,"
       Letras de México, August 15, 1943. Quoted in Schidlowsky, *Las furias y
       las penas* (2003), 1:491.

309   Ambassador Óscar Schnake wrote: Letter by Schnake to the Ministry
       of Foreign Affairs, August 30, 1943, APNF.

309   "Pablo Neruda is such a boy": Available in Quirarte, Vicente. *Pablo
       Neruda en el corazón de México: En el centenario de su nacimiento* (Mexico,
       D.F.: Universidad Nacional Autónoma de México, 2006), 95.

309   "Since you arrived in Mexico": Available in Quirarte, *Pablo Neruda en el
       corazón de México,* 102.

310   On August 30, 1943: Schidlowsky, *Las furias y las penas* (2003), 1:498.

310   "to awaken the sleeping": Falcón, Jorge. "Imagen y espíritu de Pablo
       Neruda," *Hora del hombre* (Lima), October 1943. Quoted in Schid-
       lowsky, *Las furias y las penas,* 1:510.

310   christen a rural school: Teitelboim, Volodia. "Himmo y regreso del
       poeta de América, Pablo Neruda," *El Siglo,* February 28, 1943. Quoted
       in Aguirre, *Genio y figura de Pablo Neruda,* 177.

310   "He has wanted to mix": Rueda Martinez, Pedro. "Pablo Neruda, viajero
       de la poesía," *El Siglo,* September 12, 1943. Quoted in Schidlowsky, *Las
       furias y las penas* (2003), 1:505.

310   In the following days, Neruda gave: Ibid., 508–509.

311   "I thought it held the umbilicus": *Triunfo,* November 13, 1971.

311   "The nucleus of the work": Ibid.

311   "I thought about a lot of things": Neruda, Pablo. "Algo sobre mi poesía
       y mi vida," University of Chile, January 21, 1954 (the day after he gave
       his "Infancia y poesía" discourse, part of his "Mi poesía" conference).
       Available in *Aurora,* no. 1 (July 1954), and *OC,* 4:932.

311   He wrote the poem: Ibid.

311   The poem's division into: De Costa, *Poetry of Pablo Neruda,* 115.

311   "with a series of autobiographic memories": Neruda, "Algo sobre mi
       poesía y mi vida."

312   And from Poem XIII: Hernán Loyola points out Poem XIII in his *Ser*

y morir en Pablo Neruda 1918–1945 (Santiago: Editora Santiago, 1967), 222.

313   "I felt the sense of community": *Triunfo,* November 13, 1971.

314   Neruda strove to tell the history: Author interview with José Corriel, construction engineer for the Santiago Metro, 2003.

314   He sees with their eyes: De Costa, *Poetry of Pablo Neruda,* 124.

315   "How to choose in this case?": Edwards, Magdalena. "A Conversation with Forrest Gander and Raúl Zurita About 'Pinholes in the Night: Essential Poems from Latin America,'" *Los Angeles Review of Books,* February 2, 2014, https://lareviewofbooks.org/interview/conversation-forrest-gander-raul-zurita-pinholes-night-essential-poems-latin-america.

316   "The problem of the future": Pablo Neruda interview by J. M. Cohen, *Network Three,* BBC Third Programme, July 10, 1965.

CHAPTER FIFTEEN: SENATOR NERUDA

317   "The Traitor": "El traidor," *Canto general.*

317   "I am going to Chile": Falcón, "Imagen y espíritu de Pablo Neruda."

318   "Pablo was already fat then": Sáez, *La Hormiga,* 141–142.

319   "to see beyond the usual": Poirot, *Pablo Neruda,* 122.

319   "I never thought about la Hormiga": Author interview with Inés Valenzuela, July 2003.

319   One night, Alberti saw Neruda: Poirot, *Pablo Neruda,* 112.

321   it enabled private entrepreneurs: Collier, Simon, and William F. Sater. *A History of Chile, 1808–1994,* 2nd ed. (Cambridge, UK: Cambridge University Press, 2004), 143–44.

321   a bonanza: Loveman, Brian. *Chile: The Legacy of Hispanic Capitalism,* 3rd ed. (New York: Oxford University Press, 2001), 150.

321   Many would later criticize: Collier and Sater, *History of Chile,* 144.

323   The word *pueblo:* Reid, Alastair. Introduction to *Fully Empowered,* by Pablo Neruda (New York: New Directions, 1995), vii.

324   "I enter her home": As quoted by Neruda in "Viaje al norte de Chile," *OC,* 4:560.

324   On February 24, 1945: "Antofagasta aclama a Neruda en gran acto de proclamación. Hablaron el Senador Lafertte y el Diputado César Godoy U," *El Siglo,* February 26, 1945.

324   "Salute to the North": Never published in a book, the poem was printed in *El Siglo,* February 2, 1945. Available in *OC,* 4:541.

324   Communist Party felt victorious: "Gran triunfo obtuvieron las fuerzas democráticas," *El Siglo,* March 5, 1945.

324   The poem's ability to serve: Author correspondence with María Cristina

Monsalve, PhD candidate in the University of Maryland Department of Spanish and Portuguese, 2017.

324 To raise funds, the campaign: Olivares Briones, *Pablo Neruda: Los caminos de América*, 386.

325 "This triumph over prejudice": Aguirre, *Las vidas de Pablo Neruda*, 218.

325 "In politics, not everything": Arráiz, Antonio. "Tres días con Pablo Neruda. Cartas de un director viajero," *El Nacional* (Caracas), February 8, 1946. Quoted in Schidlowsky, *Las furias y las penas* (2003), 1:577.

325 He found the social and personal: Ibid.

326 "Spoken in Pacaembú (Brazil, 1945)": "Dicho en Pacaembú (Brasil, 1945)," *Canto general*.

327 "The Corpses in the Plaza": "Los muertos de la plaza (28 de enero 1946, Santiago de Chile)," *Canto general*.

327 Neruda once again received a cable: Cable #130, "Cables cambiados con legación en Suiza," vol. 2348, 1945, Ministerio de Relaciones Exteriores de Chile, Archivo General Histórico. Quoted in Schidlowsky, *Las furias y las penas* (2003), 1:562.

327 Neruda responded through the Ministry: Ibid., cable #107.

327 That same day, August 22: Ibid., cable #170.

328 His exaggerated, flamboyant left-wing stance: Collier and Sater, *History of Chile*, 246.

328 "even into soup": Teitelboim, *Neruda: La biografía*, 297.

328 "In the north the copper worker": "El pueblo lo llama Gabriel" ["The People Call Him Gabriel"], *OC*, 4:594.

330 "I had the opportunity to compile": *OC*, 4:653–654.

331 "We thought that it would begin": Teitelboim, *Neruda: La biografía*, 302.

332 on August 22, 1947: Vergara, Angela. *Copper Workers, International Business, and Domestic Politics in Cold War Chile* (University Park: Pennsylvania State University Press, 2008), 71.

332 On October 6, the U.S. ambassador: Loveman, *Chile: The Legacy of Hispanic Capitalism*, 220.

333 "Are the Chilean miners": "Communism in Chile," *New York Times*, October 11, 1947.

334 "Nazi-style concentration camp": Neruda, Pablo. "Carta íntima para millones de hombres," *El Nacional* (Caracas), November 27, 1947. Available in *OC*, 4:697.

334 On the Senate floor on October 21: Aguirre Silva, Leonidas, ed. *Discursos parlamentarios de Pablo Neruda (1945–1948)* (Santiago: Editorial Antártica, 1997), 190.

334 "traitor. A despicable person": Lago, *Ojos y oídos*, 88.

334 "unavoidable duty, in this tragic time": *OC*, 4:681–700.

335   "to strip Senator Neruda": Olivares Briones, *Pablo Neruda: Los caminos de América*, 543.

336   On December 30, he took to: Aguirre Silva, *Discursos parlamentarios*, 233–234.

336   On January 5, the court of appeals: "La corte acordó desafuero de Neruda," *La Hora*, January 6, 1948.

336   He began his historic speech: "Yo accuso," *OC*, 4:704–729.

337   Right after Neruda gave his speech: Lago, *Ojos y oídos*, 90.

338   "give every class of help": Cable #2, vol. 2664, January 20, 1948, Ministerio de Relaciones Exteriores de Chile, Archivo General Histórico. Quoted in Schidlowsky, *Las furias y las penas* (2003), 1:644.

338   Neruda asked the Mexican ambassador: Schidlowsky, *Las furias y las penas* (2003), 1:646.

338   "You don't owe me anything": Aguirre, *Las vidas de Pablo Neruda*, 224.

338   On January 30, young members: "Simbólicamente quemaron a P. Neruda en la Plaza de Armas," *Última hora*, January 31, 1948.

CHAPTER SIXTEEN: THE FLIGHT

341   "The Fugitive: XII": "El fugitivo: XII," *Canto general*. Translated by Jack Hirschman in Neruda, *The Essential Neruda*.

341   "Nationwide Search for Neruda": Olivares Briones, *Pablo Neruda: Los caminos de América*, 608–609.

342   For most of 1948: Varas, José Miguel. *Neruda clandestino* (Santiago: Alfaguara, 2003), 41.

342   One of the homes where the couple stayed: Author interview with Aida Figueroa, July 2003.

343   It was in Aida and Sergio's house: Ibid., 2005.

343   Often, when he was writing: Varas, *Neruda clandestino*, 23.

343   In the afternoons, he would gather: Author interview with Aida Figueroa, July 2003.

343   The living situation at Lola's house: Varas, *Neruda clandestino*, 49–50.

344   "If they get me": Ibid., 85.

345   as the chief of investigations attested: Ibid., 55–56.

345   "Repeat. Repeat.": Lago, *Ojos y oídos*, 116.

345   despite the protests of Delia: Ibid., 115.

346   "As of the evening of Monday": Varas, *Neruda clandestino*, 93.

347   Delia had been told: Sáez, *La Hormiga*, 153.

347   Dr. Bulnes's wife, Lala, urged: Varas, *Neruda clandestino*, 125.

347   "Once Pablo and I": Bizzarro, *Pablo Neruda*, 145.

347   Others, though, have said: Sáez, *La Hormiga*, 153.

347   Some believed Neruda himself: Ibid., 153.

348   "From this moment on": Many of the details of Neruda's flight to San Martín de los Andes are taken from Varas's *Neruda clandestino*, as well as the author's interview with Varas in 2003 and subsequent correspondence. Varas's book includes the personal accounts of both Jorge Bellet and Victor Bianchi (including a facsimile of his journal, featuring hand-drawn maps). Additional information from Bellet's account in "Cruzando la cordillera con el poeta," *Araucaria de Chile*, nos. 47–48 (1990): 186–202 (accessed on memoriachilena.cl). Between Bianchi's, Bellet's, Neruda's, and others' accounts, there are often conflicting details about the adventure. As always, I have tried my best to discern the most valid and indicate when there may be doubt.

349   They stopped only for gas: Varas, *Neruda clandestino*, 145.

349   They took a boat across: Lago, *Ojos y oídos*, 128.

349   "they lit a bonfire": Ibid., 127. Also available in *OC*, 5:978–980.

350   Leoné Mosalvez was fifteen years old: Testimony told to Manuel Basoalto in Varas, *Neruda clandestino*, 153.

350   "You're a man I've": Ibid., 159–160.

351   Neruda carried all the pages: Aguirre, *Genio y figura de Pablo Neruda*, 199.

351   Bianchi claimed that he also: Ibid., 173.

351   volume about the birds of Chile: Pablo Neruda interview by Sun Axelsson, SVT (Swedish TV), Paris, December 1971.

352   "alongside my inscrutable colleagues": "Pablo Neruda—Nobel Lecture: Towards the Splendid City," December 13, 1971, NobelPrize.org, http://www.nobelprize.org/nobel_prizes/literature/laureates/1971/neruda-lecture.html.

353   "the wound set the poet's sentimentalism": Varas, *Neruda clandestino*, 191.

CHAPTER SEVENTEEN: EXILE AND MATILDE

357   "I End Here (1949)": "Aquí termino (1949)," *Canto general*.

357   Pablo Picasso found him: Schidlowsky, *Las furias y las penas* (2008), 2:780.

358   "to unite all the active forces": World Peace Congress. *World Peace Congress leaflet*, 1949, W. E. B. Du Bois Papers (MS 312), Special Collections and University Archives, University of Massachusetts Amherst Libraries. Available at http://credo.library.umass.edu/view/full/mums 312-b126-i237.

358   Du Bois noted the diversity: Du Bois, W. E. B. "The World Peace Congress and Colored Peoples," 1949, W. E. B. Du Bois Papers (MS 312),

Special Collections and University Archives, University of Massachusetts Amherst Libraries. Available at http://credo.library.umass.edu /view/full/mums312-b159-i430.

359   "due to the difficulties I had": Sanhueza, Jorge. "Neruda 1949," *Anales de la Universidad de Chile*, nos. 157–160 (January–December 1971): 198.

359   "Neruda was like the conscience": Fast, Howard. "Neruda en el Congreso Mundial para La Paz," *Pro arte*, June 9, 1949. Quoted in Sanhueza, "Neruda 1949."

359   "a hundred people were asking him": Ibid.

359   "Paul Robeson, a Negro and a Communist": *Report on the Communist "Peace" Offensive: A Campaign to Disarm and Defeat the United States*, prepared by the Committee on Un-American Activities, U.S. House of Representatives, Washington, D.C., April 1, 1951. Available at https:// archive.org/details/reportoncommunis00unit.

361   "efforts are being made": Airgram sent from C. Burke Elbrick, counselor of U.S. embassy in Cuba, to secretary of state (Dean Acheson), August 26, 1949, from the National Archives' General Records of the Department of State 1945–1949, file document 825.00B/8-2449, provided to author by the Textual Records Division of the National Archives in College Park, MD.

362   "None of those pages had": *OC*, 4:764.

362   "If hyenas could type": *OC*, 4:765.

362   words that brought the Eastern Bloc: Crossley, Robert. *Olaf Stapledon: Speaking for the Future* (Syracuse, NY: Syracuse University Press, 1994), 359.

363   "erotic obsessions": Quote is by Roger Garaudy, as seen in, among others, Caute, David. *The Dancer Defects: The Struggle for Cultural Supremacy During the Cold War* (Oxford, UK; New York: Oxford University Press, 2003), 310.

363   "Is that fair": Caute, David. *The Fellow-Travellers: Intellectual Friends of Communism* (New Haven, CT: Yale University Press, 1988), 315.

363   Neruda seemed sincere: Sanhueza, "Neruda 1949," 204.

363   "In the throes of death": *OC*, 4:765.

363   "when Fadeyev said in his Wrocław speech": *OC*, 4:765.

364   "Walt Whitman once wrote": Neruda, *Let the Rail Splitter Awake and Other Poems* (New York: Masses & Mainstream, Inc., 1950), 5.

365   However, as Jorge Sanhueza: Sanhueza, "Neruda 1949," 205.

365   Elsewhere, within a decade: Ibid., 206.

366   According to Volodia Teitelboim: Teitelboim, *Neruda: La biografía*, 297–298.

366   "Let the Rail-Splitter Awake": Neruda, *Let the Rail Splitter Awake*, 39.

367 in the end they extended their trip: Neruda, Pablo. *Cartas de amor: Cartas a Matilde Urrutia (1950–1973)*, ed. Darío Oses (Barcelona: Seix Barral, 2010).

367 Neruda was aroused by Matilde: Author interview with the writer Francisco Velasco, 2008.

368 "Women follow in Pablo's": Sáez, *La Hormiga*, 145.

368 He wasn't a great seducer: Author interview with Inés Valenzuela, July 2003.

368 If Delia suspected: Sáez, *La Hormiga*, 156.

369 according to an account: Sanhueza, "Neruda 1949," 207.

369 guests were given: Olivares Briones, *Pablo Neruda: Los caminos de América*, 737–742.

369 "has no illusions about Neruda": Schidlowsky, *Las furias y las penas* (2008), 2:809–810.

369 "This book is agitating me": Olivares Briones, *Pablo Neruda: Los caminos de América*, 749–750.

370 "As he still can't go down the stairs": Reyes, *Neruda: Retrato de familia*, 152.

370 "Right now his bed": Olivares Briones, *Pablo Neruda: Los caminos de América*, 747.

371 it served as a monument: Herrera, Hayden. *Frida: A Biography of Frida Kahlo* (1983; New York: HarperCollins, 1984), 312.

371 return "to the people": Suckaer, Ingrid. "Diego Rivera: Biografía," Museo Anahuacalli, http://www.museoanahuacalli.org.mx/diego rivera/index.html.

371 Rivera had influenced Neruda's interest: Felstiner, *Translating Neruda*, 186. Felstiner also astutely points out the influence of José Uriel García, the historian who took Neruda to Machu Picchu, in inspiring his interest in indigenous people and history.

371 "I've been so absorbed": Olivares Briones, *Pablo Neruda: Los caminos de América*, 751.

372 "I live, I still live": Author interview with Ariel Dorfman, 2004.

372 José Corriel, a construction engineer: Author interview with José Corriel, 2003.

372 *Canto general*—a title: González Echevarría, Roberto. Introduction to *Canto general*, by Pablo Neruda (Berkeley: University of California Press, 1991), 6.

374 This optimism, though, is dependent: Mascia, Mark J. "Pablo Neruda and the Construction of Past and Future Utopias in the *Canto general*," *Utopian Studies* 12, no. 2 (2001): 65–81. Available at http://digitalcom mons.sacredheart.edu/lang_fac/4.

375 "covering the streets": CHV, 565.

375 This directly inspired Neruda's vision: Author interview with John Felstiner, 2001, and Felstiner, *Translating Neruda*, 129.

377   Higher-quality editions: Author interview with Inés Valenzuela, July 2003. Inés helped in the distribution of the clandestine copy.

377   It's a call for the spirit: *Triunfo*, November 13, 1973.

379   "It struck me like a bomb": Author interview with Jack Hirschman, 2010.

380   Yet as he says in the poem: Cardona Peña, *Pablo Neruda y otros ensayos*, 36–37.

380   "I had two immense sources of happiness": Ibid., 37.

380   However, all this satisfaction: Ibid., 38, and Salerno, "Alone y Neruda," 324.

380   He was impressed by the poems: Alone. "Neruda," *El Mercurio*, September 7, 1947. Quoted ibid., 324–327.

380   Neruda was struck by: Cardona Peña, *Pablo Neruda y otros ensayos*, 40–41.

381   the two spent time in Prague: Hernán Loyola lists the stops in *OC*, 1:1223–1224.

381   With the help of his friends: Details of how Neruda worked with party leaders, friends, artists, etc., in different countries to schedule speaking engagements and prizes to help facilitate his being with Matilde in *OC*, 1:1224.

CHAPTER EIGHTEEN: MATILDE AND STALIN

383   "The Mountain and the River": "El monte y el río," *The Captain's Verses*.

383   "tax inspectors or people": Varas, José Miguel. "Neruda en exilio," *Mapocho* 34 (1993): 93–94.

384   "if this Chilean girl comes": Varas, José Miguel. *Nerudario* (Santiago: Planeta, 1999), 122.

384   Neruda and Delia had rented: Varas, "Neruda en exilio," 94.

385   At this point, all governments: Ibid.

385   a former Spanish Republican general: Gattai, Zélia. *Senhora Dona do Baile* (Rio de Janeiro: Ed. Record, 1985), 112–114. Quoted in Schidlowsky, *Las furias y las penas* (2008), 2:826–827.

386   "Our angel or devil": Neruda, *Cartas de amor: Cartas a Matilde Urrutia*, 26.

386   "generous and full of youthful happiness": Toledo, Manuel. "Aída Figueroa: Pablo fue un gran ejemplo," BBC Mundo, July 10, 2004, http://news.bbc.co.uk/hi/spanish/specials/2004/cien_anos_de_neruda/newsid_3868000/3868781.stm.

386   And Matilde was as Neruda hoped: Ibid.

386   Matilde was simple: Ibid.

387   He sent Matilde a welcoming telegram: Urrutia, Matilde. *My Life with Pablo Neruda*, trans. Alexandria Giardino (Stanford, CA: Stanford University Press, 2004), 44.

387   At the festival, Neruda spoke: Neruda, Pablo. "¡Hacia Berlin!" *Democracia*, August 29, 1951. Available in *OC*, 4:819.

387   "I was radiant": Urrutia, *My Life with Pablo Neruda*, 45–46.

387   This was the first of many lies: Author interview with Aida Figueroa, July 2003.

387   "You have the smell of tenderness": Urrutia, *My Life with Pablo Neruda*, 47.

388   "Always": "Siempre," *The Captain's Verses*.

389   "The Potter": "El afarero," translated by the author in Neruda, *The Essential Neruda*.

389   But the next poem in the letter: Urrutia, *My Life with Pablo Neruda*, 56.

390   "As I read those words": Ibid.

390   Ivette Joie: Friend is named in Cirillo Sarri, Teresa. *Neruda a Capri: Sogno di un'isola* (Capri: Edizioni La Conchiglia, 2001), 97.

391   "You are from the poor South": Sonnet XXIX, *One Hundred Love Sonnets*.

392   She had thought she could: Urrutia, *My Life with Pablo Neruda*, 89.

393   "I stood there like a frightened chick": Ibid., 95–96.

393   The couple was able to relax: Ibid., 104.

394   The woman he addresses: Some of this from Foster, David W., and Daniel Altamiranda, eds. *Twentieth-Century Spanish American Literature to 1960* (New York: Garland, 1997), 246.

394   In Neruda's poem "Letter on the Road": Loyola points out the location of its composition in *OC*, 1:1219.

394   "And when the sadness": "La carta en el camino" ["Letter on the Road"], *The Captain's Verses*.

395   "Neruda Urrutia": Urrutia, *My Life with Pablo Neruda*, 111.

396   when Neruda came back: Ibid., 104.

396   "In a few days when the moon": Ibid., 107–108.

397   Matilde started to feel sick: Ibid., 121.

397   "a shadow descended": Urrutia, Matilde. *Mi vida junto a Pablo Neruda* (Barcelona: Seix Barral, 1986), 113.

397   She lost her child: Urrutia, *My Life with Pablo Neruda*, 128.

397   "I'm going to give you a child": Ibid., 129.

397   an attempt to dazzle the reader: De Costa, *Poetry of Pablo Neruda*, 144.

397   constructed himself as: Cáracamo-Huechante, Luis E. "Of Commitments and Compromises: Neruda's Relationship with Ocampo and the Journal *Sur* in the Cold-War Period," *Revista Hispánica Moderna* 60, no. 1 (2007): 3, http://www.jstor.org/stable/40647351.

398   Neruda was one of the most active: Dawes, Greg. *Verses Against the Darkness: Pablo Neruda's Poetry and Politics* (Lewisburg, PA: Bucknell University Press, 2006), 281.

398 Picasso took it off: Varas, "Neruda en exilio," 97.

398 "I've been thrown out": Rodríguez Monegal, Emir. *Neruda: El viajero inmóvil* (Barcelona: Editorial Laia, 1988), 122.

398 "The future of humanity": "Palabras a Chile (Mensaje de Pablo Neruda en viaje a su patria)," *Democracia,* August 9, 1952. Available in *OC,* 4:837–838.

399 "I salute the noble people": Franulic, Lenka. "Neruda, regreso del exilio, 1952," *Ercilla,* 1952. Available in *Cuadernos* (Fundación Pablo Neruda), no. 31 (1997): 5.

399 two policemen stood outside: Franulic, "Neruda, regreso del exilio, 1952," 6.

399 "I will offer my support": Ibid.

400 "The poet isn't a lost stone": "El canto y la acción del poeta deben contribuir a la madurez y al crecimiento de su pueblo," *El Siglo,* June 21, 1954. Quoted in Schidlowsky, *Las furias y las penas* (2003), 2:805.

400 "¡Neruda! ¡Neruda!": Lago, *Ojos y oídos,* 162.

400 The Allende command: Quezada Vergara, Abraham. *Pablo Neruda y Salvador Allende: Una amistad, una historia* (Santiago: RIL Editores, 2014), 64.

401 He usually started around nine: Teitelboim, Volodia. *Voy a vivirme: Variaciones y complementos Nerudianos* (Santiago: Dolmen Ediciones, 1998), 16–17.

401 He always wrote in green ink: Author interview with Darío Oses, head of the archives and library at the Pablo Neruda Foundation, April 2015.

401 "Ever since I had an accident": Guibert, "Pablo Neruda," 59.

402 As Aida Figueroa put it: Author interview with Aida Figueroa, July 2003.

402 Inés Valenzuela commented on: Author interview with Inés Valenzuela, 2008.

402 "He made everything magical": Author interview with Aida Figueroa, July 2003.

403 "I'm not superior": "El hombre invisible," *Elemental Odes.* Translated by the author, borrowing from Stephen Kessler's translation in Neruda, *The Essential Neruda.*

403 "I've said that my first poetry": Franulic, "Neruda, regreso del exilio, 1952," 13.

404 From now on, his poetry will be: Thoughts in this paragraph are drawn from Dawes, *Verses Against the Darkness,* 100–102.

405 "The people give me my poetry": Schidlowsky, *Las furias y las penas* (2008), 2:1016.

405 "On our earth": From a speech given to the Continental Cultural Congress, Teatro Caupolicán, Santiago, May 26, 1953. Available in *OC,* 4:894.

406 his approach in the odes was experimental: Dawes notes this as well, using the words "spontaneity" and "innovation" to describe his style (*Verses Against the Darkness*, 78).

406 The poems Neruda wrote for the newspaper: Author interview with Federico Schopf, 2003.

406 Neruda's thoughtful, conceptual associations: De Costa, *Poetry of Pablo Neruda*, 147.

406 Jaime Concha, professor emeritus: Concha, Jaime. *Neruda, desde 1952: "No entendí nunca la lucha sino para que ésta termine,"* Actas del Coloquio Internacional sobre Pablo Neruda (*La obra posterior a* Canto general) (Poitiers, France: Publications du Centre de Recherche Latino-Américaines de l'Université de Poitiers, 1979), 61.

407 matrix of social relations: As described by Dawes, *Verses Against the Darkness*, 94.

407 The odes are organized alphabetically: Author interview with Federico Schopf, 2003.

408 "Some say this clarity": Alone. "Muerte y transfiguración de Pablo Neruda," *El Mercurio*, January 30, 1955. Quoted in de Costa, *Poetry of Pablo Neruda*, 147.

408 recognize their implicit virtue: Hass, *Little Book on Form*, 225.

409 "Ode to Wine": "Oda al vino," *Elemental Odes*. Translated by the author in Neruda, *The Essential Neruda*.

411 "On His Death": "En su muerte," *Las uvas y el viento* [The Grapes and the Wind].

412 Despite its strict belief: Much of this material drawn from author interview with Ariel Dorfman, 2004.

412 Had Neruda been a U.S. or French citizen: Ibid.

413 "The Man Who Ran Away": Milosz says Neruda called him "an agent of American imperialism" in his author's note to a translation of Neruda's "Three Material Songs," in the Warsaw journal *Zeszyty Literackie*, no. 64 (Fall 1998): 33–34.

413 "Anyone who was dissatisfied": Faggen, Robert. "Czeslaw Milosz, the Art of Poetry No. 70," *Paris Review*, Winter 1994.

413 "When he describes the misery": Milosz, Czeslaw. *The Captive Mind* (New York: Knopf, 1953), 234.

414 "But, Czeslaw, that was politics": Recounted to the author by Robert Hass, a colleague of Milosz's at the University of California, Berkeley, and a translator of his poetry; later confirmed in author correspondence with Renata Gorzynska, a writer and, at one point, Milosz's assistant, 2015.

414 "I don't know how": Teitelboim, *Neruda: La biografía*, 369.

414 Matilde was upset that Neruda: Sáez, *La Hormiga*, 161.

415 "What am I going to do": Urrutia, *My Life with Pablo Neruda*, 170–171.

415 "this is how it is": Ibid.

415 Matilde could buy the land: Author correspondence with Alexandria Giardino, who translated Urrutia's *My Life with Pablo Neruda*, 2012.

415 "He spoiled me to the extreme": Urrutia, *My Life with Pablo Neruda*, 174.

415 "I am very moved": "Premio a Neruda honra a Chile," *El Siglo*, December 22, 1953. Quoted in Schidlowsky, *Las furias y las penas* (2008), 2:894.

416 "When I saw that woman there": Lago, *Ojos y oídos*, 175.

416 Matilde was seen: Sáez, *La Hormiga*, 162.

416 "the girls revolved around the stars": Teitelboim, *Neruda: La biografía*, 368.

416 Neruda moved closer to: Sáez, *La Hormiga*, 163.

417 "She came dressed in white": Lago, *Ojos y oídos*, 186.

417 "At one point, the two of us": Ibid., 195.

418 "The truth of the matter": Author interview with Inés Valenzuela, July 2003.

418 Neruda sent her a telegram: Ibid.

418 "Since 1952": Bizzarro, *Pablo Neruda*, 146.

419 he asked them both to be witnesses: Sáez, *La Hormiga*, 168.

419 "Look, this is Matilde": Author interview with Inés Valenzuela, July 2003.

420 "Delia is the light": "Amores: Delia (I)," *Memorial de Isla Negra*, in Neruda, *Isla Negra*.

CHAPTER NINETEEN: FULLY EMPOWERED

421 "Fully Empowered": "Plenos poderes," in Neruda, *Fully Empowered*.

422 "Sometimes I'm a poet of nature": Author interview with Alastair Reid, 2004.

422 "a shelf of remarkable books": From Alastair Reid's introduction to his and Mary Heebner's *A la orilla azul del silencio: Poemas del mar / On the Blue Shore of Silence: Poems of the Sea* (New York: Rayo, 2003), xiii.

422 He used to say that he had: From Reid, Alastair. "Neruda and Borges," *New Yorker,* June 24, 1996.

423 "To me, the sea is an element": Pablo Neruda interview by Sun Axelsson, SVT (Swedish TV), Paris, December 1971.

424 "The Sea": "El mar," *Fully Empowered*. Translated by the author in Neruda, *The Essential Neruda*.

424 Each house was like a private stage: Ibid.

424 "The house grows and speaks": "A la Sebastiana," *Fully Empowered*.

425 As a mover hung up: Among other sources, quoted in "La Sebastiana," Fundación Pablo Neruda, https://fundacionneruda.org/museos/casa-museo-la-sebastiana/.

425 "comprises both extravagance": Gierow, Karl Ragnar. Award ceremony speech, 1971, NobelPrize.org, http://www.nobelprize.org/nobel_prizes/literature/laureates/1971/press.html.

425 Influenced by his compatriot: De Costa, *Poetry of Pablo Neruda*, 180–181.

426 "Keeping Quiet": "A callarse," *Estravagario*. Translated by Alastair Reid.

426 His favorite translator: Reid, "Neruda and Borges." *Estravagario* and "Macchu Picchu" as favorite books from author interview with Francisco Velasco, 2008.

427 The day after the rally: *CHV*, 756–757.

428 "Neruda sitting in plush suite": In Ferlinghetti, Lawrence. *Writing Across the Landscape: Travel Journals 1960–2010*, ed. Giada Diano and Matthew Gleeson (New York: Liveright, 2015), 42.

429 "still in their combat boots": Author interview with Lawrence Ferlinghetti, 2010.

429 "Those aren't hours": Edwards, *Adiós, poeta*, 146.

430 "I think about how my verses": *CHV*, 758.

430 Neruda would tell a distressed Aida: Author interview with Aida Figueroa, 2003.

430 "There is hunger": "Dijo Pablo Neruda en su conferencia de prensa: 'Las revoluciones no son exportables; Chile eligió ya su ruta de liberación,'" *El Siglo*, January 12, 1961.

431 Neruda himself didn't take the book seriously: Alastair Reid, who passed on the opportunity to translate it, attested to this in conversation with the author.

431 Sonnet XVII: Neruda, *The Essential Neruda*.

432 "lasting silence / beneath the Antarctic": The name of the poem is "The Stones of Chile," same as the book's title.

432 "monetary advance": Letter dated June 26, 1963, APNF.

432 "To whoever is not listening": "The Poet's Obligation," *Fully Empowered*.

434 "I think that China's errors": Speech quoted in *El Siglo*, November 30, 1963. Available in *OC*, 4:1165–1166.

434 "The Episode": "El medio," *Memorial de Isla Negra*, in Neruda, *Isla Negra*.

435 Alastair Reid wrote that the Spanish: Reid, Alastair. Translator's note to Neruda, *Isla Negra*, xvii.

435 Still, Neruda seems to draw: McInnis, Judy B. "Pablo Neruda: Inventing 'El mar de cada día,'" paper presentation, Latin American Studies As-

sociation, Guadalajara, Mexico, April 19, 1997. Available at http://lasa
.international.pitt.edu/LASA97/mcinnis.pdf (p. 9).

435 "formal petition; memorial": Ramondino, Salvatore, ed. *The New World Spanish-English and English-Spanish Dictionary,* 2nd ed. (New York: Signet, 1996), 307.

435 Neruda used a future-oriented word: McInnis, "Pablo Neruda: Inventing 'El mar de cada día,'" 10.

435 Both were asked by the Hungarian government: *OC,* 5:1387.

436 "to promote friendship": "The PEN World," PEN America, https://pen .org/the-pen-world/.

436 "private conversations with Washington": APNF.

437 Decades later Miller told a biographer: Feinstein, *Pablo Neruda,* 342–343.

437 "marred this country's image": Cohn, Deborah. *The Latin American Literary Boom and U.S. Nationalism During the Cold War* (Nashville, TN: Vanderbilt University Press, 2012), 53–54.

437 "It is my privilege": Recording of the evening is online courtesy of 92Y, "Pablo Neruda's First Reading in the U.S.," 92nd Street Y, New York, June 11, 1966, https://soundcloud.com/92y/pablo-neruda-1966.

437 "deeply moved": Author correspondence with Charles Simic, 2007.

437 "who had at any time been associated": Cohn, *Latin American Literary Boom,* 54.

438 The PEN Club had received money: Taubman, Howard. "Writers in Isolation: Latin Americans Face Communications Barrier—A Case in Point: Pablo Neruda," *New York Times,* July 4, 1966.

438 They held a mini-congress: "Denunció Neruda en el congreso del 'PEN' Club: '70 millones de analfabetos en América Latina,'" *El Siglo,* June 18, 1966.

438 "They sent a messenger": Vial, *Neruda vuelve a Valparaíso,* 252.

438 he seemed to disparage: Teitelboim, *Neruda: La biografía,* 173.

439 "communist provocation": "Coming to Fruition After Forty Years," Web Stories, Inter-American Development Bank, June 9, 2006, http:// www.iadb.org/en/news/webstories/2006-06-09/coming-to-fruition -after-forty-years,3117.html?actionuserstats=close&valcookie=&isaja xrequest=.

439 "learned on the spot": *CHV,* 761.

439 "jovial and very pleasant": Author interview with Georgette Dorn, March 30, 2016.

440 "spontaneous roar": Alegría, Fernando. "Talking to Neruda," *Berkeley Barb,* July 1966.

440 "Every once in a while, a few words": Letter dated June 20, 1966, APNF.

441   "We believe it is our duty": Geyer, Georgie Anne. "Cuba Has a New Gripe," *Washington Post*, August 14, 1966.

441   "Dear *compañeros:* I am": *OC*, 5:102–103.

CHAPTER TWENTY: TRIUMPH, DESTRUCTION, DEATH

443   "Right, comrade, it's the hour of the garden": From *El mar y las campanas* (*The Sea and the Bells*), published posthumously. Neruda did not title most of the poems in the book. In their absence, Matilde bracketed the first line of each poem for reference in the table of contents. This translation is by Forrest Gander in Neruda, *The Essential Neruda*.

443   "Confidential: We are getting married": APNF.

443   On a beautiful spring day: Teitelboim, *Neruda: La biografía,* 425.

444   "The Pacific Ocean overflowed the map": "El mar" ["The Sea"]. *A House in the Sand.*

444   On October 14, 1967, Neruda's play: "Anti-U.S. Play by Neruda, Chilean Poet, Opens," *New York Times,* October 16, 1967.

445   "two hours of drama": Ibid.

445   "One generalization that I": Letter dated November 2, 1967, APNF.

446   "because the same wild racism": Neruda, Pablo. "Un 'bandido' chileno," (1966) *Para nacer he nacido* (Barcelona: Seix Barral, 1985), 102.

446   "I've achieved a lucid translation": APNF.

446   Rodrigo Rojas points out: Author interview with Rodrigo Rojas, April and June 2015.

447   "Thus forgive me for the sadness": "El que cantó cantará" ["He Who Sung Will Sing"], *The Hands of the Day.*

448   "Forgive me, if when I want": "XI," *Aún.*

449   "Books and authors were discussed": Edwards, *Adiós, poeta,* 183.

450   "I am a friend of Czechoslovakia": "Invasão da Tchecoslováquia féz sofrer o poeta Neruda," *O Globo* (Rio de Janeiro), September 11, 1968. Available in Schidlowsky, *Las furias y las penas* (2008), 2:1218.

450   "The hour of Prague fell": Neruda, Pablo. "1968," *World's End,* trans. William O'Daly (Port Townsend, WA: Copper Canyon Press, 2009).

450   "I was unaware": "The Worship (II)," *World's End.*

451   "When we made that trip": Author interview with Aida Figueroa, 2005.

451   "Death of a Journalist": "Muerte de un periodista," *World's End.*

452   "There was disagreement": Author interview with Sergio Insunza, July 2003.

453   His friends saw Neruda quickly: Edwards, *Adiós, poeta,* 201.

453   *"¡Neruda, Neruda, Barrancas te saluda!"*: "'Neruda, Neruda, Barrancas te saluda,' gritan las cuatro marchas," *El Siglo,* October 10, 1969.

455   "No one was seeking absolute": Edwards, *Adiós, poeta,* 206.

455   Levine—on this first: Author conversation with Suzanne Jill Levine, 2015.

456   "I cannot really consider": Stitt, Peter A. "Stephen Spender, the Art of Poetry No. 25," *Paris Review,* Winter–Spring 1980.

456   "Listen, dammit, you know": Author interview with Francisco Velasco, 2008.

456   "if Allende should win": As said in Nixon's fourth interview with David Frost: "An Italian businessman came to call on me in the Oval Office, and, ah, he said, 'If Allende should win the election in Chile, and then you have Castro in Cuba, what you will in effect have in Latin America is a red sandwich, and eventually it will all be red.' And that's what we confronted."

457   In fact, in the run-up: U.S. Senate Select Committee to Study Governmental Operations with Respect to Intelligence Activities (Church Committee), S. Rep. No. 94-755 (1976).

457   President Johnson's administration moved to support: Church Committee, *Covert Action in Chile, 1963–1973,* 10. Available at U.S. National Archives, https://www.archives.gov/declassification/iscap/pdf/2010-009-doc17.pdf.

457   Though Chile faced few: Kornbluh, Peter. *The Pinochet File: A Declassified Dossier on Atrocity and Accountability* (New York: The New Press, 2003), 5–6.

457   It also now appears: Reid, Michael. *Forgotten Continent: The Battle for Latin America's Soul* (New Haven, CT: Yale University Press, 2007), 112.

457   "tangible economic losses": Kornbluh, *Pinochet File,* 6.

458   Following Allende's victory: Ibid., 1.

458   Helms cabled Kissinger: Ibid., 17.

458   ITT had holdings: Ibid., 18.

458   U.S. interests also schemed: Loveman, *Chile,* 248.

458   As the Church Committee report: Church Committee, *Covert Action in Chile,* 5.

458   The CIA funneled weapons: Ibid.

459   U.S. ambassador Edward Korry: Kornbluh, *Pinochet File,* 8.

459   The old orthodoxy: Most thoughts in this paragraph come from author discussion with Ariel Dorfman, 2004.

459   In a phone call: Kornbluh, *Pinochet File,* 99, as well as interview and discussion on *Democracy Now!* September 10, 2013.

460   After Allende's inauguration: Steenland, Kyle. "Two Years of 'Popu-

lar Unity' in Chile: A Balance Sheet," *New Left Review,* no. 78 (March–April 1973): 3–25.

460   The CIA, as confirmed: Church Committee, *Covert Action in Chile,* 2.

461   "foot-drag to maximum possible": Kornbluh, *Pinochet File,* 7–18.

461   "He wasn't optimistic": Edwards, *Adiós, poeta,* 210–211.

462   The writer Jay Parini: Author correspondence with Jay Parini, June 3, 2016, and from "The Home of Pablo Neruda," *Commentary Series,* Vermont Public Radio, November 13, 2007, http://vprarchive.vpr.net/commentary-series/the-home-of-pablo-neruda/.

462   "sense comes first": From a recording of the evening.

463   "one last senile love": Author interview with Aida Figueroa, July 2003.

463   While in London, Parini had dinner: Author correspondence with Jay Parini, June 3, 2016.

464   One day when Alicia had: Author interview with Francisco Velasco, 2008.

464   "I'll tell you that your friend": Teitelboim, *Neruda: La biografía,* 449. When Matilde says that Neruda is "sick," she is presumably referring to his prostate cancer, which he already had before he met Alicia; she's not saying that Alicia was the one who made him "sick down there."

464   "There is a part of the night": Ibid., 453.

464   Despite his departure for Paris: Edwards, *Adiós, poeta,* 296. Edwards doesn't mention Alicia by name, just that Neruda had fallen in love with a "considerably younger woman" right before he left for France.

CHAPTER TWENTY-ONE: THE FLOWERS THAT SLEEP

465   "Autumn": "Otoño," *Winter Garden.* The autumn the title is referring to is the autumn of April–June 1973; the tensions would break that September.

465   "My country is experiencing": Neruda interview by Axelsson, SVT.

465   As soon as they arrived in Paris: Velasco, Francisco. *Neruda: El gran amigo* (Santiago: Galinost-Andante, 1987), 121.

466   "Everything is the same": Teitelboim, *Neruda: La biografía,* 455–456.

467   "The poet is not a 'little god'": "Pablo Neruda—Nobel Lecture."

468   "hissed, laughed": Raymont, Henry. "Neruda Opens Visit Here with a Plea for Chile's Revolution," *New York Times,* April 11, 1972.

469   "return to the concerns": *OC,* 5:357–362.

469   "there [were] already ashes": Alegría, Fernando. "Neruda: Reminiscences and Critical Reflections," trans. Deborah S. Bundy, *Modern Poetry Studies* 5, no. 1 (1974): 44. Last line truncated from Bundy's translation to just "did" instead of "did know."

469 "We are sick ones": Velasco, *Neruda: El gran amigo*, 122.

470 The poet gave him: Edwards, *Adiós, poeta*, 252.

470 "I realized he was very bad": Velasco, *Neruda: El gran amigo*, 123.

470 the truckers blamed: Sigmund, Paul E. *The Overthrow of Allende and the Politics of Chile, 1964–1976* (Pittsburgh: University of Pittsburgh Press, 1977), 184.

471 one hundred thousand campesinos: Ibid., 185.

471 a letter thanking the poet: Letter dated November 16, 1972, APNF.

472 "carrying on his perpetual dialogue": Quoted in Poirot, *Pablo Neruda*, 124.

472 "bring back phenindione": Neruda, *Cartas de amor: Cartas a Matilde Urrutia*, 238.

472 In her absence, when he went: From 2012 testimony by Alicia Urrutia to Judge Mario Carroza after being summoned to answer questions about Neruda's health during the investigation of Neruda's death. Quoted in Montes, Rocío. "El último amor de Neruda: La voz de Alicia," *Caras*, December 29, 2014, http://www.caras.cl/libros/el-ultimo-amor-de-neruda-la-voz-de-alicia/.

473 Alicia was struck: Ibid.

473 Dr. Velasco remembers: Velasco, *Neruda: El gran amigo*, 124–125.

473 "The era of those classical names": Letter dated February 27, 1973, APNF.

474 "I've never been given": Letter dated March 14, 1973; copy provided to the author by Turner.

474 "Unfortunately, I must seriously protest": Letter dated August 8, 1973, APNF.

475 "The whole cultural movement": Jara, Joan. *Victor: An Unfinished Song* (New York: Ticknor & Fields, 1984), 211–212.

476 On August 31, 1973, Neruda wrote: APNF and *OC*, 5:1020.

476 "I send my best wishes": Letter dated September 4, 1973, APNF.

478 Allende shot himself: There has been controversy over the circumstances of Allende's death ever since it happened. Despite some circumstantial accounts, many insisted he would never have killed himself, but rather that he went down fighting and was shot by the military storming the building. But in 2011, the Chilean justice system investigated Allende's death, one of more than seven hundred criminal inquiries into the deaths and disappearances that took place during the dictatorship. An international forensics team conducted an autopsy. With the help of ballistics experts, the unanimous conclusion was that he had indeed shot himself. Among various sources: López, Andrés, and Javier Canales. "Informe del Servicio Médico Legal confirma

la tesis del suicidio de ex presidente Allende," *La Tercera* (Santiago), July 19, 2011, http://www.latercera.com/noticia/informe-del-servi cio-medico-legal-confirma-la-tesis-del-suicidio-de-ex-presidente -allende/.

478 "quiet; mild-mannered": Kornbluh, *Pinochet File*, 155.

478 Yet by late October, a fact sheet: Ibid., 154.

478 Instead, he seemed broken: Urrutia, *Mi vida junto a Pablo Neruda*, 7–9

479 "Look all you want": Edwards, *Adiós, poeta*, 303–304.

479 As Arévalo recalled the visit: Author interview with Hugo Arévalo, July 2003.

480 Neruda in a state of madness: Matilde's recounting is from an interview she gave in Bizzarro, *Pablo Neruda*, 155–156.

480 As Matilde wrote in her memoir: Urrutia, *My Life with Pablo Neruda*, 15–16.

480 Homero Arce asked Inés: Author interview with Inés Valenzuela, 2008.

481 "We knew what we could do": Ibid.

481 "We were afraid": Author interview with Roser Bru, 2003.

EPILOGUE

483 "coalesce in the realm of paradox": O'Daly, William. Introduction to *The Book of Questions,* by Pablo Neruda (Port Townsend, WA: Copper Canyon Press, 2001), vii.

484 "Returning": "Regresando," in Neruda, Pablo. *The Sea and the Bells*, trans. William O'Daly (Port Townsend, WA: Copper Canyon Press, 2002).

484 "Winter Garden": "Jardín de invierno," in Neruda, Pablo. *Winter Garden*, trans. William O'Daly (Port Townsend, WA: Copper Canyon Press, 2002).

487 "When I went back to Chile": Author interview with Ariel Dorfman, 2004.

488 He said the Catholic Church: Suro, Robert. "Pope, on Latin Trip, Attacks Pinochet Regime," *New York Times,* April 1, 1987.

488 The pope reportedly advised: O'Connor, Garry. *Universal Father: A Life of Pope John Paul II* (New York: Bloomsbury, 2005).

488 Under his dictatorship: Here using much of Peter Kornbluh's phrasing for the reporting of the numbers, which came from *The Report of the Chilean National Commission on Truth and Reconciliation* (*Pinochet File,* 154).

488 Their vast grassroots: National Democratic Institute for International Affairs, *Chile's Transition to Democracy: The 1988 Presidential Plebiscite*, Washington, D.C., 1988; and Kornbluh, *Pinochet File*.

489   "there was a sense": Author interview with Rodrigo Rojas, November 21, 2015.

489   The CIA, for instance: Kornbluh, *Pinochet File*, 431–432.

490   "*Compañeros,* bury me at Isla Negra": "Disposiciones" ["Dispositions"], *Canto general.*

491   "the victory of poetry": *Boletín de la Fundación Pablo Neruda,* no. 15 (Summer 1993): 23.

491   "It was very moving": Author interview with Francisco Velasco, 2008.

492   "Neruda was feverish": Matilde mentions none of this in her memoir, just that Neruda had called her at Isla Negra because he had finally learned about the realities of the coup through his friends and was in a completely agitated state.

492   That injection: There was an injection that day, which Neruda's doctor said was Dipirona, and the forensic examinations showed there had been Dipirona in Neruda's system. As explained by the Mexican journalist Mario Casasús—who at first was one of the main proponents of the allegations but has come to doubt Araya— in 1974 Matilde told a newspaper that the injection was Dolopirona. There are some differences between Dipirona and Dolopirona, and if Neruda needed Dolopirona and they gave him Dipirona, then that could cause an allergic reaction, but it wouldn't kill him. Also, according to Casasús, the medicine given to Neruda was something that the hospital already had on hand (author correspondence with Mario Casasús, February 1, 2017).

492   "evil ordered by": Note that Araya never actually saw the injection take place. Unless otherwise indicated, Araya's testimony is from an interview by Francisco Marín, published in "Neruda fue asesinado," *Proceso* (Mexico), May 12, 2011, http://www.proceso.com .mx/269909/269909-neruda-fue-asesinado.

492   it wasn't until 2004: Confirmed in Witt, Emily. "The Body Politic: The Battle Over Pablo Neruda's Corpse," *Harper's,* January 2015.

493   the regime did not begin: Taylor Branch and Eugene M. Propper wrote about the sarin attacks (Project Andrea) taking place in 1976 in their coauthored *Labyrinth: The Sensational Story of International Intrigue in the Search for the Assassins of Orlando Letelier* (New York: Viking, 1982). Actual supporting documents are found in Kornbluh, *Pinochet File,* 178–179, 201. Further insight was provided through author interview and correspondence with John Dinges, former *Washington Post* foreign news editor and author of *The Condor Years,* among other books on Pinochet, January 2017.

493   the press and others ran with it: Wills, Santiago. "Pablo Neruda May

Have Been Killed by a CIA Double Agent," ABC News, June 6, 2013, http://abcnews.go.com/ABC_Univision/pablo-neruda-killed-cia -double-agent/story?id=19332813. Through previous research on Townley for his role in a 1976 assassination (ordered by the Pinochet regime and carried out in Washington, D.C.), John Dinges, along with fellow coinvestigators, has a paper trail—including all of Town-ley's passports (and their stamps) and some personal letters he sent from Miami at the time—showing he could not have been in Santiago for the murder ("US Experts: Documents Place Michael Townley in Florida During Chilean Poet Pablo Neruda Death," Associated Press, June 3, 2013, and author correspondence with Dinges, January 2017). It has also been shown that while Townley did work for Chile's secret police, he never did work for the CIA (Kornbluh, *Pinochet File,* 401, and author interviews with Dinges, 2016 and 2017).

493   "worthy of crime fiction": Among other reports, González, Alejan-dro. "Caso Neruda: ¿Quién es el Doctor Price?" 24horas, May 30, 2013, http://www.24horas.cl/nacional/caso-neruda-quien-es-el-doctor -price--671677.

493   "results mean that there is no": Among other sources, "Expertos descartan que Pablo Neruda haya sido envenenado," CNN Español, November 8, 2013, http://cnnespanol.cnn.com/2013/11/08/expertos -descartan-que-pablo-neruda-haya-sido-envenenado/.

493   "it is clearly possible": Brief addressed to Judge Mario Carroza Espi-nosa of the Appellate Court of Santiago on behalf of the Interior Min-istry's Human Rights Program, March 25, 2015. Available at https:// ep00.epimg.net/descargables/2015/11/05/5d1ddae7d84b280f588c8dfc 710c87d1.pdf?rel=mas.

494   "No Foul Play": Lopez, Erik. "No Foul Play in Death of Chilean Poet Neruda, Researchers Say," Reuters, May 28, 2015, http://www.reuters .com/article/us-chile-neruda-idUSKBN0OD1QD20150528.

494   one last pathogen: They are testing for *Staphylococcus aureus*, which had been found in his remains. As it is not directly associated with cancer, speculation arose that Neruda may have received a lethal injec-tion containing lab-manufactured staph. Yet even in modern hospitals, natural deaths from staph infections continue to occur. A needle tip that just happens to have staph on it can be deadly when injected into a patient whose immune system is suppressed due to cancer, pneumo-nia, or other disease.

495   "rule out or prove": Doctor Aurelio Luna, a Spanish forensic specialist from the University of Murcia, as quoted in multiple sources, includ-ing "Neruda no murió producto del cáncer de próstata, concluyeron

los peritos," Cooperativa.cl (Santiago), October 20, 2017. http://www
.cooperativa.cl/noticias/cultura/literatura/pablo-neruda/neruda
-no-murio-producto-del-cancer-de-prostata-concluyeron-los-peritos
/2017-10-20/170817.html.

495   in "100% agreement": Ibid.

495   a state he was clearly not in: Author correspondence with panelist
Debi Poinar, a fellow research associate at the McMaster Ancient DNA
Centre, October 29, 2017.

495   do not believe he died from the *Staphylococcus aureus*: Author corre-
spondence and conversation with Debi Poinar, October 26–30, 2017.

495   "a long history": Author correspondence with Debi Poinar, Octo-
ber 26, 2017.

495   "enable us to rule in": Author conversation with Hendrik Poinar, the
McMaster Ancient DNA Centre's Principal Investigator (and husband
of Debi Poinar), October 28, 2017.

496   Neruda's role as the people's poet: Conway, Diana. "Neruda, Skármeta,
and *Ardiente paciencia*," *Confluencia* 7, no. 2 (Spring 1992): 141.

496   Politics are treated vaguely: Hodgson, Irene B. "The De-Chileaniza-
tion of Neruda in *Il postino*," in *Pablo Neruda and the U.S. Culture Indus-
try*, ed. Teresa Longo (New York: Routledge, 2002), 104.

496   In 2010, the renowned Plácido: Johnson, Reed. "L.A. Opera to Deliver 'Il
postino' Premiere on Thursday," *Los Angeles Times*, September 19, 2010,
http://articles.latimes.com/2010/sep/19/entertainment/la-ca-daniel
-catan-20100919.

498   "because they hit you": Author interview with Jorge Rodríguez,
2003.

500   "a component of our nationality": Lagos Escobar, Ricardo. Prologue
to *Centenario de Neruda*. Available at Archivo Chile, http://www.ar
chivochile.com/Homenajes/neruda/sobre_neruda/homenajepne
ruda0020.pdf.

500   "has touched so many different": Quoted in "Celebran los 100 de
Neruda," *La Opinión*, July 12, 2004.

501   "sign in some sense": Author interview with Ariel Dorfman, 2004.

501   "because I felt it was a way": Dorfman, Ariel. "Words That Pulse
Among Madrid's Dead," *Los Angeles Times*, March 21, 2004.

502   "You would have no idea": Seipp, Catherine. "*Times* Never Changes,"
National Review, April 1, 2004, http://www.nationalreview.com/article
/210108/times-never-changes.

503   "In some magnetic way": "El mar" ["The Sea"], *Memorial de Isla Negra*.
Note that this is a different poem from the previously quoted "The
Sea" on page 424.

503   "Let us look for secret things": "No me hagan caso" ["Forget About Me"], *Estravagario*.

504   "Lazybones": "El perezoso," *Estravagario*. Translated by Jessica Powell.

APPENDIX II: ON THE IMPORTANCE OF POETRY IN CHILE

519   "Chile has an extraordinary history": Guibert, "Pablo Neruda," 64–65.

520   The use of nature as the protagonist: Edwards, "A Conversation with Forrest Gander and Raúl Zurita."

520   "very humble origins": Author interview with Rodrigo Rojas, June 15, 2015.

Index

Credits

I am deeply grateful to the Agencia Literaria Carmen Balcells S. A. and the Fundación Pablo Neruda (© Fundación Pablo Neruda, 2017) for their permission to reprint the work of Pablo Neruda included within this biography.

Excerpts from Pablo Neruda's lecture "Towards the Splendid City" (© the Nobel Foundation, 1971) are reprinted with the kind permission of the Nobel Foundation.

And I thank the following for their gracious permission to reprint these translations of Pablo Neruda's poetry:

Farrar, Straus & Giroux for the following translations by Alastair Reid: "Where Can Guillermina Be?"; excerpts from "Forget About Me," "Keeping Quiet," from *Extravagaria*. Translation copyright © 1974 by Alastair Reid. Excerpts from "Fully Empowered," "The Poet's Obligation," "To 'La Sebastiana,'" and "The Word" from *Fully Empowered*. Translation copyright © 1975 by Alastair Reid. Excerpts from "The Birth," "The Father," "The More-Mother," and "Poetry" from *Isla Negra*. Translation copyright © 1981 by Alastair Reid.

City Lights Books for excerpts from *venture of the infinite man*, translated by Jessica Powell © 2017; and the following from *The Essential Neruda: Selected Poems*, edited by Mark Eisner, © 2004: "Canto XII" and other excerpts from "Heights of Macchu Picchu" translated by Mark Eisner with John Felstiner and Stephen Kessler; excerpts from "The Fugitive XII" and "United Fruit Co." translated by Jack Hirschman; excerpts from "Right, comrade, it's the hour of the garden (from *El mar y las campanas*) and "Ode with a Lament" translated by Forrest Gander; "Poem XV" translated by Robert Hass; "Ode to Wine," "Sonnet XVII," "The Potter," "The Sea," "Poem XX," and excerpts from "Dead Gallop" translated by Mark Eisner; "Ars Poetica" and "It Means Shadows" translated by Stephen Kessler.

The Kenneth Rexroth Trust for an excerpt of "Poem VI," from *Thirty Spanish Poems of Love and Exile*, edited and translated by Kenneth Rexroth, City Lights Books, © Kenneth Rexroth, 1968.

Copper Canyon Press for the following translations by William O'Daly: "Returning," *The Sea and the Bells*. Translation copyright © 1988, 2002 by William O'Daly. Excerpts from "1968," "The Worship (II)," and "Death of a Journalist," from *World's End*. Translation copyright © 2009 by William O'Daly. Excerpts from "I," "XIII," and "LXXII," from *The Book of Questions*. Translation copyright © 1991, 2001 by William O'Daly. "Winter Garden," from *Winter Garden*. Translation copyright © 1986, 2002 by William O'Daly.

International Publishers Co./New York for excerpts from "Let the Rail-Splitter Awake" translated by Waldeen, from *Masses and Mainstream*, © 1950.

I am also grateful to the Colchie Agency, GP, for permission to reprint "Translator to Poet" by Alastair Reid, from *Weathering: Poems and Translations* by Alastair Reid (New York: E. P. Dutton, 1978). Copyright © 1978 by Alastair Reid; and copyright © 2015 by Leslie Clark. All rights reserved. Lastly, I am grateful to Vintage Books, an imprint of the Knopf Doubleday Publishing Group, a division of Penguin Random House LLC, for permission to reprint "Spain 1937," copyright © 1940 and copyright renewed 1968 by W. H. Auden; from *Selected Poems* by W. H. Auden, edited by Edward Mendelson.